T0211080

Lecture Notes in Computer Science 14164

Founding Editors

Gerhard Goos
Juris Hartmanis

Editorial Board Members

The series Lecture Notes in Computer Science (LNCS), including its subseries Lecture Notes in Artificial Intelligence (LNAI) and Lecture Notes in Bioinformatics (LNBI), has established itself as a medium for the publication of new developments in computer science and information technology research, teaching, and education.

LNCS enjoys close cooperation with the computer science R & D community, the series counts many renowned academics among its volume editors and paper authors, and collaborates with prestigious societies. Its mission is to serve this international community by providing an invaluable service, mainly focused on the publication of conference and workshop proceedings and postproceedings. LNCS commenced publication in 1973.

Khalid Saeed · Jiří Dvorský ·
Nobuyuki Nishiuchi · Makoto Fukumoto
Editors

Computer Information Systems and Industrial Management

22nd International Conference, CISIM 2023
Tokyo, Japan, September 22–24, 2023
Proceedings

 Springer

Editors
Khalid Saeed 🆔
Bialystok University of Technology
Białystok, Poland

Jiří Dvorský 🆔
VSB - Technical University of Ostrava
Ostrava, Czech Republic

Nobuyuki Nishiuchi 🆔
Tokyo Metropolitan University
Tokyo, Japan

Makoto Fukumoto 🆔
Fukuoka Institute of Technology
Fukuoka, Japan

ISSN 0302-9743   ISSN 1611-3349 (electronic)
Lecture Notes in Computer Science
ISBN 978-3-031-42822-7   ISBN 978-3-031-42823-4 (eBook)
https://doi.org/10.1007/978-3-031-42823-4

This Springer imprint is published by the registered company Springer Nature Switzerland AG
The registered company address is: Gewerbestrasse 11, 6330 Cham, Switzerland

Preface

CISIM 2023 was the 22nd of a series of international conferences on computer information systems and industrial management applications. The conference was held during September 22–24, 2023, in Tokyo, at Tokyo Metropolitan University.

Seventy-seven works were submitted to the conference by researchers and scientists from different scientific institutions and universities around the world. They belong to Brazil, Canada, Colombia, Czechia, Germany, India, Japan, Norway, Pakistan, Poland, South Korea, Spain, Tunisia, Vietnam, and Venezuela. Most of the papers were of high quality, but only seventy-two of them were sent for peer review. Each paper was assigned to at least three referees initially, and the acceptance decision was taken after receiving at least two positive reviews. In total, more than 200 reviews and comments were collected from the referees for the submitted papers. In order to maintain the guidelines of Springer's Lecture Notes in Computer Science series, the number of accepted papers was limited. Furthermore, a number of electronic discussions were held among the Program Committee (PC) chairs to decide about papers with conflicting reviews and to reach a consensus. After the discussions, the PC chairs decided to accept for publication in the proceedings book the best 36 of the total submitted papers. The main topics covered by the chapters in this book are biometrics, kansei engineering, security systems, multimedia, classification and clustering, and industrial management. Besides these, the reader will find interesting papers on computer information systems and kansei engineering as applied to wireless networks, computer graphics, daily life, and intelligent systems. We are grateful to the three esteemed speakers for their keynote addresses. The authors of the keynote talks were Witold Pedrycz, University of Alberta, Canada; Nabendu Chaki, University of Calcutta, India, and Marina Gavrilova, University of Calgary, Canada.

We would like to thank all the members of the PC and the external reviewers for their dedicated efforts in the paper selection process. Special thanks are extended to the members of the Organizing Committee, both the International and the Local ones, and the Springer team for their great efforts to make the conference another success.

We hope that the reader's expectations will be met and that both the on-line and on-site participants had the planned benefits from the conference.

September 2023

Khalid Saeed
Jiří Dvorský
Nobuyuki Nishiuchi
Makoto Fukumoto

Organization

Conference Patrons

Marta Kosior-Kazberuk	Białystok University of Technology, Poland
Takaya Ohashi	Tokyo Metropolitan University, Japan

General Chair

Khalid Saeed	Białystok University of Technology, Poland

Conference Co-chairs

Rituparna Chaki	University of Calcutta, India
Marek Krętowski	Białystok University of Technology, Poland
Nobuyuki Nishiuchi	Tokyo Metropolitan University, Japan
Makoto Fukumoto	Fukuoka Institute of Technology, Japan

Advisory Committee

Nabendu Chaki	University of Calcutta, India
Young Im-Cho	Gachon University, South Korea
Agostino Cortesi	Ca' Foscari University of Venice, Italy
Emiro De-La-Hoz-Franco	Universidad de la Costa, Colombia
Keiko Kasamatsu	Tokyo Metropolitan University, Japan
Sławomir Wierzchoń	Polish Academy of Sciences, Warsaw, Poland

International Organizing Committee

Zenon Sosnowski (Chair)	Białystok University of Technology, Poland
Pavel Moravec	VŠB-Technical University of Ostrava, Czech Republic
Dionicio Neira	Universidad de la Costa, Colombia
Eri Shimokawara	Tokyo Metropolitan University, Japan

Local Organizing Committee

Vibol Yem (Chair)	Tokyo Metropolitan University, Japan
Attaporn Khaesawad	Tokyo Metropolitan University, Japan
Mirosław Omieljanowicz	Białystok University of Technology, Poland
Peerawat Pannattee	Tokyo Metropolitan University, Japan
Aleksander Sawicki	Białystok University of Technology, Poland
Maciej Szymkowski	Białystok University of Technology, Poland
José Escorcia Gutierrez	Universidad Autónoma del Caribe, Colombia

Program Committee

Chairs

Khalid Saeed	Białystok University of Technology, Poland
Jiří Dvorský	VŠB-Technical University of Ostrava, Czech Republic

Members

Waleed Abdulla	University of Auckland, New Zealand
Raid Al-Tahir	Univ. of the West Indies, St. Augustine, Trinidad and Tobago
Aditya Bagchi	Indian Statistical Institute, India
Valentina Emilia Balas	University of Arad, Romania
Anna Bartkowiak	Wrocław University, Poland
Daniela Borissova	Bulgarian Academy of Sciences, Bulgaria
Rahma Boucetta	University of Sfax, Tunisia
Nabendu Chaki	University of Calcutta, India
Rituparna Chaki	University of Calcutta, India
Young-Im Cho	Gachon University, South Korea
Melissa Acosta-Coll	Universidad de la Costa, Colombia
Agostino Cortesi	Ca' Foscari University of Venice, Italy
Dipankar Dasgupta	University of Memphis, USA
Pierpaolo Degano	University of Pisa, Italy
José Escorcia Gutierrez	Universidad Autónoma del Caribe, Colombia
Riccardo Focardi	Ca' Foscari University of Venice, Italy
Margarita Gamarra Acosta	Universidad del Norte, Colombia
Marina Gavrilova	University of Calgary, Canada
Jan Devos	Ghent University, Belgium

Jarosław Stepaniuk	Białystok University of Technology, Poland
Marcin Szpyrka	AGH Kraków, Poland
Hiroshi Takenouchi	Fukuoka Institute of Technology, Japan
Andrea Torsello	Ca' Foscari University of Venice, Italy
Daishi Watabe	Saitama Institute of Technology, Japan
Qiang Wei	Tsinghua University, China
Sławomir Wierzchoń	Polish Academy of Sciences, Warsaw, Poland
Michał Woźniak	Wrocław University of Technology, Poland
Kaori Yoshida	Kyushu Institute of Technology, Japan
Sławomir Zadrożny	Polish Academy of Sciences, Warsaw, Poland

Additional Reviewers

Paola Patricia Ariza Colpas
Brahim Benaissa
Takanori Chihara
Michal Choras
Hiroshi Daimoto
So Fukuhara
Yotaro Fuse
Tomasz Grześ
Yuri Hamada
Yukio Ishihara
Ken Ishibashi
Yasuo Kudo
Daisuke Miki
Tetsuya Miyoshi
Yuneidis Morales Ortega
Masao Nakagawa
Hitomi Nakamura

Abu Quwsar Ohi
Anita Pal
Danielle Pozzo
Domenec Puig
Grzegorz Rubin
Makiba Sakamoto
Dixon Salcedo
Ashis Samanta
Tatsuya Shibata
Sayaka Shiota
Hidetsugu Suto
Mio Suzuki
Kenzen Takeuchi
Kazuaki Tanaka
Xiao Xiao
Kimihiro Yamanaka

Keynotes

Berserk Detection in Distributed Ledger Systems

Nabendu Chaki

Department of Computer Science and Engineering, University of Calcutta, Kolkata, India
nabendu@ieee.org

Abstract. Emerging distributed ledger technologies are not based on Proof of Work or Proof of Stake consensus protocols. Lightweight protocols based on the voter model are often used. However, these protocols are fraught with a particular type of Byzantine adversary known as Berserk adversaries who intend to break the consensus. Besides, the existing method of Berserk detection involves the exchange of signatures which requires key servers that are subject to a single point of failure. In this lecture, the presenter a novel and recent approach to Berserk detection. Unlike most of the existing methods of detection, the proposed method does not use signatures for the detection of Berserk behavior. This opens up the possibility of a more secure distributed environment, where ensuring anonymity in terms of the identity of nodes is crucial.

An Impact of Transformative Artificial Intelligence Research on Biometric Privacy, Security and Ethics

Marina L. Gavrilova

Department of Computer Science, University of Calgary, Calgary, AB T2N 1N4
Canada
mgavrilo@ucalgary.ca

Abstract. Biometric authentication is one of the most reliable mechanisms of ensuring proper verification of an individual. Over past decade, it became a highly popular practice for government, consumer, and financial institutions to ensure authorized access to resources and information. Biometrics are also increasingly used in a cybersecurity context to mitigate online vulnerabilities, to detect possible threats and to ensure protection against an unauthorized access.

With the rise of the technological advancements, such as AI and deep learning, more and more capabilities exist to infer private information of individuals and to use aggregate data mining for commercial or other purposes. This lecture will discuss how deep learning methods can enhance biometric recognition accuracy in a variety of settings: unimodal and multi-modal systems, social behavioral biometrics, and risk assessment. The lecture will further focus on risks of privacy and ethical considerations, with discussing cancellability and de-identification as two of the mechanisms to mitigate the privacy concerns. Open problems and future directions of research will be also discussed.

Data Privacy, Energy Awareness and Credibility: Advances in Machine Learning

Witold Pedrycz

Department of Electrical and Computer Engineering, University of Alberta, Edmonton, Canada
wpedrycz@ualberta.ca

Abstract. Over the recent years, we have been witnessing spectacular achievements of Machine Learning with highly visible accomplishments encountered, in particular, in natural language processing and computer vision impacting numerous areas of human endeavours. Driven inherently by the technologically advanced learning and architectural developments, Machine Learning (ML) constructs are highly impactful coming with far reaching consequences; just to mention autonomous vehicles, control, health care imaging, decision-making in critical areas, among others.

We advocate that the design and analysis of ML constructs have to be carried out in a holistic manner by identifying and addressing a series of central and unavoidable quests coming from industrial environments and implied by a plethora of requirements of interpretability, energy aware-ness (being also lucidly identified on the agenda of green AI), efficient quantification of quality of ML constructs, their brittleness and concep-tual stability coming hand in hand with the varying levels of abstraction. They are highly intertwined and exhibit relationships with the techno-logical end of ML. As such, they deserve prudent attention, in particular when a multicriterial facet of the problem is considered.

The talk elaborates on the above challenges, offers definitions and identifies the linkages among them. In the pursuit of coping with such quests, we advocate that Granular Computing can play a pivotal role offering a conceptual environment and realizing algorithmic develop-ment. We stress and identify ways to effective assessments of credibility of ML constructs. As a detailed study, we discuss the ideas of knowledge transfer showing how a thoughtful and prudently arranged knowledge reuse to support energy-aware ML computing. We discuss passive and active modes of knowledge transfer. In both modes, the essential role of information granularity is identified. In the passive approach, information granularity serves as a vehicle to quantify the credibility of the transferred knowledge. In the active approach, a new model is constructed in the target domain whereas the design is guided by the loss function, which involves granular regularization produced by the granular model transferred from the source domain. A generalized scenario of multi-source domains is discussed. Knowledge distillation leading to model compression is also studied in the context of transfer learning.

Modeling of Real-Life Problems Using the Graph-Theoretic Approach (Invited Paper)

Anita Pal

Durgapur National Institute of Technology, India
anita.pal@maths.nitdgp.ac.in

Abstract. A graph is an efficient tool to model real-life problems. By modeling the graph, the objects and their relations are symbolized by nodes and arcs. In this article, we discuss two applications of graphs: one is a construction of a dictionary by using a binary tree, and another is selecting different programme slots telecast on various television channels in a day to reach the maximum number of viewers. The objective of the second application is to help the companies to select the programme slots, which are mutually exclusive with respect to the time schedule of telecasting time, in such a way that the total number of viewers of the selected programme slots rises to the optimum level. It is shown that the solution to this problem is obtained by solving the maximum weight colouring problem on an interval graph. An algorithm is designed to solve this optimization problem using $O(n)$ time, where n represents the total number of programmes of all channels. We have also presented some different properties of trees, rooted trees, and binary trees. We include the colouring of some special graphs, and several well-known theoretical results have been discussed. Finally, we analyze the concept of some intersection graphs like interval graphs, circular-arc graphs, trapezoid graphs, circle graphs etc.

Contents

Industrial Management and Other Applications

Machine Learning and Artificial Neural Networks

Modelling and Optimization

ICBAKE 2023 Workshop: Wellbeing and Affective Engineering

Machine Learning Using Biometric Data and Kansei Data

Biometrics and Pattern Recognition Applications

Proposal of Earprint Authentication System Considering Pressing Force

Nen Hirai[1]([⊠]), Yem Vibol[2], Lukasz Hamera[3], Lukasz Wieclaw[3], Pawel Krzempek[3], and Nobuyuki Nishiuchi[1]

[1] Faculty of Systems Design, Tokyo Metropolitan University, Tokyo, Japan
hirai-nen@ed.tmu.ac.jp, nnishiuc@tmu.ac.jp
[2] Faculty of Engineering, Information and Systems, University of Tsukuba, Tsukuba, Japan
yem@iit.tsukuba.ac.jp
[3] University of Bielsko-Biala, Bielsko-Biala, Poland
lwieclaw@ath.bielsko.pl

Abstract. Earprints are left marks when the ear is pressed against a wall or door. They are sometimes found at crime scenes, and there are some actual criminal cases in which earprints are used to identify criminals. Earprints are still being researched to find out how to use them. Among them, it has been reported that the earprint is deformed by pressing force, but the conventional study of earprint recognition does not consider the pressing force. In the existing earprint collection system based on the cooperation of the suspect, the criminal can reduce the similarity by pressing the ear with a force different from the original force. Then, our research group has developed a device that continuously acquire earprints by using acrylic blocks and a high-speed camera. In addition, a load cell is installed on the back of the acrylic block, so it is possible to get earprint images corresponding the pressing force of the ear. In this study, we obtained earprints from 10 participants by using the device we developed and verified the accuracy of authentication. As a result of an accuracy evaluation experiment, it was suggested that it is possible to identify person even in the earprints acquired using this device.

Keywords: earprint · biometrics · authentication · pressing force of ear · pattern matching · image processing · ICBAKE2023

1 Introduction

1.1 Background of Earprint Recognition

Biometric verification system can be used in criminal investigations, and there are some research on biometric information that can be used for personal authentication. Earprints are marks remaining on walls, windows, or doors by pressing one's ear and are mainly found in crime scene. Since the human ear has enough personal characteristics to identify individuals [1, 2], it is considered that earprints can be also used to verify individuals, and some research on earprint recognition has been conducted.

K. Saeed et al. (Eds.): CISIM 2023, LNCS 14164, pp. 3–13, 2023.
https://doi.org/10.1007/978-3-031-42823-4_1

Rutty, Abbas and Crossling [3] proposed a computerized earprint identification system to use earprints as evidence of crime investigation. And it has been reported that earprints are found in about 15% of crime scenes. Actually, earprints are used in criminal investigations in some countries, and it has been reported that earprints have helped to identify criminals [4]. However, research on earprint recognition is not yet sufficiently mature, and further studies are needed.

The biggest project considering possibility of earprint identification is Fear ID project. Alberink and Ruifrok [5] investigated the feasibility of verification system which uses earprints as new biometric evidence in Fear ID project. This project is conducted by some institute to confirm validity of earprint as evidence and develop earprint recognition system. In Fear ID project, a total of 7364 earprints were collected from 1229 persons to evaluate possibility of earprint verification. The earprints acquired in that experiment have been used in some studies to evaluate accuracy of personal verification and identification, but when the earprints were acquired in this study, the pressing force were not measured.

Alberink et al. [5], Junod, Pasquier and Champod, [6] and Morales et al. [7] have proposed earprint recognition system in their study by using earprints collected in Fear ID project, but there is concern that earprints can be deformed by pressing force on the ear. Abaza et al. [8], Meijerman et al. [9, 10] considered pressing force as a factor that can cause intraindividual variation in earprints in his study. Although Fear ID collects earprints by reproducing a suspect's ability to hear by installing speakers, they didn't measure pressing force. Junod et al. [6] note that this assumes that the suspect will cooperate with the police in providing his or her own evidence and therefore the earprint images collected in the Fear ID project are not applicable to police investigations. And Champod, Evett and Kuchler [11] also pointed out that there were few studies which evaluated the effects of ear pressing force in a review article.

Against this background that existing earprint recognition studies do not take such pressing forces into account, our research group member developed a device that continuously captures earprints while measuring the pressing force.

Therefore, we propose an earprint authentication system using the device that acquires earprints while measuring pressing force. The purpose of this study is to investigate the relationship between pressing force and earprint authentication and to evaluate the effectiveness of the proposed system. In this study, ear pressing force and earprints were acquired from 10 participants, and the evaluation experiments for earprint authentication were conducted using the obtained earprints data to verify its accuracy.

The remainder of this paper is organized as follows. Section 2 describes our proposed system, and Sect. 3 describes the results of the evaluation experiments for ear print authentication. The final section, Sect. 4, summarizes the contents of this paper and discusses prospects.

2 Earprint Authentication System

2.1 Device for Acquiring Earprints

In this paper, we propose the earprint authentication system by using the device developed by our research group member (Fig. 1, Left). An acrylic block and a high-speed camera were used to develop the device that can continuously capture images of participant's ears pressed against the acrylic block.

The method of acquiring the earprint is as follows; Participant stands up and presses his/her ears against the acrylic block (Fig. 1, Right). The height of the acrylic block can be adjusted according to the height of the participant so that the ear can be pressed against the acrylic block in a natural posture. LED lightings are attached to the side of the acrylic block, and when the participant presses the ear against the acrylic block, the light is reflected at the touched ear, and the participant's earprint is captured with the high-speed camera from the top of the block (Fig. 2). In addition, by a load cell attached to the back of the acrylic block, the pressing force of the ear can be also measured (Fig. 3). The waveform data of the pressing force and the earprint images are synchronized with a data logger. The dataset allows us to check all earprint images corresponding to the pressing force.

This is the way to acquire earprints by using this device. When this device is used to acquire earprints from a suspect in a real criminal investigation case, visualizing the force applied to the ear can help determine if the perpetrator is applying enough force to the ear. Also, by pressing with a force that exceeds a certain threshold, it is possible to capture earprint images corresponding to all forces from 0N to the threshold. (Actually, it becomes a discrete image that depends on the sampling rate.) Therefore, even for the earprints found at the crime scene with unknown force, it can be expected to match with the pressed earprint image.

Fig. 1. Device of acquiring earprint (Left) and usage situation of the device (Right).

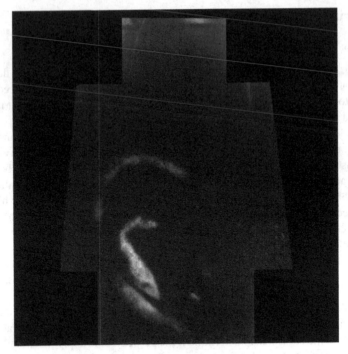

Fig. 2. Example of earprint image acquired by the device.

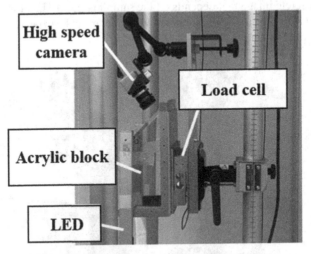

Fig. 3. Side view of the acrylic block of the device.

2.2 Preprocessing of Earprint

The Projective transformation is performed to remove distortion against the earprint images acquired by the device. Four grid marker stickers were attached to the acrylic block for the projective transformation. The distortion is eliminated by extracting the coordinates of the circle grid from the captured image and adjusting the marker grid to the correct position by the projective transformation (Fig. 4).

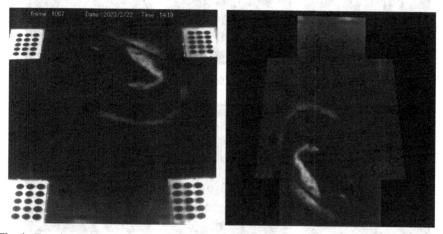

Fig. 4. Earprint before the projective transformation (Left) and earprint after the projective transformation (Right).

2.3 Acquisition of Earprint

Earprints used in this paper were acquired from 10 Japanese university students using the device. All participants press their ear five times each of the left and right ear, and all of dataset are used to create an earprint database. All participants are instructed to press with a force over 30N, and supervisor checked that the pressing force exceeded 30N.

To make template earprint images used in the evaluation experiment, we cut out the central part of the earprint image. Earprints to cut out were corresponding to the frame in which the three types of force of 10N, 20N and 30N were reached for the first time among the series of captured earprint images. And it cut out and we created a rectangle based on the value was set at predetermined coordinates. When cutting out the earprint image, part of the ear-print may protrude from the frame and the earprint may be missing. In this study, the matching score is calculated by template matching, and it is thought that earprint authentication is possible even if a part of the earprint is missing. In addition, although part of the cheek may be reflected, this information is also used for matching as a characteristic of the participant.

The actual acquired earprints are shown in Fig. 5 with the pressing force of the ear. It is possible to observe that the touched part of the ear spreads gradually along with the rising the pressing force. In addition, the antihelix of the earprint at 30N appears thicker compared with 5N. Moreover, we can observe that the earprint is slightly deformed.

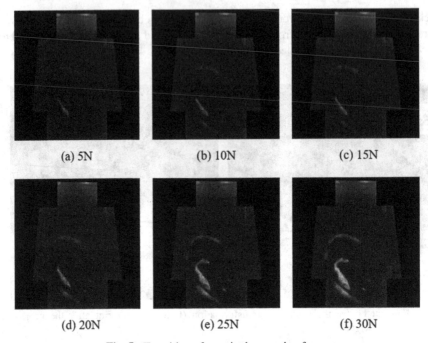

(a) 5N   (b) 10N   (c) 15N

(d) 20N   (e) 25N   (f) 30N

Fig. 5. Transition of earprint by pressing force.

2.4 Actual Usage Scene of Proposed System

This section describes the actual usage scenes of the proposed system. This system is used in criminal investigations where earprints are found at crime scenes. In this system, earprints are acquired in advance from persons who have committed crimes in the past or who are suspected of being related to the incident, as a preparation for constructing an earprint database for comparison. It is possible to check whether the suspect is pressing the ear with an appropriate force during interrogation because we can observe the current pressing force through the system. In addition, digital images of earprint can be efficiently captured without the need for items such as silver dust.

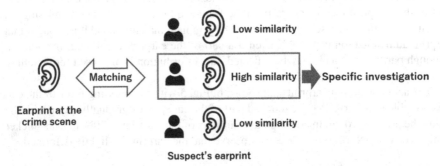

Fig. 6. Criminal investigation by earprint authentication using proposed system.

The system narrows down suspects by automatically matching all earprints in the database and earprints found at crime scenes (Fig. 6). The system outputs several earprints with high matching scores, enables experts to perform specific earprint verification of suspects.

3 Evaluation Experiment

3.1 Methodology

The purpose of this experiment is to evaluate earprint authentication system proposed in this paper and to investigate the relationship between earprints and pressing force.

By using the device, the series of earprint images (about 2,000 earprint images) were obtained in one shot. In this experiment, template image was matched with all earprint image in the database, excluding the series of earprint images of the template image (Fig. 7). 300 template images (50 images each from the left and right ears with 3 types of pressing force (10N, 20N and 30N)) were used. This means that one template image was matched with earprints of 4 series of the same participant and 45 series of other participants. Using this combination, the matching scores were calculated (Fig. 8).

Then, the earprint image having the highest score among the calculated matching scores is selected, and if the participant corresponding to the earprint is the same participant as the earprint in the template image, the authentication is considered successful. A matching score was calculated using the Zero Mean Normalized Cross-Correlation (ZNCC) used for pattern matching. The formula for calculating ZNCC is as follows [12].

$$ZNCC(x, y) = \frac{\sum_{j=1}^{N}\sum_{i=1}^{M}[I(x+i, y+j) - \mu(I_c(x, y))] \cdot [T(i, j) - \mu(T)]]}{\sqrt{\sum_{j=1}^{N}\sum_{i=1}^{M}[I(x+i, y+j) - \mu(I_c(x, y))]^2} \cdot \sqrt{\sum_{j=1}^{N}\sum_{i=1}^{M}[T(i, j) - \mu(T)]^2}} \tag{1}$$

$I(x, y)$: sub-image of size $M \times N$ located at pixel coordinates (x, y)
$T(x, y)$: sub-image of size $M \times N$ located at pixel coordinates (x, y)
$\mu(I(x, y))$: the mean intensity value of image $I(x, y)$
$\mu(T)$: the mean intensity value of image T

3.2 Results

The experimental results of the earprint authentication are shown in Table 1. As a result of the experiment, the accuracy rate of the left earprint was 92% and the accuracy rate of the right earprint was 96%. Although there is slight difference between left and right ear, both earprints acquired by the device can be used for the authentication and our proposed method is valid.

From the viewpoint of pressing force (10N, 20N and 30N), there was no large variation in accuracy. This suggests the possibility that this system can respond to various pressing forces.

Furthermore, to verify the influence of pressing force on the matching score, we referred to the pressing force with the highest matching score for all 50 template images

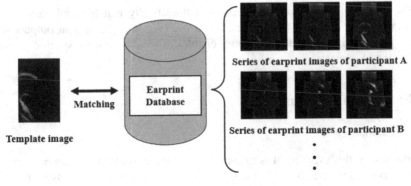

Fig. 7. Proposed system for earprint matching.

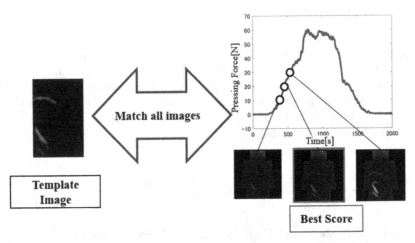

Fig. 8. Earprint matching procedure considering pressing force.

Table 1. Authentication performance in terms of Rank-1(%)

	10N	20N	30N	Average
Left	92.0	88.0	88.0	92.0
Right	96.0	96.0	96.0	96.0
Average	94.0	92.0	96.0	94.0

and investigated the relationship between the pressing force of template and the pressing force with the highest matching score. Figure 9 shows box plots of the pressing force with the highest matching score corresponding to the pressing force of the template image.

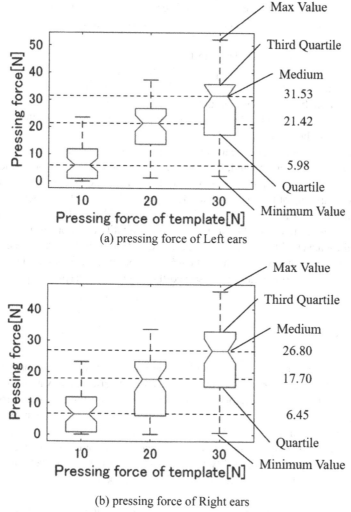

(a) pressing force of Left ears

(b) pressing force of Right ears

Fig. 9. A boxplot of pressing force with matching score

3.3 Discussion

The discrimination accuracy of this study is close to that of other earprint studies [5, 6]. However, the number of samples in the Fear ID dataset used in other studies is much larger than in this study, so making a simple comparison is inappropriate. In this study, there is a possibility that the accuracy will decrease as the number of samples increases, so in the future, we plan to increase the number of participants and verify the accuracy again. Also, when the sample size becomes large, it is necessary to consider the calculation time as well. In this study, we used all the series of images obtained from when the ear is started pressing to when the ear is released. In the actual situations, a down sampling will be needed.

In matching the earprint images, the difference between the median pressing force with the highest matching score and the pressing force of the template was confirmed, and it was within 5N (Fig. 9). This result shows that earprints which have high similarity with template image were pressed by similar force with template, so it is considered that the pressing force is important in earprint authentication.

Regarding the left and right ears, the median value of the right ear's pressing force of the highest matching score was slightly smaller than the left ear's one. It is thought that this difference is made by the posture of the participant at pressing the ear and the dominant hand of the participants.

There are some cases that the earprint is not properly shown when the pressing force is close to 0N. On the other hand, even when the pressure was over 30N, the quality of earprint image for some participants was quite poor but the matching score was also high. Skin oils are one of the factors that affect quality. Kieckhoefer, Ingleby and Lucas [13] reported that repeated pressing of the ear degrades the quality of the earprint by de-oiling the skin. Skin oil is a factor that affects the quality of earprints and even when we acquired by acrylic blocks, it can affect the reflection of light. After the evaluation experiment, we photographed additional earprints from one participant who is applied a moisturizing cream to the ear and observed them, then, the earprints appeared more clearly.

4 Conclusion

In this paper, we proposed an earprint authentication system considering pressing force and evaluated its effectiveness. From the results of the experiment, it was confirmed that the proposed system can properly identify individuals. In addition, it was confirmed that the matching score of earprint authentication tended to increase when the pressing force of the earprints was similar.

Although the past earprint authentication research did not consider pressing force, this experiment suggests a possibility that the pressing force affects earprint authentication. A more specific investigation of the relationship between earprints and pressing force is also required.

In the future, we will try to increase the number of participants in the experiment and evaluate the accuracy of earprint authentication again. And we will also try to compare earprints which were acquired by device in this study with earprints acquired by actual police method. These evaluations will enhance the feasibility of our system.

Acknowledgments. In writing this paper, we would like to express deepest gratitude to Ikumi Yamada, who was our research member and developed the device which can measure the pressing force of ear and acquire the earprint images synchronously.

References

1. Bertillon, A.: Signaletic Instructions: Including the Theory and Practice of Anthropometrical Identification. The Werner Company, Chicago (1896). R.W. McClaughry translation

2. Iannarelli, A.: Ear Identification, Forensic Identification Series. Paramount Publishing Company, Fremont (1989)
3. Rutty, G.N., Abbas, A., Crossling, D.: Could earprint identification be computerized? An illustrated proof of concept paper. Int. J. Legal Med. **119**(6), 335–343 (2005)
4. Meijerman, L., Thean, A., Maat, G.: Earprints in forensic investigations. Forensic Sci. Med. Pathol. **1**(4), 247–256 (2005)
5. Alberink, I., Ruifrok, A.: Performance of the FearID earprint identification system. Forensic Sci. Int. **166**(2–3), 145–154 (2007)
6. Junod, S., Pasquier, J., Champod, C.: The development of an automatic recognition system for earmark and earprint comparisons. Forensic Sci. Int. **222**(1–3), 170–178 (2012)
7. Morales, A., Diaz, M., Llinas-Sanchez, G., Ferrer, M.A.: Earprint recognition based on an ensemble of global and local features. In: 2015 International Carnahan Conference on Security Technology (ICCST), pp. 253–258 (2015)
8. Abaza, A., Ross, A., Hebert, C., Harrison, M.A.F., Nixson, M.S.: A survey on ear biometrics. ACM Comput. Surv. **45**(2) (2013)
9. Meijerman, L., et al.: Exploratory study on classification and individualization of earprints. Forensic Sci. Int. **140**(1), 91–99 (2004)
10. Meijerman, L., et al.: Inter- and Intra-individual variation in applied force when listening at a surface, and resulting variation in earprints. Med. Sci. Law **46**(2), 141–151 (2006)
11. Champod, C., Evett, I.W., Kuchler, B.: Earmark as evidence: a critical review. J. Forensic Sci. **46**(6), 1275–1284 (2001)
12. Di Stefano, L., Mattoccia, S., Tombari, F.: ZNCC-based template matching using bounded partial correlation. Pattern Recogn. Lett. **26**(14), 2129–2134 (2005)
13. Kieckhoefer, H., Ingleby, M., Lucas, G.: Monitoring the physical formation of earprints: optical and pressure mapping evidence. Measurement **39**(10), 918–935 (2006)

Performance Improvement of Person Verification Using Evoked EEG by Imperceptible Vibratory Stimulation

Hiroki Kobayashi[1], Hirotomo Nakashima[1], and Isao Nakanishi[2](✉) [ID]

[1] Graduate School of Sustainability Sciences, Tottori University,
4-101 Koyama-minami, Tottori 680-8550, Japan
m22j4022h@edu.tottori-u.ac.jp
[2] Faculty of Engineering, Tottori University,
4-101 Koyama-minami, Tottori 680-8550, Japan
nakanishi@tottori-u.ac.jp

Abstract. In this study, we focus on the electroencephalogram (EEG) as a biometric that can be detected continuously with high confidentiality, and aim to realize the person verification using the evoked EEG when presented with an imperceptible vibration stimulus. In previous studies, the content ratios of the power spectrum in theta (4–8 Hz), alpha (8–13 Hz), and beta (13–43 Hz) wavebands as individual features were derived from the evoked EEG data generated by imperceptible vibration stimulation, and the verification performance was evaluated by Support Vector Machine (SVM). The results showed that the Equal Error Rate (EER) was 28.2%; however, this was not a sufficient verification result. In this paper, for the purpose of improving the verification performance, the weighted (normalized) content ratios are adopted as new features and the verification performance is evaluated. Accordingly, the EER is improved to 17.0%. The verification performance is further improved by changing the feature bandwidth to 6–10 Hz, which contains many spectral components in evoked EEG, and the EER is reduced to 16.4%.

Keywords: biometrics · EEG · imperceptible vibration stimuli · content ratio · normalization

1 Introduction

Recently, biometrics, such as fingerprints and face images, have been used in personal computers (PCs) and smartphones. Biometric verification uses an individual's biometric data rather than memories or possessions, so there is no risk of loss or forgetting. However, biometric data exposed on the surface of the body, such as fingerprints or face images, can be falsified. In addition, as verification is generally only performed once at system startup, there is a possibility that someone else could impersonate the user after verification. Therefore, the EEG

K. Saeed et al. (Eds.): CISIM 2023, LNCS 14164, pp. 14–24, 2023.
https://doi.org/10.1007/978-3-031-42823-4_2

is attracting attention as a highly confidential and continuously detectable biometric [1]. We aim to verify individuals using EEG induced by specific stimuli. However, perceptible stimuli would cause stress and load on individuals. Therefore, in previous studies [2–4], imperceptible vibration stimuli were used to generate the evoked EEG. The content ratio of the power spectrum derived from the measured EEG data was used as a feature value and verification was performed by using SVM. However, verification performance was still insufficient.

In this paper, with the aim of improving the verification performance, we propose to introduce weighting into the conventional content ratio. Furthermore, based on the observation of EEG spectra, we change the bandwidth of the feature to 6–10 Hz instead of using 4–43 Hz.

2 Person Verification Using Evoked EEG from Imperceptible Vibratory Stimulation

EEG can be categorized into two types. The first is spontaneous EEG, which is generated on a daily basis. The other is induced EEG, which is generated in response to an external stimulus. In this study, induced EEG is used for person verification, as it is believed that there will be differences between responses from individuals. This section describes the previous studies [2–4] that had been conducted.

2.1 Imperceptible Vibratory Stimulation

It was thought that using tactile stimuli that could stimulate the skin directly would bring a more certain way to respond to stimuli [2]. It is known that mechanoreceptors that detect changes such as vibration have cells and corpuscles that respond to the sensation of the received stimulus, and each has different threshold properties for different vibration stimulus frequencies [5]. Therefore, in previous studies, imperceptible tactile stimulation has been achieved using high-frequency vibrational stimuli [2]. Figure 1 shows the produced stimulus presentation device. The small square part in the figure is a transducer that delivers the vibration stimulation to the palm of the hand.

The frequency of the vibration stimulus that could not be perceived varied from subject to subject. Therefore, the frequency of the vibration stimulus was gradually increased until subjects could no longer perceive the vibration and found the upper limit of frequency. The frequency added to the upper limit at 50 Hz was then used as the individual frequency (the individual stimulus).

2.2 Event-Related Potential

It is known that responses to perceptual vibratory stimuli are evoked in brain waves immediately after the stimulation, even for a short duration [6–10]. However, that is the case when the stimulation is perceptible. Thus, we investigated whether responses were evoked by imperceptible stimuli. As one of the responses,

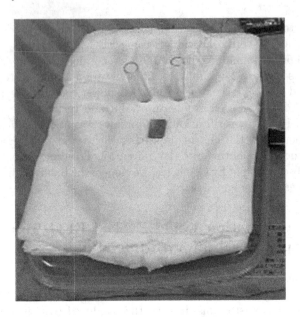

Fig. 1. Stimulus presentation device [2]

event-related potential (ERP) is known. ERPs are weak potential changes in the evoked EEG that occur in response to external stimuli and are extracted by addition-averaging many EEGs measured synchronously with stimulus presentation. To obtain many synchronized EEGs, we presented the stimulation cyclically as shown in Fig. 2, where 100 cycles of vibration stimuli were presented in a single measurement, with 0.1 s stimulation and 5.0 s blank time as one cycle shown in Fig. 2. The EEG data during 1.0 s after stimulation were extracted for each cycle and 100 EEG data were addition-averaged. The EEG was measured using an Emotiv EPOC+ with 14 electrodes; AF3, F3 F7, F3, FC5, T7, P7, O1, O2, P8, T8, FC6, F4, F8, and AF4 shown in Fig. 3. The specifications of EPOC+ are shown in Table 1.

The results showed that the evoked responses occurred during the presentation of the vibratory stimulus even when imperceptible. An example of the ERP waveform extracted at electrode F3 is shown in Fig. 4. Positive to negative changes such as P50, N70, P100, and N140 were observed for imperceptible stimuli. It has also been found that the amplitude of ERP peaks decreases as subjects become more familiar with the measurement environment [11].

2.3 Verification

The verification process is illustrated in Fig. 5. First, the measured EEG data are pre-processed by applying a 4–43 Hz band-pass filter and frequency analysis (FFT). The content ratios in the $\theta(4\text{–}8\,\text{Hz})$, $\alpha(8\text{–}13\,\text{Hz})$, and $\beta(13\text{–}43\,\text{Hz})$ wavebands are then extracted as three-dimensional features. The content ratio

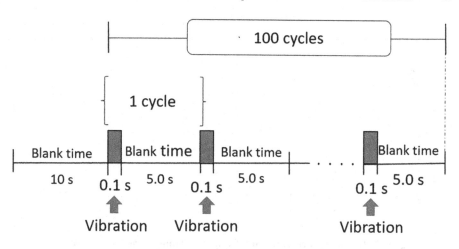

Fig. 2. Stimulation cycles for extracting ERP [2].

Fig. 3. Electroencephalograph used.

Table 1. Specifications of EPOC+

Number of Electrodes	14
	(AF3, F7, F3, FC5, T7, P7, O1,
	O2, P8, T8, FC6, F4, F8, AF4)
Sampling Method	Sequential Sampling
Sampling Rate	256 sps
Frequency Bandwidth	0:2–43 Hz (Digital notch filter at 50 Hz and 60 Hz)
Dynamic Range	8400 μV
Communication	Bluetooth

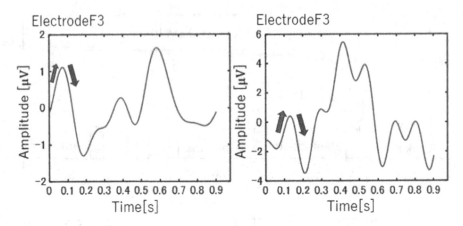

Fig. 4. ERP during presentation of imperceptible vibration stimuli [3]

Fig. 5. Flow of verification process

is the ratio of the total amount of the power spectrum in each frequency band to the total amount of the power spectrum in all wavebands. Euclidean distance matching and SVM were used as verification methods.

2.4   Performance Evaluation

A stimulus presentation cycle consisted of a 0.1 s stimulus, followed by a 5.0 s blank period, and 10 cycles of vibration stimuli were presented in a single measurement as shown in Fig. 6. The EEG data obtained when the individual stimulus was given to the subject were used as the individual data. In contrast, to evaluate the spoofing performance, the subject was given other persons' personal frequencies (other persons' stimulation), and obtained EEG data were used as the other persons' data. A database was created to evaluate the verification performance using 10 subjects. The measurement conditions are presented in Table 2.

The datasets used were 10 individual datasets and 9 other peoples' datasets. Among 10 individual datasets, 5 were used for generating a template or training for an SVM model and 5 were for testing. To reduce the effect of the combination of template and test data on verification performance, cross-validation was performed 10 times by randomising the combination. The equal error rate (EER) was used to evaluate the verification performance. The lower the EER, the better the performance.

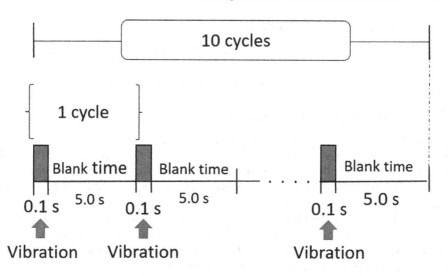

Fig. 6. Vibration stimulus presentation cycle for one subject [2].

Table 2. Measurement Condition [3]

Number of subjects	10 males
Presenting stimulus	The individual stimulus
	Another person's stimulus
Number of Measurements	The individual stimulus : ×10 times
	Another person's stimulation : ×1 time × 9 persons
Measurement time	One cycle: 0.1 s of vibration stimulus and 5.0 s of blank time
	Overall: About 50 s (10 cycles)
Environment	Resting, Eye-closed,
	Seated, Ear-plugged

The results of Euclidean distance matching and SVM are shown in Tables 3 and 4, respectively. The value for each electrode is the average of ten cross-validations. The average for all electrodes is also shown. It was 23.9% when using Euclidean distance and 28.2% when using SVM.

Table 3. EER by Euclidean distance matching [3]

Electrode	AF3	F7	F3	FC5	T7	P7	O1	O2	P8	T8	FC6	F4	F8	AF4	Average
EER [%]	21.3	20.0	26.2	22.7	34.7	17.2	23.0	26.5	23.9	21.4	24.9	26.6	21.0	25.4	23.9

Table 4. EER by SVM [3]

Electrode	AF3	F7	F3	FC5	T7	P7	O1	O2	P8	T8	FC6	F4	F8	AF4	Average
EER [%]	30.1	27.1	33.7	29.7	29.2	23.9	24.5	26.5	22.9	29.2	28.2	31.7	27.9	30.7	28.2

3   Performance Improvement

Verification performance in previous studies has not been satisfactory. Therefore, it must be improved.

3.1   Weighted Content Ratio

In previous studies, the content ratios of θ, α, and β wavebands were used as features; however, the mutual ratios of the content ratios of the θ, α, and β wavebands were found to be 17%, 55% and 28%, respectively as shown in Fig. 7, where the template data from all datasets were used. We will refer to these ratios as average content ratios to distinguish them from the content rates. The average content ratio of the α waveband is much larger than that of the other wavebands. Such a unbalance could influence the verification performance. The verification performance could be determined only by the α waveband and the effect of having three-dimension could be reduced.

Thus, to reduce the unbalance, we propose to weight the content ratios. Specifically, the content ratio of each waveband is divided by the average content ratio of the corresponding waveband. It is just like normalization as shown in Fig. 8. By using the weighting, the muted ratios of the content ratios were 99.7%, 100.4% and 99.5% and the unbalance was improved.

We evaluated the verification performance using the weighted content ratios of 4–10 Hz. The verification results are presented in Tables 5 and 6. Compared to the previous results in Tables 3 and 4, the average EER was reduced by about 0.5% for Euclidean distance matching and by about 11.2% for SVM.

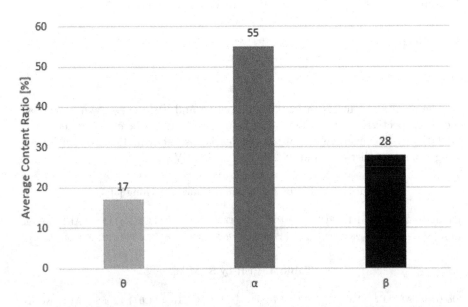

Fig. 7. Average content ratios of θ, α, and β wavebands

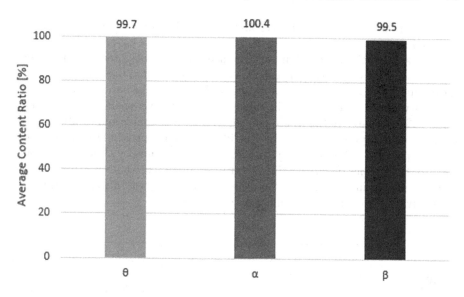

Fig. 8. Weighted content ratio of θ, α and β wavebands

This suggests that weighting (normalisation) is effective in improving verification performance.

Table 5. EER by Euclidean distance matching with weighted content ratios.

Electrode	AF3	F7	F3	FC5	T7	P7	O1	O2	P8	T8	FC6	F4	F8	AF4	Average
EER [%]	19.7	21.5	24.1	22.4	35.0	18.9	23.2	24.3	22.7	19.8	23.2	26.4	19.9	25.8	23.4

Table 6. EER by SVM with weighted content ratios.

Electrode	AF3	F7	F3	FC5	T7	P7	O1	O2	P8	T8	FC6	F4	F8	AF4	Average
EER [%]	14.8	16.7	20.6	16.1	23.6	15.8	16.3	15.6	15.4	12.6	15.6	21.6	16.9	16.2	17.0

3.2   Change of Bandwidth for Extracting Features

A power spectrum of the EEG after addition-averaging is shown in Fig. 9. It is clear that the spectral components are distributed below 10 Hz. Therefore, we propose to change the bandwidth for feature extraction from the conventional θ, α, and β wavebands (4–43 Hz) to 4–10 Hz.

Furthermore, to compare the verification performance of different bandwidths at 4–10 Hz, the average content ratios of the three bandwidths, 4–8 Hz, 5–9 Hz and 6–10 Hz were examined. The results are presented in Table 7. FFT was performed on the EEG data for 1.0 s; therefore, the frequency resolution of the EEG spectrum is 1 Hz. For example, with 4–8 Hz corresponds to the spectral components at 4, 5, 6, 7 and 8 Hz and the number of feature dimensions is increased to 5.

We evaluated the verification performance using the weighted content ratios. As a result, the best verification performance was obtained at 6–10 Hz bandwidth. The details are given in each electrode at 6–10 Hz, where the best verification performance was achieved, are given in Tables 8 and 9. The average EER decreased by about 0.9% compared to the result using θ, α and β wavebands and by about 1.4% compared to the previous result by Euclidean distance matching and by about 0.6% compared to the result using θ, α and β wavebands and by about 11.8% compared to the previous result by SVM. In both verification methods, the verification performance was improved; therefore, the change of bandwidth was confirmed to be effective in improving the verification performance.

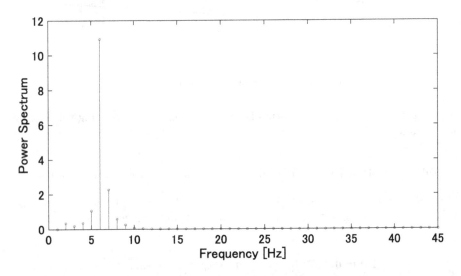

Fig. 9. A power spectrum of EEG after 10 addition-averaging

Table 7. Average content ratios of three bandwidths in 4–10 Hz and EER by Euclidean distance matching and SVM.

		4–8 Hz	5–9 Hz	6–10 Hz
Average content ratio [%]	4 Hz	8	–	–
	5 Hz	17	12	–
	6 Hz	19	13	10
	7 Hz	21	14	12
	8 Hz	35	21	18
	9 Hz	–	40	31
	10 Hz	–	–	29
EER [%]	Euclidean	30.4	27.5	22.5
	SVM	23.8	19.1	16.4

Table 8. EER by Euclidean distance matching using weighted content ratios of 6–10 Hz

Electrode	AF3	F7	F3	FC5	T7	P7	O1	O2	P8	T8	FC6	F4	F8	AF4	Average
EER [%]	21.7	21.5	19.0	20.6	28.1	20.8	21.0	23.5	25.4	23.1	21.9	20.7	23.6	23.8	22.5

Table 9. EER by SVM using weighted content ratios of 6–10 Hz

Electrode	AF3	F7	F3	FC5	T7	P7	O1	O2	P8	T8	FC6	F4	F8	AF4	Average
EER [%]	14.3	15.5	13.1	15.0	23.3	16.4	14.5	14.6	20.5	18.4	15.8	14.0	17.5	17.5	16.4

4   Conclusions

Continuous verification is necessary as a security measure in the modern information society, and EEG-based verification methods are suitable for continuous verification. In previous studies, imperceptible vibratory stimuli were used and the content ratios of an EEG spectrum evoked by the stimulation were extracted as individual features. The verification performance was evaluated using the feature; however, a sufficient verification rate could not be achieved.

To improve the verification performance, we introduced weighting into the content ratios. Verification performance was evaluated using Euclidean distance matching and SVM. Accordingly, the average EER was 23.4% for Euclidean distance matching and 17.0% for SVM, which were reduced by about 0.5% and 11.2% compared to the previous results, respectively. This suggests that weighting (normalisation) is effective for improving the verification performance.

In addition, the waveband for feature extraction from 4–43 Hz (θ, α and β wavebands) was changed to 4–10 Hz. In particular, in the waveband of 6–10 Hz, the average EER was 22.5% for Euclidean distance matching and 16.4% for SVM, which were reduced by about 1.4% and 11.8% respectively compared to the previous results. This indicates that the bandwidth of 6–10 Hz is effective for spectral feature extraction.

In the future, it will be necessary to increase the number of subjects to improve the reliability obtained in this study. Investigating novel features is required to further improve the verification performance.

References

1. Pozo-Banos, M.D., Alonso, J.B., Ticay-Rivas, J.R., Travieso, C.M.: Electroencephalogram subject identification: a review. Expert Syst. Appl. **15**, 6537–6554 (2014)
2. Shindo, Y., Nakanishi, I., Takemura, A.: A study on person verification using EEGs evoked by unperceivable vibration stimuli. In: Proceedings of the Seventh International Symposium on Computing and Networking Workshops (CANDARW), pp. 416–419, November 2019
3. Shindo, Y., Nakanishi, I.: Person verification using electroencephalograms evoked by new imperceptible vibration stimulation. In: Proceedings of 2021 IEEE 3rd

Global Conference on Life Sciences and Technologies (LifeTech 2021), pp. 286–290, March 2021

4. Nakashima, H., Shindo, Y., Nakanishi, I.: Performance improvement in user verification using evoked electroencephalogram by imperceptible vibration stimuli. In: Proceedings of the 20th International Symposium on Communications and Information Technologies (ISCIT 2021), pp. 109–113, October 2021

5. Bolanowski Jr., S.J., Gescheider, G.A., Verrillo, R.T., Checkosky, C.M.: Four channels mediate the mechanical aspects of touch. J. Acoust. Soc. Am. **84**(5), 1680–1694 (1998)

6. Adams, M.S., Popovich, C., Staines, W.R.: Gating at early cortical processing stages is associated with changes in behavioural performance on a sensory conflict task. Behav. Brain Res. **317**, 179–187 (2017)

7. Adams, M.S., Andrew, D., Staines, W.R.: The contribution of the prefrontal cortex to relevancy-based gating of visual and tactile stimuli. Exp. Brain Res. **237**(10), 2747–2759 (2019)

8. Marghi, Y.M., et al.: Signal models for brain interfaces based on evoked response potential in EEG. In: Signal Processing and Machine Learning for Brain Machine Interfaces, pp. 193–214 (2018)

9. Job, X.E., Brady, D., de Fockert, J.W., Di Bernardi Luft, C., Hill, E.L., Velzen, J.: Adults with probable developmental coordination disorder selectively process early visual, but not tactile information during action preparation. An electrophysiological study. Hum. Mov. Sci. **66**, 631–644 (2019)

10. Bolton, D.A.E., Staines, W.R.: Transient inhibition of the dorsolateral prefrontal cortex disrupts attention-based modulation of tactile stimuli at early stages of somatosensory processing. Neuropsychologia **49**(7), 1928–1937 (2011)

11. Hu, Z., Zhang, Z., Liang, Z., Zhang, L., Li, L., Huang, G.: A new perspective on individual reliability beyond group effect for event-related potentials: a multisensory investigation and computational modeling. NeuroImage **250**, Article 118937 (2022)

Biometric Gait Analysis Using Wrist-Mounted Wearable Sensors

Aleksander Sawicki(✉) 📵

Faculty of Computer Science, Bialystok University of Technology, Bialystok, Poland
a.sawicki@pb.edu.pl

Abstract. The paper presents a proposed gait biometrics system using wearable sensors. The work carried out verified the possibility of building systems using motion sensors located on the right and left wrist. The biometric system presented used input data in the form of accelerometer and gyroscope measurement values. The classifier was trained with fragments of a time series known as gait cycles - periods of time between which the participant touched his right foot against the ground. A CNN classifier with a multi-input architecture was used to validate the proposed approach. Experiments were conducted using the author's 100-person human gait database. The results of the experiments show that the system based on the sensor located on the right wrist achieved the highest metric of 0.750 ± 0.012 F1-score, while the left wrist sensor reached 0.571 ± 0.030 F1-score.

In addition, the presented approach includes a data mechanism that increased the performance of the right wrist biometric system to 0.92 ± 0.050 and the left wrist to 0.81 ± 0.030 F1-score metrics. As a result of the augmentation experiments, it was observed that for the right and left wrist, signal perturbations should follow a different parameter selection. For the right wrist, we observed a major advantage in modeling greater tilts during movement and higher sensor vibrations. According to the literature, most people (72%) have a right dominant hand. It can be concluded that this limb is more expressive during movement and thus has greater biometric information.

Keywords: biometrics · gait · accelerometer · augmentation

1 Introduction

In recent years, the dominance of methods from the so-called deep learning group of methods in a variety of artificial intelligence applications has been noticeable. These algorithms are being successfully applied also in the field of biometrics, but in the case of behavioral biometrics they are used rather in a limited scope. Deep networks with special emphasis on Convolutional Neural Networks (CNNs) indicates very high performance in classification problems, especially in the case of availability of numerous training datasets. However, their application is challenging when only a limited number of training samples are accessible [1].

Data augmentation can be an effective solution to data shortages when additional data acquisition involves high financial costs or is not possible for other reasons [2].

K. Saeed et al. (Eds.): CISIM 2023, LNCS 14164, pp. 25–35, 2023.
https://doi.org/10.1007/978-3-031-42823-4_3

Augmentation of learning sets using affine transformations is a common practice in the field of image recognition, while augmentation of motion signals is not standardized. The presented study is a continuation of the research described in [3], where algebraic augmentation of accelerometer and gyroscope data was applied with very promising results.

With the increasing popularity of devices such as smart watches/smart bands (which have built-in motion sensors), this work addresses the aspect of sensor location selection. This paper attempts to answer the question of whether the use of sensors around the right and left wrist can affect the accuracy of a biometric system.

2 Related Works

The literature of the construction of behavioral biometric systems using sensors at different mounting locations is relatively small. Existing approaches are very often based on single motion sensors, for example, embedded in a smart-phone [4] or a proprietary electronic solution [5]. On the other hand, the solutions presented in the literature are even less relevant to sensor sets [6]. Moreover, even taking into account the disproportions in the popularity of the presented approaches, extensive analyses of sensor placement impact on a biometric system metrics are published occasionally.

It can be assumed that this is mainly due to the fact that it is very difficult to achieve high subject verification rates in the field of behavioral biometrics. If only information on signals from an additional sensor becomes available, the authors will almost certainly use it to improve the performance of the presented systems.

Nevertheless, there are publications in literature arising from the scheme. In [7], a comprehensive study is described in which researchers conduct experiments involving a multi-sensor set of signals. The authors of [7] used the proprietary data corpus, in which they studied the effect of the location and number of accelerometers on the subjects' verification rates. Data acquisition was realized with the involvement of sensors located at a total of five locations - right wrist, upper arm, right side of pelvis, left thigh, right ankle. As can be predicted, the authors achieved the highest measures of system effectiveness when the whole set of sensors was used.

The authors indicated that for the single-sensor solution, the lowest verification rates were achieved for the sensor located on the right wrist, and the highest for the right thigh. On the other hand, in the case of a two-sensor solution, the highest number of errors was achieved for the right wrist and forearm. Whereas system performed best for the right pelvis and right ankle. The presented study, ignores the real-world applicability entirely. It is difficult to imagine a system that works in so-called real-life scenarios based on all five sensors. In addition, the study completely omit data acquisition issues involving the sensor located on the right/left wrist.

Author's previous work [8] focused on investigating the effect of sensor pair location on the effectiveness of a biometric system. Experiments were carried out using a publicly available corpus of data with the unique feature of different substrate types. Data acquisition was performed using sensors located at a total of five sites - torso, right and left thigh, right and left calf, and right wrist. The experiments showed that in concept using a pair of sensors in general (considering different types of substrate), the right wrist and trunk achieved the lowest verification rates. On the other hand, the best results were achieved for the right thigh and right shin. Again, the aspect of real-world use was neglected for the described studies. Due to the lack of a sensor located on the left wrist, the issue of left/right wrist selection was also ignored.

Finally, it should be noted that other researchers have conducted experiments that take into account whole sets of sensors, but are not directly connected with biometrics field. In [9], the authors realized the issue of detecting individual moments of gait cycles -heel strike, toe off, using sensors located on the: feet, calves and torso. The results of the study indicated that it the sensors located on the feet and calves allowed to achieve the best results. The conclusion can be drawn that the sensors mounted in these areas conveyed the most relevant information.

The publications listed above allow us to observe a number of general trends. First of all, the installation of sensors in the area of the feet, i.e. ankles, shins, allows the acquisition of signals that maintain the most information. Moreover, the use of a sensor in the wrist area typically degraded the performance of the biometric system.

The current article, in contrast to previous work [7, 8], primarily aims to test whether a biometric system working on the right wrist sensor will achieve higher verification rates than one operating on the left wrist. Additionally it was verified whether the data augmentation process could change existing relationships.

Finally, it should be stressed that the choice of sensors - right thigh, right and left wrist - was made since the data can approximate the signals recorded by smartphones or smartwatches. Conversely, it was decided to omit experiments involving the sensor located at the left thigh. According to the study [10], if a sensor is worn in a trouser pocket, it is more likely to be worn in the right pocket.

3   Methodology

The research carried out makes it possible to determine whether, in the case of a biometric gait analysis system, higher metric values will be obtained by placing the sensor in the right or left wrist area. The choice of classifier is due to the fact that a CNN (Multi-input CNN with early fusion) of this type has achieved very promising identification rates in the work of other authors [11] (in the field of gait biometrics). It was dedicated to work with two different sensors that measured two separate physical quantities (a triaxial accelerometer, and a triaxial gyroscope). It should be noted that the use of CNNs for this type of data is an unpopular solution, since architectures of this type mainly touched on the aspect of image processing. In this study, no comparison was made between different types of classifiers, e.g. Vanilla CNN, Graph Neural Network (GNN), Capsule Neural Network (CNN), for the reason that most of the attention of the paper wanted to focus on the issue of data augmentation.

A major part of the work addresses the issue of data augmentation. The performed experiments are run with a limited amount of input data. Only about 30 gait cycles are available for a single participant. As part of the conducted experiments, various config-urations of the author's data augmentation mechanism were examined. The conducted experiments allow to answer the question whether multiplication of training samples can influence the preferred location of sensor mounting.

The study conducted included 3 experiments:

- In the first elementary one, classification metrics were compared for three different sensor locations. No data augmentation mechanism was applied.
- The second examined whether data augmentation could benefit the performance of the biometric system. In this stage of the experiment, the effect of the number of samples generated on the indicators of the biometric system was investigated.
- The last experiment investigated the impact of the settings of the author's data augmentation mechanism on the effectiveness of the biometric system. It allowed us to answer the question: should data augmentation be performed in the same way for both sensor locations?

It should be noted that the conducted experiments involve a scenario in which training of classifiers takes place with data collected during one day, and validation is performed with data collected during the second day. Clearly, this is a much more challenging case and reflects a situation more similar to 'real-life scenarios'.

3.1 Dataset Description

The research used a proprietary data corpus created for the evaluation of biometric gait verification systems. A distinctive feature of our dataset is the participation of the 100 participants, the availability of two motion tracking sessions (for two separate days). The data acquisition took place in a laboratory setting with a constant ground type and fixed shoes types for each participant. Data acquisition was performed with a Perception Neuron 32 motion tracking system, which allows synchronized recording of up to 17 motion sensors. Single IMU measurement data can be understood as triaxial accelerometer and gyroscope recording data.

For the experiments described in this paper, measurement data from sensors located on the right and left wrist were selected. However, indirect use was made of measurement data from the sensor located on the right thigh, which was used to segment the gait cycles. Due to the different walking styles as well as the different heights of the subjects, a variation in the number of segmented gait cycles was observed. During the first session, 3376 gait cycles were acquired (for each participant 33.8 ± 6.1), whereas during the second one, a total of 3321 gait cycles were accumulated (for each participant 33.2 ± 6.6 gait cycles). The individual gait cycles were interpolated to a fixed number of 100 samples so that they could form the input of the neural network. The database is made available on request and contains metadata in the form of timestamps of the start and end of each gait cycle. Due to this availability of the database, the learning of classifiers can be reproduced by other researchers, and the process itself can be described as reproducible (Fig. 1).

It should be noted that this choice of sensors from the entire set of 17 is not accidental. The sensors located on the right and left wrist can successfully reflect the measurement values of the sensor embedded in smartwatch devices. The sensor used on the right thigh, on the other hand, can approximately mirror the sensor located in a smartphone device placed in a trouser pocket.

Fig. 1. Location and indication of sensor use. The yellow color of the cuboid indicates an unused sensor, while the pink color indicates a sensor in use. (Color figure online)

3.2 Data Augmentation Mechanism

In this study, the influence of data augmentation on the performance of behavioral biometric identification systems was examined. The elementary algorithm of the Delegato-Escano et al. [11] group was used as a baseline method. This method is dedicated to signals coming from an accelerometer and a gyroscope and consists of three steps. In the first, Gaussian noise is added to the signal, in the second the magnitude of the signal is scaled. In the last, sampling inequality is modelled using interpolation.

The second augmentation mechanism verified is the author's algorithm described in detail in [3] (Fig. 2). This algorithm, thanks to the use of quaternion algebras, makes it possible to model disturbances such as: different ways of mounting the sensor on the body (*offset*), vibration of the sensor (*noise*), slow rotation of the sensor during the gait cycle (*drift*).

3.3 Classifier Architecture and Data Validation Method

The decision-making module of the biometric system consisted of a deep CNN in a so-called multi-input configuration [11]. Figure 3 illustrates the schematic diagram of the architecture. The classifier has two inputs to which the accelerometer and gyroscope readings are applied separately. The presented approach has the following advantages:

- first layers of the CNN do not combine data from the two modalities
- (each of the sensors have different processing characteristics).
- it is possible to set a specific number of kernels separately for the accelerometer data and separately for the gyroscope data.

The experiments were conducted as follows, the data collected during the first day fully formed the training set (3376 gait cycles). Meanwhile, the data collected during the second day (3321 gait cycles) constituted the test set. Due to the random selection of the initial network weights, each experiment was repeated 10 times.

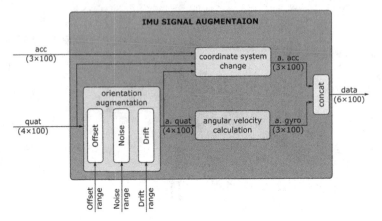

Fig. 2. The flow chart of the data augmentation mechanism [3].

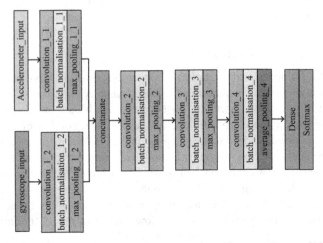

Fig. 3. Simplified multi-input CNN network architecture diagram [11].

4 Results of Experiments

Table 1 presents the results of the first experiment. It concerned the case of three sensor locations and the absence of any data augmentation form. The rows present the sensor locations, while the columns present the basic metrics - *F1-score*, *Accuracy*, *Precision* and *Recall*. The individual measures are described in Eq. (1). The formulas directly describe the differences between the respective metrics.

$$Precision = \frac{TP}{TP+FP}$$
$$Recall = \frac{TP}{TP+FN}$$
$$Accuracy = \frac{TP+TN}{TP+TN+FP+FN} \qquad (1)$$
$$F_1 = 2 \cdot \frac{Precision \cdot Recall}{Precision+Recall}$$

where:

TP – True Positive;
TN – True Negative;
FP – False Positive;
FN – False negative.

Table 1. Biometric system metrics in the baseline case (without augmentation)

	F1-score	Accuracy	Precision	Recall
Right Thigh	0.680 ± 0.009	0.722 ± 0.009	0.682 ± 0.009	0.722 ± 0.009
Left Wrist	0.571 ± 0.030	0.610 ± 0.035	0.587 ± 0.019	0.610 ± 0.035
Right Wrist	0.750 ± 0.012	0.780 ± 0.010	0.764 ± 0.017	0.780 ± 0.010

From Table 1, it can be observed that the highest F1-score metrics values accurse using right wrist (0.750) measurement data whereas lowest for the left wrist (0.571) signals. Using data collected with a sensor located in the right thigh area (0.680), average metrics be achieved.

Given the unbalanced data, the *Accuracy* coefficient takes on "optimistic values" relative to the *F1-score* measure, which is more restrictive. In addition, it can be observed that the *Recall* indicator takes on larger values than *Precision* (in all examined cases). This is associated with a higher count of False Positive indications.

In the next experiment II, a study involving the data augmentation process was performed. In this case, augmentation mechanisms described in [3] and [11] was applied with additional changes in the number of generated samples. Figure 4 shows the performance scores of the biometric system for the two sensor placement cases (Left wrist A) and Right wrist B)). The results are presented as a box plot based on the 10 learning and validation iterations of the performed experiments.

In Fig. 4 following convention is applied - the vertical axes show the value of the F1-score metric and the horizontal presents the number of new generated samples (for each original gait cycle). The first left blue box plot refers to the absence of data augmentation - baseline case (no generated samples). The results are presented for two data augmentation methods - proposed by 'Delegato-escano' [11] and the author's method [3]. The first algorithm in each subplots was colored in orange. Proposed method was highlighted in green or red (depending on the parameter settings).

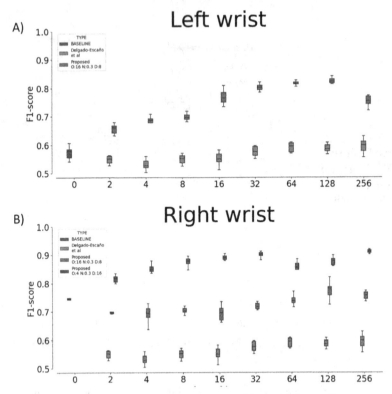

Fig. 4. Impact of data augmentation on the performance of biometric systems for a sensor mounted on the left A) and right wrist B).

First of all, data augmentation will not always lead to an improvement in the performance of the biometric system. The Delegato-Escano method, which achieve high verification rates within one day data [11], worsens the verification rates in the case of two days' data (current study). Furthermore, a continuous increase in the number of generated samples will not be associated with a continuous increase in the accuracy of the biometric system. In the case of Fig. 4A), a downward trend is observed for a large number of generated samples.

The augmentation while capable of improving metrics, is not a 'remedy' able to raise verification rates significantly. In the case of the Left Wrist, the proposed augmentation method allowed an increase from approximately 0.57 to 0.8, for the right wrist it was an increase from approximately 0.75 to 0.9.

Finally, it should be noted that using the same data augmentation settings for the Right wrist sensor (Fig. 4B) as for the left sensor resulted in a decrease in system efficiency. Changing the *Offset* parameter settings from 16 to 4, and increasing the *Drift* parameter from 8 to 16, improved the performance of the system. The interpretation of these parameters is that in the case of the right wrist, slow changes in sensor orientation during movement are typical, and a large initial offset related to a variance in the way the device is mounted is rather unlikely.

The last most challenging experiment concerned the use of a grid-search approach to check which parameters of the augmentation mechanism are relevant to the biometric system. In this case, again the results of the experiment represent the average value of the 10 performed iterations (simple validation repeated 10 times).

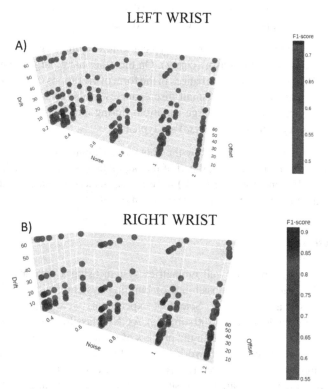

Fig. 5. Influence of augmentation algorithm parameters on biometric system metrics A) Left Wrist B) Right Wrist

Figure 5 provides scatter plots that graphically illustrate the impact of augmentation parameters on the performance of biometric verification systems. Each graph represents a set of points in 3D space. Each axis reflects a different parameter - *Offset* (mounting method), *Noise* (vibration), and *Drift* (slow changes in orientation over the length of gait cycles).

Several differences can be seen from Fig. 5. First of all, for the Left Wrist sensor, the drift parameter (Fig. 5A Z-axis) should assume low values. This is in contrast to the Right Wrist (Fig. 5B Z-axis) sensor where even very significant values of the Drift parameter can provide high F1-score metrics. This indicates that large values of sensor orientation changes during movement (*Drift*) is more typical of the right hand.

On the other hand, some differences can be observed with the Offset parameter (Fig. 5 Y-axis). For the Left Wrist sensor, the best verification rates were achieved when the parameter took values from about 8 to 32 (Fig. 5A Y-axis), and the lowest for values outside this range. For the Right wrist senor (Fig. 5B Y-axis), in contrast the best achieved measures were for an *Offset* parameter close to zero.

Finally, it is important to note the differences for the noise parameter (Fig. 5B X axis). For the left wrist sensor (Fig. 5A X-axis), the highest measurements were obtained for small values of the parameter. In contrast, for the right wrist sensor (Fig. 5B X-axis), good results were achieved for large parameter values.

From the experiments, the following correlation can be seen:

- In the case of the left wrist sensor, it is typical to have quite large discrepancies in the initial mounting of the sensor (*Offset*). On the other hand, large changes during movement (*Drift*) as well as disturbances in the form of vibrations (*Noise*) are atypical
- For the right wrist sensor, very small discrepancies in the initial sensor assembly (*Offset*) are typical. In contrast, large variations during movement (*Drift*) as well as noise in the form of vibrations (*Noise*) are typical

It is worth asking what is caused by the above correlations? It can be concluded it is related to the fact that the dominant part of the population is right-handed. According to the literature [10], most people (72%) have a right-hand dominant hand. It can be assumed that this limb is more expressive during movement.

5 Conclusions

This paper presents a proposed gait biometrics system using a wearable sensor. The conducted study examined the possibility of building systems using motion sensors located on the right and left wrist. Scientific experiments were conducted using the author's human gait cycles dataset (100 subjects). A CNN classifier with two independent inputs (multi-input CNN) was used in the process of subject classification [11].

The main part of the conducted work concerned the possibility of using data augmentation to improve the generative properties of artificial neural network models. The carried out experiments compared the results of using two augmentation mechanisms [11] and [3]. The first of these is the base-reference algorithm. The second of the described mechanisms is of our authorship, and the presented work is an extension of it.

The present study examined which augmentation settings have a beneficial effect on the performance of the biometric system. In the case of a sensor located on the Right Wrist, data augmentation in the form of modeling the slow movement of the sensor (*Drift*) and vibration (*Noise*) allowed to increase the metrics of the system. We speculate that this is related to the right-handedness of the majority of the population, which may increase limb expression during movement.

In the results of the experiments conducted without data augmentation, it can be seen that the system based on the sensor located on the right wrist allowed to achieve the highest measure of F1-score (0.750 ± 0.012) (Table 1). The use of sensors located on the right thigh in the system was characterized by lower metric (0.680 ± 0.009), while the left wrist sensors had the lowest metric (0.571 ± 0.030).

The use of data augmentation [3] allowed to increase the performance of the biometric system of the left wrist to 0.81 ± 0.030 and of the right wrist to 0.92 ± 0.050 (Fig. 5). The algorithm described in [3] outperformed the competing method [11].

Acknowledgment. This work was supported by grant 2021/41/N/ST6/02505 from Białystok University of Technology and funded with resources for research by National Science Centre, Poland. For the purpose of Open Access, the author has applied a CC-BY public copyright license to any Author Accepted Manuscript (AAM) version arising from this submission.

References

1. Um, T.T., Pfister, F.M., Pichler, D., et al.: Data augmentation of wearable sensor data for Parkinson's disease monitoring using convolutional neural networks. In: Proceedings of the 19th ACM International Conference on Multimodal Interaction, Glasgow, UK, 13–17 (2017)
2. Eyobu, O.S., Han, D.: Feature representation and data augmentation for human classification based on wearable IMU sensor data using a deep LSTM neural network. Sensors **18**, 2892 (2018)
3. Sawicki, A.: Augmentation of accelerometer and gyroscope signals in biometric gait systems. In: Saeed, K., Dvorský, J. (eds.) Computer Information Systems and Industrial Management, CISIM 2022. LNCS, vol. 13293, pp. 32–45. Springer, Cham (2022). https://doi.org/10.1007/978-3-031-10539-5_3
4. Zou, Q., Wang, Y., Wang, Q., Zhao, Y., et al.: Deep learning-based gait recognition using smartphones in the wild, arXiv:1811.0033 (2018)
5. Gadaleta, M., Merelli, L., Rossi, M.: Human authentication from ankle motion data using convolutional neural networks. In: 2016 IEEE Statistical Signal Processing Workshop (SSP), Palma de Mallorca, Spain, pp. 1–5 (2016). https://doi.org/10.1109/SSP.2016.7551815
6. Giorgi, G., Martinelli, F., Saracino, A., Sheikhalishahi, M.: Try walking in my shoes, if you can: accurate gait recognition through deep learning. In: Tonetta, S., Schoitsch, E., Bitsch, F. (eds.) Computer Safety, Reliability, and Security, SAFECOMP 2017. LNCS, vol. 10489, pp. 384–395. Springer, Cham (2017). https://doi.org/10.1007/978-3-319-66284-8_32
7. Zhang, Y., Pan, G., Jia, K., et al.: Accelerometer-based gait recognition by sparse representation of signature points with clusters. IEEE Trans. Cybern. **45**(9), 1864–1875 (2015)
8. Sawicki, A.: Influence of accelerometer placement on biometric gait identification. In: Zamojski, W., Mazurkiewicz, J., Sugier, J., Walkowiak, T., Kacprzyk, J. (eds.) New Advances in Dependability of Networks and Systems, DepCoS-RELCOMEX 2022. Lecture Notes in Networks and Systems, vol. 484, pp. 255–264. Springer, Cham (2022). https://doi.org/10.1007/978-3-031-06746-4_25
9. Panebianco, G.P., Bisi, M.C., Stagni, R., et al.: Analysis of the performance of 17 algorithms from a systematic review: influence of sensor position, analysed variable and computational approach in gait timing estimation from IMU measurements. Gait Posture **66**, 76–82 (2018)
10. Cui, Y., Chipchase, J., Ichikawa, F.: A cross culture study on phone carrying and physical personalization. In: Aykin, N. (ed.) Usability and Internationalization. HCI and Culture. UI-HCII 2007. LNCS, vol. 4559, pp. 483–492. Springer, Heidelberg (2007). https://doi.org/10.1007/978-3-540-73287-7_57
11. Delgado-Escaño, R., Castro, F.M., Cózar, J.R., et al.: An end-to-end multi-task and fusion CNN for inertial-based gait recognition. IEEE Access **7**, 1897–1908 (2019). https://doi.org/10.1109/ACCESS.2018.2886899 (2018)

Finger Minutiae Extraction Based on the Use of YOLO-V5

Krzysztof Trusiak[1]([✉])[iD] and Khalid Saeed[1,2][iD]

[1] Faculty of Computer Science, Białystok Technical University,
ul. Wiejska 45 A, 15-351 Bialystok, Poland
`krzysztof.trusiak@pb.edu.pl`
[2] Department of Electronics and Computation Sciences, Universidad de la Costa,
Barranquilla, Colombia

Abstract. In this study, we propose a novel method for detecting minutiae in fingerprint images using YOLOv5, a state-of-the-art object detection algorithm. Our approach utilizes a convolutional neural network (CNN) to identify and locate minutiae points, such as ridge endings and bifurcations, within a fingerprint image. We trained the CNN on a dataset of fingerprint images and corresponding minutiae annotations, and evaluated its performance using standard metrics such as precision, recall, mAP 0.5 and mAP 0.5:0.95. Our results indicate that the proposed method is able to accurately detect minutiae in fingerprint images with high precision - 91%, recall - 82%, mAP 0.5 - 89% and mAP 0.5:0.95 - 39%. Furthermore, we demonstrate that the YOLOv5-based approach is significantly faster than traditional minutiae detection methods, making it suitable for real-time applications. In conclusion, this study presents a promising approach for the automated detection of minutiae in fingerprint images using YOLOv5.

Keywords: Fingerprints · Minutia · Artificial intelligence

1 Introduction

Biometric identification has become increasingly important in our rapidly advancing world. With the growth of digital transactions and the increasing need for secure authentication methods, biometric technologies are being used more and more frequently in various applications. Fingerprint recognition is one such biometric technology that has received a lot of attention in recent years.

Fingerprint recognition relies on the extraction and matching of unique features, known as minutiae, the unique ridge endings and bifurcations in a fingerprint. Minutiae extraction is a critical step in the fingerprint recognition process and has traditionally been performed using hand-crafted algorithms. However, the increasing demand for high accuracy, fast solution and the availability of large amounts of training data have motivated researchers to explore deep learning techniques for minutiae extraction.

K. Saeed et al. (Eds.): CISIM 2023, LNCS 14164, pp. 36–48, 2023.
https://doi.org/10.1007/978-3-031-42823-4_4

Convolutional Neural Networks (CNNs) have been the dominant method for object detection and classification, and have been applied to biometric problems with great success. One such CNN is YOLO v5, which has been used for various applications, including object detection, image segmentation, and semantic segmentation. It showed remarkable performance and great accuracy (see Fig. 1).

Fig. 1. Fingerprint image with minutiae marked and classified by YOLOv5 [1]

In this study, we investigate the feasibility of using YOLO v5 for finger minutiae extraction. Our experiments involve training the network on a dataset of finger minutiae and evaluating its performance using various metrics, such as precision, recall, mAP 0.5 and mAP 0.5:0.95. The results of our experiments indicate that YOLO v5 can effectively extract finger minutiae with high accuracy and speed, outperforming traditional hand-crafted methods and other deep learning-based approaches.

The use of YOLO v5 for finger minutiae extraction has several advantages, including its ability to handle complex and variable fingerprint images, its real-time processing capability, and its potential for use in practical fingerprint recognition systems. Our study provides a foundation for further research on the use of YOLOv5 and other architectures from YOLO family in fingerprint recognition and other biometric recognition tasks.

2 Related Work

Before deciding to use YOLOv5 as a minutiae detector in our solution, we conducted a review of solutions based on convolutional neural networks for minutiae detection and classification. Several related works were considered, including:

1. FingerNet: An Unified Deep Network for Fingerprint Minutiae Extraction [3]: The authors proposed a specialized network for fingerprint analysis that combined the strengths of conventional handcrafted techniques and deep learning. They transformed traditional methods into convolutional kernels and integrated them into a shallow network with predefined weights. The process involved normalization, orientation estimation, segmentation, Gabor enhancement, and minutiae extraction.
2. A Direct Fingerprint Minutiae Extraction Approach Based on Convolutional Neural Networks [4]: This study introduced a novel approach for minutiae extraction using multiple deep convolutional neural networks. During the training stage, two networks, namely JudgeNet and LocateNet, were trained. These networks were subsequently employed in the prediction stage to estimate minutiae positions in fingerprint images.
3. Robust Minutiae Extractor: Integrating Deep Networks and Fingerprint Domain Knowledge [5]: The authors proposed a framework for minutiae extraction comprising two distinct modules. The first module, CoarseNet, was a residual learning-based convolutional neural network that generated candidate patches containing minutiae from the original fingerprint image. The second module, FineNet, was an inception-resnet-based network architecture that served as a robust minutiae classifier, categorizing the candidate patches generated by CoarseNet. Additionally, these networks provided minutiae orientation and location information as outputs.
4. "Fingerprint Feature Extraction by Combining Texture, Minutiae, and Frequency Spectrum Using Multi-Task CNN." [6]: This paper proposes a method that combines texture information, minutiae, and frequency spectrum using a Multi-Task Convolutional Neural Network (CNN). The approach aims to extract comprehensive and discriminative features from fingerprint images by leveraging multiple modalities. By integrating texture, minutiae, and frequency spectrum analysis, the proposed method offers a more robust and accurate approach for fingerprint feature extraction.

These related works demonstrate various approaches to leveraging convolutional neural networks for fingerprint minutiae detection. The proposed methods incorporate domain expertise, integrate traditional techniques, and exploit the representational power of deep learning. Each work focuses on different aspects of the minutiae extraction process, such as normalization, segmentation, orientation estimation, and classification. By analyzing these approaches, we gained valuable insights into the existing solutions and their potential applicability to our research problem. Ultimately, after careful consideration, we decided to employ YOLOv5 as the minutiae detector in our solution.

3 Proposed Method

Our minutiae extraction solution consists of two parts. First part is data pre-processing in form of Gabor enhancement. We do this to make data easier to process by neural network and acquire better results in the end. Main part of our solution is finger minutiae extraction in form of YOLO v5, a state-of-the-art object detection model that is trained to find minutiae on image and classify them. Main database used to train model is "Fingerprint Color Image Database .v1" [8] containing 250 fingerprint acquired from 50 people.

3.1 Data Enhancement

First step in out algorithm is data enhancement. We enhance our data for many reasons. First of all we want to unify our data. Fingerprint images can be very different, even the same fingerprint can look different depending on the reader or the condition of the finger. That's why we want to make sure all data we passing to neural network looks the same way and have the same size (see Figs. 2 and 3).

Fig. 2. Base fingerprint image [8]   **Fig. 3.** Image after enhancement [7]

To achieve these results we use fingerprint Gabor enhancement [2]. Gabor enhancement is a technique used to enhance the visibility and distinguishability of minutiae features in fingerprint images. By applying Gabor enhancement to the input data, the contrast of minutiae features is increased, making it easier for a minutiae extraction algorithm, such as YOLOv5, to accurately detect and locate these features. Algorithm use oriented Gabor filters to enhance a fingerprint image. The orientation of the Gabor filters are based on the orientation of the ridges. The shape of the Gabor filter is based on the frequency and wavelength of the ridges. Algorithm has 5 main steps. The first one is normalization.

Input fingerprint image is normalized to get a predetermined mean and variance. Second step is local orientation estimation where the orientation image is estimated from normalization result. In the next step - local frequency estimation, algorithm computes the frequency image based on results from previous steps. Forth step is region mask estimation. Algorithm creates the region mask by classifying each block in the normalized input fingerprint image into a recoverable or a unrecoverable block. Last step is filtering. An enhanced fingerprint image is obtained by applying a bank of Gabor filters, which are adjusted for the local ridge orientation and ridge frequency of the ridge-and-valley pixels, to the normalized input fingerprint image. After enhancement all images looks in the same way and have the same size.

3.2   Data Augmentation

Data augmentation is a technique used to increase the size and diversity of a training dataset by generating new, slightly modified versions of the original data. In the case of fingerprint images, data augmentation can be used to create new images that are similar to the original ones but have different variations in terms of orientation, scale, and other characteristics.

When training a YOLOv5 model for object detection on fingerprint images, data augmentation can be particularly useful because it can help to improve the robustness and generalization capabilities of the model. By exposing the model to a larger and more diverse set of training data, data augmentation can help to reduce overfitting and improve the model's ability to detect minutiae in a wide range of conditions.

Some of the specific types of data augmentation that we applied to fingerprint images for training a YOLOv5 model include:

- Rotation: image is randomly rotated 90° clockwise, counter-clockwise and upside down to help model be insensitive to image orientation.
- Cropping: image is randomly zoomed from 0% to 20%. We are doing it to add variability to positioning and size to help model be more resilient to subject translations and finger position.
- Flipping: - flipping the fingerprint image horizontally or vertically to simulate mirror images. It help model be insensitive to subject orientation.

By applying these and other types of data augmentation to fingerprint images, we can create a more diverse and robust training dataset that can help to improve the accuracy and reliability of our YOLOv5 model for minuti detection.

3.3   Model

To detect and classify minutia on fingerprint image we use YOLOv5. In the beginning it is worth mentioning that The YOLOv5 repository is a natural extension of the YOLOv3 PyTorch repository by Glenn Jocher [9]. The decision to use this architecture was made based on many reasons. First of all YOLOv5 is

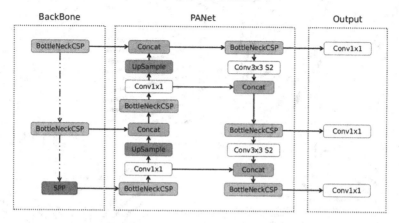

Fig. 4. Overview of YOLOv5 model structure

based on PyTorch library and not on darknet like previous versions. This results in easier use and configuration. Another reason is speed, YOLOv5 is very fast in both training and prediction. This architecture is also very performant achieving better results than previous versions of YOLO and other object detection solutions. The YOLO network comprises three essential components: a Backbone, a Neck, and a Head (see Fig. 4). The Backbone is a Convolutional Neural Network (CNN) that extracts and compiles image features at various levels of detail. The Neck is a series of layers that blend and merge image features, which are then passed on to the prediction stage. The Head, in turn, uses the features from the Neck to make predictions about the bounding boxes and class labels. The steps involved in training a model are just as crucial to the final outcome of an object detection system as any other factor, despite often receiving less attention. Let's delve into the two main training procedures in YOLOv5. Loss Calculations: In YOLO, a comprehensive loss function is computed by combining the GIoU, obj, and class loss functions. This loss function can be designed carefully to maximize the mean average precision objective. Data Augmentation: This process involves modifying the original training data to expose the model to a broader range of semantic variations than it would experience with the training set alone. So in addition to our augmentation YOLOv5 also augments the data. In each training iteration, YOLOv5 processes the training data through a data loader that performs online data augmentation. The data loader applies three types of augmentations: scaling, color space adjustments, mosaic augmentation (see Fig. 5).

Next topic worth discussing is auto learning bounding box anchors. In the YOLOv3 PyTorch repository, Glenn Jocher introduced the concept of using K-means and genetic learning algorithms to determine anchor boxes based on the distribution of bounding boxes in a custom dataset. This is particularly

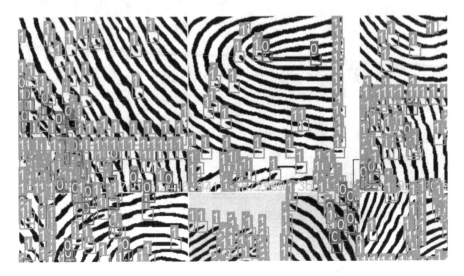

Fig. 5. An example of mosaic augmentation generated by YOLOv5 with marked minutia

significant for custom tasks, as the distribution of bounding box sizes and locations can vary greatly from the pre-set bounding box anchors. The YOLOv5 network makes predictions about bounding boxes by estimating how they deviate from a set of pre-defined anchor box dimensions. In backbone YOLOv5 utilizes the CSP Bottleneck to construct image features. The CSP resolves the issue of duplicated gradients in other extensive ConvNet backbones, leading to fewer parameters and computational operations for equivalent significance. This is crucial for the YOLO family, where efficient inference speed and a compact model size are of paramount importance. In the neck section YOLOv5 implement the PA-NET neck for feature aggregation. YOLOv5 comes in different sizes, each optimized for a specific use case. The YOLOv5 sizes are named according to their number of layers: YOLOv5s, YOLOv5m, YOLOv5l, and YOLOv5x. These sizes range from 85 in S version to 430 layers in X version. The larger the model size, the better the results should be, but at the cost of speed and computational resources (see Fig. 6). Therefore, it is important to properly select the size of the model for the appropriate task [11].

4   Training and Metrics

The training process involved a series of experiments that differed in terms of training time, model versions and data forms. This experiments allowed us to acquire information what influences results in a good way and what makes our model work worse. Biggest impact on result have data. Some ways of augmenting like bounding box area flip and rotate can result to creating false minutiae which influence result in a bad way. The amounts of the two minutiae types that

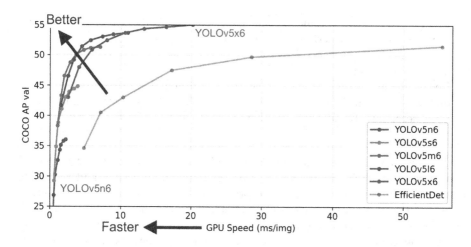

Fig. 6. YOLOv5 sizes comparison + EfficientDet [10]

we classify differ significantly in favor of the ridge ending. The ratio of endings to bifurcations in used dataset is seven to one. Attempts to balance the data by reducing the number of ending markings isn't a good decision because all minutiae occurrences in the image must be marked. Another important parameter that was tested is model size. The size of the model significantly affects the final outcome, as a result of which the metric values can vary significantly even within the same experiment. Last parameter to adjust is a number of epochs that should be set according to dataset size. YOLOv5 Training have early stopping mechanism so we can't overtrain model. mAP 0.5, mAP 0.5:0.95, precision, and recall are common metrics used to evaluate the performance of object detection models such as YOLOv5.

- mAP 0.5: mAP stands for mean average precision. It is a metric that calculates the average precision across different levels of confidence scores for detected objects. mAP 0.5 is the mAP calculated with a minimum IoU (Intersection over Union) threshold of 0.5 between predicted bounding boxes and ground-truth objects. An IoU of 0.5 means that the predicted bounding box overlaps with the ground-truth object by at least 50%. This metric is commonly used to evaluate the detection accuracy of object detection models.
- mAP 0.5:0.95: mAP 0.5:0.95 is the mAP calculated with a range of IoU thresholds from 0.5 to 0.95. This metric provides a more complete picture of the detection accuracy of an object detection model as it considers a wider range of IoU thresholds.

- Precision: Precision is a metric that measures the proportion of true positive predictions (i.e., correctly detected objects) out of all the predicted positives (i.e., all detected objects). Precision indicates how accurate the model's positive predictions are.
- Recall: Recall is a metric that measures the proportion of true positive predictions out of all the ground-truth positives (i.e., all objects that should have been detected). Recall indicates how well the model can detect all relevant objects.

In summary, mAP 0.5 and mAP 0.5:0.95 are used to evaluate the overall detection accuracy of an object detection model, while precision and recall are used to evaluate the model's positive prediction accuracy and ability to detect all relevant objects, respectively. These metrics are commonly used to compare different object detection models and to track the performance of a model during training and testing. Best result among all experiments is chosen based on metrics values and their importance (see Eq. 1).

- mAP 0.5 - 0.9 importance
- mAP 0.5:0.95 - 0.1 importance
- precision - 0 importance
- recall - 0 importance

$$X = mAP0.5 * 0.9 + mAP0.5 : 0.95 * 0.1 \tag{1}$$

5   Results

After series of experiments the best model was selected. Model of size L was trained for 500 epochs, batch size was automatic. Model was trained, validated and tested on augmented dataset consisting 516 training images, 50 validation images and 25 testing images. Detailed model structure is placed on Ultralytics github page [10].

Result of the best model are:

- mAP 0.5 - 0.8901945404277702
- mAP 0.5:0.95 - 0.38812467373225934
- precision - 0.910365749520557
- recall - 0.8179159270468729
- speed on GPU - 13 ms

Charts of above metrics and losses during training and validation are shown on Fig. 7 and F1 curve is shown on Fig. 8. Figure 9 shows the confusion matrix of our model. On The results for the YOLOv5 model for minutiae detection show that the model has achieved an mAP (mean average precision) of 0.890 for a confidence threshold of 0.5, indicating that the model is able to accurately detect minutiae in an image with a high degree of confidence. For a wider range of confidence thresholds from 0.5 to 0.95, the mAP drops to 0.388, indicating

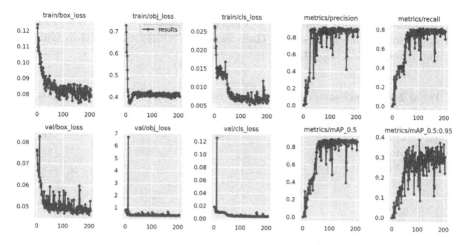

Fig. 7. A charts of metrics and loses - bounding box regression loss, objectness loss and classification loss during training and validation process

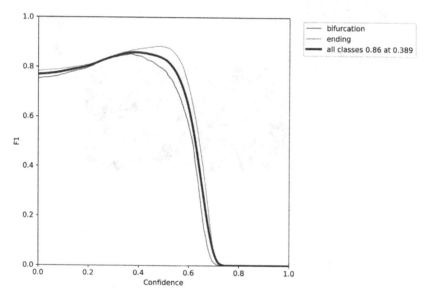

Fig. 8. F1 curve

that the model has a lower precision for detecting minutiae with lower confidence scores.

The model's precision is reported to be 0.910, which indicates that it has a low rate of false positive predictions, while the recall is reported to be 0.818, indicating that the model is able to detect a high proportion of actual positive instances of minutiae. We compared our work to other CNN-based solutions mentioned in a related work section - CoarseNet + FineNet, JudgeNet + LocateNet, Finger-Net and one commercial system - Gafis, which is widely employed in Chinese criminal investigation departments.

Table 1. Comparison of our method and other minutiae extraction solutions

	Proposed method	CoarseNet + FineNet [5]	JudgeNet + LocateNet [4]	FingerNet [3]	Gafis [4]
Precision	91%	86%	95%	87%	74%
Recall	81%	85%	92%	91%	93%
Performance	13 ms	1.2–1.5 s	–	0.6 s	–

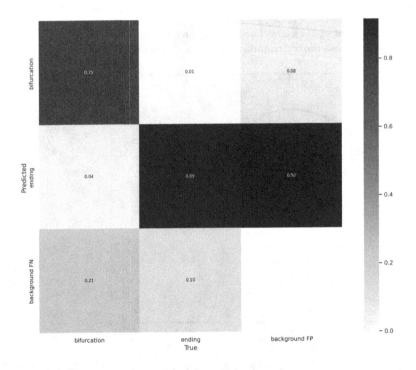

Fig. 9. Model confusion matrix

Observing comparison in Table 1, there are few interesting conclusions. First is that other solutions achieved better results in recall metric so our model has lowest percentage of actual positives that the model correctly identified as positives. In Case of precision metric, proposed method ranked second after JudgeNet + LocateNet. Where the our model performed best compared to other solutions was performance. YOLOv5 method achieved greatly outperformed competition in terms of speed. It is worth remembering that the model was trained on a very small amount of data, largely lower compared to other solutions but still achieved competitive results. Overall, these results suggest that the YOLOv5 model is effective in minutiae detection tasks, particularly for detecting minutiae with a high degree of confidence. However, as with any machine learning model, it is important to evaluate its performance in the specific task at hand, as minutiae detection may have its own unique challenges and requirements.

6   Conclusion

In conclusion, our study has demonstrated the effectiveness of the YOLO-V5 object detection algorithm for the extraction and classification of finger minutiae. By using YOLOv5, we were able to accurately and efficiently locate and classify the minutiae points from a database of finger images. Our solution show that YOLOv5 even with small amount of training data can generate great result that are competitive to other systems. With more training data and by using newer versions of YOLO architecture, results can be greatly improved. Another place for improvement is data enhancement step where artificial intelligence could generate enhanced images faster, with more details and with lower quality input images.

The use of YOLOv5 has several advantages, including its ability to handle real-time image processing. Moreover, the algorithm has a relatively low computational cost and can be easily deployed on resource-constrained devices, making it ideal for applications in mobile devices and other embedded systems.

Overall, our study provides valuable insights into the use of deep learning algorithms for finger minutiae extraction and highlights the potential of YOLOv5 for this task. Our findings suggest that YOLOv5 (and other YOLO family architectures) can be a promising solution for improving the accuracy and efficiency of biometric identification systems that rely on finger minutiae extraction. We hope that our study will inspire further research in this area and encourage the development of more advanced deep learning techniques for biometric applications.

Acknowledgments. The work was supported by grant no. WZ//I-IIT/5/2023 from Bialystok University of Technology and funded with resources for research by the Ministry of Education and Science in Poland.

References

1. Result of algorithm presented in paper
2. Hong, L., Wan, Y., Jain, A.K.: Fingerprint image enhancement: algorithm and performance evaluation. IEEE Trans. Pattern Anal. Mach. Intell. **20**(8), 777–789 (1998)
3. Tang, Y., Gao, F., Feng, J., Liu, Y.: FingerNet: an unified deep network for fingerprint minutiae extraction. In: Proceedings of IEEE IJCB (2017)

4. Bai, C., Yong, A., Wu, M., Jiang, L., Zhao, T.: A direct fingerprint minutiae extraction approach based on convolutional neural networks. In: 2016 International Joint Conference on Neural Networks (IJCNN) (2016)
5. Cao, K., Nguyen, D., Jain, A.K.: Robust minutiae extractor: integrating deep networks and fingerprint domain knowledge. In: 2018 International Conference on Biometrics (ICB) (2018)
6. Ito, K., Aoki, T., Takahashi, A., Koda, Y.: Fingerprint feature extraction by combining texture, minutiae, and frequency spectrum using multi-task CNN. In: 2020 IEEE International Joint Conference on Biometrics (IJCB) (2020)
7. Results of database image after Gabor enhancement in proposed algorithm
8. Gawande, U., Hajari, K., Golhar, Y.: Fingerprint Color Image Database .v1 (2023). https://www.mathworks.com/matlabcentral/fileexchange/52507-fingerprint-color-image-database-v1, MATLAB Central File Exchange. Accessed 19 Feb 2023
9. Ultralytics YOLOv3 github page. https://github.com/ultralytics/yolov3. Accessed 19 Feb 2023
10. Ultralytics YOLOv5 github page. https://github.com/ultralytics/yolov5. Accessed 19 Feb 2023
11. What is YOLOv5. https://blog.roboflow.com/yolov5-improvements-and-evaluation/. Accessed 19 Feb 2023

Computer Information Systems
and Security

Towards a Blockchain, Smart Contract, and NFT Based Waste Treatment System for Developing Countries: A Case Study in Vietnam

Bang L. Khanh[1(✉)], Hong K. Vo[1], Phuc N. Trong[1], Khoa T. Dang[1],
Khiem H. Gia[1], Nguyen D. P. Trong[1], Hieu L. Van[1], Loc V. C. Phu[1],
Duy N. T. Quoc[1], Nguyen H. Tran[1], Anh N. The[1], Huynh T. Nghia[1],
Hieu M. Doan[1], Bao Q. Tran[1], Ngan N. T. Kim[2], and Luong H. Huong[1(✉)]

[1] FPT University, Can Tho, Vietnam
banglkce160155@fpt.edu.vn, huonghoangluong@gmail.com
[2] FPT Polytechnic, Can Tho, Vietnam

Abstract. The problem of waste treatment (i.e., industrial waste, domestic waste, medical waste) is a serious problem for the whole world and developing countries in particular. In developing countries (i.e., Vietnam) with large populations and inadequate waste treatment infrastructure, solving this problem is essential. Most of these types of waste are not composted, and the only treatment method is destruction. This seriously affects people's health and the environment. The waste treatment plants that do not meet the current requirements are also a reason for the increased amount of waste in the environment. Another solution to be considered is reusing them instead of destroying them all. However, in Vietnam, this process has not been taken seriously - the individual/organization has not yet complied with the waste separation requirements. In this paper, we propose a model of waste classification and treatment based on blockchain technology and smart contracts. In addition, complying/violating the garbage classification requirements is also considered to reward/penalize individuals and organizations.

Keywords: Waste treatment in Vietnam · Blockchain · Smart contracts · NFT · Ethereum · Fantom · Polygon · Binance Smart Chain

1 Introduction

Domestic, industrial and medical waste is a concern for the economic development of a country [24], as well as a burden for the environment [5]. Currently, developed countries have a strict process in the process of inspecting, classifying and destroying waste from the above sources [18]. Most hazardous waste is converted into electricity in the form of incineration plants. However, in developing countries (i.e., Philippines, Vietnam), where the economy is small and the population structure is large, the classification and treatment of waste has not been given enough attention methodical way. Currently, traditional waste treatment methods, i.e., do not include segregation of waste at the starting sources (eg., in residential areas, hospitals or industrial sites) [21]. The pre-treatment and waste separation stages at these initial sources have not been given due attention and investment. Most of the waste is not sorted and dumped directly into the ecological environment, causing serious pollution to the environment and surrounding areas. These types of waste are then collected and destroyed in the traditional way (i.e., no treatment of smoke and odors). This leads to air and water pollution in the waste disposal area.

For hazardous solid waste such as rubber (eg., tires), electronic components (eg., computers, phones) need to be sorted and treated with special processes that do not harm the environment. For example, a thermal power plant in Germany uses old tires to fuel a thermal power plant. To solve this problem, the stage of sorting (i.e., pre-treatment of waste) is extremely important. Specifically, the size of developed countries, industrial zones and households will classify waste into 4 categories, including i) paper (eg., paper box, packaging); ii) recyclable wastes (eg., rubber, glass, metal cans); iii) organic food (eg., feed); and iv) other types of waste. Each type of waste has a different treatment and classification process so that it can be reused or discarded to avoid causing harm to the environment or people's health. However, this process cannot be applied in developing countries due to cultural differences and processing procedures. In particular, the limitations in waste treatment in developing countries are not only limited to infrastructure but also to people's consciousness. For example, in Vietnam, wastes are not classified and only one method of disposal is applied, which is to dispose of them outside the environment (see Sect. 3 for more details).

In addition, the end of the Covid-19 epidemic has revealed many shortcomings in the health system around the world [6]. Health systems (i.e., infrastructure, medical supplies, and equipment) are already dealing with a huge influx of patients - affecting care and treatment services. Thereby, the disease becomes more difficult to control and the number of deaths increases. Especially for developing countries (i.e., Vietnam), which has seen a record increase in the number of positive cases from the end of 2020 to the beginning of 2021. One of the reasons for this serious situation is the basis. infrastructure for treatment is limited (i.e., especially the waste treatment process). Indeed, studies conducted by [7] have all concluded that unsafe medical waste handling procedures during the epidemic period also contribute to the spread of the Covid-19 epidemic.

To solve the problem of waste classification and treatment, many approaches have proposed a management model based on Blockchain technology and Smart Contracts. Specifically, for each type of waste and treatment scope, these approaches offer a different treatment and transportation process: such as medical waste [33], solid waste (eg., electronic components, computers, phones) [12], household waste [23], and waste from industrial areas [13] (see Related work for details). Several other research directions have focused on developing a waste treatment process for developing countries (eg., India [3]; Brazil [13]; and Vietnam [16]). For the covid-19 epidemic, the above approaches also suggest a model of waste management and classification between stages (i.e., hospital/isolation zone - transportation company or transport company - company). process rubbish). However, the above studies only support the government to easily track and trace types of waste (eg., weight, type of waste, etc.).

To solve this problem, we aim for a waste classification and treatment model based on Blockchain technology, Smart contract, and NFT, which is applicable to Vietnam. Specifically, the proposed model supports parties to assess the level of waste treatment at the output - all information stored on the chain is processed and validated by the relevant parties. On-chain storage makes information more transparent than traditional storage [14]. In addition, ensuring the system works well without being overloaded is also supported by an approach based on decentralized storage (i.e., distributed ledger). Smart contract technology, supporting parties to manage the waste treatment process from sorting to transporting and treating waste. NFT technology helps to store information about a garbage bag, making it easy to determine the weight, time, original place, and type of waste (i.e., garbage, industrial, medical, domestic). In addition, we also apply NFTs to identify compliance/violations with waste classification requirements, thereby sanctioning/rewarding the above behaviors.

The main contribution in this paper consists of 4 aspects: i) introducing the waste classification and treatment model in Vietnam based on Blockchain technology and Smart Contract; ii) apply NFT to store content (i.e., compliance/violation of garbage classification requirements) and corresponding metadata; iii) proof-of-concept implementation based on Ethereum platform; and iv) deploy the proposed model on four EVM and ERC721 enabled platforms (i.e., BNB Smart Chain, Fantom, Polygon, and Celo) to select the most suitable platform for our proposal.

2   Related Work

2.1   Waste Sorting and Treatment Solutions Based on Blockchain Technology

There are many different approaches to dealing with each type of household waste in our daily lives. For e-waste, for example, Gupta et al. [12] has proposed an Ethereum-based waste management system for electrical and electronic equipment. In the proposed model, the authors focus on three user groups, namely producers, consumers and retailers. Direct constraints between related objects are shown on the smart contracts of the system. In it, the retailer plays the role of distributing and collecting used products from users and returning them to manufacturers. These activities, if done correctly, will receive a fixed reward (i.e., ETH). Through the above proposed model, product developers do not have to collect their used products again.

For solid waste types (eg., computers and smartphones), to be able to monitor the stages of transportation from waste sources to waste treatment centers, Laura et al. [15] introduced a management system based on a combination of Ethereum and QR codes. In addition, the authors focus on exploiting a system that supports four actors, including a collection manager, an archive manager, a transaction manager, and a processing manager. For the process of determining the type of waste to be destroyed, each garbage bag will be identified with a QR code that links directly to the data stored on the chain. In this way, stakeholders can trace and determine the current location and expected time to complete the processing. Besides, the problem of overcrowding in the waste treatment areas is also ensured because the transport companies can determine the remaining amount of waste consumed each day based on the expected date of extraction from the garbage bag. corresponding.

Another Ethereum-based study that can track cross-border garbage in a secure, tamper-proof and privacy-preserving way is introduced by Schmelz et al. [22]. Specifically, the information can only be accessed by authorized parties based on encryption technology. For cross-border waste transport matters, authorities can trace the location, volume of transport and the estimated time that a unit of waste (eg., vehicle, bag) can be transported. Transfers between exchange locations based on information stored on distributed ledgers. In addition, shipping processes can be run by predefined smart coins. However, one disadvantage with this process is that they do not support penalties for violations in the transportation and disposal of waste. Similarly, Francca et al. [9] proposes an Etherem-based model for solid waste management in small municipalities.

For models developed on the Hyperledger Fabric platform, Trieu et al. [16] proposes a Hyperledger Fabric-based waste treatment model called MedicalWast-Chain. This proposed model is aimed at the treatment of medical waste from medical centers, reuse of tools, the process of transferring medical supplies waste (i.e., protective gear, gloves, masks, etc.) pages), and waste treatment processes in factories. They aim for a solution to help parties trace the source of waste and toxic levels during the pandemic. Similar to the above approach, Ahmad et al. [1] aims at the traceability model of personal protective equipment for healthcare workers (i.e., doctors, nurses, testers) during the pandemic. In addition, the above approach also identifies (not) allowed behaviors in the process of garbage classification and collection. Specifically, they will take pictures of medical waste collection sites and compare them to identify the above behaviors. To assist with validation of waste treatment processes (i.e., stakeholder interactions), Dasaklis et al. [8] proposed a blockchain-based system set up on smartphones.

2.2   The Approaches Apply to Specific Regions

To the best of our knowledge, there are currently no specific studies applying Blockchain technology to a specific region. Therefore, we conduct a survey of traditional waste treatment approaches.

For traditional problems, the travel route directly affects the efficiency of the waste collection process (i.e., pretreatment step). For this problem, some approaches have calculated the time and cost (i.e., vehicle route) that manage the path of the garbage collection vehicle. To solve this problem, some solutions have applied Geographic Information System (GIS) technology to manage the path of moving vehicles, for example in the city of Asansol in India, Ghose et al. [11] has developed a solid waste collection and treatment route by combining it with the best route based on GIS. For an area larger than a city (i.e., region), Nuortio et al. [20] proposed a route (i.e., well-scheduled and routed) waste collection for Eastern Finland using the neighborhood threshold metadata approach. As another example in the Brazilian city of Porto Alegre, a truck planning model for solid waste collection purposes was proposed by Li et al. [17]. For countries in Europe (eg., Castellón (Spain)) Gallardo et al. [10] proposed a Municipal Solid Waste (MSW) management system designed in a combination of ArcGIS[1] with a planning approach to optimize travel time between locations when collecting waste in the city. This approach has been shown to be optimal and more effective than traditional approaches (Bonomo et al. [4]; Avila-Torres et al. [2]).

2.3 Analysis of Approaches Based on Blockchain Technology Applied to Vietnam

The above approaches do not pay too much attention to the process of reproduction/refurbishment. Neither of the above approaches provide a reasonable solution for handling (i.e., rewarding and handling violations) the behavior of user (eg., household, company). For models based on Blockchain and smart contracts, the above solutions (for both Hyperledger and Ethereum platforms) focus only on the waste management model from the beginning to the end. waste treatment plant. Besides, the application of a specific approach and implementation for a territory (i.e., Vietnam) must consider many aspects. For that reason, we aim at a solution to change people's medical waste sorting habits (not only for companies/enterprises/medical centers but also for households). For traditional waste classification and treatment problems applied to a specific geographical area, modern technologies have not been applied much to reduce labor time and fill current gaps. (i.e., overloading, shipping process, information validation). In this paper, we not only offer a model to manage the waste sorting process but also provide a solution for rewarding and handling violations of users/companies/enterprises via NFT tokens.

3 Approach

3.1 Traditional Waste Treatment Model in Vietnam

To the best of our knowledge, the treatment process in urban (eg., cities in Vietnam) and rural areas (eg., Cho Lach district - Ben Tre province) is completely different. In urban areas or densely populated areas, people collect garbage in a fixed area and treat it by waste treatment companies. For rural areas, people have a direct way to treat garbage by destroying all of it in the natural environment.

In addition, in industrial or medical care areas, all kinds of waste are gathered in a certain area and collected by the cleaning company daily or twice a day.

---

[1] A command line based GIS system for manipulating data https://www.arcgis.com/index.html.

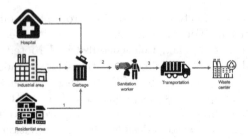

Fig. 1. Traditional waste treatment model in Vietnam

Since the classification of waste in urban areas and rural areas is different, we develop a model of waste classification and treatment in urban areas (i.e., similar to the steps taken in industrial parks). industry and health care). Figure 1 shows the five steps of traditional waste treatment common in urban areas, industrial parks and hospitals. Most of these wastes are collected at a fixed location (step 1). Corresponding to each type of waste, the collection procedures are different. For example, for household waste (i.e., leftovers), the health protection requirements of sanitation workers are lower when compared to medical waste collection. The cleaners collect the waste at step 2 and transfer it to the waste sorting and recycling plants step three and step 4 respectively. Finally, it depends on the type of waste that the plant treats. Waste will carry out the process of recycling or destroying them (step 4).

In this paper, we focus on exploiting the waste treatment process at the garbage collection place (i.e., residential area, factory, hospital). Indeed, the recycling and waste treatment process is less stressful when people separate their waste into the right categories (i.e., paper, bio, metal and glass). However, this role is being overlooked in Vietnam. In particular, it is difficult for waste collectors to distinguish the corresponding type of waste because it has not been classified. Therefore, we recommend NFTs to store evidence of behavior related to the violation/compliance with people's waste classification requirements. The next section presents the detailed steps of our proposal.

3.2 Waste Treatment Model Based on Blockchain, Smart Contract and NFT

Figure 2 shows 6 steps of waste classification and treatment based on blockchain technology, smart contract and NFT. Specifically, the only difference in our proposed model compared to the traditional process (Fig. 1) is in step 2. Waste types after sorting must be divided into 4 groups (i.e., paper, bio, metal and glass) corresponding to the labels or colors at different bins. Hygienists conduct an inspection of an individual/organization's classification process to confirm their behavior is in compliance/violation (step 3). These proofs are then updated to the respective functions provided in the smart contracts (step 4). Step 5 generates NFTs corresponding to the individual/organization's

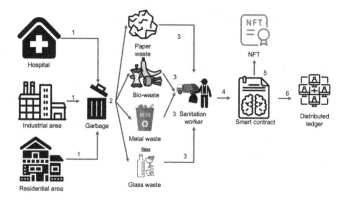

Fig. 2. Waste treatment model based on blockchain, smart contract and NFT

waste classification violation/compliance and associated information (i.e., metat-data - see Implementation for details). Finally, the entire process is updated and stored on the distributed ledger and easily validated by the parties involved.

4 Implementation

Our reality model focuses on two main purposes i) data manipulation (i.e., garbage) - initialization, query and update - on blockchain platform and ii) generation of NFTs for each action rewards and violations by users (i.e., individuals/organizations) based on their behavior in the sorting/disposal of waste.

4.1 Initialize Data/NFT

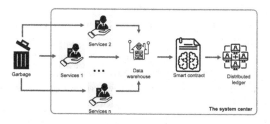

Fig. 3. Initialize data/NFT

Figure 3 shows the garbage data initialization steps. These types of waste include wastes in industrial zones; domestic waste; or medical waste. These types of waste are required to be classified into different categories (i.e., discard, reuse) depending on their level of toxicity. Then descriptions of the type of waste are added to each specific garbage bag. Each trash bag has a unique address to separate them with the type of waste. In addition, information about the sorter as well as which household/company/enterprise, time, and location are also added to the metadata of the trash bag. As for the storage process, services support concurrent storage (i.e., distributed processing as a peer-to-peer network) on a distributed ledger - supporting more than one user for concurrent storage. reduce system latency. In general, waste data is organized as follows:

```
garbageDataObject = {
"garbageID": medicalWasteID,
"userID": userID,
"type": type of waste,
"address": address,
"quantity": quantity,
"unit": unit,
"packageID": packageID,
"time": time,
"location": location,
"state": null,
"reUse": Null};
```

Specifically, in addition to information to extract content (i.e., place of origin, weight, type of waste, etc.), we also store information related to the status of garbage bags in residential areas, factories, hospitals, etc. (i.e., "state" and "reUse" - defaults to Null). Specifically, "state" changes to a value of 1 if the corresponding garbage bag has been removed from the original collection location (i.e., for the type of waste to be treated); value 0 - pending. Meanwhile, "reUse" presents the value 1 when the garbage type is reused (i.e., value 0 - pending). Non-hazardous wastes (i.e., non-toxic to the environment and user's health). After the waste sorting phase, the cleaning staff will check if they are in accordance with the process and wait for validation before synchronizing on the chain (i.e., temporarily stored on the data warehouse). Then the pre-designed constraints in the Smart Contract are called through the API (i.e., name of function) to sync them up the chain. This role of accreditation is extremely important because they directly affect the waste treatment process, as well as the premise for rewarding or sanctioning individuals and organizations.

For processes that initiate NFTs (i.e., reward, sanction), the content of the NFT is defined as follows:

```
NFT GARBAGE = {
"garbageID": garbageID,
"userID": userID,
"address": address,
"packageID": packageID,
"type": true/false,
"quantity": true/false,
```

```
"time": time,
"verifier": staffID}; // Cleaning staff
```

If the values on the checked trash bags are correct then the sorter is rewarded and vice versa if they are penalized for violations. In case the verifier does not provide correct information, the person penalized is the verifier.

4.2   Data Query

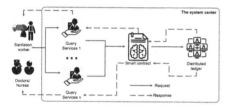
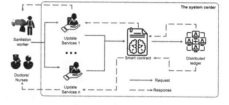

Fig. 4. Data query   **Fig. 5.** Data updated

Similar to the data initialization steps, the data query process also supports many simultaneous participants in the system for access (i.e., distributed model). Support services receive requests from Cleaning staff or individuals/organizations to access data. Depending on the query object we have different access purposes. Specifically, Cleaning staff queries with the purpose of checking the process of sorting or transferring wastes (eg., recyclable, hazardous) to the shipping company. In contrast, individuals/organizations can query the data to find information related to the waste treatment process. Figure 4 shows the steps of querying garbage data. These requests are sent as requests (i.e., pre-designed services as API calls) from the user to the smart contracts available in the system (i.e., name of function) before retrieving the data from the distributed ledger. All retrieval requests are also saved as query history for each individual or organization. In case the corresponding information is not found (eg., wrong ID), the system will send a message not found results. For the NFT query process, all support services are provided as APIs.

4.3   Data Updated

The data update routine is invoked only after verifying that the data exists on the thread (i.e., after executing the corresponding data query procedure). In this section, we assume that the search data exists on the string. Where none exists, the system sends the same message to the user (see Sect. 4.2 for details). Similar to the two processes of query and data initialization, we support update services in the form of APIs to receive requests from users before passing them to smart contract (i.e., name of function) for processing. The purpose of this process is to update the time and location of the garbage bags during the transportation and sorting/disposal of the waste. Thereby, the administrator can track the status of waste treatment/transportation from medical centers/residential areas/factories to waste treatment companies. Figure 5 shows the garbage data update process. For NFTs (i.e., available) the update process includes only moving from the owner's address to the new (i.e., new owner). If any information is updated on an existing NFT, it will be stored as a new NFT (see Sect. 4.1 for details).

5   Evaluation

Fig. 6. The transaction info (e.g., BNB Smart Chain)

Since the proposed model rewards/penalizes compliance/waste-sorting violations, we implement the recommendation model on EVM-enabled blockchain platforms instead of mining platforms belonging to the Hyperledger eco-system. In addition, assessments based on system responsiveness (i.e., number of requests responded successfully/failed, system latency - min, max, average) have been evaluated by us in the previous research paper. Therefore, in this paper, we determine the suitable platform for our proposed model. Specifically, we install a recommendation system on four popular blockchain platforms today, supporting Ethereum Virtual Machine (EVM), including Binance Smart Chain (BNB Smart Chain)[2]; Polygon[3]; Fantom [4]; and Celo [5]. Our implementations on these four platforms are also shared as a contribution to the article to collect transaction fees corresponding to the four platforms' supporting coins[6], i.e., BNB[7]; MATIC[8]; FTM[9]; and CELO[10]. For example, Fig. 6 details our three assessments of a successful installation on BNB Smart Chain (i.e., similar settings are shown for the other three platforms). Our implementations to evaluate the execution

---

[2] https://github.com/bnb-chain/whitepaper/blob/master/WHITEPAPER.md.
[3] https://polygon.technology/lightpaper-polygon.pdf.
[4] https://whitepaper.io/document/438/fantom-whitepaper.
[5] https://celo.org/papers/whitepaper.
[6] Implementation of theme models our release at Nov-24-2022 04:37:14 AM.
[7] https://testnet.bscscan.com/address/0x741c8dc8630dbde529466eec066fe5f98b1f6 ee4.
[8] https://mumbai.polygonscan.com/address/0x3253e60880ce432dded52b5eaba9f75b 92ca530a.
[9] https://testnet.ftmscan.com/address/0x3253e60880ce432dded52b5eaba9f75b92ca 530a.
[10] https://explorer.celo.org/alfajores/address/0x3253e60880cE432DdeD52b5EAba9f7 5b92Ca530A/transactions.

cost of smart contracts (i.e., designed based on Solidity language) run on testnet environments of four platforms in order to choose the most cost-effective platform to deploy reality. Our detailed assessments focus on the cost of performing contract creation, NFT generation, or NFT retrieval/transfer (i.e., updating NFT ownership address) presented in the respective subsections related to i) Transaction Fee; ii) Gas limit; iii) Gas Used by Transaction; and iv) Gas Price.

5.1   Transaction Fee

Table 1. Transaction fee

	Contract Creation	Create NFT	Transfer NFT
BNB Smart Chain	0.02731184 BNB ($8.43)	0.00109162 BNB ($0.34)	0.00057003 BNB ($0.18)
Fantom	0.009576994 FTM ($0.001837)	0.000405167 FTM ($0.000078)	0.0002380105 FTM ($0.000046)
Polygon	0.006840710030099124 MATIC ($0.01)	0.000289405001389144 MATIC ($0.00)	0.000170007500884039 MATIC ($0.00)
Celo	0.0070974384 CELO ($0.004)	0.0002840812 CELO ($0.000)	0.0001554878 CELO ($0.000)

Table 1 shows the cost of creating contracts for the four platforms. It is easy to see that the highest transaction fee of the three requirements is contract creation for all four platforms. In which, the cost of BNB Smart Chain is the highest with the highest cost when creating a contract is 0.02731184 BNB ($8.43); whereas, the lowest cost recorded by the Fantom platform with the highest cost for contract initiation is less than 0.009576994 FTM ($0.001837). Meanwhile, the cost to enforce Celo's contract initiation requirement is lower than Polygon's with only $0.004 compared to $0.01. For the remaining two requirements (Create NFT and Transfer NFT), we note that the cost of implementing them for all three platforms, Polygon, Celo, and Fantom is very low (i.e., negligible) given the cost close to $0.00. However, this cost is still very high when deployed on BNB Smart Chain with 0.00109162 BNB ($0.34) and 0.00057003 BNB ($0.18) for Create NFT and Transfer NFT, respectively.

5.2   Gas Limit

Table 2. Gas limit

	Contract Creation	Create NFT	Transfer NFT
BNB Smart Chain	2,731,184	109,162	72,003
Fantom	2,736,284	115,762	72,803
Polygon	2,736,284	115,762	72,803
Celo	3,548,719	142,040	85,673

Table 2 shows the gas limit for each transaction. Our observations show that the gas limits of the three platforms (i.e., BNB, Polygon, and Fantom) are roughly equivalent - where Polygon and Fantom are similar in all three transactions. The remaining platform (i.e., Celo) has the highest gas limit with 3,548,719; 142,040; and 85,673 for all three transaction types.

5.3   Gas Used by Transaction

Table 3. Gas Used by Transaction

	Contract Creation	Create NFT	Transfer NFT
BNB Smart Chain	2,731,184 (100%)	109.162 (100%)	57,003 (79.17%)
Fantom	2,736,284 (100%)	115,762 (100%)	68,003 (93.41%)
Polygon	2,736,284 (100%)	115,762 (100%)	68,003 (93.41%)
Celo	2,729,784 (76.92%)	109.262 (76.92%)	59,803 (69.8%)

Table 3 shows the amount of gas used when executing the transaction (i.e., what percentage of gas in total gas is shown in Table 2). Specifically, three platforms BNB, Polygon, and Fantom use 100% of Gas Limit for two transactions Contract Creation and Create NFT. Meanwhile, Celo uses 76.92% of the Gas limit for the above two transactions. For the last transaction of Transfer NFT, the highest Gas level was recorded by Fantom and Polygon with 93.41% of Gas limit; while BNB and Celo use 79.17% and 69.8% of Gas limit.

5.4   Gas Price

Table 4. Gas Price

	Contract Creation	Create NFT	Transfer NFT
BNB Smart Chain	0.00000001 BNB (10 Gwei)	0.00000001 BNB (10 Gwei)	0.00000001 BNB (10 Gwei)
Fantom	0.0000000035 FTM (3.5 Gwei)	0.0000000035 FTM (3.5 Gwei)	0.0000000035 FTM (3.5 Gwei)
Polygon	0.000000002500000011 MATIC (2.500000011 Gwei)	0.000000002500000012 MATIC (2.500000012 Gwei)	0.000000002500000013 MATIC (2.500000013 Gwei)
Celo	0.0000000026 CELO (Max Fee per Gas: 2.7 Gwei)	0.0000000026 CELO (Max Fee per Gas: 2.7 Gwei)	0.0000000026 CELO (Max Fee per Gas: 2.7 Gwei)

Table 4 shows the value of Gas for all four platforms. Specifically, BNB, Fantom, and Celo have the same Gas value in all three transactions with values of 10 Gwei (i.e., the highest of the three platforms), 3.5 Gwei, and 2.7 Gwei, respectively. Meanwhile, the Gas value of the Polygon platform (i.e., MATIC) has the lowest value and fluctuates around 2.5 Gwei.

6 Discussion

According to our observation, the transaction value depends on the market capitalization of the respective coin. The total market capitalization of the 4 platforms used in our review (i.e., BNB (Binance Smart Chain); MATIC (Polygon); FTM (Fantom); and CELO (Celo)) are \$50,959,673,206; \$7,652,386,190; \$486,510,485; and \$244,775,762.[11] This directly affects the coin value of that platform - although the number of coins issued at the time of system implementation also plays a huge role. The total issuance of the four coins BNB, MATIC, FTM, and CELO, is 163,276,974/163,276,974; 8,868,740,690/10,000,000,000; 2,541,152, 731/3,175,000,000; and 473,376,178/1,000,000,000 coins, respectively. The value of the coin is conventionally based on the number of coins issued and the total market capitalization with a value of \$314.98; \$0.863099; \$0.1909; and \$0.528049 for BNB, MATIC, FTM, and CELO respectively. Based on the measurements and analysis in Sect. 5 section, we have concluded that the proposed model deployed on Faltom brings many benefits related to system operating costs. In particular, generating and receiving NFTs has an almost zero (i.e., negligible) fee. Also, the cost of creating contracts with transaction execution value is also meager (i.e., less than \$0.002).

In future work, we proceed to implement more complex methods/algorithms (i.e., encryption and decryption) as well as more complex data structures to observe the costs for the respective transactions. Deploying the proposed model in a real environment is also a possible approach (i.e., implementing the recommendation system on the FTM mainnet). In our current analysis, we have not considered issues related to the privacy policy of users (i.e., access control [26,27], dynamic policy [25,34]) - a possible approach would be implemented in upcoming research activities. Finally, infrastructure-based approaches (i.e., gRPC [19,30]; Microservices [28,31]; Dynamic transmission messages[32] and Brokerless [29]) can be integrated into the model of us to increase user interaction (i.e., API-call-based approach).

7 Conclusion

The article proposes a waste treatment model in Vietnam that exploits Blockchain technologies, and smart contracts to increase data processing capacity (i.e., decentralized storage and processing) as well as easy data retrieval with high reliability (i.e., on-chain data transparency). In addition, to deal with compliance/violation of waste classification and disposal requirements, we store the evidence (i.e., images, metadata) as NFTs that cannot be altered/eliminated. To realize our proof-of-concept, we mine the Ethereum platform. For smart contracts we implement based on Solidity language - scripts (i.e., contract creation, NFT creation, NFT transfer) are deployed on 4 EVM-enabled platforms including BNB, MATIC, FTM, and CELO. Our assessments and analysis revolve around execution fees and gas usage (i.e., presented in the evaluation section).

---

[11] Our observation time is 12:00 PM - 11/26/2022.

Our observations indicate that smart contract deployments on the Faltom platform provide the best economic benefits - suitable for deployment in a real-world environment in Vietnam.

References

1. Ahmad, R.W., et al.: Blockchain-based forward supply chain and waste management for Covid-19 medical equipment and supplies. IEEE Access **9**, 44905–44927 (2021)
2. Avila-Torres, P., et al.: The urban transport planning with uncertainty in demand and travel time: a comparison of two defuzzification methods. J. Ambient. Intell. Humaniz. Comput. **9**(3), 843–856 (2018)
3. Awasthi, A.K., Zeng, X., Li, J.: Environmental pollution of electronic waste recycling in India: a critical review. Environ. Pollut. **211**, 259–270 (2016)
4. Bonomo, F., Durán, G., Larumbe, F., Marenco, J.: A method for optimizing waste collection using mathematical programming: a Buenos Aires case study. Waste Manage. Res. **30**(3), 311–324 (2012)
5. Chisholm, J.M., et al.: Sustainable waste management of medical waste in African developing countries: a narrative review. Waste Manage. Res. **39**(9), 1149–1163 (2021)
6. Danh, N.T.: Electronic waste classification in Vietnam and some solutions to protect clean and green environment. Int. J. Mech. Eng. **7**(2) (2022)
7. Das, A.K., et al.: Covid-19 pandemic and healthcare solid waste management strategy-a mini-review. Sci. Total Environ. **778**, 146220 (2021)
8. Dasaklis, T.K., Casino, F., Patsakis, C.: A traceability and auditing framework for electronic equipment reverse logistics based on blockchain: the case of mobile phones. In: 2020 11th International Conference on Information, Intelligence, Systems and Applications, IISA, pp. 1–7. IEEE (2020)
9. França, A., et al.: Proposing the use of blockchain to improve the solid waste management in small municipalities. J. Clean. Prod. **244**, 118529 (2020)
10. Gallardo, A., Carlos, M., Peris, M., Colomer, F.: Methodology to design a municipal solid waste pre-collection system. A case study. Waste Manage. **36**, 1–11 (2015)
11. Ghose, M., et al.: A GIS based transportation model for solid waste disposal-a case study on Asansol municipality. Waste Manage. **26**(11), 1287–1293 (2006)
12. Gupta, N., Bedi, P.: E-waste management using blockchain based smart contracts. In: 2018 International Conference on Advances in Computing, Communications and Informatics (ICACCI), pp. 915–921. IEEE (2018)
13. Hakak, S., et al.: Industrial wastewater management using blockchain technology: architecture, requirements, and future directions. IEEE Internet Things Mag. **3**(2), 38–43 (2020)
14. Hepp, T., et al.: On-chain vs. off-chain storage for supply-and blockchain integration. IT -Inf. Technol. **60**(5–6), 283–291 (2018)
15. Laouar, M.R., Hamad, Z.T., Eom, S.: Towards blockchain-based urban planning: application for waste collection management. In: Proceedings of the 9th International Conference on Information Systems and Technologies, pp. 1–6 (2019)
16. Le, H.T., et al.: Medical-waste chain: a medical waste collection, classification and treatment management by blockchain technology. Computers **11**(7), 113 (2022)
17. Li, J.Q., Borenstein, D., Mirchandani, P.B.: Truck scheduling for solid waste collection in the City of Porto Alegre, Brazil. Omega **36**(6), 1133–1149 (2008)

18. Moldovan, M.G., Dabija, D.C., Pocol, C.B.: Resources management for a resilient world: a literature review of Eastern European countries with focus on household behaviour and trends related to food waste. Sustainability **14**(12), 7123 (2022)
19. Nguyen, L.T.T., et al.: BMDD: a novel approach for IoT platform (broker-less and microservice architecture, decentralized identity, and dynamic transmission messages). PeerJ Comput. Sci. **8**, e950 (2022)
20. Nuortio, T., et al.: Improved route planning and scheduling of waste collection and transport. Expert Syst. Appl. **30**(2), 223–232 (2006)
21. Salvia, G., et al.: The wicked problem of waste management: an attention-based analysis of stakeholder behaviours. J. Clean. Prod. **326**, 129200 (2021)
22. Schmelz, D., et al.: Technical mechanics of a trans-border waste flow tracking solution based on blockchain technology. In: 2019 IEEE 35th International Conference on Data Engineering Workshops (ICDEW), pp. 31–36. IEEE (2019)
23. Sen Gupta, Y., et al.: A blockchain-based approach using smart contracts to develop a smart waste management system. Int. J. Environ. Sci. Technol. **19**(8), 7833–7856 (2022)
24. Singh, N., Ogunseitan, O.A., Tang, Y.: Medical waste: current challenges and future opportunities for sustainable management. Crit. Rev. Environ. Sci. Technol. **52**(11), 2000–2022 (2022)
25. Son, H.X., Dang, T.K., Massacci, F.: REW-SMT: a new approach for rewriting XACML request with dynamic big data security policies. In: Wang, G., Atiquzzaman, M., Yan, Z., Choo, K.-K.R. (eds.) SpaCCS 2017. LNCS, vol. 10656, pp. 501–515. Springer, Cham (2017). https://doi.org/10.1007/978-3-319-72389-1_40
26. Son, H.X., Hoang, N.M.: A novel attribute-based access control system for fine-grained privacy protection. In: Proceedings of the 3rd International Conference on Cryptography, Security and Privacy, pp. 76–80 (2019)
27. Son, H.X., Nguyen, M.H., Vo, H.K., Nguyen, T.P.: Toward an privacy protection based on access control model in hybrid cloud for healthcare systems. In: Martínez Álvarez, F., Troncoso Lora, A., Sáez Muñoz, J.A., Quintián, H., Corchado, E. (eds.) CISIS/ICEUTE - 2019. AISC, vol. 951, pp. 77–86. Springer, Cham (2020). https://doi.org/10.1007/978-3-030-20005-3_8
28. Thanh, L.N.T., et al.: IoHT-MBA: an Internet of Healthcare Things (IoHT) platform based on microservice and brokerless architecture. Int. J. Adv. Comput. Sci. Appl. **12**(7) (2021)
29. Thanh, L.N.T., et al.: SIP-MBA: a secure IoT platform with brokerless and microservice architecture (2021)
30. Thanh, L.N.T., et al.: Toward a security IoT platform with high rate transmission and low energy consumption. In: Gervasi, O., et al. (eds.) ICCSA 2021. LNCS, vol. 12949, pp. 647–662. Springer, Cham (2021). https://doi.org/10.1007/978-3-030-86653-2_47
31. Nguyen, T.T.L., et al.: Toward a unique IoT network via single sign-on protocol and message queue. In: Saeed, K., Dvorský, J. (eds.) CISIM 2021. LNCS, vol. 12883, pp. 270–284. Springer, Cham (2021). https://doi.org/10.1007/978-3-030-84340-3_22
32. Thanh, L.N.T., et al.: UIP2SOP: a unique IoT network applying single sign-on and message queue protocol. IJACSA **12**(6) (2021)
33. Wang, H., et al.: Research on medical waste supervision model and implementation method based on blockchain. Secur. Commun. Netw. **2022**, 16 (2022)
34. Xuan, S.H., et al.: REW-XAC: an approach to rewriting request for elastic ABAC enforcement with dynamic policies. In: 2016 International Conference on Advanced Computing and Applications (ACOMP), pp. 25–31. IEEE (2016)

A New File Format for Binarized Images

Patryk Milewski[1]([✉])(iD) and Khalid Saeed[1,2](iD)

[1] Faculty of Computer Science, Bialystok University of Technology,
Wiejska 45A, 15-351 Białystok, Poland
{patryk.milewski,k.saeed}@pb.edu.pl
[2] Department of Computer Science and Electronics – CUC, Universidad de la Costa,
Barranquilla, Colombia
https://pb.edu.pl/

Abstract. In this paper we present a new lossless file format specialized in binarized images. The proposed algorithm creates files smaller in average than standard lossless formats. We propose a modification to the algorithm which allows it to be used in every type of images, not only the binarized ones. We compare the file sizes with the PNG format. In order to encourage the use and compatibility with the most common image libraries, we provided the implementation details and the idea behind the algorithm.

Keywords: file · format · binarize · image · picture · run length · encode · decode · deflate · png · jpg · gif

1 Introduction

File format is a way of organizing data in the operating system. Before the advent of complex computer systems, hardware and software were intertwined to such a degree that image formats had no place due to the immediate display of programmed images with no option for loading data. As operating system and hardware were separated, the need to have a common interface to communicate between them have arisen. Initially, the first image formats were distinguished from text file by ending files with ".img" extension, as a shortcut for image. As more and more formats were developed, non-standard file extensions were used and the first file headers were introduced. File header is a unique sequence of bits at the start of the file which identifies a file format. One of the most common image formats used nowadays are:

- BMP – straightforward and heavy lossless image format created by Microsoft. On older machines loading data from BMP achieves high performance because of the BMP data structure which is padded to 4 bytes in order to be fast to read for 32-bit microprocessors. Furthermore, this format is unique due to being still in use today in spite of the minimal to none compression. Currently used because of the simplicity and availability on Windows platforms.
- GIF – image format commonly used on the Web. Uses Lempel-Ziv-Welch lossless compression method. This compression method was patented till 2004 and those patents were the main motivation behind creation of PNG. This file format supports animations.

K. Saeed et al. (Eds.): CISIM 2023, LNCS 14164, pp. 66–76, 2023.
https://doi.org/10.1007/978-3-031-42823-4_6

- PNG [1,2] – lossless, main competitor to GIF format which uses the deflate algorithm instead of LZW.
- JPEG – the most popular image format with lossy compression which was very important in enabling image transmit on the Web.

There are many additional file formats used as a native format for graphics editors. It includes (Table 1):

Table 1. File formats native to various graphic editors.

Application	File Format
GIMP	.xcf
Krita	.kra
Adobe Illustrator	.ai
Adobe InDesign	.indd
Photoshop	.psd
Paint.NET	.pdn

As those file formats are designed specifically for given application, they are not implemented by other applications as a common link, so their usage is limited. Another issue is the lack of formalization and the possibility of unexpected changes to the algorithms.

2   State of the Art

The first, successful and very popular data compression algorithm could be attributed to Huffman [3] and further improvements with dynamic Huffman coding [4]. Dynamic length can be seen in Golomb encoding [5], further improved in [6]. Huffman encoding designed specifically for PNG format is seen in [7] Modern approaches are visible in TMW algorithm [8] which adopts a multiple pass to analyze data. As shown in [9], data compression often consists of two phases – modeling part, where data is analyzed as is read and coding part, where it is compressed in the best possible way.

In [10] there is an evaluation of standard PNG, JPEG and TIFF image formats. We can see an application for a single channel images representing topographic data. Comparison of lossless compression ratios proves that PNG format compares reasonably well to the other algorithms, although the format JPEG-LS outperforms in terms of compression and execution time. The JPEG-LS format was firstly introduced in [11] and further improved upon in [12,13].

Table 2. Compression ratio comparison with standard image formats as shown in [10]. Higher is better.

Image	TIFF (LZW)	JPEG2000	JPEG-LS	PNG
Peaks	1.9	2.64	2.91	2.8
Lake	11	16.2	19.4	18.8
Valley	12.6	12.5	15.5	30.8
Ridges	2.28	4.97	4.98	3.25
Average	6.95	9.08	10.7	13.91

As shown in Table 2, on average PNG format achieves the best compression ratio when compared to compression methods used in TIFF and JPEG formats (Table 3).

Table 3. Proprietary compression ratio comparison with PNG format as shown in [10]. Higher is better.

Image	WinRAR	WinZIP	WinACE	PNG
Peaks	2.7	2.04	2.00	2.80
Lake	12	11.2	13.4	18.8
Valley	15.6	17.5	13.5	30.8
Ridges	3.28	3.07	2.80	3.25
Average	8.38	8.45	7.92	13.91

It is clear that PNG format weakness does not lie within it's Deflate compression algorithm, as it is shown in the proprietary compression method comparison table that PNG achieves far better compression ratio.

As shown in Table 4, lossless JPEG-LS variation is faster. The JPEG-LS algorithm with LOCO-I lossless image compression is further described in [9]. There are algorithms which were developed specifically for grayscale images, as shown in lossless compression of grayscale medical images [14].

The JPG variants can achieve lossy and lossless compression. [16] The lossy compression variants are a lot better in terms of compression ratio. JPEG-LS is not widely known and is proprietary and license protected as many other variants of JPEG. Standard JPG compression is based on discrete cosine transform, while JPEG2000 [23] has compression based on discrete wavelet transform (DWT) [17].

In terms of lossy compression methods, research is being made on numerical analysis of quality loss after the compression. [18] and quality assessment with artifacts when very low quality factors are used [19].

In terms of JPG, there are tools for identification of used quality factor as described in [20], they are present in GIMP and ImageMagick. In terms of PNG, there are ways to optimize file size, as shown in [21,22].

Table 4. Execution time of standard image formats as shown in [10]. Lower is better.

Image	TIFF (LZW)	JPEG2000	JPEG-LS	PNG
Peaks	5.0	4.1	0.77	2.19
Lake	3.7	2.7	0.33	0.89
Valley	3.1	2.8	0.86	0.74
Ridges	6	4.3	0.49	1.77
Average	4.45	3.48	0.61	1.39

3 A New File Format – RLBG

In order to make a unique identifier for our file format we propose to call it Run-Length Binary Graphics, with file extension "rlbg".

Proposed compression and file format is specialized in binarized images. The file format structure consists of a header which is **4 bytes** for format detection. Next **8 bytes** are reserved for the image width and height. Next **6 bits** are reserved for the maximum $\log_2$ of number of occurrences described below. Another bit is used in order to signal whether or not the data part is compressed by the Deflate algorithm and the last bit is reserved for future modifications and user-specific changes. The other bits are used for the compressed data.

Algorithm's first step is to count the occurence of repeated bit patterns. Instead of writing multiple zeros and ones, they are packed into integers. Consider the following examples:

$$\mathbf{0011\ 1000} \rightarrow 23$$
$$\mathbf{0100\ 0101} \rightarrow 113111$$
$$\mathbf{1011\ 1110} \rightarrow 0115$$

The last zeroes are omitted. Next step consists of coding data. For every number of occurence n, compute $\log_2 n$. For every n, coding number c needs to be computed. Consider the following coding pattern:

$$
\begin{array}{llll}
n = 0 \vee \log_2 n \in [0, 1) & \Rightarrow & c = 0, & \text{binary:} \quad 0 \\
\log_2 n \in [1, 2) & \Rightarrow & c = 2, & \text{binary:} \quad 10 \\
\log_2 n \in [2, 3) & \Rightarrow & c = 6, & \text{binary:} \quad 110 \\
\log_2 n \in [3, 4) & \Rightarrow & c = 14, & \text{binary:} \quad 1110 \\
\log_2 n \in [4, 5) & \Rightarrow & c = 30, & \text{binary:} \quad 11110 \\
\log_2 n \in [5, 6) & \Rightarrow & c = 62, & \text{binary:} \quad 11110 \\
\log_2 n \in [6, 7) & \Rightarrow & c = 126, & \text{binary:} \ 111110
\end{array}
$$

If the maximum value of $\log_2 n = 8$, then the following compression can be used:

$$\log_2 n \in [7, 8) \quad \Rightarrow \quad c = 128, \text{ binary: } 11111$$

If the value is greater, in order to increase the number of options and add further encodings, the following compression should be used:

$$\log_2 n \in [7,8) \quad \Rightarrow \quad c = 254, \text{ binary: } 1111110$$

If $\max(\log_2 A) = 5$, where A is a set of every occurence number, then it can be shortened accordingly in this row:

$$\log_2 n \in [4,5) \quad \Rightarrow \quad c = 7, \text{ binary: } 111$$

Note that the last bit of every number n can be omitted due to the log ranges. Consider the following:

$$n \in \mathbb{N} \wedge \log_2 n \in [4,5) \Rightarrow n \in [16,32) \tag{1}$$

If we consider a number n with property $n \,\&\, 16 = 0$, where & is binary AND then the greatest, closest numbers to this range would be 32 and 15, so it does not fulfill the condition $x \in [16,32)$.

After computing c value, all of the numbers are written sequentially with omition of the greatest bit of n. Using the previously introduced 3 examples, all of the steps are presented below:

0011 1000 → 23
→ c=2 n=2, c=2, n=3
→ c=2 n=0, c=2, n=1
→ 100,101
→ 100101

0100 0101 → 113111
→ c=1 n=1, c=1 n=1, c=2 n=3, c=1 n=1, c=1 n=1, c=1 n=1
→ c=1 n=1, c=1 n=1, c=2 n=1, c=1 n=1, c=1 n=1, c=1 n=1
→ 11, 11, 101, 11, 11, 11
→ 1111101111111

1011 1110 → 0115
→ c=1 n=0, c=1 n=1, c=1 n=1, c=6 n=5
→ c=1 n=0, c=1 n=1, c=1 n=1, c=6 n=1
→ 10, 11, 11, 11001
→ 10111111001

After computing the run-length encoding for all of the data, as an optional part, we may compress the data by the Deflate algorithm.

Table 5. The structure of proposed file format.

Header	Image Width	Image Height	Max Log	Deflate	Reserved	Data
4 bytes	4 bytes	4 bytes	6 bits	1 bit	1 bit	Vary
RLBG					Always 0	

In Table 5 we present the structure of proposed file format, name for every part, length and, if possible, the default value. Note that the header is written in ASCII, so the equivalent ASCII numbers are 82 76 71 66. All of the data are placed most-significant bit first, so the value "5" in Max log_2 part would be written as 000101 in binary form. In "Deflate" part, Deflate algorithm is used if the bit is set to one. Our experiments have shown that using the Deflate compression, shrinks the data on average by 8%, so this step is not a significant step although it is a reliable method to slightly decrease the file size. Note that this algorithm will work for non binarized images, but the nature of the data would greatly increase the size.

4   Experiments and Results

Our experiments show that increase of coding by 1 bit is better in terms of compression size than by any other, due to the fact that the most number of occurences are below 4 bits, so best compression of smaller occurences is of the upmost priority.

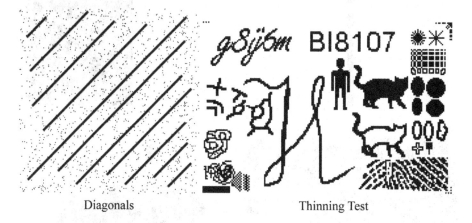

Diagonals   Thinning Test

Fig. 1. Samples used in the experiments – diagonal lines with infrequent noise and thinning test image

The algorithm best works for images which have frequent occurence of sequences of same value bits with length between 3 and 63, or which have great repetitions. Our analysis has shown that the first type of data it is the most common pattern.

In Figs. 1 and 2, we present samples used for the experiments. The "Diagonals" picture was specifically chosen to represent the run-length encoding weakness to regular data with applied noise. Moreover, as the algorithm runs horizontally, horizontal lines would be the most suited for the compression.

The best compression scenario could be seen in "Half" and "Line" pictures, as they have great horizontal repetition pattern. The first sample represents a single vertical stroke which tests suitability for intertwined long and short repetitions, whereas the latter represents half-white, half-black scenario with repeating values of the same number of occurence.

The hardest data to compress is represented in "Noise" picture which is a pseudo-random Gaussian noise. In this picture there are unpredictable bit repetitions of usually short length. As this algorithm uses lossless compression, the noise has to be compressed without modifications.

The "Apple" and "Thinning Test" images are practical examples of binarized images. Thinning test image was designed specifically in [15] for testing biometric systems and image processing algorithms.

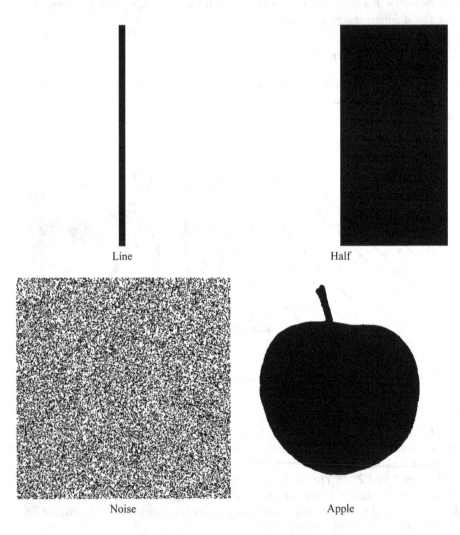

Line   Half

Noise   Apple

Fig. 2. Samples used in the experiments

We present below a comparison of compression sizes of our algorithm with the most common ones:

Table 6. Size results of chosen algorithms.

Image	PNG (8-bit)	PNG (1-bit)	GIF	JPG (lossless)	RLBG (proposed algorithm)
Line	379 B	181 B	843 B	1536 B	29 B
Half	376 B	177 B	873 B	2079 B	40 B
Noise	14213 B	8318 B	9551 B	76441 B	8416 B
Apple	2014 B	1301 B	2040 B	15537 B	1035 B
Diagonals	3777 B	3044 B	3836 B	81688 B	3096 B
Thinning Test	2413 B	1760 B	2146 B	30050 B	1735 B
Average	4634 B	2956 B	3858 B	41466 B	2870 B

As shown in the table, our algorithm achieves similar result in terms of compression to the PNG file format and in many cases it can surpass PNG format in terms of compression size, yet our algorithm is a lot simpler and faster. Note that those results were obtained with the Deflate algorithm. In terms of compression, the Deflate algorithm usually shrinks the data by additional 6–12%.

All of the results were obtained from open source applications. 1-bit PNG sizes were obtained by using Paint.NET 5.0.3. 8-bit PNG, GIF and JPG were obtained by using GIMP 2.10.22. In every case, the best compression method were used. As it is a comparison of lossless image formats, JPG were set to 100% quality. Lossy JPG usually achieves better size than PNG. As this format is specialized in binarized images, lossy compression methods are not acceptable due to the usual applications of those type of images. In biometrics, changes applied to the image because of the lossy compression can drastically alter the result so it is very important to preserve the original, binarized image. Lossy compression can be mitigated by upscaling or by using any of the cyclic correction codes but then it defeats the purpose of using this type of compression due to inevitable size increase.

Table 7. Compression ratios for given algorithms. Lower is better.

Image	Pixel count	PNG (8-bit)	PNG (1-bit)	GIF	JPG (lossless)	RLBG (proposed algorithm)
Line	65 536	0,58%	0,28%	1,29%	2,34%	0,04%
Half	65 536	0,57%	0,27%	1,33%	3,17%	0,06%
Noise	65 536	21,69%	12,69%	14,57%	116,64%	12,84%
Apple	262 144	0,77%	0,5%	0,78%	5,93%	0,39%
Diagonals	65 536	5,76%	4,64%	5,85%	124,65%	4,72%
Thinning Test	25 600	9,43%	6,88%	8,38%	117,38%	6,78%
Average	109 978	7,76%	5,05%	6,44%	74,02%	4,97%

In the Table 7 we see a compression ratios for given algorithms. Our algorithm on average achieves very similar compression ratio as 1-bit PNG algorithm. We can see that the standard lossless JPG with 100% quality performs the worst in terms of file size.

In all of the tests, GIF achieved on average slightly worse results than PNG. On the first edge cases, "Line" and "Half" images, as it is expected the run-length algorithms will perform much better in terms of compression size than more complex algorithms. As they are designed with good compression of any type of image in mind, it is much harder to achieve better performance than algorithms specifically designed for such, as our method with run-length encoding. Complex "Noise" and "Diagonals" test images were chosen specifically in order to test images where it would be advantageous to use the general-purpose algorithms. As it is visible in Tables 6 and 7, the PNG format is better although the difference is negligible (Table 8).

Table 8. A file format comparison chart.

File Format	Size	Speed	Implementation	Purpose	Popularity
PNG	Best	Fast	Hard	General	Widespread
Standard JPEG	Average	Fast	Hard	Photography	Widespread
JPEG-LS	Best	Fast	Hard	General	Specialized Users
BMP	Worst	Very Fast	Easy	General	Mainly Windows
GIF	Average	Fast	Hard	General, Animation	Widespread
RLBG (proposed format)	Best	Best	Easy	Binarized Images	New

4.1 Applications

The proposed file format is specialized in binarized images. It is format with easy implementation and execution speed. In biometrics, binarized images are used as a crucial step for next phases of the algorithms. This file format can significantly reduce the file size.

Fig. 3. Minutiae image used in biometrics

In the Fig. 3 is visible a part of the binarized fingerprint image. This type of image has little to no noise and is structurally sound, so our algorithm will be very suitable to use for this kind of images.

As the implementation is short and the algorithm is not very demanding in terms of hardware requirements, this type of file format can be used in embedded systems, especially for the communication with any operating system. In real-time applications without using the Deflate compression this algorithm can be read by many threads further increasing the performance. As the data can be read sequentially, it is suited for applications where only a part of data is needed to be read.

4.2 Conclusions

We have presented a novel file format. This format uses run-length encoding and the Deflate algorithm to achieve simple yet effective results. Our file format is specialized in single-channel 1-bit images. This type of images has numerous applications in biometrics and other science fields. We hope to further improve it to be a general purpose algorithm. In order to encourage the usage of our algorithm, its implementation will be publicly available.

Acknowledgements. The work was supported by grant no. WZ//I-IIT/5/2023 from Bialystok University of Technology and funded with resources for research by the Ministry of Education and Science in Poland.

References

1. Randers-Pehrson, G., Boutell, T.: PNG (Portable Network Graphics) Specification Version 1.2 (1997)
2. Roelofs, G.: PNG: The Definitive Guide (1999). ISBN 9781565925427
3. Huffman, D.: A method for the construction of minimum redundancy codes. Proc. IRE **40**, 1098–1101 (1952)
4. Knuth, D.E.: Dynamic Huffman coding. J. Algorithms **6**, 163–180 (1985)
5. Golomb, S.W.: Run-length encodings. IEEE Trans. Inform. Theory **IT-12**, 399–401 (1966)
6. Seroussi, G., Weinberger, M.J.: On adaptive strategies for an extended family of Golomb-type codes. In: Proceedings of Data Compression Conference Snowbird, UT, pp. 131–140 (1997)
7. Liao, T.: The design of high speed Huffman decoder in PNG image decoding process. Microelectronics & Computer (2009)
8. Meyer, B., Tischer, P.: TMW-a new method for lossless image compression. In: Proceedings of International Picture Coding Symposium, Berlin, Germany (1997)
9. Weinberger, M.J., Seroussi, G., Sapiro, G.: The LOCO-I lossless image compression algorithm: principles and standardization into JPEG-LS. IEEE Trans. Image Process. **9**(8), 1309–1324 (2000). https://doi.org/10.1109/83.855427
10. Scarmana, G.: Lossless data compression of grid-based digital elevation models: a PNG image format evaluation (2014). https://doi.org/10.5194/isprsannals-II-5-313-2014
11. Weinberger, M.J., Seroussi, G., Sapiro, G.: LOCO-I: a low complexity, context-based, lossless image compression algorithm. In: Proceedings of 1996 Data Compression Conference, Snowbird, UT, pp. 140–149 (1996)
12. Proposed Modification of LOCO-I for Its Improvement of the Performance. ISO/IEC JTC1/SC29/WG1 Doc. N297 (1996)
13. Fine-Tuning the Baseline. ISO/IEC JTC1/SC29/WG1 Doc. N341 (1996)
14. Clunie, D.: Losssless compression of grayscale medical images. In: Proceedings of SPIE, vol. 3980 (2000)

15. Milewski, P., Saeed, K.: A new approach for image thinning. In: Saeed, K., Dvorský, J. (eds.) CISIM 2022. LNCS, vol. 13293, pp. 18–31. Springer, Cham (2022). https://doi.org/10.1007/978-3-031-10539-5_2

16. Taubman, D., Marcellin, M.: JPEG2000 Image Compression Fundamentals, Standards and Practice. The Springer International Series in Engineering and Computer Science, Springer, New York (2004). https://doi.org/10.1007/978-1-4615-0799-4

17. Matsuoka, R.: Quantitative analysis of image quality of lossy compression images. ISPRS, Istanbul (2004)

18. Al-Otum, H.M.: Qualitative and quantitative image quality assessment of vector quantization, JPEG, and JPEG2000 compressed images. J. Electron. Imaging 12(3), 511–521 (2003)

19. Baig, M.A., Moinuddin, A.A., Khan, E., Ghanbari, M.: A versatile blind JPEG image quality assessment method. Multimedia Tools Appl. 1–18 (2023). https://doi.org/10.1007/s11042-023-14983-0

20. Cogranne, R.: Determining JPEG Image Standard Quality Factor from the Quantization Tables (2018)

21. Mao, H., Hu, Z., Zhu, L., Qin, H.: PNG File Decoding Optimization Based Embedded System, pp. 1–4 (2012). https://doi.org/10.1109/WiCOM.2012.6478619

22. Pu, H., Sun, Y.: Research on PNG file compression. Modern Computer (2007)

23. Santa-Cruz, D., Ebrahimi, T.: An analytical study of JPEG 2000 functionalities. In: Proceedings of the International Conference on Image Processing, vol. 2, pp. 49–52 (2000)

A New Approach to the Architecture of Hybrid and Multilayer Steganographic Methods

Jerzy Pejaś[ID] and Łukasz Cierocki[✉][ID]

Department of Software Engineering and Cybersecurity, Faculty of Computer Science
and Information Technology, West Pomeranian University of Technology,
49 Żołnierska Street, 71-210 Szczecin, Poland
jpejas@wi.zut.edu.pl, lukasz.cierocki@zut.edu.pl

Abstract. Audio steganography is a rapidly growing aspect of broad information protection. However, most of the designed steganographic algorithms are vulnerable to stegoanalysis and detecting the presence of hidden messages in stegoobjects. High hopes for solving this problem are associated with multilayer and hybrid secret message embedding techniques because such mixed techniques can withstand a wide range of attacks. The proposed article expands the knowledge of multilayer methods and introduces the concept of a hybrid method based on the embedding place in different domains of steganographic methods. A comparative analysis of a single-layer, operating in two domains, and a hybrid method that combines the two embedding methods, was made. The comparative analysis shows the advantage of hybrid methods over single-layer methods. The hybrid methods have the exciting potential of creating more flexible methods better suited to a specific purpose or improving one parameter at the expense of another. In addition, combined hybrid and multilayer methods are more secure due to the greater difficulty in extracting a secret message by an intruder.

Keywords: Steganography architecture · Data Hiding · Transparency · Imperceptibility

1 Introduction

Audio steganography is a rapidly growing aspect of information protection methods. The name steganography itself comes from Greek words meaning "hidden writing" [7,10]. On the implementation side, it means embedding information in information. Audio steganography can be used as a method of providing security as well as a way to mark products digitally, i.e. watermarking [7]. Based on the medium used, we can distinguish many types, where the most popular include audio, video, image and text-based steganography. This article will focus on steganography using audio as a medium [8,17].

Along with cryptography, steganography is one of the main ways to protect data. Cryptography hides the meaning of information, and steganography hides the very fact of its existence [5].

© The Author(s), under exclusive license to Springer Nature Switzerland AG 2023
K. Saeed et al. (Eds.): CISIM 2023, LNCS 14164, pp. 77–91, 2023.
https://doi.org/10.1007/978-3-031-42823-4_7

A well-developed steganographic method should achieve acceptable transparency, robustness and capacity [14]. The parameters of steganographic methods have in common that a change in one of the parameters does not leave the other parameters unaffected. Changing capacitance affects transparency, and changing resistance affects capacitance and so on [8].

Among all steganographic techniques, audio steganography is one of the most challenging. The human auditory system is often more sensitive to signal changes than vision. However, this stonewalls an interesting research gap [14].

This article is organized as follows. Section 2 describes the general architecture of steganographic methods. The literature on methods that describe hybrid and multilayer methods is reviewed. Section 3 describes the motivations for addressing this issue. The following section proposes a systematic way of naming steganography methods. Section number 5 tests the proposed method. The last 6 section describes conclusions and further anticipated work.

This paper brings a new architecture of steganographic methods to classify and compare different techniques for hiding information in multimedia signals. The article proposes criteria for distinguishing between hybrid and multilayer methods and provides examples of such methods for audio files. The article proposes and tests a new hybrid method in terms of transparency and capacity. The results of the study may be useful for designers and users of steganographic systems, as well as for researchers involved in information protection.

2   Related Works

Many articles have recently been published on multilayer and hybrid methods. The primary purpose of creating methods with an architecture different from the classic one is to improve its performance in terms of resistance, capacity and transparency. The articles selected for this review were based on the fact that the authors themselves called them hybrid or multilayer methods or articles treating the architecture of steganography methods directly.

A fascinating article was prepared by Al-Najjar [3]. This article deals with the multilayer architecture of steganographic methods. According to the proposed architecture, any created stegoobject acts as a decoy.

The second interesting article was prepared by Krishna Bhowal [6]. This article expands the concept presented by Al-Najjar and presents two embedding methods that develop the concept of multilayering. The proposed algorithms feature enhanced security during transmission over public channels.

We must start the description of multilayer steganographic methods by introducing primary designations. Let us take M_i as the designation of the part of the transmitted message, C_i as the intermediate carrier and I_i as the intermediate stegoobject [6]. T_i was adopted as an intermediate form of transformation (e.g. (Discrete Fourier Transform - DFT, Discrete Wavelet Transform - DWT). The embedding/extraction operation designation was adopted f, and f' [6].

2.1   Single Message Multiple Cover - Type 1

The message is concealed in multiple media, using multiple embedding functions. This type of embedding increases the security of the stegosystem by making it more transparent, but the capacity of the method may be limited in most cases [6].

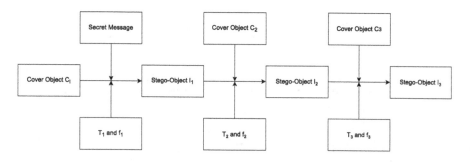

Fig. 1. Type 1 embedding method taken from [6]

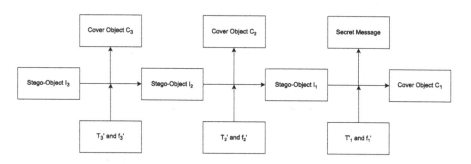

Fig. 2. Type 1 extraction method taken from [6]

The Figs. 1 and 2 show type 1 of multilayer steganographic model for insertion and extraction as well.

Example for 2 Layer Type 1 Stegosystem. As an example of this type of steganography methods, we can assume that the C_1 carrier is an audio file, such as WAV type, and the message is a string of bits denoted as a secret message. As T_1, we specify, for example, a compression method or other form of transformation of the embedded message. Then, using the LSB algorithm (f_1), the individual bits are sequentially embedded in the carrier, generating an intermediate stegoobject. In the next step ($i = 2$), the previously created intermediate stegoobject is converted to a bit string, which is subjected to embedding with the help of the f_2 mechanism in the next carrier, on the Fig. 1 denoted as C_2. Thus, the resulting stegoobject is obtained, which can be delivered to the recipient.

2.2   Single Cover Multiple Messages - Type 2

For type two, the message is embedded using related steganography methods. This allows more data to be embedded, but may not be unaffected by transparency. As a carrier, a stegoobject is used, which was obtained by the previous deposition method.

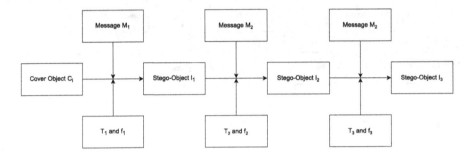

Fig. 3. Type 2 embedding method taken from [6]

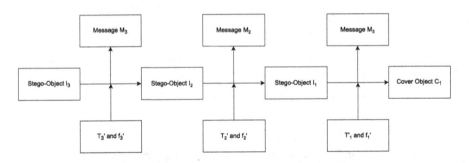

Fig. 4. Type 2 extraction method taken from [6]

The Figs. 3 and 4 show type 2 of multilayer steganography model for extraction and insertion as well.

Example for 2 Layer Type 2 Stegosystem. As an example of type two layering, one can cite a steganographic scheme where, in the first step, part of the secret M_1 is embedded in the carrier C_1, for example, using the LSB method T_1 which gives us an intermediate stegoobject I_1. Then, in this intermediate stegoobject, the another part of secret denoted as M_2 is embedded using an already different steganographic technique T_2. Thus, the resulting stegoobject is obtained.

Hybrid Techniques. In [18], a steganography method based on spread spectrum uses a discrete redundant wavelet transform. In addition, this method uses a new way of detecting pauses in the speech signal (IPDP, intelligent pause detection protocol). The deposition process for this method is presented in Fig. 5. Using this method, transmitting messages in the speech signal using LBC (low-bit coding, i.e. reduced memory) with a pause removal mechanism is possible. According to this article's author, hybridity involves combining a way to detect pauses along with an embedding mechanism based on the spread spectrum and a redundant discrete wavelet transform.

In a paper by [16], a fascinating one called by the authors as a multilayer steganography algorithm based on the Fourier transform and pseudo-random LSB selection is presented. The method has been tested by measures such as PSNR, MSE, and MOS for different types of music. This article defines hybridity as using two embedding domains, i.e. the time domain and the frequency domain However, in our opinion, the following article uses only the frequency domain where, by modifying the coefficients of the transform, the data are embedded by LSB method. In addition, In addition, the authors treat multilayeredness as "layers" of bits used in the LSB technique, which is confounding.

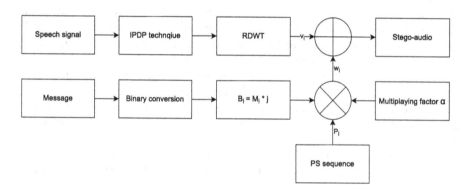

Fig. 5. Insertion process presented in [18]

The paper [15] presents another hybrid method where, this time, hybridity refers to the binding of two different domains of operation, i.e. the time domain and the frequency domain. The algorithm is based on several steps, executed sequentially after each other. First, the data is converted from text to binary form. Then the data is embedded into an image using the LSB technique, after which the image is encrypted into an intermediate image using a basic cypher. Then, using a discrete cosine transform and embedding in the coefficients of this transform, the intermediate image is injected into the final stegoimage (Fig. 6).

Another interesting method called hybrid by the authors is the one presented in the [20]. This method, also indicates its hybridity through the use of cryptography and steganography. In addition, compression is used.

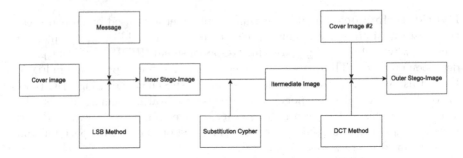

Fig. 6. Insertion process presented in [15]

3 Motivation

This article focuses on the architecture of steganographic methods. We want to describe and systematize the knowledge of multilayer and hybrid steganographic methods. In addition, make a comparative analysis of classical steganographic algorithms and their hybrid versions. As we can see, defining the conditions for multilayer or hybridity is exceptionally complicated. Some methods call themselves hybrid, although they do not have signs of hybridity, or they call themselves multilayer and do not have multiple layers. **Both hybridity and multilayeredness in steganography should refer only to how each method embeds information.** As we believe, this should not apply to techniques and methods that can be understood as post-processing or pre-processing, as it does not apply at all, to the process of embedding/extraction of steganographic methods. Therefore, it is impossible to speak of a multilayer steganographic method if it does not meet the conditions outlined by the Al-Najjar in [3] and extended by Bhowal in [6].

In hybridity, we should adopt specific conditions that a method must meet to be called hybrid. As we can quote from the Cambridge Dictionary and the igi-global dictionary:

Hybrid
- *something that is a combination of two different things, so it has qualities relating to both of them* [1]
- *methods or approaches that consist of a combination of two or three methods or algorithms* [2]

Thus, it can be assumed that hybridity should be called algorithms that use two steganographic techniques fundamentally different from each other. There can be no hybridity when discussing a method that integrates steganography and cryptography because although both techniques move in the field of information protection, they serve different purposes. Cryptography changes the meaning of a message, while steganography hides that message.

As for multilayering, the conditions proposed by Al-Najjar in [3] and extended by Bhowal in [6] should be met. Only this kind of categorization will allow us to identify methods as hybrid and multi-layered unambiguously.

4   Proposed Architecture - From the General to the Specific

In general, we can present the steganographic system as a sequence of sequentially performed steps, where we can distinguish two phases - the embedding phase and the information extraction phase (Fig. 7). Before the embedding itself, there is often a step in the methods that we can call preprocessing. It assumes the processing of the signal of the carrier or secret using various techniques, e.g. compression, cryptography, noise reduction, etc. Thus, for example, in the technique presented in [18] first, as part of the preprocessing, the carrier's signal is subjected to an intelligent pause detection algorithm.

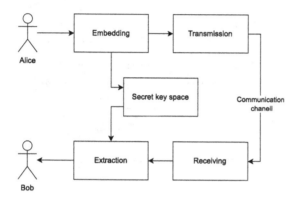

Fig. 7. Typical stegosystem with two phases

Another great technique using preprocessing is the method proposed by Ali et al. in [4]. In pre-processing, pseudo-random indexes are generated using chaotic maps where the information will be embedded. Just after embedding and even before transmission, there may be a post-processing stage, which may include cryptographic, error correction or compression techniques.

Figure 8 shows a block diagram of the proposed architecture. We can distinguish several blocks in it:

– **Transform** - Included in this block are various types of transformation that the carrier/secret can undergo. In steganographic methods operating in the transformation domain, it is almost necessary to use this block. We can distinguish different types of transformations used to create steganographic methods, i.e. Discrete Cosine Transform (DCT), Discrete Fourier Transform (DFT), or Discrete Wavelet Transform (DWT).
– **Domain** - The deposition process proceeds differently depending on the method used. To date, many methods have been proposed for embedding information that differ from each other in parameters. These methods can be categorized in several ways, for example, from the domain of embedding

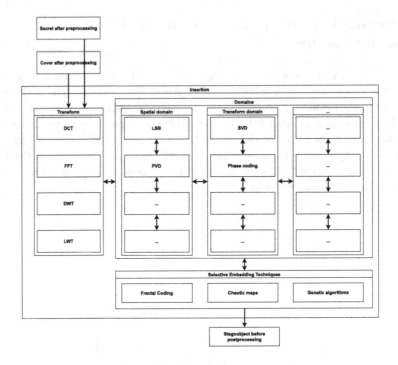

Fig. 8. Proposed architecture

or from the method of embedding. For the purpose of the architecture under development, we propose to use a method of categorization against different embedding domains.

- **Selective embedding techniques** - Some methods have a selective model for choosing the places of embedding information, and this happens non sequentially. I.e. a block of information is read in, then on the basis of various mechanisms (depending on the method) the most sensible placement is typed. The corresponding site determination module, must be sewn into the embedding algorithm, so to speak. Various ways of determining the embedding place are known, for example, on the basis of fractal coding, chaotic maps, or genetic algorithms.

4.1   Example 1 - Hybrid Method

Figure 9 presents the proposed block diagram for the hybrid methods. As we can see, a method classified as hybrid embeds data sequentially (in this case) first in the time domain. In the next step, with the help of the DCT (Discrete Cosine Transform), there is a transition to the transformation domain where then with the help of SVD (Singular Value Decomposition) the data is embedded.

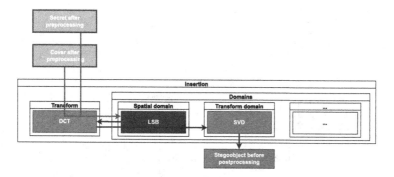

Fig. 9. Hybrid method on block diagram

4.2   Example 2 - Multilayer Method

Figure 10 shows the block diagram of the multilayer method. As we can see, the secret and the carrier pass through the method layers within a single domain. No transformation is performed, and the carrier remains in a uniform form throughout the embedding process.

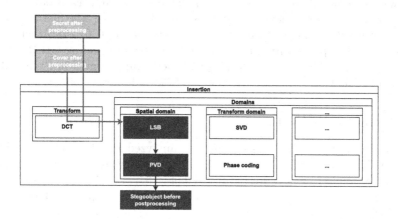

Fig. 10. Multilayer method on block diagram

4.3   Example 3 - Hybrid - Multilayer Method

A method that is simultaneously multilayered and hybrid appears to be the most complicated. For example, this method embeds data in the first step using the LSB method then within the same domain the data is embedded using PVD (Pixel Value Differencing). In the next step, with the help of the DCT (Discrete Cosine Transform), there is a transition to the transformation domain where then with the help of SVD (Singular Value Decomposition) the data is embedded (Fig. 11).

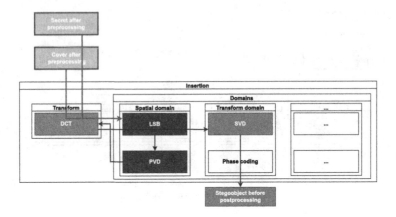

Fig. 11. Hybrid Multilayer method on block diagram

5 Performed Tests

As part of the testing phase, the method classified as hybrid was tested. The tests were conducted on 10 audio files available in the NOIZEUS database [9]. All files represent human speech and are sampled 44100 Hz. The files are single-channel files with a bit width of 16 bits per sample of 10 to 20 s in length. A desktop-class computer with an Intel i7-7600U processor and 32 GB RAM was used as a testing platform. All schemes have been implemented in Python 3.8.6 in Visual Studio Code environment under Windows 11 x86-64 operating system.

5.1 Imperceptibility Test

Further, the audio quality of stegoaudio is analyzed by MSE, PSNR. **PSNR** (Peak to Signal Noise Ratio) is used to evaluate the stegoaudio quality compared to the cover audio and is expressed in decibels (dB) [12]. A higher PSNR value means higher audio quality, and more than 30 dB is acceptable. The formula gives PSNR:

$$PSNR = 10 \times log\left(\left(\frac{max^2}{MSE}\right)\right) \quad \text{where} \quad MSE = \frac{1}{M \times N} \sum_{0}^{M-1} \sum_{0}^{N-1} \|c - s\|^2$$

(1)

where M, N are the width and height of the audio and c, s are the carrier and stegoaudio, respectively. Max means the possible maximum value in the signal.

5.2 Robustness

Robustness has been checked by the BER (Bit Error Ratio). We can read in [13], BER is the proportion between transmitted and recovered incorrectly bits.

BER is calculated according to the equation:

$$BER = \frac{\sum_{i=1}^{N} E \oplus E'}{N} \times 100\% \qquad (2)$$

where E and E' describe embedded and recovered message bit vectors, $\oplus$ is a XOR binary operation and N denotes the number of message bits. Lower BER value describes better accuracy of message extraction.

5.3   Capacity

Capacity is one of the basic requirements for steganographic methods. The creation of hybrid and multilayer methods should have a significant impact on the capacity of steganographic methods.

This test uses a capacity evaluation measure that captures the ratio of the number of embedded bits, to the number of carrier bits.

$$cr = \frac{cs}{eb} \times 100\% \qquad (3)$$

where cr is the capacity ratio and cs carrier size in bits, eb embedded bits, respectively.

5.4   Tested Methods

Two steganographic methods, operating in two different domains, were tested. The first is the classic LSB method, which operates in the time domain, while the second is the SVD-DCT method, which careens in the transformation domain.

LSB Method is almost the canonical method in steganography. It has a very rich literature and is widely used. The LSB method uses the k the least significant bit of the carrier to embed k bits of information [19]. These methods, are simple to implement and fast but have significant drawbacks like high vulnerability [21].

The SVD-DCT Method is the second approach tested. This method operates in the transformation domain and uses the DCT (Discrete Cosine Transform) to decompose the signal into DCT coefficients. Then, using singular value decomposition (SVD), the data is embedded [11]. This method, has one major drawback. It is necessary to store large amounts of information in order to recover the embedded information.

5.5   Results

Table 1 shows results of transparency and robustness analysis for LSB method, SVD method and hybrid LSB + SVD-DCT, respectively. The coefficients were chosen experimentally to maintain a similar high level of transparency while maximizing the other parameters. As can be seen, the hybrid method has the best capacity/transparency ratio while having an error rate of about 8.5%. The hybrid method allowed embedding 100% more information than the classic LSB method with similar transparency but a higher BER. It is necessary to note that the two embedding domains affect each other. It is necessary to consider the appropriate selection of the proportion of embedded information in the case of hybrid systems. Wanting to increase the method's capacity, we can embed a more significant part of it in the time domain. When we care about greater resilience, we can embed a more significant data stream in the transformation domain. This allows the creation of more flexible methods.

Table 1. The comparison of methods transparency and robustness

Methods	Results			
	CR	MSE	PSNR	BER
Hybrid method (LSB + SVD-DCT)	53	42.81	73.99	8.58
One - Layer Method SVD-DCT	46	55.22	72.95	12.53
One - Layer Method LSB	25	42.53	74.02	0

In addition, spectral analysis of the carrier, the LSB method and the hybrid method were performed (Figs. 12, 13 and 14). In the spectral plots of the LSB method and the hybrid method, it is possible to see constant noise, which may indicate embedded data. However, it is noteworthy that in the case of the hybrid method, almost 100% more information was embedded than in the case of LSB alone.

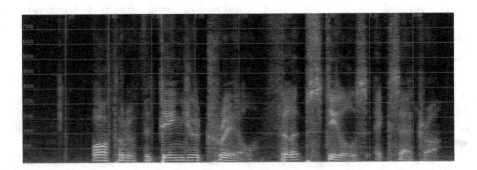

Fig. 12. LSB method spectral analysis

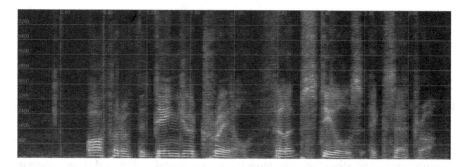

Fig. 13. SVD-DCT method spectral analysis

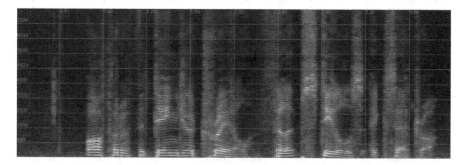

Fig. 14. Hybrid method spectral analysis

6   Conclusions

The proposed article expands the knowledge of multilayer methods and introduces the concept of a hybrid method based on the embedding place in different domains of steganographic methods. A comparative analysis was made of single-layer, operating in two domains, and a hybrid method that combines the two. The comparative analysis made shows the advantage of hybrid methods over single-layer methods. Hybrid methods have the exciting potential of creating more flexible methods better suited to a specific purpose or improving one parameter at the expense of another.

Further research on the present issue will be related to the comparative analysis of hybrid, hybrid-multilayer, and single-layer methods to select the best methods for different applications. In addition, an essential element of further work is the appropriate categorization of methods in the context of the way of embedding information and the domain of embedding.

References

1. Hybrid. https://dictionary.cambridge.org/dictionary/english/hybrid
2. What is Hybrid Methods — IGI Global. https://www.igi-global.com/dictionary/hybrid-genetic-metaheuristic-for-two-dimensional-constrained-guillotinable-cutting-problems/13485
3. Al-Najjar, A.: The decoy: multi-level digital multimedia steganography model. In: Proceedings of the 12th WSEAS International Conference on Communications (2008)
4. Ali, A.H., George, L.E., Zaidan, A.A., Mokhtar, M.R.: High capacity, transparent and secure audio steganography model based on fractal coding and chaotic map in temporal domain. Multimedia Tools Appl. **77**(23), 31487–31516 (2018). https://doi.org/10.1007/s11042-018-6213-0. https://linkinghub.elsevier.com/retrieve/pii/S1574013720304160
5. AlSabhany, A.A., Ali, A.H., Ridzuan, F., Azni, A., Mokhtar, M.R.: Digital audio steganography: systematic review, classification, and analysis of the current state of the art. Comput. Sci. Rev. **38**, 100316 (2020). https://doi.org/10.1016/j.cosrev.2020.100316. https://linkinghub.elsevier.com/retrieve/pii/S1574013720304160
6. Bhowal, K.: Multilevel Steganography to Improve Secret Communication (2019)
7. Dutta, H., Das, R.K., Nandi, S., Prasanna, S.R.M.: An overview of digital audio steganography. IETE Tech. Rev. **37**(6), 632–650 (2020). https://doi.org/10.1080/02564602.2019.1699454. https://www.tandfonline.com/doi/full/10.1080/02564602.2019.1699454
8. Hassaballah, M.: Digital Media Steganography: Principles, Algorithms, Advances (2020). https://doi.org/10.1016/C2018-0-04865-3
9. Hu, Y., Loizou, P.C.: Subjective comparison and evaluation of speech enhancement algorithms. Speech Commun. **49**(7), 588–601 (2007). https://doi.org/10.1016/j.specom.2006.12.006. https://www.sciencedirect.com/science/article/pii/S0167639306001920
10. Kahn, D.: The history of steganography. In: Anderson, R. (ed.) IH 1996. LNCS, vol. 1174, pp. 1–5. Springer, Heidelberg (1996). https://doi.org/10.1007/3-540-61996-8_27
11. Kanhe, A., Aghila, G.: A DCT-SVD-based speech steganography in voiced frames. Circuits Syst. Signal Process. **37**(11), 5049–5068 (2018). https://doi.org/10.1007/s00034-018-0805-9
12. Kumar, K.P., Kanhe, A.: Secured speech watermarking with DCT compression and chaotic embedding using DWT and SVD. Arab. J. Sci. Eng. **47**(8), 10003–10024 (2022). https://doi.org/10.1007/s13369-021-06431-8
13. Mahmoud, M.M., Elshoush, H.T.: Enhancing LSB using binary message size encoding for high capacity, transparent and secure audio steganography-an innovative approach. IEEE Access **10**, 29954–29971 (2022). https://doi.org/10.1109/ACCESS.2022.3155146
14. Manjunath, K., Kodanda Ramaiah, G.N., GiriPrasad, M.N.: Backward movement oriented shark smell optimization-based audio steganography using encryption and compression strategies. Digit. Signal Process. **122**, 103335 (2022). https://doi.org/10.1016/j.dsp.2021.103335. https://www.sciencedirect.com/science/article/pii/S1051200421003742

15. Narula, M., Gupta, M., Garg, M.: Implementation of hybrid technique from spatial and frequency domain steganography: along with cryptography to withstand statistical attacks. In: 2020 2nd International Conference on Advances in Computing, Communication Control and Networking (ICACCCN), pp. 803–808. IEEE (2020). https://doi.org/10.1109/ICACCCN51052.2020.9362754. https://ieeexplore.ieee.org/document/9362754/

16. Pal, D., Goswami, A., Chowdhury, S., Ghoshal, N.: A novel high-density multilayered audio steganography technique in hybrid domain. In: Bhattacharjee, D., Kole, D.K., Dey, N., Basu, S., Plewczynski, D. (eds.) Proceedings of International Conference on Frontiers in Computing and Systems. AISC, vol. 1255, pp. 721–730. Springer, Singapore (2021). https://doi.org/10.1007/978-981-15-7834-2_67

17. Pilania, U., Tanwar, R., Gupta, P.: An ROI-based robust video steganography technique using SVD in wavelet domain. Open Comput. Sci. **12**(1), 1–16 (2022). https://doi.org/10.1515/comp-2020-0229. https://www.degruyter.com/document/doi/10.1515/comp-2020-0229/html

18. Rao, R.C., Jayasree, P.V.Y., Rao, S.S.: Hybrid speech steganography system using SS-RDWT with IPDP-MLE approach. Soft Comput. **27**(2), 1117–1129 (2023). https://doi.org/10.1007/s00500-021-05970-4

19. Sánchez Rinza, B.E., Munive Morales, L.G., Jaramillo Núñez, A.: LSB algorithm to hide text in an audio signal. Computación y Sistemas **26**(1), 39–44 (2022). https://doi.org/10.13053/cys-26-1-4150. https://cys.cic.ipn.mx/ojs/index.php/CyS/article/view/4150

20. Teotia, S., Srivastava, P.: Enhancing audio and video steganography technique using hybrid algorithm. In: 2018 International Conference on Communication and Signal Processing (ICCSP), pp. 1059–1063 (2018). https://doi.org/10.1109/ICCSP.2018.8524182

21. Wahab, O.F.A., Khalaf, A.A.M., Hussein, A.I., Hamed, H.F.A.: Hiding data using efficient combination of RSA cryptography, and compression steganography techniques. IEEE Access **9**, 31805–31815 (2021). https://doi.org/10.1109/ACCESS.2021.3060317

Towards a Blockchain, Smart Contract, and NFT Based Medical Waste Classification System: A Case Study in Vietnam

N. T. Phuc[1(✉)], Q. L. Khoi[1], L. H. Huong[1], T. D. Khoa[1], H. G. Khiem[1],
N. D. P. Trong[1], V. C. P. Loc[1], N. T. Q. Duy[1], T. Q. Bao[1], D. M. Hieu[1,2],
N. T. Anh[1], H. T. Nghia[1], N. T. K. Ngan[2], and V. H. Khanh[1(✉)]

[1] FPT University, Can Tho City, Vietnam
nguyentrongphuchcm191@gmail.com, KhanhVH@fe.edu.vn
[2] FPT Polytecnic, Can Tho City, Vietnam

Abstract. Medical waste is classified as hazardous waste because most of it is discarded after six months of usage, and very little of it is capable of being reused. This statement is also proven during the Covid-19 epidemic when the ineffective treatment of medical waste is one of the direct causes of infections worldwide. For developing countries (i.e., Vietnam), the problem of waste treatment is a difficult problem to solve in a short time. Currently, the medical waste treatment process is a combination of medical staff - transport staff - waste treatment staff. Thus the wrongdoings in the first stage (i.e., waste sorting) seriously affect the last steps. Therefore, we propose a model of waste classification and treatment for Vietnam, applying Blockchain technology, smart contract, and NFT to raise individual/collective awareness of garbage classification in the medical environment. Specifically, our work contributes four-fold, (a) propose a blockchain-based mechanism for the classification and treatment of medical waste; (b) propose a model to create reward/punishment decisions for individuals/organizations; (c) implement the proposed model based on smart contracts; and (d) deploying proof-of-concept on 4 EVM&NFT-supported platforms (i.e., ERC721 and ERC20) including BNB Smart Chain, Fantom, Polygon, and Celo.

Keywords: Medical waste treatment · Blockchain · Smart contract · NFT · Ethereum · Fantom · Polygon · Binance Smart Chain

1 Introduction

Medical waste is considered a hazardous waste that needs strict supervision during classification and treatment [34]. These types of waste are highly infectious, so 99% of items (including medical equipment and supplies) become garbage after use within the first six months of first use [17]. In addition, single-use wastes also pose many environmental hazards (eg, medical gloves, protective gear, masks, etc.) [33]. Because of the above reason, countries around the world have applied a strict process in the classification and treatment of these types of waste.

K. Saeed et al. (Eds.): CISIM 2023, LNCS 14164, pp. 92–107, 2023.
https://doi.org/10.1007/978-3-031-42832-4_8

This is extremely important for economic development. There have been many studies on the consequences of waste treatment in economic development [5]. Besides, the pressure on the environment is also very high because the components are difficult to decompose causing environmental pollution [11]. For developing countries, there are numerous studies that have investigated each link between waste disposal and environmental pollution (eg, India [4], Brazil [10]) or infection due to medical supplies used a lot during the epidemic season (eg, medical protective equipment [6], vaccination [7]). In Vietnam, systematic studies have explored the risks of waste segregation with the prevention of the Covid 19 epidemic. It is worth mentioning that these studies only focus on the results/consequences of waste management rather than offering an improved model which focuses on transparency and decentralized storage.

To solve these problems, a series of new research papers have been born to propose a model of waste treatment and classification based on Blockchain technology and management based on the smart contracts system [16,18]. These research directions focus on determining the origin and composition of trash bags (called bags). In addition, these approaches focus mainly on four user groups: healthcare workers, patients (in isolation and treatment areas), waste collectors, and waste treatment companies (see related work for details). The information related to the three groups of users and bags is all validated before saving the information on the chain. This information helps to identify the source and limit contact between the parties (eg, medical staff - collectors or collectors - waste treatment staff) [8]. Limiting contact between parties also reduces the risk of disease transmission. Therefore, this model can replace traditional waste treatment methods during the epidemic period.

In addition, the support and awareness raising of the people should also be considered in order to limit the waste treatment time. Figure 2 shows the medical waste treatment process during the pandemic in Vietnam [21]. The first step is self-classification. This seems simple enough and has developed as a habit among people in developing countries. However, in developing countries, this regulation began to be implemented immediately after the outbreak of the Covid-19 epidemic. In Vietnam, most types of waste are not classified and have a great impact on their treatment process. Therefore, in addition to applying a model to support the state in the treatment of medical waste based on Blockchain technology and smart contracts, we aim to change people's perception in waste classification (i.e., the first step Fig. 2). We have also developed a series of waste treatment models before, but in this article, we aim to raise people's awareness in Vietnam by exploiting NFT technology. This study aims to evaluate the current waste treatment model in developing countries (i.e., research focused on Vietnam) during the Covid-19 pandemic, thereby providing an appropriate approach for similar epidemics in the future. Specifically, the main contribution of the paper is to present an NFT-based approach (ERC 721) and penalties for people's waste classification violations.

Therefore, our work contributes on four aspects. (a) Propose a mechanism for classification and treatment of medical waste based on blockchain technology and smart contract for the Vietnamese environment; (b) propose a model to create reward/punishment decisions for individuals/organizations based on NFT technology; (c) implementing the proposed model based on smart contracts and the proposed model (i.e., proof-of-concept); and (d) deploying proof-of-concept on 4 supporting platforms (ERC721 - NFT of ETH) and EVM (deploying smart contract implemented in solidity language) including BNB Smart Chain, Fantom, Polygon, and Celo.[1]

2   Related Work

In this section, we summarize previous research directions focusing on waste treatment processes based on Blockchain technology and smart contracts [15, 22]. The following sections summarize the state-of-the-art in treatment of medical waste based on Blockchain technology - focusing on two main approaches before analyzing the pros and cons in the last subsection.

2.1   Waste Treatment Model to Achieve Circular Economy (CE)

CE is considered a model of the future of a green economy. Specifically, all waste is treated in a closed manner and optimizes their use time. For example, to reduce waste and increase recycling. This definition is also pursued by leading companies in the technology sector, such as Amazon introduced Amazon CE [2], where, Amazon created a loop of using their products based on partnerships and service offerings. Amazon also offers more choices to users when they want to reuse their own products instead of buying a new product (i.e., options for customers to reuse, repair, and recycle their products). surname).

There are many different approaches to dealing with each type of household waste in our daily lives. For e-waste, for example, Gupta et al. [12] has proposed an Ethereum-based waste management system for electrical and electronic equipment. In the proposed model, the authors focus on three user groups, namely producers, consumers, and retailers. Direct constraints between related objects are shown on the smart contracts of the system. These activities, if done correctly, will receive a fixed reward (i.e., ETH). Through the above-proposed model, product developers do not have to collect their used products again.

For solid waste types (eg, computers and smartphones), to be able to monitor the stages of transportation from waste sources to waste treatment centers, Laura et al. [14] introduced a management system based on a combination of Ethereum and QR codes. For the process of determining the type of waste to be destroyed, each garbage bag will be identified with a QR code that links directly to the data stored on the chain. In this way, stakeholders can trace and determine the current location and expected time to complete the processing. Besides, the problem of overcrowding in the waste treatment areas is also ensured because the transport

---

[1] We do not deploy smart contracts on ETH because the execution fee of smart contracts is too high.

companies can determine the remaining amount of waste consumed each day based on the expected date of extraction from the garbage bag.

Another Ethereum-based study that can track cross-border garbage in a secure, tamper-proof and privacy-preserving way is introduced by Schmelz et al. [23]. Specifically, the information can only be accessed by authorized parties based on encryption technology. For cross-border waste transport matters, authorities can trace the location, volume of transport and the estimated time that a unit of waste (eg, vehicle, bag) can be transported. In addition, shipping processes can be run by predefined smart coins. However, one disadvantage of this process is that they do not support penalties for violations in the transportation and disposal of waste.

2.2   Model of Waste Treatment in Medical Environment

Positive environmental benefits cannot be attributed to the application of binding CE conditions in production and economic development (especially within a country) [13]. However, as noted above the majority (99%) of medical items (including medical equipment and supplies) cannot be reused after 6 months from the date of first use [17]. Therefore, applying CE in a practical environment is extremely difficult, especially in a medical environment. A good example drawn from the Covid-19 pandemic is the asynchronous waste treatment process, resulting in a huge amount of medical waste and personal protective equipment. sheehan2021use, Covid-19 vaccine [1]) also contributed to many subsequent infections [19].

Because of these challenges, Trieu et al. [16] propose a Hyperledger Fabric-based waste treatment model called MedicalWast-Chain. This proposed model is aimed at the treatment of medical waste from medical centers, the reuse of tools, the process of transferring medical supplies waste (i.e., protective gear, gloves, masks, etc.) pages), and waste treatment processes in factories. Similar to the above approach, Ahmad et al. [3] aims at the traceability model of personal protective equipment for healthcare workers (i.e., doctors, nurses, testers) during the pandemic. In addition, the above approach also identifies (not) allowed behaviors in the process of garbage classification and collection. Specifically, they will take pictures of medical waste collection sites and compare them to identify the above behaviors. To assist with the validation of waste treatment processes (i.e., stakeholder interactions), Dasaklis et al. [9] proposed a blockchain-based system set up on smartphones.

The above approaches do not pay too much attention to the process of reproduction/refurbishment. Neither of the above approaches provides a reasonable solution for handling (i.e., rewarding and handling violations) nor the behavior of users (i.e., patients, and healthcare workers). Specifically, the above solutions (for both Hyperledger Eco-system and Ethereum platforms) only focus on the management model of the waste treatment chain from the place of origin (i.e., medical centers) to factories process rubbish. Besides, the application of a specific approach and implementation for a territory (i.e., Vietnam) must consider many aspects. For that reason, we aim to change people's habit of sorting medical waste (not only for medical centers but also for households). This research can be the foundation for responding to respiratory diseases (eg, Covid 19) applied in the future, where each household has a responsibility to protect people body and people around through the re-sorting of hazardous waste. In this paper, we not only offer a model to manage the waste sorting process, but also provide a solution for rewarding and handling user violations based on NFT technology. The following section will detail the processing process and implementation steps.

3   Approach

3.1   Traditional Model of Treatment and Classification of Medical Waste

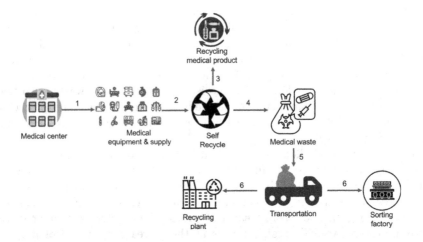

Fig. 1. Traditional model of treatment & classification of medical waste

To build the current model of treatment and classification of medical waste, we refer to the classification and treatment of medical waste during the Covid-19 pandemic in Vietnam - signed by the Ministry of Health in 2019 [21]. The steps are shown in Fig. 2 [21]. Figure 2 shows five sources of medical waste classification and five treatment steps. Sources of medical waste include treatment places (i.e., hospitals, military barracks), testing, vaccination, and the personal place under quarantine (eg, households, apartments). For medical waste classification, the first three steps are carried out at healthcare centers (i.e., classification, separation, and collection) where all hazardous waste is sent to factories for treatment (i.e., destruction) including transportation and treatment.

In the real environment (i.e., care and treatment of diseases in medical centers), the amount of waste can be divided into two categories: reuse and complete disposal. For each type, we have different treatment. Figure 1 shows the steps of

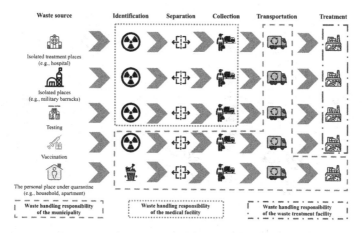

Fig. 2. The Covide-19 pandemic-related medical waste treatment sample in Vietnam [21]

traditional garbage classification and treatment. Step 1 presents the waste collection process in departments in medical facilities (eg, hospitals). These types of waste include medical equipment and supply. Step 2 presents the process of self-segmentation and reuse in the medical environment. At the end of this process, products belonging to the recycling medical product group are reused (step 3) while medical waste is disposed of (step 4). All medical waste is sent to the waste treatment area (step 5). Here, depending on the treatment requirements, the medical waste is classified into the corresponding treatment processes (i.e., recycling plant and sorting factory - step 6).

The risks in the traditional medical waste treatment process have been summarized and presented in Sect. 1 and 2. However, in order to improve people's sense of self-segregation and treatment of medical waste, we propose a model that combines blockchain, smart contracts, and NFT technologies to create certificates in classification waste at medical centers thereby identifying compliance/violation with medical waste classification requirements.

3.2 Model of Treatment and Classification of Medical Waste Based on Blockchain Technology, Smart Contract and NFT

Figure 3 presents nine steps of classification and treatment of medical waste using blockchain, smart contract, and NFT technologies. In particular, doctors and nurses should consult the requirements and regulations of waste segregation before implementing them (step 1). These requirements are extremely important as they will be assessed based on the level of violation/compliance to penalize/reward the implementer (eg, nurse, doctor). Then, steps are taken by medical personnel (called self recycle) - step 2. Hazardous waste must be removed and located outside the care and treatment area of the hospital or center medical center (step 3). Cleaning staff is also familiar with the process of checking the

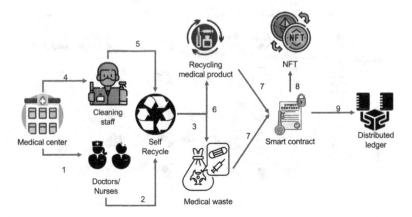

Fig. 3. Model of treatment and classification of medical waste based on blockchain technology, smart contract and NFT

waste sorting behaviors (i.e., compliance/violation) of medical staff carried out in step 4. The inspection process will include two steps (i.e., 5,6). Specifically, the cleaning staff looks at the sorting processes of medical staff to remove hazardous waste during treatment (step 5) - no direct inspection; meanwhile, step 6 presents a process for assessing reused waste in a medical environment. Confirmations about the compliance/violation classification behavior of an individual or organization (i.e., in the hospital) are updated based on the corresponding functions - predefined on the smart contract (i.e., naming the functions). functions). This step is confirmed by the cleaning staff. Step 8 generates NFTs that correspond to the individual/organization's compliance/violation behavior (i.e., including relevant evidence and information - see Sect. 4 for details). Finally, all evaluation and validation steps are stored on distributed ledgers (step 9).

4   Implementation

Our reality model focuses on two main purposes: i) data manipulation (i.e., medical waste) - initialization, query and update - on blockchain platform and ii) creation of NFTs for each user's (i.e., individual/organization) reward and violation behavior based on their behavior in waste sorting/disposal.

4.1   Initialize Data/NFT

Figure 4 shows the steps to initialize medical waste data. These types of waste include medical equipment (i.e., expired/damaged) or medical supplies (eg, masks, PPE, injections). These types of waste are required to be classified into different categories (i.e., discard, reuse) depending on their level of toxicity. Then descriptions of the type of waste are added to each specific garbage bag. Each trash bag has a unique address to separate them with the type of waste.

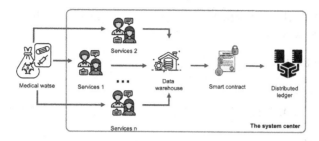

Fig. 4. Initialize data/NFT

In addition, information about the sorter as well as in which department, time, and location is also added to the metadata of the trash bag. As for the storage process, services support concurrent storage (i.e., distributed processing as a peer-to-peer network) on a distributed ledger - supporting more than one user for concurrent storage reduce system latency. In general, the medical waste data is organized as follows:

```
medicalWasteDataObject = {
"medicalWasteID": medicalWasteID,
"staffID": staffID,
"type": type of waste,
"apartmentID": apartmentID,
"quantity": quantity,
"unit": unit,
"packageID": packageID,
"time": time,
"location": location,
"state": null,
"reUse": Null};
```

Specifically, in addition to the information to extract the content (i.e., place of origin, weight, type of waste, etc.), we also store information related to the status of the garbage bags at the hospital (i.e., "state" and "reUse" - defaults to Null). Specifically, "state" changes to 1 if the corresponding garbage bag has been shipped out of the medical center (i.e., for the type of waste to be treated); value 0 - pending. Meanwhile, "reUse" presents the value 1 when the type of waste (i.e., medical device) is reused (i.e., value 0 - pending). Non-hazardous wastes (i.e., non-toxic to the environment and user's health). After the waste sorting phase, the cleaning staff will check if they are in accordance with the process and wait for validation before synchronizing on the chain (i.e., temporarily stored on the data warehouse). Then the pre-designed constraints in the Smart Contract are called through the API (i.e., name of function) to sync them up the chain. This role of accreditation is extremely important because they directly affect the waste treatment process, as well as the premise for rewarding or sanctioning individuals and organizations.

For processes that initiate NFTs (i.e., reward, sanction), the content of the NFT is defined as follows:

```
NFT WASTE_TREATMENT = {
"medicalWasteID": medicalWasteID,
"staffID": staffID,
"apartmentID": apartmentID,
"packageID": packageID,
"type": true/false,
"quantiy": true/false,
"time": time,
"verifier": staffID // Cleaning staff};
```

If the values on the checked trash bags are correct then the sorter is rewarded and vice versa if they are penalized for violations. In case the verifier does not provide correct information, the person penalized is the verifier.

4.2 Data Query

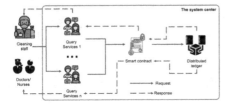 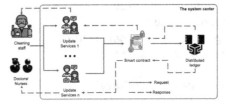

Fig. 5. Data query   **Fig. 6.** Data updated

Similar to the data initialization steps, the data query process also supports many simultaneous participants in the system for access (i.e., distributed model). Support services receive requests from Cleaning staff or nurses/doctors to access data. Depending on the query object we have different access purposes. Specifically, Cleaning staff queries with the purpose of checking the classification process or transferring hazardous medical waste to the shipping company. In contrast, healthcare professionals can query data to find reusable medical tools (i.e., out of stock). Figure 5 shows the steps to query medical waste data. These requests are sent as requests (i.e., pre-designed services as API calls) from the user to the smart contracts available in the system (i.e., name of function) before retrieving the data from the distributed ledger. All retrieval requests are also saved as query history for each individual or organization. In case the corresponding information is not found (eg, wrong ID), the system will send a message not found results. For the NFT query process, all support services are provided as APIs.

4.3   Data Updated

The data update routine is invoked only after verifying that the data exists on the thread (i.e., after executing the corresponding data query procedure). In this section, we assume that the search data exists on the string. Where none exists, the system sends the same message to the user (see Sect. 4.2 for details). Similar to the two processes of query and data initialization, we support update services in the form of APIs to receive requests from users before passing them to smart contracts (i.e., name of function) for processing. The purpose of this process is to update the time and location of the garbage bags during transportation and handling of medical waste. Thereby, the administrator can trace the status of medical waste treatment/transportation from medical centers to waste treatment companies. Figure 6 shows the procedure for updating medical waste data. For NFTs (i.e., available) the update process includes only moving from the owner's address to the new one (i.e., new owner). If any information is updated on an existing NFT, it will be stored as a new NFT (see Sect. 4.1 for details).

5   Evaluation

5.1   EVM-Supported Platforms

Fig. 7. The transaction info (e.g., BNB Smart Chain)

Since the proposed model rewards/penalizes for compliance/violation of the medical waste classification process, we implement the recommendation model on EVM-enabled blockchain platforms instead of mining platforms under the Hyperledger eco-system. In addition, assessments based on system responsiveness (i.e., number of requests responded successfully/failed, system latency - min, max, average) have been evaluated by us in the previous research paper.

Therefore, in this paper, we determine the suitable platform for our proposed model. Specifically, we install a recommendation system on four popular blockchain platforms today, supporting Ethereum Virtual Machine (EVM), including Binance Smart Chain (BNB Smart Chain)[2]; Polygon[3]; Fantom[4]; and

---

[2] https://github.com/bnb-chain/whitepaper/blob/master/WHITEPAPER.md.
[3] https://polygon.technology/lightpaper-polygon.pdf.
[4] https://whitepaper.io/document/438/fantom-whitepaper.

Celo[5]. Our implementations on these four platforms are also shared as a contribution to the article to collect transaction fees corresponding to the four platforms' supporting coins[6], i.e., BNB[7]; MATIC[8]; FTM[9]; and CELO[10]. For example, Fig. 7 details our three assessments of a successful installation on BNB Smart Chain (i.e., similar settings are shown for the other three platforms). Our implementations to evaluate the execution cost of smart contracts (i.e., designed based on Solidity language) run on testnet environments of four platforms in order to choose the most cost-effective platform to deploy. Our detailed assessments focus on the cost of performing contract creation, and NFT retrieval/transfer (i.e., updating NFT ownership address presented in the respective subsections related to i) Transaction Fee; ii) Gas limit; iii) Gas Used by Transaction.

Table 1. Transaction fee

	Contract Creation	Create NFT	Transfer NFT
BNB Smart Chain	0.02731376 BNB ($8.41)	0.00109162 BNB ($0.34)	0.00057003 BNB ($0.18)
Fantom	0.009577666 FTM ($0.001840)	0.000405167 FTM ($0.000078)	0.0002380105 FTM ($0.000046)
Polygon	0.006841190030101236 MATIC($0.01)	0.000289405001041858 MATIC($0.00)	0.000170007500612027 MATIC($0.00)
Celo	0.0070979376 CELO ($0.004)	0.0002840812 CELO ($0.000)	0.0001554878 CELO ($0.000)

5.2 Transaction Fee

Table 1 shows the cost of creating contracts for the four platforms. It is easy to see that the highest transaction fee of the three requirements is contract creation for all four platforms. In which, the cost of BNB Smart Chain is the highest with the highest cost when creating a contract is 0.02731376 BNB ($8.41); whereas, the lowest cost recorded by the Fantom platform with the highest cost for contract initiation is less than 0.009577666 FTM ($0.001840). Meanwhile, the cost to enforce Celo's contract initiation requirement is lower than Polygon's with only $0.004 compared to $0.01. For the remaining two requirements (Create NFT and Transfer NFT), we note that the cost of implementing them for all three platforms, Polygon, Celo, and Fantom is very low (i.e., negligible) given the cost. trades close to $0.00. However, this cost is still very high when deployed on BNB Smart Chain with 0.00109162 BNB ($0.34) and 0.00057003 BNB ($0.18) for Create NFT and Transfer NFT, respectively.

---

[5] https://celo.org/papers/whitepaper.

[6] Implementation of theme models our release at Nov-24-2022 04:19:05 AM +UTC.

[7] https://testnet.bscscan.com/address/0x94d93a5606bd3ac9ae8b80e334dfec74d007 5ece.

[8] https://mumbai.polygonscan.com/address/0x48493a3bb4e7cb42269062957bd541d 52afc0d7a.

[9] https://testnet.ftmscan.com/address/0x48493a3bb4e7cb42269062957bd541d52 afc0d7a.

[10] https://explorer.celo.org/alfajores/address/0x48493A3bB4E7cB42269062957Bd541 D52aFc0d7A/transactions.

5.3 Gas Limit

Table 2. Gas limit

	Contract Creation	Create NFT	Transfer NFT
BNB Smart Chain	2,731,376	109,162	72,003
Fantom	2,736,476	115,762	72,803
Polygon	2,736,476	115,762	72,803
Celo	3,548,968	142,040	85,673

Table 2 shows the gas limit for each transaction. Our observations show that the gas limits of the three platforms (i.e., BNB, Polygon, and Fantom) are roughly equivalent - where Polygon and Fantom are similar in all three transactions. The remaining platform (i.e., Celo) has the highest gas limit with 3,548,968; 142,040; and 85,673 for all three transaction types.

5.4 Gas Used by Transaction

Table 3. Gas Used by Transaction

	Contract Creation	Create NFT	Transfer NFT
BNB Smart Chain	2,731,376 (100%)	109.162 (100%)	57,003 (79.17%)
Fantom	2,736,476 (100%)	115,762 (100%)	68,003 (93.41%)
Polygon	2,736,476 (100%)	115,762 (100%)	68,003 (93.41%)
Celo	2,729,976 (76.92%)	109.262 (76.92%)	59,803 (69.8%)

Table 3 shows the amount of gas used when executing the transaction (i.e., what percentage of gas in total gas is shown in Table 2). Specifically, three platforms BNB, Polygon, and Fantom use 100% of Gas Limit for two transactions Contract Creation and Create NFT. Meanwhile, Celo uses 76.92% of the Gas limit for the above two transactions. For the last transaction of Transfer NFT, the highest Gas level was recorded by Fantom and Polygon with 93.41% of Gas limit; while BNB and Celo use 79.17% and 69.8% of Gas limit.

6 Discussion

According to our observation, the transaction value depends on the market capitalization of the respective coin. The total market capitalization of the 4 platforms used in our review (i.e., BNB (Binance Smart Chain); MATIC (Polygon); FTM (Fantom); and CELO (Celo)) are $50,959,673,206; $7,652,386,190; $486,510,485; and $244,775,762.[11] This directly affects the coin value of that plat-

---

[11] Our observation time is 12:00 PM - 11/26/2022.

form - although the number of coins issued at the time of system implementation also plays a huge role. The total issuance of the four coins BNB, MATIC, FTM, and CELO, is 163,276,974/163,276,974; 8,868,740,690/10,000,000,000; 2,541,152, 731/3,175,000,000 and 473,376,178/1,000,000,000 coins. The coin's value is conventionally based on the number of coins issued and the total market capitalization with a value of $314.98; $0.863099; $0.1909; and $0.528049 for BNB, MATIC, FTM, and CELO, respectively.

Based on the measurements and analysis in Sect. 5 section, we have concluded that the proposed model deployed on Faltom brings many benefits related to system operating costs. In particular, generating and receiving NFTs has an almost zero (i.e., negligible) fee. Also, the cost of creating contracts with transaction execution value is very low (i.e., less than $0.002). In our current analysis, we have not considered issues related to the privacy policy of users (i.e., access control [25, 26, 32], dynamic policy [24, 35]) - a possible approach would be implemented in upcoming research activities. Finally, infrastructure-based approaches (i.e., gRPC [20, 29]; Microservices [27, 30]; Dynamic transmission messages [31] and Brokerless [28]) can be integrated into the model of us to increase user interaction.

7   Conclusion

Our proposal is to develop a classification and treatment system for medical waste applicable to the Vietnamese environment. The risks associated with infection people and pollution of the environment are the main virulence factors for this work. Specifically, we propose a model that combines blockchain and smart contracts to manage the process of sorting and treating waste from medical facilities to medical waste treatment companies. In addition, the model we aim to include rewards/penalties for compliance/violation behaviors of individuals/organizations that are stored pieces of evidence in the form of NFTs. Our proof-of-concept is implemented on the Ethereum platform; while, smart contracts exploit Solidity language to define three transactions (i.e., contract creation, NFT creation, NFT transfer). Our smart contract implementations are performed on four popular platforms that currently support EVM, including BNB, MATIC, FTM, and CELO. Based on our analysis looking at a wide range of criteria (i.e., Transaction Fee; Gas limit; Gas Used by Transaction; and Gas Price), the Fantom platform has the lowest execution fee compared to the other three platforms. Some of the reasons are mentioned in the discussion. In this section, we also present future development directions of current work.

References

1. The circular economy in detail. https://www.cdc.gov/vaccines/covid-19/hcp/wastage-operational-summary.html#vaccine-wastage-best-practices. Accessed 30 Oct 2022
2. How amazon is investing in a circular economy. https://www.aboutamazon.com/news/sustainability/how-amazon-is-investing-in-a-circular-economy. Accessed 30 Oct 2022
3. Ahmad, R.W., et al.: Blockchain-based forward supply chain and waste management for Covid-19 medical equipment and supplies. IEEE Access 9, 44905–44927 (2021)
4. Awasthi, A.K., Zeng, X., Li, J.: Environmental pollution of electronic waste recycling in India: a critical review. Environ. Pollut. 211, 259–270 (2016)
5. Bakhsh, K., Rose, S., Ali, M.F., Ahmad, N., Shahbaz, M.: Economic growth, CO2 emissions, renewable waste and FDI relation in Pakistan: new evidences from 3SLS. J. Environ. Manage. 196, 627–632 (2017)
6. Benson, N.U., et al.: Covid-19 pandemic and emerging plastic-based personal protective equipment waste pollution and management in Africa. J. Environ. Chem. Eng. 9(3), 105222 (2021)
7. Chen, Z., et al.: The independent effect of Covid-19 vaccinations and air pollution exposure on risk of Covid-19 hospitalizations in Southern California. Am. J. Respir. Crit. Care Med. 207, 218–221 (2022)
8. Das, A.K., et al.: Covid-19 and municipal solid waste (MSW) management: a review. Environ. Sci. Pollut. Res. 28(23), 28993–29008 (2021)
9. Dasaklis, T.K., Casino, F., Patsakis, C.: A traceability and auditing framework for electronic equipment reverse logistics based on blockchain: the case of mobile phones. In: 2020 11th International Conference on Information, Intelligence, Systems and Applications (IISA), pp. 1–7. IEEE (2020)
10. Echegaray, F., et al.: Assessing the intention-behavior gap in electronic waste recycling: the case of Brazil. J. Clean. Prod. 142, 180–190 (2017)
11. Gaur, N., Narasimhulu, K., PydiSetty, Y.: Recent advances in the bio-remediation of persistent organic pollutants and its effect on environment. J. Clean. Prod. 198, 1602–1631 (2018)
12. Gupta, N., Bedi, P.: E-waste management using blockchain based smart contracts. In: 2018 International Conference on Advances in Computing, Communications and Informatics (ICACCI), pp. 915–921. IEEE (2018)
13. Jiao, W., et al.: Policy durability of circular economy in China: a process analysis of policy translation. Resour. Conserv. Recycl. 117, 12–24 (2017)
14. Laouar, M.R., Hamad, Z.T., Eom, S.: Towards blockchain-based urban planning: application for waste collection management. In: Proceedings of the 9th International Conference on Information Systems and Technologies, pp. 1–6 (2019)
15. Le, H.T., Nguyen, T.T.L., Nguyen, T.A., Ha, X.S., Duong-Trung, N.: Bloodchain: a blood donation network managed by blockchain technologies. Network 2(1), 21–35 (2022)
16. Le, H.T., et al.: Medical-waste chain: a medical waste collection, classification and treatment management by blockchain technology. Computers 11(7), 113 (2022)
17. Leonard, A.: The story of stuff: How our obsession with stuff is trashing the planet, our communities, and our health-and a vision for change. Simon and Schuster (2010)

18. Li, J., Kassem, M.: Applications of distributed ledger technology (DLT) and blockchain-enabled smart contracts in construction. Autom. Constr. **132**, 103955 (2021)
19. Manninen, K., et al.: Do circular economy business models capture intended environmental value propositions? J. Clean. Prod. **171**, 413–422 (2018)
20. Nguyen, L.T.T., et al.: BMDD: a novel approach for IoT platform (broker-less and microservice architecture, decentralized identity, and dynamic transmission messages). PeerJ Comput. Sci. **8**, e950 (2022)
21. Nguyen, T.D., et al.: Estimation of Covid-19 waste generation and composition in Vietnam for pandemic management. Waste Manag. Res. **39**(11), 1356–1364 (2021)
22. Quynh, N.T.T., et al.: Toward a design of blood donation management by blockchain technologies. In: Gervasi, O., et al. (eds.) ICCSA 2021. LNCS, vol. 12956, pp. 78–90. Springer, Cham (2021). https://doi.org/10.1007/978-3-030-87010-2_6
23. Schmelz, D., et al.: Technical mechanics of a trans-border waste flow tracking solution based on blockchain technology. In: 2019 IEEE 35th International Conference on Data Engineering Workshops (ICDEW), pp. 31–36. IEEE (2019)
24. Son, H.X., Dang, T.K., Massacci, F.: REW-SMT: a new approach for rewriting XACML request with dynamic big data security policies. In: Wang, G., Atiquzzaman, M., Yan, Z., Choo, K.-K.R. (eds.) SpaCCS 2017. LNCS, vol. 10656, pp. 501–515. Springer, Cham (2017). https://doi.org/10.1007/978-3-319-72389-1_40
25. Son, H.X., Hoang, N.M.: A novel attribute-based access control system for fine-grained privacy protection. In: Proceedings of the 3rd International Conference on Cryptography, Security and Privacy, pp. 76–80 (2019)
26. Son, H.X., Nguyen, M.H., Vo, H.K., Nguyen, T.P.: Toward an privacy protection based on access control model in hybrid cloud for healthcare systems. In: Martínez Álvarez, F., Troncoso Lora, A., Sáez Muñoz, J.A., Quintián, H., Corchado, E. (eds.) CISIS/ICEUTE -2019. AISC, vol. 951, pp. 77–86. Springer, Cham (2020). https://doi.org/10.1007/978-3-030-20005-3_8
27. Thanh, L.N.T., et al.: IoHT-MBA: An internet of healthcare things (IoHT) platform based on microservice and brokerless architecture. Int. J. Adv. Comput. Sci. Appl. **12**(7) (2021)
28. Thanh, L.N.T., et al.: Sip-MBA: a secure IoT platform with brokerless and microservice architecture. Int. J. Adv. Comput. Sci. Appl. **12**(7) (2021)
29. Thanh, L.N.T., et al.: Toward a security IoT platform with high rate transmission and low energy consumption. In: Gervasi, O., et al. (eds.) ICCSA 2021. LNCS, vol. 12949, pp. 647–662. Springer, Cham (2021). https://doi.org/10.1007/978-3-030-86653-2_47
30. Nguyen, T.T.L., et al.: Toward a unique IoT network via single sign-on protocol and message queue. In: Saeed, K., Dvorský, J. (eds.) CISIM 2021. LNCS, vol. 12883, pp. 270–284. Springer, Cham (2021). https://doi.org/10.1007/978-3-030-84340-3_22
31. Thanh, L.N.T., et al.: UIP2SOP: a unique IoT network applying single sign-on and message queue protocol. IJACSA **12**(6) (2021)
32. Thi, Q.N.T., Dang, T.K., Van, H.L., Son, H.X.: Using JSON to specify privacy preserving-enabled attribute-based access control policies. In: Wang, G., Atiquzzaman, M., Yan, Z., Choo, K.-K.R. (eds.) SpaCCS 2017. LNCS, vol. 10656, pp. 561–570. Springer, Cham (2017). https://doi.org/10.1007/978-3-319-72389-1_44
33. Turner, J.M., Nugent, L.M.: Charging up battery recycling policies: extended producer responsibility for single-use batteries in the European Union, Canada, and the United States. J. Ind. Ecol. **20**(5), 1148–1158 (2016)

34. Wafula, S.T., Musiime, J., Oporia, F.: Health care waste management among health workers and associated factors in primary health care facilities in Kampala City, Uganda: a cross-sectional study. BMC Public Health **19**(1), 1–10 (2019)

35. Xuan, S.H., et al.: Rew-XAC: an approach to rewriting request for elastic ABAC enforcement with dynamic policies. In: 2016 International Conference on Advanced Computing and Applications (ACOMP), pp. 25–31. IEEE (2016)

A Game-Based Approach for Mitigating the Sybil Attacks on Blockchain Applications

Ashis Kumar Samanta$^{(\boxtimes)}$ (iD) and Nabendu Chaki$^{(\boxtimes)}$ (iD)

Department of Computer Science and Engineering, University of Calcutta,
Kolkata, India
aksdba@caluniv.ac.in, nabendu@ieee.org

Abstract. The data explosion of this digital century encourages the necessity of data security and maintaining privacy. The generated data through online transactions in different sectors have been increased a million times. Therefore, the trustful transaction and reliability of data became necessary for its analysis and future use in the online platform. The change of data platform from a centralized to distributed nature enhances the utility of the data use, and the security threats are also increased side by side. The Sybil attack is one of the significant security threats in the distributed network environment. Blockchain is a peer-to-peer distributed ledger that works in a distributed environment. However, the blockchain framework, which aims to provide tamper-proof security on data suffers from Sybil attacks too. This paper aims to analyze the implementation of blockchain technology in different applications and propose a new game-based model to effectively detect and mitigate Sybil attacks on the blockchain.

Keywords: Blockchain · Smart Contract · Sybil Attack · Security Threats · Game theory

1 Introduction

The various wireless sensor network (WSN) applications are integrated with many sensors. This network's deployment area is so large and dynamic that there is an immense possibility to become the network venerable [1]. Sybil attack is one of the significant threats to the WSN, and the attacker wants to access and control the system by introducing multiple legitimate identities. The blockchain is a framework that runs in the distributed network using cryptographic technology. Each node within the blockchain network possesses a public key and a private key. This key-value technology or hash-key is the primary tool of security of blockchain because it is cryptographically based. On the other hand, this hash-key is also one of the main issues of the blockchain for its security threats for its unauthorized access or loss. Therefore, in the blockchain framework, Sybil attack chances are much higher due to multiple nodes in the blockchain network.

K. Saeed et al. (Eds.): CISIM 2023, LNCS 14164, pp. 108–123, 2023.
https://doi.org/10.1007/978-3-031-42823-4_9

1.1 Why Sybil Attack is Threat to Blockchain

The implementation of blockchain is to secure the data and maintain privacy and trustworthiness. The Sybil attack may raise different threats to the blockchain as described below.

The mining nodes of the blockchain do the mining or writing operations in the blockchain. When a block is generated, the miners are selected for mining. The miners' pool may work as an honest and dishonest miner, and if the miners' response exceeds 50% consent, they will act accordingly.

1. Therefore, in the case of a Sybil attack, when several fake identities or dishonest nodes exist, that can generate the issues of 51% attack.
2. The dishonest node can partially complete the mining work by generating another block withhold attack.

Therefore, the Sybil attack draws significant attention in the domain of prospective research work. In this paper, the objective is to analyze the Sybil attack and the probable reason for the Sybil attack on smart contract. It also tries to address the attack by using Gambler's Ruin game theory. The authentication of the generated block and the block-generated node is done. In the case of honest mining of the block in the longest chain, the miner is offered incentive and in case of attack, the attacker is charged a penalty value by the blockchain administrator for the malicious behaviors.

2   Literature Review

A. Bochem et al.(2021) proposed to address the Sybil attack of a distributed network. The proposed model recommends financially punishing the Sybil nodes instead of incentives. The system frames an upper and lowers bound of the cost to identify Sybil nodes. The efficiency and accuracy of the recommended algorithm are analyzed using "coloredPetri nets." The performance of Proof of concepts is ultimately evaluated using IoT [2]. The paper published by M. Platt et al. (2021) proposed a method IdAPoS ("Identity augmented proof of stake"). The mechanism addresses the Sybil attack by resisting the attacker's prolonged timing to attack [3]. An article proposed by T. Rajabi et al. (2020) identified the research gap of the famous addressing model (Elastico) of Sybil's attack on blockchain. The Proof of Work (PoW) takes much longer to produce an identifier, which would increase the venerability of the said chain. More Sybil IDs' are generated by the nodes having more hash power. The author analyzed two types of Sybil attacks, i) Break Consensus Protocol (BCP) attack to spoil the consensus process, ii) Generate Fake Transaction (GFT) attack to identify the fake transactions into the blockchain [4].

An analysis of comparing and mapping of Sybil attacks is presented by U.S.R.K. Dhamodharan et al. (2015) in [5]. The authors also proposed an algorithm to mitigate the Sybil attack through message-passing authentication. R. Pacori et al. recommend a solution model for Sybil attack that may generate the

"Spartacus" attack [6]. The authors proposed the up-gradation of distributed hash table Sybil attack and want to save the routing table data from tampering. The recommended trust solution model mitigates the Sybil attack for storing and retrieving routing data through recursive and non-recursive processes. P. Swathi et al. [7] proposed a solution to mitigate the Sybil attack. The authors suggested that each node has been brought under the close monitoring of other nodes. Therefore, every item a node forwards under the vigil of other nodes. A particular node can quickly be identified if it only forwards the blocks to a specific user. The paper by A. Begum et al. [8], highlighted different reasons for double-spending attack and their targeted area of cryptocurrency. An article published by B. Kumar et al. introduces a zero-sum game model to mitigate the Sybil attack by decreasing the reputation of the malicious node. The attacker has to spend an amount of 'cost' to get back its reputation and optimised the attacking level. The mechanism proposed, thus protects the controlling authorities towards handling the Sybil attack [9]. M. B. Shareh et al. proposed a mechanism to address the Sybil attack. This increases stability and incorporates robustness in the incentive system as a whole. An evolutionary game is used in system [10].

2.1   Findings of Literature Review

As evident in the discussion above, several researchers have worked towards handling the Sybil attack. It may further be inferred from the study that the excessive time consumption for mining a block by the proof of work (pow), IdAPoS, and inappropriate consensus algorithm are the main reasons for the Sybil attack. Some new consensus algorithms like proof of concept (poc) are also proposed in the existing literature to avoid pow. In order to mitigate the Sybil attack, some of the researchers have emphasized for reducing the cost of blockchain transactions by introducing internet-independent low-power consumption IoT devices.

2.2   Gap Analysis

The lack of central monitoring and centralized control are among the root causes of the Sybil attack in a blockchain. Therefore, the introduction of a central controlling agent is the out of scope of the proposed solutions as mentioned. Therefore, there is a scope for introducing a blockchain administrator to ensure vigilance on the attack.

2.3   Problem Statement

This works aims to propose a Game-based mechanism such that the blockchain administrator would identify the Sybil node in advance and determine its penalty depending upon the intensity of its malicious performances. The penalty may also depend on the transnational values of the block that the miner mined maliciously.

3 Methodology

3.1 Proposed Solutions

The two primary reasons for Sybil's attack are trying to address many issues. The first is the false identity of the generated block and the second issue that has been addressed is the dishonest mining of the block by the miner (Fig. 1).

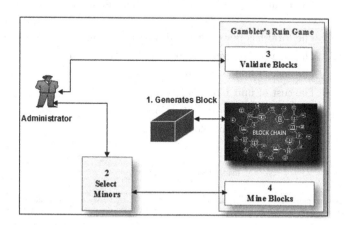

Fig. 1. The Addresing of Sybil Attack Using Gambler's Ruin Game

3.2 The Game Model

The Gambler's Ruin Problem is one of the famous two-contestant problems of two players' honest user (u_h) and attacker (u_a). The game is a probabilistic game that can play multiple times one player against the other player. The player can play the game indefinitely until they exhaust all of their hash power to invest (Table 1).

The basic assumptions that have been made to play the game are

1. All the players are logical and can take independent decisions to maximize their respective pay-off.
2. The player can take a logical decision within the given set of actions.
3. The game shall be closed to its end then the value of the probability of either 0 or 1.

Table 1. The Symbol used in Proposed Solution

Symbol	Descriptions
p_v	winning probability of validation of player $u_h, p_v (0 \le p_v \le 1)$
$q_v = 1 - p_v$	winning probability of validation of player $u_a, q_v (0 \le p_v, q_v \le 1)$
p_m	winning probability of mining of player $u_h, p_v (0 \le p_v \le 1)$
$q_m = 1 - p_m$	winning probability of mining of attacker $u_a, q_m (0 \le q_m \le 1)$
H_v	The total has power invested for the validation of block generation node
H_m	The total has power invested for the mining of the data block
H_a	The total has power invested by the attacking node
c_v	The cost of node verification
c_m	The cost of unit block mining
r_v	The revenue of node verification
r_m	The revenue of unit block mining

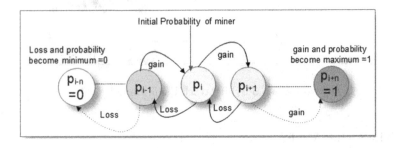

Fig. 2. The Gambler's Ruin Game Strategy

Initially, if it is imagined that both players have the probability is $p = q = (\frac{1}{2})$, then both players are in a stable stage. If it is found at any stage that $p > (\frac{1}{2})$, the user u_h is in the winning stage and the attacker u_a is in the losing stage. Otherwise, if it is found at any stage that $p < (\frac{1}{2})$, the attacker u_a is in the winning stage and the honest user u_h is in the losing stage. The game ends either when $p_n = 1$ or $p_n = 0$. Therefor at any instant $\tau_i = \min\{ n \ge 0 : p_n \in \{0,1\} \| p_0 = i \}$.

Let it consider at any instant of iteration-i of the game P_i is the probability and if the player win in this iteration the probability is represented as P_{i+1} and in case of the losing the probability is denoted as P_{i-1} (Fig. 2). Therefore the probability after the first iteration of the game is shown as

$$P_i = pP_{i+1} + (1 - p)P_{i-1} \tag{1}$$

The total probability of winning the game by the honest user and losing the game by the attacker is 1, then the Markov property the gambler can be written as

$$pP_i + (1-p)P_i = pP_{i+1} + (1-p)P_{i-1} \tag{2}$$

$$\therefore P_{i+1} - P_i = \frac{(1-p)}{p}(P_i - P_{i-1}) \tag{3}$$

Taking the initial value $P_0 = 0$

$$\equiv P_{i+1} - P_i = \left(\frac{(1-p)}{p}\right)^i (P_1), \{0 \le i \le 1\} \tag{4}$$

$$\equiv P_{i+1} - P_i = \sum_{n=1}^{n}(P_{n+1} - P_n) \tag{5}$$

$$\equiv P_{i+1} - P_i = \sum_{n=1}^{n}\left(\frac{(1-p)}{p}\right)^n P_1 \tag{6}$$

$$\equiv P_{i+1} = \left(\frac{(1-p)}{p}\right)^i (P_1), \{0 \le i \le 1\} \tag{7}$$

$$\therefore P_n = \begin{cases} P_1 \frac{1-\left(\frac{1-p}{p}\right)^n}{1-\left(\frac{1-p}{p}\right)}, & \text{if } p \ne q \\ P_1 n, & \text{if } p = q = \frac{1}{2} \end{cases} \tag{8}$$

The (Eq. 8) can be written for i^{th} iteration as (Eq. 9)

$$\therefore P_i = \begin{cases} \frac{1-\left(\frac{1-p}{p}\right)^i}{1-\left(\frac{1-p}{p}\right)^n}, & \text{if } p \ne q \\ \frac{i}{n}, & \text{if } p = q = \frac{1}{2} \end{cases} \tag{9}$$

Authentication of Block Generation Node: The blockchain administrator has the database of all the public-key hash value of all the nodes of the blockchain network. The public-key of the node of the generated block is broadcasted by the blockchain administrator to all nodes in the network except the block-generated node of the blockchain network. The nodes of the network acknowledge the broadcasted public-key to the blockchain administrator along with their respective identity (public-key). if the accumulated acknowledge value is more than 50% then the node of the generated block is successfully authenticated (Algorithm 1), otherwise, the block is discarded and no mining is done. The input of Algorithm 1 is the number of nodes (n–1) in the blockchain (except the block-generated node) and the public-key (pk_b) of the respective node. The probability of a node in the blockchain honestly or dishonestly identifying the node of the generation block is $\frac{1}{(n-1)}$ in this particular case (Fig. 3).

1. The probability distribution of the entire blockchain using the Poisson distribution can be written as (Eq. 10), where $\lambda = \sum_{i=1}^{i=(n-1)} n_i \times \frac{1}{(n-1)}$, the value of e = 2.71828 (approx),

$$p(x, \lambda) = \frac{e^{-\lambda} \times \lambda^x}{x!} \tag{10}$$

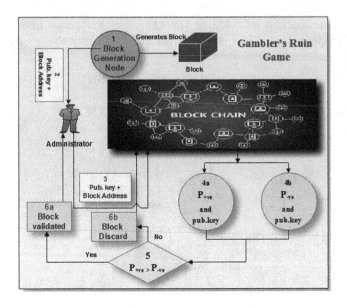

Fig. 3. The Validation of Block Generation Node

2. In case all the nodes in the system take the honest participation in the verification of the block generation node, then the $p_v = 1$ and $q_v = 0$. The generated revenue dishonest nodes ($r_{va1} = 0$), the revenue of the honest node (r_{vh1}) and the entire revenue in the system (r_{v1}) respectively shown in Eqs. 11i and 11ii respectively.

$$r_{vh1} = r_v \times p_v - H_v \times c_v \times p_v \text{ where } p_v = \sum_{i=1}^{i=(n-1)} \frac{1}{(n-1)} \tag{11i}$$

$$r_{v1} = r_{vh1} - r_{va1} \text{ where } r_{va1} = 0 \tag{11ii}$$

3. In case if much of the nodes(say n_1) in the system take honest participation in the verification of the block generation node, and some nodes (say n_2 such that $n_1 > n_2$) are behaving maliciously then the probability of honestly behaved nodes is greater than the probability of dishonest nodes ($p_v\,q_v$). The generated revenue honest nodes (r_{vh2}), the revenue of the dishonest node (r_{va2}) and the entire revenue in the system (r_{v2}) respectively shown in Eqs. 12i, 12ii and 12iii respectively.

$$r_{vh2} = r_v . \sum_{i=1}^{i=n_1} \frac{1}{(n-1)} - c_v.(H_v . \sum_{i=1}^{i=n_1} \frac{1}{(n-1)} + H_a . \sum_{i=1}^{i=n_2} \frac{1}{(n-1)}) \tag{12i}$$

$$r_{va2} = r_v . \sum_{i=1}^{i=n_2} \frac{1}{(n-1)} - c_v.H_a . \sum_{i=1}^{i=n_2} \frac{1}{(n-1)} \tag{12ii}$$

$$r_{v2} = r_{vh2} - r_{va2}, \text{ such that } (n_1 > n_2) \tag{12iii}$$

Algorithm 1. The Verification of Block Generation Node

Input: The number of nodes (n-1) in the blockchain network, pk_b
Output: Successfully verified or Discard the block

1: $i \leftarrow 1, p_{+ve} \leftarrow 0, p_{-ve} \leftarrow 0$
2: **while** $i \leq (n-1)$ **do**
3:     **if** pk_b exist in n_i **then**
4:         $p_{+ve} = p_{+ve} + \frac{1}{(n-1)}$
5:         $pk_i \leftarrow pk_{n_i}$
6:         $L_{pve} \leftarrow pk_i$
7:         $i = i + 1$
8:     **else**
9:         $p_{-ve} = p_{-ve} + \frac{1}{(n-1)}$
10:        $pk_i \leftarrow pk_{n_i}$
11:        $L_{nve} \leftarrow pk_i$
12:        $i = i + 1$
13:    **end if**
14: **end while**
15: **if** $p_{+ve} > 0.5$ **then**
16:     Successfully Verified the block-generated node
17: **else**
18:     Fake identity of block generated node
19:     Discard the generated block
20: **end if**
21: Return$(p_{+ve}, p_{-ve}, L_{pve}, L_{nve})$

---

4. In case some of the nodes (say n_1) in the system take the honest participation in the verification of the block generation node, and some of the nodes (say n_2 such that $n_1 \leq n_2$) are behaving maliciously then the probability of honestly behaved nodes is less than or equal to the probability of dishonest nodes ($p_v \leq q_v$). The generated revenue honest nodes (r_{vh3}), the revenue of the dishonest node (r_{va3}) and the entire revenue in the system (r_{v3}) respectively shown in Eqs. 13i, 13ii and 13iii respectively.

$$r_{vh3} = r_v . \sum_{i=1}^{i=n_1} \frac{1}{(n-1)} - c_v.(H_v . \sum_{i=1}^{i=n_1} \frac{1}{(n-1)} + H_a . \sum_{i=1}^{i=n_2} \frac{1}{(n-1)})$$
(13i)

$$r_{va3} = r_v . \sum_{i=1}^{i=n_2} \frac{1}{(n-1)} - c_v . H_a . \sum_{i=1}^{i=n_2} \frac{1}{(n-1)}$$
(13ii)

$$r_{v3} = r_{vh3} - r_{va3}, \text{ such that } (n_1 \leq n_2)$$
(13iii)

5. In case all the nodes in the system take the participation dishonestly in the verification of the block generation node, then the $p_v = 0$ and $q_v = 1$. The generated revenue honest nodes ($r_{vh4} = 0$), the revenue of the dishonest node

(r_{va4}) and the entire revenue in the system (r_{v4}) respectively shown in Eqs. 11i and 11ii respectively.

$$r_{va4} = r_v \cdot \sum_{i=1}^{i=(n-1)} \frac{1}{(n-1)} - c_v.H_a \times q_a \tag{14i}$$

$$r_{v4} = r_{vh4} - r_{va4} \tag{14ii}$$

Table 2. The gambler's ruin Pay-off of node validation in Proposed Solution

u_h		The Attacker (u_a)	
		(H)	(A)
Honest	**(H)**	$r_{vh1}, 0$ [1]	r_{vh2}, r_{va2} [2]
User	**(A)**	r_{vh3}, r_{va3} [3]	$0, r_{va4}$ [4]

The pay-off of the block generation node using the gambler's ruin is shown in Table 2. The nodes accumulated in the positive acknowledgment of the validation process are referred to as honest nodes and the nodes that increased the negative acknowledgment (as shown in Algorithm 1) are to be referred to as the attacking nodes or dishonest nodes.

Mining of Generated Block: The miners then mine the block into the longest chain of the network. The number of miners is (n-1) except for the block greeted node (G). Let it be considered that the corresponding probabilities of miners that they can solve the crypto-puzzle of hash power are $p_1, ..., p_{(n-1)}$.

The miners need to mine the block in a fixed time quantum during the mining process. The primary objective is to add the block into the longest chain of the network. The longest chain contains the consensus algorithm and the effort of creating any sub-branches of the chain would consider an attack and would be the waste of time. In the real situation, all the miners in the network do not try to mine the block by extending the longest branch of the chain in a given time quantum. Therefore there may be a chance to get benefit by the miners by adding the block in some sub-branches or sometimes withholding the block for later use.

Algorithm 2. Public Blockchain Mining using Gambler's Ruin Game
___

Input: $G_{pub-key}, B_{add}, LI_{add}, t, c_m, m, r_m, H_a$
Output: Successfully Mined or transfer the block to other miner
1: Label Do:
2: $Type \leftarrow public, S_c \leftarrow 0, L_c \leftarrow 0, time \leftarrow 0$
3: $OS_{ret} \leftarrow \{\}, OL_{ret} \leftarrow \{\}$
4: bool Solve()   ▷ Temporary mine the block
5: bool List()   ▷ List the block in the Longest Chain
6: **if** $time \leq t$ **then**
7:     $OS_{ret} \leftarrow$ Solve($G_{pub-key}, c_m, m, r_m, H_a$)
8:     $OL_{ret} \leftarrow$ List(B_{add}, LI_{add})
9: **else**
10:     **if** $OS_{ret}.S_c = 0$ And $OL_{ret}.LI_c = 0$ **then**
11:         Can not Incomplete in Time
12:         Provide Penalty for $m_{pub-key}$
13:         Goto LabelDo   ▷ Block forwarded to next miner
14:     **else**
15:         **if** $OS_{ret}.H_{val} = L_{add}$ And $OS_{ret}.S_c = 1$ And $OL_{ret}.LI_c = 1$ **then**
16:             Block Mined Successfully
17:             Initialize and Release Incentives
18:         **else**
19:             Provide Penalty for $m_{pub-key}$
20:             Goto LabelDo   ▷ Block forwarded to next miner
21:         **end if**
22:     **end if**
23: **end if**
24:
___

1. The gambler's ruin game is considered for the mining process of the generated block.

2. The public-key of the block generator nodes, the block address, and the longest address of the blockchain is contained by all the nodes of the network as those are the public information.

3. The node that takes part in the mining of the block with minimum time within the specified time quantum and mined the block in the longest chain will be a success miner and will be eligible for revenue as mentioned in equation.

4. Any miner node that does not want to participate in the mining process may keep salient without investing any mining power. In this case, the silent miner will not be eligible for any incentives as their respective investment is nil for mining.

5. In case a miner cannot complete the mining process within the specified time quantum, then the mining process will automatically get rid of the control of that node. After the expiry of time, the expenditure of the said unsuccessful node will be taken into account without providing any incentives to that node.

Algorithm 3. Solve function of mining of Public Blockchain

    Procedure: Solve()
    Input: $G_{pub-key}, B_{add}, LI_{add}, t, c_m, m, r_m, H_a$
    Output: Successfully return Hash-value,$m_{pub.key}$, Prev.hash

1: **if** $H_m = 0$ **then**

2:     $P_m = \lim_{H_m \to 0} \dfrac{\left(\frac{(1-p)}{p}\right)^{-H_m} - 1}{\left(\frac{(1-p)}{p}\right)^{-H_m} - \left(\frac{(1-p)}{p}\right)^g} = \dfrac{1-1}{1-\left(\frac{(1-p)}{p}\right)^g} = 0$ ▷ Referring (eq-18)

3:     $R_m = 0$ ▷ Referring (eq-18)

4: **else**

5:     **if** $H_m = g$ **then**

6:       $P_m = \lim_{H_m \to g} \dfrac{\left(\frac{(1-p)}{p}\right)^{-H_m} - 1}{\left(\frac{(1-p)}{p}\right)^{-H_m} - \left(\frac{(1-p)}{p}\right)^g} = \dfrac{1}{1+\left(\frac{(1-p)}{p}\right)^g}$ ▷ Referring (eq-19)

7:       $R_m = \sum_{i=1}^{t} \cdot(\frac{1}{2}).m.(r_m - c_m)$ ▷ Referring (eq-20)

8:     **else**

9:       When $H_m = \infty$ ▷ Referring (eq-21)

10:       $P_m = \lim_{H_m \to \infty} \dfrac{\left(\frac{(1-p)}{p}\right)^{-H_m} - 1}{\left(\frac{(1-p)}{p}\right)^{-H_m} - \left(\frac{(1-p)}{p}\right)^g} = \dfrac{-1}{-\left(\frac{(1-p)}{p}\right)^g} = \left(\frac{p}{(1-p)}\right)^g$

11:       $R_m = \sum_{i=1}^{t} \cdot p_i.m.(r_m - c_m) = \sum_{i=1}^{t} \frac{e^{-\lambda} \times \lambda^t}{t!} m.(r_m - c_m)$ Referring (eq-21)

12:     **end if**

13: **end if**

14: Hash= SHA256($B_{add}.Data$)

15: $B_{add}.Hash.Value =$ Hash

16: $B_{add}.Prev.Hash = m_{address}$

17: $S_c \leftarrow 1$

18: Return($c_m, m_{pub.key}, LI_{address}$, Prev.hash, Hash.Value)

---

6. In the case of public blockchain, a node takes part in the mining process and mines the block in any sub-branch rather than the main long branch. In that case the miner will expense its energy without getting any incentive. Those miners are considered as attacker and the same mining process will be repeated for that block by forwarding the block to the next miner node of the network.

7. In the case of public blockchain, the miner uses two functions solve(Ψ_{pvt}) and list($\mathcal{L}_{pub}$). The Ψ_{pvt} function, the miner solves the puzzle of the block and temporarily and privately mine it in its own chain. After that the address of the longest chain is available publicly, and the block is listed as the main longest chain, using function $\mathcal{L}_{pub}$ refereed in Algorithm 2 and the block previous hash-key value, hash-key value, and miner public-key($miner_{pub}$) are acknowledged to the blockchain administrator for the verification of payment.

8. In the case of private blockchain, the miner uses the function ($\mho_{pvt}$) to solve the puzzle of the block and privately mine it in its own chain refereed in Algorithm 3 and the block previous hash-key value, hash-key value and miner public-key($miner_{pub}$) are acknowledged to the blockchain administrator for the verification of payment.

Algorithm 4. List function of mining of Public Blockchain

    Procedure: List()
    Input: $G_{pub-key}, B_{add}, LI_{add}, t, c_m, m, r_m, H_a$
    Output: Successfully return Hash-value, $m_{pub.key}$, Prev.hash
1: $B_{add}.Hash.Value =$ Hash
2: $B_{add}.Prev.Hash = LI_{address}$
3: $LI_c \leftarrow 1$
4: Return($S_c, m_{pub.key}$, Prev.hash, Hash.Value)

---

9. After getting acknowledgment from the blockchain administrator verify the block chaining sequence and after proper verification, the blockchain administrator releases the payment. The payment is released to the miner according to the longest depth of the mining into the chain.
10. At the time of verification of mining acknowledgment, if it is found that the blocks are mined by the miner in the wrong chain or in the wrong sequence, then the miner is identified as an attacker, and no payment is released to the miner. In addition, a penalty will be charged to the miner (Fig. 4).

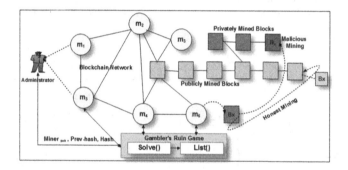

Fig. 4. The Mining of Block Using Gambler's Ruin Game

Initially, the miner nodes compete to mine the generated block. Under the purview of this applicable Gambler's Ruin game, an eligible node started to mine the block by investing the computation energy H_i in a particular cycle of point (i) of a game with intending to gain an extra amount of incentive $g = H_m - H_i$. The revenue of the miner also depends upon d, c_m and also r_m. The probability of the i_{th} cycle can be written from the (Eq. 9) as

$$P_i = \begin{cases} \frac{1-\left(\frac{1-p}{p}\right)^{H_i}}{1-\left(\frac{1-p}{p}\right)^{H_i+g}}, & \text{if } p_m \neq q_m \\ \frac{H_i}{H_m}, & \text{if } p_m = q_m = \frac{1}{2} \end{cases} \tag{16}$$

When the node approaches for honest mining the (Eq. 16) can be written by multiplying numerator and denominator by $\left(\frac{(1-p)}{p}\right)^{-H_i}$, when $(p \neq q)$ as (Eq. 17)

Algorithm 5. Private Blockchain Mining using Gambler's Ruin Game

---

Input: $G_{pub-key}, B_{add}, LI_{add}, t, c_m, m, r_m, H_a$
Output: Successfully Mined or transfer the block to other miner

1: LabelDo:
2: $Type \leftarrow Private, S_c \leftarrow 0, L_c \leftarrow 0, time \leftarrow 0$
3: $OS_{ret} \leftarrow \{\}, OL_{ret} \leftarrow \{\}$
4: bool Solve()   ▷ Temporary mine the block
5: bool List()   ▷ List the block in the Longest Chain
6: **if** $time \leq t$ **then**
7:     $OS_{ret} \leftarrow$ Solve($G_{pub-key}, c_m, m, r_m, H_a$)
8: **else**
9:     **if** $OS_{ret}.S_c = 0$ And $OL_{ret}.LI_c = 0$ **then**
10:        Can not Incomplete in Time
11:        Provide Penalty for $m_{pub-key}$
12:        Goto LabelDo   ▷ Block forwarded to next miner
13:     **else**
14:        **if** $OS_{ret}.H_{val} = L_{add}$ And $OS_{ret}.S_c = 1$ And $OL_{ret}.LI_c = 1$ **then**
15:            Block Mined Successfully
16:            Initiale and Release Incentives
17:        **else**
18:            Provide Penalty for $m_{pub-key}$
19:            Goto LabelDo   ▷ Block forwarded to next miner
20:        **end if**
21:     **end if**
22: **end if**
23:

$$P_i = \frac{\left(\frac{(1-p)}{p}\right)^{-H_i} \cdot \left(1 - \frac{(1-p)}{p}^{H_i}\right)}{\left(\frac{(1-p)}{p}\right)^{-H_i} \cdot \left(1 - \left(\frac{(1-p)}{p}\right)^{H_i+g}\right)} = \frac{\left(\frac{(1-p)}{p}\right)^{-H_i} - 1}{\left(\frac{(1-p)}{p}\right)^{-H_i} - \left(\frac{(1-p)}{p}\right)^{g}} \quad (17)$$

- If the honest node invest nothing i.e. $H_i = 0$ then it reduce to (Eq. 18)

$$P_i = \lim_{H_i \to 0} \frac{\left(\frac{(1-p)}{p}\right)^{-H_i} - 1}{\left(\frac{(1-p)}{p}\right)^{-H_i} - \left(\frac{(1-p)}{p}\right)^{g}} = \frac{1-1}{1 - \left(\frac{(1-p)}{p}\right)^{g}} = 0 \quad (18)$$

Therefore, if any miner wants to keep the ideal without participating ($H_i = 0$) in the mining activities, then the miner would not gain any incentives (i.e. $R_i = 0$).

$$P_i = \lim_{H_i \to g} \frac{\left(\frac{(1-p)}{p}\right)^{-H_i} - 1}{\left(\frac{(1-p)}{p}\right)^{-H_i} - \left(\frac{(1-p)}{p}\right)^{g}} = \frac{1}{1 + \left(\frac{(1-p)}{p}\right)^{g}} \quad (19)$$

Algorithm 6. Solve function of mining of Private Blockchain

Procedure: Solve()

Input: $G_{pub-key}, B_{add}, LI_{add}, t, c_m, m, r_m, H_a$

Output: Successfully return Hash-value,$m_{pub.key}$, Prev.hash

1: **if** $H_m = 0$ **then**

2: $\quad P_m = \lim_{H_m \to 0} \dfrac{\left(\frac{(1-p)}{p}\right)^{-H_m} - 1}{\left(\frac{(1-p)}{p}\right)^{-H_m} - \left(\frac{(1-p)}{p}\right)^g} = \dfrac{1-1}{1-\left(\frac{(1-p)}{p}\right)^g} = 0$ ▷ Referring (eq-18)

3: $\quad R_m = 0$ ▷ Referring (eq-18)

4: **else**

5: $\quad$ **if** $H_m = g$ **then**

6: $\quad\quad P_m = \lim_{H_m \to g} \dfrac{\left(\frac{(1-p)}{p}\right)^{-H_m} - 1}{\left(\frac{(1-p)}{p}\right)^{-H_m} - \left(\frac{(1-p)}{p}\right)^g} = \dfrac{1}{1+\left(\frac{(1-p)}{p}\right)^g}$ ▷ Referring (eq-19)

7: $\quad\quad R_m = \sum_{i=1}^{t} \cdot(\frac{1}{2}).m.(r_m - c_m)$ ▷ Referring (eq-20)

8: $\quad$ **else**

9: $\quad\quad$ When $H_m = \infty$ ▷ Referring (eq-21)

10: $\quad\quad P_m = \lim_{H_m \to \infty} \dfrac{\left(\frac{(1-p)}{p}\right)^{-H_m} - 1}{\left(\frac{(1-p)}{p}\right)^{-H_m} - \left(\frac{(1-p)}{p}\right)^g} = \dfrac{-1}{-\left(\frac{(1-p)}{p}\right)^g} = \left(\frac{p}{(1-p)}\right)^g$

11: $\quad\quad R_m = \sum_{i=1}^{t} \cdot p_i.m.(r_m - c_m) = \sum_{i=1}^{t} \frac{e^{-\lambda} \times \lambda^t}{t!} m.(r_m - c_m)$ Referring (eq-21)

12: $\quad$ **end if**

13: **end if**

14: Hash= SHA256($B_{add}.Data$)

15: $B_{add}.Hash.Value = $ Hash

16: $B_{add}.Prev.Hash = m_{address}$

17: $S_c \leftarrow 1$

18: $LI_c \leftarrow 1$

19: Return($c_m, m_{pub.key}, LI_{address}$, Prev.hash, Hash.Value)

The incentive gain by the miner is

$$R_i = \sum_{i=1}^{t} \cdot(\frac{1}{2}).m.(r_m - c_m) \tag{20}$$

- If the honest node invest nothing i.e. $H_i = \infty$ then it reduce to (Eq. 21)

$$P_i = \lim_{H_i \to \infty} \frac{\left(\frac{(1-p)}{p}\right)^{-H_i} - 1}{\left(\frac{(1-p)}{p}\right)^{-H_i} - \left(\frac{(1-p)}{p}\right)^g} = \frac{-1}{-\left(\frac{(1-p)}{p}\right)^g} = \frac{1}{\left(\frac{(1-p)}{p}\right)^g} = \left(\frac{p}{(1-p)}\right)^g \tag{21}$$

$$R_i = \sum_{i=1}^{t} \cdot p_i.m.(r_m - c_m) = \sum_{i=1}^{t} \frac{e^{-\lambda} \times \lambda^t}{t!} m.(r_m - c_m) \tag{22}$$

3.3 Simulated Result and Analysis

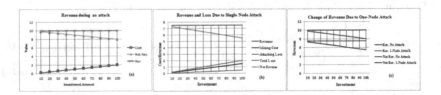

Fig. 5. (a) Revenue and cost during no attack, (b) Revenue, cost and attacking loss during 1-Node attack and (c) The change in revenue and net revenue due to 1-Node attack

- The first cell (1), of Table 2, represents the cooperation of all the nodes of the blockchain networks and the maximum generated revenue is distributed equally among the validator node.
- The Nash equilibrium is represented by cells (2) and (3) of Table 2, where the revenue earned by the honest node is decremented in the validation phase of the block generation node. The reduction of revenue depends on the number of validator nodes that behaves maliciously.
- In case the percentages of attack become more than 50% as described in cell (3) of Table 2, and cell (4) of Table 2 (in this case, the attacking probability is p_a=1), then for both the cases, the generated block is discarded and no mining will be done.
- The miner wants to keep idle as shown in (Eq. 18) without participating ($H_i = 0$) into the mining activities then the miner would not gain any incentives.
- If the miner has the mining or attacking probability ($\frac{1}{2}$), and in case of honest mining still the miner suppose to gain (Eq. 20) the respective incentives. In case of a miner is functioning maliciously would not get its mining incentives. In addition, the blockchain administrator would fine the malicious minor.
- The gross mining revenue, mining cost, and net mining revenue are shown in Fig. 5a. The mining cost will be increased with the increment of the investment. This indicates that the more reputed miners can invest more for the mining work to get proportionate incentives.
- The change of net revenue from the gross revenue due to the attack of a single node can be shown in Fig. 5b. The loss due to the attack of the single node increases the losses in revenue earning of the honest miners.
- The comparison of change of revenue (both the gross and net) earning in case of without attack and due to the attack of a single node is shown in Fig. 5c. The gross and the net revenue is decreased due to a single node attack by 2.5 irrespective of investments.

4   Conclusion

The work starts with a focused study of Sybil attack on blockchain and identifies the probable causes based on the existing literature. Instead of following the more conventional approaches, this paper aims to mitigate the threats due to the Sybil attack by introducing a novel methodology based on the Gambler Ruins game. The proposed approach works well for both public and private blockchain applications. The analysis is done for the verification of the generated block for all the states of the game. The states are described when the nodes are used for honest validation - some nodes responded honestly and some responded maliciously. Evaluation is also done for an extreme situation when all the nodes in the system behave like attackers. In the mining operation, the miner nodes that do not take part in the mining operations are also taken into account.

This work sets the foundation for developing a new consensus algorithm to mitigate the Sybil attack and ensure the mining of data faster. In future, there is a plan to explore the work for semi-structured big data using the Hyper ledger framework.

References

1. Arifeen, M.M., Al Mamun, A., Ahmed, T., Kaiser, M.S., Mahmud, M.: A blockchain-based scheme for sybil attack detection in underwater wireless sensor networks. Adv. Intell. Syst. Comput. **1309**, 467–476 (2021)
2. Bochem, A., Leiding, B.: Rechained: Sybil-resistant distributed identities for the internet of things and mobile ad hoc networks. Sensors **21**(9), 1–27 (2021)
3. Platt, M., McBurney, P.: Sybil attacks on identity-augmented proof-of-stake. Comput. Netw. **199**, 108424 (2021)
4. Rajab, T., Manshaei, M.H., Dakhilalian, M., Jadliwala, M., Rahman, M.A.: On the feasibility of sybil attacks in shard-based permission less blockchains (2020)
5. Wadii, J., Rim, H., Ridha, B.: Detecting and preventing Sybil attacks in wireless sensor networks. In: Mediterranean Microwave Symposium, vol. 2019, October 2019
6. Pecori, R., Veltri, L.: A balanced trust-based method to counter sybil and spartacus attacks in chord. Secur. Commun. Netwo. **2018**, 1–16 (2018)
7. Swathi, P., Modi, C., Patel, D.: Preventing sybil attack in blockchain using distributed behavior monitoring of miners. In: 2019 10th International Conference on Computing, Communication and Networking Technologies, ICCCNT 2019, pp. 1–6 (2019)
8. Begum, A., Tareq, A.H., Sultana, M., Sohel, M.K., Rahman, T., Sarwar, A.H.: Blockchain attacks, analysis and a model to solve double spending attack. Int. J. Mach. Learn. Comput. **10**(2), 352–357 (2020)
9. Kumar, B., Bhuyan, B.: Game theoretical defense mechanism against reputation based sybil attacks. Procedia Comput. Sci. **167**(2019), 2465–2477 (2020). https://doi.org/10.1016/j.procs.2020.03.299
10. Shareh, M.B., Navidi, H., Javadi, H.H.S., HosseinZadeh, M.: Preventing Sybil attacks in P2P file sharing networks based on the evolutionary game model. Inf. Sci. **470**, 94–108 (2019). https://doi.org/10.1016/j.ins.2018.08.054

Industrial Management and Other Applications

Dynamic Adaptive Capacity of Metalworking Companies in Barranquilla - Colombia: Analysis from the Export Process in the 4.0 Era

Osvaldo Arevalo[1], Margel Parra[2], Jhony García-Tirado[3], Javier Ramírez[3(✉)], Marlene Ballestas[4], and Carlos Rondón Rodríguez[1]

[1] Universidad de la Costa, 58 Street #55 66, Barranquilla, Colombia
oarevalo1@cuc.edu.co

[2] Corporación Universitaria Reformada, 38 Street #74 -179, Barranquilla, Colombia

[3] Corporación Universitaria Taller Cinco, Km 19, Chía, Colombia
Jramirez07papers@gmail.com

[4] Institución Universitaria de Barranquilla, 18 Street # ##39-100, Soledad, Colombia

Abstract. This article presents a methodology for analyzing the Dynamic Adaptive Capacity in the Export Process of metal-mechanical Small and medium-sized enterprises (SMEs) in Barranquilla - Colombia. In the new environments that are being developed in the 21st century, companies in different sectors have had the need to implement mechanisms that allow them to be able to face the constant changes that exist in the environment, especially in the 4.0 era. For its development, research of a documentary nature is proposed, which aims through the reports presented by four key informants that are part of 4 SMEs of the metal-mechanic sector in the city of Barranquilla, Colombia and are in charge of the export process. This establishes the following categories of analysis: strategic flexibility, intellectual flexibility, digital governance, leadership in virtual environments, technological resources and resilience. Due to this study, it was possible to recognize that based on the results of the qualitative analysis of the six dimensions of dynamic adaptive capacities (strategic flexibility, intellectual flexibility, resilience, leadership, resources and governance), a content analysis can be established, making possible to filter the main qualitative categories associated with flexibility, exporting, international, capacity, dynamics, adaptation, leadership, innovation, organization, resources, solutions, strategic, markets and SMEs.

Keywords: Dynamic Adaptive Capacity · Era 4.0 · SME · export

1 Introduction

Dynamic capabilities are the skills that organizations develop to reinvent, reconfigure, innovate, and restructure their resources to create a sustainable competitive advantage that is developed in response to environmental changes and current market disruption caused by changes in market dynamics. This makes companies to rapidly change their decisions to stay informed and adapt quickly through a flexible and intelligent architecture [1, 2].

K. Saeed et al. (Eds.): CISIM 2023, LNCS 14164, pp. 127–138, 2023.
https://doi.org/10.1007/978-3-031-42823-4_10

Currently, it is important to recognize how major changes in worldwide industries require companies to be able to respond effectively to new market demands, so that they can stay afloat and be competitive within their ecosystem. It is especially in the era of Industry 4.0 where organizations have had to streamline their ability to respond to these changes in the international market, taking advantage of new technologies as catalysts for achieving business objectives [3, 4].

Thus, one of the sectors to be considered within this current dynamic is the metal-mechanic sector [5], which plays an important role in the generation of employment and development of the country, since it tends to offer shorter delivery times, as well as the capacity to produce small batches and deliver lower value shipments than international competitors. However, although most of the companies in the production chain are small and medium-sized, domestic production is concentrated in large companies [6].

At the level of the city of Barranquilla, there are three trainings at the level of technological innovation in the metal-mechanical industries of the export sector, one is high level, one is medium level, and one is low level [7]. These profiles were defined by the Joint Industrial Opinion Survey where the dynamic capacity has specific implications, since metallurgists from Barranquilla are defined by innovation to achieve the strategic objectives set by the organization [8].

It is important that SMEs in the metal-mechanic sector can develop dynamic skills to respond to market demands and not wait for the market to force them to change their strategy. Considering the above, this study is developed with the aim of analyzing the Dynamic Capacity for Adaptation in the Export Process of metal-mechanical SMEs in Barranquilla - Colombia.

2 Literature Review

To address the concept of dynamic capacity for innovation, the authors Camargo, Díaz, Velandia and Navarro are mentioned, who mention that this is the intrinsic capacity of organizations to create new processes, procedures, products, and services based on the changes and demands that occur within the external context and the market. This concept implies that these processes and procedures, supported by tools, allow organizations to generate new opportunities for development and competitive positioning [6].

These authors mention that developing a dynamic capacity for innovation in modern companies requires the following fundamental elements [6]: Capture opportunities; Referring to attention to the local and global context, which depends to a large extent on effective communication with stakeholders, in turn said information and informants become generators of opportunities. Detect problems; As a result of this observation process, the possibility arises of detecting the various problems in the form of weaknesses and threats for their adequate attention by the company. Design; It is the phase where those problems and opportunities are taken and transformed into organizational strategies to optimize growth and sustainability. Finally, experiment: it is based on the process of creativity and how it is, when implemented through testing, allows to verify the effectiveness of tools, processes, and procedures [6].

3   Materials and Method

For the estimation of the sample, the development of the census estimation was considered, given the limited character of the sample conformed by small and medium companies of the metal-mechanic sector of Barranquilla with activities in export process, considering that it does not work on a sample but on the total population. Thus, a research sample of 4 companies of the metal-mechanic sector that carry out export operations was selected, such as while the implementation time depends on the purpose of the requested data.

The types of censuses are: "De Jure, or de facto: implies the census of the entire population present in the territory under study. The population census: population count that is carried out periodically (statistics): count of elements of a population in descriptive statistics, which is the one that applies to the present work" [9]. Given the above, it can be determined that the present study correspond to an intended sample, as a list of pre-selected companies.

For the development of this study, a non-probabilistic sample was selected according to expert criteria, derived from the group of metal-mechanical companies in Barranquilla, with criteria that include:

1) the target population in the sector of the SMEs
2) the study focuses on the SME sector with existing export business operations (Fig. 1).

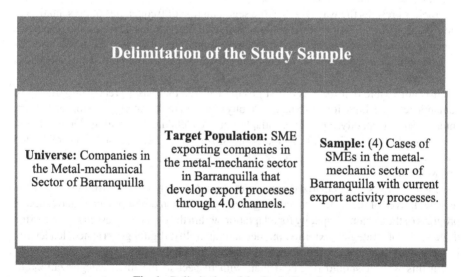

Fig. 1. Delimitation of the Study Sample.

Taking the figure one as a reference, it is highlighted that the information source of the study comes from the development of interviews with representatives of four (4) SMEs in the metal-mechanic sector of Barranquilla with current export activity processes. These companies were selected based on the criteria of their years of existence in the market for more than ten years, as well as their relevance in the regional context.

For the information-gathering process, the Assessment Scale of the Level of Development of the Dynamic Adaptive Capacity within the Export Process in SMEs of the Metalworking Sector in environments is used as a reference. This scale is semi-structured (qualitative and quantitative) and refers to the six components or elements inherent to the organizations that provide them with the capacity to respond to long-term or short-term impacts, either by planning measures or facilitating and encouraging responses. For these, they develop strategic flexibility, intellectual flexibility, digital governance, leadership in virtual environments, technological resources, and resilience.

The information analysis process is carried out with the support of information from the Atlas.ti software and, in turn, information processed in SPSS for its final presentation, taking as a reference the statistical frequencies and the percentages that these values represent over the total.

4 Results

The following are the findings from the study of dynamic adaptive capacity at the time of exporting, based on the reports of the managers of each of the (4) SMEs. For this purpose, an emerging categorization was established that corresponds to the assessment dimensions of the range of development of the dynamic adaptive capacity, namely strategic flexibility, intellectual flexibility, digital governance, leadership in virtual environments, technological resources, and resilience:

Table 1 presents the way in which the segmentation of frequencies of presentation of the emerging classification of the study was carried out. All this based on the respective contents of the answers established by the representatives of each of the SMEs in comparison with the dimensions of the Dynamic Adaptive Capacity in the export process in the 4.0 era.

It is noticeable that there is a first group of words that has a greater importance of semantic relationship with the dynamic faculty of adaptation, namely: Flexibility, Export, International, Capacity, Dynamic, Adaptation, Leadership, Innovation, Organization, Resources, Solutions, Strategic, Markets and SMEs. Likewise, a second group of related categories is recognized: Competence, Decisions, Governance, Intellectual, Resilience and Marketing.

Table 2 offers a schematized version of the main participations formulated by the representatives of the SMEs, concerning their appreciation of the practices and range of progress of the dynamic capacity for adaptation within the export process in relation to the dimensions of strategic flexibility, intellectual flexibility, digital governance, leadership in virtual environments, technological resources and resilience.

In this way, it should be noted that, with respect to the main categorizations of semantic association with the dimension of strategic flexibility, emphasis is placed on the constant study of the competitive nature, the processes of innovation and development, the consecutive configuration of the productive and administrative process, as well as the monitoring of the quality standard and the change of prices compared to the market competition.

Table 1. Qualitative Content Analysis

Word	Word length	Frequency	%	Range
Flexibility	12	8	5,48	1
Export	11	8	5,48	1
International	12	7	4,79	2
Capacity	9	7	4,79	2
Dynamics	8	7	4,79	2
Adaptability	10	7	4,79	2
Leadership	9	6	4,11	3
Innovation	10	6	4,11	3
Organization	12	6	4,11	3
Resources	8	6	4,11	3
Solutions	10	6	4,11	3
Strategic	11	6	4,11	3
Markets	7	6	4,11	3
SME	4	6	4,11	3
Competition	11	5	3,42	4
Decisions	10	5	3,42	4
Governance	14	5	3,42	4
Intellectual	11	5	3,42	4
Resilience	11	5	3,42	4
Marketing	8	4	2,74	5
Obstacles	10	3	2,05	6
Pricing	7	3	2,05	6
Production	10	3	2,05	6
Control	7	2	1,37	7
Command	5	2	1,37	7
Matrix	6	2	1,37	7
Measurement	6	2	1,37	7
Offer	6	2	1,37	7
Products	9	2	1,37	7
System	7	2	1,37	7
Vanguard	10	2	1,37	7
	Totals	146	100,00	

Table 2. Analysis of the Dimensions of Dynamic Adaptive Capacity

Code	Beginning	End	Segment	Area	Percentage %
Strategic flexibility	4	4	Constantly analyzing the competition in terms of prices, production and penetration in international markets, in order to innovate based on them, trying to overcome them in order to obtain advantages	195	5,42
	17	17	With an innovation and product development department to keep us ahead of the competition	123	3,42
	30	30	Constantly reconfiguring production and administrative processes, with excellent marketing strategies, allowing us to stay one step ahead of the competition	173	4,81
	43	43	By constantly monitoring the prices and quality of international competition, we are able to analyze for innovation and marketing decisions	178	4,95
Intellectual flexibility	6	6	Encouraging group work, taking advantage of individual knowledge to obtain the synergy of its application to the collective	129	3,59
	19	19	Constant training to be prepared for market demands	77	2,14
	32	32	To the extent that the organization contributes by providing tools to its employees, they are able to provide solutions that contribute to the solution of the obstacles that arise	209	5,81

(continued)

Table 2. (*continued*)

Code	Beginning	End	Segment	Area	Percentage %
	45	45	Undoubtedly, training in this aspect is the order of the day in order to have a highly trained team in decision-making	132	3,67
Digital governance	53	53	We must reach the construction of a command control to help us make decisions	103	2,86
	40	40	The organization's goal for the coming year is to develop an intelligent system that will contribute to the solution of obstacles	135	3,75
	27	27	We should have a command control, i.e. a matrix to establish solutions	91	2,53
	14	14	Despite the marked hierarchies, we have a matrix model as an element for decision-making	109	3,03
Leadership in virtual environments	10	10	We maintain our leadership through product innovation, marketing policy and pricing strategy, which has allowed us to be present in the South American market	177	4,92
	23	23	Leadership is gained to the extent that there is innovation, which is why the organization aimed at this strategy	124	3,45
	36	36	In the region where we export, innovation plays an important role, and that is the reason why we are playing our part in this regard	120	3,34

(*continued*)

Table 2. (*continued*)

Code	Beginning	End	Segment	Area	Percentage %
	49	49	Innovation is constantly at the forefront of maintaining leadership as an organization	103	2,86
Technological resources	51	51	The organization should seek credits to solve this impasse, which sometimes occurs	104	2,89
	38	38	Resources are a must and this aspect is always elusive in the organization	90	2,50
	25	25	Resources to respond to needs are limited	64	1,78
	12	12	That is what we are constantly aiming at, since the management system allows us to solve any inconveniences that may arise	125	3,47
Resilience	8	8	We have slowed down production a little, due to market impacts, but because of these obstacles, we have had to adjust in terms of production costs to reduce the economic impact	215	5,98
	21	21	Undoubtedly, looking for new marketing methods to dynamize the low supply in the international market	111	3,09
	34	34	When there is a drop in supply, it has been up to us to devise new routes to expand the customer base in terms of numbers	117	3,25
	47	47	Open new international market niches to diversify sectors	79	2,20

In addition, concerning the dimension of intellectual flexibility, it is possible to highlight that its objective is the promotion of collaborative work, the constant development of updating processes and specialized growth, the creation and use of strategies and tools at the business level to adjust to demand and market needs, especially within the innovative contemporary environments that challenge the ability of organizations to adapt.

On the other hand, the resilience dimension, the dynamic capacity to adapt is associated, in the first place, with the use of certain "conservative" protection strategies in comparison with the unstable condition of the market, the need to search for international markets, the possibility of innovating to respond to the relationship between supply and demand, and the opportunity to generate new markets internationally.

Also, it is mentioned that in the dimension of leadership in virtual environments, the dynamic capacity for adaptation is generally related to conditioning factors such as entrepreneurship, product updating, market policy and price tactics, in a strategic process of maintenance, productivity and competitiveness in the market.

Subsequently, in the analysis corresponding to the dimension of resource management related to the dynamic capacity for adaptation in the export process, it is highlighted that resource management consists of a complex process of permanent management of inputs and adequate situations for an optimized operation, with the need to access them in a restricted space, and to expose the eventualities of prevention in order to be able to respond to unforeseen events.

Finally, concerning the analysis of the governance dimension, in which the dynamic adaptive capacity is mainly related to the difficulty present in hierarchically ordered structures, the implementation of processes allows a functional nature that requires matrix measurement structures. In the same way, it offers the possibility of designing and carrying out the development of intelligent management systems that are based on functionally controlling the command. This way, the dynamic capacity of adaptation requires development processes that are in accordance with the flexible character of the SMEs to adopt the changing conditions of the market, especially in the contexts of exporting with productivity, innovation, competitiveness and leadership.

5   Discussions

In this way, it should be noted that, with respect to the main categorizations of semantic association with the dimension of strategic flexibility, emphasis is placed on the constant study of the competitive nature, the processes of innovation and development, the consecutive configuration of the productive and administrative process, as well as the monitoring of the quality standard and the change of prices compared to the market competition [10].

In addition, concerning the dimension of intellectual flexibility, it is possible to highlight that its objective is the promotion of collaborative work, the constant development of updating processes and specialized growth, the creation and use of strategies and tools at the business level to adjust to demand and market needs, especially within the innovative contemporary environments that challenge the ability of organizations to adapt [11].

On the other hand, the resilience dimension, the dynamic capacity to adapt is associated, in the first place, with the use of certain "conservative" protection strategies in comparison with the unstable condition of the market, the need to search for international markets, the possibility of innovating to respond to the relationship between supply and demand, and the opportunity to generate new markets internationally [12]. Also, it is mentioned that in the dimension of leadership in virtual environments, the dynamic capacity for adaptation is generally related to conditioning factors such as entrepreneurship, product updating, market policy and price tactics, in a strategic process of maintenance, productivity and competitiveness in the market [13].

Subsequently, in the analysis corresponding to the dimension of resource management related to the dynamic capacity for adaptation in the export process, it is highlighted that resource management consists of a complex process of permanent management of inputs and adequate situations for an optimized operation, with the need to access them in a restricted space, and to expose the eventualities of prevention in order to be able to respond to unforeseen events.

Finally, concerning the analysis of the governance dimension, in which the dynamic adaptive capacity is mainly related to the difficulty present in hierarchically ordered structures, the implementation of processes allows a functional nature that requires matrix measurement structures. In the same way, it offers the possibility of designing and carrying out the development of intelligent management systems that are based on functionally controlling the command [14–17].

This way, the dynamic capacity of adaptation requires development processes that are in accordance with the flexible character of the SMEs to adopt the changing conditions of the market, especially in the contexts of exporting with productivity, innovation, competitiveness and leadership.

As a last point, it is possible to conclude that certainly the new dynamics make organizations see the need to evolve and adapt to said changes [18–20]; especially in the current era 4.0 where technologies serve as the main tool for interaction between human beings [21]. This reality shows to be faced by Colombian organizations in their effort to remain current within the markets [22–24].

6 Conclusions

Como cierre del proceso investigativo, es posible concluir que las capacidades dinámicas de adaptación son el eje central para que las organizaciones modernas tengan la oportunidad de tomar los constantes cambios presentes en el contexto dentro de la sociedad 4.0 para tomarlos como una oportunidad de desarrollo y crecimiento, de forma que se logran acortar brechas y se dan nuevos mercados donde dichas organizaciones hacen vida.

Due to this study, it was possible to recognize that based on the results of the qualitative analysis of the six dimensions of dynamic adaptive capacities (strategic flexibility, intellectual flexibility, resilience, leadership, resources and governance), a content analysis can be established, making possible to filter the main qualitative categories associated with flexibility, exporting, international, capacity, dynamics, adaptation, leadership, innovation, organization, resources, solutions, strategic, markets and SMEs.

As a point of contribution, it is recommended to the organizations of the metal-mechanical sector of the city of Barranquilla that make exports that they work hard to develop an institutional policy aimed at managing change towards the strengthening of dynamic capacities. of adaptation.

References

1. Cockburn, I., Henderson, R., Stern, S.: Untangling the origins of competitive advantage. Strateg. Manag. J. **21**(10–11), 1123–1145 (2000)
2. Hodgkinson, G., Healey, M.: Psychological foundations of dynamic capabilities. Strateg. Manag. J. **32**(13), 1500–1516 (2011)
3. Helfat, C., Raubitschek, R.: Dynamic and integrative capabilities for profiting from innovation in digital platform-based ecosystems. Res. Policy **47**(8), 1391–1399 (2018)
4. Lay, N., et al.: Uso de las herramientas de comunicación asincrónicas y sincrónicas en la banca privada del municipio Maracaibo (Venezuela). Revista Espacios **40**(4) (2019)
5. García Guiliany J.E., Duran, S., Pulido, R.P.: Politicas de gestion de talento humano para el desarrollo de competencias gerenciales en empresas metalmecanica. FACE: Revista de la Facultad de Ciencias Económicas y Empresariales **17**(2) (2017)
6. Camargo, A., Díaz, R., Velandia, G., Navarro, E.: Capacidad dinámica de innovación en las PyME exportadoras metalmecánicas en Colombia. Espacios **38** (2017)
7. Ovallos, D., Amar, P.: Perfil innovador de la industria manufacturera colombiana. Caso del sector metalmecánico de Barranquilla. Revista Ingenierías Universidad de Medellín **13**, (25) (2014)
8. EOIC: Encuesta de Opinión Industrial Conjunta. Clean (2015)
9. Ayala, O.: Competencias informacionales y competencias investigativas en estudiantes universitarios. Revista Innova Educación **2**(4), 668–679 (2020)
10. Valencia-Rodríguez, M.: Relación entre la innovación de productos y capacidades organizacionales. Ingeniería Industrial **40**(2), 194–201 (2019)
11. Bernal, C.A., Fracica, G., Frost Gonzalez, J.: Análisis de la Relación entre la Innovación y La Gestión del Conocimiento con la Competitividad Empresarial en Una Muestra de Empresas en La Ciudad De Bogotá. Estudios Gerenciales **28**, 303–315 (2012)
12. Herrera, L., Hernández, G., Castillo, K., Arriola, O.: Diagnóstico del uso de herramientas tecnológicas para la gestión y apoyo del liderazgo en las PYMES. Revista GEON (Gestión, Organizaciones y Negocios) **6**(1), 69–83 (2019)
13. Hernández, H., Cardona, D., Del Rio, J.: Direccionamiento Estratégico: Proyección de la Innovación Tecnológica y Gestión Administrativa en las Pequeñas Empresas. Información Tecnológica **28**(5), 15–22 (2017)
14. Salas-Navarro, K., Meza, J., Obredor-Baldovino, T., Mercado-Caruso, N.: Evaluación de la Cadena de Suministro para Mejorar la Competitividad y Productividad en el Sector Metalmecánico en Barranquilla, Colombia. Información tecnológica **30**(2), 25–32 (2019)
15. Toala-Toala, G., Mendoza-Briones, A., Vinces-Menoscal, D.L.: La oferta exportable de las PYMES de la provincia de Manabí. Polo del Conocimiento **4**(4), 71–87 (2019)
16. Cujilema, C., Yungán, J., Pérez, M.: La imagen corporativa en las PYMES y su relación con la responsabilidad social empresarial. Observatorio de la Economía Latinoamericana (2019)
17. Pérez, C.: Hacia la PYME latinoamericana del futuro: Dinamismo Tecnológico e Inclusión Social. Mayéutica Revista Científica de Humanidades y Artes **5**, 17–42 (2017)
18. Zhang, X., Gao, C., Zhang, S.: The niche evolution of cross-boundary innovation for Chinese SMEs in the context of digital transformation-Case study based on dynamic capability. Technol. Soc. 101870 (2022)
19. García, J.: La gerencia financiera una visión práctica para la creación de valor. Corporación Universitaria Taller Cinco Publicaciones (2020)

20. Mendoza-Ocasal, D., Navarro, E., Ramírez, J., García-Tirado, J.: Subjective well-being and its correlation with happiness at work and quality of work life: an organizational vision. Pol. J. Manag. Stud. **26**(1), 202–216 (2022)
21. Parejo, I., Nuñez, L., Nuñez, W.: Análisis de la transformación digital de las empresas en Colombia: dinámicas globales y desafíos actuales. Aglala **12**(1), 160–172 (2021)
22. Parejo, I., Núñez, W., Núñez, L.: Inserción del análisis financiero en PyMes colombianas como mecanismo para promover la sostenibilidad empresarial. Desarrollo Gerencial **13**(2), 1–19 (2021)
23. Fernández, J., Barrero, D., Rojas, L.: Industria 4.0: el reto para las pymes manufactureras de Bogotá, Colombia. Revista Mutis **12**(1) (2022)
24. Marín, C.: Organizaciones públicas frente a cambios en su entorno: implicaciones de las capacidades de respuesta y de adaptación. Revista Opera **1**(30), 231–249 (2022)

An Ecological Unmanned Hot-Air Balloon for the Agricultural Lands' Inspection

Rahma Boucetta[1,2(✉)] [iD]

[1] Department of Physics, Faculty of Sciences of Sfax, Soukra Road, 3000 Sfax, Tunisia
rahma.boucetta@macs.tn
[2] Lab-STA, LR11ES50, ENIS, Sfax, Tunisia

Abstract. The current paper presents an ecological design of an autonomous hot-air balloon used for the continuous inspection of large agricultural lands ensuring low power consumption, noise free and long endurance. Currently, growers and cultivators use cars and trucks to examine harvest and trees, evenly to monitor human or animal intruders. These means remain slow, noisy and energy-intensive to produce much more difficulties and pollution problems. Furthermore, farmers receive a limited outlook between trees and plants. For these reasons, and for the imperative need of a rapid and ecological answer, an autonomous unmanned vehicle based on a hot-air balloon powered by photovoltaic panels was proposed to guarantee a permanent supervision of wide fields, and to give a clear expanded view. Therefore, this paper is dedicated to establishment of an autonomous Montgolfier with a detailed description of its different features. Thermodynamic and aerodynamic laws are developed to generate a mathematical model used in the control process. To analyze the system performances, an open-loop numerical simulation is initially carried out with an on/off relay applied to the heater temperature. Then, a feedback control is drawn with a PID to reach a desired altitude. Finally, the PID is replaced by a Sugeno-like fuzzy controller to enhance the balloon performances in a climb phase. The paper is ended with a conclusion and prospects.

Keywords: Hot-air Balloon · Design · Heat Transfer · Aerodynamics · PID · Fuzzy Logic

1 Introduction

Agriculture in Tunisia, is prevalent from north to south, and carried out using traditional procedures that results in extremely irregular making levels. Tunisia is the fourth-largest producer of olive oil in the world, the production of olives and olive oil is of great socio-economic impact.

Olive is considered the most suitable and best-adapted crop to the Mediterranean environment, where it encompasses 80% of the worldwide olive tree area. Spain is the world's largest producer of olive oil with more than 35% of global production, followed by Greece, Italy, and Tunisia (Fig. 1). These four countries, together with Portugal, are also the largest exporters of olive oil [1]. Olive is the pillar of the Mediterranean agro-ecosystems, given its great economic, social and cultural importance [2]. The crop is

K. Saeed et al. (Eds.): CISIM 2023, LNCS 14164, pp. 139–150, 2023.
https://doi.org/10.1007/978-3-031-42823-4_11

cultivated on more than 12 million hectares worldwide, displaying a wide variability witnessed by more than 2600 different varieties for oil and/or table fruits, which are conserved at the World Olive Germplasm Bank [3].

These 50 million hectares of olive tree forests in Sfax City require regular examination by farmers and landlords in order to inspect thieves, insects or trees' state... Actually, they use cars, trucks or tractors to move in the tree-line pathways along the panoramic fields. This operation is considered tiring and much expensive. Furthermore, it spends a long time to get around the whole forest.

To overcome the current trouble and to attempt to help farmers and landowners to inspect rapidly, efficiently and inexpensively their crop, the design of an unmanned autonomous hot-air balloon called also Montgolfier is proposed and studied.

Contrary to standard drones that remain heavier than air aircrafts and their lift requires powerful motors such as bicopters, quadcopters, octacopters or helicopters..., Hot-air Balloons (LTA aircrafts) can maintain their flight for a long time using light hot gas (air) and consuming much less power supply. Their particular characteristics can deliver a long flight duration compared to traditional drones.

The paper is composed as follows: The next section describes the literature review to indicate the most famous productions of Montgolfier. The third section describes the design of the proposed unmanned Montgolfier with its specific features. The development of a mathematical model taking account of aerodynamics and heat transfer is given in the Sect. 4. Performances and control law synthesis are illustrated in Sect. 5. Finally, the paper is ended with a conclusion and some future perspectives.

Fig. 1. 350.000 hectares of olive trees in Sfax City in the middle East of Tunisia.

2   Literature Review

Since 300 AD, Chinese invented hot air balloons (called Lanterns) for military and communication purposes, but they never enlarged the dimensions to carry animals or humans. In the 13th century, A. Magnus and R. Bacon developed separately hypothetical flying machines based on Archimedes principle [4].

In the 18th century, the Montgolfier brothers designed a large hot-air balloon. After animals' flight achievements, humans experimented these aircrafts with success. Especially P. de Rozier, in 1784, continued as a pioneer to set speed, altitude and distance records (70 km/h, 3000 m and 52 km respectively). Likewise, Rozier invented incorporating Hydrogen in the balloon for the first time [5].

Traditional balloon aircrafts have enjoyed renaissance in the early 1960s through E. Yost and his Raven Industries that designed and built hot air balloons for the US Navy's Office and Naval Research Centre. They employed propane burner, new envelope material, light-bulb style envelope shape and some safety features.

Although historically the first aircrafts overall less research and development has been conducted in lighter than air (LTA) compared to heavier than air (HTA) flying machines. The development of dynamic and thermal models of balloon flight was worked out in 1960s and 1970s with the launching of space age and the increasing use of high-altitude applications and researches.

Furthermore, the future space exploration of planets and moons could employ LTA balloons and airships where aerobots and robotic balloons are applied for extra-terrestrial atmospheric flights related to planetary explorations [6, 7, 10, 11]. Mentioned proposals can be given for using unmanned hot-air balloons to explore Titan planet (a largest moon of Saturn). Due to obvious short coming, HTA aircraft would be likely more difficult to deploy, launch and control in space missions [12, 13].

3   Design of the Oliver

The Oliver is the name of the tiny hot-air balloon proposed to inspect wide olive trees fields in the City of Sfax. It consists of three main components (Fig. 2):

- The envelope that is a single-layered ripstop polyamide fabric reinforced with polyester straps in the principal part. The bottom section of the envelope is open and made of Nomex (heat resistant fabric). Fixed and mobile objects sensors are attached throughout the balloon mid.
- The basket or the gondola that is constructed of four photovoltaic panels to collect solar energy necessary for the electric balloon supply.
- A heater in a cylindrical shape placed in the lower balloon aperture is served as a heat source to increase the temperature of the air inside the envelope.

The principle behind the operation of a Montgolfier is the use of the hot air to produce buoyancy force which in turn creates lift. The heater placed in the basket produces the increase of the temperature of the air inside the envelope through an orifice. The density gradient between the air inside and outside the envelope results in a buoyant force that lifts the balloon off the ground based on Archimedes' principle.

The upward force acting on the hot-air balloon is equal to the weight of the surroundings air displaced by the balloon. The heater air in the envelope is less dense than the surrounding air due to the lighter temperature which in turn results in a buoyant force. In order to generate lift, the buoyant force must exceed the weight of the Montgolfier and its components. The balloon is usually unconditionally stable during flight because the weight of the balloon is always concentrated at the bottom, below the centre of buoyancy.

The descent of the Montgolfier is realized by either stopping the heater to cool naturally the hot air in the envelope or opening a small vent at the top of the envelope to release some of the inside hot air.

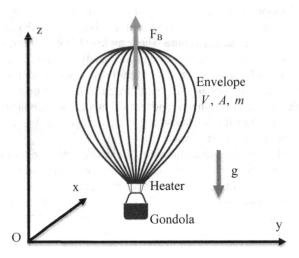

Fig. 2. The scheme of the Hot-air Balloon.

4 Mathematical Models of the Oliver

To develop the fundamental equations of motion describing both vertical and horizontal balloon's displacement as well as the thermal equations describing the gas temperature behaviour inside the balloon on a very basic level, two balance equations are required: the Newton's law and the conversation of energy.

The vertical acceleration of the balloon is described by the vertical force balance equation. The balloon's buoyance force is function of both internal gas temperature and the encircling atmosphere's density and temperature. Moreover, Newton's law applied to balloon's motion requires the inclusion of an additional term to account for apparent mass involved in the acceleration process.

The envelope is assumed to be a sphere and the motion of the hot-air balloon depends on the heat transfer between the balloon and its surroundings. The energy balance between the lifting gas inside and the ambient temperature consists on computing the difference between the heat gain and loss.

The heat gain of the envelope is given as follows:

$$\frac{\delta Q_{in}}{\delta t} = mc_{air}(T_h - T_g) \tag{1}$$

where m is the envelope mass, T_h and T_g are respectively the heater and the gas temperatures, c_{air} indicates the specific heat capacity of the air. Furthermore, the heat loss by convection, conduction and radiation occurrences has the following expression:

$$\frac{\delta Q_{out}}{\delta t} = h_i A(T_g - T_s)^{\frac{4}{3}} + \varepsilon_i \sigma A(T_g^4 - T_s^4) + \frac{KA}{D}(T_s - T_a)$$
$$+ h_e A(T_s - T_a)^{\frac{4}{3}} + \varepsilon_e \sigma A(T_s^4 - T_a^4) \tag{2}$$

where h_i, h_e, ε_i and ε_e are respectively internal and external convection coefficients and emissivities. K and σ are respectively thermal conductivity and Stefan's constant. A and D are the area and the thickness of the envelope respectively. T_s is the envelope temperature derived from the following equation:

$$\frac{\delta T_s}{\delta t} = \frac{1}{mc_e}\left(h_e A(T_a - T_s)^{4/3} + \varepsilon_e \sigma A(T_a^4 - T_s^4)\right) \tag{3}$$

The gas temperature can be determined from the net heat of the envelope which is the difference between the heat gain and loss such as:

$$\frac{\delta T_g}{\delta t} = \frac{1}{mc_e}\left(\frac{\delta Q_{in}}{\delta t} - \frac{\delta Q_{out}}{\delta t}\right) \tag{4}$$

The upward buoyancy-driven lift force, denoted L, may be generated from the temperature produced from the heat transfer (heater). Theoretical buoyancy is only affected by the mass of the ambient air and the local gravitational constant. Using Archimedes' principle of displacement, the net of effective lift is the difference between the buoyancy force and the weight of the lifting gas replacing the ambient atmospheric air in the balloon envelope:

$$L = Vg(\rho_a - \rho_g) = \frac{Vg}{R}\left(\frac{p_a}{T_a} - \frac{p_g}{T_g}\right) \tag{5}$$

where $\rho_a - \rho_g = \Delta\rho = \rho_0(\sigma_a - \sigma_g) \geq 0$. Fully inflated envelope volumes are practically constant. The net lift changes with altitude. The internal and external envelope gas are assumed to have the same pressure $p_a = p_g$. Therefore, the Eq. (5) can be simplified as:

$$L = \rho_a Vg\left(1 - \frac{T_a}{T_g}\right) \tag{6}$$

The equation of movement can be determined using the Newton's second law as:

$$m\frac{d^2 z}{dt^2} = L - G \tag{7}$$

The introduction of the expressions of the mass m and the lift L in the Eq. (7) gives us the altitude acceleration equation as follows:

$$\frac{d^2 z}{dt} = \frac{1}{V\rho_g + \frac{G}{g}}\left(\rho_a Vg(1 - \frac{T_a}{T_g}) - G\right) \tag{8}$$

where $\rho_g = \rho_a\frac{T_a}{T_g}$ and G is the weight of the balloon.

From the previous differential equations governing the plant's dynamics, a block diagram was created using Simulink/Matlab. The mathematical model comprises a heat transfer model and a buoyancy model and considering that the flight of the system is produced by heat transfer between the balloon and its surroundings. The entire model is illustrated by Fig. 3.

In order to develop a model for drone applications, the properties of classical drones can define two adjustable key parameters: the volume of the drone that can occupy and the gross weight that a drone can carry.

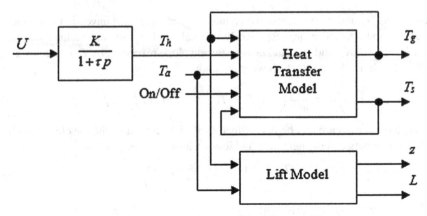

Fig. 3. The block diagram of the Oliver model.

5   Control of the Oliver

The goal of the section is to describe the methodology applied to the analysis and design of a controller based on PID in a first study and Fuzzy logic theory in a second study to compare between them.

After the development of the dynamic model, a controller will be synthesized based on the features of the system. The control strategy is based on the error signal resulting from the difference between the measure and the reference signal (in a closed loop) in order to turn the feedback information to a control signal which is transmitted to the plant to attain the desired output and reduce the error signal Fig. 4. Three types of feedback control will be used for the hot air balloon:

- On/Off control: This type of control uses the error signals to determine the "On" or the "Off" control.
- PID controller: Three actions are added to produce the control input signal. The proportional gain will tend to accelerate the plant's response. The integral action allows the signal to be nonzero even if the feedback error tends to zero. The derivative signal anticipates the system response.
- Fuzzy logic: A fuzzy controller is formed of a concept of linguistic statements derived from human expertise. These statements are used to define a set of "If-Then" rules between different inputs and outputs. The result, deduced from an inference mechanism, will be transformed to a crisp value applied to the controlled plant.

The numeric simulation of the developed model allows to display some significant signals to observe the dynamic behaviour of the plant ant examine the different features and performances (Table 1).

The operation of the system requires a heater temperature chosen as $T_h = 450$ K and a switcher (relay) to give On or Off signals that can modify the heater temperature application with a binary signal (0 or 1), to enable or to prohibit the order to heat the air

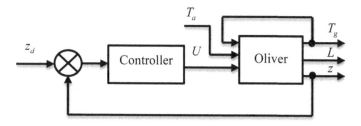

Fig. 4. The control scheme of the Oliver.

Table 1. The Oliver's parameters.

Variable	Value
c_{air}	1005.4 J/kg.K^{-1}
c_f	1700 J/kg.K^{-1}
h_i	16 W/m^2.K^{-1}
h_e	3.37 W/m^2.K^{-1}
K	0.0265 J/ms^{-1}.K^{-1}
D	10^{-3} m
ε_i	0.85
ε_e	0.87
σ	5.67×10^{-8} W/m^2.K^{-4}
V	4.18 m^3
G	9.81 N

inside the envelope. The ambient temperature is chosen as $T_a = 300$ K. The different signals are given by Figs. 5, 6 and 7.

The On/Off command seems to be insufficient to allow the balloon to reach the desired altitude. In order to improve the plant's performances, a PID is tuned in a first stage to adjust the control signal depending on the error between desired and measured heights. The different signals are shown in Figs. 8, 9 and 10.

As noticed in Fig. 8, the height signal response reached its desired value chosen as $z_d = 3$ m after a settling time $t_{r\pm5\%} \simeq 2.13$ mn and an overshoot $D_1\% = 3.5\%$. These obtained results are accepted because the hot air balloon is considered as a system that has slow dynamics in lift-off, landing and during hover movements.

To enhance the control system and to improve simulation results, a Sugeno FIS controller is synthesized from the altitude error and the balloon velocity. The two controller inputs have symmetric triangular memberships, furthermore, the output has two values 0 or 1 to generate the adequate order to apply or not the heater temperature that produce lift of the balloon. The rule base is composed of 9 rules "If-Then" that give the order to stop heating the envelope gas if the altitude is reached, and to continue if not. The numerical

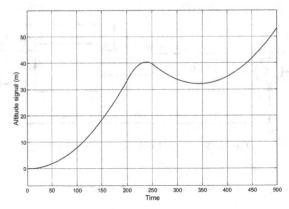

Fig. 5. Evolution of the altitude of the balloon with an On/Off command.

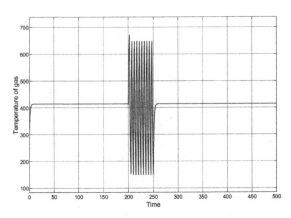

Fig. 6. Evolution of gas temperature in the envelope with an On/Off command.

simulation of the closed loop of the hot air balloon yields the responses illustrated by Figs. 11, 12 and 13.

The altitude response becomes rapid with a settling time $t_{r\pm5\%} \simeq 62s$ and an overshoot around $D_1\% \simeq 6.56\%$. We can notice that the fuzzy controller gives a remarkable rapidity to the dynamic of the system in spite of a low growth of the overshoot that can be improved with other approaches of control.

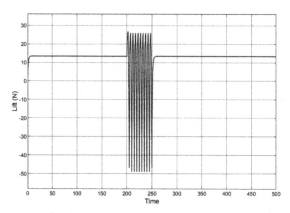

Fig. 7. Evolution of lift force of the balloon with an On/Off command.

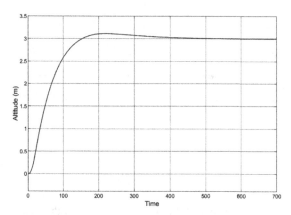

Fig. 8. Evolution of the altitude of the balloon with a PID.

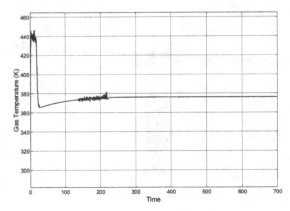

Fig. 9. Evolution of the gas temperature of the balloon with a PID.

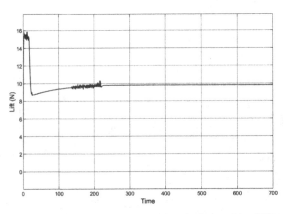

Fig. 10. Evolution of lift force of the balloon with a PID.

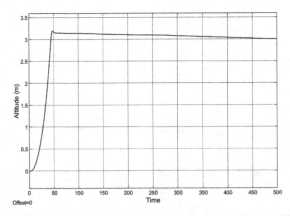

Fig. 11. Evolution of altitude of the balloon with a Sugeno FIS.

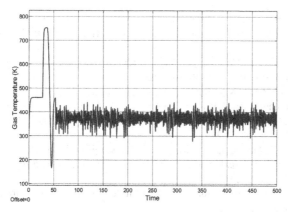

Fig. 12. Evolution of altitude of the balloon with a Sugeno FIS.

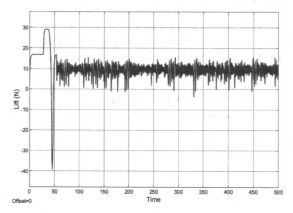

Fig. 13. Evolution of lift force of the balloon with a Sugeno FIS.

6 Conclusion

The main contribution of this paper is the proposition of a specific design of a drone inspired from hot air balloons or Montgolfier. This kind of drone will be used to inspect large agriculture fields, especially olive trees. A reduced-size hot-air balloon is first designed and specified. The mathematical model based on heat transfer and Newton's second law was generated and analyzed to develop control laws that can allow the balloon to reach the desired altitude. The future work consists on the making of the Montgolfier and the implementation of the strategy control taking into account the lift, the horizontal displacement and the wind effect.

References

1. Bagues, M., Nagaz, K., Ben Rouina, B.: Comportement écophysiologique et biochimique de l'olivier variété "Chemlali Sfax" cultivé en plein champ en relation avec les conditions hydriques et édaphiques. Revue des Régions Arides **35**, 1247–1253 (2013)

2. Debbabi, O.S., Ben Amar, F., Rahmeni, S.M., Taranto, F., Montemurro, C., Marilena, M.: The status of genetic resources and olive breeding in Tunisia. Plants (Basel) **11**(13), 1759, 1–12 (2022)

3. Besnard, G., Terral, J.F., Cornille, A.: On the origins and domestication of the olive: a review and perspectives. Ann. Bot. **121**, 385–403 (2018)

4. Garg, K.: Autonomous Navigation System for High Altitude Balloons, Doctoral thesis, Luleå University of Technology, November 2019

5. Daidzic, N.E.: Mathematical model of hot-air balloon steady-state vertical flight performance. Aviation **25**(3), 149–158 (2021)

6. Azeta, J., Ishola, F., Akinpelua, T., Dirisua, J.O., Okokpujiea, I.P., Ibhadodeb, O.: Performance evaluation of developed mathematical models of hot air balloon for drone application. Proc. Manuf. **35**, 1073–1078 (2019)

7. Azeta, J.: An experimental evaluation of LTA on the performance of a drone. Proc. Manuf. **35**, 1135–1140 (2019)

8. De Bruijn, E.I.F., Bosveld, F.C., De Haan, S., Heusinkveld, B.: Measuring low-altitude winds with a hot-air balloon and their validation with Cabauw tower observations. J. Atmos. Ocean. Tech. **37**, 263–277 (2020)

9. Manoj Kumar, R., Haribalan, S., Abinash Nataraj, S., Adithya, S.: Design and Analysis of Solar Heated Hot Air Balloon for Mars Exploration. AIAA SCITECH Forum, January 2022

10. Blackwell, D.: Hot-Air Balloon Navigation, Aerospace Engineering, December 2010

11. Bowman, D.C., et al.: Multihour stratospheric flights with the heliotrope solar hot-air balloon. J. Atmos. Ocean. Tech. **37**(6), 1051–1066 (2020)

12. De Bruijn, E.I.F, De Haan, S., Bosveld, F.C., Holtslag, B.: Wind measurements from hot-air balloon flights. In: 22nd Symposium on Boundary Layers and Turbulence, Salt Lake City, June 2016

13. Edmonds, I.: Hot air balloon engine. Renew. Energy **34**(4), 1100–1105 (2009)

SE-Coins System: Software for Supporting Gamification-Based Educational Processes

Margarita Gamarra[1] (ID), Jan Charris[2], Asly Cantillo[2], Jaime Daza[2], Brandon Llamas[2], Mauricio Vásquez-Carbonell[3] (ID), Anderson Dominguez[4] (ID), and José Escorcia-Gutierrez[2(✉)] (ID)

[1] Department of System Engineering, Universidad del Norte, Barranquilla 081007, Colombia
mrgamarra@uninorte.edu.co
[2] Department of Computational Science and Electronic, Universidad de la Costa, CUC, Barranquilla 080002, Colombia
jescorci56@cuc.edu.co
[3] System Engineering Program, Universidad Simón Bolívar, Barranquilla 081002, Colombia
[4] Corporación Universitaria Minuto de Dios, UNIMINUTO, Barranquilla 081002, Colombia

Abstract. The importance of strategies that facilitate the teaching-learning process is discussed, particularly in the context of digital technologies and the COVID-19 pandemic. Gamification, a popular methodology that incorporates game elements into the classroom to motivate students and improve learning, is the focus of this research. The paper describes the development of a web application based on gamification to assist in teaching Software Engineering. It follows an agile software development methodology and uses UML diagrams to describe the operation and user interaction. A prototype of the SE-Coins App was developed to support the gamification strategy, allowing the teacher to keep track of student progress and reward them accordingly. The functional and quality requirements of the software were implemented with a focus on user requirements to facilitate the implementation of gamification in the classroom. The software is intended for use by both teachers and students, supporting a gamification strategy based on roles, points, recognition, and prizes. The prototype complements the requirements and serves as a starting point for this strategy.

Keywords: Engineering education · Gamification · Software Engineering · UML diagrams · Web applications

1 Introduction

The COVID-19 health emergency has caused a significant shift in societal customs, particularly in the education sector. With confinement and other safety measures, higher education institutions were compelled to adopt remote learning to continue their activities [1]. This shift has necessitated the implementation of teaching methodologies and strategies that rely on technological tools to enhance student performance and interest in the subjects being presented [2]. These strategies are being implemented in remote learning and face-to-face learning as institutions gradually return to the classroom. Gamification has emerged as one of the most used methodologies.

K. Saeed et al. (Eds.): CISIM 2023, LNCS 14164, pp. 151–165, 2023.
https://doi.org/10.1007/978-3-031-42823-4_12

The gamification methodology incorporates game-like elements into non-game activities. The authors of a preliminary work developed a gamification strategy that includes challenges, levels of complexity, and rewards. Challenges are associated with student activities both inside and outside the classroom [3]. Levels represent academic periods where previously acquired knowledge is combined with knowledge at the next level to development challenges. Rewards, which may be intangible, are associated with achieving learning objectives and can range from earning points to obtaining bonuses or privileges for top performers [4].

Various gamification strategies have been applied across different stages of the education process, from preschool to higher education [5], and have even been targeted toward individuals with disabilities [6].

Despite the proven benefits of gamification in educational processes and the digital tools that support it, many teachers who implement gamification in the classroom still have to track student progress and activities manually. Furthermore, students may need help understanding the activity's development because, in some cases, they rely on Learning Management Systems (LMS) designed for traditional teaching models [7]. Students attending institutions without LMS must listen carefully and record the instructions in their class notes.

Therefore, this study proposes the implementation of the SECoins System (Software Engineering Coins), a software solution to support teachers and students who take courses that implement the gamification methodology. Initially developed for the subjects Software Engineering I and II at the Universidad de la Costa, the system will allow teachers to track student progress in their subjects, publish activities, communicate important information, and grant rewards. Similarly, students will be able to monitor their progress in each subject, receive instructions for each activity, and check the status of their work team.

The system will initially focus on teaching Computer Science, specifically Software Engineering and related disciplines. This is because the implementation of gamification in this subject has yielded positive results, motivating students to excel in practical activities, build effective teamwork, and develop social and critical thinking skills, which are essential tools for the professional performance of a software engineer. However, the system is designed to be scalable, enabling its implementation in any subject at any educational institution.

The article is structured into eight sections. In Sect. 2, several bibliographic sources of interest are consulted to support the development of the methodological proposal presented in Sect. 3. Afterward, Sect. 4 outlines the proposal's planning, while Sects. 5, 6, and 7 address the software design, architecture, and implementation, respectively. Finally, Sect. 8 presents the conclusions reached in this research.

2 Related Work

The existing literature extensively documents the gamification methodology and its applications in various areas. For this research, we will focus on the literature related to the applications of this methodology in Software Engineering and related disciplines, along with similar proposals.

An example of gamification implementation in the face-to-face modality is presented in [4]. A gamification strategy was successfully implemented and evaluated among a representative group of electronic and systems engineers from two higher education institutions in Barranquilla, Colombia. The score-based gamification strategy was well-received and resulted in increased participation in the course, greater interest in the proposed activities, and improved group participation, leading to valuable findings on the effective use of gamification design elements in learning contexts in higher technical education institutions. Survey results indicated a positive reception of the strategy, with students suggesting its application in other courses.

Due to the pandemic-induced confinement, educational institutions were compelled to adopt technology-enhanced learning strategies to ensure students' successful continuation of studies through suitable remote or virtual learning modes.

The literature review found that gamification has the potential to mitigate the impact of the transition in the educational sector caused by the SARS-CoV-2 virus pandemic [8]. However, it is also noted that supporting gamification mechanics with a solid theoretical framework and research is essential, which should be further developed in future studies on this methodology.

Gamification has been utilized in software engineering to enhance the quality and results by elevating people's motivation and commitment. A methodological map has revealed research gaps in this field, including the challenge of creating an integrated gamified environment that encompasses all the tools of an organization. This is because most existing gamified tools are customized developments or prototypes. In the case study addressed in [9], it is demonstrated that gamification technology enables a company to build a granular workplace by integrating custom and pre-built tools, such as Redmine, TestLink, or JUnit with this methodology, under an architecture where a REST API is used to facilitate the exchange of information between these tools and a gamification engine. Two primary benefits of this work can be highlighted: (1) the proposed solution allows the organization to retain its existing tools, and (2) the rewards earned in any tool are accumulated in a centralized gamified environment.

Developing software that supports gamification and computer science is essential to enhance the knowledge acquired in any field of study, mainly as the world increasingly relies on digital environments. The work described in [10] presents a software engineering learning application that addresses this need by utilizing two approaches. Firstly, the application is implemented as an Android app to increase accessibility, allowing students to use it anywhere, anytime. Secondly, a gamification system with different itineraries is implemented to adapt to each learner's learning style, motivating students to compete with their classmates. The application is structured in stages or content units, each with different difficulty levels assigned to various topics. The game has four levels: Boot, Bronze, Silver, and Gold, and the student's objective is to reach the highest level possible in each unit. To pass a level, the student must answer a test consisting of 10 main questions, with 10 alternatives for each main question, within 30 s. If the time is exceeded, the system moves on to the next question and counts it as a failure.

Although there has been much research on gamification methodology and its implementation, software implementations that assist in teaching using this methodology are very scarce. One of the few examples is *Classroom Live* [11], developed by the United

States Air Force Academy. It is a desktop application based on a two-tier client-server architecture. Although it was still under development at the time, the results of the applied tests were outstanding. However, since it was designed as a desktop application, adapting it for information sharing with other devices would be costly. The architecture only presents a data flow between the desktop client and the server where the database is located. Therefore, several improvements were necessary for the development of the system. From an educational point of view, the system is conceived as a tool to implement the "learning by doing" strategy, in which the teacher can perform various activities, such as practice tests, to reinforce knowledge on a particular topic.

The SEcoins System, our software proposal, is designed for gamified and reward-based environments. This tool aims to provide teachers with better resource management and help students achieve greater motivation and commitment to the subject.

3 Methodology

The ideal methodology for this software development project is the agile Scrum approach because it allows for the generation of incremental results through collaborative efforts between the development team and stakeholders in the system's development. This methodology involves establishing development cycles called sprints, which focus on the incremental development of different functionalities while maintaining the general objectives of the system [12].

The advantage of using this methodology is its applicability to various types of companies, especially those focused on software engineering. This aligns with the gamification strategy, as a clear list of objectives must be prioritized beforehand, called the product backlog. This list depends on the project requirements and is essential in defining the application development roadmap. For instance, the teacher, in addition to assigning regular class activities, may allow students to propose activities that earn more points for participation, increasing the possibility of obtaining better rewards.

In the design phase, the system's persistence will be based on the relational diagram for the database. This diagram was created using the MySQL Workbench tool, which specializes in modeling databases that follow the relational model. It also allows the database model to be translated into SQL code for creating a data schema in MySQL. Additionally, various UML (Unified Modeling Language) diagrams were created to describe different elements of the system and its interaction with the user, including use case diagrams, state diagrams, collaboration diagrams, and component diagrams.

In the coding stage, we will follow the Scrum methodology guidelines, considering its incremental nature and the need to adapt the project requirements to any changes that stakeholders wish to apply to the system.

4 Proposal's Planning

The implementation largely follows the gamification guidelines described in [1]. It was decided to call the points "SECoins," a name derived from Software Engineering Coins since this unit is specifically designed for Software Engineering subjects. However, the system allows each subject to specify its units to measure the score obtained by students, providing great flexibility to teachers and universities in using the system.

4.1 Requirements Analysis

We followed the FURPS model [13] for the requirements analysis, which addresses the functional and non-functional or quality requirements that the software being developed must have. Regarding software quality, the reference model should focus on monitoring and evaluating each phase of the software product construction process [14]. Table 1 presents the requirements defined for the SE-Coins System software.

Table 1. Requirements according to the FURPS model.

Quality Factor	Attributes
Functionality	• Assist in communication of course activities • Administer bonuses (SEcoins) awarded by the teacher • Ensure a well-organized rewards store • Allow requests for reports from participating groups • Organize activities according to the stipulated schedule
Ease of use	• It has a user-friendly interface • It is adaptable to operating systems such as Android and Windows • It contains support documentation or helpful resources
Reliability	• The delivery of activities and rewards depends on the roles of the users • Includes support for potential failures • The failover capability should be at least one day
Performance	• The software's technology platforms will ensure adequate performance
Support capacity	• Adaptable • Compatible • It has the ability to be configured • Testing capability

4.2 Risk Assessment

When developing a project, it is necessary to assess the potential risks that may arise. This allows for the generation of strategies to anticipate and mitigate the occurrence of such risks. As part of the planning for this project, the risks and their potential impact have been considered in Table 2.

Table 2. Software risks and their potential impact.

Risks	Impact
Missing or poorly defined requirements	Moderate
Delays due to inadequate requirements analysis	Moderate
Underestimation of application size	Low
User difficulty with application usage and resistance to change	Low
Possible software failures during development	Moderate
Inadequate information provided by the application	Low
Security breaches leading to unauthorized access or manipulation of bonuses and ratings	Moderate

5 Software Design

UML diagrams have been adopted for the software design phase, serving as a link between the requirements analysis and implementation phases.

5.1 Use Case Diagram

Four actors were identified for the development of the system, of which two are main actors (students and teachers), one is supporting (global administrators), and the last one is passive (the university). Each stakeholder has specific objectives, as shown in Table 3. Additionally, Fig. 1 displays the use case diagram of the software platform.

Table 3. Stakeholder with specific objectives.

Administrator	Teacher	Student
Manage teacher information	Create or delete companies	Manage company information
Manage student information	Allocate SECoins	View individual SECoin amounts
Manage company information	Manage the rewards store	View the total SECoin amount of the company
Manage SECoins	Accept or reject SECoins donation requests	Donate SECoins to company members
		Redeem SECoins in the rewards store

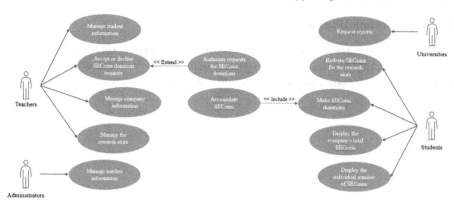

Fig. 1. Use case diagram for the SEcoins system software.

5.2 State Diagram

Figure 2 presents a state diagram illustrating redeeming rewards in the SEcoins store. In this process, the student decides which reward for selecting for redeeming their points. If the student has enough points, the redemption is completed immediately. Otherwise, they may request points from their classmates and seek authorization from the teacher. If the teacher rejects the request, the process is canceled, and the student request is terminated. If the request is approved, the student is authorized to redeem the SEcoins. In either case, the administrator is notified, and the process is terminated.

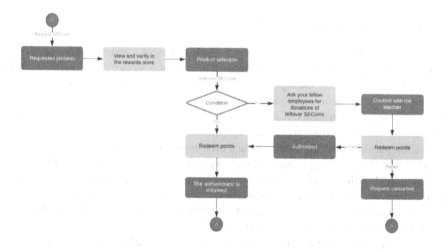

Fig. 2. State diagram for the SEcoins system software.

5.3   Collaboration Diagram

This diagram illustrates some of the actions that a teacher can perform using the SEcoins System application. The teacher can manage groups, create or delete them, and accept or reject requests for point donations. The collaboration diagram is shown in Fig. 3.

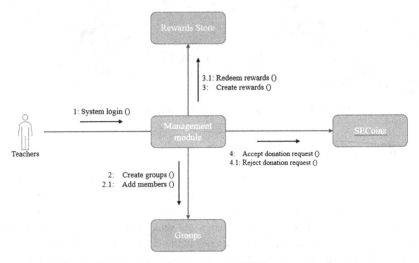

Fig. 3. Collaboration diagram for the SECoins system software.

5.4   Components Diagram

The component diagram displayed in Fig. 4 illustrates eight components that depict the main modules accessible to a user assigned the role of a student. In this context, the concerned user can solely manage the system and their data after registering. Therefore, they must utilize the login component and its provided interface named "validate data" to verify their registration status. If the user is not registered, the system has the "register" component, which provides the "send registration" interface. This interface is used to submit the user's data to the database once they have filled out the registration form.

The "My Profile" component manages user profile data and provides students with the "Manage Profile" interface. This component, in turn, depends on two other components to perform its task: "Manage Profile" and "Manage Password". Both of these components require interfaces to function provided by the main component. These interfaces are "Change Names" and "Change Password".

In order to exchange SEcoins for a prize, there is a "Store" component that contains all available prizes and their SEcoin cost. This component offers the "Request Redemption" interface. Meanwhile, the "My Courses" component allows students to view their enrolled courses through the "Manage Courses" interface. This component depends on the "Course" component, which can be viewed through the "View Course" interface provided by the "My Courses" component.

In short, the student uses and relies on the following interfaces: *validate data, submit the registration, manage profile, manage courses, and request SEcoin exchange.*

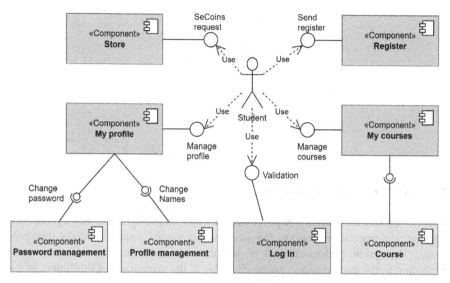

Fig. 4. Diagram of SECoins system software components.

6 Software Architecture

The software presented was developed using the MVC (Model-View-Controller) architectural pattern as its base. In this model, applications are composed of three main components: the Model, where all system logic, primary system operations, and data storage forms are specified; the View, which is responsible for displaying the application interface; and the controller, which allows for the connection between the view and the model through user input data. Due to the interactive nature of the system proposed in this work, a rapid display of information is required.

Laravel is one of the most used frameworks to develop applications using this architectural pattern. It is based on PHP and is used to build the application's backend.

The Model View Controller (MVC) software architecture separates application data, user interface, and control logic into three distinct components. This mature model has been proven over the years in various applications and across many development languages and platforms.

However, for this application, a variant of the MVC model was chosen, in which the controller executes the REST services that perform the requests to the API used by the application. This approach makes the application scalable, allowing communication between the server and multiple clients using the API. Instead of sending information directly to the views, the Controller exchanges data with the REST services, which then return the requested resources (data). This data is made available through URLs that client applications access to use. The workflow is described in Fig. 5.

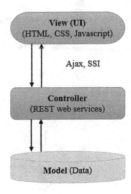

Fig. 5. MVC pattern with REST API.

7 Software Implementation

After completing the planning, requirements analysis, and design process, we proceeded with the implementation phase of the gamification system to support educational processes. The system performed well in the unit tests of the functional requirements. According to the requirements exposed in Table 1, the percentage of fulfillment in the preliminary version are reported in Table 4.

Table 4. Evaluation of the software functionality.

Attributes	Implementation	Percentage of fulfillment
Assist in communication of course activities	The software includes a visualization of activities published by the instructor	100%
Administer bonuses (SEcoins) awarded by the teacher	The instructor can assign SEcoins according to the performance of the students, but the information is off-line	70%
Ensure a well-organized rewards store	The rewards are associated with the SEcoins obtained by the students, but the purchase is not online	70%
Allow requests for reports from participating groups	The instructor can report the SEcoins obtained by group or individual	100%
Organize activities according to the stipulated schedule	The instructor can create and update activities for groups	100%

Some limitations of the software are associated with the availability of the web server, as the current version is off-line.

Figures 6, 7, and 8 display some elements of the SeCoins System software interface, which allow users to register, log in, and view available courses.

Fig. 6. SECoins app student registration form design.

Fig. 7. SECoins app course room design.

Additionally, we tested our software with 10 users (instructors) and we created and applied a survey to evaluate the usability of our software. According to [15], we can test a software with 10 users to have an idea about the usability. The question tries to collect background information (with Q1, Q2, and Q3), to observe user behavior (with Q4 and Q5) and to evaluate the overall user impression (with Q6).

The survey includes the following questions:

1. How often do you use a gamification software tool in your class?

a. Never	b. Occasionally (1–2 times/period)
c. Frequently (3–4 times/period)	d. Very Frequently (4 + times/period)

2. What tools do you use, if any, to implement gamification?

a. Kahoot	b. Moodle XP
c. Wooclap	d. Others

3. How do you manage badges, leaderboard, points, or rewards?

a. I don't use these elements	b. With some informatics tools (e.g. Word, Excel, Power Point, etc.)
c. With some design tools (e.g. Genially, Canvas, etc.)	d. Others

4. How easy was it to navigate into SEcoins APP?

a. Very easy	b. Easy
c. Difficult	d. Very Difficult

5. How useful did you find the software tools?

a. Very useful	b. Useful, but not complete
c. Useful, but hard to use	d. Useless

6. How frequently would you use this software?

a. Never	b. Occasionally (1–2 times/period)
c. Frequently (3–4 times/period)	d. Very Frequently (4 + times/period)

The results of this survey are summarized in Fig. 8, 9, 10 and 11. The graph in Fig. 8 exposes a comparison between the use of gamification tools before test SEcoins App and after. These values show that the 20% of instructors that don't use any gamificiation tool would be willing to use SEcoins App and 90% of instructors would use the software. Figure 9 shows that 70% of instructor have used Kahoot, 30% Wooclap and 40% other tools to implement gamification in class. Figure 10 shows that 60% of instructors use some informatics tools to manage some gamified elements. Figure 11 shows the results for Q4 and Q5 which evaluate the easy to use and the usefulness. The 100% of the surveyed considered that SEcoin App is easy or very easy to use and the 80% considered that it is a very useful tool.

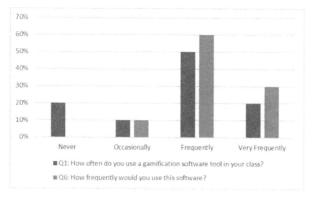

Fig. 8. Results of Q1 and Q6.

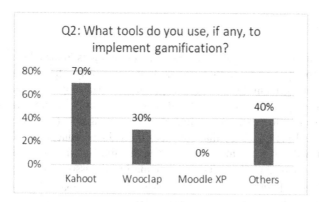

Fig. 9. Results of Q2.

Fig. 10. Results of Q3.

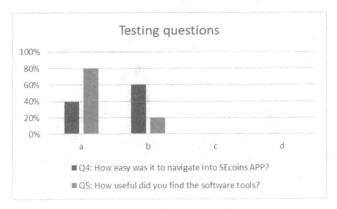

Fig. 11. Results of Q4 and Q5.

8   Conclusions

Gamification has become one of the essential methodologies in the educational process because of its ability to improve students' skills and positively influence their motivation and academic engagement through various gaming and learning activities.

The preliminary study conducted for this development [4] demonstrated that gamification positively affects students' motivation and engagement. Consequently, it represents a practical methodology that enhances individuals' educational experiences. It is well-established that when methodologies are flexible and interactive for their users, they tend to improve their knowledge, particularly in classrooms where most of the audience are young people who typically prefer these learning methods because they motivate them and increase their competitiveness.

The development process of the gamification strategy support system involved three phases: requirements analysis, system design, and implementation. During the design phase, several UML diagrams were used, including a use case diagram to characterize the system users, a state diagram to illustrate the system's processes, a collaboration diagram to describe user interactions, and a component diagram to outline the main modules available to specific users. Each of these diagrams enhances the system's comprehension for customers and developers.

The application's architecture combines the Model View Controller (MVC) pattern with the REST pattern, enabling simple scalability of the application to other platforms without compromising the MVC pattern's principles. This is necessary since it facilitates the creation of applications with constant user interaction, where data loading is crucial and needs to occur as quickly as possible.

The development team should be aware of the research related to the methodology in order to ensure that the implementation is suitable for the needs of each institution and teacher. This makes the Scrum methodology the most suitable development methodology, as it allows for great adaptation to changes in requirements that may occur when new elements are incorporated into the gamification methodology.

SECoins Systems is a project that is still under development, but all the functions required was fulfilled. Additionally, the survey applied to instructors demonstrated that the software has a good potential to be implemented as a gamification tool. The current results allow for reasonable use of the application by students to access their information. However, future research may influence the development, and therefore the system's evolution may vary after the project's completion. As such, the definition of the diagrams, methodology, and architecture is fundamental for ensuring good performance during the development and implementation of this system.

References

1. Villarroel, V., Pérez, C., Rojas-Barahona, C.A., García, R.: Educación remota en contexto de pandemia: caracterización del proceso educativo en las universidades chilenas. Formación Universitaria **14**, 65–76 (2021). https://doi.org/10.4067/S0718-50062021000600065
2. Estrada, F.J.R., Flores, E.G.R.: Docentes universitarios frente al confinamiento académico: un análisis exploratorio. Texto Livre **15** (2022). https://doi.org/10.35699/1983-3652.2022.38234
3. Alhammad, M.M., Moreno, A.M.: Gamification in software engineering education: a systematic mapping. J. Syst. Softw. **141**, 131–150 (2018). https://doi.org/10.1016/j.jss.2018.03.065
4. Gamarra, M., Dominguez, A., Velazquez, J., Páez, H.: A gamification strategy in engineering education—A case study on motivation and engagement. Comput. Appl. Eng. Educ. **30**, 472–482 (2022). https://doi.org/10.1002/CAE.22466
5. Becker, K., Nicholson, S.: Learning, education and games volume two: bringing games into educational contexts. In: Schrier, K. (ed.) Learning, Education and Games. ETC Press (2015)
6. Gasca-Hurtado, G.P., Gomez-Alvarez, M.C., Hincapie, J.A., Zepeda, V.V.: Gamification of an educational environment in software engineering: case study for digital accessibility of people with disabilities. Revista Iberoamericana de Tecnologias del Aprendizaje. **16**, 382–392 (2021). https://doi.org/10.1109/RITA.2021.3137372
7. Altamar, M.S.O., Arregocés, M.V.M., Perico, J.Y.M.: Descripción del uso de las herramientas del Learning Management System (LMS) en el aula: relaciones y diseños de entornos de aprendizaje. Paradigmas Socio-Humanísticos **3**, 12–24 (2021). https://doi.org/10.26752/REVISTAPARADIGMASSH.V3I2.614
8. Nieto-Escamez, F.A., Roldán-Tapia, M.D.: Gamification as online teaching strategy during COVID-19: a mini-review. Front. Psychol. **12** (2021). https://doi.org/10.3389/fpsyg.2021.648552
9. Pedreira, O., Garcia, F., Piattini, M., Cortinas, A., Cerdeira-Pena, A.: An architecture for software engineering gamification. Tsinghua Sci. Technol. **25**, 776–797 (2020). https://doi.org/10.26599/TST.2020.9010004
10. Sarasa-Cabezuelo, A., Rodrigo, C.: Development of an educational application for software engineering learning. Computers **10** (2021). https://doi.org/10.3390/computers10090106
11. De Freitas, A.A., De Freitas, M.M.: Classroom live: a software-assisted gamification tool (2013). https://doi.org/10.1080/08993408.2013.780449.
12. Pressman, R.S., Maxim, B.R.: Software Engineering: A Practitioner's Approach. McGraw-Hill Education (2015)
13. Moreno, J.J., Bolaños, L.P., Navia, M.A.: Exploración de modelos y estándares de calidad para el producto software. Revista UIS Ingenierías **9**, 39–53 (2010)
14. Castaño, J.F., Castillo, W.: Metrics in the evaluation of software quality. Comput. Electron. Sci.: Theory Appl. **2**, 21–26 (2021). https://doi.org/10.17981/CESTA.02.02.2021.03
15. Nielsen, J., Landauer, T.K.: Mathematical model of the finding of usability problems. In: Conference on Human Factors in Computing Systems - Proceedings, pp. 206–213 (1993). https://doi.org/10.1145/169059.169166

The Effects of Buyer-Supplier Collaboration on Supply Chain Performance: A Study in the Brazilian Electronics Sector

Danielle Nunes Pozzo[1]([✉]) [ID], Alexandre Vargas Duarte[2] [ID],
Isamar Paola Gutierrez Roa[3] [ID], Carlos Alfonso Gonzalez Beleño[4] [ID],
Hussein Serjan Jaafar Orfale[3] [ID], Aydaluz Villanueva Vasquez[3] [ID],
and Lainet Maria Nieto Ramos[3] [ID]

[1] Universidad de la Costa - CUC, Barranquilla, ATL 080002, Colombia
dnunez8@cuc.edu.co
[2] Universidade de São Paulo – USP, São Paulo, SP 01246-904, Brazil
[3] Institución Universitaria de Barranquilla, Barranquilla, ATL 080002, Colombia
[4] Corporación Universitaria Americana, Barranquilla, ATL 080001, Colombia

Abstract. Supply chain collaboration is still a challenge in emerging economies due to the predominant low level of maturity in most sectors. The specific literature that could enlighten the context factors as well as provide empirical data is still not conclusive, leading to a relevant gap to explore. Specifically in Brazil, previous literature shows the struggles of most companies to establish a solid and sustainable collaboration in their supply chains, therefore emphasizing successful cases as the outliers to be studied. Therefore, this study aims to analyze how the buyer-supplier collaboration between manufacturer and retailer affects the performance of the supply chain based on a case in the Brazilian electronics sector. As specific objectives, this research analyze the perception of retail and industry managers about the benefits of collaborative sales planning (i), the influence of this phenomenon on inventory management (ii) as well as identify the formative aspects of collaborative behavior based on an adaptation of Spekman and Carraway's framework [31]. Results evidence that sales planning in collaboration is strongly influenced by the macroeconomic factors, among other variables outside of the supply chain more than the strategic orientation of the involved companies. Trust appears as a key factor, as well as volume of inventory, in order to provide the perception of collaboration as beneficial. Aspects such as power of negotiation, intent to enhance control and perception of 'fairness' can interfere with both the sustainability of the collaborative model and its performance results.

Keywords: Collaboration · Supply chain management · Buyer-supplier relations

1 Introduction

Supply chain performance is a fundamental element of competitiveness that constitutes a continuous challenge, both to achieve and maintain [13, 25]. Although the general parameters of the field have already been established for a significant number of years,

K. Saeed et al. (Eds.): CISIM 2023, LNCS 14164, pp. 166–176, 2023.
https://doi.org/10.1007/978-3-031-42823-4_13

the constant changes of the market and the increasing complexity of operations keep this topic as one of the primary management concerns [35]. Among many variables, collaboration presents itself as a highlight as relational aspects – such as culture, information sharing and strategic orientation - are more complex and abstract to manage than other functional performance dimensions [37].

In less mature supply chains, studies on collaboration is a relatively rare finding, which results in a lack of empirical studies in emerging countries where traditionally supply chain operations are not yet or not properly integrated to a point in which collaboration can be properly observed [1, 11]. In the same sense, the level of maturity and its relation to the performance of the collaboration is also still ambiguous in current literature [11].

Moreover, supply chain performance and collaboration models are primarily designed considering the context of developed countries, in which internal and external variables differ from developing ones [21, 27]. Therefore, in-depth studies of collaboration in developing countries' environments may lead to contributions in terms of models adjusted to the context and a clearer understanding of variable interactions in this scenario. So far, literature has not been conclusive, which constitutes a research opportunity.

More specifically, current studies regarding supply chain collaboration in Latin America are still limited and add an additional layer of gap in context-specific studies on the topic [32].

Based on this perspective, the present study aims to contribute to the discussion by analyzing how the buyer-supplier collaboration between manufacturer and retailers affects the performance of a supply chain in the Brazilian electronics sector. As specific objectives, this research analyze the perception of retailer and manufacturer's managers about the benefits of collaborative sales planning (i), the influence of this phenomenon on inventory management (ii) as well as identify the formative aspects of collaborative behavior based on an adaptation of Spekman and Carraway's framework [31].

2 Buyer-Supplier Collaboration

Collaboration in supply chains is a known key-aspect to achieve and maintain high levels of performance. Although it can be analyzed among the entire supply chain, differences in the object of collaboration as well as specificities of the organizations involved lead to analysis per links, in dyads and triads [30, 36].

Regarding buyer-supplier collaboration, the models so far proposed on the literature are not excessive in quantity, with few efforts applicable to large portions of supply chains as the majority of discussions focused on more sector and case-specific approaches [22].

Among the efforts to propose a general framework for buyer-supplier collaboration, Spekman and Carraway [31] present a largely accepted and applied model that base the relationship on two extremes: traditional and collaborative. According to this approach, drivers, enablers, and capabilities are required to develop a collaborative relationship, that can be achieved in different intensities [31] as shown on Fig. 1.

Spekman and Carraway's framework [31] has been updated to actual days not in terms of key variables, *per se*, but according to changes in context: current studies based

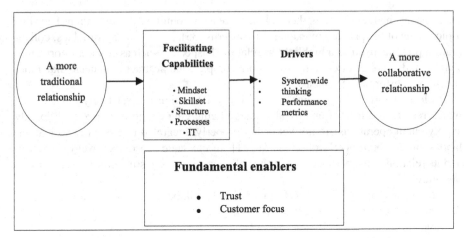

Fig. 1. Towards an understanding of buyer – seller relationships—Transitioning to a more collaborative model [31].

on the same constructs are now adding aspects of the digital era, as well as the outcomes in sustainability and innovation capabilities [19, 24, 29]. Therefore, its application to analyze supply chains is still valid, however context variables need to be taken into consideration as well as the expansion of some construct-related discussions. The quality of the buyer-supplier relationship and the way information is managed are elements that are guiding current research and still require deeper analysis on specific industries [14].

Current literature has also been emphasizing that task involvement and joint planning are drivers that can not only lead to better knowledge about the customer, but also lead to inputs to develop and launch new and innovative products [4, 29].

Li et al. [16] provides an updated overview of the collaboration between buyers and suppliers by connecting macro and micro level variables. In this perspective, the propensity for employee collaboration is associated with internal collaborative behaviors as an integrated micro level force that is paralleled with strategic intention to explain buyer-supplier collaboration [16]. On a different approach, Kashyap and Lakhanpal [13] have improved the buyer-supplier collaboration analysis by structuring levels according to integration and interaction, reinforcing that collaboration is a case-specific phenomenon leading to a variety of outcomes.

Due to current literature discussions on multilevel variables (macro and micro) as stated in Li et al. [16] and Kashyap and Lakhanpal [13], constructs are now represented in parallel and not as a sequence. Considering the definition of mindset of Spekman and Carraway [31], it includes a broad spectrum of elements that configures the organizational willingness to collaborate, which would also include joint planning [4]. As for task involvement, although it is partially involved in skillset as it can be considered a soft skill, it is also a behavioral aspect of the capabilities [4, 29], which is why the variable was included in the proposed updated version. Taking into consideration the definition of drivers in the original framework, it can be seen as analogue to the macro level of Li et al. [16], which is why strategic intention was added as a variable to this construct. The

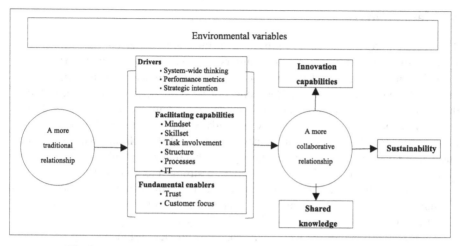

Fig. 2. An updated approach on buyer-supplier collaboration analysis

outputs reflect elements mentioned in Sikombe and Phiri, [29], Patrucco et al., [24], and Mujianto et al. [19].

In terms of buyer-supplier relationships, the literature in Latin America is quite limited [32, 34] - especially due to empirical limitations, since the phenomenon is not easily found in this context - and major databases show only 23 papers on this topic as the center of discussion in the brazilian scenario.

Although Brazil shares characteristics with other emerging countries and, more specifically, with other countries in Latin America, brazilian business environment presents a set of specific cultural aspects – also mentioned as the 'brazilian way' or the 'brazilian jeitinho' - that could deeply affect the dynamics and results of collaboration [15, 30].

Latest publications on buyer-supplier collaboration in brazilian supply chains are mostly focused on the food sector [2, 6, 26, 28].

More recently, Costa et al. [6] studied buyer-supplier dyads in the brazilian food sector evidencing a significant presence of communication, flexibility, innovation, knowledge management and highly effective leadership. However, the performance outcomes present a counter-intuitive reality in which performance can be decreased by the level of flexibility and resilience.

In a different approach, Domenek et al. [7] showed the relevance and the mediating role of operational capabilities in the relationship between collaborative management and operational performance based on brazilian managers' perceptions. This point of view provides a point of view in which capabilities are critical to high-level performance results in collaboration.

F. Ayala et al. [8] work suggests that collaboration in different sectors of the brazilian environment may present different configurations and behaviors, which reinforces the opportunity for studies such as this one. To our knowledge, no specific study has been conducted on buyer-supplier collaboration in the brazilian electronics sector as major databases do not present a paper with similar approach to the present research.

3   Methodology

This research has a qualitative approach, as it intends to understand the influence of collaborative planning between manufacturers and retail on supply chain performance. Therefore, it requires an in-depth analysis of the phenomenon that can only be obtained through this type of research [10]. Data collection was conducted on a manufacturer that, due to non-disclosure requirements, will be presented with the alias "E.L.". E.L. is a large multinational electronics company, currently present in more than 150 countries and ranked on the top 10 largest digital companies in the world [9]. The company was chosen due to its relevance on the market and the high number of reported collaborative relations established with retailers. That condition was a strong reference that the case was a significant scenario for the phenomenon to be studied. Although this is a multinational company, it sustains a solid manufacturing operation in Brazil. The analyzed relations were focusing on brazilian retailers.

Three dyadic relationships were analyzed, one from each customer group. Customers groups are divided by E.L. considering the volume of purchased products per year (small, medium and large). The customers selected to participate on this research are the most important players from each group, according to E.L. managers. The decision to include companies from different groups was made considering the intention to amplify case comprehension and reduce elite bias [18]. Although expanding to more cases was first considered, the saturation (later presented on the results) was considered proof of suitable sampling. Table 1 presents the details of the relationships studied.

Table 1. Subjects' profiles

Relationship	Customer Group	Person ID	Current Position	Status and Experience
Dyad 1	Small	Subject 1	Sales manager at E.L	Senior manager. 3 years
		Subject 2	Purchasing manager at company A	Senior manager. 10 years
Dyad 2	Medium	Subject 3	Sales manager at E.L	Senior manager. 4 years
		Subject 4	Purchasing manager at company B	Senior manager. 12 years
Dyad 3	Large	Subject 5	Sales manager at E.L	Senior manager. 4 years
		Subject 6	Purchasing manager at company C	Senior manager. 1 year

As displayed on Table 1, E.L.'s managers, retailer brands and their respective pur-chasing managers will also be referred by numbers and letters to avoid disclosing identity. These identifications will be used during the next chapters as references. It is also rel-evant to highlight that the aforementioned experiences refer only to the timeframe the specific subject is being involved in the dyad as main responsible for their respective company, not the total years of experience in the market.

A semi structured interview was applied as the main source of data. The instruments (one for E.L. managers and other for retailers) were developed based on the theoretical framework previously presented. Additional in loco observation was conducted to verify possible nuances and complementary data regarding managers' interactions. Also, documents (reports, e-mails, and agreements) were analyzed for confirmatory purposes. The dynamic of data collection from different sources and approaches configures the triangulation required for this methodological strategy [18].

Interviews were recorded and later transcribed for analysis. Subsequently, content analysis was applied following the protocol of Miles et al. [18], which included data condensation, display and verification. *A priori* categorization was applied using the framework's respective variables and constructs.

4   Results and Discussions

Table 1 presents the main integrated findings of this research, highlighting the results that affect the analyzed dyads.

Besides the main topics presented on Table 2, volume of operations and stable order levels also seems to be critical for the manufacturer to consider higher levels of collaboration, since collaboration requires investments in resources and sharing of sensitive information, which leads to a higher risk perception. This perception is not seen as instinctive but as an outcome based on historical data and can be connected to the Transaction Cost Theory [3, 5, 12], as E.L. does not see compensation in the transaction cost brought by collaboration in smaller buyers. This is also supported in previous literature [23, 39].

In terms of culture, some aspects of the Brazilian way or "brazilian jeitinho" as previously stated in Lee Park et al. [15] were found as part of the dynamics, however with low impact on performance and formal processes. The high level of policies and external control (international supervision and regulation as well as outside audits) may explain the limited the interference of this variable in the observed dyads.

Another relevant context aspect is that both manufacturer and retailers emphasized macroeconomic factors as more critical to affect planning than strategic orientation itself. This finding suggests that planning and decision-making among these players might be presented differently in a scenario with less uncertainty and market instability.

Overall, the analyzed dyads refer to an asymmetric scenario between the manufacturer and retailers [17, 33].

In terms of performance, two key factors are taken into consideration by both parties: systemic environment and indicators. Performance is strictly controlled by manufacturer, that establishes non-negotiable contractual parameters. Therefore, although planning is a shared process, the final decisions are, if necessary, imposed by manufacturer, which is usually detached from retailers' projections. The rather strict dynamic, although counter-intuitive for collaborative relations can be partially caused by a managerial response to cultural and context elements, since Costa et al. [6] has evidenced that a flexible environment can be a source of reduction in performance in the brazilian context.

Table 2. Main findings

Highlighted aspects	Integrated results
Mutual benefit	Collaboration is unanimously seen as a key factor to improve performance, especially in inventory management, even in dyads with lower collaboration levels
Sustainability	Managers believe collaboration as it is reduces risks and align expectations, contributing directly to a more sustainable operation, both between buyer and supplier and within the supply chain as a whole
Customer focus	Customer focus is clear and shared by the involved parties. This allow sales strategies to flow easily and obtaining consensus in deciding the majority of customer-related initiatives
Trust	Trust is perceived as an antecedent of collaboration and as a determinant to establish the level of collaboration between buyer and supplier. However, it is shown that power dynamics may affect in a way that trust is only measured from the manufacturer's point of view
Co-dependency	Power in negotiation represents a relevant aspect, as dependency is not equal, reinforcing previous studies [37, 39]. The manufacturer may, even in highly collaborative environments, create unilateral strategies that may affect retailers when critical performance indicators are affected, without previous notice. That scenario shows that, although co-dependency is present, negotiation power is biased and resulting in a perception of eventual "unfairness", even in scenarios with a general win-win assessment, similar to Newman et al. [20] findings
Distinction of cooperative factors	Managers are aware of the cooperative factors involved and can clearly separate the competences and level of collaboration per indicator, evidencing a high level of technical assessment, as opposite to previous studies [15]
Shared knowledge	Information sharing is limited to functional aspects and even manufacturer's antecedents are removed from documents to reduce risk in information sharing. Since information sharing is critical to customization, responsiveness, cooperation and innovation [6, 30] a limited dynamic leads to fewer benefits than potentially showed by previous literature in analogous scenarios

(continued)

Table 2. (*continued*)

Highlighted aspects	Integrated results
Innovation capabilities	Results show that, although collaboration affects performance levels, it does not impact innovation capabilities, since the supplier limits collaboration to the functional aspects of operation and restricts access to its strategy
Facilitating capabilities	Structures and systems are shared only with top-seller retailers. Factors such as trust, consistency, potential sustainability are considered only as additional elements applied after the 'order-based cut-off'

Additionally, although innovation capabilities do not seem to be affected by these collaborations, extracts from retailers from dyads 1 and 3 might support the possibility of innovations in procedures caused by requirements of the dynamics, similar to the findings by Costa et al. [6] which could, as a non-intentional factor, impact the development of innovation capabilities on retailers.

Analyzing the performance *per se*, managers were oriented to compare scenarios, highlighting before and after collaboration with the other party as well as interactions with other supply chains. Results show unanimously the perception of higher performance clearly focused on the accuracy of inventory management as well as sales projections, planning and point of sale strategies.

Finally, considering performance is maintained even without the development of critical capabilities, it is suitable to highlight this phenomenon as different from previous data obtained by Domenek et al. [7].

5 Conclusions

The present paper aimed to analyze the perception of retail and industry managers about the benefits of collaborative sales planning (i), the influence of this phenomenon on inventory management (ii) as well as identify the formative aspects of collaborative behavior based on an adaptation of Spekman and Carraway's framework [31].

Considering the majority of companies in Brazil are SMEs, it may sound counterintuitive to develop the research based on a large company, especially in this case that is not a local founded business. However, the level of maturity of supply chains in Brazil is considered generally low and its early stages would present a difficult scenario to study collaboration.

Regarding the main findings, the highly regulated scenario was an important factor to impulse retailers into taking a more mature posture. It also potentially allowed the reduction of the so called 'brazilian way' [15] in the buyer-supplier dynamics. But while the culture did not have a direct impact on dynamics, the macroeconomic factors – also in an environmental dimension – is critical to constantly define parameters more than strategic orientation itself, which reinforces that context-specific variables can change how collaboration occurs and affects performance in supply chains.

If organized hierarchically, macroeconomic factors lead the collaboration, followed by the volume of orders from each retailer. Only after these parameters are met, internal characteristics are taken into consideration in order to manage the collaboration. These findings, along with the observed asymmetry and the restrictions on information sharing present a scenario of low-level collaboration. Interestingly enough, managers do not see it as such a limited interaction and rather defend as a win-win dynamic with a potential to improve. These outcomes can be a response to a scenario where some level of collaboration is already a positive alternative to a general non-collaborative standard. Also, the power dynamics can impact perception as well, since retailers that could be in an inflexible and distant relationship with the manufacturer are at least achieving some level of close collaboration, even if it is strictly related to inventory.

Although the perception of improved performance is mostly based on cost reduction, sales precision and inventory efficiency, in a scenario of macroeconomic uncertainty, these elements might constitute the best outcomes possible. Previous literature has already stated how biased inventory decisions can be when economic aspects external to the supply chain are impacting directly the outputs of the operation [38]. This opens the door for additional questions in terms of value perception and performance measurements to compare cases, variables that deserve complementary discussions on future research.

In terms of contribution, the proposed updated framework consists of a preliminary exercise to support current discussions on the topic. However, it requires further research – especially empirical multi-case and multi-country studies – to be properly consolidated as a model. As a single case study, results are merely providing an initial overview on the topic in Brazil as local literature referring to supply chains in the country as well as in Latin America is still very limited. Empirical studies in different sectors can help enlighten the discussion about the impact of industry-specific variables on buyer-supplier collaboration. Also, the scenario of predominant low-maturity supply chains can be used as a fortuitous opportunity to amplify studies regarding the relationship between collaboration, maturity and performance [11].

References

1. Alamsjah, F., Yunus, E.N.: Achieving supply chain 4.0 and the importance of agility, ambidexterity, and organizational culture: a case of Indonesia. J. Open Innov.: Technol. Mark. Complex. **8**(2) (2022). https://doi.org/10.3390/joitmc8020083
2. Azevedo, S.G., Silva, M.E., Matias, J.C.O., Dias, G.P.: The influence of collaboration initiatives on the sustainability of the cashew supply chain. Sustainability (Switzerland) **10**(6) (2018). https://doi.org/10.3390/su10062075
3. Bromiley, P., Harris, J.: Trust, transaction cost economics, and mechanisms. In: Bachmann, R., Zaheer, A. (eds.) Handbook of Trust Research, 4th edn., pp. 124–143. Edward Elgar, Northampton (2006)
4. Chang, J.: The effects of buyer-supplier's collaboration on knowledge and product innovation. Ind. Mark. Manag. **65**, 129–143 (2017). https://doi.org/10.1016/j.indmarman.2017.04.003
5. Chiles, T.H., McMackin, J.F.: Integrating variable risk preferences, trust, and transaction cost economics. Acad. Manag. Rev. **21**(1), 73–99 (1996)

6. Costa, F.H.D.O., de Moraes, C.C., da Silva, A.L., Delai, I., Chaudhuri, A., Pereira, C.R.: Does resilience reduce food waste? Analysis of Brazilian supplier-retailer dyad. J. Clean. Prod. **338** (2022). https://doi.org/10.1016/j.jclepro.2022.130488

7. Domenek, A.C., Moori, R.G., Vitorino Filho, V.A.: The mediating effect of operational capabilities on operational performance. Revista De Gestao **29**(4), 350–366 (2022). https://doi.org/10.1108/REGE-01-2021-0016

8. Ayala, N.F., Gaiardelli, P., Pezzotta, G., Le Dain, M.A., Frank, A.G.: Adopting service suppliers for servitisation: which type of supplier involvement is more effective? J. Manuf. Technol. Manag. **32**(5), 977–993 (2021). https://doi.org/10.1108/JMTM-09-2020-0374

9. Forbes: Top digital companies (2021). https://www.forbes.com/top-digital-companies/list/

10. Hennink, M., Hutter, I., Bailey, A.: Qualitative Research Methods, 2nd edn. SAGE Publications Ltd., Thousand Oaks (2020)

11. Ho, T., Kumar, A., Shiwakoti, N.: Supply chain collaboration and performance: an empirical study of maturity model. SN Appl. Sci. **2**, 726 (2020). https://doi.org/10.1007/s42452-020-2468-y

12. Hobbs, J.E.: A transaction cost approach to supply chain management. Supply Chain Manag.: Int. J. **1**(2), 15–27 (1996)

13. Kashyap, A., Lakhanpal, P.: Development of levels of buyer-supplier collaboration: a Delphi study. Int. J. Bus. Perform. Supply Chain Model. **13**(1), 27 (2022). https://doi.org/10.1504/IJBPSCM.2022.10046566

14. Kros, J.F., Kirchoff, J.F., Falasca, M.: The impact of buyer-supplier relationship quality and information management on industrial vending machine benefits in the healthcare industry. J. Purchas. Supply Manag. **25**(3) (2019). https://doi.org/10.1016/j.pursup.2018.06.005

15. Lee Park, C., Fracarolli Nunes, M., Muratbekova-Touron, M., Moatti, V.: The duality of the Brazilian jeitinho: an empirical investigation and conceptual framework. Crit. Perspect. Int. Bus. **14**(4), 404–425 (2018). https://doi.org/10.1108/CPOIB-04-2017-0022

16. Li, M., Falcone, E., Sanders, N., Choi, T.Y., Chang, X.: Buyer-supplier collaboration: a macro, micro, and congruence perspective. J. Purch. Supply Manag. **28**(1), 100723 (2022). https://doi.org/10.1016/j.pursup.2021.100723

17. Michalski, M., Montes, J.L., Narasimhan, R.: Relational asymmetry, trust, and innovation in supply chain management: a non-linear approach. Int. J. Logist. Manag. **30**(4), 1211–1231 (2018). https://doi.org/10.1108/IJLM-01-2018-0011

18. Miles, M.B., Huberman, A.M., Saldana, J.: Qualitative Data Analysis: A Methods Sourcebook. SAGE Publications Inc., Thousand Oaks (2013)

19. Mujianto, M., Hartoyo, H., Nurmalina, R., Yusuf, E.Z.: The unraveling loyalty model of traditional retail to suppliers for business sustainability in the digital transformation era: insight from MSMEs in Indonesia. Sustainability **15**(3), 2827 (2023). https://doi.org/10.3390/su15032827

20. Newman, C., Gligor, D., Cho, Y.N.: A multi-tier approach to supply chain collaboration: implications of shopper solutions. Int. J. Logist. Manag. (2022). https://doi.org/10.1108/IJLM-08-2021-0403

21. Nguyen, H., Onofrei, G., Truong, D.: Supply chain communication and cultural compatibility: performance implications in the global manufacturing industry. Bus. Process. Manag. J. **27**(1), 253–274 (2021). https://doi.org/10.1108/BPMJ-08-2019-0314

22. Nikulina, A., Wynstra, F.: Understanding supplier motivation to engage in multiparty performance-based contracts: the lens of expectancy theory. J. Purchas. Supply Manag. **28**(2) (2022). https://doi.org/10.1016/j.pursup.2022.100746

23. Nurhayati, K., Tavasszy, L., Rezaei, J.: Joint B2B supply chain decision-making: drivers, facilitators and barriers. Int. J. Prod. Econ. **256**, 108721 (2023). https://doi.org/10.1016/j.ijpe.2022.108721

24. Patrucco, A., Moretto, A., Trabucchi, D., Golini, R.: How do Industry 4.0 technologies boost collaborations in buyer-supplier relationships? Res.-Technol. Manag. 65(1), 48–58 (2022). https://doi.org/10.1080/08956308.2021.1999131

25. Paulraj, A., Lado, A.A., Chen, I.J.: Inter-organizational communication as a relational competency: antecedents and performance outcomes in collaborative buyer-supplier relationships. J. Oper. Manag. 26(1), 45–64 (2008). https://doi.org/10.1016/j.jom.2007.04.001

26. Pohlmann, C.R., Scavarda, A.J., Alves, M.B., Korzenowski, A.L.: The role of the focal company in sustainable development goals: a Brazilian food poultry supply chain case study. J. Clean. Prod. 245 (2020). https://doi.org/10.1016/j.jclepro.2019.118798

27. Pouly, M., Greber, M., Glardon, R.: Network structure analysis for multicultural industrial CNO. In: Camarinha-Matos, L.M., Picard, W. (eds.) PRO-VE 2008. IFIPAICT, vol. 283, pp. 399–406. Springer, Boston (2008). https://doi.org/10.1007/978-0-387-84837-2_41

28. Prim, A.L., Sarma, V., de Sá, M.M.: The role of collaboration in reducing quality variability in Brazilian breweries. Prod. Plann. Control (2021). https://doi.org/10.1080/09537287.2021.1992528

29. Sikombe, S., Phiri, M.A.: Exploring tacit knowledge transfer and innovation capabilities within the buyer-supplier collaboration: a literature review. Cogent Bus. Manag. 6(1) (2019). https://doi.org/10.1080/23311975.2019.1683130

30. Silva, E.M., Paiva, E.L., Neto, M.S., de Freitas, K.A.: Developing operational capabilities in the collaborative practice-adoption process through different triadic structures. BAR - Braz. Adm. Rev. 18(4) (2021). https://doi.org/10.1590/1807-7692bar2021210025

31. Spekman, R.E., Carraway, R., Carraway, R.: Making the transition to collaborative buyer-seller relationships: an emerging framework. Ind. Mark. Manag. 35(1), 10–19 (2006). https://doi.org/10.1016/j.indmarman.2005.07.002

32. Tanco, M., Escuder, M., Heckmann, G., Jurburg, D., Velazquez, J.: Supply chain management in Latin America: current research and future directions. Supply Chain Manag. 23(5), 412–430 (2018). https://doi.org/10.1108/SCM-07-2017-0236

33. Thomas, R., Esper, T.: Exploring relational asymmetry in supply chains: the retailer's perspective. Int. J. Phys. Distrib. Logist. Manag. 40(6), 475–494 (2010)

34. Tseng, M.-L., Bui, T.-D., Lim, M.K., Tsai, F.M., Tan, R.R.: Comparing world regional sustainable supply chain finance using big data analytics: a bibliometric analysis. Ind. Manag. Data Syst. 121(3), 657–700 (2021). https://doi.org/10.1108/IMDS-09-2020-0521

35. Um, K.-H., Oh, J.-Y.: The interplay of governance mechanisms in supply chain collaboration and performance in buyer–supplier dyads: Substitutes or complements. Int. J. Oper. Prod. Manag. 40(4), 415–438 (2020). https://doi.org/10.1108/IJOPM-07-2019-0507

36. Veile, J.W., Schmidt, M.-C., Müller, J.M., Voigt, K.-I.: The transformation of supply chain collaboration and design through industry 4.0. Int. J. Logist. Res. Appl. (2022). https://doi.org/10.1080/13675567.2022.2148638

37. Vlachos, I., Dyra, S.C.: Theorizing coordination, collaboration and integration in multi-sourcing triads (B3B triads). Supply Chain Manag. 25(3), 285–300 (2020). https://doi.org/10.1108/SCM-01-2019-0006

38. Wu, D., Sepehri, M., Hua, J., Xu, F.: Uncertainty shocks, network position, and inventory. J. Model. Manag. (2022). https://doi.org/10.1108/JM2-02-2022-0043

39. Zhang, X., Liang, X.: How does the power dynamics in the information technology outsourcing supply chain influence supplier's talent retention: a multiple case study. Pers. Rev. (2022). https://doi.org/10.1108/PR-12-2020-0912

Relationship Between Degree of Appropriation of ICT and Learning Styles of Teachers in Training

Olga Martínez Palmera[1](✉) ⓘ, Ever Mejía Leguia[1] ⓘ, Hilda Guerrero Cuentas[1] ⓘ, Yuneidis Morales-Ortega[1] ⓘ, Gilma Camargo Romero[1] ⓘ, Carmen I. Imitola[2] ⓘ, and Estella I. Imitola[3] ⓘ

[1] Universidad de la Costa CUC, 08003 Barranquilla, Colombia
ymorales4@cuc.edu.co
[2] Escuela Normal Superior del Distrito, 08003 Barranquilla, Colombia
[3] Institución Educativa Distrital Para el Desarrollo del Talento Humano, 08003 Barranquilla, Colombia

Abstract. The incursion of Information Technology and Communications (ICT) in education is shaping and modifying teaching-learning processes. Therefore, educational institutions have been forced to offer contextualized training programs according to the personal characteristics of the actors. The article presents the results of a research carried out at Barranquilla-Colombia, whose objective was to analyze the relationship between the appropriation of ICT mediations and learning styles in an initial teacher training program. For this, the process of appropriation of ICT was characterized from the profile of mediation agents in initial teacher training, and the learning styles of students who are being trained as teachers were identified. Under a quantitative approach, non-experimental design, and a sample of 63 teachers in training for the first and fourth semester to whom a REATIC (Cognitive and Affective Reactions to Information and Communication Technology) questionnaire and a CHAEA (Honey-Alonso Questionnaire of Learning Styles) questionnaire. Data was analyzed using R Studio statistical software. The Pearson, Kendall, T-Student, Wilcoxy ANOVA (Analysis of Variance) tests were applied. The results indicate a higher degree of educational appropriation of ICT in individuals with a pragmatic learning style.

Keywords: Learning Style · Technology of the Information and Communication · Teacher Training

1 Introduction

The incursion of Information Technology and Communications (ICT) in education is shaping and modifying teaching-learning processes, methodologies, materials and educational tools, giving it a fundamental role in the educational context [26], which currently demands that the actors in the educational process, teachers and students have digital skills and competencies to achieve better performance during a teaching-learning

K. Saeed et al. (Eds.): CISIM 2023, LNCS 14164, pp. 177–192, 2023.
https://doi.org/10.1007/978-3-031-42823-4_14

process; Therefore, institutions of all educational levels have been forced to offer contextualized training programs according to the personal characteristics of the actors, their learning styles, needs and interests to achieve the development of digital skills that lead to awareness by the teacher immersed into the digital society, on the relevance of appropriating ICT mediations in order to be successfully incorporated into educational processes with a true pedagogical intention and the use of didactic and methodological strategies according to the context of action.

The ICTs have become an essential part of the construction of knowledge, generation of learning, exchange of knowledge and socialization, that is why, they have pierced strongly in education, more specifically in the learning process of students, making easy the dissemination of information and knowledge [27]. Faced with these challenges, it is considered convenient to generate educational processes that boost the acquisition and development of digital competence in students and teachers, not as an use of the technological device, but as a true planned process, designed from a critical perspective of the ICTs that make them advance from a social conscience [22].

This has made important that many of the teachers are not capable of giving a real educational use to technology becoming into a wall to the development of skills based on knowledge, knowing how to do and how to be, which are required from training teacher's initial. For this reason, it is necessary to generate learning scenarios that lead to the strengthening of both technological and pedagogical skills for their effective incorporation into the classroom. However, it is still evident that many of the new teachers are not being trained in the proper pedagogical use of ICT, while this concept only focuses on learning from computers and projectors to support traditional teaching practices [29]. In the same way, traditional pedagogical and educational models based on continuity discourses are still evident in a context screened by sudden and abrupt migration processes towards virtual environments, supported using technological tools as a consequence of the serious, unprecedented health crisis, caused by COVID 19 [10].

Appropriation of ICT

The process of appropriation of ICT must take place from the initial training of teachers, through qualification routes adapted both to their learning style and to the needs of current education and society, which allows teachers to assume an active role in relation to the adequacy of an identity specific to their area of study in the search for equity in the practice of their role, in the teaching exercise. [6, 13, 15, 30]. Faced with these challenges, there is an increase in curricular proposals that try to respond to the development of digital competence of teachers in training; However, even these processes are not very successful and do not meet the expectations of the teachers, because generalized training is offered to everyone, without taking into account the way they learn and the pedagogical intentions of the area where they work.

It could be assumed that making people digitally literate implies not only teaching how to use technologies in an accelerated manner, but also developing the ability to select them according to the empirical context where their use is needed. The role of future teachers must be reconsidered, since they have the responsibility of educating digital natives, young people exposed to communication and information technologies from birth [29], that is, teachers have the mission of adjusting educational processes through innovations based on activities mediated by ICTs, the reliability of Internet information and digital platforms, through an inclusive process that lead theories towards the digital age, but it must also be a transformation where teachers develop the ability to educate, promoting suitable and adequate learning environments and activities [4, 16, 21] suitable and appropriated.

Consequently, from what was stated above, it would be said that the ideal in the development of the formative dynamics is to have an educational environment where there is clear knowledge of the characteristics that are be able to influence the development of the teaching-learning process and performance of students, knowing the personality of students, as well as the relationship between the predominant personality type, their learning style, the type of motivation that influences them, which will allow the generation of favorable conditions to give better attention to the students and therefore better results in the process [24], as well as in their learning. In the same way, the existence of multiple accurate tools to each predominant style of the students must be considered, hence the need to identify their learning styles, to establish how the student will benefit from more specific actions that really impact their knowledge acquisition, in order to enhance their teaching-learning process [27].

In this regard, Alonso, Gallego and Honey, identify four types of learning styles: theoretical, reflective, active, and pragmatic, each of these styles presents specific characteristics, for example the theoretical style, represents people with thoughts that come from logical stages, whereby they adjust their observations and experiences to logical and complex theories, they tend to analyze, synthesize, seek rationality and objectivity in everything. People with a reflective style are characterized by being analytical, observant, compiler, data recorder, exhaustive, report writer, argument builder, alternative foresight, conscientious, careful, detailed, slow, assimilative, receptive, investigative, and prudent; people with this active style involve themselves fully and without prejudice in new experiences, are intolerant of long terms, and prefer immediate results, they are open-minded and with a low level of skepticism. Finally, the characteristics of people with a pragmatic learning style prefer active experimentation and the search for practical applications, discovering the positive aspects of new theories and technologies in order to put them. These types of students are experimenters, practical, direct, realistic, technical, and attached to reality [2, 23].

Based on what has been stated, thus, this research is conceived as an alternative for the continuous improvement of the academic processes that are developed in the beneficiary institution of the project, since it allowed us to analyze how future teachers learn, generating positive changes in their professional training, in their pedagogical practice and, Therefore, in the approach to knowledge and concretion in the classroom, finally allowing the construction of more significant and lasting learning in the future teachers of preschool, basic primary, basic secondary and secondary education in the country.

2 Methodology

The research carried out was framed within the positivist paradigm [14], from a quantitative investigative approach and with a descriptive-correlational scope [17], following a non-experimental design of transactional or transversal cut, four stages were established in the development of the research: one of a theoretical type applying documentary review as information collection techniques through a content analysis matrix instrument, as well as digital ethnography that allows study the systems and environments of interactivity favored by the Internet and explore the interrelationships between technologies and the daily life of teachers in the classroom or in any setting to understand the behavior and interaction of teachers in training in the digital society. A second stage empirical, from which the object of study was analyzed in the field of action, a third phase of analysis of results where techniques were used for data processing from descriptive and inferential statistics, through the statistical software RStudio version 1.1.383 for Windows and a last stage where conclusions were derived from the discussion and established recommendations for other studies.

The population was defined as the students of the I and IV semester of the Complementary Training Program (PFC) of the Normal Superior School of the District of Barranquilla from the period 2019-2. Groups constituted in that period by 167 students, organized into 93 students for the first semester and 74 students for the fourth semester. A stratified probabilistic sample was selected, specifically, made up of 63 students, 35 from the first semester and 28 from the fifth semester of the Complementary Training Program in the period 2019-2 belonging to the morning (23.8%), afternoon (31.7%) and nocturnal (44.4%). 56% belong to the first semester and 44% are from the fourth semester. The stratified sampling is with proportional allocation without replacement, with a confidence level of 95% and a standard error in the estimate of the parameter of interest of 5%. The age range is between 16 and 51 years with an average of 26.94 years.

Initially, the first three sections of the REATIC (Cognitive and Affective Reactions to Information and Communication Technology) questionnaire [9] were used, a standardized instrument validated by experts and with internal consistency determined by Cronbach's alpha ($\alpha = 0.92$). With this, the degree of appropriation of ICT mediations by teachers in training was measured. However, it was considered to carry out a new reliability analysis of the instrument, since only the first 44 items were required for the present investigation, grouped into three parts: I know ($\alpha = 0.93$), referring to the dimension of knowledge of ICT mediations (items 1–14), the use ($\alpha = 0.85$) concerning the dimension of the use of ICT mediations (items 15–28), the I consider ($\alpha = 0.75$) associated with the assessment of ICT mediations (items 29–44). The questionnaire uses a Likert-type scale, from 1 (not at all) to 4 (a lot).

Consecutively, the learning styles variable was measured through the application of the CHAEA (Honey-Alonso Questionnaire of Learning Styles) questionnaire [2], widely known for its validity and reliability to identify the various ways of learning in higher education students. It is made up of 80 items, divided into four sections corresponding to twenty questions for each learning style. To answer this, the participants showed a greater or lesser degree of identification with the stated statement using the + and – signs, respectively. Each question corresponds to a learning style, determining a student's preference for a specific style through the largest number of questions answered with +.

Regarding to the data collection, the instruments were uploaded to the Google Forms online application. Then, the questionnaires were administered during the students' academic day using the school's infrastructure (computer rooms, computers, tablets, and Wi-Fi networks). The participants were informed about the objective of the research and informed consents were signed to authorize the processing of personal data and voluntary participation in favor of improving the training offered in the program. The information was collected objectively by the researchers, who did not interfere, avoiding giving appreciations about the answers given by the students. Each student used between 15 and 20 min to solve the questionnaires.

Finally, the data was quantified through descriptive and inferential statistical analysis from the statistical software R Studio version 1.1.383 from the matrix generated in the Excel program version 2016, applying the Pearson and Tau-Kendall coefficient tests. Also, ANOVA (Analysis of Variance) statistical tests were performed to establish the analysis of variance between the degree of appropriation of ICT mediations and each learning style and T-Student and Wilcox assigned range distributions, in order to compare the strata of the sample and determine if there are significant differences between them.

2.1 Research Results and Findings

2.2 Statistical Analysis

The analysis of the results carried out using the R Studio statistical software and the statistical tests of the Pearson and Kendall Coefficient, T-Student, Wilcox, and an analysis of variance (ANOVA) for repeated measures, the results found on socio-economic aspects are detailed academics through the application of the REATIC and CHAEA questionnaires, information that allows characterizing the selected sample, skipping data such as semester, day, and age intervals. Likewise, the characteristics of the ICT appropriation process are shown from their profile as mediation agents in the initial training of teachers. Based on the analysis of the answers given to the different questions of the REATIC questionnaire, for which tables and figures are shown that explain the results produced by items for the dimensions of knowledge used and assessment. In addition, an analysis of the characteristics of the process of appropriation of ICT mediations focused on the pedagogical practice of teachers in initial training was established.

For the first objective referring to the characterization of the ICT appropriation process from its profile of mediation agents, the frequencies (F) and means (M) obtained for each item of the REATIC questionnaire were determined. These are shown in Tables 1, 2 and 3 according to the 3 levels that make up the degree of appropriation: knowledge, use and valuation, respectively.

According to the results shown in Table 1, the students of first and fifth semester show knowledge in most of the items, considering the Likert scale used in the questionnaire (1–4); This is how, in 7 of 14 statements an average above 3 was obtained according to the scale. On the other hand, the items that registered the highest score above 3.50 were those referring to web search engines, online video portals and personal interaction programs, such as Messenger, email, Facebook, among others. In contrast, it was evidenced that students present low knowledge in educational programs and authoring tools and guided Internet search activities, with scores below 2.50, as described in Table 1.

Table 2 describes the level of use of ICT mediations, the students reported having a lower score in reference to the level of knowledge.

Table 1. Knowledge of ICT mediations.

N°	Items	F	M
1	I know basic programs such as word processor (Word), spreadsheet (Excel), slideshow (PowerPoint)	215	3.41
2	I am familiar with personal interaction programs (Messenger, email, Tuenti, Facebook, Hi5)	229	3.63
3	I know what a blog, a chat a forum is	212	3.36
4	I am familiar with educational portals (Campus network, Moodle, Webct)	145	2.30
5	I know image editing programs (Paint, Photoshop), video (Windows media maker, Pinnacle, Adobe Premier), audio (Windows Media, Winamp)	175	2.77
6	I am familiar with web search engines (Google, Yahoo, Altavista)	225	3.57
7	I know online translators (elmundo.es)	183	2.90
8	I know online video portals (YouTube)	224	3.55
9	I am familiar with virtual libraries and encyclopedias (Wikipedia, Encarta, Royal Academy of Language, Miguel de Cervantes)	211	3.34
10	I know editors to make web pages (FrontPage, Dreamweaver)	136	2.15
11	I know some web browsers (Explorer, Mozilla, Fire Fox, Netscape)	200	3.17
12	I am familiar with author educational programs (Clic, JClic, Hot Potatoes, Neobook)	134	2.12
13	I am familiar with guided Internet search activities (Webquest, Miniwebquest, Hunttreasure)	133	2.11
14	I know multimedia devices (Pc, projector, Pda, Scanner, WebCam	181	2.87

As it is evidenced by Table 2, regarding the level of use of ICT mediations, the students reported having a lower score in reference to the level of knowledge, in such a way that only 4 of 14 items showed average scores above 3.00, according to the Likert scale (1–4) defined for the questionnaire. On the other hand, the items that registered the highest score above 3.50 were those referring to the use of personal interaction programs and the use of image editing programs. On the contrary, it was found that students present low use in online translators, editors to build web pages and guided Internet search activities, with scores below 2.00, according to the questionnaire scale.

Table 2. Use of ICT mediations.

N°	Items	F	M
15	I use basic programs such as word processor (Word), spreadsheet (Excel), slideshow (Powerpoint)	204	3.23
16	I use personal interaction programs (Messenger, email, Tuenti, Facebook, Hi5)	200	3.17
17	I use a blog, a chat, a forum	173	2.74
18	Use of educational portals (Campus Network, Moodle, Webct)	121	1.92
19	I use image editing programs (Paint, Photoshop), video (Windows media maker, Pinnacle, Adobe Premier), audio (Windows Media, Winamp)	200	3.17
20	I use Internet search engines (Google, Yahoo, Altavista)	173	2.74
21	I use online translators (elmundo.es)	121	1.92
22	I use of online video portals (YouTube)	158	2.50
23	I use virtual libraries and encyclopedias (Wikipedia, Encarta, Royal Academy of Language, Miguel de Cervantes)	199	3.15
24	I use editors to make web pages (FrontPage, Dreamweaver)	123	1.95
25	I use some web browsers (Explorer, Mozilla, Fire Fox, Netscape)	179	2.84
26	I use author educational programs (Clic, JClic, Hot Potatoes, Neobook)	170	2.69
27	I use guided Internet search activities (Webquest, Miniwebquest, Hunttreasure)	122	1.93
28	I use multimedia devices (PC, projector, Pda, Scanner, WebCam	140	2.22

Table 3 shows the assessment that students (teachers in initial training) have regarding ICT mediations.

Table 3 shows the assessment that students have regarding ICT mediations. In general, a level is shown on the scales of much and enough, in 16 items, 9 registered an average score above 3.00 on the Likert scale (1–4) defined for the questionnaire. Likewise, the items referring to the role of ICT as important mediators in academic training, in the learning process and in helping to search for information were those that presented

Table 3. Assessment of ICT mediations.

N°	Ítems	F	M
29	I consider that ICTs are an important element in my academic training	239	3.79
30	I consider that ICT help me in my learning process	237	3.76
31	I consider that ICTs harm me more than help me in my academic training	116	1.84
32	I consider that ICTs are important for their educational application	229	3.63
33	I consider that ICT helps me improve my academic results	225	3.57
34	I consider that ICTs are a means to foster personal relationships among my classmates	209	3.31
35	I consider that ICTs are difficult to understand and use it	127	2.01
36	I consider that ICTs are a support to complete my academic and training knowledge	236	3.74
37	I consider that ICTs do not offer me sufficient security in my privacy	130	2.06
38	I consider that ICT make me lose a lot of time	112	1.77
39	I believe that ICTs do not replace traditional educational resources	150	2.38
40	I consider that ICTs are essential in today's society	207	3.28
41	I consider that ICTs are an aid to search for information	240	3.80
42	I consider that ICTs are a useful tool for preparing jobs	237	3.76
43	I consider that ICTs are not fully reliable in the information they provide	151	2.39
44	I consider that ICTs help me to occupy my leisure and free time	187	2.96

the highest average ratings. However, the items in which it is considered that ICT mediations make me lose a lot of time and ICT mediations harm me more than help me in my academic training, presented scores below 2.00.

On the other hand, for the objective focused on identifying the learning styles of the sample of students of the program from the application of the CHAEA questionnaire, results shown in Fig. 1 were obtained.

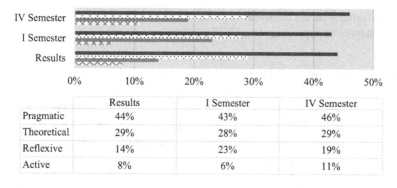

	Results	I Semester	IV Semester
Pragmatic	44%	43%	46%
Theoretical	29%	28%	29%
Reflexive	14%	23%	19%
Active	8%	6%	11%

■ Pragmatic   ·· Theoretical   ■ Reflexive   ＼ Active

Fig. 1. Comparison of learning styles of PFC students.

Figure 1, which describes the comparison of the percentages obtained for each learning style in the selected sample and in the two groups (I and IV semester), in which it was stratified for the purposes of the study, shows a quite marked preference towards a pragmatic learning style in students (teachers in training) by obtaining percentages of 44%, 43% and 46%, respectively.

Regarding the third objective of this study, the levels of knowledge, use and assessment of ICT mediations were described as the basis of the degree of appropriation that the students have of the program. On this matte, Fig. 2 shows their distribution. For this, the response options given by the REATIC questionnaire were used as a scale to present the description: nothing (up to 25%), little (up to 50%), a lot (up to 75%) and quite a lot (up to 100%). A higher score is evident in the assessment level with a percentage of 75% (a lot), corresponding to the sample of 63 students. Immediately below is the level of knowledge with a percentage of 74% (a lot) and finally, the level of use with a percentage equal to 65% (a lot).

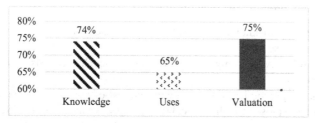

Fig. 2. Description of appropriation of ICT mediations/students/levels/knowledge/use and assessment.

On the other hand, to determine the relationship between the appropriation of ICT mediations with learning styles as part of the last research objective, parametric and non-parametric tests were applied: Pearson's linear correlation coefficients (r) and Kendall (tau), T-student, Wilcox, and ANOVA.

Firstly, Table 4 shows the linear correlation analysis between the variables learning styles and degree of appropriation of ICT mediations.

Table 4. Matrix of correlations of Learning Styles vs degrees of appropriation of ICT mediations.

Style	Knowledge	Use (r)	Valoration
Active	0.1293 r (0.3124)	0.0450 r (0.7261)	0.1187 r (0.354)
Reflexive	0.0480 tau (0.6044)	0.1319 tau (0.1565)	0.1768 tau (0.0601) *
Theoretical	0.1925 r (0.1307)	0.2408 r (0.0573) *	0.3049 r (0.0151) *
Pragmatic	−0.0421 r (0.7433)	−0.0165 r (0.8981)	0.0536 r (0.6767)

Based on the results obtained and shown in Table 4, the following significant findings were found:

Weak directly proportional relationships:

- Between the dimension of theoretical learning style with the level of use of ICT mediations, since when positive r is obtained ($r = 0.2408$), a weak directly proportional relationship is demonstrated, and the p-value (0.0573) is very close to 0. This means that, despite presenting a directly proportional relationship, it is not significant enough to affirm that there is a linear correlation between these two dimensions.
- Between the reflective learning style dimension with the assessment of ICT mediations, since when positive tau is obtained ($tau = 0.1768$) a weak directly proportional relationship is demonstrated, which indicates that, despite presenting a directly proportional relationship, it is not significant enough to affirm that there is a linear correlation between these two dimensions.
- Between the theoretical learning style dimension and the assessment of ICT mediations $r = 0.3049$, p-Value $= 0.0151$), the latter being the one with the greatest statistical significance.

Strong directly proportional relationships:

- Between the level of knowledge and the level of use of ICT mediations, since $r = 0.8108$ is very close to 1.
- Between the reflective learning style with the theoretical learning style ($tau = 0.37829$, p-Value < 0.001).
- Between the pragmatic learning style with the rest of the styles, since the r and tau coefficients were close to 1 [theoretical ($r = 0.3845$, p-Value $= 0.002$), reflective ($tau = 0.3121$, p-Value $= 0.001$) and active ($r = 0.3928$, p-Value $= 0.0014$)].

For their part, the means (T-student) and medians (Wilcox assigned range) comparison tests between two groups, being a stratified sample (I and IV semester) were required to establish significant differences between them. Table 5 describes that, for the knowledge dimension, the p-value of 0.687 indicates that there was no significant difference, because the value is greater than the significance level (0.05). In the same way, regarding the level of use, a p-value of 0.1809 was obtained, showing that no relevant differences were found either. Likewise, for the assessment level, the p-value obtained shows that there were no differences between I and IV semester, as the p-value was greater than 0.05. Thus, it is concluded that two equal groups were found.

Table 5. Comparison test of the degree of appropriation of ICT by semester.

Dimension vs Semester	Stadistical	p-Valoration
Knowledge vs Semester	T = 0.4052	0.6867
Use vs Semester	T = 1.3535	0.1809
Valoration vs Semester	W = 519.5	0.6871

Likewise, the analysis of variance or ANOVA was applied to establish if the degree of appropriation of ICT mediations varies according to a certain learning style, the results shown in Table 6 and Fig. 3 determined that the degree of appropriation in its dimensions of knowledge, use and assessment is statistically the same for the four learning styles. Average appropriation percentages above 60% and low variations are evident. This allows us to affirm that regardless of the learning style identified in the student, there will be a degree of appropriation above 60%.

Table 6. Analysis of variance of the degree of appropriation of ICTs by learning style by levels.

Levels	F	g.l	p-Valoration
Knowledge	0.7163*	3;59	0.5462
Use	0.4560	3;59	0.7140
Valoration	1.3960	3;59	0.2530

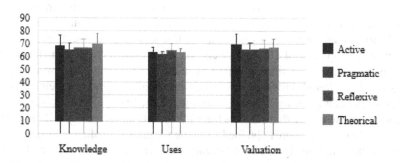

Fig. 3. Comparison of the degree of appropriation of ICT by learning style.

3 Discussion

The analysis of the results shows that despite the fact that future teachers during the Complementary Training Program receive pedagogical training in ICT mediations (one curricular unit per semester), their degree of appropriation of ICT within the assessment scale, I cannot place myself in the "enough" value of this. The low level of knowledge and educational use of technological tools for content development, specialized search tools and web page editors is notorious since the scores for these items show the lowest value in the knowledge dimension, it is ideal that it is in correspondence with what was proposed by Vahos, Muñoz, and Londoño-Vásquez [29], that there is evidence that shows that new teachers are not being trained in the pedagogical use of ICT, while this concept only focuses on learning the use of computers and projectors to support traditional teaching practices. This is how investigative proposals should be made to guide teachers to reconsider their praxis through innovations based on activities mediated by ICTs, the reliability of information from the Internet and digital platforms is an inclusive process that mobilizes theories towards the digital era.

Regarding the results obtained for the dimension of using, it is shown that the spotted items with the highest value were those referring to social interaction programs and video editing, contrasting with low scores for educational programs supported by authoring tools and guided internet search activities. Thus, it agrees on what has been pointed out by some authors who consider that there is a high self-perception in teachers regarding the application of the digital competences evaluated, however, in a minority in some of them it was observed that sometimes or even almost never or never are applied [31].

It should be pointed out the presence of some findings obtained for the assessment dimension, whose statistics reflect a greater degree of acceptance towards ICT mediations, that is, out of 16 items, 9 registered an average score above 3.00 on the Likert scale (1–4) defined for the questionnaire. Likewise, the items referring to the role of ICT as important mediators in academic training, in the learning process and in helping to search for information were those that presented the highest average ratings. Aspect that makes notorious the opening of the new generations of teachers towards ICT mediations, as tools that facilitate their personal and professional development.

Thus, a favorable outlook is opened to generate changes, from the training institutions, in the pedagogical strategies for the appropriation of ICT mediations, which positively affect their future work performance. That is, to explore the didactic use that can be given to computer tools, focusing them on the achievement of learning for both the teacher and the student. Confirming what was stated by Colina and Tua, by stating that teachers who have digital skills may be resource providers, designers of their own material, organizers of online learning spaces, tutor-guide-facilitator and researcher, aspects that are necessary to ensure that students learn in contexts permeated by technology [7].

In the same way, the scores obtained from the means and median comparison tests showed that there are no significant differences between the students of the I and IV semesters, an aspect that allows us to reflect on the fact that the students of the I semester may have a better projection over those of the fourth semester, who are close to graduating, to the extent that they are just beginning their training and must go through a study plan that will allow them to develop their digital teaching competence. Hence, their performance in pedagogical practices could show a higher degree of appropriation and even more, because there is a prior identification of their learning styles, which motivates them to learn and teach with the use of ICT mediations.

On the other hand, a pragmatic learning style predominates, which allows us to characterize them as people who prefer active experimentation and the search for practical applications, discovering the positive aspect of new theories and technologies to put them into practice. These types of students are experimenters, practical, direct, realistic, technical, and attached to reality [23]. Since a high preference for a particular learning style was found. The identification of this reality allows teachers from their training to become aware of the way they learn and the abilities they have. The above is based on the perspective of Ausubel, Novak and Hanesian in his theory of significant learning, when he considers that: "the information of the content must integrate the logical meaning and the psychological meaning" [5]. For the specific case of the identification of learning styles, a psychological meaning would be given to the objects and concepts.

From this analysis, the identification of learning styles in future teachers becomes a favorable process for the construction of learning, since it allows them to know what is the best way to face educational experiences, with the use of ICT mediations that are introduce you Simultaneously, the teacher also benefits, since he has an overview of how his students build knowledge and, at the same time, an input for planning their strategies, activities and, consequently, the resources that will be made available to them. It is important then, to identify the learning style from a multi-modal approach and apply them to practical situations considering the environment of an intelligent classroom [8, 15].

It is important to point out that through the use of association and grouping rules techniques, it has been possible to identify two sets of relationships among students, namely, the first between IQ and multiple intelligences and the second between emotional intelligence and learning styles [3], and on the other hand, that if students used a mixed domain learning style, this could contribute to the development of their emotional intelligence [12]. But it cannot be overlooked that on many occasions there is a discrepancy between what teachers say and what they do in the classroom with respect to their learning styles, so adequate training on learning styles would increase skills, techniques, and instruments of the teacher [11, 25].

Besides, the correlations between the variables of appropriation of ICT mediations and learning styles, scored for the most part, as weak, revealing weak relationships. These results show that due to the current positioning of ICT mediations in many areas of daily life, future teachers are faced with a training that requires different and faster processing of a large amount of information.

Likewise, this makes it possible to demonstrate the presence of other factors that are affecting the variables, which, in this case, could be age, working hours, or previous pedagogical training, which were not considered in this investigation. Thus, [1], highlight the fact that learning will always be subject to the conditions of the learner's context, either around their possibilities or environmental resources, and framed in the characteristics of each person. The educational project is required to institutionalize such needs, through their integration as fundamental components. This has implications for the availability of physical - environmental conditions that contribute to the achievement of the purpose [20].

The identification of learning styles constitutes a strategy that helps to obtain information about the way students learn. Precisely, it coincides with the idea of Acosta, Quiroz, and Rueda while affirming that recognizing the learning styles at a certain moment can help to determine the strategies to obtain better results in the academic performance of the students [1]. The level of knowledge of ICT mediations in the Complementary Training Program was located at much (74%), while the use scored lower (65%), contrasting these with the results on the scale of much (75%) obtained for the valuation level; weak correlations were established between the dimensions of the variables: appropriation of ICT mediations and learning styles, since the r (Pearson) and tau (Kendall) coefficients were between −0.0421 and 0.3049.

Finally, for the authors it is necessary to search for and implement pedagogical strategies according to the new modality of education advocates for the implementation of ICT, but this requires teachers to adapt their teaching methodologies to provide effective learning through digital media [18]. This paradigm shift was generated during the pandemic, as many educational institutions were forced to adopt online learning technologies to continue education, leading to an increase in the number of students participating in virtual courses [19].

4 Conclusion

According to the results obtained, the following main conclusions can be set out:

1) The process of appropriation of ICT mediations in teachers in initial training is characterized by being a more recreational than pedagogical use, since they value the importance in their professional training and personally, however the knowledge and educational use of the variety of ICT tools still has its back to pedagogical intentions.
2) The identification of the learning styles of teachers in initial, training provides relevant information to develop more relevant teaching styles in them, which contributes to their progress as professionals. It is observed how ICTs are appropriate to a high degree when the individual presents a pragmatic learning, which is closely related to a functional teaching style, therefore, these teachers in training will be, in the future, teachers who grant greater relevance to the process with greater feasibility functionality, and concretion; that is to say, they will end up giving greater importance to the most practical contents and close to the reflection of reality using ICT mediations.
3) The description of the level of knowledge, use and assessment of ICT mediations as a basis for the degree of appropriation that the students of the program have (teachers in initial training), allow describing the appropriation of ICT mediations as a process under construction that requires intervention for its strengthening as part of a high quality initial teacher training process.
4) The correlation between the appropriation of ICT mediations with the different learning styles of the Complementary Training Program, show little close relationships. This reveals the existence of other factors that are affecting them and that were not taken into account in this investigation.
5) From the results of the tests for the comparison of means, it is concluded that homogeneous groups were found, when it was statistically determined that there were no significant differences between the strata of the sample, for which the semester does

not become a variable that is influencing in the acquisition of a certain degree of appropriation of ICT mediations.

References

1. Acosta, J., Quiroz, L., Rueda, M.: Learning styles, learning strategies and their relationship with the use of ICT in secondary school students. Revista de Estilos de Aprendizaje **11**(21) (2018)
2. Alonso, C., Gallego, D., Honey, P.: Learning Styles: Diagnosis and Improvement Procedures. 7th edn. Messenger, Bilbao (2007)
3. Agyei, D., Voogt, J.: Examining factors affecting beginning teachers' transfer of learning of ICT-enhanced learning activities in their teaching practice. Australas. J. Educ. Technol. **30**(1), 92–105 (2014)
4. Arevalo, P., et al.: Educational data mining to identify the relationship between IQ, learning styles, emotional intelligence and multiple intelligences of engineering students. Iberian J. Informacao Syst. Technol.-RISTI **17**(1), 48–63 (2019)
5. Ausubel, D., Novak, J., Hanesian, H.: Educational Psychology: A Cognitive Point of View. 2nd edn. Trillas, México (1983)
6. Beach, D.: Teacher education cultural diversity, social justice and equality: policies, challenges and abandoned possibilities in Swedish teacher education. Curriculum J. Teach. Formation **23**(4), 26–44 (2019)
7. Colina, A., Tua, J.: Appropriation of ICT in university teaching: status quo in a complex panorama. Spaces Mag. **39**(43), 21–27 (2018)
8. Cordero, J., Aguilar, J., Aguilar, K.: Intelligent approaches to identify student learning styles through emotions in a classroom. Iberian J. Informacao Syst. Technol.-RISTI **17**(1), 703–716 (2019)
9. De Moya, M., Hernández, J., Hernández, J., Cózar, R.: Analysis of learning styles and ICT in the personal training of university students through the REATIC questionnaire. J. Educ. Res. **29**(1), 137–156 (2011)
10. Díaz, L., García, J., Alvarado, G., Verges, I.: Challenges of university education in the face of virtuality in times of the pandemic. Soc. Sci. J. **27**(4), 32–48 (2021)
11. Domínguez, J., López, S., Andion, M.: The opinions of teachers of Spanish as a foreign language about learning styles. Anish J. Appl. Linguistics **32**(2), 419–454 (2019)
12. Estrada, M., Monferrer, D., Moliner, M.: The relation between learning styles according to the whole brain model and emotional intelligence: a study of university students. Stud. Educ. **36**, 85–111 (2019)
13. Falcón, C., Arraiz, A.: Construction of teaching professional identity during initial training as teachers. Complutense J. Educ. **31**(3), 329–340 (2020)
14. Flores, M.: Implications of research paradigms in educational practice. Univ. Digit. Mag. **5**(1), 2–9 (2004)
15. Giron, V., Cósar, R., González, J.: Analysis of self-perception on the level of teachers' digital competence in teacher training. Interuniversity Electron. J. Teach. Train. **22**(3), 193–218 (2019)
16. Haydn, T.: The impact of social media on History education: a view from England. Yesterday Today **17**, 23–37 (2017)
17. Hernández, R., Fernández, C., Baptista, P.: Research Methodology. 6th edn. Mc Graw Hill Education, México (2014)
18. Hrastinski, S.: Teaching in the digital age: how educators adapt to online learning. Educ. Res. Rev. **36**, 100485 (2022)

19. Liu, F., Cavanaugh, C.: Virtual learning and COVID-19: a review of the effects on academic performance and mental health. J. Educ. Technol. Dev. Exch. **15**(1), 1–15 (2022)
20. Marín, F., Inciarte, A., Hernández, H., Pitre, R.: Strategies of higher education institutions for the integration of information and communication technology and innovation in teaching processes. Study District Barranquilla Colombia Univ. Educ. **10**(6), 29–38 (2017)
21. Núñez, C., et al.: Teaching practice mediated by ICT: a significance construction. Spaces J. **40**(5), 4–18 (2019)
22. Pascual, M., Ortega-Carrillo, J., Pérez-Ferra, M., Fombona, J.: Digital competences in the students of the grade of teacher of primary education. The case of three Spanish universities. Univ. Educ. **12** (6), 141–150 (2019)
23. Pérez, A., Méndez, C., Pérez, P., Yris, H.: Learning styles as a strategy for teaching in higher education. Learn. Styles Mag. **12**(23), 96–122 (2019)
24. Ramírez, M., Soto, M., Rojas, E.: Computer simulation modeling for the identification of the relationship between the predominant personality type and learning styles of university students. Iberian J. Inf. Syst. Technol. **46**(11), 58–68 (2021)
25. Romero, A., Jordan, G., Ilaquiche, R., Garcia, G., Tapia, H.: Teachers' perceptions on the use of learning styles in the development of competencies of learning to think and think to learn. Spaces J. **40**(5), 23–29 (2019)
26. Sola-Martínez, T., Cáceres-Reche, M., Romero-Rodríguez, J., Navas-Parejo, M.: Bibliometric study of documents indexed in Scopus on ICT teacher training that are related to educational quality. Interuniversity Electron. J. Teach. Train. **23**(2), 10–35 (2020)
27. Tapia-Jara, J., Sánchez-Ortiz, A., Vidal-Silva, C.: Learning styles and intent of using YouTube academic videos in the Chilean university context. Formación Universitaria **13**(1), 3–12 (2020)
28. UNESCO: ICT competencies and standards from the pedagogical dimension: A perspective from the levels of appropriation of ICT in the teaching educational practice. Pontifical Javeriana University, Colombia (2016)
29. Vahos, L., Muñoz, L., Londoño-Vásquez, D.: The role of the teacher to achieve significant learning supported by ICT. Encounters **17**(2), 118–131 (2019)
30. Van Den Beemt, A., Diepstraten, I.: Teacher perspectives on ICT: a learning ecology approach. Comput. Educ. **92–93**, 161–170 (2016)

Efficacy of Flipped Learning in Engineering Education of India

Soumyabrata Saha(✉) and Suparna DasGupta

JIS College of Engineering, Kalyani, West Bengal 741235, India
soumyabrata.saha@jiscollege.ac.in

Abstract. This fast proliferation of interactive technology has enabled creative techniques in higher education that foster collaborative learning, exploration, inquiry in interactive learning environments. Flipped learning turns the classroom into an active learning environment by emphasizing higher order thinking abilities like assessing, analyzing, and producing to involve students in the learning process. It creates a dynamic, interactive learning environment by transforming the group learning space into an individual learning space. Flipped learning bridges the gap between students' abilities to comprehend knowledge and apply it in a cohesive and intelligent manner. Flipping the classroom signifies an ongoing paradigm shift in engineering education from teacher-centric to learner-centric instructional strategies. The outcomes of flipped learning reveal an improvement in student performance. Our study identifies that 81.8% engineering students are benefitted from this pedagogical approach and persuaded on their life skills and professional skills.

Keywords: Flipped Learning · Flip Classroom · Teacher-centric · Learner-centric · Engineering Education · Paradigm Shift

1 Introduction

Recent advances in active learning pedagogical methodologies and instructional design and technology have led to the development of flipped learning [1, 2], a paradigm for education that is dynamic and innovative. The innovative structure of flipped learning allows for the provision of individualized instruction tailored to the specific requirements of each learner. This blended learning method combines behaviorism, cognitivism, social learning theory, constructivism, and connectivism. The four pillars [3] of flipped learning are:

- **Flexible Environment**: It lets students to engage and reflect on their learning in appropriate settings and times; continually watch and listen to the students so you can make changes as needed; provide web-based learning and assessment to students.
- **Learning Culture**: Involve students in relevant work without making the instructor the focal point; using differentiation and feedback, scaffold these exercises and make them accessible to all students.

K. Saeed et al. (Eds.): CISIM 2023, LNCS 14164, pp. 193–208, 2023.
https://doi.org/10.1007/978-3-031-42823-4_15

- **Intentional Content**: Emphasize direct teaching principles for independent learning; curate relevant content for the students; differentiate content to engage students.
- **Professional Educators**: The instructor is constantly accessible to students; observation-based formative evaluations throughout class; collaborate and reflect with other educators to change practice.

Learner-centered [4] pedagogies that successfully engage students in the learning process have a long and illustrious history. Flipped learning is an instructional method and form of blended learning that inverts the conventional educational arrangement by distributing instructional material, often online, outside of the classroom. It moves activities, including some that may have been considered homework in the past, into the classroom.

The flipped classroom [5] concept is gaining popularity worldwide due to its innovative approach to learning and many advantages. The flipped classroom lets instructors spend less time imparting core information and more time utilizing their skills to explore subjects and ideas. In the flipped classroom, students take part in online discussions, or do research at home. In class, they talk about the ideas they've learned and get help from the teacher. This innovative technique has been well received by instructors and students since it reduces lecture time and allows students to participate in group activities. Flipped learning in the classroom provides the environments as; promotes comprehension in students; allows for distinctiveness; assures access to knowledgeable assistance; engages students in learning; creates a welcoming atmosphere for learning; offers opportunity for teamwork.

Three distinct phases make up the flipped learning [6] methodology: pre-class, in-class, and post-class activities. Before coming to class for a doubt clearing session, students may complete quired pre-class assignments. The most typical pre-class activity is to view lecture videos. After completion of the in-class activities, each learner is responsible for completing the post-class assignments within due time.

The contextualization of the relevance of implementing flipped learning [7] in the population are mentioned herewith. This pedagogical approach helps to improve students' higher-order thinking abilities including analysis, application, assessment, and invention via its focus on active learning activities and meaningful student-instructor interactions in-class. Enabling a customized learning speed during pre-class preparation and prompt facilitator feedback during in-class cooperation might boost students' self-efficacy during flipped learning by minimizing task complexity and learning anxiety. The possible advantages of this pedagogy [8] include greater one-on-one contact time between instructor and students, active learning and collaboration, and self-paced learning. The technique also allows instructors to choose from a variety of learning activities, such as mastery learning, peer teaching, cooperative learning, role-playing, inquiry-based learning etc.

The main contribution of the paper is evidence-based advice for instructors having an affinity towards leveraging the flipped teaching model of engineering education. Implementation of flipped pedagogy at flipped classroom environments presents a sea changing performance of the learners of JIS College of Engineering. Designing the flipped evaluation guidelines based on World Economic Forum [9] is one of the key aspects for this study. The presented recommendations are grounded on the authors' own case study based on the students' performance of JIS College of Engineering.

From the study it is evident that the communication skills, competency skills, core skills of engineering students are improved and that helps them to industry ready for their carrier purposes. Students can achieve proficiency in verbal and nonverbal communication and communicate successfully in both personal and professional contexts. They can critically assess all circumstances, whether they be personal or professional, and act appropriately. Recognize the significance of engineering related morals and ethics and put them into practice. Students become familiar with the techniques of effective leadership.

The rest of the paper is organized as follows. Existing techniques on pedagogical approaches presented in Sect. 2. In Sect. 3, we have presented the case study based Flipped Learning execution at JIS College of Engineering and present how this pedagogical approach is effective for learners. In Sect. 4, this paper concludes and identifies some of the future directions with open research issues.

2 Literature Survey

Since 2012, flipped learning has piqued the interest of several scholars as an educational strategy based on the concept of switching the sequence of assignment and teaching.

In [10] authors concluded that online resources and activities about computations and sketching in STEM courses improve communication and teamwork, which increases knowledge retention. Flipped learning improves student satisfaction, particularly with algebra video lectures, and allows students to access them anytime, anyplace [11]. Authors [12] found that self-study with activities improves students' subject knowledge and makes them engaged learners in flipped courses. In [13] authors agreed that flipped films encourage active learning and cooperation and enable students to critically assess content in a more learner-centered way. Flipped learning in teacher education needs instructors to consider how to integrate it into educational technology course curriculum [14]. In [15] authors identified five key mechanisms via which the flipped classroom model is effective. Students are more invested in their learning, their teamwork skills are honed, students get more supervision, more classroom discussion is stimulated, and instructors are given more opportunity to foster these outcomes.

The flipped class is an active, student-centered strategy that increases class quality [16], offers organized, active learning [17] and encourages students to investigate and engage with professors, classmates, employers, and learning resources. It may also help instructors develop students' critical and independent thinking, lifelong learning, and workforce development [18]. As a pedagogical approach, the flipped demands students to commit and actively participate in learning activities before and during class, with the use of technology [19]. Due to the COVID-19 epidemic and most HEIs adopting to online instruction, the flip class has become more appealing, but the flipped learning potential is still not being completely realized [20]. Throughout the massive transition to online education, there have been indications that students favored passive learning methods including webinars, presentations, and demonstrations [21]. Neither a meta-analysis nor an SLR on the use of FCs during the COVID-19 pandemic have been reported.

University programs must continue to deliver quality education despite obstacles [22]. In light of the present crisis, academics in many fields have reassessed their teaching materials and sought new ways to engage students. During this time of enormous strain, creative ways based on distant conferencing technology and internet tools are crucial [23]. In [24] authors proposed numerous ways to reduce the danger of viral propagation, including the FC model, teleconferencing, and online practice. Participants were happy with the format and wanted to keep learning without attending lectures. Authors [25] found that participants were more likely to actively participate in their own learning by developing 21st century abilities like critical thinking and creativity under the FC model than passively listening to direct instruction. Several researchers noted the use of videos, recorded lectures, and group discussions, among other digital tools, to promote debate, learning, and distraction from the pandemic [26].

It has always been the norm to instruct students in classrooms and assign them practice problems such as homework to cement their understanding of the material. The current generation of students in India are digital natives, yet traditional approaches to education have not kept up with the advances. Using flipped learning, students may more easily transition from being passive information consumers to active, reflective users of that information. Table 1, shows a comparison between Traditional learning and Flipped learning, outlining several distinguishing features of both.

Table 1. Flipped Learning vs. Traditional Learning

Parameter	Flipped Learning	Traditional Learning
Knowledge Dissemination	Proactive	Passive
Performance Evaluation	Continuous	Periodic
Communication Skills	Improved	No checks
Teamwork	Improved	No chance
Leadership Qualities	Improved	No chance
Group discussions	Mandatory	No chance
Attitude	Checks available	No checks
Aptitude	Checks available	No checks
Grades	Much improved	Average
Availability of Performance Evaluation Results	Instantaneous that alerts students for improvement	Periodic

From the previous discussion, it is apparent that many studies have been done on flipped learning, but very few have focused on engineering education in India. In this study we aimed to create a flip learning mechanism for engineering education. For this purpose, we have incorporated some key aspects identified from the above discussion. It has been shown that the activity based self-learning mechanism is very effective information of student knowledgebase. We have integrated a variety of student-centered activities in our execution model, where less classroom teaching and more student engagement is required. It has also been shown that appropriately assigning a flip class based on the indicated necessary activities is an essential component of the execution process. Proper designing evaluation metrics is crucial for ensuring trustworthy assessment of student learning. The highlights provided here served as inspiration for the development of a methodology and implementation strategy for the introduction of a flip learning mechanism.

3 Methodology and Execution

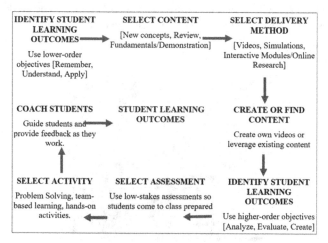

Fig. 1. Design Process of Flipped Classroom

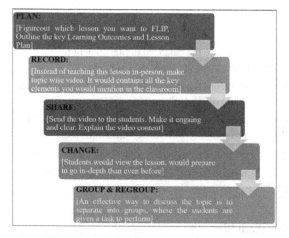

Fig. 2. Steps for Flipping the Classroom

JIS College of Engineering has always strived to include innovative concepts throughout the entire teaching learning process. From the beginning of 2017, the flipped learning methodology has been implemented at JISCE. The entire case study is presented based on every day's teaching learning at the institution. At first, we highlighted the design process of flipped classroom, followed by the guidelines how to flipped the class (Figs. 1 and 2).

- **Design a FLIPPED Classroom**
- **Steps for 'FLIPPING the Classroom'**
- **Flipped Learning Activities**

Different flipped learning activities have been performed by both facilitator and learners; Pre-Class Activities; In-Class Activities; Post-Activities. The guidelines for all these activities have clearly been specified in each flipped classroom.

- **Pre-Class Activities**

Fig. 3. Guidelines of Flipped Learning Activities

The Pre-Class activities have been identified for both facilitator and learners (Fig. 3).

- **Facilitator Centric Activities**

Step 1:	Faculty members create the balanced digital content for each class at the Blend Space Digital Platform as per the lesson plan.
Step 2:	Faculty concerns record the introductory video (2–3 min) of their own of each topic at the Digital Studio of JIS College of Engineering.
Step 3:	The digital content would comprise mandatorily one short video (2–3 min), PPT notes, PDF materials along with the few questions based on the above topic.
Step 4:	Faculty members prepare the digital contents of all the classes.
Step 5:	Faculty concern share the 4-digit unique class code to all the registered students of the said class to join in the class.

- **Learner Centric Activities**

Step 1:	Each registered student has joined in the class by using the 4-Digit unique code.
Step 2:	Students will watch the Introductory video along with all other digital contents of each topic before attending the next class.
Step 3:	After watching digital contents, they will attempt the quizzes.

Students can also access the digital content through the said URL.
https://www.jisgroup.net/erp/forms/frmcommonlogin.aspx

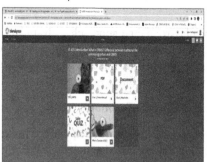

Fig. 4. Balanced Digital Content

Fig. 5. Digital Contents of All Modules

Fig. 6. 4-digit Class Joining Code

Fig. 7. Digital Content Repository

- **In-Class Activities**

Facilitators lead in-class activities in the designated flip classroom where assessment has been completed as learning activities (Figs. 4, 5, 6, 7, 8 and 9).

- **Team Formation**

First year learners would create a group with three members and would sit at the 'Round Table'. As the 1st year learners are the new entrants in this system, to provide more attention of their in-class activities three members groups have arranged in each round table. Second-Third-fourth year students would sit on a 'Hexagonal' table of six people.

Fig. 8. Flipped Classroom: 1st Year Program   **Fig. 9.** Flipped Classroom: 2nd–4th Year Program

The facilitator would stand in the middle of the classroom and approach each student at each table in both types of classes. Think-Pair-Share, Debate, Seminar, Quiz, and other student-centered group-based activities have been carried out. Students would take their seats in the classroom while according to the seating guidelines.

- **Relationship between Flipped Learning and Blooms Taxonomy**

Flipped learning, on the contrary hand, inverts Bloom's taxonomy such that the bottom portions are designated for student self-instruction via organized activities, while class time is focused on the higher parts, which are best served by a rich social environment (Fig. 10).

Fig. 10. Flipped Learning Interlinked with Blooms Taxonomy [27]

Conventional training assumes no prior knowledge of new subjects and concentrates on the lower half of Bloom in class and the upper half after class. Instead of flipping the halves, it's better to split Bloom's Taxonomy into thirds for flipped instruction.

- **Flipped Evaluation Technique**

Facilitators would do day-to-day evaluation based on the following 'Flip Learning Evaluation' guidelines. The following guidelines have been designed based on the world economic forum's 21st century skills, industry demand and in the line of Blooms' Taxonomy Level. The said guidelines have duly approved by Institutional Academic Council and Board of Governors.

The flipped evaluation criteria are developed in accordance with Bloom's Taxonomy. These fundamental abilities or core skills as tested by pre-class exercises, are strongly associated with the lower levels of Blooms' taxonomy, as Remembering, Understanding, and Applying. Competency is evaluated on a scale that includes such factors as the ability to learn and work well with others, adapt to new situations, and demonstrate leadership. These are all closely connected to Bloom's Taxonomy's Analyze intermediate level. The assessment criteria of communication skills are connected to the higher order Bloom's Taxonomy level as Evaluate and Create.

During the course of the year, we have used the flipped approach in all of our engineering classes at JIS College of Engineering. Here we have presented the case study of the two different subjects of B.Tech. Information Technology program. Each facilitator has evaluated the learner's activity of each class in each paper code. The three core skills (Par1 to Par3) are evaluated based on the Pre-class activities of each learner. Remaining Competency Skills (Par4 to Par6) and Communication Skills (Par7 to Par10) during In-Class activity. Based on the learner's performance the grade value is evaluated at the end of each class. At the end of the month, each facilitator can easily find out the monthly performance of learners. The grading system is calculated in 10-point scale.

❖ **Guidelines for Evaluating the Students Grading: [0 to 10]**

Par 1:	**Digital Content-Critical Thinking [Remembering]**	
Par 2:	**Flow, Quality and Balanced of Digital Content-Creativity [Understanding]**	**Core Skills**
Par 3:	**Understanding of the Digital Content Including Complex Problem Solving [Applying]**	
Par 4:	**Collaborative Learning-Group Discussion and Negotiation [Analyzing]**	
Par 5:	**Cognitive Flexibility-Attitude and Aptitude [Analyzing]**	**Competency Skills**
Par 6:	**Leadership Qualities Including Judgement and Decision Making [Analyzing]**	
Par 7:	**Audience Engagement [Evaluation]**	
Par 8:	**Pitching-To Succeed in Achieving [Create]**	**Communication Skills**
Par 9:	**Body Language**	
Par10:	**Voice Modulation**	

Grading System (10 Scale)

A = 10	B = 9	C = 8
D = 7	E = 6	Absent = 0

Grade Value = Average of Ten Parameters

Based on the evaluation report Weak Students-Slow Learners (Score < 6.0, marked in 'Yellow Colour') and Bright Students-Advanced Learners (Score > = 8.0) have been identified and proactive measured would be taken care.

- **For Weak Students-Slow Learners:** Topics have discussed in the application classes, and hands on execution has conducted in those classes. Special attention has given to the slow learners. Conducting Doubt clearing session, Remedial classes, arranging Motivational Talks, providing the opportunity for accessing MOOCs courses, participating in Projects and Co-curricular activities.
- **For Bright Students-Advanced Learners:** They were advised to help their peers and additional problems have given them to solve as a team. Additional facilities would be arranged for them, such as special class for GATE exam, opportunity for Advanced MOOCs courses, participation in Seminars/Conferences/Educational Campus etc.
- **Post-Class Activities**

Students submit a PPT file on the discussed topic and prepare 3 min video assignment at digital studio; participate in online quiz activities.

- **Sample Case Study: Flipped Evaluation**

Case-I-A: [Class Wise Daily Evaluation: Paper Code: IT301]

JIS College of Engineering											
Department:	Information Technology						Year: 2ND				
Subject: Data Structure and Algorithm							Stream: IT				
Code:IT301		Credit:3					Group:1				
Faculty: Soumyabrata Saha							Date of Evaluation : 05.08.2019				
Sl	College Roll	Par. 1	Par. 2	Par. 3	Par. 4	Par. 5	Par. 6	Par. 7	Par. 8	Par. 9	Par. 10	Grade Value
1	123180704001	0	0	0	0	0	0	0	0	0	0	0
2	123180704002	0	0	0	0	0	0	0	0	0	0	0
3	123180704003	7	7	7	7	7	6	6	6	6	6	6.5
4	123180704004	0	0	0	0	0	0	0	0	0	0	0
5	123180704005	7	7	8	7	8	7	7	6	6	6	6.9
6	123180704006	0	0	0	0	0	0	0	0	0	0	0
7	123180704007	8	8	8	8	7	7	7	7	7	7	7.4
8	123180704008	7	8	8	7	8	7	8	7	7	7	7.4
9	123180704009	7	7	8	7	8	7	7	7	7	7	7.2
10	123180704010	9	9	9	9	9	8	8	8	8	8	8.5
11	123180704011	9	9	9	9	9	9	9	9	8	9	8.9
12	123180704012	8	9	8	8	9	8	8	8	8	8	8.2
13	123180704013	8	8	8	8	8	7	7	7	7	7	7.5
14	123180704014	8	8	8	8	8	8	8	8	8	8	8
15	123180704015	8	7	8	7	8	7	7	7	7	7	7.3
16	123180704016	0	0	0	0	0	0	0	0	0	0	0
17	123180704017	8	8	8	8	8	8	8	8	8	8	8
18	123180704018	8	8	8	8	8	8	8	8	8	8	8
19	123180704019	8	8	8	8	8	7	7	7	7	7	7.5
20	123180704020	0	0	0	0	0	0	0	0	0	0	0
21	123180704021	8	7	7	7	8	8	7	7	7	7	7.3
22	123180704022	8	9	9	8	8	8	8	8	8	8	8.2
23	123180704023	8	8	9	8	9	8	8	8	8	8	8.2
24	123180704024	7	7	7	7	7	7	7	7	7	7	7
25	123180704025	7	7	7	7	7	7	7	7	7	7	7
26	123180704026	9	7	8	8	7	8	7	7	7	7	7.5
27	123180704027	9	9	9	9	8	8	8	8	8	8	8.4
28	123180704028	0	0	0	0	0	0	0	0	0	0	0
29	123180704029	9	8	8	9	8	8	8	8	8	8	8.2
30	123180704030	0	0	0	0	0	0	0	0	0	0	0
31	123180704031	0	0	0	0	0	0	0	0	0	0	0
32	123180704032	7	7	8	8	7	8	8	7	7	7	7.4

Fig. 11. Daily Evaluation Report of IT301

4 Result Analysis

Faculty members have conducted flipped classes and conducted the flipped evaluation in each class based on the evaluation guidelines. In Fig. 11 [Class wise daily evaluation report of paper code IT301], there are 9 students who are marked as '0' as all of them

Case-I-B: [Class Wise Monthly Evaluation: Paper Code: IT301]

Department: Information Technology				Semester: 3rd	
Subject: Data Structure and Algorithm				Stream: IT	
Code: IT301				Group: A	
Credit: 4				Month:August (2019)	

Sl. No	College ID No / Roll No	Day 1 05.08.19	Day2 19.08.19	Day 3 26.08.19	Monthly Grade Value (10 scale)
1	123180704001	0	0	0	0.0
2	123180704002	0	0	7	2.2
3	123180704003	6.5	7	0	4.5
4	123180704004	0	0	0	0.0
5	123180704005	6.9	7	7	6.8
6	123180704006	0	8	9	5.7
7	123180704007	7.4	8	8	7.6
8	123180704008	7.4	0	7	4.7
9	123180704009	7.2	0	0	2.4
10	123180704010	8.5	9	9	8.7
11	123180704011	8.9	9	0	6.0
12	123180704012	8.2	8	8	8.2
13	123180704013	7.5	8	7	7.5
14	123180704014	8	8	8	7.9
15	123180704015	7.3	8	7	7.3
16	123180704016	0	7	7	4.6
17	123180704017	8	8	7	7.7
18	123180704018	8	8	7	7.8
19	123180704019	7.5	8	7	7.2
20	123180704020	0	0	0	0.0
21	123180704021	7.3	7	7	7.2
22	123180704022	8.2	0	8	5.2
23	123180704023	8.2	8	0	5.5
24	123180704024	7	0	7	4.6
25	123180704025	7	0	0	2.3
26	123180704026	7.5	0	0	2.5
27	123180704027	8.4	8.6	8.3	8.4
28	123180704028	0	8.4	8.1	5.5
29	123180704029	8.2	8.4	8.1	8.2
30	123180704030	0	0	0	0.0
31	123180704031	0	0	0	0.0
32	123180704032	7.4	7.6	7.2	7.4

Fig. 12. Monthly Evaluation Report of IT301

were absent in the corresponding classes. Figure 12 represents the class wise monthly evaluation report, where 17 students have scored below the benchmark and 5 students were absent in all classes and marked as '0'. All the defaulters are marked in yellow color. Monthly evaluation is calculated based on the all the individual class evaluation.

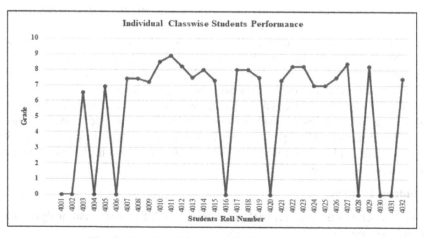

Fig. 13. Individual Class wise Students' Performance

Figure 13 represents the individual class wise students' performance where performance is measured based on the 10 evaluating parameters. Based on the slow/advanced learners corresponding action would be taken care of to improve the students' performance.

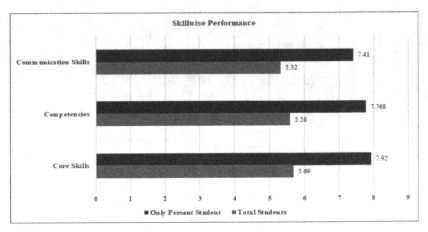

Fig. 14. Skill-wise Students' Performance

Figure 14 represents the students' performance based on three different types of skills. It is identified that students [in this class students] have acquired more 'Core Skills' in comparison with 'Competencies' and 'Communication Skills'. Learners can apply the acquired knowledge for complex problem solving which is highly important for engineering study. Learners have also acquired a good number of competencies skills that help for analyzing in cognitive flexibility, collaborative learning and decision making. Students would improve their communication skills in comparison with the other two skills.

Figure 15 identifies the monthly class performance of all students along with the individual class wise students' performance. From the above fig, it is noted that overall performances of the students depend on the individual class performances. Any student can improve his/her performance in the next class if his/her current class performance is not up to the mark or he/she was absent in the class. The flipped study helps to improve every day's performance in comparison with existing performance.

In Fig. 16, we have presented the parameter wise-class wise individual students' performance. Here we have considered one individual student's performance. This is observed that monthly class performance is dependent on all the existing class performances. The student is not always performing the same, but his/her monthly class performance is scored better.

- **Students Feedback**

We have conducted the feedback mechanism on 338 learners and analyzed their feedback opinion (Fig. 17).

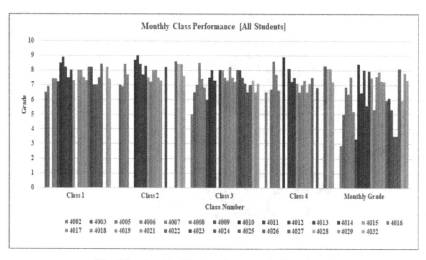

Fig. 15. Monthly Class Performance [All students]

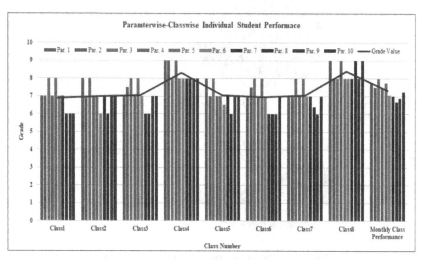

Fig. 16. Individual Students Performance [Class wise-Parameter wise]

It is identified that more than 81.8% students identified that flipped Learning is useful for them. 71.4% of students have remarked that flipped Learning is more interesting than traditional learning. 61.7% preferred flipped learning over traditional teaching. 62.2% students have recommended flipped learning to their junior batches.

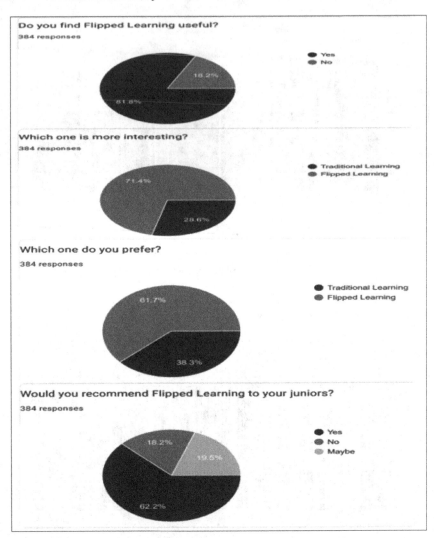

Fig. 17. Students Feedback on Flipped Learning

5 Conclusions

The flipped learning has been a major factor in the shift from more conventional teaching techniques to those that make use of technological advances. Students benefit in the areas of accomplishment, attitude, cognitive abilities, and soft skills while using this approach since it encourages them to become active participants in their own education. Learners take part in pre-class activities before attending the assigned class at college premises. They have fundamental ideas of the topics that would be discussed in the next scheduled class. The facilitator conducted in-class activities to measure the learner's performance in class. Learners would clear their doubt from the corresponding subject experts or facilitator. The total allotted time is used to clear the doubt of each learner which helped them to acquire more knowledge on the topics. The interaction behavior is a strong predictor of students' test scores and their learning outcomes when they worked together in the classroom.

This study shows how students may become more engaged in learning via a range of in-class activities when the traditional lecture format is flipped. The flipped classroom model also gives educators more leeway in how they present lessons to students. We may infer that students in flipped classes perform better on assessments and are equally satisfied with the learning environment. This study presents that the engineering students' performance is improved through flipped learning approaches in the theorical subjects. In the future, we would introduce this pedagogy for the practical courses of all engineering disciplines. In accordance with the Indian National Educational Policy of India, we would apply this paradigm in outcome-based education.

References

1. Bergmann, J., Sams, A.: Flip your classroom: reach every student in every class every day. International Society for Technology in Education, Alexandria, Va (2012)
2. Hew, K.F., Lo, C.K.: Flipped classroom improves student learning in health professions education: a meta-analysis. BMC Med. Educ. **18**(1), 1–12 (2018). https://doi.org/10.1186/s12909-018-1144-z
3. van Alten, D.C.D., Phielix, C., Janssen, J., Kester, L.: Effects of flipping the classroom on learning outcomes and satisfaction: a meta-analysis. Educ. Res. Rev. **28** (2019). https://doi.org/10.1016/j.edurev.2019.05.003
4. Cheng, L., Ritzhaupt, A.D., Antonenko, P.: Effects of the flipped classroom instructional strategy on students' learning outcomes: a meta-analysis. Educ. Tech. Res. Dev. **67**, 793–824 (2019). https://doi.org/10.1007/s11423-018-9633-7
5. Chen, K.S., et al.: Academic outcomes of flipped classroom learning: a meta-analysis. Med. Educ. **52**(9), 910–924 (2018). https://doi.org/10.1111/medu.13616
6. Akçayır, G., Akçayır, M.: The flipped classroom: a review of its advantages and challenges. Comput. Educ. **126**, 334–345 (2018). https://doi.org/10.1016/j.compedu.2018.07.021
7. Hodges, C., Moore, S., Lockee, B., Trust, T., Bond, A.: e-difference between emergency remote teaching and online learning. Educause Rev. **27** (2020)
8. Stöhr, C., Demazière, C., Adawi, T.: The polarizing effect of the online flipped classroom. Comput. Educ. **147** (2020). https://doi.org/10.1016/j.compedu.2019.103789
9. https://www.weforum.org/agenda/2016/03/21st-century-skills-future-jobs-students/
10. Nouri, J.: The flipped classroom: for active, effective and increased learning – especially for low achievers. Int. J. Educ. Technol. High. Educ. **13**(1), 1 (2016). https://doi.org/10.1186/s41239-016-0032-z
11. Ogden, L., Shambaugh, N.: The continuous and systematic study of the college algebra flipped classroom. In: Keengwe, J., Onchwari, G. (eds.) Handbook of Research on Active Learning and the Flipped Model Classroom in the Digital Age, pp. 41–71. Information Science Reference, Hershey (2016)
12. Guraya, S.: Combating the COVID-19 outbreak with a technology-driven e-flipped classroom model of educational transformation. J. Taibah. Univ. Med. Sci. **15**(4), 253–254 (2020). https://doi.org/10.1016/j.jtumed.2020.07.006. Epub 2020 Aug 8. PMID: 32837509; PMCID: PMC7414784

13. Amhag, L.: Mobile technologies for student centred learning in a distance higher educa-tion program. In: Information Resources Management Association (ed.) Blended Learning: Concepts, Methodologies, Tools, and Applications, pp. 802–817. IGI Global (2017)

14. Chellapan, L., Van der Meer, J., Pratt, K., Wass, R.: To flip or not to flip, that's the question – findings from an exploratory study into factors that may influence tertiary teachers to consider a flipped classroom model. J. Open Flexible Distance Learn. **22**(1), 6–21 (2018). Distance Education Association of New Zealand. https://www.learntechlib.org/p/184659/. Accessed 21 Mar 2023

15. Alghamdi, A., Karpinski, A.C., Lepp, A., Barkley, J.: Online and face-to-face classroom multitasking and academic performance: moderated mediation with self-efficacy for self-regulated learning and gender. Comput. Hum. Behav. **102**, 214–222 (2020). https://doi.org/10.1016/j.chb.2019.08.018

16. Ozdamli, F., Asiksoy, G.: Flipped classroom approach. World J. Educ. Technol. Current Issues. **8**(2), 98–105 (2016)

17. Strelan, P., Osborn, A., Palmer, E.: The flipped classroom: a meta-analysis of effects on student performance across disciplines and education levels. Educ. Res. Rev. **30**, 100314 (2020). ISSN 1747-938X. https://doi.org/10.1016/j.edurev.2020.100314

18. O'Flaherty, J., Phillips, C.: The use of flipped classrooms in higher education: a scoping review. Internet High. Educ. **25**, 85–95 (2015). ISSN 1096-7516. https://doi.org/10.1016/j.iheduc.2015.02.002

19. Aguilera-Ruiz, C., Manzano-León, A., Martínez-Moreno, I., Lozano-Segura, M.C., Yanicelli, C.C.: El Modelo flipped classroom. Int. J. Dev. Educ. Psychol. **4**, 261–266 (2017). https://doi.org/10.17060/ijodaep.2017.n1.v4.1055

20. Hoshang, S., Hilal, T.A., Hilal, H.A.: Investigating the acceptance of flipped classroom and suggested recommendations. Procedia Comput. Sci. (2021). https://doi.org/10.1016/j.procs.2021.03.052

21. Oadowicz, A.: Modified blended learning in engineering higher education during the COVID-19 lockdown—building automation courses case study. Educ. Sci. **10**(10), 292 (2020)

22. Barrot, J.S., Llenares, I.I., del Rosario, L.S.: Students' online learning challenges during the pandemic and how they cope with them: the case of the Philippines. Educ. Inf. Technol **26**, 7321–7338 (2021). https://doi.org/10.1007/s10639-021-10589-x

23. Divjak, B., Rienties, B., Iniesto, F., et al.: Flipped classrooms in higher education during the COVID-19 pandemic: findings and future research recommendations. Int. J. Educ. Technol. High Educ. **19**, 9 (2022). https://doi.org/10.1186/s41239-021-00316-4

24. Chick, R.C., et al.: Using technology to maintain the education of residents during the COVID-19 pandemic. J. Surg. Educ. **77**(4), 729–732 (2020). https://doi.org/10.1016/j.jsurg.2020.03.018. Epub 2020 Apr 3. PMID: 32253133; PMCID: PMC7270491

25. Campillo-Ferrer, J.M., Miralles-Martínez, P.: Effectiveness of the flipped classroom model on students' self-reported motivation and learning during the COVID-19 pandemic. Humanit. Soc. Sci. Commun. **8**, 176 (2021). https://doi.org/10.1057/s41599-021-00860-4

26. Agarwal, S., Kaushik, J.S.: Student's perception of online learning during COVID pandemic. Indian J. Pediatr. **87**, 554 (2020). https://doi.org/10.1007/s12098-020-03327-7

27. https://rtalbert.org/re-thinking-blooms-taxonomy-for-flipped-learning-design/

Hybrid Recommender System Model for Tourism Industry Competitiveness Increment

Andres Solano-Barliza[1,2]([envelope]) [ID], Melisa Acosta-Coll[1] [ID], Jose Escorcia-Gutierrez[1] [ID], Emiro De-La-Hoz-Franco[1] [ID], and Isabel Arregocés-Julio[1,2] [ID]

[1] Department of Computational Science and Electronics, Universidad de la Costa, CUC, 080002 Barranquilla, Colombia
{asolano21,macosta10,jescorci56,iarregoc,edelahoz}@cuc.edu.co
[2] Faculty of Engineering and Economics and Administrative Sciences, Universidad de La Guajira, Riohacha-La Guajira, Colombia

Abstract. In the tourism industry, recommender systems (RS) are information technology (IT) tools used to strengthen competitiveness indicators since allow interaction with tourists, generate mobility in the environment and with other users, and provide helpful information about the destination. However, recommender systems applied to tourism tend to focus mainly on the indicator of destination promotion and management, neglecting other competitiveness indicators that make destinations more attractive, such as tourist safety. This study proposes a model to strengthen various indicators of competitiveness, such as destination management, tourism promotion, marketing, and safety tourism, following a three-step methodology. First, the documentation and analysis of sources in scientific databases to identify the fields of uses of recommender systems in the tourism industry; second selection of techniques and models of recommender systems applied in the tourism industry; third, the construction of a model for the improvement of indicators in a tourist destination. The developed model uses a hybrid recommender system strengthen indicators such as promotion and visitor growth but also provides safe recommendations to users while contributing to the promotion of the tourism offer.

Keywords: Recommender System · Machine Learning · Tourism Competitiveness

1 Introduction

The tourism industry makes a significant contribution to the world economy due to the wide range of economic opportunities that this activity offers, and is becoming a source of great resources for developing countries, which need to meet the demands of this industry through diversification and competitiveness in the products and services offered [1]. In this sense, the main challenge for destinations today is to strengthen their tourism competitiveness indicators to attract new tourists.

K. Saeed et al. (Eds.): CISIM 2023, LNCS 14164, pp. 209–222, 2023.
https://doi.org/10.1007/978-3-031-42823-4_16

Tourism competitiveness indicators are measurable criteria for assessing the performance of a tourism destination. According to the UNWTO - World Tourism Organization, a specialised agency of the United Nations - "tourism competitiveness is the ability of a destination to create and integrate value-added products that preserve local resources and maintain its market position vis-à-vis its competitors" [2]. Similarly, as stated in [3], tourism competitiveness should aim to "create harmony among tourists and ensure well-being in terms of health, environment and safety, implementing sustainability indicators focusing on the positive impact on competitiveness" [4].

The competitiveness indicators proposed by the World Economic Forum (WEF) establish sub-indices and pillars for the Tourism and Travel (T&T) Tourism Competitiveness Benchmark Index [9], see Fig. 1.

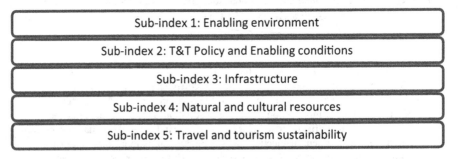

Fig. 1. Subindexes used to measure tourism competitiveness by the WEF. Source: [5]

Of the first subindex, enabling environment, safety and security is a critical pillar as it affects the promotion and diversification of supply in tourism destinations. Therefore, in the tourism sector, the use of technology is required to promote these indicators. Implementing Information and communication technologies (ICT) is the primary strategy to become tourist destinations more competitive [6].

In the tourism sector, ICTs, in particular recommender systems (RS), contribute to innovation, development, and accessibility of destinations, improving competitiveness indicators such as the strengthening of supply and destination management. RS are algorithms that optimize the analysis of data and the collection of information according to user criteria, in order to make predictions in the form of recommendations [7] that facilitate the tourist's interaction with the environment and other users.

In this sense, recommender systems contribute to the innovation, development, and accessibility of destinations, improving competitiveness indicators such as the strengthening of supply and destination management [8]. This technology also promotes the tourist's interaction with the environment and other users.

In the tourism sector, recommender systems contribute to the innovation, development, and accessibility of destinations, improving competitiveness indicators such as the strengthening of supply and destination management. This technology also promotes the tourist's interaction with the environment and other users. This information is useful for government agencies to develop strategies that help strengthen the destination and make timely decisions, transforming it into a smart destination.

In tourism, a project developed by Spanish researchers, using data from the Museum of Modern Art (MoMA) in New York [9], designed recommender systems to promote cultural tourism offered in Museums and other cultural elements. It uses a synthetic dataset generator for CARS evaluation, called DataGenCARS to build recommendation scenarios based on real and synthetic data using the context-aware typology (Collaborative filtering and context), and a data source the Sqlite-JDBC, SQLite database management. In this project, performed an evaluation of context-sensitive recommender systems to assign a geographic location for each artwork.

Additionally, [10] used a context-aware recommender system with two stages. The first stage suggests services using a user-based ranking with majority voting. The second stage presents the service with contextual information using the neighbourhood's method. This technological development applies User-Based Classification techniques, a neighbourhood-based methodology that seeks to strengthen the promotion of the offer and uses quality of services (QoS) datasets from real-world data as a data source. This recommender system addresses destination management issues. And aspect about context.

In turn, [11] presented a recommender system for groups, which takes the preferences of all users and creates a travel recommendation framework that receives a set of preferred points of interest from each tourist and forms multi-day travel plans that cover all points of tourists' preferences. It uses Foursquare from two major cities, New York, and Tokyo, as a data source. The technique used is ontology. It is used as variables to make the recommendation, distance, and time, intending to stay within the monetary budget. This recommender system addresses destination management issues.

However, although tourism rating systems are useful for most indicators, such as promotion and destination management, other competitiveness indicators that make destinations more attractive, such as tourism safety, are neglected.

This study presents a hybrid model of a recommender system that uses different techniques within machine learning to strengthen and increase tourism competitiveness indicators, such as destination management, tourism promotion, marketing, sustainable tourism, and security tourism.

This paper describes in Sect. 2 the research methodology. Section 3 presents the research findings and Sect. 4 shows the research results.

2 Methodology

In this study, a methodology was used to construct the hybrid model in three steps, see Fig. 2: 1) Literature review for theoretical documentation of the topic under study. 2) Identification of the most used techniques and models of recommender systems in tourism for tourism promotion and security, and 3) Configuration of the hybrid model to address tourism competitiveness indicators such as tourism promotion and security.

2.1 Literature Review for Theoretical Documentation of the Topic Under Study

In this step, scientific databases were consulted on the research topic of recommender systems applied to tourism. In this sense, this work started with a structured search in

Fig. 2. Steps methodological route used in the research.

Scopus, IEEE, WOS, and Google Academic using the keywords of the two thematic axes (TITLE-ABS-KEY ("Recommender system") OR TITLE-ABS-KEY ("Competitiveness") AND TITLE-ABS-KEY ("tourism")) in a 5-year window, comprised between 2017–2022.

After consulting the databases, this step served to identify the areas of tourism that use recommender systems, i.e., the typologies and techniques of recommender systems applied to tourism.

2.2 Identification of the Most Used Techniques and Models of Recommender Systems in Tourism for Tourism Promotion and Security

In this second step, once the recommender systems applied to tourism had been identified, the recommender systems were analysed to identify which indicators they addressed, which machine learning techniques they used and which characteristics, such as data sources, they used.

These classifications were used to identify which technical characteristics were most relevant for addressing competitiveness indicators.

2.3 Configuration of the Hybrid Model to Address Tourism Competitiveness Indicators Such as Tourism Promotion and Security

Once the techniques had been identified, they were analysed and combined to see which ones addressed the indicators to be addressed in the project, which focused on safety. In this case, the recommender system models were analysed and compared with the tourism competitiveness indicators to be promoted, and a hybrid RS model was proposed to help tourist destinations increase their indicators and improve the tourist experience.

In this step, the objective or problem to be addressed by the recommender system was defined, data sources, data collection and data processing were identified. Next, the machine learning algorithms that would be generated to process the data and generate personalized recommendations to tourists based on their tastes and preferences were defined. This data was used in the model that combines the characteristics of two typologies, contextual and location-based recommender systems.

3 Results

The results of the methodological process proposed for the development of the proposed hybrid recommender system model are presented below.

3.1 Fields of Uses of Recommender Systems in Tourism

The reviewed documents found that the main types of tourism that used recommender systems are Tourist attractions, Gastronomic Tourism, Nature Tourism, and Cultural tourism. Table 1 shows a classification of tourism activities that use that used recommender systems.

Table 1. Fields of uses of recommender systems in tourism

Uses of recommender systems in tourism	References
Restaurant	[12, 13]
Cultural item	[14],
Hotels	[15, 16]
Tourist attractions	[17]

For the above tourist activities, the recommender systems stand out for the use of features such as location, temperature, weather, traffic conditions, time of day, week, season, nearby resources, and people accompanying the user, which can be helpful in the tourism context [18]. In this sense, the interaction between users, the system, and the context helps to shape preferences by forming a contextual dataset.

3.1.1 Models and Techniques Classification of Recommender Systems Applied in Tourism

Within tourism, recommender systems provide accurate recommendations to tourists based on the opinions or preferences of users that allow for greater personalization of recommendations. From the analysed scientific literature, Table 2 presents the most used recommender systems models applied in tourism such as collaborative filtering, Content-based filtering, Location-based, Context-aware, and hybrid models.

Figure 3 show the prevalence of techniques employed in every model is Machine learning models, Clustering, sentiment analysis, KNN, Deep neural networks, Recurrent Neural Networks, Fuzzy, ontology.

Recommender system for data processing, recommender systems employ different techniques and algorithms. The machine learning technique that prevailed most in the review was Clustering.

Among the models of recommender systems that can help strengthen competitiveness indicators are:

Table 2. Types of recommender systems

Types of recommender systems	References
Collaborative filtering RS	[16, 19]
Content-based filtering RS	[12, 29]
Location-based RS	[22–29]
Context-aware RS	[31, 32]
Hybrid RS	[26, 29, 44]

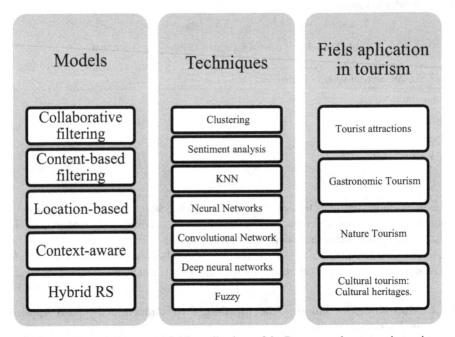

Fig. 3. Models, techniques, and fields applications of the Recommender system in tourism.

3.2 Identification of the Most Used Techniques and Models of Recommender Systems in Tourism for Tourism Promotion and Security

The following are the models of recommender systems and techniques most used in the tourism sector to improve competitiveness indicators such as tourism promotion and security.

Location-Based Recommender Systems

This recommender system uses geographic location property, usually employing technologies such as GPS or social networks, to improve recommendations of places or activities in which a target user may be interested. According to [39, 40], there is currently a classification of these types of systems, among which there are two groups.

Table 3 shows a review of articles according to the type of location-based recommender system.

Table 3. Analysis of research on the use of location-based recommender systems

Type of SR based on location	Techniques/algorithms used	Dataset	References
Autonomous location-based recommender systems	Hypertext-induced	Instagram, foursquare	[41]
	Convolution matrix factorization	Foursquare/ Gowalla	[42]
GPS-based trajectory	Collaborative, naïve Bayes	GeoLife	[43]
Stand-alone point	Content-based, collaborative, matrix factorization, deep learning, neural networks	Foursquare, Gowalla	[44]
	Collaborative	Foursquare	[45]

This model of recommender system has had a great growth in its use for tourism, as it helps tourists to move around different points of their destination. In recent years, location-based recommender systems have used data from platforms such as Facebook, Instagram and Twitter, which are representative services of the social media sector [32]. This type of recommender system has seen an increase in algorithms for the tourism sector, as it allows the analysis and prediction of tourist movements in tourist destinations.

-Context-aware recommender systems

Context-aware recommender systems become an opportunity to provide personalized and more relevant recommendations that consider variables of the contextual situation where the user develops the activity, be it tourism or any other kind of activity. This system considers contextual information to provide recommendations [46] and categorizes context information into five general categories: individual, space, time, activity, and communication.

The context's elements are temperature, location, activity, lighting, traffic conditions, climate, time of day, week, season, nearby resources, network connectivity, communication bandwidth, and people accompanying the user. Table 4 shows the articles reviewed on this typology of context-aware recommender systems. The variables analysed were a contextual factor, Techniques/algorithm employed, the data source,

Table 4 shows the contextual factor used in this recommender system, such as social variables, multidimensional variables, geolocation, temporality, climate, and emotions. Among the techniques used by this type of recommender systems are those related to supervised and unsupervised algorithms, such as clustering, neural networks, and deep recurrent neural networks. An important element for the configuration of this type of models is the source of the data that must help the training of the model, and therefore the exercises reviewed have built the data collection from internal and external sources.

Table 4. Analysis of research on recommender systems.

Contextual factor	Techniques/algorithm	Dataset	References
Social	Machine learning model	Created subjective	[47]
Multidimensional	Clustering	Gowalla, Weeplace	[27]
Emotion records	Neural Network	Weibo	[48]
	Deep recurrent neural network	NYC Restaurant Rich Dataset	[13]

- Hybrid models Recommender Systems

Hybridizations of two or more techniques in the field of recommender systems are used to improve the accuracy of the recommendations given by the system. This hybridization is conducted within the recommender systems to make up for the limitations of one or another typology or technique used, seeking a complementary way to improve the accuracy of the recommendations given by the system. Table 5 presents the classification of hybrid recommender systems according to the variables Type of main RS, Type of RS to be hybridized with, the purpose of the R.

Table 5. Research on hybrid recommender systems

Type of the main RS	RS hybridized with	Purpose of the RS	References
Collaborative filtering	Location-based	Travel routes	[14]
	Location-based recommender system	Search for information on the internet	[29]
Location-based recommender system	Context-based recommender system	Hybrid Deep Neural Networks for Friend Recommendations	[49]
Multi-criteria-based recommender system	Hybridization in techniques	Multi-criteria recommendation for tourist areas	[50]

From Table 5, hybridization between different recommender system approaches provided a solution to specific needs. The project developed by [37] presented a hybridization between collaborative and content-based filtering, which meets the needs of the user requesting the service in a particular way. The design of hybrid recommender models among its different typologies, using Machine Learning techniques, is a trend that reinforces specific problems in the tourism sector, contributing to the management and transformation into smart destinations.

Nowadays, there are an excellent variety of hybridized techniques for tourism and other sectors. We find that the most hybridized typology is Collaborative Filtering. One of the hybrid forms that can help the solution of specific problems in the tourism sector is through the combination of location-based and context-aware recommender systems since there is a high relevance because it combines characteristic elements of this sector, as proposed in research such as [25].

According to the above specific cases on the use of hybrid recommender systems, it is evident that their features and characteristics contribute to the innovation, development, and accessibility of destinations, as they can improve competitiveness indicators such as strengthening the supply, and destination management, among others [51]. In this sense, the main advantages of recommender systems are that 1) they facilitate the tourist's interaction with the environment and other users, and 2) they provide information about the destination services. These actions developed by users contribute to consolidating data on the tourist compartment, which is helpful for government agencies to make decisions that allow them to propose strategies that help strengthen the destination.

3.3 Configuration of the Hybrid Model to Address Tourism Competitiveness Indicators

The main advantages of the use of recommender systems are that they facilitate the interaction of the tourist with the environment, with other users, plans to make, provide information about the destination, interactive services and this contributes to the consolidation of data from the tourist compartment, which is useful for government agencies to make decisions that allow them to propose strategies that help strengthen the destination. In this way, and with the interaction with this technology, we can contribute to the consolidation of an intelligent tourist destination. Figure 4 shows an architecture of a hybrid recommender system for an intelligent tourist destination.

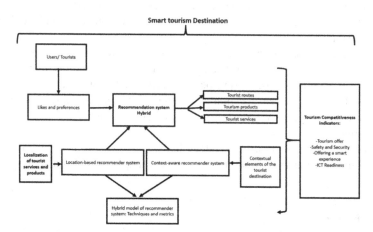

Fig. 4. Architecture of a Hybrid recommender system for a smart destination

Figure 4 presents the architecture of the proposed RS. The system performs the characterization of the tourists' profile based on their tastes and preferences, then this information is sent to the RS, which makes use of the hybridization of techniques so that it can recommend the shortest routes, products, and security services within the tourist destination, which are under the framework of formality before the competent entities.

The proposed model will be trained and evaluated with information from databases related to the registration of service providers, registered with the entity that regulates tourism in the destination, geolocated points and previous valuations of products and services. As a result of the use of the RS and the information recorded in the characterization form, a dataset will be created.

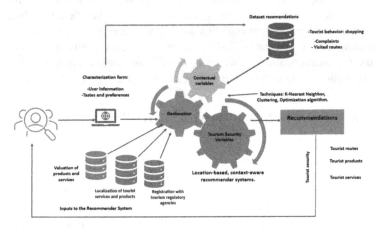

Fig. 5. Hybrid model of recommender system for competitiveness tourism

The model presented in Fig. 5 considers characteristics and functionalities of recommender systems that contribute to innovation, development, and accessibility of destinations, since they can improve competitiveness indicators such as supply and tourism safety in a destination.

The presented model incorporates innovative context-aware and location-based recommender systems that use machine learning techniques and optimisation algorithms to improve the accuracy of delivering personalised and relevant recommendations to tourists based on their current location and context. The recommender system allows tourists to receive suggestions specific to them in real time, increasing their satisfaction and enhancing their tourism experience.

In terms of competitiveness, these systems help to collect data on tourists' preferences and behaviour, allowing tourism service providers to adapt their offers and improve their indicators.

4   Conclusion

Current tourism advisory systems mainly contribute to issues related to destination management and although they contribute to competitiveness indicators, there is still a challenge to design systems that strengthen and address different indicators to strengthen tourism destinations.

To present dynamic tourism recommendations that consider the preferences and tastes of users, it is not enough to implement a single recommendation system model, but it is necessary to resort to the hybridisation of different typologies and techniques in recommendation systems as an alternative that can generate an innovative contribution in the construction of accurate recommendation models.

The presented recommender system model allows the improvement of recommendations in tourism contexts, with innovative elements through the hybridisation of location-based and context-aware models, using machine learning techniques and optimisation algorithms to improve the accuracy in the delivery of recommendations and strengthen competitiveness indicators.

References

1. Gof, G., Cucculelli, M., Masiero, L.: Fostering tourism destination competitiveness in developing countries: the role of sustainability. J. Clean. Prod. **209** (2019). https://doi.org/10.1016/j.jclepro.2018.10.208
2. Crouch, G.I.: Destination competitiveness: an analysis of determinant attributes (2011). https://doi.org/10.1177/0047287510362776
3. Firgo, M., Fritz, O.: Does having the right visitor mix do the job? Applying an econometric shift-share model to regional tourism developments. Ann. Reg. Sci. **58**(3), 469–490 (2017). https://doi.org/10.1007/s00168-016-0803-4
4. World Economic Forum: The Travel & Tourism Competitiveness Report 2019 (2019)
5. World Economic Forum: Travel & Tourism Development Index 2021: Rebuilding for a Sustainable and Resilient Future. Travel & Tourism Development Index 2021: Rebuilding for a Sustainable and Resilient Future (2021). https://www.weforum.org/reports/travel-and-tourism-development-index-2021/in-full/about-the-travel-tourism-development-index/
6. Ghorbani, A., Danaei, A., Zargar, S.M., Hematian, H.: Heliyon designing of smart tourism organization (STO) for tourism management: a case study of tourism organizations of South Khorasan province, Iran. Heliyon **6**, e01850 (2020). https://doi.org/10.1016/j.heliyon.2019.e01850
7. Isinkaye, F.O., Folajimi, Y.O., Ojokoh, B.A.: Recommendation systems: principles, methods and evaluation. Egypt. Informatics J. **16**(3), 261–273 (2015). https://doi.org/10.1016/j.eij.2015.06.005
8. Solano-Barliza, A.: Revisión conceptual de sistemas de recomendación y geolocalización aplicados a la seguridad turística Conceptual review of recommendation and geolocation systems applied to tourism security. J. Comput. Electron. Sci. Theory Appl. **2**(2), 37–43 (2021)
9. del Carmen Rodríguez-Hernández, M., Ilarri, S., Trillo, R., Hermoso, R.: Context-aware recommendations using mobile P2P. In: The 15th International Conference, pp. 82–91, October 2017. https://doi.org/10.1145/3151848.3151856
10. Naser, R.S.: Context aware web service recommender supported by user-based classification, pp. 131–135 (2019)
11. Kargar, M., Lin, Z.: A socially motivating and environmentally friendly tour recommendation framework for tourist groups. Expert Syst. Appl. **180**, 115083 (2021). https://doi.org/10.1016/j.eswa.2021.115083
12. Unger, M., Tuzhilin, A., Livne, A.: Context-aware recommendations based on deep learning context-aware recommendations based on deep, May 2020. https://doi.org/10.1145/3386243
13. Boppana, V., Sandhya, P.: Web crawling based context aware recommender system using optimized deep recurrent neural network. J. Big Data (2021). https://doi.org/10.1186/s40537-021-00534-7

14. Ravi, L., Subramaniyaswamy, V., Vijayakumar, V., Chen, S., Karmel, A., Devarajan, M.: Hybrid location-based recommender system for mobility and travel planning. Mob. Networks Appl. **24**(4), 1226–1239 (2019). https://doi.org/10.1007/s11036-019-01260-4

15. Alrehili, M., Alsubhi, B., Almoghamsi, R., Almutairi, A.-A., Alansari, I.: Tourism mobile application to guide Madinah visitors. In: 2018 1st International Conference on Computer Applications & Information Security (ICCAIS), pp. 1–4, October 2018. https://doi.org/10.1109/CAIS.2018.8442023

16. Shambour, Q.Y., Abu-Shareha, A.A., Abualhaj, M.M.: A hotel recommender system based on multi-criteria collaborative filtering. Inf. Technol. Control, 390–402 (2022). https://doi.org/10.5755/j01.itc.51.2.30701

17. Herzog, D., Laß, C., Wörndl, W.: Tourrec - a tourist trip recommender system for individuals and groups. In: RecSys 2018 - 12th ACM Conference on Recommender Systems, pp. 496–497 (2018). https://doi.org/10.1145/3240323.3241612

18. Al-Ghobari, M., Muneer, A., Fati, S.M.: Location-aware personalized traveler recommender system (lapta) using collaborative filtering KNN. Comput. Mater. Contin. **69**(2), 1553–1570 (2021). https://doi.org/10.32604/cmc.2021.016348

19. Alhijawi, B., Kilani, Y.: A collaborative filtering recommender system using genetic algorithm. Inf. Process. Manag. **57**(6), 102310 (2020). https://doi.org/10.1016/j.ipm.2020.102310

20. Al Fararni, K., Nafis, F., Aghoutane, B., Yahyaouy, A., Riffi, J., Sabri, A.: Hybrid recommender system for tourism based on big data and AI: a conceptual framework. Big Data Min. Anal. **4**(1), 47–55 (2021). https://doi.org/10.26599/BDMA.2020.9020015

21. Lavanya, R., Khokle, T., Maity, A.: Review on hybrid recommender system for mobile devices. In: Hemanth, D., Vadivu, G., Sangeetha, M., Balas, V. (eds.) Artificial Intelligence Techniques for Advanced Computing Applications. LNNS, vol. 130, pp. 477–486. Springer, Singapore (2021). https://doi.org/10.1007/978-981-15-5329-5_44

22. Ojagh, S., Malek, M.R., Saeedi, S., Liang, S.: A location-based orientation-aware recommender system using IoT smart devices and social networks. Futur. Gener. Comput. Syst. **108**, 97–118 (2020). https://doi.org/10.1016/j.future.2020.02.041

23. Bahulikar, S., Upadhye, V., Patil, T., Kulkarni, B., Patil, D.: Airline recommendations using a hybrid and location based approach. IEEE Access, 972–977 (2017)

24. Huang, Z., Lin, X., Liu, H., Zhang, B., Chen, Y., Tang, Y.: Deep representation learning for location-based recommendation. IEEE Access **7**(3), 648–658 (2020)

25. Artemenko, O., Pasichnyk, V., Kunanec, N.: E-tourism mobile location-based hybrid recommender system with context evaluation. In: 2019 IEEE 14th International Scientific and Technical Conference on Computer Sciences and Information Technologies (CSIT), pp. 114–118, October 2019. https://doi.org/10.1109/STC-CSIT.2019.8929775

26. Gao, K., et al.: Exploiting location-based context for POI recommendation when traveling to a new region. IEEE Access **8**, 52404–52412 (2020). https://doi.org/10.1109/ACCESS.2020.2980982

27. Baral, R., Iyengar, S.S., Zhu, X., Li, T., Sniatala, P.: HiRecS: a hierarchical contextual location recommendation system. IEEE Access **6**(5), 1020–1037 (2019)

28. Amirat, H., Fournier-Viger, P.: Recommendation in LBSN. IEEE Access (2018)

29. Suguna, R., Sathishkumar, P., Deepa, S.: User location and collaborative based recommender system using Naive Bayes classifier and UIR matrix. IEEE Access, 0–4 (2020)

30. Abu-Issa, A., et al.: A smart city mobile application for multitype, proactive, and context-aware recommender system (2020)

31. Abbasi-Moud, Z., Hosseinabadi, S., Kelarestaghi, M., Eshghi, F.: CAFOB: context-aware fuzzy-ontology-based tourism recommendation system. Expert Syst. Appl. **199**, 116877 (2022). https://doi.org/10.1016/j.eswa.2022.116877

32. Ko, H., Lee, S., Park, Y., Choi, A.: A survey of recommendation systems: recommendation. Electronics **11**(141), 1–18 (2022)
33. Hosseini, S., Yin, H., Zhou, X., Sadiq, S., Kangavari, M.R., Cheung, N.M.: Leveraging multi-aspect time-related influence in location recommendation. World Wide Web **22**, 1001–1028 (2019)
34. Fernández-García, A.J., Rodriguez-Echeverria, R., Carlos, J., Perianez, J., Gutiérrez, J.D.: A hybrid multidimensional recommender system for radio programs. Expert Syst. Appl. **198**, 116706 (2022). https://doi.org/10.1016/j.eswa.2022.116706
35. Wayan, N., Yuni, P., Permanasari, A.E., Hidayah, I., Zulfa, M.I.: Collaborative and content-based filtering hybrid method on tourism recommender system to promote less explored areas. Int. J. Appl. Eng. Technol. **4**(2), 59–65 (2022)
36. Maru'ao, M.: Tourism recommender system using hybrid multi- criteria approach tourism recommender system using hybrid multi-criteria approach. IOP Conf. Ser. Earth Environ. Sci. **729** (2021). https://doi.org/10.1088/1755-1315/729/1/012118
37. Wayan, N., Yuni, P.: Designing a tourism recommendation system using a hybrid method (Collaborative Filtering and Content-Based Filtering), pp. 298–305 (2021)
38. Kolahkaj, M., Harounabadi, A., Nikravanshalmani, A., Chinipardaz, R.: A hybrid context-aware approach for e-tourism package recommendation based on asymmetric similarity measurement and sequential pattern mining. Electron. Commer. Res. Appl. **42**, 100978 (2020). https://doi.org/10.1016/j.elerap.2020.100978
39. Rehman, F., Khalid, O., Madani, S.: A Comparative Study of Location Based Recommendation Systems (2017)
40. Yochum, P., Chang, L., Gu, T., Zhu, M.: Linked open data in location-based recommendation system on tourism domain: a survey. IEEE Access, 16409–16439 (2020)
41. Aliannejadi, M., Crestani, F.: 1 Personalized context-aware point of interest recommendation. ACM Trans. Inf. Syst. **1**(1), 1–29 (2017)
42. Chen, J., Zhang, W., Zhang, P., Ying, P., Niu, K., Zou, M.: Exploiting spatial and temporal for point of interest recommendation. Complexity **2018** (2018)
43. Cui, G., Luo, J., Wang, X.: Personalized travel route recommendation using collaborative filtering based on GPS trajectories. Int. J. Digit. Earth **8947**, 284–307 (2018). https://doi.org/10.1080/17538947.2017.1326535
44. Ding, R., Chen, Z.: RecNet: a deep neural network for personalized POI recommendation in location-based social networks. Int. J. Geogr. Inf. Sci. **00**(00), 1–18 (2018). https://doi.org/10.1080/13658816.2018.1447671
45. Rios, C., Schiaffino, S., Godoy, D.: A study of neighbour selection strategies for POI recommendation in LBSNs. J. Inf. Sci., 1–16 (2018). https://doi.org/10.1177/016555151876 1000
46. Villegas, N.M., Sánchez, C., Díaz-cely, J., Tamura, G.: Knowledge-base d systems characterizing context-aware recommender systems: a systematic literature review. Knowl.-Based Syst. **140**, 173–200 (2018). https://doi.org/10.1016/j.knosys.2017.11.003
47. Lasmar, E.L., De Paula, F.O., Rosa, R.L., Abrahão, J.I., Rodríguez, D.Z., Member, S.: RsRS: ridesharing recommendation system based on social networks to improve the user's QoE, 1–13 (2019). https://doi.org/10.1109/TITS.2019.2945793
48. Li, G., et al.: Group-based recurrent neural networks for POI recommendation **1**(1) (2020)
49. Wang, S., Bhuiyan, Z.A., Peng, H.A.O., Du, B.: Hybrid deep neural networks for friend recommendations in edge computing environment, pp. 10693–10706 (2020)

50. Forouzandeh, S., Rostami, M., Berahmand, K.: A hybrid method for recommendation systems based on tourism with an evolutionary algorithm and Topsis model. Fuzzy Inf. Eng. **14**(1), 26–50 (2022). https://doi.org/10.1080/16168658.2021.2019430
51. Liu, Y., et al.: Interaction-enhanced and time-aware graph convolutional network for successive point-of-interest recommendation in traveling enterprises. IEEE Trans. Ind. Informatics **19**(1), 635–643 (2023)

Machine Learning and Artificial Neural Networks

Insect Detection on High-Resolution Images Using Deep Learning

Mateusz Choiński[1]([✉]), Marcin Zegarek[2], Zuzanna Hałat[2], Tomasz Borowik[2],
Jenna Kohles[3], Melina Dietzer[3], Katrine Eldegard[4], Reed April McKay[4],
Sarah E. Johns[4], and Ireneusz Ruczyński[2]

[1] Faculty of Computer Science, Bialystok University of Technology, Bialystok, Poland
mateusz.choinski100@gmail.com

[2] Mammal Research Institute Polish Academy of Sciences, Stoczek 1, 17-230 Białowieża, Poland

[3] Max Planck Institute of Animal Behavior, Am Obstberg 1, 78315 Radolfzell, Germany

[4] Faculty of Environmental Sciences and Natural Resource Management, Norwegian University of Life Sciences, 1432 Ås, Norway

Abstract. Dramatic regional or even global decline in insect abundance has emerged as a critical concern. Effective but simple methods are needed for monitoring changes in insect abundance. Most monitoring methods are labor-intensive and selective. Recently camera traps were described as a tool to monitor changes in the nocturnal and seasonal activity of flying insects. However, visually counting the insects on the images is time-consuming and dramatically limits the usefulness of this method. We have developed a method to use deep learning for the automatic detection of insects in photos. The method incorporates artificial neural networks with representation learning to automatically discover the representations needed for feature detection or classification from raw data. The resulting counts were highly accurate, respectively. We compared our automatic results carried out with precision and recall indicators at the levels of 0.819 and 0.826 with visual counts of insects on photos from Poland, Panama, Germany, and Norway, and correlations varied between 0.73 and 0.93. This indicates that automatic counting can be successfully used to monitor nocturnal insect activity. However, rain and the presence of objects such as plants in the photos may substantially decrease the correctness of insect identification. The method we present here will allow researchers to monitor insects, a crucial indicator of ecosystem health and an important resource for many animals at higher trophic levels, and to compare standardized counts across habitats, countries, and seasons.

Keywords: Computer Vision · Convolution Neural Networks · Faster R-CNN · Object detection · Wildlife · Insects

K. Saeed et al. (Eds.): CISIM 2023, LNCS 14164, pp. 225–239, 2023.
https://doi.org/10.1007/978-3-031-42823-4_17

1 Introduction

1.1 A Subsection Sample

In recent years, evidence for a dramatic regional or even global decline in insect abundance has emerged as a critical concern [1]. Insect populations are challenging to study, and most monitoring methods are labor-intensive and selective [2, 3]. However, methods using cameras and other sensors to effectively, continuously, and noninvasively describe insect abundance in space and time are being developed [3–6]. Camera trap transects, for example, can function as a tool to monitor temporal and spatial changes in the nightly and seasonal activity of nocturnal flying insects, including differences between habitats and the influence of environmental conditions [5]. The cameras can be programmed to take flash photos at set time intervals and insects can be counted as white reflections against a dark sky. This method of monitoring flying insects is simple to implement, but time-consuming when insects in photos must be counted visually [5]. The development of deep learning tools designed for object detection provides new solutions which may be used for the automation of insect counting in photos [4].

Deep learning is a machine learning method based on artificial neural networks with representation learning [7], which is a set of techniques that allows a system to automatically discover the representations needed for feature detection or classification from raw data. Deep learning requires large amounts of computational power for processing high-resolution images [8].

1.2 Usage of Deep Learning in Camera Traps and Insects Detection

Some deep learning models have previously been used to process camera trap images. The Megadetector model was successfully developed for the task of detecting animals in various environments and detecting multiple species [9]. However, this model could not detect insects in our images because of the large size difference between animals in camera traps and insects in our images.

There were also previous attempts to use Deep Learning for the purpose of insect detection in images. One of the first approaches was described in *A Vision-Based Counting and Recognition System for Flying Insects in Intelligent Agriculture* [10]. The author's approach was to use the YOLO network for the detection of insects in insect traps and then SVM for the classification of species. The results achieved were 92.5% of mAP using 7 insect classes. Another approach is described in *Remote insects trap monitoring system using deep learning framework and IoT* [11]. The authors used Faster RCNN neural network architecture. The resolution of images processed with their method was small (640px × 480px) and the observations on their images were large and clearly visible relative to the image size. With this method they prioritized species classification of insects. The researchers reached 88.79% of mAP and 96.08% accuracy for 14 insect species. Yet another approach was presented in *Application of Deep Learning in Integrated Pest Management: A Real-Time System for Detection and Diagnosis of Oilseed Rape Pests* [12]. The researchers used the SSD neural network architecture for real-time detection and classification of the insects placed on plants. The results of detection reached 77.1% of the mAP score using 12 insect species.

These three methods were not suitable for detecting insects in our camera trap images for several reasons. The images used in these studies contained much larger insects relative to the image size, which makes it easier to detect and classify them. Additionally, the images with insects were taken within a closed camera trap, or of an insect on a plant. Insects flying in the open air present different detection challenges. The camera trapping methods themselves are also more invasive and require a more complicated set-up reducing their feasibility for field ecologists studying natural insect abundance and distribution. Most popular deep learning models, in fact, are not tuned to detect small objects due in part to their internal structure and usage of convolution layers. Small objects are detected by the first layers of the network, and their features disappear as network depth increases. To overcome this issue, a deep learning model must be trained specifically for detecting small objects and optimized for this problem (i.e., using the Feature Pyramid Network (FPN) [13] backbone for the encoder network).

1.3 The Paper Contribution

In this paper, we present a method of insect detection and counting developed and tested with camera trap photos collected in Białowieża Forest, Poland for which visual counts were already available [5]. The novel deep learning-based method uses state-of-the-art machine learning methods to detect and count insects. We subsequently evaluated the accuracy of the algorithm's ability to correctly identify and count insects using three additional annotated datasets of insect monitoring in Panama, Germany, and Norway, spanning temperate and tropical regions and various habitat types.

These contributions have important implications for ecological research, allowing for more efficient and cost-effective monitoring of insect populations. Additionally, our method can be easily scaled to larger areas and populations, making it a valuable tool for insect conservation efforts.

2 Materials and Methods

2.1 Dataset Acquisition

Monitoring of insects with camera transects was conducted in Poland [5], Germany, Norway, and Panama in the years 2016–2021. Camera lenses were directed toward the sky and took photos every 1–5 min, usually from dusk to dawn. Each image had a resolution of 4608×2592 pixels or 12 megapixels.

For the training setup, we used 265 images from Poland taken under different weather conditions (rain, dust, fog, clear and cloudy skies, or strong wind), both with and without the presence of leaves and tree branches in the frame, and covering all parts of the night (including dusk and dawn). Insects appearing in images were visually annotated by a biologist from the Mammal Research Institute, Polish Academy of Sciences. We received the data with annotations in COCO (Common Objects in Context) format [14]. The number of insects on images ranged from 0 to 307, with a mean of 31.43 insects per image (Fig. 1). See examples of images containing trees and leaves or with a clear sky (Fig. 2).

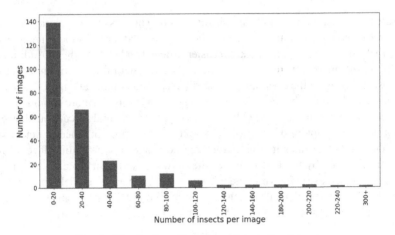

Fig. 1. Distribution of insect numbers in the dataset.

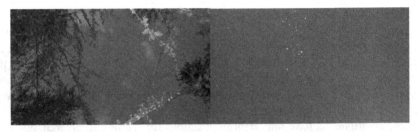

Fig. 2. Examples of images with trees in the background and with a clear sky.

Some images contained objects that can cause difficulties for an automated counting algorithm, such as raindrops, dust, or seeds. A few images also contained dried water droplets on the lens, which could be misidentified as insects (Fig. 3). These non-insect elements can affect the performance of the model.

Fig. 3. Examples of stains or dust/pollen on the lens.

Additionally, insects appeared in different shapes and sizes in the images. Most of this variation was caused by species identity, flight phase, and the distance between an insect and the camera (Figs. 4 and 5).

Fig. 4. Examples of insects detected in images.

Fig. 5. Example of the potential size difference between two insects on the same image.

2.2 Data Processing

Creating Training and Testing Datasets

We split our dataset images into two parts, the first for training and validation of the model, and the second for testing the performance and accuracy of the model. The training and validation part contained 85% of the images in the dataset, while the remaining 15% of images were reserved for the testing part. The dataset was split visually, not randomly, to ensure that both parts contained the same proportion of specific types of images, e.g., night versus dusk images and small versus large numbers of insects (>100) contained within the same image. We chose to split the images this way due to the large amounts of variation between images in the dataset.

Subdividing Images

Individual images were subdivided for processing and feature assessment to avoid the problem of small objects vanishing with neural networks. Each input image was split into 25 separate sub-images (grid of 5 × 5) with 10% overlap (Fig. 6). After testing several different splitting methods, a split into 25 sub-images gave the best results for the applied neural network architecture. In the subsequent steps, each sub-image was treated as a separate image for training, validation, and testing. We removed sub-images without insects.

Data Augmentation

Data augmentation introduces some small changes to the processed image, each time it goes through the neural network. Those changes may include random shearing, resizing, cropping, color modification, etc. We used data augmentation to increase the training dataset's diversity and improve trained model generalization capabilities.

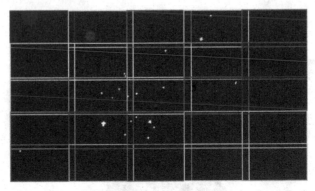

Fig. 6. An example image is split into sub-images, using the grid size 5 × 5. Each color represents a single sub-image. Images overlap by 10%.

The augmentation process was applied during the training and validation phases. In the training phase, we randomly applied five transformations to each training image:

- resizing the image (to 648px × 648px)
- random vertical and horizontal image mirror reflections
- changing brightness and contrast
- random image shifts
- random image scaling

To improve inference results we used Test Time Augmentation (TTA) [21], the technique of making multiple predictions on the same image but with little transformation for each predicted image. In our case, those transformations consisted of different scaling of the images and vertical flips.

2.3 Deep Learning Architecture

The architecture we chose was the Faster R-CNN [15] with the Feature Pyramid Network (FPN) [13] backbone. The architecture was selected because it performs best for the challenge of detecting small objects in images. Other architectures considered were YOLOv4 [19] and SSD [18]. For our project, the most important goal was to achieve highest possible accuracy in small objects detection. Here the YOLOv4 and SSD networks performed worse in accuracy metrics compared to the Faster RCNN, despite the fact that they have shorter inference times. If we had planned to deploy our models on edge devices, the most appropriate architecture would likely have been YOLOv4 or SSD.

The Faster RCNN [15] architecture with the FPN [13] backbone allows the network to preserve features from small as well as large objects because the FPN backbone network extracts the feature maps from the input image at different scales (Fig. 7). This feature of the FPN was well-suited to our datasets because the size of the insects in source images varied greatly. The features extracted by the FPN network were then used by the Faster R-CNN network.

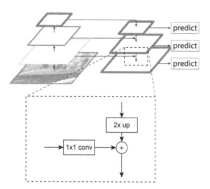

Fig. 7. The FPN network simplified schema. The building block illustrates the lateral connection and the top-down pathway merged by addition. Published with author permission [10].

We decided to use Faster R-CNN [15] because of its versatility and its capacity to detect high numbers of objects relative to other architectures [20]. At the moment of release (2016), this architecture (Faster R-CNN + RPN) achieves state-of-the-art single model results on the COCO detection benchmark.

2.4 Model Training and Validation Process

We prepared the Python script for model training which was parameterized to run multiple tests in the hyperparameter tuning process. To speed up the training process we used pre-trained weights for the network, called Transfer Learning [16]. This allows us to reduce the training time and increase model generalization capabilities despite using a small training dataset to train the model from scratch. In the hyperparameter tuning process, we tuned the most relevant parameters for the Faster R-CNN architecture. The parameters we tuned for the network were:

- Batch per image size - number of Region of Interests (ROI) heads for each image
- Batch size - how many images are in a single training batch
- Anchor sizes - the sizes of the anchors for ROI
- Learning rate
- Learning rate steps - at which training iteration will learning rate be decreased according to applied policy
- Training iterations number - number of training iterations for model

We treated grid size used for subsetting images as a parameter that should be tuned. For the first set of experiments, we used a grid-search approach for hyperparameter tuning to build the intuition (Table 1). After finishing the grid-search analysis, we ran the model training based on intuition gained from the grid-search results and the experience. The final training was run for 10000 iterations. The single iteration flowchart is presented in Fig. 8.

The validation of the model was done using similar steps, the only difference was that the augmentation did not contain random modifications to the image. The flowchart for image prediction using the Deep Learning model is presented in Fig. 9.

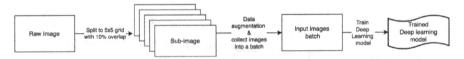

Fig. 8. Single interaction of preprocessing image and training Deep Learning model.

Fig. 9. Prediction of the single image using Deep Learning – flowchart.

Metrics

For evaluating the performance and accuracy of the trained model, we used Recall, Precision, and F1 Score (Powers 2007). In our implementation, we calculated Recall and Precision globally. This means that the calculation was done by taking all True Positives, False Negatives, and False Positives from all images, summing them up, and then calculating the metrics from those sums. Calculating the metrics per image and average would strongly bias the results because of the differences between insect numbers on the images. Both precision and recall were equally important for evaluating the performance of the model – to detect as many insects as possible while remaining accurate in detecting insects and discriminating them from non-insect elements.

2.5 Software and Hardware Used During Experiments

We used the implementation of the Faster R-CNN network from the Detectron2 [17]. This runs on Python 3.8.5, Nvidia CUDA 10.1, Pytorch 1.4.0, and Torchvision 0.5.0. The experiments were run on a machine with a single i7 CPU 16 GB of RAM and Nvidia GTX 1080Ti GPU. This setup allows for training the model in the timespan of 8 h. The full inference time for a single image was 1.5 s considering that the single image requires the prediction of 25 sub-images.

2.6 Testing of the Model

We used four datasets of photos collected from four countries – Poland, Germany, Panama, and Norway – to validate our automated counting with visual counting. First, for the dataset from Poland (n = 61,758), we compared the effect of varying values of the recall level (0.90, 0.93, 0.95, 0.97, 0.98) on similarities between visual and automatic counting. The highest similarity was observed on recall levels 0.95 and 0.97, so for further validation of the model we used recall on the level 0.95. Photos for testing were arbitrarily selected but included photos with and without insects, with different weather conditions, and in different habitats.

3   Results

The best-trained model had a precision value of 0.819, a recall value of 0.826, and an F1 Score of 0.822 (Table 1) achieved on a test dataset. Precision and Recall are at a comparable level which means that the trained model is not biased toward precision or recall and is balanced between the number of detected insects and the accuracy of the prediction. After the 7000th iteration of training, training loss strongly plateaus (Fig. 10), which means the model learned everything that it could from the current training configuration.

Table 1. Final model metrics results on a test set.

Precision	0.819
Recall	0.826
F1 Score	0.822

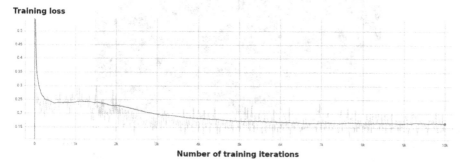

Fig. 10. Training loss plot for the final model training process.

3.1   Correct Predictions

The trained model performed best on pictures with a clear sky and several insects (Fig. 11). On such images, precision and recall are nearly 1.0, meaning almost all insects were detected with 100% accuracy. Predictions for images containing a large number of insects (>100 insects) but still clear sky were slightly lower (between 0.90–0.98 of F1-Score) (Fig. 12). The model made few false negatives (insects present in photos but were undetected by the algorithm) and few false positives (the algorithm made insect detections where insects were not actually present) indicating that the trained model performed well.

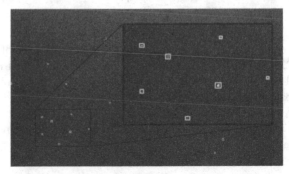

Fig. 11. Example of correct predictions for a clear sky and small amounts of insects. Green boxes are correct predictions. The blue box represents zoomed-in areas. Recall: 1.0, Precision: 1.0, F1 Score: 1.0 on both images. (Color figure online)

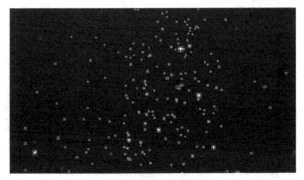

Fig. 12. A large number of insects with a clear background. Green boxes are correct predictions, blue boxes are false positives (the model incorrectly predicts insects), and red boxes are not detected insects. Recall: 0.98, Precision: 0.99, F1 Score: 0.98. (Color figure online)

3.2 Incorrect Predictions

Images which decreased the accuracy and precision of the model were those that contained high amounts of non-insect objects, i.e., flying seeds, raindrops, lens smudges (Fig. 13). Figure 13 represents an extreme and rare case when the model was unable to detect any insects in the image because of their small size compared to the sizes of non-insect objects – raindrops and the water smudges on the lens. Another type of non-insect object that decreased model accuracy and precision was trees in the background. Occasionally buds or branches were incorrectly classified as insects (Fig. 14).

Lastly, the model can struggle to detect multiple insects when they are close to each other or overlapping in the image. In such a situation, the algorithm typically detected all clustered insects as a single insect (Fig. 15).

Fig. 13. Image contaminated with raindrops. No insects were correctly detected in the image. Blue boxes are false positives (the model incorrectly predicts insects), and red boxes are insects not detected. Recall: 0.0, Precision: 0.0, F1 Score: 0.0. (Color figure online)

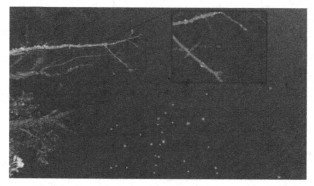

Fig. 14. Image with tree branches in the background. One tree bud was incorrectly detected as an insect. Recall: 1.0, Precision: 0.82, F1 Score: 0.90. (Color figure online)

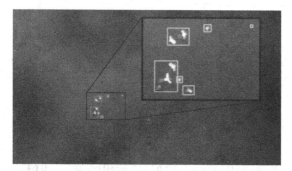

Fig. 15. A group of adjacent insects was detected as a single insect. Recall: 0.83, Precision: 0.90, F1 Score: 0.87.

3.3 Validation of the Automatic Counting

We calculated correlations between visual and automated counting at different recall levels in models describing the relationship between ambient temperature and insect abundance in different habitats of Białowieża Forest [5]. The highest correlations between visual and automated counting were observed at recall levels of 0.95 and 0.97 (Fig. 16, Table 2). In habitats with a high number of insects (Lake and Wetland), the correlation between visual and automatic counting was higher than when the insect number was low (Forest and Open Habit).

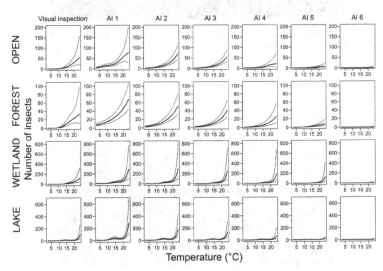

Fig. 16. Relationship between the ambient temperature and the number of insects on photos counted visually (data from Białowieża Forest [5]) and by AI at a recall level AI1- 0.8, AI2 – 0.9, AI3 – 0.93, A4 – 0.95, A5 – 0.97, A6 – 0.99 in different habitats (Blue lines represent 95% confidence interval).

Table 2. Correlation between the number of insects counted visually (data from Białowieża Forest, [5]) and by AI at the different recall levels (0.8, 0.9, 0.93, 0.95, 0.97, 0.99) in Open habitat (O), Forest (F), Wetlands (W), Lake (L).

Sensitivity						
Habitat	0.8	0.9	0.93	0.95	0.97	0.99
O	0.54	0.62	0.66	0.69	0.67	0.12
F	0.52	0.58	0.62	0.65	0.64	0.08
W	0.58	0.66	0.70	0.74	0.74	0.19
L	0.77	0.80	0.81	0.83	0.85	0.45

Comparisons of insect numbers detected during visual and automated counting indicated high positive correlations for the datasets from Germany (N = 2090, Spearman Rank Correlation 0.7309), Panama (N = 1177, Spearman Rank Correlation 0.8000), and Poland (N = 61758 Spearman Rank Correlation 0.74). The dataset from Norway indicates an even higher correlation (N = 185, Spearman Rank Correlation 0.93).

4 Discussion and Conclusions

The results of the developed models and their validation indicate that Machine Learning for the automation of counting insects is efficient and can be used for counting nocturnal flying insects in camera trap photos, especially when large data sets make visual counting time-consuming.

4.1 Comparison to Other State-of-the-Art Research Results

The performance of the model developed in our research, as evaluated on the test set, yielded an F1 Score of 0.822, which is comparable to the outcomes achieved in related studies [10–12]. Nonetheless, it should be noted that our research objectives differ somewhat from those of prior work. Specifically, our study focused on processing images with high resolution that contain a large number of insects. In addition, our model was designed to detect insects of varying sizes.

Our results demonstrate that our model is capable of accurately detecting insects within images, even when the insects differ considerably in size. These findings suggest that our approach holds potential for a range of applications, particularly those in which the ability to rapidly and accurately detect insects in high-resolution images is essential. However, further research is needed to assess the effectiveness of our model across diverse insect species and in varied environmental conditions.

4.2 Challenges in Annotating Data for Model Training

The most significant challenge in model training was data annotations. The dataset was challenging to annotate due to the massive number of objects within a single image. The current version is designed to work on a server to process the collected data from the camera traps on high computationally capable machines. Using lighter models SSD [18] or YOLO [19] probably will open the possibility to run insect detection on edge devices (i.e. smart camera traps) directly in the forest.

4.3 Limitations and Considerations for Increasing Model Accuracy and Precision

To increase the accuracy and precision of insect detection and counting, it is necessary to take into account the method's limitations. Weather conditions and the presence of leaves or branches in photos substantially decrease the accuracy of insect identification, and the model generates errors connected with the misclassification of insects and non-insect objects. Excluding photos from nights with rain is necessary as well as controlling stands with the presence of leaves or branches on photos. Additionally, validation of automatic counting with visual counting on a limited dataset is recommended to determine error and uncertainty levels specific to each unique dataset. The model allows for adjusting the recall level which can be helpful if the researcher prefers a more or less conservative approach (e.g. less misclassified insects but fewer detected or otherwise). Our tests with images taken in different geographical regions indicate that the methods and algorithms can be applied widely, despite climatic differences.

4.4 Validation of Automatic Counting

The highest correlation between visual and automatic counting on the dataset from Białowieża Forest was at recall levels of 0.95 and 0.97, and the correlation was very low at 0.99. The model did not identify many insects at such a high recall level. This indicates that selecting the correct recall level is crucial for accurate results. It is unknown if there are differences in response to the recall level between regions. However, the high correlation between visual and automatic counting at the recall level of 0.95 in Poland, Germany, and Panama indicates that this value can be used in studies across different geographic regions. Our data also showed that the correlation between values from visual and automatic counting was higher in habitats with more detected insects compared to habitats with fewer detected insects [5].

4.5 Applicability and Potential of the Algorithm for Large-Scale Insect Monitoring

In conclusion, the developed models and their validation indicate that machine learning for the automation of counting insects is effective. Our algorithm paves the way for large-scale non-invasive insect monitoring to be carried out and analyzed in an efficient and cost-effective way. In light of the rapidly increasing changes in climate and landscape structure and the correlated declines in insect abundance, a camera transect method [5] paired with automated insect counting could prove highly informative regarding changes in flying nocturnal insects across landscapes, at various temporal and spatial scales, from minutes to years, and from local to continental scales.

Acknowledgment. We thank Dina Dechmann for her critical comments and language corrections. This work was funded by the Polish National Science Centre Grant DEC-2013/10/E/NZ8/00725.

5. References

1. Benton, T.G., Bryant, D.M., Cole, L., Crick, H.Q.P.: Linking agricultural practice to insect and bird populations: a historical study over three decades: farming, insect and bird populations. J. Appl. Ecol. **39**(4), 673–687 (2002). https://doi.org/10.1046/j.1365-2664.2002.00745.x
2. Kunz, H.T.: Methods of assessing the availability of prey to insectivirous bats. In: Kunz, H.T., (ed.), Ecological and Behavioral Methods for the Study of Bats, pp. 191–210. Smithsonian Institution Press, Washington, D.C.; London (1990)
3. Hausmann, A., et al.: Toward a standardized quantitative and qualitative insect monitoring scheme. Ecol. Evol. **10**, 4009–4020 (2020). https://doi.org/10.1002/ece3.6166

4. Høye, T.T., Arje, J., Bjerge, K., Hansen, O.L.P., Iosifidis, A.,Leese, F., et al.: Deep learning and computer vision will transform entomology. Proc. Natl. Acad. Sci. **118**(2), e2002545117 (2021) https://doi.org/10.1073/pnas.2002545117

5. Ruczyński, I., Hałat, Z., Zegarek, M., Borowik, T., Dechmann, D.K.N.: Camera transects as a method to monitor high temporal and spatial ephemerality of flying nocturnal insects. Methods Ecol. Evol. **11**, 294–302 (2020). https://doi.org/10.1111/2041-210X.13339

6. van Klink, R., August, T., Bas, Y., et al.: Emerging technologies revolutionise insect ecology and monitoring. Trends Ecol. Evol. **37**(10), 872–885 (2022). https://doi.org/10.1016/j.tree.2022.06.001

7. Bengio, Y., Courville, A., Vincent, P.: Representation learning: a review and new perspectives. IEEE Trans. Pattern Anal. Mach. Intell. **35**, 1798–1828 (2013) https://doi.org/10.1109/TPAMI.2013.50

8. Desislavov, R., Martínez-Plumed, F., Hernández-Orallo, J.: Compute and Energy Consumption Trends in Deep Learning Inference (2021) (_eprint: 2109.05472)

9. Beery, S., Morris, D., Yang, S., Simon, M., Norouzzadeh, A., Joshi, N.: Efficient pipeline for automating species ID in new camera trap projects. Biodiver. Inform. Sci. Stand. **3**, e37222 (2019). https://doi.org/10.3897/biss.3.37222

10. Zhong, Y., Gao, J., Lei, Q., Zhou, Y.: A vision-based counting and recognition system for flying insects in intelligent agriculture. Sensors (Basel) **18**(5), 1489 (2018). https://doi.org/10.3390/s18051489.PMID:29747429;PMCID:PMC5982143

11. Ramalingam, B., Mohan, R.E., Pookkuttath, S., et al.: Remote Insects Trap Monitoring System Using Deep Learning Framework and IoT. Sensors (Basel). 2020 Sep 15 **20**(18), 5280. https://doi.org/10.3390/s20185280. PMID: 32942750; PMCID: PMC7571233

12. He, Y., et al.: Application of deep learning in integrated pest management: a real-time system for detection and diagnosis of oilseed rape pests. Mob. Inf. Syst. 4570808, 1–4570808:14 (2019)

13. Lin, T.Y, et al.: Feature pyramid networks for object detection. In: 2017 IEEE Conference on Computer Vision and Pattern Recognition (CVPR), pp. 936–944. Honolulu, HI, USA (2017). https://doi.org/10.1109/CVPR.2017.106

14. Lin, T.Y., et al.: Microsoft COCO: Common Objects in Context. European Conference on Computer Vision (2014)

15. Ren, Shaoqing, He, Kaiming, Girshick, Ross, Sun, Jian: Faster R-CNN: towards real-time object detection with region proposal networks. IEEE Trans. Pattern Anal. Mach. Intell. **39**(6), 1137–1149 (2017). https://doi.org/10.1109/TPAMI.2016.2577031

16. Zhuang, F., et al.: A comprehensive survey on transfer learning. Proc. IEEE **109**(1), 43–76 (2021). https://doi.org/10.1109/JPROC.2020.3004555

17. Facebook AI Research. Detectron2. GitHub (2019). https://github.com/facebookresearch/detectron2. Accessed 15 May 2023

18. Liu, W., et al.: SSD: single shot multibox detector. In: Computer Vision–ECCV 2016: 14th European Conference, Amsterdam, The Netherlands, October 11–14, 2016, Proceedings, Part I 14, pp. 21–37. Springer International Publishing (2016)

19. Bochkovskiy, A., Wang, C., Liao, H.M.: YOLOv4: Optimal Speed and Accuracy of Object Detection. ArXiv abs/2004.10934 (2020)

20. Groener, A.M., Gary, C., Mark, D.P.: A comparison of deep learning object detection models for satellite imagery. In: 2019 IEEE Applied Imagery Pattern Recognition Workshop (AIPR), pp. 1–10 (2019)

21. Shanmugam, D., Blalock, D.W., Balakrishnan, G., Guttag, J.V.: When and Why Test-Time Augmentation Works. arXiv preprint arXiv:2011.11156 (2020)

Grading Diabetic Retinopathy Using Transfer Learning-Based Convolutional Neural Networks

José Escorcia-Gutierrez[1](✉) [iD], Jose Cuello[2] [iD], Margarita Gamarra[3] [iD],
Pere Romero-Aroca[4] [iD], Eduardo Caicedo[5] [iD], Aida Valls[6] [iD], and Domenec Puig[6] [iD]

[1] Department of Computational Science and Electronic, Corporación Universitaria de la Costa,
CUC, 080001 Barranquilla, Colombia
jescorci56@cuc.edu.co
[2] Electronic and Telecommunications Engineering Program, Universidad Autónoma del Caribe,
080001 Barranquilla, Colombia
[3] Department of System Engineering, Universidad del Norte, 080001 Barranquilla, Colombia
[4] Ophthalmology Service, Universitari Hospital Sant Joan, Institut de Investigacio Sanitaria
Pere Virgili [IISPV], 43204 Reus, Spain
[5] School of Electrical and Electronic Engineering, Universidad del Valle, 760032 Cali, Colombia
[6] Departament d'Enginyeria Informàtica i Matemàtiques, Escola Tècnica Superior
d'Enginyeria, Universitat Rovira i Virgili, 43007 Tarragona, Spain

Abstract. Diabetic Retinopathy (DR) is a disease that affect the retina, consequence of a diabetes complication. An accurate an on time diagnosis could delay
severe damage in the eye or vision loss. Currently, the diagnosis is supported by
a retinography and visual evaluation by a trained clinician. However, retinography evaluation is a difficult task due to differences in contrast, brightness and
the presence of artifacts. In this work we propose a convolutional neural network
(CNN) model to detect and grading DR to support the diagnosis from a fundus
image. Moreover, we used the transfer learning technique to reuse the first layers
from deep neural networks previously trained. We carried out experiments using
different convolutional architectures and their performance for DR grading was
evaluated on the APTOS database. The VGG-16 was the architecture with higher
results, overcoming the other networks and other related works. The best experimentation we obtained reached an accuracy value of 83.52% for DR grading
tasks. Experimental results show that the CNN based transfer learning achieve
high performance taking the knowledge learning from pretrained network and
saving computational time in the training process, which turns out suitable for
small dataset as DR medical images.

Keywords: convolutional neural network · Deep learning · Diabetic
retinopathy · Image recognition · Retinal imaging · Transfer learning

1 Introduction

Diabetes Mellitus is a disease with a high affectation for patients and it is a major concern
among the clinicians and medical field. Diabetes is a chronic disease that occurs when
the pancreas does not produce enough insulin, or the body cannot use the insulin it

K. Saeed et al. (Eds.): CISIM 2023, LNCS 14164, pp. 240–252, 2023.
https://doi.org/10.1007/978-3-031-42823-4_18

produces [1, 2]. Long-term diabetes can affect the retina of the eye with deterioration in vision, even more, they can cause blindness if not diagnosed in time [3], associated with diseases as Diabetic Retinopathy (DR) [4] and Diabetic Macular Edema (DME) [5].

The early diagnosis of diverse pathologies in the retina and a suitable treatment can lead to avoid complications in the patient vision. Generally, the diagnosis is accomplished by experts using a medical protocol using a visual inspection of retina images, based in identification of lesions associated with abnormalities in the blood vessels caused by diabetes. However, the visual diagnosis is a hard task, due to the color similarities and the background information in the images, which makes abnormalities are not perceptible to the human eye. The expertise and equipment needed to alleviate blindness caused by DR will be even more scarce due to the growing rate of people with diabetes [6].

Deep learning techniques have demonstrated a high performance in disease detection through image analysis. Particularly, Convolutional Neural Networks are a powerful tool with diverse applications, including the lesion detection in fundus images [7]. CNN has a deep architecture which enable the network to learn mid-level and high-level abstraction from the input images. The training of CNN requires a dataset with a big number of samples to achieve the demanded performance. It is a big challenge in a medical environment, where the representative samples are limited. Additionally, the training of CNN requires large computational and memory resources such as expensive GPUs (Graphics Processing Unit). Then, to overcome these drawbacks the transfer learning is a suitable solution for medical imaging applications, such as the diabetic retinopathy diagnosis. The transfer leaning technique requires the use of a stage for fine-tuning which trains a CNN from a set of weights pre-trained using new and different data.

Considering the context exposed previously, the objective of this work is to implement different pre-trained CNN and adjust a fine-tuning stage to compare the results and obtain the best configuration for diabetic retinopathy grading using fundus images.

The main contribution of this work is the implementation of a DR grading system based on deep transfer learning through different pre-entrained convolutional neural network in APTOS database. More than thirteen CNN models are tested to determine high performance in DR detection. Hence, this article is organized as follows. Section 2 exposes the related works in the DR grading using CNN. Section 3 exposes our proposed solution methodology for the problem of DR grading in retinal images. In Sect. 4 we describe the evaluation metrics to compare our work with other approaches. Finally, Sect. 5 describes our conclusions about automated DR detection through Deep Learning and the recommendations for future lines of research.

2 Related Work

In the literature, several works have been developed for DR and DME detection. The last three decades, the ophthalmic imaging has had significant advancements [8], which represents a great contribution in the medical field to support the diagnosis and treatment of eye diseases. Nevertheless, the DR classification is a hard task, because it includes an accurate detection of abnormalities in the retina. Although several studies have an approach to DR detection or grading, a limited number of publications report a retina abnormalities detection approach, which involve microaneurysm, exudates and hemorrhages.

Recent advancements in software development and computational resources have allowed developing Deep Learning (DL) techniques for an improved DR detection and classification. An overview about DL techniques applied to DR detection and classification is presented in [9]. In that review, authors include an analysis of the publicly available datasets used to that purpose, a comparative technical information regarding DL architectures, the commonly used preprocessing pipelines, and the models that have been applied in real clinical settings.

The work developed in [10] is based on a deep residual convolutional neural network for extracting discriminatory features with no prior complex image transformations. They used a residual pretrained network to detect and grading DR in fundus images. They tested the ResNet-18 and ResNet-50b architectures, AlexNet, ZhangNet, SqueezeNet and two versions of VGGnet as baseline experiments under the same conditions. After experimentations, the best results were found using a ResNet50-based architecture, showing an AUC of 0.93 for grades 0 + 1, AUC of 0.81 for grade 2 and AUC of 0.92 for grade 3 labelling.

Authors in [11] designed a Source-Free Transfer Learning (SFTL) method for DR detection, without use annotated retinal images and only employs source model in the training process. They proposed a target generation module and the collaborative consistency module. They obtained an accuracy of 91.2%, a sensitivity of 0.951 and a specificity of 0.858 for APTOS dataset.

The transfer learning method can be used with a fine tuning, training the CNN from the weights pretrained using the new dataset or directly use pre-trained CNN models as feature extractors. Following this second line, the work developed in [12] implements deep neural network for feature extraction and these features are further ensembled with statistical feature selection module and SVM classifier for DR grading. The model was tested in IDRiD dataset with accuracy of 90.01% for Inception V3 network.

Authors in developed a severity grading system for DR by transfer learning with the pretrained CNN EfficientNet-B3 and the APTOS 2019 dataset. Additionally, they used image processing technique for lesion detection. The results in severity grading showed that the accuracy was 0.84, 0.95, and 0.98 for the 1st, 2nd, and 3rd predicted labels, respectively.

Finally, the work developed in [13] proposes a deep learning model based on global average pooling (GAP) technique with different pre-trained convolutional neural network (CNN) models. GAP is used as a regularization layer that reduces the overfitting and increases the generalization of the results. The experiments demonstrated that the best model achieved 82.4% quadratic weighted kappa (QWK).

After a preliminary work exposed in [14] where a CNN based DR detector was developed with suitable results, the study was extended to a multiclass classifier for DR grading using transfer leaning with different pretrained architectures. The model was validated in APTOS dataset.

3 Methodology

3.1 Work Environment

All the development, testing, and improvement of the model presented in this research work was carried out in the Google Colaboratory environment [15]. It should be noted that this environment has its limitations in terms of processing capacity, storage, and active session duration. However, the hardware acceleration made available by Google Colaboratory through GPU was fundamental in processing a large number of images in a short time.

3.2 Dataset Description and Processing

For this research, we used a set of images provided by the Kaggle platform [16] for the APTOS 2019 Blindness Detection competition [17]. This set is ideal for our work because the images are acceptable. The set size is large enough to train convolutional neural networks without saturating the available memory in the Google Colab environment. The set includes 3662 fundus images for training and validation and 1928 images for testing, but they are not labeled, making it impossible to compare the network performance using them. Therefore, we only used the 3662 labeled images mentioned above.

Regarding the preprocessing of the images, it was found that they had varying sizes, dimensions, fundus centering, sharpness, and contrast. A dark edge cropping algorithm was implemented to address this issue to remove any irrelevant fundus information. Furthermore, all images were adjusted to a size of 320 × 320 pixels.

Finally, the Contrast Limited Adaptive Histogram Equalization (CLAHE) technique [18] was applied to each of the images, which allows for improving aspects such as brightness and contrast of the photograph in order to enhance the quality of retinal features. Figure 1 shows the improvement in quality, contrast, and sharpness of the images before and after applying the preprocessing steps described in this section.

A characteristic feature of this dataset is that the images provided for training and validation tasks, despite being labeled in the different levels 0, 1, 2, 2, 3, and 4, corresponding to the classes "No DR", "Mild", "Moderate", "Severe" and "Proliferative DR", show a significant imbalance in terms of the number of photographs that make up each level (see Fig. 2a). This is a significant factor in separating the set of images into the groups designated for use in training, validation, and testing. When dividing each level, for data stratification, special care was taken to maintain the proportions specified in Fig. 2b.

3.3 Proposed Approach

Regarding the process of developing, constructing, and implementing the CNN model, we started with the work developed by [14] and the various works enunciated by [19], which employed techniques such as transfer learning and data augmentation. These techniques enable us to leverage models previously created for the same scientific and research line to create new CNN-type networks without excessively using the hardware and software resources required to train the network.

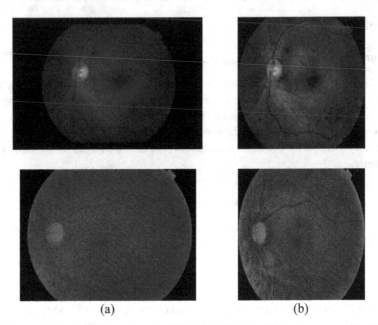

Fig. 1. Images before and after processing: (a) Original image, (b) Image processed with black border cropping, resizing, and CLAHE algorithm. [17]

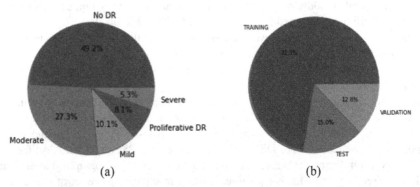

Fig. 2. Distribution of the image set: (a) Percentage of images per DR level, and (b) percentage of images for training, validation, and testing.

– **Transfer Learning:** It is a machine learning technique that involves using a pre-trained model on a large dataset, made available to the public, to solve a similar problem in a different domain or task. This approach helps reduce the training data and time needed to build a new model from scratch [14].

Considering the objective of this research, using pre-trained networks is a good starting point for structuring models used in image processing and classification. The training was performed with various pre-trained networks, including Xception, VGG16, VGG19, DenseNet121, DenseNet169, InceptionV3, ResNet50,

ResNet101, InceptionResNetV2, EfficientNetB0, EfficientNetB1, EfficientNetB2, and EfficientNetB3.

– **Feature Extraction:** The process consists of utilizing the patterns that the pre-trained network has learned for recognizing the characteristics of an image based on generic concepts such as shapes, contours, colors, etc. Then, the CNN pretrained is considered a feature extractor, and these features are the input to the final classifier represented in Fig. 3. For this purpose, a technique called "layer freezing" is implemented, which specifies that the weights in the layers of the pre-trained network will be maintained, preserving the knowledge they have acquired for interpreting the information in the images [14].

For our work, we disregarded the "layer freeze" technique. We decided to train the elaborated networks from start to finish, allowing them to learn to recognize the fundamental features of fundus images more precisely, even though the training would take a relatively long time. Using the work environment described in Sect. 3.1, the training time was about 22.25min. Nevertheless, replacing the default classifier of the imported network with a custom classifier for the task remained essential. Figure 3 illustrates the structure of the network using the pre-trained neural network.

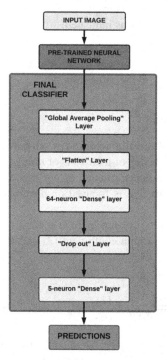

Fig. 3. Diagram depicting the construction of the network to be used for transfer learning training

Our proposal includes a "Flatten" layer that helps to interpret the images as data vectors for greater ease of interpretation by the network and a "Dense" layer of 64 Neurons so that the network analyzes the image information before reaching the last layer of predictions. In addition, it is extremely important to highlight the number of Neurons in the last "Dense" layer, now being 5, corresponding to the 5 levels of Retinopathy that are to be recognized.

- **Data augmentation:** It is a highly beneficial technique for this work as it increases the number of images the model observes during training. The algorithm enables the network to study the same image from different perspectives by making modifications such as rotations within a 180° range and inversions vertically and horizontally. In the training stage we used a batch size of 32, updating the average gradient of the batch by Backpropagation. Data augmentation was performed on these batches by means of four image parameter modifications. The possibility of combining with four options is 24, therefore the increase in data per batch resulted in a total of 32 * 24 = 768 images.

Finally, it is necessary to indicate the conditions and parameters under which the training of the networks was carried out. These would be:

- Adam type optimizer with a fixed Learning Rate of 1e-4.
- The batch size (Batch Size) was 32.
- 30 epochs were stipulated for each training.
- Loss function set to binary_crossentropy.
- For "metrics" only "accuracy" was indicated.

The specified methodological design for creating the networks is shown in Fig. 4. In the following section, we will present the results and compare them with those of different state-of-the-art works in the same line.

3.4 Performance Indicators

To establish a comparison of the results achieved by our network for the DR classification task, evaluating them using a series of metrics is of utmost importance. This evaluation will allow us to determine the performance of our model and compare it with other research in the state of the art that is focused on developing a solution for the same problem.

The metrics chosen for this research include accuracy, sensitivity, specificity [20], precision, F1 score [19], and kappa coefficient [21]. These metrics are described by Eqs. 1 to 6.

$$Accuracy\ (Acc) = \frac{TP + TN}{TP + TN + FP + FN} \quad (1)$$

$$Specificity\ (Sp) = \frac{TN}{TN + FP} \quad (4)$$

$$Precision\ (P) = \frac{TP}{TP + FP} \quad (2)$$

$$F1 - Score = 2 * \frac{Precision * Se}{Precision + Se} \quad (5)$$

$$Sensitivity\ (Se) = \frac{TP}{TP + FN} \quad (3)$$

$$Kappa\ coef = \frac{(Obs\ Acc - Exp\ Acc)}{(1 - Exp\ Acc)} \quad (6)$$

Here, TN corresponds to true negatives, TP to true positives, FP to false positives, and FN to false negatives.

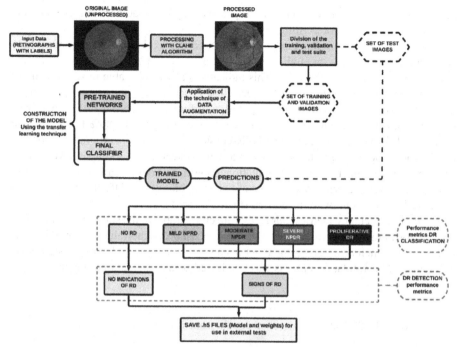

Fig. 4. A Proposed Model for Diabetic Retinopathy Classification Using Deep Learning Techniques and Pre-Trained Networks.

4 Results and discussion

4.1 Comparative Between Evaluated Models

Table 1 shows the results achieved by all models after training and validation. It was found that the model trained with the VGG16 neural network as a pre-trained base network provided more accurate predictions than the other models. These metrics were calculated using the confusion matrix shown in Fig. 5, which displays true positives (TP), true negatives (TN), false positives (FP), and false negatives (FN) for each level. However, the system faced significant difficulties in detecting images labeled as grade 3, indicating severe DR, which is also level with the lowest number of images (only 5.3% of the total value of images in the set, as shown in Fig. 2a). This data imbalance indicates that categorical distribution significantly influences the quality of the training of a convolutional neural network for feature detection and image classification.

4.2 Comparative with Related Works

Table 2 summarizes the results achieved by our approach and a comparison with other works available in the state of the art that also used the APTOS 2019 Blindness Detection image set [17] for DR classification tasks. This comparison allows us to measure the performance of our system against those proposed by other authors and evaluate our approach in the context of existing research.

The results show that our model outperformed the works of Bodapati et al. [22], Nguyen et al. [23], Kassani et al. [21], Harikrishnan et al. [24], and Dekhil et al. [25] in terms of precision and accuracy. This indicates that we were able to surpass almost all authors. Furthermore, our model is very close in accuracy to the highest-performing model achieved by Bodapati et al. [22], with a difference of only 0.79%, considering that our work only used a 70% of the images for training versus 80% from Bodapati et al. [22]. It is worth noting that our study employed a feature incorporation approach in addition to network pre-training. Despite being executed in a simple development environment without significant computational power, this demonstrates that our model solution achieves the primary objective of correctly classifying DR and surpasses this objective by competing with the current state-of-the-art results.

Regarding accuracy metrics, our results are comparable to the state-of-the-art. However, performing a statistical comparison was impossible, as the values reported in other works did not include information about a standard deviation to determine significant differences. The validation process was conducted using new data not included in the training stage.

Table 1. Evaluation results of models for diabetic retinopathy classification.

Pre-trained networks	*Acc (%)*	*P (%)*	*Se (%)*	F1-Score (%)	Kappa coef. (%)
Xception	81.87	81.60	81.87	81.47	72.50
VGG16	**83.52**	**82.68**	**83.52**	**82.52**	**74.71**
VGG19	81.32	81.74	81.32	79.93	71.23
DenseNet121	82.05	82.61	82.05	81.78	72.81
DenseNet169	82.05	82.32	82.05	81.52	72.64
InceptionV3	81.87	81.81	81.87	81.50	72.45
ResNet50	81.87	82.04	81.87	81.14	72.37
ResNet101	82.78	82.57	82.78	82.00	73.64
InceptionResNetV2	82.42	81.85	82.42	81.87	73.30
EfficientNetB0	80.95	80.71	80.95	80.41	70.90
EfficientNetB1	81.50	82.27	81.50	80.62	71.87
EfficientNetB2	78.02	77.03	78.02	76.92	66.19
EfficientNetB3	79.49	79.80	79.49	79.13	68.91

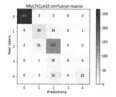

Fig. 5. Confusion matrix for DR classification using the VGG16 network.

Table 2. Comparison between our model and the state-of-the-art.

Reference	Model	*Acc*	*P*	*Sn*	*Sp*	*F1-Score*	*Kappa Coef*
Our Model	**VGG16**	83.52	82.68	83.52		82.52	74.71
Bodapathi et. al. [22]	VGG16	82.54	82.00	83.00	–	82.00	–
Pak et al. [26]	DenseNet 121	–	–	–	–	–	69.00
Pak et al. [26]	ResNet50	–	–	–	–	–	70.80
Pak et al. [26]	ResNet101	–	–	–	–	–	73.40
Nguyen et al. [27]	VGG16 and VGG19	82.00	–	80.00	82.00	–	–
Kassani et al. [20]	Xception modified	83.09	–	88.04	87.00	–	–
Harikishnan et al. [28]	NASNet	82.00	–	–	–	–	–
Gangwar et al. [29]	Hybrid from Inception and ResNet-v2	82.18	–	–	–	–	–
Dekhil et al. [30]	VGG16	77.00	–	–	–	–	78.00
Bodapathi et al. [21]	Features incorporation approach	84.31	–	–	–	84.00	75.87
Mungloo et al. [31]	Resnet-50	82.00	–	–	–	–	–

5   Conclusions

Diabetic retinopathy is a complication of diabetes that results in pathology. It is one of the most common conditions worldwide. Due to the failure to detect and classify it early, more and more people suffer from higher levels of diabetic retinopathy. This can potentially lead to vision loss for many patients who cannot have a screening test in time because of the large influx of people with this complication of diabetes around the world. Therefore, in this research work, we propose an alternative, robust, and low-cost solution in the field of computer vision that focuses on classifying DR into its different levels of severity.

We developed a final classifier adapted to the task, along with the implementation of pre-trained neural networks. These networks (the primary network and the final custom classifier) were trained using the publicly available dataset provided by the APTOS 2019 Blindness Detection competition. We obtained very satisfactory and competitive results compared to other works available in the state of the art that also used the same dataset as us. However, we required significantly more computing power and resources. Our research focused on achieving fast and accurate graded classification using pre-trained models and techniques such as Transfer Learning and Data Augmentation. We employed a range of pre-trained models, including Xception, VGG16, VGG19, DenseNet121, DenseNet169, Inception V3, ResNet50, ResNet101, InceptionResNetV2, EfficientNetB0, EfficientNetB1, EfficientNetB2, and EfficientNetB3.

Among the different results obtained using the networks mentioned above, the best network yielded 83.52% accuracy, 82.68% precision, 83.52% sensitivity, 82.52% F1-score, and 74.71% Kappa Coefficient. These results overcome most of the works presented in the state-of-the-art, demonstrating the robustness and level of competence provided by this network, despite being a simple approach compared to other more elaborate methods that required a large number of resources to classify DR in its different levels of severity.

6   Funding Statement

This work has received funding from the Spain Ministry of Universities, NextGenerationEU - European Union, and Recovery, Transformation and Resilience Plan, as well as from research projects PI21/00064 and PI18/00169 (ISCIII and Fondos FEDER) funds and the URV grant 2019-PFR-B2-6, which partially support this research.

References

1. Romero-Aroca, P., et al.: Cost of diabetic retinopathy and macular oedema in a population, an eight year follow up. BMC Ophthalmol. **16** (2016). https://doi.org/10.1186/S12886-016-0318-X
2. Pelullo, C.P., Rossiello, R., Nappi, R., Napolitano, F., Di Giuseppe, G.: Diabetes prevention: knowledge and perception of risk among Italian population. Biomed Res Int. (2019). https://doi.org/10.1155/2019/2753131
3. Sneha, N., Gangil, T.: Analysis of diabetes mellitus for early prediction using optimal features selection. J. Big Data. https://doi.org/10.1186/s40537-019-0175-6
4. Diabetic Retinopathy | National Eye Institute. https://www.nei.nih.gov/learnabout-eye-health/eye-conditions-and-diseases/diabetic-retinopathy. Accessed 1 March 2022
5. Mathews, M.R., Anzar, S.M.: A comprehensive review on automated systems for severity grading of diabetic retinopathy and macular edema. Int. J. Imaging Syst. Technol. **31**, 2093–2122 (2021). https://doi.org/10.1002/IMA.22574

6. Yu Wang, G., Wang, A., Fan, W., Li, J.: A deep learning based pipeline for image grading of diabetic retinopathy. In: Chen, H., Fang, Q., Zeng, D., Jiang, W. (eds.) Smart Health: International Conference, ICSH 2018, Wuhan, China, July 1–3, 2018, Proceedings, pp. 240–248. Springer International Publishing, Cham (2018). https://doi.org/10.1007/978-3-030-03649-2_24

7. Alyoubi, W.L., Shalash, W.M., Abulkhair, M.F.: Diabetic retinopathy detection through deep learning techniques: a review. Inform. Med. Unlocked **20**, 100377 (2020). https://doi.org/10.1016/J.IMU.2020.100377

8. Ajaz, A., Kumar, H., Kumar, D.: A review of methods for automatic detection of macular edema. Biomed. Signal Process Control **69**, 102858 (2021). https://doi.org/10.1016/J.BSPC.2021.102858

9. Tsiknakis, N., et al.: Deep learning for diabetic retinopathy detection and classification based on fundus images: a review. Comput. Biol. Med. **135**, 104599 (2021). https://doi.org/10.1016/J.COMPBIOMED.2021.104599

10. Martinez-Murcia, F.J., Ortiz, A., Ramírez, J., Górriz, J.M., Cruz, R.: Deep residual transfer learning for automatic diagnosis and grading of diabetic retinopathy. Neurocomputing **452**, 424–434 (2021). https://doi.org/10.1016/J.NEUCOM.2020.04.148

11. Zhang, C., Lei, T., Chen, P.: Diabetic retinopathy grading by a source-free transfer learning approach. Biomed. Signal Process Control **73**, 103423 (2022). https://doi.org/10.1016/J.BSPC.2021.103423

12. Bhardwaj, C., Jain, S., Sood, M.: Transfer learning based robust automatic detection system for diabetic retinopathy grading. Neural Comput. Appl. **33**, 13999–14019 (2021). https://doi.org/10.1007/S00521-021-06042-2/FIGURES/8

13. Al-Smadi, M., Hammad, M., Bani Baker, Q., Al-Zboon, ad A.: A transfer learning with deep neural network approach for diabetic retinopathy classification. Int. J. Electrical Comput. Eng. **11**, 3492–3501 (2021). https://doi.org/10.11591/ijece.v11i4.pp3492-3501

14. Escorcia-Gutierrez, J., et al.: Analysis of Pre-trained Convolutional Neural Network Models in Diabetic Retinopathy Detection Through Retinal Fundus Images. Lecture Notes in Computer Science (including subseries Lecture Notes in Artificial Intelligence and Lecture Notes in Bioinformatics), LNCS, vol. 13293, pp. 202–213 (2022). https://doi.org/10.1007/978-3-031-10539-5_15/COVER

15. Google colab is a free cloud notebook environment, Biochemistry Computational Research Facility (BCRF), 5 de febrero de 2021. https://bcrf.biochem.wisc.edu/2021/02/05/google-colab-is-a-free-cloud-notebook-environment/. Accessed 25 March 2023

16. Kaggle: Your Machine Learning and Data Science Community. https://www.kaggle.com/. Accessed 25 March 2023

17. APTOS 2019 Blindness Detection. https://kaggle.com/competitions/aptos2019-blindness-detection. Accessed 25 March 2023

18. OpenCV: Histograms - 2: Histogram Equalization. https://docs.opencv.org/4.x/d5/daf/tutorial_py_histogram_equalization.html. Accessed 25 March 2023

19. Cuello-Navarro, J., Peña, C.B., Escorcia-Gutiérrez, J.: Una revisión de los métodos de Deep Learning aplicados a la detección automatizada de la retinopatía diabética. Revista SEXTANTE **23**, 12–27 (2020). https://doi.org/10.54606/Sextante2020.v23.02

20. Kassani, S.H., Kassani, P.H., Khazaeinezhad, R., Wesolowski, M.J., Schneider, K.A., Deters, R.: Diabetic retinopathy classification using a modified xception architecture. In 2019 IEEE International Symposium on Signal Processing and Information Technology (ISSPIT), pp. 1–6. IEEE (2019)

21. Bodapati, J.D., Shaik, N.S., Naralasetti, V.: Deep convolution feature aggregation: an application to diabetic retinopathy severity level prediction. Signal Image Video Process. **15**(5), 923–930 (2021). https://doi.org/10.1007/s11760020-01816-y

22. Bodapati, J.D., Shaik, N.S., Naralasetti, V.: Composite deep neural network with gated-attention mechanism for diabetic retinopathy severity classification. J. Ambient Intell. Human. Comput. **12**(10), 9825–9839 (2021). https://doi.org/10.1007/s12652-020-02727-z

23. Gangwar, A.K., Ravi, V.: Diabetic retinopathy detection using transfer learning and deep learning. In: Bhateja, V., Peng, S.-L., Satapathy, S.C., Zhang, Y.-D. (eds.) Evolution in Computational Intelligence: Frontiers in Intelligent Computing: Theory and Applications (FICTA 2020), Volume 1, pp. 679–689. Springer Singapore, Singapore (2021). https://doi.org/10.1007/978-981-15-5788-0_64

24. Minarno, A.E., Mandiri, M.H.C., Azhar, Y., Bimantoro, F., Nugroho, H.A., Ibrahim, Z.: Classification of diabetic retinopathy disease using convolutional neural network. JOIV: Int. J. Inform. Visual. **6**(1), 12–18 (2022)

25. Dekhil, O., Naglah, A., Shaban, M., Ghazal, M., Taher, F., Elbaz, A.: Deep learning based method for computer aided diagnosis of diabetic retinopathy. In: 2019 IEEE International Conference on Imaging Systems and Techniques (IST), pp. 1–4. IEEE (2019)

26. Pak, A., Ziyaden, A., Tukeshev, K., Jaxylykova, A., Abdullina, D.: Comparative analysis of deep learning methods of detection of diabetic retinopathy, vol. 7 (2020) https://doi.org/10.1080/23311916.2020.1805144. http://www.editorialmanager.com/cogenteng

27. Nguyen, Q.H., et al.: Diabetic retinopathy detection using deep learning. In: ACM International Conference Proceeding Series, pp. 103–107 (2020). https://doi.org/10.1145/3380688.3380709

28. Harikrishnan, V.K., Vijarania, M., Gambhir, A.: Diabetic retinopathy identification using autoML. Comput. Intell. Appl. Healthcare 175–188 (2020). https://doi.org/10.1016/B978-0-12-8206041.00012-1

29. Gangwar, A.K., Ravi, V.: Diabetic retinopathy detection using transfer learning and deep learning. Adv. Intell. Syst. Comput. **1176**, 679–689 (2021). https://doi.org/10.1007/978-981-15-5788-0_64/COVER

30. Dekhil, O., Naglah, A., Shaban, M., Ghazal, M., Taher, F., Elbaz, A.: Deep learning based method for computer aided diagnosis of diabetic retinopathy. In: IST 2019 - IEEE International Conference on Imaging Systems and Techniques, Proceedings (2019). https://doi.org/10.1109/IST48021.2019.9010333

31. Mungloo-Dilmohamud, Z., Khan, M.H.M., Jhumka, K., Beedassy, B.N., Mungloo, N.Z., Peña-Reyes, C.: Balancing data through data augmentation improves the generality of transfer learning for diabetic retinopathy classification. Appl. Sci. **12**, 5363 (2022). https://doi.org/10.3390/APP12115363

Evaluating Techniques Based on Supervised Learning Methods in Casas Kyoto Dataset for Human Activity Recognition

Johanna-Karinna García-Restrepo[1], Paola Patricia Ariza-Colpas[1(✉)],
Shariq Butt-Aziz[2], Marlon Alberto Piñeres-Melo[3], Sumera Naz[4],
and Emiro De-la-hoz-Franco[1]

[1] Department of Computer Science and Electronics, Universidad de La Costa CUC, 080002
Barranquilla, Colombia
{jgarcia3,pariza1,edelahoz}@cuc.edu.co
[2] Department of Computer Science, University of South Asia, Lahore, Pakistan
[3] Department of Systems Engineering, Universidad del Norte, 081001 Barranquilla, Colombia
pineresm@uninorte.edu.co
[4] Department of Mathematics, Division of Science and Technology, University of Education,
Lahore, Pakistan
sumera.naz@ue.edu.pk

Abstract. One of the technical aspects that contribute to improving the quality of life for older adults is the automation of physical spaces using sensors and actuators, which facilitates the performance of their daily activities. The interaction between individuals and their environment enables the detection of abnormal patterns that may arise from a decline in their cognitive abilities. In this study, we evaluate the CASAS Kyoto dataset from WSU University, which provides information on the daily living activities of individuals within an indoor environment. We developed a model to predict activities such as Cleaning, Cooking, Eating, Washing hands, and Phone Call. A novel approach is proposed, which involves preprocessing and segmenting the dataset using sliding windows. Furthermore, we conducted experiments with various classifiers to determine the optimal choice for the model. The final model utilizes the regression classification technique and is trained on a reduced dataset containing only 5 features. It achieves outstanding results, with a Recall of 99.80% and a ROC area of 100%.

Keywords: Human Activity Recognition · Activity of Daily Living · Selection Methods · Classification Methods · Smart home

1 Introduction

Older adults usually have problems with their health and managing their quality of life. There are studies [2–6] that have made it possible to strengthen the social welfare of the elderly using technology. One of the technologies that contribute to improving the quality of life of older adults consists of remote monitoring of the activities carried out

K. Saeed et al. (Eds.): CISIM 2023, LNCS 14164, pp. 253–269, 2023.
https://doi.org/10.1007/978-3-031-42823-4_19

by individuals due to their interaction with sensors deployed in the environment. This facilitates the identification of human behavior patterns generated from the movement and interaction of individuals with the environment, recognizing situations that may put them at risk. Smart Home (SH) technology is considered a way to promote health care, helping to improve the autonomous development of daily activities and social conditions of people with special care needs, due to mobility difficulties and cognitive impairment of these [7]. The technology has been applied in many fields for energy saving [8], security and protection [8], fall detection [9], light control [10], and smoke and fire detection [11] among others. Through various technological solutions that involve video monitoring [12], alarm deployment [13], and the use of intelligent schedulers [14]. These solutions usually use different equipment for the process of data collection and generation of physical responses (sensors, video surveillance equipment, and actuators). Human Activity Recognition (HAR) aims to discover patterns of human activities by analyzing the data generated from the movement and interactions of individuals with the environment. HAR has several potential applications, to facilitate data monitoring and understanding of human activity in technology-based surveillance environments [15], to automatically detect abnormal patterns in the development of activities. Thanks to the data collection processes, the sensors integrated into the home allow the reading of the interactions of individuals with said sensors, while the residents carry out their daily routines. The sensor readings are collected by devices deployed in the indoor environment, which use different technologies and communication protocols. The data collected is stored in databases from which predictive models are built and used to generate useful knowledge, based on analyzing patterns and identifying behavior trends.

The Washington State University developed the Center for Advanced Studies in Adaptive Systems (CASAS) project which compiled a repository of data related to activities of daily living in indoor environments, one of the datasets contained in the said repository is Daily Life 2010–2012 Kyoto, one of the most widely used to evaluate the daily activities of an individual in an SH, the aforementioned dataset contains data that represents sensor events that detected the movement of individuals in the indoor environment. In the research project from which this article arises, several techniques based on artificial intelligence were used to build predictive models that integrated feature selection and classification techniques. The comparative analysis of the quality metrics generated by the different models allowed us to identify the one that generated the best hit rates. The paper proposes a new model that performs a pre-processing of the dataset, a segmentation using sliding windows, and a selection of features to improve the efficiency of the model. In addition, experimentation with the main classifiers is carried out individually to determine the best option for the model, and to test the level of improvement of the different parts of the model: preprocessing and segmentation. With this experimentation, the reliability of artificial intelligence-based techniques to be able to support people with neurodegenerative diseases can be evidenced. The design and implementation of different classification scenarios can show the impact of the selection of the characteristics and the different processing algorithms in the selection of the classifier.

2 Related Research

As a result of the review of the literature, a series of works related to HAR has been identified, regarding 1) the implementation of preprocessing techniques [16–21]; 2) the application of techniques based on supervised and unsupervised learning [22–25]; and 3) the different areas of development of the HAR that allow the processing of the data extracted from the sensors, to solve problems related to human activities in different contexts: SH [26, 27, 29], behavior [28] or even diseases such as dementia [29]. This work has focused primarily on preprocessing techniques. In [16], a study based on the selection of features is carried out, there Convolutional Neural Networks (CNN) are proposed that allowed the extraction of features and their classification, using smartphone sensors. A multilayer CNN contains alternating convolution and pooling membranes, considering that the outer layers allow input capture, and the inner layers have transformation functions. In [16] it is shown how the different architectures of a CNN affect the overall performance and how this system does not require advanced preprocessing or tedious manual construction functions and can outperform other next-generation algorithms in the field of HAR.

On the other hand, in [17] they determined the characteristics of the signals that are more suitable for the recognition of human activities, using smartphones, carried on the waist by different individuals. Capela performed the feature selection independently of the classifier. The identification of feature subsets that favor activity classification and improve mobility monitoring models, for use in future classifiers. Feature subsets with classifier performance like the full feature set should reduce the computational load, thus facilitating real-time implementations. This research is an important step in the development of an accurate and robust HAR system for diverse populations. The analysis presented by [20] proposes the collection of data from different sources using one device and the use of a modified version of the Adaptive Boosting algorithm (AdaBoost) for feature selection. Similar work has been proposed [21] using hidden Markov models (HMM) to classify certain activities. A relevant example of this technique is the one proposed by Sean Eddy, who built a model called the Discriminative Conditional Restricted Boltzmann Machine (DCRBM). This model combines a discriminant approach with the capabilities of the Conditional Restricted Boltzmann Machine (CRBM). The model enables the discovery of actionable components of Essential Social Interaction Predicates (ESIPs) to train the DCRBM model and use it to generate low-level, ESIP-corresponding data with a high degree of accuracy.

Regarding the category of the HAR development field, the long-term analysis of the activities can provide information regarding the performance of basic tasks, such as eating, sleeping, and cooking, among others. Monitoring people in their natural environment enables data collection using sensors deployed at multiple locations in a smart home. From the approach based on activity recognition, ontological and semantic reasoning models are applied, which according to Chen et al. [27] can be combined. Another knowledge-based approach is that of user interaction information, which within the context is combined with the sensors available in the smart home, to generate a Markov decision model that allows the recognition of daily life activities. and its impact on the well-being of older adults [28]. The Kyoto dataset is described with the instances and the information of the activities, in addition, a balance of a proposed model is shown and the comparison with other datasets can be observed in Table 1 where the dataset of Kyoto has the best results in about the model proposed by Fahad et al. [29]. Most of these studies present datasets, collected by different types of sensors. In addition, Du et al. [30] propose a methodology that is based on the recognition of the activity being carried out and a prediction of the following activity using RFID technology.

Table 1. Comparison of the approach proposed in [29] with ET-KNN, without selection of characteristics and data balancing, using the dataset Kyoto and Kasteren.

Datasets	Folds	Approach	Precision (%)	Recall (%)	F1score [0, 1]	Accuracy (%)
Kyoto1	Three folds	Proposed approach	97.33	96.67	0.97	96.67
		ET-KNN	95.85	95.00	0.95	95.00
	One day out	Proposed approach	98.11	97.44	0.97	97.44
		ET-KNN	97.22	96.15	0.95	96.15
Kyoto7	Three folds	Proposed approach	79.00	76.79	0.77	80.00
		ET-KNN	72.35	69.59	0.69	74.15
	One day out	Proposed approach	76.60	80.09	0.77	81.00
		ET-KNN	70.72	75.74	0.71	76.07
Kasteren7	Three folds	Proposed approach	90.10	93.11	0.91	94.21
		ET-KNN	89.89	87.77	0.87	92.27
	One day out	Proposed approach	94.13	94.13	0.94	95.28
		ET-KNN	93.41	89.66	0.90	93.06
Kasteren10	Three folds	Proposed approach	88.80	88.40	0.87	92.54
		ET-KNN	90.70	84.31	0.85	90.04
	One day out	Proposed approach	88.10	89.14	0.88	92.00
		ET-KNN	83.62	83.32	0.82	90.77

In this study, a dataset containing activities of daily living (ADL) collected in a single resident indoor environment from three data sources (binary, proximity, and motion sensors) was evaluated. The goal of this work is to propose a supervised methodology using pre-processing and segmentation of the dataset. In addition, a reduction of the feature set of the dataset is searched to provide a fast model that can be transposed to a real-time system. This feature reduction also allows us to focus on the most important sensors.

3 Methodology

The methodology used in this research for the prediction of ADL is Knowledge Discovery in Databases (KDD) since it allows the extraction and analysis of previously unknown and potentially useful information. This methodology consists of extracting patterns that allow the user to obtain information from massive datasets. This is through preprocessing and data mining, then the results are presented through a trained model, which will estimate the activity performed by a person in an indoor environment. Finally, the quality metrics of the different models generated are evaluated to identify the model with the best performance. The Daily Life 2010–2012 Kyoto dataset has been used as input for the construction of the predictive model. This involved proposing a series of experimentation scenarios. Previously, it was necessary to implement a methodology for data preparation, which involved the consolidation of different sources (motion, binary, and proximity sensors) with different types of data (binary and numerical). In particular, the numerical data was preprocessed using feature representation techniques. The resulting dataset was segmented using 3-s sliding windows. After segmentation, different models based on Machine Learning (ML) techniques were trained and tested. The model with the highest quality metrics has been selected as the one with the best performance after making a comparative analysis between different experimentation scenarios. Finally, a traditional methodology is followed for the validation of the model in which the data set is divided into two parts: training set (70%) and test set (30%). A summary of the proposed methodology can be seen in Fig. 1.

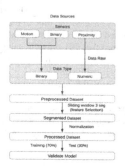

Fig. 1. Model Representation.

4 Data Preparation

Washington State University WSU collected data for 86 days from 20 volunteers for the construction of the dataset called CASAS Kyoto. This is made up of 120 files with information generated from the interactions of individuals in an indoor environment.

The activities carried out by these individuals in the environment were: cooking, eating, washing hands, cleaning, and making phone calls. To do this, different types of sensors were used: contact (in cabinets, kitchen utensils, and medicine containers, among others) and to measure proximity due to movement. The integration of the 120 files generated a total of 6,425 instances, which were ordered in descending order by the TimeStamp column. The original dataset consisted of five types of data columns (TimeStamp, Motion Sensors, Binary Sensors, Proximity Sensors, and Phone Usage), with 26 features in all. Using aggregation functions, the representation process of the numerical characteristics (which come from the proximity sensors) was carried out. All the characteristics, both those generated because of the representation, as well as the original ones, were integrated into a dataset called preprocessing. Data instances were then grouped through sliding windows. The data instances were then grouped into sliding windows. The size used is 3 s due to the reactivity of the recognition decreased and the computational load is increased if the time window is too large because it may contain information from multiple activities [32]. However, if the time window is too small, some activity may be divided into multiple consecutive windows, and the recognition task will be triggered too frequently without producing high recognition results.

After the previous process, the preprocessed dataset is obtained, and the process of generating new features continues, taking the attribute values corresponding to the sensors (AD1-A, AD2-B, and AD1-C), and applying functions of aggregation, such as mean, standard deviation, maximum, minimum, range, skewness, and kurtosis. As a result, 21 new features were obtained and a segmented dataset with 45 features including activity and 5,736 instances were generated. See Table 2.

Table 2. Description of the characteristics of the segmented dataset

Feature	Qty	Description
TimeStamp	1	Contains the date and time of the sequence of activities
Motion sensors	11	Identified as follows: M01, M07 to M09, from o M18, and M23. Each one takes ON and OFF values
Binary sensors	10	Identified as follows: from I01 to I08 and D01. Each takes values ABSENT and PRESENT
Proximity sensors	21	For each of the THREE initial proximity characteristics (AD1-A, AD2-B, and AD1-C) the aggregation functions were applied: standard deviation, mean, range, max, min, kurtosis, and bias
Telephone usage	1	It takes values of START and END
Activity	1	Cleaning, Cooking, Eating, Washing hands, and Phone call
Total	45	

The dataset after segmentation is unbalanced, that is, the proportion of the number of instances of each activity is different. One solution to this is class balancing. For this process, the SMOTE (Synthetic Minority Oversampling Technique) technique [24] was used, and the result is a balanced dataset as shown in Fig. 2. When balanced, the symmetry of each class can be observed.

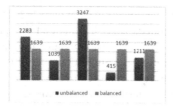

Fig. 2. Class unbalanced and balanced using SMOTE Techniques.

5 Experimentation

In this section, we present an experimentation scenario in which the model is evaluated using the preprocessed dataset. This dataset was segmented into 3-s sliding time windows, obtaining a segmented dataset. Different classification techniques were applied, assessing which one yields the best results. Each of these classification techniques is characterized by the use of supervised machine learning. In this case, the following classifiers have been selected (see Tables 3 and 4): Via Regression, One Rule, Attribute selected, J48, Random SubSpace, Random Forest, Bagging, RandomCommittee, REP Tree, and Long Term Memory. Previously, the best hyperparameters have been searched for each of these classifiers.

Table 3. Segmented dataset classification technique results

	Classification Technique	FPR (%)	Precision (%)	Recall (%)	ROC Area (%)
1	Classification Via Regression	0.1	99.8	99.8	100
2	OneR	0.3	99.5	99.5	99.6
3	Attribute Selected	0.9	97.1	97.1	98.5
4	J48	0.9	96.8	96.8	98.6
5	Random SubSpace	3.8	91.5	91.1	98.7
6	Random Forest	3.2	90.3	90.4	98.4
7	Bagging	3.5	89.8	90	98.8
8	RandomCommittee	3.3	89.8	89.9	95.9
9	REP Tree	3.6	89	89.2	97.8
10	LTM	3.9	88.3	88.6	97.1

One of the classifiers used that has better performance is the Classificator Via Regression, which is based on the operation of the regression algorithm that is based on the principles of linear regression and decision trees to achieve the objectives of the algorithm. The functionality of this algorithm is divided into two stages: 1) A normal decision tree is built based on both the difference and the existing variations in the attributes according to the output values. During the construction of this tree, it tends to reduce the deviation that is evaluated in the construction of the tree. 2) Subsequently, the process of pruning the tree is carried out, obtaining a set of subtrees that are merged through the regression

function. It is later during the classification training process that huge numbers of decision trees are massively generated. 3) Each generated tree provides information about
its classification that is taken as a vote that is assigned to the class; The highest rating
is assigned to the class that receives the highest number of votes. This algorithm is very
useful for predicting the incidence of a class compared to the rest of the generated classes
and has been widely used in the literature, demonstrating its efficiency.

The evaluation of the segmented and balanced dataset was carried out, establishing
which classifier obtained the best results in the quality metrics (see Table 5). Finally,
the model was evaluated by hybridizing feature selection and classification techniques
with the segmented and balanced dataset (see Tables 10 and 11). In the experimental
scenario, the segmentation of the dataset was performed in sliding time windows of three
seconds, thus going from 6425 instances of the preprocessed dataset to 5736 instances in
the segmented dataset. The same classification techniques, used in the experimentation
scenario carried out in [31], were applied. As a result, the 10 classifiers that yielded the
best results were identified, see Table 3.

It can be pointed out that the classifiers with which the best ROC area and recall rates
were obtained were Classification Via Regression, OneR, and Attribute Selected. Other
classifiers that were previously ranked in the top ten positions, changed their position
as we can see with the OneR classifier, this one in the first scenario was in the seventh
position, and with the segmentation process, it goes to second place, which indicates that
the segmentation process favors this classifier, proof of this is the area ROC of 99.6%
and recall of 99.5%.

Table 4. Comparison best results scenario 1 vs scenario 2.

Classifier	Scenario 1 Preprocessed dataset			Scenario 2 Segmented dataset		
	FPR (%)	Recall (%)	ROC Area (%)	FPR (%)	Recall (%)	ROC Area (%)
Classification Via Regression	1.2	97.69	99.7	0.1	99.8	100
Random SubSpace	4.1	89.9	98.6	3.8	91.1	98.7
Bagging	5.2	86.4	97.4	3.5	90	98.8
Random Forest	4.1	87.4	97.2	3.2	90.4	98.4
Attribute Selected	2.7	91.8	96.9	0.9	97.1	98.5

In a third scenario, balancing is performed concerning the class criterion, and several
data instances per class change, thanks to the application of the balancing technique
called SMOTE, see Table 5. We can see that in the unbalanced dataset, there is a greater
number of instances of the cooking and cleaning class, these have 67.97% of the total

instances referenced in the table. As a result of the balancing, the same number of instances is evidenced in the dataset.

Table 5. Comparison best results scenario 1 vs scenario 2.

Class	Scenario 1 Segmented dataset				Scenario 2 Segmented and Balanced dataset			
	Train		Test		Train		Test	
	Num	%	Num	%	Num	%	Num	%
Make phone call	822	14.33	389	15.81	1147	20	491	19.97
Handwashing	297	5.17	118	4.80	1147	20	492	20.01
Cook	2299	40.08	948	38.55	1147	20	492	20.01
Eat	719	12.53	320	13.01	1147	20	492	20.01
Clean up	1599	27.89	684	27.83	1148	20.01	492	20.01

In this scenario, the segmented dataset (with sliding time windows of a fixed size of 3 seconds) and balanced (consisting of 45 characteristics, including the class criterion) the same classification techniques, previously listed in the first scenario, were applied. As a result, the 10 classifiers that yielded the best results were identified, see Table 6. To determine which of these classification techniques generated better results, the different quality metrics were evaluated. With the Classification Via Regression classifier, the highest ROC area was 99.96% and the Recall was 99.95%, and the FPR was 0.28%. In the same way, we can show an improvement in the different classifiers concerning the previous scenarios, as shown in Table 7.

Table 6. Results classification techniques complete the dataset.

Classifier Technique	FPR (%)	Precision (%)	Recall (%)	ROC Area (%)
Classification Via Regression	0.28	99.55	99.95	99.96
OneR	0.14	99.75	99.75	99.80
Random SubSpace	2.15	95.06	94.75	99.47
Bagging	3.42	90.14	90.28	98.80
J48	0.77	97.62	97.64	98.75
Attribute Selected	0.69	97.90	97.92	98.74
Random Forest	3.10	90.93	91.09	98.35
REP Tree	3.52	89.39	89.54	97.56
Random Committee	3.18	90.49	90.64	95.84
LTM	3.35	89.39	89.67	97.33

Table 7. Comparison best results scenario 1, scenario 2, and scenario 3.

Classifier	Scenario 1 Preprocessed Dataset			Scenario 2 Segmented Dataset			Scenario 3 Segmented and Preprocessed Dataset		
	FPR (%)	Recall (%)	ROC Area (%)	FPR (%)	Recall (%)	ROC Area (%)	FPR (%)	Recall (%)	ROC Area (%)
Classification Via Regression	1.2	97.6	99.7	0.1	99.8	100	0.28	99.5	99.96
OneR	2.8	94.8	96	0.3	99.5	99.6	0.14	99.75	99.80
Attribute Selected	2.7	91.8	96.9	0.9	97.1	98.5	0.69	97.92	97.92
J48	2.7	91.6	96.8	0.9	96.8	98.6	0.77	97.64	98.75
Random SubSpace	4.1	89.9	98.6	3.8	91.1	98.7	2.15	94.75	99.47
Random Forest	4.1	87.4	97.2	3.2	90.4	98.4	3.1	91.09	91.09
Bagging	5.2	86.4	97.4	3.5	90	98.8	3.42	90.28	98.80

Table 8. Dataset attributes

Id	Attribute	Id	Attribute	Id	Attribute
0	DATE	15	I04	30	AD1-B-MAX
1	M01	16	I05	31	AD1-B-MIN
2	M07	17	I06	32	AD1-B-RANGE
3	M08	18	I07	33	AD1-B-MEAN
4	M09	19	I08	34	AD1-B-STD
5	M13	20	D01	35	AD1-B-KURT
6	M14	21	asterisk	36	AD1-B-SKEW
7	M15	22	E01	37	AD1-C-MAX
8	M16	23	AD1-A-MAX	38	AD1-C-MIN
9	M17	24	AD1-A-MIN	39	AD1-C-RANGE
10	M18	25	AD1-A-RANGE	40	AD1-C-MEAN
11	M23	26	AD1-A-MEAN	41	AD1-C-STD
12	I01	27	AD1-A-STD	42	AD1-C-KURT
13	I02	28	AD1-A-KURT	43	AD1-C-SKEW
14	I03	29	AD1-A-SKEW	44	Activity

Table 9. Priority of characteristics according to attribute selection technique

Id	GainRatio	Id	InfoGain	Id	OneR	Id	ReliefF	Id	Symmetrical Uncert	Id	ChiSquared
21	0.3294	0	2.0407	0	99.546	23	0.0597	0	0.4758	0	22.943
5	0.3173	5	0.1328	5	45.571	26	0.0597	5	0.1080	5	12.793
3	0.3133	26	0.0955	33	44.334	24	0.0597	26	0.0793	24	63.906
0	0.3121	24	0.0955	31	44.334	9	0.0226	24	0.0793	26	63.906
1	0.3059	23	0.0955	30	44.316	5	0.0183	23	0.0793	23	63.906
4	0.304	30	0.0728	6	41.945	30	0.0108	30	0.0572	31	57.157
2	0.2999	33	0.0727	40	41.945	33	0.0108	33	0.0571	30	57.106
11	0.2956	31	0.0727	38	41.945	31	0.0107	31	0.0571	33	57.022
23	0.2598	9	0.0606	37	41.945	6	0.0085	9	0.0442	9	35.162
24	0.2598	6	0.0435	10	41.631	21	0.0069	6	0.0376	6	34.508
26	0.2598	38	0.0321	21	40.777	37	0.0067	38	0.0279	21	24.080
19	0.2558	40	0.0321	3	40.603	40	0.0067	40	0.0279	40	22.934
17	0.1621	37	0.0321	1	40.533	38	0.0067	37	0.0279	37	22.934
6	0.1586	10	0.0246	4	40.516	20	0.0055	10	0.0220	38	22.934
30	0.1437	21	0.0197	2	40.481	10	0.0052	21	0.0188	10	20.445
33	0.1436	7	0.0165	19	40.463	3	0.0040	7	0.0150	3	18.028
31	0.1435	8	0.0150	11	40.446	7	0.0035	3	0.0141	1	15.613
25	0.1319	3	0.0147	7	40.411	2	0.0034	8	0.0135	7	15.405
27	0.1319	1	0.0127	8	40.394	13	0.0034	1	0.0122	4	15.010
10	0.1246	4	0.0122	17	40.271	17	0.0033	4	0.0118	8	14.029
38	0.122	2	0.0113	34	40.237	19	0.0029	2	0.0108	2	13.804
40	0.122	11	0.0103	32	40.237	4	0.0028	11	0.0099	11	12.600
37	0.122	19	0.0099	36	40.080	1	0.0026	19	0.0096	19	11.835
18	0.1202	7	0.0091	39	40.080	11	0.0023	17	0.0086	17	68.299
7	0.1005	20	0.0080	41	40.080	15	0.0022	20	0.0073	20	43.105
9	0.0864	18	0.0040	12	40.080	18	0.0021	18	0.0038	13	25.566
8	0.0822	13	0.0039	9	40.080	14	0.0020	13	0.0037	18	24.830
13	0.0775	15	0.0035	14	40.080	8	0.0017	15	0.0033	25	22.483
15	0.0766	27	0.0034	13	40.080	12	0.0008	27	0.0033	27	22.483
16	0.0763	25	0.0034	16	40.080	27	0.0006	25	0.0033	16	21.984
14	0.0625	16	0.0033	15	40.080	25	0.0006	16	0.0032	15	21.071
20	0.0481	14	0.0030	28	40.08	16	0.0001	14	0.0029	14	18.359

In the last scenario, the model was evaluated by hybridizing selection and classification techniques with the segmented dataset. In the first instance, a numbering was established for each of the attributes (see Table 8), to establish the incidence of the attributes. After the application of the feature selection techniques (see Table 9).

Table 10. Hybridization results in classification and selection techniques

Classifier	Atr	FPR (%)	Precision (%)	Recall (%)	ROC area (%)	Selection
Classification Via Regression	5	0.25	99.95	99.95	99.96	Gain Ratio
	5	0.25	99.95	99.95	99.96	Info Gain
	5	0.25	99.95	99.95	99.96	OneR
	5	0.25	99.95	99.95	99.96	Symmetrical lUncert
	5	0.25	99.95	99.95	99.96	ChiSquared
OneR	5	0.14	99.75	99.75	99.80	Gain Ratio
	5	0.14	99.75	99.75	99.80	Info Gain
	5	0.14	99.75	99.75	99.80	OneR
	5	0.14	99.75	99.75	99.80	Symmetrical Uncertain
	5	0.14	99.75	99.75	99.80	ChiSquared

Table 11. Comparative result between the classification via regression + gain ratio and OneR + gain ratio

Class	Classification Via Regression + Gain ratio (5 characteristics)				OneR + Gain ratio (5 characteristics)			
	FP-Rate (%)	Precision (%)	Recall (%)	ROC area (%)	FP-Rate (%)	Precision (%)	Recall (%)	ROC area (%)
Eat	0	100	100	100	0	100	99.8	99.8
Clean	0	100	100	100	0.1	99.9	99.9	100
Cook	1	99.9	99.9	100	0.3	99.5	99.7	99.8
Phone Call	0	100	100	100	0	100	100	100
Washing Hands	0	100	99.6	99.4	0	100	97.8	97.9
Total	0.25	99.95	99.95	99.96	0.14	99.75	99.75	99.8

The model was then evaluated using the classification techniques with the best results obtained from scenario 3-s, hybridizing the following feature selection techniques: Gain Ratio, Info Gain OneR, Symmetrical Uncert, and ChiSquared (see Table 10). To determine which of these classification techniques generated better results, the different quality metrics were evaluated.

The selection techniques used do not ostensibly affect generating a differential value in the ROC Area, Recall, and Precision metrics, their incidence is reflected in determining the number of most appropriate characteristics. There is evidence of a decrease in the number of characteristics that have a greater incidence in the model, but no significant result was obtained by applying the different selection techniques. However, by reducing the number of features we improve the computational time for the realization of the model. It is confirmed that the Classification Via Regression and OneR classifiers with five characteristics (asterisk, M13, M08, DATE, M01) with any of the selection techniques yield important results for Classification Via Regression the ROC area is 99.96% and Recall 99.95%, for OneR the ROC area is 99 .80% and Recovery 99.75%. Below is a comparison between the Classification Via Regression classifier and OneR for each of the classes (see Table 11).

6 Conclusions

This article shows that because of the segmentation process in sliding time windows of 3-s, a notable improvement has been observed in classifiers with the highest rates, among which we can highlight Classification Via Regression, OneR, and Random SubSpace generating an increase in the ROC area, Recall and Precision metrics, in the same way, a decrease in the false positive rate of 0.92% is also observed concerning the first classifier. Table 12 shows for the first scenario the Classification Via Regression classifier had a Recall of 97.60%, after performing the segmentation process this same metric had a result of 99.80%. The Random SubSpace classifier in the first scenario was in second place with a ROC area of 98.60%, in the second scenario it was in fifth place with a ROC area of 98.7%, and after load balancing it was in third place with a ROC area of 99.47%. It should be noted that OneR shows a decrease in the rate of false positives of 2.4%, with which we can indicate that it performs better concerning Classification Via Regression.

In the fourth scenario, the prioritization of the attributes was carried out and after the hybridization of the classification and selection techniques, it was established that the most significant process concerning the best results obtained was load balancing, because the attributes of the greatest incidence on the model are those that do not have aggregation functions, which are generated by the segmentation process. Table 13 shows the prioritization of the attributes with the Gain Ratio selection technique, of which the first five are used to generate the model (asterisk, M13, M08, DATE, M01). Load balancing considerably favored the activity of washing hands. In Table 11 we can see that in the first scenario where load balancing had not been performed, the Recall is 71.20%, in scenario two after load balancing, the Recall improved considerably to 99.80%, With these results, we can say that washing hands was the activity that had the best benefits after load balancing.

Table 12. Comparison of the quality metrics of Scenario 1, Scenario 2, and Scenario 3

Classifier	Scenario 1 Dataset Preprocessed		Scenario 2 Dataset Segmented		Scenario 3 Dataset Segmented and Processed	
	FPR (%)	Recall (%)	FPR (%)	Recall (%)	FPR (%)	Recall (%)
Classification Via Regression	1.2	97.6	0.1	99.8	0.28	99.95
Random SubSpace	4.1	89.9	3.8	91.1	2.15	94.75
Bagging	52	86.4	3.5	90	3.42	90.28
Random Forest	4.1	87.4	3.2	90.4	3.1	91.09
Attribute Selected	2.7	91.8	0.9	97.1	0.69	97.92
J48	2.7	91.6	0.9	96.8	0.77	97.64
OneR	2.8	94.8	0.3	99.5	0.14	99.75
LMT	5.5	85.2	3.9	88.6	3.35	89.67
REP Tree	5.7	84.5	3.6	89.2	3.52	89.54
Random Committee	4.2	87.2	3.3	89.9	3.18	90.64

As a result of the experimentation of the three scenarios shown in the article: preprocessed dataset, segmented dataset, and segmented and processed dataset, it has been possible to demonstrate the results of the Classification Via Regression classifier, having as configuration the delimitation of 5 characteristics. The behavior of the selected classifier is shown below using the ROC curves, generated by using the WEKA software, differentiating them in each of the activities selected for the experimentation scenarios, see Figs. 3, 4, and 5.

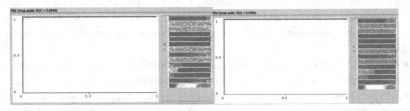

Fig. 3. a) ROC curve characteristic **Clean** b) ROC curve characteristic **Cook**

The recognition of human activities in real life is of vital importance as it allows us to understand and analyze people's behavior in their environment. This information is valuable in various fields such as healthcare, security, artificial intelligence, and human-computer interaction. By identifying and understanding the activities individuals perform, we can design more efficient systems, personalize services, improve decision-making, and ensure a better quality of life for individuals.

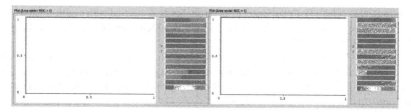

Fig. 4. a) ROC curve characteristic **Eat** b) ROC curve characteristic **Phone Call**

Fig. 5. ROC curve characteristic **Wash Hands.**

Table 13. Prioritization of characteristics according to attribute selection technique

Id	GainRatio	Atr.
21	0.3294	asterisk
5	0.3173	M13
3	0.3133	M08
0	0.3121	DATE
1	0.3059	M01
4	0.304	M09
2	0.2999	M07
11	0.2956	M23
23	0.2598	AD1-A-MAX
24	0.2598	AD1-A-MIN

References

1. Welcome to CASAS. http://casas.wsu.edu/datasets/. Accessed 11 Sep 2022
2. Fettes, L., Bone, A.E., Etkind, S.N., Ashford, S., Higginson, I.J., Maddocks, M.: Disability in basic activities of daily living is associated with symptom burden in older people with advanced cancer or chronic obstructive pulmonary disease: a secondary data analysis. J. Pain Symptom Manage. **61**(6), 1205–1214 (2021). https://doi.org/10.1016/J.JPAINS YMMAN.2020.10.012

3. Carlozzi, N.E., et al.: Daily variation in sleep quality is associated with health-related quality of life in people with spinal cord injury. Arch. Phys. Med. Rehabil. (2021). https://doi.org/10.1016/J.APMR.2021.07.803

4. Vich, G., Delclòs-Alió, X., Maciejewska, M., Marquet, O., Schipperijn, J., Miralles-Guasch, C.: Contribution of park visits to daily physical activity levels among older adults: evidence using GPS and accelerometer data. Urban Forestry Urban Green. **63**, 127225 (2021). https://doi.org/10.1016/J.UFUG.2021.127225

5. Ariza-Colpas, P.P., et al.: Human activity recognition data analysis: History, evolutions, and new trends. Sensors **22**(9), 3401 (2022)

6. Itoh, S., et al.: Acceptance of care technologies to support activities of daily living by middle-aged and older adults in Japan: a cross-sectional study. Int. J. Nurs. Stud. Adv. **3**, 100042 (2021). https://doi.org/10.1016/J.IJNSA.2021.100042

7. Ding, D., Cooper, R.A., Pasquina, P.F., Fici-Pasquina, L.: Sensor technology for smart homes. Maturitas **69**(2), 131–136 (2011). https://doi.org/10.1016/j.maturitas.2011.03.016

8. Khalifa, S., Lan, G., Hassan, M., Seneviratne, A., Das, S.K.: HARKE: human activity recognition from kinetic energy harvesting data in wearable devices. IEEE Trans. Mob. Comput. **17**(6), 1353–1368 (2018). https://doi.org/10.1109/TMC.2017.2761744

9. Cardoso, H.L., Moreira, J.M.: Human activity recognition by means of online semi-supervised learning. In: 2016 17th IEEE International Conference on Mobile Data Management (MDM), pp. 75–77 (2016). https://doi.org/10.1109/MDM.2016.93

10. Calabria-Sarmiento, J.C., et al.: Software applications to health sector: a systematic review of literature (2018)

11. Islam, A.: Android application based smart home automation system using Internet of Things. In: 2018 3rd International Conference for Convergence in Technology (I2CT), pp. 1–9 (2018). https://doi.org/10.1109/I2CT.2018.8529752

12. Jalal, A., Kamal, S., Kim, D.: A depth video-based human detection and activity recognition using multi-features and embedded hidden markov models for health care monitoring systems. Int. J. Interact. Multimedia Artific. Intell. **4**(4), 54 (2017). https://doi.org/10.9781/ijimai.2017.447

13. He, Y., Li, Y., Yin, C.: Falling-incident detection and alarm by smartphone with multimedia messaging service (MMS). E-Health Telecommun. Syst. Networks **01**(01), 1–5 (2012). https://doi.org/10.4236/etsn.2012.11001

14. Tabuenca Dopico, P., Sánchez Espeso, P.P., Villar Bonet, E.: Realisation of an intelligent planner for high-level synthesis. In: 8th Integrated Circuit Design Conference, pp. 315–319 (1993). https://dialnet.unirioja.es/servlet/articulo?codigo=6418065&info=resumen&idioma=SPA. Accessed 11 Sep 2022

15. Chen, Y., Shen, C.: Performance analysis of smartphone-sensor behavior for human activity recognition. IEEE Access **5**, 3095–3110 (2017). https://doi.org/10.1109/ACCESS.2017.2676168

16. Ronao, C.A., Cho, S.B.: Human activity recognition with smartphone sensors using deep learning neural networks. Expert Syst. Appl. **59**, 235–244 (2016). https://doi.org/10.1016/j.eswa.2016.04.032

17. Capela, N.A., Lemaire, E.D., Baddour, N.: Feature selection for wearable smartphone-based human activity recognition with able bodied, elderly, and stroke patients. PLoS ONE **10**(4), e0124414 (2015). https://doi.org/10.1371/journal.pone.0124414

18. Gudivada, V.N., Ding, J., Apon, A.: Data Quality Considerations for Big Data and Machine Learning: Going Beyond Data Cleaning and Transformations Flow Cytometry of 3-D structure View project Data Quality Considerations for Big Data and Machine Learning: Going Beyond Data Cleaning and Transf," no. October, pp. 1–20 (2017) https://www.researchgate.net/publication/318432363. Accessed 11 Sep 2022

19. Ren, X., Malik, J.: Learning a classification model for segmentation. In: Proceedings of the IEEE International Conference on Computer Vision, vol. 1, pp. 10–17 (2003). https://doi.org/10.1109/iccv.2003.1238308

20. Galván-Tejada, C.E., et al.: An analysis of audio features to develop a human activity recognition model using genetic algorithms, random forests, and neural networks. Mob. Inf. Syst. **2016**, 1 (2016). https://doi.org/10.1155/2016/1784101

21. Eddy, S.R.: Profile hidden Markov models, academic.oup.com, vol. 144, no. 9, pp. 755–63 (1998). https://academic.oup.com/bioinformatics/article-abstract/14/9/755/259550. Accessed 11 Sep. 2022

22. Shah, C.: Supervised Learning. In: A Hands-On Introduction to Data Science, pp. 235–289 (2020). https://doi.org/10.1017/9781108560412.010

23. Nettleton, D.F., Orriols-Puig, A., Fornells, A.: A study of the effect of different types of noise on the precision of supervised learning techniques. Artif. Intell. Rev. **33**(4), 275–306 (2010). https://doi.org/10.1007/s10462-010-9156-z

24. Caruana, R., Niculescu-Mizil, A.: An empirical comparison of supervised learning algorithms. In: ACM International Conference Proceeding Series, vol. 148, pp. 161–168 (2006). https://doi.org/10.1145/1143844.1143865

25. Mejia-Ricart, L.F., Helling, P., Olmsted, A.: Evaluate action primitives for human activity recognition using unsupervised learning approach. In: 2017 12th International Conference for Internet Technology and Secured Transactions, ICITST 2017, pp. 186–188 (2018). https://doi.org/10.23919/ICITST.2017.8356374

26. Crandall, A.S. Cook, D.J.: Behaviometrics for Identifying Smart Home Residents, pp. 55–71 (2013). https://doi.org/10.2991/978-94-6239-018-8_4

27. Chen, L., Nugent, C.D., Wang, H.: A knowledge-driven approach to activity recognition in smart homes. IEEE Trans. Knowl. Data Eng. **24**(6), 961–974 (2012). https://doi.org/10.1109/TKDE.2011.51

28. Hoey, J., Pltz, T., Jackson, D., Monk, A., Pham, C., Olivier, P.: Rapid specification and automated generation of prompting systems to assist people with dementia. Pervasive Mob. Comput. **7**(3), 299–318 (2011). https://doi.org/10.1016/j.pmcj.2010.11.007

29. Fahad, L.G., Tahir, S.F., Rajarajan, M.: Feature selection and data balancing for activity recognition in smart homes. In: 2015 IEEE International Conference on Communications (ICC), pp. 512–517 (2015). https://doi.org/10.1109/ICC.2015.7248373

30. Du, Y., Lim, Y., Tan, Y.: A novel human activity recognition and prediction in smart home based on interaction. Sensors **19**(20) (2019). https://doi.org/10.3390/s19204474

31. Johanna, G.R., et al.: Predictive model for the identification of activities of daily living (ADL) in indoor environments using classification techniques based on Machine Learning. Procedia Comput. Sci. **191**, 361–366 (2021). https://doi.org/10.1016/J.PROCS.2021.07.069

32. Ma, C., Li, W., Cao, J., Du, J., Li, Q., Gravina, R.: Adaptive sliding window based activity recognition for assisted livings. Inform. Fus. **53**, 55–65 (2020). https://doi.org/10.1016/j.inffus.2019.06.013

A Novel Self-supervised Representation Learning Model for an Open-Set Speaker Recognition

Abu Quwsar Ohi[(✉)] and Marina L. Gavrilova

Department of Computer Science, University of Calgary, Calgary, AB T2N 1N4, Canada
{mdabuquwsar.ohi,mgavrilo}@ucalgary.ca

Abstract. Speaker recognition is an important problem in behavioral biometric domain. Supervised speaker recognition systems have rapidly evolved since the development of deep learning (DL) architectures. Despite advancements in supervised speaker recognition, an open-set speaker clustering remains a challenging problem. This paper proposes a novel self-supervised representation learning architecture that laverages bi-modal architecture based on CNN and MLP sub-networks. A novel combination of angular prototypical loss and cosine similarity loss ensure an excellent clustering parity, while data augmentation results in a better generalization of the model. The experimental results convincingly demonstrate that the proposed archietcture outperforms state-of-the-art speaker verification methods on VoxCeleb1 and LibriSpeech datasets.

Keywords: Representation Learning · Self-supervised Learning · Deep Neural Network · Open-set Speaker Recognition · Behavioral Biometric

1 Introduction

Speaker recognition is the process of identifying a person from their speech. As speech is a wide-spread medium of communication, speaker recognition is one of the fundamental approaches to human authentication. Speaker recognition has become an exciting research domain due to its applications in voice command recognition, voice authentication, smart homes, remote communication, and e-learning [20].

Speaker recognition systems rapidly evolved over past few years due to the arrival of advanced DL architectures and large-scale training datasets [18]. Supervised learning strategies can achieve high performance upon the availability of a labeled data [10]. At the same time, labeling of large datasets incurs substantial expenses. Therefore, self-supervised speaker recognition methods are becoming highly popular [8].

Self-Supervised Learning (SSL) is a machine learning method that relies on data itself instead of its labels for training [26]. SSL methods are similar to DL as

K. Saeed et al. (Eds.): CISIM 2023, LNCS 14164, pp. 270–282, 2023.
https://doi.org/10.1007/978-3-031-42823-4_20

they identify the similarity and dissimilarity of input [26]. Open-set recognition is the problem where a system is trained based on a specific set of speakers and can recognize both previously seen and unseen speakers during its deployment [5].

Clusterable speaker embeddings allow to estimate the number of speakers, identify similar speakers, discover data representation, and even provide better performance for other downstream tasks during speaker recognition [25]. However, current self-supervised speaker representation learning methods do not focus on creating speaker embeddings.

This study presents a novel self-supervised, open-set speaker representation learning architecture that not only determines the similarity between speakers but also generates embeddings suitable for clustering. The method develops a CNN and MLP neural network architecture and utilizes a simple siamese network that does not require negative data samples for training. To improve the clustering performance, a unique combination of Angular prototypical (AP) loss and cosine distance (CDist) loss is introduced. To the best of our knowledge, this is the first work that develops a self-supervised DL architecture to realize an open-set clusterable speaker representation learning. The paper makes the following contributions:

- A novel deep-learning architecture, which utilizes a combination of CNN and MLP networks, has been proposed for an open-set speaker recognition.
- A simple siamese training architecture that does not require negative sampling has been utilized for speaker clustering.
- A proposed architecture is suitable for self-supervised speaker representation learning and surpasses state-of-the-art deep-learning speaker recognition systems in both clustering parity and speaker verification, while requiring less number of parameters.

The proposed novel architecture is fully implemented and validated on two benchmark datasets: VoxCeleb1 [18] and LibriSpeech [19]. Due to its low number of parameters, it is well suitable for real-time speaker recognition.

The rest of the paper is organized as follows: Sect. 2 highlights the related works in self-supervised learning and speaker recognition systems. Section 3 describes the proposed self-supervised representation learning system. Section 4 provides experimental analysis to validate the efficiency of the proposed method. Finally, Sect. 5 draws conclusions and proposes future work.

2   Related Works

Speaker recognition is one of the fundamental research problems, studies from the communication as well as biometric point of views. From speech synthesis for virtual reality and consumer applications [28], to advanced multi-modal systems based on speech and face recognition [12], this is an ever-growing domain with numerous applications.

The speaker recognition domain of research was traditionally relying on classical machine learning models [6]. Early speaker recognition systems highly depended on speech feature extraction using Gaussian mixture models and Markov models [6]. DL methods demonstrated their superiority by replacing classical machine learning models with neural networks [24]. Further improvements lead the system to be independent of the feature extraction, resulting in end-to-end speaker recognition systems [14].

DL methods can learn similarity from data without labels with the help of similarity learning networks. Siamese networks [1] are commonly used for this task, and can learn data representation from a shared weight architecture receiving a pair of inputs. A similar data pair is called a positive input pair, and dissimilar data pair a negative pair. While training a siamese network with unlabelled data, positive samples can be generated using augmentation, while negative examples require pre-processing [3]. Further improvement in the self-supervised methods alleviates the need for negative samples. Grill et al. [8] introduced a BYOL architecture that uses a momentum encoder and a DL architecture in the siamese network. Caron et al. [2] introduced cluster assignment codes to learn the feature representation indirectly from the input data. The problem with such architectures is that they only perform well with large batch sizes. Simple siamese [4] is a powerful self-supervised model that uses an encoder, a typical DL architecture for feature extraction, and a shallow multi-layer perceptron as a predictor network. Additionally, the siamese network does not require an increased batch size for achieving a good accuracy.

Recently, Huh et al. [11] introduced an adversarial approach for speaker recognition. Like adversarial architectures, the training involves an embedding model and a discriminator model. A pair of non-overlapping audio segments with the same and different noise augmentation is used for training. Although the method is promising as it generates noise-invariant embeddings, it is only suitable for speaker verification.

Mun et al. [17] proposed a self-supervised speaker embedding extractor called contrastive equilibrium learning (CEL). The method uses uniformity loss and AP loss to maintain an equilibrium state of the embeddings. The limitation of the model is the uniformity loss uses a radial basis function that is sensitive to its kernel width as well as the parameter. Scaling such models with a higher number of embeddings can cause model overfitting.

Sang et al. [21] proposed a self-supervised speaker recognition system based on simple siamese [4] architecture that consists of an encoder and a shallow predictor model. Simple siamese architecture can automatically learn the dissimilarity of speaker representations due to its training strategy. However, the model is highly dependent on the regularization, and data augmentation strategies, which does not generalize well for different datasets.

As seen from the above discussion, practically no work focused on producing clusterable embedding that leads to better speaker representation learning. Our method offers the following advantages: it does not depend on hyperparameter tuning while scaling the model and embedding dimension and does not require an extensive regularization network. Moreover, the proposed neural network architecture is faster and requires less memory than the existing speaker representation learning methods. The proposed methodology is described in the following section.

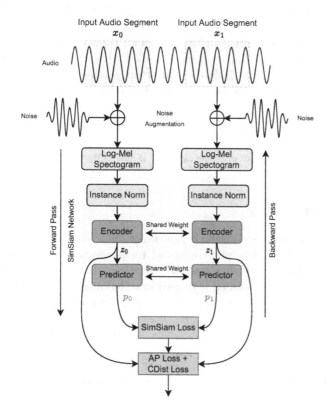

Fig. 1. The training flowchart of the proposed architecture.

3   Methodology

The novel self-supervised speaker clustering system based on residual learning paradigm described in this section. It is rooted in a simple siamese network, which enables training the network without requiring negative samples, with smaller batch size and fewer memory requirements. In order to produce clusterable embeddings, AP loss and CDist loss are added to the output of the encoder. In each mini-batch, the architecture is trained with two randomly cropped utterance segments x_1 and x_2 from the same speaker (see Fig. 1). The utterance segments are augmented, which allows the model to learn speech variations and provides an excellent generalization. In the subsequent sections, we describe the training strategy, introduce the loss functions, and explain the advantages of the proposed architecture.

3.1 Self-supervised Network

Figure 1 depicts the training process of the proposed network. The encoder generates an encoding of the given input, which is further processed by the predictor model. The standard encoder model is built using CNN, followed by a three-layer MLP.

The model receives positive audio samples for training. The encoder and predictor models are placed in a siamese network with shared weights, and half of the network's weight is not updated using stop gradients. The proposed architecture is trained with cosine loss function derived as,

$$\mathcal{L}_{simsiam} = \frac{1}{2}\mathcal{C}(p_0, z_1) + \frac{1}{2}\mathcal{C}(p_1, z_0) \tag{1}$$

Here z_i is the output of the encoder, and p_i is the output of the predictor when z_i. $\mathcal{C}(\cdot, \cdot)$ is the cosine distance between two datapoints.

3.2 Cluster Criterion

While the typical siamese network loss function is designed to discriminate between pairs of data, it is not optimized for generating clusterable outputs. Therefore, to perform clustering, a separate criterion is required. A recently proposed AP loss [5] has performed very well in differentiating data similarity. AP loss is calculated by computing the softmax loss between the centroids and the embeddings,

$$\mathcal{L}_{proto} = -\frac{1}{N}\sum_i^N log\frac{e^{\mathcal{D}(y_i,c_i)}}{\sum_{k=1}^N e^{\mathcal{D}(y_k,c_i)}} \tag{2}$$

The centroids c_i are the embeddings that are calculated by taking the mean of the available support set,

$$c_i = \frac{1}{M-1}\sum_m^{M-1} x_{i,m} \tag{3}$$

Here, M is the number of data available in the support set. $M = 2$ has been evaluated to perform better for metric learning [5], hence we use the same value of M. In Eq. 2, $\mathcal{D}(\cdot, \cdot)$ is the angular cosine distance between two data points, which can be calculated as,

$$\mathcal{D}(p, q) = \mathcal{C}(p, q) \times w + b \tag{4}$$

In the equation, w and b are learnable real-value parameters. We further add the value of all possible cosine distance (CDist) as loss so that the model can emphasize maintaining distance from the other centroids. It is defined as follows,

$$\mathcal{L}_{cdist} = \sum_{i\neq j}^N \mathcal{D}(y_i, e_j) \tag{5}$$

The clustering module is trained using loss functions derived from Eqs. 1, 2, and 5. The final weighted loss is,

$$\mathcal{L} = \lambda_1 \mathcal{L}_{simsiam} + \lambda_2 \mathcal{L}_{proto} + \lambda_3 \mathcal{L}_{cdist} \tag{6}$$

Here, the value of λ_1, λ_1, and λ_1 is 0.7, 0.3, and 3, respectively.

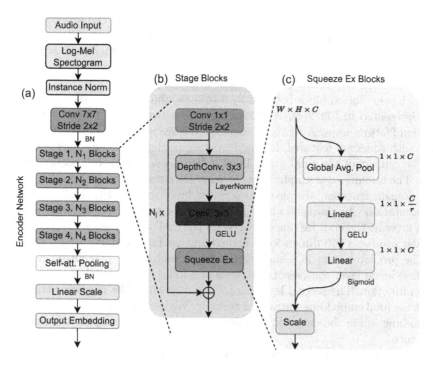

Fig. 2. The overall flowchart of the proposed deep learning architecture. Left to right: (a) the CNN pipeline used for the encoder architecture; (b) a single block of the CNN; (c) an excitation block.

3.3 Model Architecture

The proposed deep-learning architecture consists of an encoder and a shallow decoder model. The encoder receives a log-mel spectrogram which is a powerful audio feature extractor that perceives similar feature intensities to the human ear. Instance normalization [27] is performed after computing the log-mel spectrogram to reduce the covariance shift of the input data, to smoothen the learning process. The inputs are augmented with noise and room impulses to ensure better generalization in noisy environments [5].

Figure 2 demonstrates the model architecture. The encoder network begins with a convolution layer with a kernel size of 7 and a stride of 2, followed by a batch norm layer. The convolution layer is followed by four stages of convolution blocks, each having N_i number of convolutions. The number of convolutions for the four stages are $\{2, 2, 6, 2\}$, which follows the 1:1:3:1 convolution block ratio used in the state-of-the-art vision models [15]. The channel dimensions for the four blocks are $\{16, 32, 64, 128\}$. Similar to Fast-ResNet-34 [5], the strides of 2 are placed in the second and third blocks to reduce computational complexity and memory demands.

Each of the convolution blocks is illustrated in Fig. 2(b). The proposed architecture utilized the layer norm instead of batch norm, as layer norm helps to reduce bias on training data. The channel dimensions are increased at the first depthwise separable convolution block. In addition, the number of norms is reduced, in order to create a light-weight system.

Each convolution block is tailed by a squeeze and excitation block (SEblock) [9], represented in Fig. 2(c). A SEblock provides better calibration to the convolution feature maps. A SEblock contains average pooling, followed by a linear layer with squeezed features, followed by a sigmoid-gated linear layer.

The output of the final stage block follows a self-attentive pooling (SAP) layer. The pooling layer emphasizes the most important features from the overall time domain features. We also add a linear layer to scale the final embedding representation. As simple siamese networks tend to work better with a batch norm layer at the end, we place it between the SAP and linear scaler layer. The encoder produces 256 dimensional embeddings as final output.

The predictor layer is a shallow two-layer, multi-layer perceptron network. The first linear layer consists of 64 dimensions, followed by a batch norm and activation function. The second layer is of 256 dimensions. The predictor layer produces the final embedding output for training. We use SiLU [7] as the default activation function in the network, as it avoids dead neurons and provides smoother gradients.

The proposed network combines two loss functions to represent speech as clusterable embeddings. The encoder architecture is redesigned based on state-of-the-art strategies to improve the network's performance while reducing time and memory complexity.

4   Experimental Results

4.1   Datasets

The proposed deep-learning architecture was validated on two benchmark datasets. VoxCeleb1 [18] dataset contains 1251 speakers, with 1,211 speakers in the training set and 40 speakers in the testing set. The speakers in training and testing sets do not overlap. We further use the LibriSpeech dataset's [19] test-clean subset, containing 40 speakers, for verifying the effectiveness of the method in an open-set scenario. The models are trained on the VoxCeleb1 training set without any labels.

4.2 Experimental Setup

The model is trained using a batch size of 128 with 1.8-s audio speech pairs. The log-mel spectrogram is generated using 40 mel filterbanks with 25 ms frame length and 10 ms shift. The model is trained using Adam optimizer with an automatic weight decay [16], with a 0.001 learning rate. In order to simulate real world conditions, the Musan [23] noise dataset was used for noise augmentation during training. A learning rate scheduler was used with a 3% decay in every 10 epochs. All of the hyper-parameters were chosen after thorough experimentation. To compare the proposed system with state-of-the-art methods, we re-implemented CEL [17] and SimSiamReg [21] self-supervised methods and used similar augmentation procedures for training all architectures. All of the models were trained without any data labels from random initial weights. Pytorch library is used to implement the DL architectures and trained on NVIDIA GeForce RTX 3090 graphics with 64 gigabyte random access memory.

Table 1. Ablation study of the proposed method.

Method	VoxCeleb1			LibriSpeech	
	ARI	NMI	EER	ARI	NMI
Without an additional linear layer	0.7317	0.9081	27.8	0.7031	0.8541
Without CDist loss	0.8709	0.9766	18.2	0.8781	0.9272
Without augmentation	0.8664	0.9756	18.6	0.8625	0.9171
Without proposed model	0.9575	0.9798	15.1	0.8907	0.9374
The proposed model with an additional linear layer, AP loss, CDist loss, and data augmentation	**0.9626**	**0.9855**	**15.4**	**0.9065**	**0.9564**

4.3 Ablation Study

We first investigate the effectiveness of the various components of the proposed method based on clustering performance, shown in Table 1. K-means clustering has been used to identify the cluster regions. For measuring clustering performance, we computed normalized mutual information (NMI) score [13] that is a measure of the mutual dependence among clusters on a scale [0, 1]. We also computed the adjusted rand index (ARI) [22], which provides the cluster similarity of all possible cluster pairs on a scale [0, 1]. We computed equal error rate (EER) to measure the recognition performance of the system. The standard simple siamese architecture uses three linear layers at the encoder. With the default setup, the model does not perform well in the VoxCeleb1 and LibriSpeech datasets. Adding a linear layer provided better performance. Further, excluding the AP loss results in worst cluster performance, as the network loses its ability to center similar embeddings. CDist loss emphasizes pushing cluster points farther so that cluster groups avoid overlap. Its removal results in a reduction of NMI and ARI values, but to the smaller degree than the removal of AP loss. Augmenting data improves the generalization of the model. Training the model with Fast-ResNet [5] architecture results in reduced model performance. The conducted experiment clearly demonstrates that each component of the proposed system is essential and contributes to the optimal performance.

Table 2. Comparison of the clustering performance of different self-supervised methods with the proposed architecture.

Method	VoxCeleb1		LibriSpeech	
	ARI	NMI	ARI	NMI
CEL [17]	0.8385	0.9645	0.7939	0.9083
SimSiamReg [21]	0.8535	0.9667	0.8004	0.9077
Proposed method	**0.9626**	**0.9855**	**0.9065**	**0.9564**

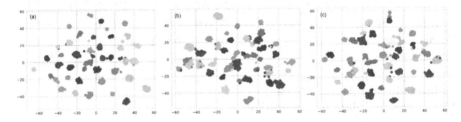

Fig. 3. Embeddings of the VoxCeleb1-test dataset generated by (a) the proposed method, (b) CEL [17], and (c) SimSiamReg [21].

4.4   Speaker Clustering

Table 2 provides a performance comparison of the proposed method with the state-of-the-art methods. The proposed method outperforms the comparators by a 0.10 ratio in ARI score on both datasets. Additionally, the method performs better by a ratio of 0.05 on LibriSpeech dataset. Figure 3 provides a visualization of the embeddings of the models for VoxCeleb1-test dataset. It can be observed that the embeddings of the proposed method tightly group together for each of the clusters (Fig. 3(a)). Moreover, the distance between each cluster group is efficiently maintained. Compared to the proposed method, the embeddings produced by CEL and SimSiamReg are not tightly bound and contain overlappings (Fig. 3(b), 3(c), respectively).

Table 3. A comparison of the methods for speaker verification task on VoxCeleb1-test set.

Method	Precision	Recall	F1-score	EER	AUC
SimSiamReg [21]	64.3	91.3	75.5	22.4	85.4
CEL [17]	65.2	95.6	77.5	17.8	90.1
Proposed method	**68.9**	**96.0**	**80.2**	**15.4**	**92.8**

4.5 Speaker Verification

Table 3 shows performance of the model for speaker verification task on VoxCeleb1-test set. The proposed SSRL architecture delivers 3% improvement in precision and F1-score over CEL model and 4% over SimSiamReg model. The proposed model gains 2.4% improvement in EER over other methods.

Figure 4 provides additional insight into the AUC score and EER for speaker verification on VoxCeleb1-test. Our method outperforms CEL by 3% and SimSiamReg by 8% in AUC score, indicating that it is highly effective for speaker verification tasks.

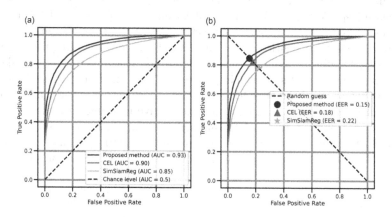

Fig. 4. Comparison of different methods based on (a) AUC and (b) EER.

4.6 Computational Complexity

Table 4 presents the number of parameters and computational complexity scores of the compared architectures. The proposed method requires 1.1 million parameters, which is substantially less than the comparators. The table also provides a comparison of the computational complexity of models based on the multiply-accumulate (MAC) operations. The proposed method requires 0.14G MAC, which is 0.34G MAC less than the lightest deep neural network architecture Fast-ResNet. As our method requires substantially less time than the

Table 4. Comparison of parameters and complexity of different self-supervised speaker representation learning methods.

Method	Network	Parameters	MAC	Inference Time (ms)
SimSiamReg [21]	Thin ResNet-34	1.4M	0.93G	6.81
CEL [17]	Fast-ResNet	1.4M	0.45G	2.56
Proposed method	**Custom-ResNet**	**1.1M**	**0.14G**	**1.92**

input stream timeline, we can infer that it can be utilized for real-time speaker embeddings.

5 Conclusion

In this paper, we propose the novel self-supervised speaker representation model for an open-set clustering and a speaker verification problems. With the introduction of a deep learning architecture, powered by a combination of two powerful loss functions, the method achieves better performance then its comparators in an open-set speaker clustering and verification on VoxCeleb1 and LibriSpeech datasets. Moreover, the encoder architecture is fast, allowing the possibility for real-time speaker authentication. The method also does not require negative samples for training, making it easier to train and resistant to class imbalance. The experimental results convincingly demonstrate that the proposed method performs better in all the clustering and verification scenarios then most recent state-of-the-art methods. In the future, alternative loss functions that mitigate the effect of a noisy data can be examined. A comparative user study can be conducted to evaluate the model performance compared to human perception. In addition, the architecture can be adapted for speaker diarization problem.

Acknowledgment. The authors acknowledge the Natural Sciences and Engineering Research Council (NSERC) Discovery Grant funding, as well as the NSERC Strategic Partnership Grant (SPG) and the Innovation for Defense Excellence and Security Network (IDEaS) for the partial funding of this project.

References

1. Bromley, J., Guyon, I., LeCun, Y., Säckinger, E., Shah, R.: Signature verification using a Siamese time delay neural network. In: Proceedings of the 6th International Conference on Neural Information Processing Systems, pp. 737–744 (1993)
2. Caron, M., Misra, I., Mairal, J., Goyal, P., Bojanowski, P., Joulin, A.: Unsupervised learning of visual features by contrasting cluster assignments. Adv. Neural. Inf. Process. Syst. **33**, 9912–9924 (2020)
3. Chen, T., Kornblith, S., Norouzi, M., Hinton, G.: A simple framework for contrastive learning of visual representations. In: International Conference on Machine Learning, pp. 1597–1607. PMLR (2020)

4. Chen, X., He, K.: Exploring simple Siamese representation learning. In: Proceedings of the IEEE/CVF Conference on Computer Vision and Pattern Recognition, pp. 15750–15758 (2021)
5. Chung, J.S., et al.: In defence of metric learning for speaker recognition. In: Proc. Interspeech 2020, pp. 2977–2981 (2020)
6. Dehak, N., Kenny, P.J., Dehak, R., Dumouchel, P., Ouellet, P.: Front-end factor analysis for speaker verification. IEEE Trans. Audio Speech Lang. Process. **19**(4), 788–798 (2010)
7. Elfwing, S., Uchibe, E., Doya, K.: Sigmoid-weighted linear units for neural network function approximation in reinforcement learning. Neural Netw. **107**, 3–11 (2018)
8. Grill, J.B., et al.: Bootstrap your own latent-a new approach to self-supervised learning. Adv. Neural. Inf. Process. Syst. **33**, 21271–21284 (2020)
9. Hu, J., Shen, L., Sun, G.: Squeeze-and-excitation networks. In: Proceedings of the IEEE Conference on Computer Vision and Pattern Recognition, pp. 7132–7141 (2018)
10. Jung, J.w., Kim, Y.J., Heo, H.S., Lee, B.J., Kwon, Y., Chung, J.S.: Pushing the limits of raw waveform speaker recognition. arXiv preprint 2203 (2022)
11. Kang, J., Huh, J., Heo, H.S., Chung, J.S.: Augmentation adversarial training for self-supervised speaker representation learning. IEEE J. Sel. Top. Signal Process. **16**(6), 1253–1262 (2022)
12. Kuśmierczyk, A., Sławińska, M., Żaba, K., Saeed, K.: Biometric fusion system using face and voice recognition: a comparison approach: biometric fusion system using face and voice characteristics. Adv. Comput. Syst. Secur. **10**, 71–89 (2020)
13. Kvålseth, T.O.: On normalized mutual information: measure derivations and properties. Entropy **19**(11), 631 (2017)
14. Li, C., et al.: Deep speaker: an end-to-end neural speaker embedding system. arXiv preprint arXiv:1705.02304 (2017)
15. Liu, Z., et al.: Swin transformer: hierarchical vision transformer using shifted windows. In: IEEE/CVF International Conference on Computer Vision, pp. 10012–10022 (2021)
16. Loshchilov, I., Hutter, F.: Decoupled weight decay regularization. arXiv preprint arXiv:1711.05101 (2017)
17. Mun, S.H., Kang, W.H., Han, M.H., Kim, N.S.: Unsupervised representation learning for speaker recognition via contrastive equilibrium learning. arXiv preprint arXiv:2010.11433 (2020)
18. Nagrani, A., Chung, J.S., Zisserman, A.: VoxCeleb: a large-scale speaker identification dataset. Telephony **3**, 33–039 (2017)
19. Panayotov, V., Chen, G., Povey, D., Khudanpur, S.: LibriSpeech: an ASR corpus based on public domain audio books. In: 2015 IEEE International Conference on Acoustics, Speech and Signal Processing (ICASSP), pp. 5206–5210. IEEE (2015)
20. Saeed, K.: New Directions in Behavioral Biometrics. CRC Press, Boca Raton (2016)
21. Sang, M., Li, H., Liu, F., Arnold, A.O., Wan, L.: Self-supervised speaker verification with simple Siamese network and self-supervised regularization. In: ICASSP 2022–2022 IEEE International Conference on Acoustics, Speech and Signal Processing (ICASSP), pp. 6127–6131. IEEE (2022)
22. Santos, J.M., Embrechts, M.: On the use of the adjusted rand index as a metric for evaluating supervised classification. In: Alippi, C., Polycarpou, M., Panayiotou, C., Ellinas, G. (eds.) ICANN 2009, Part II. LNCS, vol. 5769, pp. 175–184. Springer, Heidelberg (2009). https://doi.org/10.1007/978-3-642-04277-5_18

23. Snyder, D., Chen, G., Povey, D.: MUSAN: a music, speech, and noise corpus. arXiv preprint arXiv:1510.08484 (2015)
24. Snyder, D., Garcia-Romero, D., Povey, D., Khudanpur, S.: Deep neural network embeddings for text-independent speaker verification. In: Interspeech, vol. 2017, pp. 999–1003 (2017)
25. Tanveer, M.I., Casabuena, D., Karlgren, J., Jones, R.: Unsupervised speaker diarization that is agnostic to language, overlap-aware, and tuning free. In: Proceedings of the Interspeech 2022, pp. 1481–1485 (2022)
26. Tao, R., Lee, K.A., Das, R.K., Hautamäki, V., Li, H.: Self-supervised speaker recognition with loss-gated learning. In: ICASSP IEEE International Conference on Acoustics, Speech and Signal Processing (ICASSP), pp. 6142–6146. IEEE (2022)
27. Ulyanov, D., Vedaldi, A., Lempitsky, V.: Instance normalization: the missing ingredient for fast stylization. arXiv preprint arXiv:1607.08022 (2016)
28. Yanushkevich, S.N., Stoica, A., Srihari, S.N., Shmerko, V.P., Gavrilova, M.: Simulation of biometric information: the new generation of biometric systems. In: Modeling and Simulation in Biometric Technology, pp. 87–98 (2004)

How to Boost Machine Learning Network Intrusion Detection Performance with Encoding Schemes

Marek Pawlicki[1,3]([✉]), Aleksandra Pawlicka[1,2], Rafał Kozik[1,3], and Michał Choraś[1,3]

[1] ITTI, Poznań, Poland
mpawlicki@itti.com.pl
[2] University of Warsaw, Warsaw, Poland
[3] Bydgoszcz University of Science and Technology, Bydgoszcz, Poland

Abstract. Network Intrusion Detection is one of the major components of maintaining cybersecurity. This is especially crucial in Soft Targets, important places which are easily accessible, and thus more vulnerable. Real-time machine-learning-based network intrusion detection is an increasingly more relevant field of study offering important benefits to the practice of securing against cyberthreats. This paper contributes to this growing body of research by evaluating one of the problems prevailing in all machine-learning-based detectors - the notion of encoding categorical values. The use of different encoding schemes is thoroughly evaluated with the use of three different classifier types, and statistical analysis of the results is performed. The best-performing solution is proposed.

Keywords: Machine Learning · Network Intrusion Detection · Deep Neural Networks

1 Introduction

In the security nomenclature, a 'soft target' refers to an important location accessible to the public but lacking the protections characteristic of critical infrastructure, rendering it significantly harder to protect. Recently, the topic of the soft target cybersecurity has gained prominence following various incidents. In one case in September 2022, a hacktivist group GhostSec claimed control over some of the operational technology (OT) pool controllers for a hotel in Israel. The following investigation concluded that two controllers responsible for the dispersion of chloride and the pool pH levels could be affected [3]. Another example reported in Forbes [2] involved hackers using a smart fish tank to infiltrate a casino network. The cybersecurity breach allowed them to exfiltrate 10 GB of data, masking it as video streaming. An attack reported in [5] hit a Water Plant in the city of Oldsmar, Florida. While the intrusion itself lasted for no more than five minutes, it caused a 111-fold increase in sodium hydroxide level in the water going to the city, which was only remedied after almost six hours. As reported, sodium hydroxide can cause vomiting, chest and abdominal pain, skin burns and hair loss. The study presented in [20] gathers and analyses fifteen cyberincidents related to the water sector. The authors conclude that the industry has to both face new threats like ransomware or crypto-jacking and handle already-known attack vectors.

Industries face emerging threats. A ransomware attack described in [6] impacted over 440,000 customers of SmarterASP.NET hosting provider customers, causing downtime for some of the services the company customers were hosting on their infrastructure, which includes websites and app backends. As a result, the attack impacted the SmarterASP.NET brand, causing some of its clients to look for other providers. Similar attacks in 2019 hit Cencosud, a multinational retail operator based in Chile. Reportedly, as the attack hit, printers in some of the operator's stores started printing notes about the ransomware automatically. In an attack on Landry's restaurant chains, some of the customers' credit card credentials were exfiltrated. This leak included the names, card numbers, expiration dates and verification codes [4]. In October 2020, Universal Health Services, which is one of the largest health systems in the US was subject of a cyberattack [7], affecting multiple hospitals, causing outages to computer systems, phone services, internet connectivity, and as consequence delaying medical procedures. Furthermore, an estimated 450 million cyberattacks against the Tokyo Olympics and Paralympics were attempted and thwarted by the Olympics SOC team and affiliated parties, as reported in [1].

The rapid digitization accelerated by the recent pandemic has underscored the immense importance of cybersecurity [29]. The latest cyberattacks, causing financial losses, disruptions in operation and damage to the organisation's reputation, delineate the developing importance of soft target cybersecurity. Machine-Learning Based Network Intrusion Detection is a broad area of research, where various attempts are made to squeeze better performance out of the application of ML algorithms to detect network threats. The fields of study include acquiring proper datasets [28,34,38], various data preprocessing methods [8,13,15,23], application of numerous ML and Deep Learning (DL) algorithms [9,12,27,31,37,40].

The following paper contributes to this growing body of research by evaluating and proposing a simple solution to one of the aspects prevalent in ML-based Network Intrusion Detection Systems (NIDS): efficient categorical feature encoding, which allows for the same or better results in terms of performance metrics and for much more streamlined and elegant processing of data.

The paper is structured as follows: Sect. 2 presents the related works, the materials and methods are presented in Sect. 3, the experiments and achieved results are described in Sect. 4, and Sect. 5 contains the conclusions. Table 1 contains the glossary of abbreviations and full forms used in this paper.

2   Related Works

The notion of using machine learning in intrusion detection systems has been widely researched in recent years. The authors of [18] perform a meta-analysis of a series of surveys on the utilisation of deep learning in NIDS. The study covers collectively over 150 research pieces. Having performed the state-of-the-art analysis, the authors conduct their own evaluation of the application of four different Artificial Neural Network types and compare them with the baseline set up with the Random Forest algorithm, formulating models on four different IDS benchmark datasets.

Table 1. List of abbreviations and their full forms

Abbreviation	Full Form
ANN	Artificial Neural Network
CICIDS2017	Canadian Institute for Cybersecurity Intrusion Detection Dataset 2017
DL	Deep Learning
DoS	Denial of Service
DDoS	Distributed Denial of Service
IDS	Intrusion Detection System
ML	Machine Learning
NIDS	Network Intrusion Detection System
NSL-KDD	Network Security Laboratory - Knowledge Discovery Dataset
OHE	One-Hot Encoding
OT	Operational Technology
SOC	Security Operations Center

In [16], different neural network types are evaluated over the NSL-KDD and CICIDS2017 datasets. The hyperparameters for the networks are optimised with a procedure proposed by the authors, which involves a double particle swarm optimisation.

In [41], using NetFlow for an IDS has been proposed. The proposed anomaly detector has the ability to detect DoS and DDoS attacks, as well as network worms. In [21], NetFlows are used to mitigate DoS and DDoS attacks. The anomaly detector leveraging NetFlows is built as a direct extension of the NetFlow/IPFIX collector, which allows to mitigate the effects of malicious traffic in real-time, by moving the detection directly to the observation point. The approach has been test run on a backbone link of CESNET.

The authors of [14] present a system that dynamically defines and extracts network features from data with the use of clustering algorithms. The advantage of their approach is that the proposed solution defines the set of used features dynamically at run time.

In [35] and [24], the authors attempt to define the most effective set of Net-Flow features for ML-based NIDS. In [35], the authors convert four benchmark NIDS datasets to the NetFlow format, and evaluate two different NetFlow feature sets with the use of the Extra Tree classifier. This research fosters a more rigorous and thorough evaluation of ML-based NIDS. The authors of [24] extend [35] significantly by performing feature selection and testing the obtained feature set on a range of ML algorithms, like Random Forest, a Deep Neural Network, Adaptive Boosting algorithm and Naive Bayes classifier. The most effective feature set is reported.

The topic of encoding categorical features has not been very prominent in the latest IDS research.

The authors of [25] evaluate six different categorical feature encoding schemes in the field of heart disease prediction. The authors note the importance of categorical feature encoding as a crucial preprocessing step in machine learning, as adequate encoding can emphasise the expressiveness of the encoded feature. In [33], seven encoding schemes are evaluated with neural networks in the classification task with the use of the car evaluation dataset.

In their survey on the use of categorical values in artificial neural networks, the authors of [19] identify a wide range of different encoding schemes. The authors divide the schemes into three categories: determined encoding, automatic encoding and algorithmic encoding. Some of the described techniques are code counting, one-hot encoding, label encoding, leave-one-out encoding, and hash-encoding.

In [22], the effect of encoding categorical features is evaluated. The encoding schemes tested are 'Label Encoding', 'One-Hot Encoding' and 'Binary Encoding'. The approaches are tested with six different ML algorithms. The comparison of research in related works can be found in Table 2.

Table 2. Comparison of research in related works

Ref.	Research Focus	Contributions/Findings
[18]	Deep learning in NIDS	SOTA analysis and evaluation of ANN types
[16]	Neural network evaluation	Hyperparameter optimization
[41]	NetFlow-based IDS	Detection of DoS, DDoS, and network worms
[21]	NetFlow-based mitigation	Real-time mitigation
[14]	Dynamic feature extraction	Clustering algorithms for runtime feature definition
[35]	Effective NetFlow feature sets	Evaluation with Extra Tree classifier
[24]	Feature selection in ML-based NIDS	Evaluation with various ML algorithms
[25]	Categorical feature encoding	Emphasizing expressiveness of encoded features
[33]	Encoding schemes in classification	Evaluation with neural networks
[19]	Categorical values in ANNs	Categorization of encoding schemes
[22]	Encoding categorical features	Testing with six different ML algorithms

3   Materials and Methods

Some categories in collected data are not quantitative and are represented in nominal form, often human-readable. In the NetFlow schema, there are categorical values which carry important information. These features carry information about, for example, the protocol used or the utilised destination port. Different than expected destination port number or abnormal protocol usage could indicate an incoming attack. This introduces the notion of proper encoding of those values in the field of NIDS.

3.1   Encoding Schemes

In order for machine learning to be able to make use of this text-format categorical data in needs to be converted to a format that ML can work with. It is an essential step in preparing data for ML. The following are four ways of handling categorical data.

Label Encoding assigns a unique integer value to each distinct class in a particular feature, commencing from 0. While this method posesses the ease of implementation, it can introduce difficulties when encountering novel labels, particularly in features which have numerous different values. This is due to high integer value assigned to a class potentially causing the ML algorithm to value it as more significant [32].

Table 3. Results of Random Forest, ANN and K-NN over the test set, Frequency Encoding

	Random Forest			ANN			K-NN		
	P	R	F1	P	R	F1	P	R	F1
Benign	0.99	1.00	1.00	0.99	1.00	1.00	0.99	1.00	1.00
Bot	1.00	1.00	1.00	0.98	1.00	0.99	1.00	1.00	1.00
Brute Force-Web	0.59	0.92	0.72	0.00	0.00	0.00	0.58	0.94	0.72
Brute Force-XSS	0.41	0.05	0.08	0.38	0.46	0.42	0.48	0.06	0.11
DDOS-HOIC	0.41	0.35	0.38	0.00	0.00	0.00	0.40	0.35	0.37
DDOS-LOIC-UDP	0.83	0.84	0.83	0.72	0.99	0.83	0.82	0.89	0.86
DDoS-LOIC-HTTP	1.00	1.00	1.00	0.98	1.00	0.99	1.00	1.00	1.00
DoS-GoldenEye	1.00	1.00	1.00	0.97	0.81	0.88	1.00	1.00	1.00
DoS-Hulk	1.00	1.00	1.00	0.99	1.00	0.99	1.00	1.00	1.00
DoS-SlowHTTPTest	0.00	0.00	0.00	0.00	0.00	0.00	0.00	0.00	0.00
DoS-Slowloris	1.00	1.00	1.00	0.92	0.97	0.94	1.00	1.00	1.00
FTP-BruteForce	0.65	1.00	0.79	0.64	1.00	0.78	0.65	1.00	0.79
Infilteration	0.27	0.05	0.09	1.00	0.00	0.00	0.50	0.07	0.12
SQL Injection	0.33	0.29	0.31	0.00	0.00	0.00	0.00	0.00	0.00
SSH-Bruteforce	1.00	1.00	1.00	1.00	1.00	1.00	1.00	1.00	1.00

In **One-Hot Encoding (OHE)**, each category is represented by a binary value, where 1 is assigned to the position where the particular feature manifested and 0 in all other positions. Although OHE mitigates the issue of order importance inherent in Label Encoding, OHE introduces its own challenges. OHE increases the dimensionality of input data, often significantly increasing the computational cost.

Frequency Encoding transforms categorical data by substituting each category with the number of occurrences of a particular label in the training set. This approach preserves low dimensionality compared to OHE, and the highest numerical value is assigned to the feature with the highest frequency. One drawback of frequency encoding is that if the high-value feature is more prevalent in one class, this can bias the model towards that class [39].

Dropping Categories is the baseline for handling categorical features, and refers to not using those features altogether. This maintains the low dimensionality of the input data but also rids the model of some potentially important information.

3.2   Classifiers

Table 4. Results of Random Forest, ANN and K-NN over the test set, Label Encoding

	Random Forest			ANN			K-NN		
	P	R	F1	P	R	F1	P	R	F1
Benign	0.99	1.00	1.00	0.99	1.00	0.99	0.99	1.00	1.00
Bot	1.00	1.00	1.00	1.00	1.00	1.00	1.00	1.00	1.00
Brute Force-Web	0.60	0.93	0.72	0.59	0.92	0.72	0.61	0.77	0.68
Brute Force-XSS	0.43	0.05	0.08	0.00	0.00	0.00	0.46	0.26	0.34
DDOS-HOIC	0.41	0.35	0.38	0.00	0.00	0.00	0.38	0.35	0.36
DDOS-LOIC-UDP	0.83	0.84	0.83	0.00	0.00	0.00	0.82	0.89	0.86
DDoS-LOIC-HTTP	1.00	1.00	1.00	0.98	1.00	0.99	1.00	1.00	1.00
DoS-GoldenEye	1.00	1.00	1.00	0.96	0.79	0.87	1.00	1.00	1.00
DoS-Hulk	1.00	1.00	1.00	0.96	0.96	0.96	1.00	1.00	1.00
DoS-SlowHTTPTest	0.00	0.00	0.00	0.00	0.00	0.00	0.00	0.00	0.00
DoS-Slowloris	1.00	1.00	1.00	0.91	0.86	0.88	0.99	1.00	1.00
FTP-BruteForce	0.65	1.00	0.79	0.61	1.00	0.76	0.65	1.00	0.79
Infilteration	0.28	0.06	0.10	0.30	0.02	0.04	0.46	0.05	0.09
SQL Injection	0.33	0.29	0.31	0.00	0.00	0.00	0.00	0.00	0.00
SSH-Bruteforce	1.00	1.00	1.00	0.96	0.98	0.97	1.00	1.00	1.00

Random Forest is an extension of the Decision Trees algorithm. Described in [11] as a way to increase the accuracy and mitigate overfitting of the decision trees. It is a highly-regarded ensemble algorithm, which combines the outputs of multiple decision trees, which are trained using bootstrap aggregation of the training set. It is very well suited for NIDS due to fast execution time and high accuracy on NIDS data [30].

K-Nearest Neighbours uses the similarity between datapoints to assign a label to an incoming sample at test time. The similarity can be expressed as one of a range of distance metrics, including Euclidean and Manhattan distance. The 'k' refers to the number of evaluated samples, with small 'k' causing the classification to be more sensitive to local variations in data, and larger 'k's tend to smooth out the classifications [17].

Artificial Neural Networks (ANN) are a family of versatile algorithms comprising of multiple layers of neural nodes and weighted edges between those nodes. Many scientists refer to them as a sort of computational expression of what biological neural networks are believed to be. The weights connecting neural layers determine the way the inputs are combined to form the output. The neural pathways which lead to minimised error on the received data are arrived at via training, where the error is propagated backwards using the chain rule, allowing to adjust the sets of weights incrementally [26,31]. The hyperparameters of the used models are reported in Table 5.

Table 5. Summary of Hyperparameters for TensorFlow Keras Model, Random Forest Classifier, and K-Nearest Neighbors Classifier

Model	Hyperparameters	Value
Model	Optimizer	Nadam
	Loss	Categorical Crossentropy
	Metrics	Accuracy
	Dense (Input): Units	512
	Dense (Input): Kernel initializer	Uniform
	Dense (Input): Activation	ReLU
	Dropout: Rate	1%
	Dense (Hidden): Units	512
	Dense (Hidden): Activation	ReLU
	Dense (Output): Kernel initializer	Uniform
	Dense (Output): Activation	Softmax
	Batch size	10
	Epochs	10
	GPU	Enabled
Random Forest	n_estimators	200
K-NN	n_neighbors	5

10-Fold Cross Validation. Cross-Validation (CV) is a technique used to evaluate the performance of a model on unseen data. In a k-fold CV, the dataset is divided into k equal parts, then the model is trained on k-1 parts and the final part is used for testing. The procedure is repeated so each subset becomes the testing set once [10]. The CV used in this work was also stratified.

4 Experiments and Results

4.1 Datasets

This research is conducted with the use of the well-regarded NIDS benchmark dataset, CSE-CIC-IDS2018, which is a collection of NIDS data released by the Canadian Institute for Cybersecurity [36]. In its original form, the dataset contains over 80 features; however, the version used in this paper has been converted to the NetFlow format by [34].

4.2 Experimental Procedure

The dataset is split into training and testing sets, using 80% for the training set. The split is stratified to get samples from all target labels into both training and testing sets.

Table 6. Results of Random Forest, ANN and K-NN over the test set, Dropping Features

	Random Forest			ANN			K-NN		
	P	R	F1	P	R	F1	P	R	F1
Benign	0.98	1.00	0.99	0.94	1.00	0.97	0.98	1.00	0.99
Bot	1.00	1.00	1.00	0.00	0.00	0.00	1.00	1.00	1.00
Brute Force-Web	0.58	0.94	0.72	0.40	0.02	0.04	0.50	0.20	0.28
Brute Force-XSS	0.43	0.04	0.08	0.00	0.00	0.00	0.38	0.73	0.50
DDOS-HOIC	0.42	0.37	0.40	0.23	0.26	0.24	0.41	0.35	0.38
DDOS-LOIC-UDP	0.83	0.83	0.83	0.77	0.99	0.86	0.82	0.89	0.86
DDoS-LOIC-HTTP	1.00	0.77	0.87	0.97	0.77	0.86	1.00	0.77	0.87
DoS-GoldenEye	0.86	0.76	0.81	0.76	0.72	0.74	0.86	0.75	0.80
DoS-Hulk	0.97	0.96	0.97	0.95	0.92	0.93	0.97	0.96	0.97
DoS-SlowHTTPTest	0.00	0.00	0.00	0.00	0.00	0.00	0.00	0.00	0.00
DoS-Slowloris	0.99	0.72	0.83	0.79	0.21	0.33	0.98	0.72	0.83
FTP-BruteForce	0.62	1.00	0.76	0.00	0.00	0.00	0.62	1.00	0.76
Infilteration	0.20	0.02	0.04	0.00	0.00	0.00	0.55	0.02	0.04
SQL Injection	0.33	0.29	0.31	0.00	0.00	0.00	0.00	0.00	0.00
SSH-Bruteforce	1.00	1.00	1.00	0.96	1.00	0.98	1.00	1.00	1.00

The training set is balanced using random subsampling on the majority class ('*benign*').

Four different categorical encoding procedures are performed on the categorical variables in the training set: Label Encoding, One-Hot Encoding, Frequency Encoding and Dropping Columns. The encoded features are: '*L7_PROTO*', '*PROTOCOL*', '*L4_DST_PORT*' and '*TCP_FLAGS*'

The resulting encoded training sets are then used to formulate models with the use of RandomForest, KNN and DNN algorithms. RandomForest and DNN have been chosen as they displayed very promising results in earlier research in NIDS with NetFlow. To complete the evaluation, k-NN was included, as it relies on the similarity of datapoints, and is a good supplement to the gradient and tree-based methods. The models are tested on copies of the testing set, which have categorical variables encoded congruently with the training of the model. The results are reported in Table 3, Table 4, Table 6 and Table 7.

A similar procedure is conducted to perform 10-fold cross-validation of the models, the results are reported in Table 8.

One major setback surfaced during evaluation of the OHE approach. Of the four categorical features usable in NIDS, one had 237 different values, and one had 65092 different values. Encoding those features with OHE caused significant memory and computational cost, and the columns had to be dropped due to multiple freezes of the machine the training was performed on. This only emphasises the unwieldiness of OHE in the context of NIDS.

4.3   Metrics

For performance evaluation, a set of established metrics derived from the confusion matrix has been used. These values are Accuracy (ACC), Balanced Accuracy (BCC), Matthews Correlation Coefficient (MCC), Precision (P), Recall (R) and their harmonic mean, the F1-Score. The values found in the confusion matrix are True Positives (TP), True Negatives (TN), False Positives (FP) and False Negatives (FN).

$$ACC = \frac{TP + TN}{TP + FP + FN + TN} \tag{1}$$

$$P = \frac{TP}{TP + FP} \tag{2}$$

$$R = \frac{TP}{TP + FN} \tag{3}$$

$$F1 = 2 * \frac{Recall * Precision}{Recall + Precision} \tag{4}$$

$$BCC = \frac{\frac{TP}{TP+FN} + \frac{TN}{TN+FP}}{2} \tag{5}$$

$$MCC = \frac{TN * TP - FN * FP}{\sqrt{(TP + FP)(TP + FN)(TN + FP)(TN + FN)}} \tag{6}$$

4.4 Results

Table 7. Results of Random Forest and ANN over the test set, One-Hot Encoding

	Random Forest			ANN		
	P	R	F1	P	R	F1
Benign	0.98	1.00	0.99	0.94	1.00	0.97
Bot	1.00	1.00	1.00	0.00	0.00	0.00
Brute Force-Web	0.59	0.94	0.72	0.00	0.00	0.00
Brute Force-XSS	0.00	0.00	0.00	0.00	0.00	0.00
DDOS-HOIC	0.11	0.11	0.11	0.00	0.00	0.00
DDOS-LOIC-UDP	0.81	0.82	0.81	0.00	0.00	0.00
DDoS-LOIC-HTTP	1.00	0.77	0.87	1.00	0.77	0.87
DoS-GoldenEye	0.99	0.99	0.99	0.78	0.63	0.70
DoS-Hulk	1.00	1.00	1.00	0.99	0.88	0.93
DoS-SlowHTTPTest	0.00	0.00	0.00	0.00	0.00	0.00
DoS-Slowloris	1.00	1.00	1.00	0.52	0.65	0.58
FTP-BruteForce	0.65	1.00	0.78	0.00	0.00	0.00
Infilteration	0.28	0.03	0.06	0.00	0.00	0.00
SQL Injection	0.10	0.14	0.12	0.00	0.00	0.00
SSH-Bruteforce	1.00	1.00	1.00	0.93	1.00	0.97

The multiclass detection results for Random Forest, ANN and k-NN are gathered in Table 3, Table 4, Table 6 and Table 7, sorted by encoding schema. Upon inspection, it is evident that Random Forest has achieved better performance across the board on data with categorical variables encoded via Label Encoding and Frequency Encoding. The effects of encoding schemes are more extensive in the case of ANN, where dropping or one-hot-encoding values results in the classifier not picking up on some of the attacks at all, like the 'Bot' class or the 'FTP-Brute Force' class. For k-NN the results are similar, however the high dimensionality of the one-hot-encoded training set was too much of a demand for the k-NN algorithm on the experimental setup. The results of the 10-fold CV are contained in Table 8, Table 9 and Table 10. Upon inspection, the Frequency-Encoded Random Forest achieved the best results across the board, with the highest mean ACC, BACC and MCC from the 10 folds, highest maximum values and highest minimum values. For RandomForest, the minimum values of results for frequency encoded set were higher than the mean results for other encoding types (ACC, BACC and MCC).

Statistical Analysis. To establish the statistical significance of the results, the Wilcoxon signed-rank test was performed, with the null hypothesis expressed as 'Frequency Encoding has the same effect on the classification results as X encoding scheme'. The results of the CV evaluation were used as the basis for the Wilcoxon test. For Random Forest in terms of ACC, Frequency Encoding vs Label Encoding the test rejects the null hypothesis with p = 0.0488. Same for Frequency Encoding vs Dropping categories at p = 0.002 and with p = 0.002 the null hypothesis is rejected for Frequency Encoding vs One-Hot-Encoding. In terms of BCC, the Wilcoxon test fails to reject the null hypothesis of Frequency Encoding vs Label Encoding at p = 0.322. Then it rejects the null hypothesis for Frequency Encoding vs Dropping Categories with p = 0.002. Same for Frequency Encoding vs OHE at p = 0.002. For MCC the test fails to reject the null hypothesis on Frequency Encoding vs Label Encoding at p = 0.084, same for Frequency Encoding vs Dropping Values, and rejects the null hypothesis for Frequency Encoding vs OHE at p = 0.002. Similar tests were performed for ANN and k-NN.

Table 8. Results of stratified 10-fold cross validation, Random Forest

Encoding:	Frequency	Label	Dropping	One-Hot
ACC Max:	**0.979**	0.966	0.966	0.969
ACC Min:	**0.979**	0.964	0.964	0.968
ACC Mean:	**0.979**	0.965	0.965	0.969
BACC Max:	**0.778**	0.719	0.719	0.666
BACC Min:	**0.696**	0.639	0.639	0.642
BACC Mean:	**0.740**	0.683	0.683	0.650
MCC Max:	**0.906**	0.841	0.841	0.860
MCC Min:	**0.905**	0.834	0.834	0.853
MCC Mean:	**0.905**	0.837	0.837	0.854

Table 9. Results of stratified 10-fold cross validation, ANN

Encoding:	Frequency	Label	Dropping
ACC Max:	0.978	0.976	0.940
ACC Min:	0.977	0.974	0.936
ACC Mean:	0.978	0.976	0.938
BACC Max:	0.690	0.688	0.440
BACC Min:	0.535	0.577	0.340
BACC Mean:	0.615	0.658	0.398
MCC Max:	0.902	0.894	0.700
MCC Min:	0.897	0.884	0.673
MCC Mean:	0.900	0.891	0.686

Table 10. Results of stratified 10-fold cross validation, K-NN

Encoding:	Frequency	Label	Dropping
ACC Max:	0.980	0.980	0.966
ACC Min:	0.969	0.969	0.955
ACC Mean:	0.977	0.978	0.961
BACC Max:	0.780	0.779	0.718
BACC Min:	0.702	0.700	0.652
BACC Mean:	0.734	0.736	0.682
MCC Max:	0.908	0.908	0.843
MCC Min:	0.862	0.861	0.790
MCC Mean:	0.898	0.898	0.820

5   Conclusions

This paper evaluated the usefulness of different categorical variable encoding schemes in machine-learning-based network intrusion detection using NetFlows. Overall, Frequency Encoding in IDS has produced similar or better results than other evaluated encoding schemes in terms of ACC, BCC and MCC on three evaluated types of ML classifiers. This was established with extensive tests, 10-fold CV and evaluated with the Wilcoxon signed-rank test. Frequency Encoding also does not increase the dimensionality of the dataset, keeping the computational requirements lower than OHE, especially for features with a large number of unique values. This makes Frequency Encoding a good fit for real-time NIDS using NetFlow. The work presented in this paper is significant in comparison to existing works as the aspect of the influence of value encoding has not been widely explored in the literature in the context of NIDS, making it a valuable addition to the field. For future directions, the research could be extended by investigating more encoding techniques, like hashing. The research could also explore the effect of encoding schemes in conjunction with different feature extraction and selection methods, using a wider range of ML algorithms, like support vector machines or boosting methods, to better understand the effect of encoding on ML performance in the context of NIDS. The study could also be extended to include real-world evaluation of Frequency Encoding in operational environments, such as SOCs. Future research could also investigate the effect of Frequency Encoding on different types of datasets.

Acknowledgements. This research is funded under the Horizon 2020 APPRAISE Project, which has received funding from the European Union's Horizon 2020 research and innovation programme under grant agreement No. 101021981.

References

1. About 450m cyberattacks prevented during Tokyo olympics. https://www.aa.com. tr/en/asia-pacific/about-450m-cyberattacks-prevented-during-tokyo-olympics/ 2383969. Accessed 20 Feb 2023
2. Criminals hacked a fish tank to steal data from a Casino. https://www.forbes. com/sites/leemathews/2017/07/27/criminals-hacked-a-fish-tank-to-steal-data-from-a-casino/#3bc82bd032b9. Accessed 20 Feb 2023
3. Cyberattackers make waves in hotel swimming pool controls. https://www. darkreading.com/attacks-breaches/breached-controllers-let-attackers-breach-hotel-pools-in-israel. Accessed 20 Feb 2023
4. Data breach affects 63 Landry's restaurants — threatpost. https://threatpost.com/ data-breach-affects-63-landrys-restaurants/151503/. Accessed 20 Feb 2023
5. Lessons learned from Oldsmar water plant hack – security today. https:// securitytoday.com/articles/2021/04/05/lessons-learned-from-oldsmar-water-plant-hack.aspx. Accessed 20 Feb 2023
6. Ransomware attack on smarterasp.net impact 440,000 customers - cybersecurity insiders. https://www.cybersecurity-insiders.com/ransomware-attack-on-smarterasp-net-impact-440000-customers/. Accessed 20 Feb 2023
7. Update: UHS health system confirms all us sites affected by ransomware attack. https://healthitsecurity.com/news/uhs-health-system-confirms-all-us-sites-affected-by-ransomware-attack. Accessed 20 Feb 2023
8. Ahmad, T., Aziz, M.N.: Data preprocessing and feature selection for machine learning intrusion detection systems. ICIC Express Lett. **13**(2), 93–101 (2019)
9. Ahmad, Z., Shahid Khan, A., Wai Shiang, C., Abdullah, J., Ahmad, F.: Network intrusion detection system: a systematic study of machine learning and deep learning approaches. Trans. Emerg. Telecommun. Technol. **32**(1), e4150 (2021)
10. Arlot, S., Celisse, A.: A survey of cross-validation procedures for model selection (2010)
11. Breiman, L.: Random forests. Mach. Learn. **45**, 5–32 (2001)
12. Chowdhury, M.N., Ferens, K., Ferens, M.: Network intrusion detection using machine learning. In: Proceedings of the International Conference on Security and Management (SAM), p. 30. The Steering Committee of The World Congress in Computer Science, Computer ... (2016)
13. Davis, J.J., Clark, A.J.: Data preprocessing for anomaly based network intrusion detection: a review. Comput. Secur. **30**(6–7), 353–375 (2011)
14. Dias, L., Valente, S., Correia, M.: Go with the flow: clustering dynamically-defined NetFlow features for network intrusion detection with DynIDS. In: 2020 IEEE 19th International Symposium on Network Computing and Applications (NCA), pp. 1–10 (2020). https://doi.org/10.1109/NCA51143.2020.9306732
15. Dutta, V., Choras, M., Pawlicki, M., Kozik, R.: Detection of cyberattacks traces in IoT data. J. Univers. Comput. Sci. **26**(11), 1422–1434 (2020)
16. Elmasry, W., Akbulut, A., Zaim, A.H.: Evolving deep learning architectures for network intrusion detection using a double PSO metaheuristic. Comput. Netw. **168**, 107042 (2020). https://doi.org/10.1016/j.comnet.2019.107042. https://www. sciencedirect.com/science/article/pii/S138912861930800X
17. Fix, E.: Discriminatory Analysis: Nonparametric Discrimination, Consistency Properties, vol. 1. USAF School of Aviation Medicine (1985)

18. Gamage, S., Samarabandu, J.: Deep learning methods in network intrusion detection: a survey and an objective comparison. J. Netw. Comput. Appl. **169**, 102767 (2020). https://doi.org/10.1016/j.jnca.2020.102767. https://www.sciencedirect.com/science/article/pii/S1084804520302411

19. Hancock, J.T., Khoshgoftaar, T.M.: Survey on categorical data for neural networks. J. Big Data **7**(1), 1–41 (2020). https://doi.org/10.1186/s40537-020-00305-w

20. Hassanzadeh, A., et al.: A review of cybersecurity incidents in the water sector. J. Environ. Eng. **146**(5), 03120003 (2020)

21. Hofstede, R., Bartoš, V., Sperotto, A., Pras, A.: Towards real-time intrusion detection for NetFlow and IPFIX. In: Proceedings of the 9th International Conference on Network and Service Management (CNSM 2013), pp. 227–234 (2013). https://doi.org/10.1109/CNSM.2013.6727841

22. Jackson, E., Agrawal, R.: Performance evaluation of different feature encoding schemes on cybersecurity logs. In: 2019 SoutheastCon, pp. 1–9 (2019). https://doi.org/10.1109/SoutheastCon42311.2019.9020560

23. Jo, W., Kim, S., Lee, C., Shon, T.: Packet preprocessing in CNN-based network intrusion detection system. Electronics **9**(7), 1151 (2020)

24. Komisarek, M., Pawlicki, M., Kozik, R., Hołubowicz, W., Choraś, M.: How to effectively collect and process network data for intrusion detection? Entropy **23**(11), 1532 (2021)

25. Kosaraju, N., Sankepally, S.R., Mallikharjuna Rao, K.: Categorical data: need, encoding, selection of encoding method and its emergence in machine learning models–a practical review study on heart disease prediction dataset using Pearson correlation. In: Saraswat, M., Chowdhury, C., Kumar Mandal, C., Gandomi, A.H. (eds.) ICDSA 2022, vol. 1, pp. 369–382. Springer, Singapore (2023). https://doi.org/10.1007/978-981-19-6631-6_26

26. Leung, H., Haykin, S.: The complex backpropagation algorithm. IEEE Trans. Signal Process. **39**(9), 2101–2104 (1991)

27. Li, J., Qu, Y., Chao, F., Shum, H.P.H., Ho, E.S.L., Yang, L.: Machine Learning Algorithms for Network Intrusion Detection, pp. 151–179. Springer, Cham (2019)

28. Mihailescu, M.E., et al.: The proposition and evaluation of the RoeduNet-SIMARGL2021 network intrusion detection dataset. Sensors **21**(13), 4319 (2021)

29. Pawlicka, A., Choraś, M., Pawlicki, M., Kozik, R.: A $10 million question and other cybersecurity-related ethical dilemmas amid the COVID-19 pandemic. Bus. Horiz. **64**(6), 729–734 (2021)

30. Pawlicki, M., Choraś, M., Kozik, R., Hołubowicz, W.: On the impact of network data balancing in cybersecurity applications. In: Krzhizhanovskaya, V.V., et al. (eds.) ICCS 2020. LNCS, vol. 12140, pp. 196–210. Springer, Cham (2020). https://doi.org/10.1007/978-3-030-50423-6_15

31. Pawlicki, M., Kozik, R., Choraś, M.: A survey on neural networks for (cyber-) security and (cyber-) security of neural networks. Neurocomputing **500**, 1075–1087 (2022)

32. Pedregosa, F., et al.: Scikit-learn: machine learning in Python. J. Mach. Learn. Res. **12**, 2825–2830 (2011)

33. Potdar, K., Pardawala, T.S., Pai, C.D.: A comparative study of categorical variable encoding techniques for neural network classifiers. Int. J. Comput. Appl. **175**(4), 7–9 (2017)

34. Sarhan, M., Layeghy, S., Moustafa, N., Portmann, M.: NetFlow datasets for machine learning-based network intrusion detection systems. In: Deze, Z., Huang, H., Hou, R., Rho, S., Chilamkurti, N. (eds.) BDTA/WiCON 2020. LNICST, vol. 371, pp. 117–135. Springer, Cham (2021). https://doi.org/10.1007/978-3-030-72802-1_9

35. Sarhan, M., Layeghy, S., Portmann, M.: Towards a standard feature set for network intrusion detection system datasets. Mobile Netw. Appl. **27**, 357–370 (2022)

36. Sharafaldin, I., Gharib, A., Lashkari, A.H., Ghorbani, A.A.: Towards a reliable intrusion detection benchmark dataset. Softw. Netw. **2018**(1), 177–200 (2018)

37. Sinclair, C., Pierce, L., Matzner, S.: An application of machine learning to network intrusion detection. In: Proceedings 15th Annual Computer Security Applications Conference (ACSAC 1999), pp. 371–377 (1999). https://doi.org/10.1109/CSAC.1999.816048

38. Szumelda, P., Orzechowski, N., Rawski, M., Janicki, A.: VHS-22-a very heterogeneous set of network traffic data for threat detection. In: Proceedings of the 2022 European Interdisciplinary Cybersecurity Conference, pp. 72–78 (2022)

39. Uyar, A., Bener, A., Ciray, H.N., Bahceci, M.: A frequency based encoding technique for transformation of categorical variables in mixed IVF dataset. In: 2009 Annual International Conference of the IEEE Engineering in Medicine and Biology Society, pp. 6214–6217. IEEE (2009)

40. Zaman, M., Lung, C.H.: Evaluation of machine learning techniques for network intrusion detection. In: NOMS 2018–2018 IEEE/IFIP Network Operations and Management Symposium, pp. 1–5 (2018). https://doi.org/10.1109/NOMS.2018.8406212

41. Zhenqi, W., Xinyu, W.: NetFlow based intrusion detection system. In: 2008 International Conference on MultiMedia and Information Technology, pp. 825–828 (2008). https://doi.org/10.1109/MMIT.2008.213

Neural Networks and Saliency Maps in Diabetic Retinopathy Diagnosis

Maciej Szymkowski[✉]

Faculty of Computer Science, Bialystok University of Technology, Bialystok, Poland
m.szymkowski@pb.edu.pl

Abstract. Diabetes is one of the most dangerous illnesses. Sometimes it can be observed faster by experienced ophthalmologist rather than general practitioner. It is related to the fact that it leads to the small changes in the form of exudates visible in retina color images. Such amendments are known under name of "diabetic retinopathy". However, it needs to be claimed that, in most of the cases, when detected it is too advanced to preserve patient's eyesight. This is the main reason why it is urgent to work-out novel ideas and approaches that can detect these changes in their early stages. In this work we propose a neural network-based algorithm for diabetic retinopathy recognition. For the aim of classification, we consumed well-known CNN's architectures as ResNet50 or VGG-16 but also, new ones as InceptionV4. The best results reached 95% in the task of diabetic retinopathy recognition. Moreover, to increase confidence, saliency maps were introduced – by this solution we observed which parts of the image had the highest impact on the classifier decisions. Our observations confirmed that exudates were the most important in the classification process.

Keywords: retina color images · diabetic retinopathy · machine learning · saliency maps · InceptionV4 · convolutional neural networks

1 Introduction

Nowadays, Machine Learning (ML) and Artificial Intelligence (AI) are one of the key-words in computer science and computer engineering. We observe fast development of the methodologies based on these algorithms. It is related to the fact that they can guarantee high accuracy, efficiency, and precision. One of the latest examples showing that ML and AI provide satisfactory results is ChatGPT3 [1]. This solution can even write a book or publication on its own (on the provided topic).

Previously mentioned ML is also being developed in the medical images analysis and classification. We can observe that plenty of solutions are consumed for the aim of pathological changes detection within diversified samples. On the one hand it can be used to diagnose cardiology issues [2] whilst it is also useful for analysis of human mental state [3]. This statement shows that Machine Learning can be applied to different issues and health problems (in the diversified areas of medicine) as well as it can improve the diagnosis process (make it much faster and even more reliable).

© The Author(s), under exclusive license to Springer Nature Switzerland AG 2023
K. Saeed et al. (Eds.): CISIM 2023, LNCS 14164, pp. 298–309, 2023.
https://doi.org/10.1007/978-3-031-42823-4_22

One of the areas where AI can also be applied is retina color images analysis (or Optical Coherence Tomography images). This statement is true when it comes to diabetic retinopathy or hard exudates recognition. In the literature one can find diversified approaches – especially based on deep learning and hybrid approaches [4] – where the final decision is made with artificial neural network results combined with the information gathered from contextual data. However, in most of the cases we can observe that these approaches are not effective and efficient enough. Moreover, they do not apply one of the latest trends in ML that is explainability. It means that, in fact, we are not aware which part of the image was selected as the pathological change (we know only about final classification result). Explainable AI [5] allows user (and software developer) to better understand which part of the image was classified as changed – it makes the AI models much more reliable.

In this work we propose a natural combination – on the one side we apply convolutional neural networks for detection of the samples with diabetic retinopathy (we consume here both well-known ideas as ResNet50 [6] or VGG-16 [7] as well as novel approaches as InceptionV4 [8]) whilst we also prepared an explainability module based on saliency maps. By such an approach we can observe whether the changes were marked appropriately and whether our model understands images correctly.

This work is organized as follows: in the second section we present recent approaches to automatic (or semi-automatic) diabetic retinopathy recognition whilst in the third section proposed approach is described (especially in the terms of Machine Learning algorithms and architectures). Information about experiments is given in the fourth section. In this section we also describe what kind of analytical approach was used to reach the result. Finally, conclusions and future work are given in the fifth section.

2 Related Works

In the literature one can find plenty of diversified approaches connected with detection of diabetic retinopathy (DR). On the one hand, different types of samples are consumed – e.g., retina color images or Optical Coherence Tomography (OCT) pictures (also from multiple devices – with varied quality and resolution). It also leads to the fact that much more sophisticated approaches are needed to deal with these images (low- and high-quality samples can be both used in one algorithm). It is why, one can find approaches where traditional image analysis and processing algorithms are used to deal with the problem of diabetic retinopathy recognition. On the other hand, in the literature we can also observe papers that consume Machine Learning (Artificial Intelligence) models for this aim. Finally, hybrid methodologies (that combine traditional and ML pipelines) are also under consideration. To be precise enough, we would like to present the most important representatives of each group. At the end of this chapter, we will also provide our conclusions and remarks related to the recent state of the art.

The first group that we would like to analyze is the set of methodologies based on traditional image processing and analysis pipelines. In this area we can find one primary, general pipeline that is consumed by different approaches. It was presented in Fig. 1. At the beginning the image is filtered. It is done to remove noise from the image (it can be observed as the result of image acquisition process). After that process, in most of the cases, veins are detected and removed (it is done because, it is impossible to observe exudates around veins [9, 10]), the same removal operation is made with the optic disk (the reason is the same as in the case of veins [11]). Finally, the remaining area is being analyzed with different tools. For example, these can be segmentation (even the simplest one – Otsu [12, 13]), anomalies detection (also with usage of the newest frameworks in Python programming language) [14, 15] or comparison with ground truth elements [16]. However, all these approaches have one huge disadvantage – it is the fact that they are extremely slow. The second reason is that the results can be precise but when the sample is even slightly different than the well-known base, the recognition can be done with unsatisfactory results.

The second group of approaches is related to Machine Learning and Artificial Intelligence. In this case we can observe two types of algorithms – those that are based on deep learning and the ones that consume "shallow" learning models. In both groups we can find approaches both to detection of early-stage pathologies [16, 17] and changes that are clearly visible [18, 19]. It needs to be pointed out that deep learning models based on convolutional neural networks give much more precise results in the terms of initial-stage illnesses recognition. It is related to the fact that at the very beginning the low-level features are considered whilst general (high-level features) ones are built upon the results collected earlier [20]. It means that we will first observe pathological changes and then place them within the whole area of the retina color image. Significant example of such an approach was presented in [21].

The last group of approaches that is also described in the literature is related to the idea of Hybrid Artificial Intelligence. This concept was given by Gary Marcus in his work published in 2020 [22]. In this case, the approach for diabetic retinopathy recognition is based on two general pillars. The first of them are retina color images collected with specialized devices (e.g., Kova-VX10) whilst the second one is related to contextual information provided by the patient – e.g., his medical data or self-determined health status. It can lead to an approach where Computer Vision algorithm can be aligned with Natural Language Processing methodology. In the literature we cannot find plenty of approaches that consume Hybrid Artificial Intelligence, however, one of the most important was described in work [23].

As a conclusion observed within the performed experiments, we can say that there is no other approach like the one proposed by the Authors. It means that saliency maps were not yet used in the process of retina color image analysis for detection of the most important image area (to ensure which part of the sample needs to be carefully analyzed to detect pathological changes). This solution provides evidence that the selected architectures can guarantee high accuracy and efficiency when it comes to the detection of pathological changes (in our case especially diabetic retinopathies) within the area of retina.

3   Proposed Approach

The proposed approach is based on one general assumption. The goal is to obtain Machine Learning-based algorithm that can detect even early stage of diabetic retinopathy. To be precise enough we consumed a dataset that is available within Kaggle challenges system [24]. In this case we can find more than 35000 labelled retina color images. It needs to be claimed that both left and right eye are observable in the dataset. Database consists of around 25000 normal images (no diabetic retinopathy is observable, even early stages are not visible) and around 9500 samples representing different types of DR. Moreover, diversified stages of diabetic retinopathy were provided – no diabetic retinopathy, mild stage, moderate level, severe stage, and proliferative diabetic retinopathy. In the case of proposed approach, we analyzed the images and then classified them. It means that we distinguish whether symptoms of diabetic retinopathy are observable or not – the stage of the illness is not analyzed. Differentiation of illness stages will be the next step in our work. The samples that are provided in the dataset are presented in Fig. 1 and Fig. 2. It also needs to be claimed that during experiments we do not consume the whole database – only 15000 images were considered (10000 "normal" and 5000 with illness). It is related to the fact that the neural network should not be overtrained to the dataset. We would like to provide the solution that can swiftly generalize.

During our experiments we consumed three general convolutional neural networks models. It was related to the fact that (as was observed during literature analysis), these models can guarantee much more precise results when it comes to observation of diabetic retinopathy and retina illnesses (even in their early stage). We selected three architectures that were trained (from the beginning, without transfer learning approach) and the results were collected – the first of them is ResNet50, the second VGG-16, whilst the last one is InceptionV4. The architectures of each model are given in Fig. 4.

It needs to be claimed that during our experiments we also consumed different approaches to dataset division. Three ideas were checked – the first one where 50% of the initial database was used as a train dataset and 50% as testing part; the second where 70% of samples were consumed as a training one and 30% as testing; and the third – 80% training and 20% testing. These splits were checked to obtain information which of them can guarantee the most precise model – in the literature we cannot find one general way of splitting (different splits were described as the most precise), it is why we also checked how does it look like in the case of Kaggle dataset. However, it also needs to be pointed out that in the case of training and testing datasets, we tried to obtain balanced amount of the samples from both groups (normal and with illness). It means that if our set consists of 80% of samples (training) we use 80% of normal dataset and 80% of samples with illness. The same statement is true in the case of different splits (50/50 and 70/30). It guarantee us that the balance between sick and healthy samples is preserved.

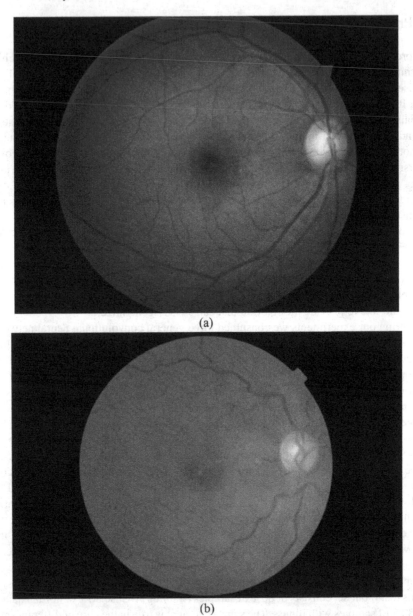

(a)

(b)

Fig. 1. Samples from the Kaggle database [24] – healthy retina (a), retina with early diabetic retinopathies (b)

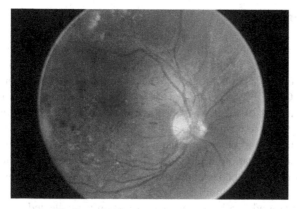

Fig. 2. Sample with diabetic retinopathy

Within our experiments we would also like to observe whether the neural model detects appropriate structures (diabetic retinopathies). It was done with saliency maps [28]. Within these images we can mark which parts of an image were the most important in the final decision. We would like to obtain classifier that will be able to carefully analyze the image and select only the regions that really contains diabetic retinopathy (rather than some small, non-pathological changes – e.g., light reflexes). The general scheme of the whole approach is given in Fig. 3.

Fig. 3. The general scheme of the proposed approach

It also needs to be pointed out that we did not apply any preprocessing methods. It is related to the fact that the images were of high-quality (they were collected with professional, medical tools rather than simple devices as d-Eye [29]). Moreover, we would like to obtain an efficient and general classifier that can be precise also with different datasets (generalization of the classifier) – e.g., collected with different tools and devices (also those that can be used not in the hospitals but rather than general practitioners) – it was another reason why no preprocessing methodologies were applied. The general outcomes of the work show that such an approach was justified (the results are satisfactory enough – they were checked by the experienced ophthalmologist). These outcomes are presented in Sect. 4 of this paper.

4 Experiments

All tests described within this section were performed with the computing device with the following parameters: Intel Core i9-11900K, 32 GB RAM, 1 TB SSD and graphics card Nvidia GeForce RTX 3080. It needs to be pointed out that training procedures were performed with GPU. The experiments included in this research were mostly related to two areas. The first of them was selection of an appropriate convolutional neural network architecture (from three selected at the beginning – ResNet50, VGG-16 and InceptionV4). The second outcome related to splitting of the dataset into testing and training parts (for observation of how many samples are needed to train precisely and efficiently the model). We need to claim that each experiment (training) was repeated 25 times (it was hard to enlarge number of repetitions due to the time needed for even one training – it was around 4–5 h). From each execution we collected information about model precision – the results in the Table 1 presents the mean value of the accuracy calculated as a sum of all precisions divided by 25. The general formula is given in (1). Moreover, it is important to point out that the dataset for each experiment was divided equally. Both datasets were considered in the way in which the number of samples relates to the percentage of the data set (50% of the dataset, means that we will include 50% of healthy samples and 50% of samples with pathological changes).

$$accuracy = \frac{TP + TN}{TP + FP + TN + FN} \tag{1}$$

where TP means true positives, TN is responsible for true negatives, FP relates to true negative and FN is false negatives.

Table 1. The results collected with different architectures and data splits.

Architecture/Data split	50% training/50% testing	70% training/30% testing	80% training/20% testing
ResNet50	84.30%	**95.20%**	90.31%
VGG-16	72.25%	88.45%	82.35%
InceptionV4	65.35%	71.45%	70.05%

The last stage of our work was related to generation of saliency maps. It is an important step by which we can observe whether pathological changes were appropriately assigned or not. It can be claimed that our work can guarantee precise enough results as pathological changes were marked within the saliency map – it means that the classifier was also trained on these structures – so it is possible to recognize them also in different images (outside of the training dataset). Example of saliency map (it provides the strength for each pixel contribution to the final output) is shown in Fig. 5.

It needs to be claimed that the highest accuracy of the algorithm was observed in the case of ResNet50 architecture and data split - 70% for training and 30% testing. It relates to the fact that our classifier was not too much aligned with the data (it is why we consumed smaller dataset, consisting of 15000 samples) – also evaluation on completely different dataset (collected with Medical University of Białystok where 1500 samples are included – 500 with diabetic retinopathy and 1000 healthy) provided information that these settings were the most precise. Appropriate recognition (metric – accuracy – given in (1)) level reach 95% also in the case of additional dataset. It means that our model can be also generalizable and be consumed also with different databases. It is also important that we can align our algorithm with different datasets and devices (Table 1).

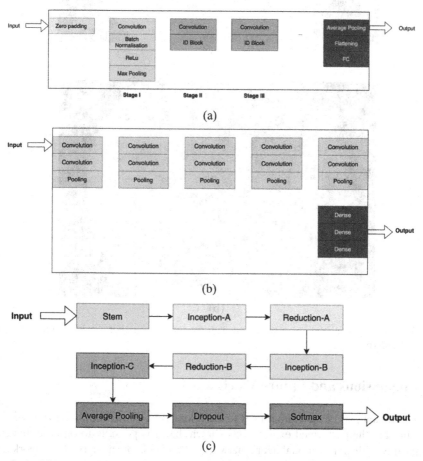

Fig. 4. Architectures of the consumed convolutional neural networks – ResNet50 based on [25] (a), VGG-16 prepared with [26] (b) and InceptionV4 described in [27] (c)

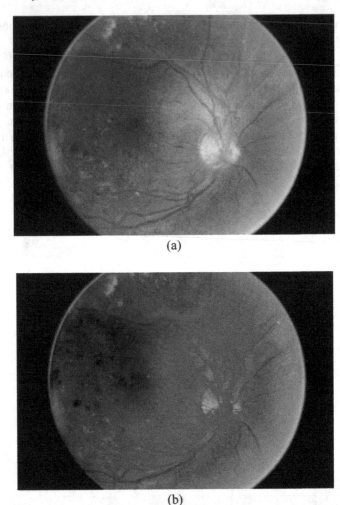

(a)

(b)

Fig. 5. Example of saliency map generated with the trained classifier – original image (a), its saliency map (b).

5   Conclusions and Future Work

The significant part of the work relates to the testing procedure. The authors would like to claim that the performed experiments shown that it is possible to observe diabetic retinopathy with convolutional neural networks classifiers. The novelty of this work lies not in the classification itself but rather in visual evaluation of the worked-out models (the saliency map shows which part of the image was the most important – by that we can also consider some changes in the acquisition procedure – just to concentrate on better quality of that part). It means that saliency maps can guarantee us that the model observed appropriate structures and that it was trained on sufficient parts of a sample. It is important to train it with sufficient data as it can be then easily generalized. One of the major mistakes made by Machine Learning engineers is that their models are too much trained to the data and then their precision and efficiency rates decrease with the datasets outside of the training samples. We would like to omit such situation and it is why the proposed neural networks models were checked also in the terms of generalization.

Neural networks and their usage for diabetic retinopathy recognition was previously described in the literature. The most important work with which we can compare our results is [36]. In this paper the Authors obtained worse results with ResNet-50 than those presented in this work. However, it is probably related to the fact that they trained their model with the whole database – we only used a part of it (15000 from the whole 35000 samples – where 10000 represented "normal" retina and 5000 unhealthy ones).

The author current work is to retrain the models – so that they can evaluate samples also in the terms of diabetic retinopathy advancement (as it was stated the images in the database present at least four different stages). Moreover, the next step in this process is to prepare explainability module – so that the model will not only provide information about classification but also will generate justification of its decision. It needs to be clearly pointed out that Explainable and Trustworthy AI is one of the major trends nowadays.

On the other hand, the Author would like to check other different architectures [30] of neural networks – e.g., AlexNet [31], SqueezeNet [32] and MobileNet [33]. Moreover, we would like to check whether it is possible to obtain satisfactory results with different algorithms – as Fuzzy Logic [34] or Genetic Algorithms [35].

Acknowledgment. This work was supported by grant W/WI/4/2022 from Białystok University of Technology and funded with resources for research by the Ministry of Science and Higher Education in Poland.

The Author is grateful to experienced ophthalmologists who checked the results and provided their opinions about the processing pipeline and the marked regions within saliency maps.

References

1. https://openai.com/blog/chatgpt. Accessed 11 Feb 2023
2. Quer, G., Arnaout, R., Henne, M., Arnaout, R.: Machine learning and the future of cardiovascular care: JACC state-of-the-art review. J. Am. Coll. Cardiol. **77**(3), 300–313 (2021)
3. Chung, J., Teo, J.: Mental health prediction using machine learning: taxonomy, applications and challenges. Appl. Comput. Intell. Soft Comput. **2022**, Article no. 9970363 (2022). https://doi.org/10.1155/2022/9970363
4. Goodfellow, I., Bengio, Y., Courville, A.: Deep Learning. MIT Press, Cambridge (2016)
5. Molnar, C.: Interpretable machine learning: a guide for making black box models explainable (2022). ISBN: 979-8411463330
6. He, K., Zhang, X., Ren, S., Sun, J.: Deep residual learning for image recognition. arXiv: 1512.03385 [cs.CV], 10 December 2015
7. Simonyan, K., Zisserman, A.: Very deep convolutional networks for large-scale image recognition. arXiv: 1409.1556 [cs.CV], 10 April 2015
8. Szegedy, C., Ioffe, S., Vanhoucke, V., Alemi, A.: Inception-v4, Inception-ResNet and the impact of residual connections on learning. arXiv: 1602.07261v2 [cs.CV], 23 August 2016
9. Monemian, M., Rabbani, H.: Exudate Identification in retinal fundus images using precise textural verifications. Sci. Rep. **13**, Article no. 2824 (2023)

10. Malhi, A., Grewal, R., Pannu H.: Detection and diabetic retinopathy grading using digital retinal images. Int. J. Intell. Robot. Appl. (2023)

11. Basit, A., Moazam Fraz, M.: Optic disk detection and boundary extraction in retinal images. Appl. Opt. **54**(11), 3440–3447 (2015)

12. Bahadar, K., Khaliq, A., Shahid, M.: A morphological hessian based approach for retinal blood vessels segmentation and denoising using region based otsu thresholding. PLoS ONE **11**(7) (2016). PMCID: PMC4956315

13. Galdran, A., Anjos, A., Dolz, J., Chakor, H., Lombaert, H., Ayed, I.: State-of-the-art retinal vessel segmentation with minimalistic models. Sci. Rep. **12**, Article no. 6174 (2022)

14. https://www.projectpro.io/article/anomaly-detection-using-machine-learning-in-python-with-example/555. Accessed 11 Feb 2023

15. Du, Y.: Anomaly detection in fundus images by self-adaptive decomposition via local and color based sparse coding. Biomed. Opt. Express **13**(8), 4261–4277 (2022)

16. Gadekallu, T., Khare, N., Bhattacharya, S., et al.: Deep neural networks to predict diabetic retinopathy. J. Ambient Intell. Humaniz. Comput. (2020). https://doi.org/10.1007/s12652-020-01963-7

17. Wu, H., Zhao, S., Zhang, X., et al.: Back-propagation artificial neural network for early diabetic retinopathy detection based on a priori knowledge. J. Phys. Conf. Ser. Article no. 012019 (2020). https://doi.org/10.1088/1742-6596/1437/1/012019

18. Benzamin, A., Chakraborty, C.: Detection of hard exudates in retinal fundus images using deep learning. arXiv: 1808.03656 [cs.CV] (2018)

19. Patil, A., Chakravorty, C.: Detection of hard exudate using retinal optical coherence tomography (OCT) images. Glob. Transit. Proc. **2**(2), 566–570 (2021)

20. Ekman, M.: Learning Deep Learning. Addison-Wesley (2022). ISBN: 978-0-13-747035-8

21. Yasashvini, R., Vergin Raja Sarobin, M., Panjanathan, R., Graceline Jasmine, S., Jani Anbarasi, L.: Diabetic retinopathy classification using CNN and hybrid deep convolutional neural networks. Symmetry **14**(9) (2022). https://doi.org/10.3390/sym14091932

22. Marcus, G.: The next decade in AI: four steps towards robust artificial intelligence. arXiv:2002.06177 [cs.AI] (2020)

23. Ghnemat, R.: Hybrid framework for diabetic retinopathy stage measurement using convolutional neural network and fuzzy rules inference system. Appl. Syst. Innov. **5**(102) (2022). https://doi.org/10.3390/asi5050102

24. https://www.kaggle.com/competitions/diabetic-retinopathy-detection/data. Accessed 12 Mar 2023

25. https://www.educba.com/keras-resnet50/. Accessed 12 Mar 2023

26. https://www.analyticsvidhya.com/blog/2021/06/transfer-learning-using-vgg16-in-pytorch/. Accessed 12 Mar 2023

27. https://www.geeksforgeeks.org/inception-v4-and-inception-resnets/. Accessed 12 Mat 2023

28. Simonyan, K., Vedaldi, A., Zisserman, A.: Deep inside convolutional networks: visualising image classification models and saliency maps. arXiv: 1312.6034v2 [cs.CV]

29. https://www.d-eyecare.com. Accessed 12 Mar 2023

30. Shen, Z., Yang, H., Zhang, S.: Neural network architecture beyond width and depth. arXiv: 2205.09459 [cs.LG], 14 January 2023

31. Krizhevsky, A., Sutskever, I., Hinton, G.E.: ImageNet classification with deep convolutional neural networks. In: Advances in Neural Information Processing Systems 25, NIPS 2012 (2012)

32. Iandola, F., Han, S., Moskewicz, M., Ashraf, K., Dally, W., Keutzer, K.: SqueezeNet: AlexNet-level accuracy with 50x fewer parameters and <0.5 MB model size. arXiv: 1602.07360 [cs.CV], 4 November 2016

33. Howard, A., et al.: MobileNets: efficient convolutional neural networks for mobile vision applications. arXiv: 1704.04861 [cs.CV], 17 April 2017

34. Moraga, C.: Introduction to fuzzy logic. Facta Universitas Series Electronics and Energetics, vol. 18, no. 2, pp. 319–328 (2005)
35. Katoch, S., Chauhan, S., Kumar, V.: A review on genetic algorithm: past, present and future. Multimedia Tools Appl. **80**, 8091–8126 (2021)
36. Lin, C., Wu, K.: Development of revised ResNet-50 for diabetic retinopathy detection. BMC Bioinform. **24**(157) (2023). https://doi.org/10.1186/s12859-023-05293-1

Towards Rough Set Theory for Outliers Detection in Questionnaire Data

Vojtěch Uher[(✉)] and Pavla Dráždilová

Department of Computer Science, VŠB – Technical University of Ostrava, 17.
listopadu 15/2172, 708 33 Ostrava, Czech Republic
{vojtech.uher,pavla.drazdilova}@vsb.cz

Abstract. Manual processing of questionnaire surveys takes a lot of
time and effort. This article aims at the automatic detection of cor-
rupted or inappropriate responses in questionnaire data using unsupervised outliers detection methods. Unlike numerical data, which are usually assessed by distance-based methods, the entries in questionnaires
need to be assessed from multiple perspectives. This paper proposes a
novel algorithm utilizing the rough sets that capture relations among
attributes/questions. The rough set theory is based on the granularity
of data and is used to find combinations of attributes identifying the
discernible questionnaires. The method is compared with standard and
recent outlier detection algorithms that are based on distance, entropy,
correlation, and probability. The tests are computed on the real-world
HBSC dataset using several experiments. The rough set score computed
on combinations of three attributes is preferred as it returns significant outliers that even reflect multiple perspectives investigated by other
types of methods.

Keywords: Outliers detection · Questionnaire data · Rough set
theory · HBSC

1 Introduction

Anomaly detection, also known as outlier detection, is the process of identifying
observations in a dataset that appear to be inconsistent with the majority of
the data. As described by Hawkins [8], an outlier is an observation that deviates
significantly from the rest of the data and raises suspicion that it was generated by a different mechanism. Outliers can arise due to various reasons such
as measurement errors, coding errors, system failure, or unusual or infrequent
events that the dataset does not capture correctly. Outliers can negatively impact
data distribution, weaken the reliability and credibility of statistical results, and
therefore need to be detected, assessed, and excluded from the analysis if they
cannot be corrected [11,24,28,29].

The specific type of data that often needs to be preprocessed and cleaned
from the outliers is the questionnaire data produced by surveys used e.g. in
social, behavioral research, and psychology [21]. This kind of data is represented

K. Saeed et al. (Eds.): CISIM 2023, LNCS 14164, pp. 310–324, 2023.
https://doi.org/10.1007/978-3-031-42823-4_23

by mixed attributes (categorical and numerical) storing the answers of respondents that are heavily affected by human factors. Besides, the independence of attributes or the normal distribution cannot be assumed. Due to the named specifics, the outliers can be defined in various ways and the proximity-based methods (e.g. k-nearest neighbors, local outlier factor) are not always satisfactory. The authors specifically examine data from the Health Behaviour in School-aged Children (HBSC) 2020 study, which focuses on the health and health behaviors of 11-, 13-, and 15-year-olds [10,18].

This paper aims to develop and test a novel method based on the rough set theory [14,20] using a completely different approach. The rough sets capture relations among attributes/questions of the input data. Our method uses this theory to find combinations of attributes to identify the discernible questionnaires with weak relations to the rest of the data. Several variants of this method are computed and compared with older and recently published methods such as k-nearest neighbors, local outlier factor, Mahalonobis distance, and methods based on entropy, correlation, and probability [27]. All the tested algorithms including the rough sets are unsupervised machine learning algorithms.

Despite the importance of outliers in questionnaires, there are not many articles focused on the automatic detection in this type of data. A rare example is the probability score introduced by Zijlstra et al. [32] called $O+$ which computes the outlier score on the basis of the number of infrequent answers per questionnaire, which is also tested here. An ensemble method combining results of different algorithms was also proposed [27], and the final suggestions are considered here as well.

Rough set theory and granularity are two approaches that have been used to detect outliers in various domains [12,13,16]. Yuan et al. [31] provided a mixed attribute outlier detection method based on multigranulation relative entropy with the application of the neighborhood rough set. Suri et al. [25] proposed rough k-modes clustering algorithm for outlier detection in categorical data sets. The article [16] presents a computationally efficient algorithm for the detection of outliers based on rough set theory in large volumes of information. Mixed attribute data (numerical and categorical) are used in [30] where outlier detection is solved by fuzzy rough granules. An idea to search infrequent itemsets for distributed outlier detection in mixed attribute data was presented by Otey et al. [19]. Most of the existing solutions based on the rough sets rely on a specific concept or a decision attribute. Here, we propose a blind method applying the general rules of the rough set theory to find outlying observations.

The method is described in Sect. 2. The procedure preprocessing the data and the tested related algorithms are depicted in Sect. 3. Finally, the model setup, experiments, and results comparing the methods and evaluating the rough set-based method are summarized in Sect. 4.

2   Rough Set Theory for Outliers Detection

First, the theoretical background for the rough sets is explained in Sect. 2.1. Next, our proposed method for outliers detection using the rough set theory is introduced in Sect. 2.2.

2.1   Rough Set Theory in a Nutshell

Although the mathematical foundations of the rough set theory have been defined [14,20], the following definitions are used for the explanation of anomaly detection based on rough sets. The *information system* is an ordered tuple $\mathcal{A} = (U, A, f, V)$, where U is a non-empty set of objects called the universe and A is a non-empty set of attributes such that mapping $f : U \times A \to V$ assigns a value to each pair of object and attribute. The set V is called the value set of attributes. The information system is usually represented by an information table where rows represent objects and columns represent attributes. A decision system is any information system of the form $\mathcal{A} = (U, A \cup \{d\}, f, V)$, where $d \notin A$ is the decision attribute. The elements of A are called conditional attributes or simply conditions.

Let $\mathcal{A} = (U, A, f, V)$ be an information system, then with any $A_i \subseteq A$ is associated an equivalence relation ρ_i, where

$$\rho_i = \{(x, y) \in U \times U; \forall a \in A_i \ [f(x, a) = f(y, a)]\}.$$

This equivalence relation is called the A_i-indiscernibility relation. If $(x, y) \in \rho_i$ then objects x and y are indiscernible from each other by attributes from A_i.

Let U/ρ_i be the set of equivalence classes $[y]_{\rho_i} = \{x \in U; (x, y) \in \rho_i\}$ induced by ρ_i in U. Two approximations are defined to characterize some $X \subseteq U$ via equivalence classes:

Upper approximation: $\overline{\rho_i}(X) = \cup\{[y]_{\rho_i}; \ [y]_{\rho_i} \cap X \neq \emptyset\}$. The union of all equivalence classes is induced by ρ_i in U whose intersection with X is not empty.

Lower approximation: $\underline{\rho_i}(X) = \cup\{[y]_{\rho_i}; \ [y]_{\rho_i} \subseteq X\}$. The union of all equivalence classes induced by ρ_i in U that are contained in X.

In the Fig. 1, there is the class of equivalence ρ_i induced by subset $A_i \subset A$ such that element z_1 is indiscernible from element z_2 ($|[z_1]_{\rho_i}| \geq 2$). For the finer equivalence ρ_j induced by subset $A_j \subset A$, such that $A_i \subset A_j$, the class of equivalence with element z_1 is smaller ($|[z_1]_{\rho_i}| > |[z_1]_{\rho_j}| \geq 1$).

2.2   Proposed Method for Outlier Detection

The proposed method for outlier detection inspired by the rough set theory is based on the observation that the object $x \in U$ (respondent in the questionnaire) is discernible from all other objects via selected attributes $A_k = \{a_{i1}, \ldots, a_{ik}\}$ if the class of equivalence induced by A_k contains just one object x (i.e. $|[x]_{\rho_{A_k}}| = 1$). The method uses all subsets with k attributes. Three variants are tested: RSk for $k \in \{2, 3, 4\}$.

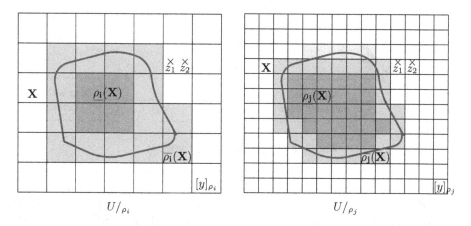

Fig. 1. Visual description of the terms in rough set theory.

The algorithm for RSk score computation goes as follows:

1. For all $A_{ik} = \{a_{i1}, \ldots, a_{ik}\} \subset A$, where $i \in \{1, \ldots, \binom{|A|}{k}\}$, and for all objects are calculated absolute numbers of relation indiscernibility that distinguish the discernible object

$$aRSk(x) = |\{\rho_{ik}; |[x]_{\rho_{ik}}| = 1\}|.$$

   Relation of indiscernibility: $\rho_{ik} = \{(x, y) \in U \times U; [f(x, a_{ij}) = f(y, a_{ij})]\ \forall j \in \{1, \ldots, k\}\}$.
2. Normalization of an outlier score to the interval $\langle 0, 1 \rangle$:

$$RSk(x) = \frac{aRSk(x)}{\max_{\forall x} aRSk}$$

3. Adjusted box-plot method is used for the outlier score threshold computation (more in Sect. 3.2).

3 Overview of the Tested Pipeline

This section summarizes the procedure for outliers detection in questionnaire data represented by categorical attributes that was proposed earlier [27]. It goes from raw data, through data preprocessing and cleaning (Sect. 3.1) to outlier scores computation and outliers detection (Sect. 3.2) as illustrated in Fig. 2.

3.1 HBSC Data Cleaning and Preprocessing

The questionnaire data is a matrix where rows represent the respondents and columns represent the attributes. The attributes are defined by multiple-choice questions with a single answer selected from a predetermined list of options.

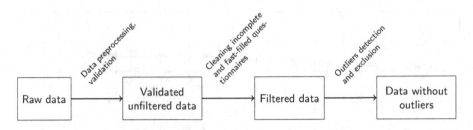

Fig. 2. Flowchart of data processing

The attributes represent categorical variables with a low count of options. To get to this state, the raw data has to be validated and cleaned [4,7]. The data is validated and cleaned according to the procedure defined in article [27]. It consists of several steps including a selection of categorical attributes, elimination of fast respondents and questionnaires with many missing answers ($\geq 70\%$), replacement of missing and open-ended responses by zeros, elimination of poorly distributed attributes with $\geq 80\%$ of the same values, the renumbering of option indices, and attribute normalization (for some methods). The described preprocessing produces the filtered data containing the categorical attributes required for outliers detection.

In this paper, the questionnaire-based survey from the Health Behaviour in School-aged Children (HBSC) study is tested. The HBSC collaborates with World Health Organization and monitors trends in the health and health behaviours of 11-, 13-, and 15-year-old people. The survey was conducted in the Czech Republic in June 2020 during the final stage of the first COVID-19 epidemic wave. It assesses the impact of the lockdown (i.e. ban of sports and leisure-time activities, or school closure) on young people's lives [2]. The survey contains 7082 unique entries with 232 variables gathered from 141 schools from 14 administrative regions of the Czech Republic. After the preprocessing and cleaning, it was reduced to 3255 entries and 113 multiple-choice questions with a single answer. The number of possible options is between 3 to 16 options per question. Such a reduction was achieved due to many missing answers and infeasible non-categorical attributes.

3.2 Outlier Score Methods

The filtered data is used to detect outliers that affect the distribution and results of statistical methods. While the outlying points in the real space are usually detected by some proximity-based methods, the categorical variables of questionnaires can be assessed from different perspectives. Various types of outliers existing in the questionnaire data can be defined [27]:

1. Significantly longer response times.
2. Predictable patterns, and repetitive answers (such as "a, b, c, d").
3. Self-contradictory responses to related questions detecting lack of understanding or cheating of respondents.

4. Preserved inconsistent responses that are out of the distribution and can represent a rare cluster of data.
5. Graphic interpretation of data for visual verification.

All the named approaches are unsupervised methods for outliers detection as they do not require any a priori knowledge about data. Each tested method computes an outlier score $\omega_i \in \langle 0, 1 \rangle$ for each i-th questionnaire of the data matrix such that a greater score represents a more suspicious entry. The outlier score is analyzed to identify the final outliers.

The tested methods have been defined in detail [27] and only a brief overview is presented here:

1. **k-th order empirical entropy** [23] can detect predictable patterns of answers using the moving window of k subsequent questions on a row basis. The low entropy is signaling biased answers and such a respondent is suspicious. Besides, the k-th order empirical entropy is also used specifically for batteries of questions (partial entropy) that are consolidated and bring respondents to cheat more often.
2. **Correlation of attributes.** It is assumed that the highly correlated attributes relate in some way. The linear regression of correlated attributes is computed and the distance of values from the line represents how much the answers disrupt the estimated trend. The distance is computed for each significantly correlated pair of attributes ($\geq corrMin$). The final score of a questionnaire is an average of the τ greatest distances computed for the corresponding row of answers.
3. **Probability score** [32] called $O+$ is a question/attribute-based score computed as a number of individual's frequency of unpopular answers. It is a non-parametric method. Basically, the relative frequencies of existing options within a question are computed. The more improbable answers are detected, the more suspicious the respondent is.
4. **Mahalanobis distance** [17] is a non-parametric method measuring a distance of a sample to the distribution of data in the multidimensional space using the covariance matrix.
5. **Local outlier factor (LOF)** [3] is a density-based method judging the consistency with the data distribution from the perspective of a local neighborhood defined by the $MinPts$ nearest neighbors. As the LOF depends on a spherical neighborhood, the reduction by Principal component analysis (PCA) to 10 dimensions is computed.
6. **k-Nearest Neighbors (kNN)** [5] computes the outlier score as the average distance to the k nearest objects.
7. **Rough sets** [20] represent the method described in this paper detecting the lonely observations assigned to single-element equivalence classes. The parameter k defines the size of the tested subset of attributes.

The outlier scores of all questionnaires of the data define a random variable of scores ω. The distribution of ω needs to be analyzed and the final outliers have to be selected. Traditionally, some threshold of scores is set or the k observations with the greatest scores are selected as outliers [1,15,22]. Both approaches are tricky in unsupervised methods as they are based on user-estimated parameters. A widely-used statistical method is the box-plot [26] which uses the interquartile range but it assumes a normal distribution of scores. According to our experiments, most of the outlier scores have the right skewness. Therefore, the *adjusted box-plot (ABP)* [9] modified for skewed distributions is preferred, and all the scores greater than the high limit of ABP are selected as outliers. The only exception is the LOF method which has its own decision-making approach.

4   Experiments

The experiments evaluate the summarized outliers detection methods tested on the filtered HBSC 2020 data. The following sections describe the model setup and selected parameters of methods (Sect. 4.1), outlier scores distribution and comparison (Sect. 4.2), and the impact of the excluded outliers on the data properties (Sect. 4.3).

4.1   Model Setup

The methods are based on those tested in article [27] and extended by a rough set-based approach. The methods and their parameters are summarized in Table 1. Some configurations were excluded on the basis of the results published in article [27]. Their names are used in all charts and tables. The parameters were set experimentally for the HBSC 2020 data set.

Two orders of the k-th order empirical entropy and two partial ones are tested. The k is reasonably small as the data has only 113 variables (batteries are even smaller). If a questionnaire is incomplete only the initial complete part of the answers is used [27]. The Mahalanobis distance and probability score ($O+$) are non-parametric. The only correlation-based method uses the linear regression of correlated attributes. Spearman correlation is used with threshold $corrMin = 0.7$ for $\tau = 12$ greatest distances. The threshold detects 15 significant correlations. The LOF method uses the neighborhood of $MinPts = 100$ observations and is applied to PCA-reduced data in 10-dimensional space. Also, the kNN method is set to $k = 100$ neighbors. Finally, the rough sets for combinations of 2, 3, and 4 attributes are computed.

4.2   Outlier Scores Distribution and Relation

The filtered HBSC2020 dataset is used to test the introduced methods with selected parameters summarized in Table 1. Each method defines an outlier in a different way and they complement each other. The aim of this section is to compare the outlier scores computed by different methods, especially to evaluate the outliers detected by our novel approach based on the rough set theory. All the scores are normalized and inverted eventually so that the score value 1 represents the observation with the greatest outlierness.

Table 1. Tested methods and their parameters and types of outliers they reveal.

Name	Description	Outlier types	Parameters
en$k$	k-th order empirical entropy	predictable patterns, missing values	$k \in \{1, 2\}$
pen$k$	partial en$k$ of batteries	predictable patterns, missing values	$k \in \{1, 2\}$
Maha	Mahalanobis distance	inconsistent responses	–
$O+$	Probability score	inconsistent responses	–
rc12	Correlation (linear regression)	self-contradictory responses	$corrMin = 0.7 \ \tau = 12$
LOF10	Local outlier factor	inconsistent responses	PCA dims $d = 10 \ MinPts = 100$
kNN100	k-Nearest Neighbors	inconsistent responses	$k = 100$
RSk	Rough sets	self-contradictory responses	$k \in \{2, 3, 4\}$

The correlation matrix in Fig. 3 shows Spearman correlations between scores produced by all tested methods. It illustrates several groups of methods with similar properties. Most of the scores correlate positively. Only the entropy-based methods correlate negatively, esp. with rc12 and $O+$ methods. The RSk methods lead to very similar scores and they are highly correlated with kNN, LOF, Maha, and $O+$ methods.

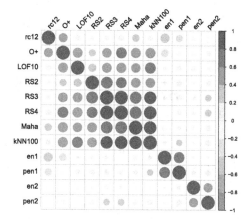

Fig. 3. Comparison of Spearman correlations between outlier scores computed by tested methods on the filtered HBSC 2020 data

The outlier scores are reasonably distributed for the filtered HBSC 2020 data, so that, the majority of questionnaires are assigned with low scores. The right tail of score distributions is represented by a relatively small amount of questionnaires with high scores. Figure 4 illustrates the distribution of the tested scores. As the scores have positive skewness of distribution, they can be approximated by the continuous gamma function which fits the scores very well. This fact proves that the normal distribution is generally not reachable, therefore the adjusted box-plot (ABP) is a more representative method for the statistical identification of outliers than the simple box-plot. The red line marks the ABP threshold cutting off the outliers.

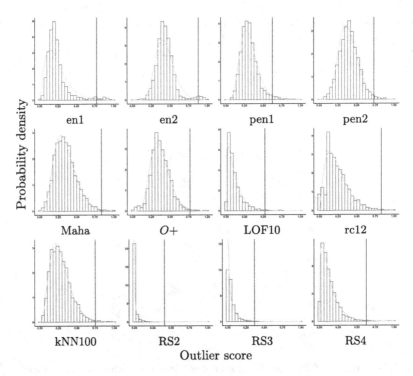

Fig. 4. Histograms and approximated gamma function for distributions of outlier score methods on filtered HBSC 2020 data.

The next experiment examinates a number of unique and common outliers detected according to different scores as it is shown in Table 2. The intersection table corresponds to the correlation matrix described before. A high intersection is between methods of the same type. The diagonal shows the number of outliers detected by each method. These numbers vary a lot. Especially, the entropy-based methods return many suspicious observations which are affected by many missing answers increasing the entropy-based outlier score. The last row represents numbers of unique outliers that are specific for each method.

The methods such as en2, pen1, rc12, and LOF10 find many outliers that are not covered by any other method. The rough set-based methods are highly intersected one by another. The RS2 is completely included in the RS3 which represents an extreme outlierness of these observations. The RS4 detects fewer outliers than RS3. This is because four attributes distinguish the observations better and produce many single-element equivalence classes pushing the whole distribution to higher scores. The threshold computed by the ABP method is also pushed to a higher score. However, the single-element equivalence classes detected by RS2 and RS3 are implicitly included in RS4. The RS3 and RS4 have common outliers, especially with kNN100, Maha, en1, and pen1. The size of the intersection corresponds with the number of detected outliers. The correlation matrix better reflects the relative context of score trends.

Table 2. Intersection table displaying the numbers of outliers detected by multiple methods. The diagonal shows the numbers found by particular methods and the last row represents unique outliers that are not captured by any other method. The RS3 is highlighted as the preferred variant of the RSk methods.

	en1	en2	pen1	pen2	Maha	O+	rc12	LOF10	kNN100	RS2	RS3	RS4
en1	**73**	19	50	14	4	12	0	9	16	3	13	8
en2	19	**62**	21	16	1	0	0	2	2	3	5	4
pen1	50	21	**74**	20	4	9	0	5	12	3	10	7
pen2	14	16	20	**40**	2	3	0	3	5	1	3	2
Maha	4	1	4	2	**20**	5	3	3	12	1	11	9
O+	12	0	9	3	5	**28**	1	5	12	1	5	6
rc12	0	0	0	0	3	1	**19**	0	2	0	1	0
LOF10	9	2	5	3	3	5	0	**30**	8	1	4	4
kNN100	16	2	12	5	12	12	2	8	**28**	3	16	11
RS2	3	3	3	1	1	1	0	1	3	**8**	8	6
RS3	13	5	10	3	11	5	1	4	16	8	**40**	25
RS4	8	4	7	2	9	6	0	4	11	6	25	**27**
Unique	8	22	10	9	3	8	16	17	1	0	5	1

4.3   Importance of Outliers

To evaluate the impact of the detected outliers, the change of the data distribution before and after outliers exclusion needs to be assessed. Two statistics are monitored: the variance of the total score and Cronbach's alpha coefficient. The total score of a questionnaire is computed as a sum of all normalized response values of the whole questionnaire (one row). Total scores computed for all questionnaires form a random variable $A+$. The variance σ^2 of $A+$ shows how compact the data set is. Cronbach's alpha [6] is a well-known coefficient that computes the covariance between each pair of attributes and shows the dependence between attributes.

The computed statistics are examined to see the importance of the specific K excluded outliers. The statistical significance is based on 1000 omissions of K randomly selected questionnaires from the original data. For each omission, a statistic is computed, and the 1000 statistics form a random variable. The omission of the detected K outliers is statistically significant if the statistic is out of the interval between the 2.5th and the 97.5th percentiles of the random variable distribution for a significance level equal to 5%. The influence of the K outliers is the same as the influence of any K randomly deleted questionnaires if the statistic is within this interval. The resulting variances and Cronbach's alphas are summarized in Table 3 for all tested methods.

The Table 3 shows that the $O+$ and the rc12 methods increase the statistics while the others decrease them. The RSk methods significantly decrease both statistics. While the pen1 method eliminates 74 questionnaires that are statistically insignificant the RS2 method finds only 8 outliers but they are significant. Comparing the RS3 and RS4 methods, the RS3 finds 40 significant outliers while preserving a lower complexity of triplets. The RS4 uses combinations of 4 attributes and finds 27 outliers that are mostly covered by RS3. The number of existing combinations of attributes can be computed as $\binom{113}{2}$, $\binom{113}{3}$, $\binom{113}{4}$ for RS2, RS3, and RS4 respectively, therefore $\binom{113}{4} = 27.5 \cdot \binom{113}{3}$.

Table 3. Statistical significance of outliers found by outlier detection methods. **Columns**: K- number of outliers identified by ABP method; $K\%$- percentage of suspected observations; $\alpha_{2.5p^{th}}$, $\alpha_{97.5p^{th}}$, $\alpha(K)$, $s_{\alpha(K)}$- Cronbach's alpha statistics, and $\sigma^2_{2.5p^{th}}$, $\sigma^2_{97.5p^{th}}$, $\sigma^2(K)$, $s_{\sigma^2(K)}$- total score variance σ^2_{A+} (lower/upper percentiles of 1000 random omissions, value for the K found outliers and significance); ++: significant value increase over random elimination, +: insignificant value increase over random elimination, −−: significant value decrease over random elimination, −: insignificant value decrease over random elimination.

Methods	K	$K\%$	$\alpha_{2.5p^{th}}$	$\alpha_{97.5p^{th}}$	$\alpha(K)$	$s_{\alpha(K)}$	$\sigma^2_{2.5p^{th}}$	$\sigma^2_{97.5p^{th}}$	$\sigma^2(K)$	$s_{\sigma^2(K)}$
en1	73	2.24	.90383	.90656	.88297	−−	77.74972	80.09752	62.66853	−−
en2	62	1.91	.90366	.90639	.87281	−−	77.59456	79.94232	58.03576	−−
pen1	74	2.27	.90375	.90658	.90404	−	77.65353	80.09816	77.79473	−
pen2	40	1.23	.90413	.90612	.89301	−−	77.97641	79.68803	69.18034	−−
Maha	20	0.61	.90443	.90578	.90455	−	78.23596	79.39965	77.80248	−−
$O+$	28	0.86	.90422	.90591	.90669	++	78.05610	79.52942	79.21280	+
rc12	19	0.58	.90449	.90576	.90595	++	78.27367	79.38607	79.33506	+
LOF10	30	0.92	.90426	.90594	.90493	−	78.08243	79.55177	78.02416	−−
kNN100	28	0.86	.90428	.90592	.90364	−−	78.12332	79.52470	76.59394	−−
RS2	8	0.25	.90527	.90554	.90413	−−	78.93187	79.18174	77.84670	−−
RS3	40	1.23	.90502	.90607	.90102	−−	78.71686	79.65009	74.78089	−−
RS4	27	0.83	.90508	.90587	.90319	−−	78.79098	79.49044	76.67091	−−

The difference between methods is visualized in Fig. 5 using the 3D PCA-reduced data space with outliers highlighted by black color. We emphasize that the data space is reduced from 113 attributes to 3D visualization which is very lossy. Despite the loss, the outliers of all methods are visualized outside of the central mass of the distribution as was expected.

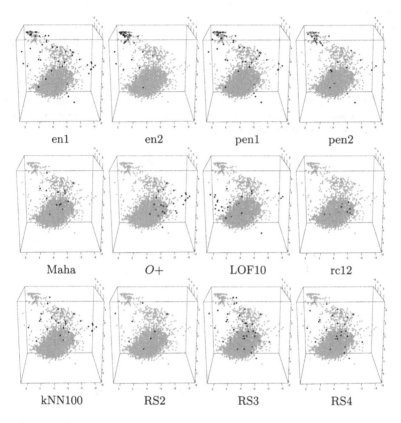

Fig. 5. Outliers detected by selected methods (black points) visualized in PCA-reduced 3D visualization of filtered HBSC 2020 data.

4.4 Computation Times

The experiments show that the rough sets can detect outliers relevant from various perspectives without a priori knowledge in the questionnaire data. However, their complexity significantly rises with the number of tested attributes. Table 4 shows computation times of separate outlier detection methods based on different principles and parameters that are summarized in Table 3 and measured on the HBSC2020 data. The table also contains the preprocessing time which is common for all methods and it includes loading the data file, cleaning missing values, renumbering of answers, normalization, computation of correlation matrix, and statistics of individual variables that are used in the tested framework of methods. The shortest times are reached by simple methods such as kNN, Maha, and $O+$, while the rough set methods are computationally very expensive as they are based on computing many combinations of attributes. The code was written in Python using public libraries that are not precisely optimized for large-scale optimizations.

The program was implemented in Python 3.10.11, Pandas 1.4.1, Scikit-learn 1.0.2, and Roughsets-base 1.0.1.1. All experiments run on the following hardware: Intel Core i7-1185G7 @ 3.0 GHz, 32 GB RAM, Windows 10 64-bit.

Table 4. Computation times measured in seconds (average and standard deviation of 10 measurements) of preprocessing (common for all methods), and each standalone method for HBSC2020 data (3255 respondents).

Method/time(s)	Avg.	St.dev.
preprocessing	47.6000	2.5123
en1	2.0953	0.1625
en2	2.8078	0.1956
pen1	7.6344	0.5288
pen2	8.1000	0.5557
Maha	0.7234	0.0748
$O+$	0.2000	0.0161
rc12	2.6703	0.2067
kNN100	0.5391	0.0552
LOF10	2.9219	0.0612
RS2	69.0750	1.6886
RS3	5153.2688	185.7533
RS4	384825.9857	24791.4936

5   Conclusion

This paper aims at unsupervised outliers detection in real-world questionnaire data that usually negatively affect the statistical methods. The main contribution of the paper is a novel method based on the rough set theory that captures relations among attributes. A subset of k attributes is selected from the original data to identify the discernible entries by rough sets (RSk). Three variants RS2, RS3, and RS4 are tested and compared with other recently published methods. The RS3 (40 significant outliers) is finally chosen as it covers all the outliers detected by RS2 (8 significant outliers) and most ones detected by RS4 (27 significant outliers). It correlates with most of the tested methods and also has many common outliers with other methods, especially kNN and Maha. Moreover, the RS3 is cheaper than RS4 as it computes only triplets of attributes. The entropy-based methods have a significant intersection with RS3 but the correlation of scores is weak. The mentioned indicates that the RS3 finds outliers that are relevant from different perspectives. Unlike proximity- and density-based methods, the RSk is not based on the distance, and therefore, it is suitable for mixed attribute data (numerical and categorical).

Acknowledgment. This work was supported by SGS, VŠB – Technical University of Ostrava, Czech Republic, under the grant No. SP2023/12 "Parallel processing of Big Data X".

References

1. Aggarwal, C.C., Sathe, S.: Theoretical foundations and algorithms for outlier ensembles. SIGKDD Explor. Newsl. **17**(1), 24–47 (2015)
2. Badura, P., et al.: After the bell: adolescents' organised leisure-time activities and well-being in the context of social and socioeconomic inequalities. J. Epidemiol. Community Health **75**, 628–636 (2021)
3. Breunig, M.M., Kriegel, H.P., Ng, R.T., Sander, J.: LOF: identifying density-based local outliers. In: Proceedings of the 2000 ACM SIGMOD International Conference on Management of Data, pp. 93–104 (2000)
4. Van den Broeck, J., Argeseanu Cunningham, S., Eeckels, R., Herbst, K.: Data cleaning: detecting, diagnosing, and editing data abnormalities. PLoS Med. **2**(10), e267 (2005)
5. Chandola, V., Banerjee, A., Kumar, V.: Outlier detection: a survey. ACM Comput. Surv. **14**, 15 (2007)
6. Cronbach, L.J.: Coefficient alpha and the internal structure of tests. Psychometrika **16**(3), 297–334 (1951)
7. García, S., Luengo, J., Herrera, F.: Data Preprocessing in Data Mining, vol. 72. Springer, Cham (2015). https://doi.org/10.1007/978-3-319-10247-4
8. Hawkins, D.M.: Identification of Outliers, vol. 11. Springer, Dordrecht (1980)
9. Hubert, M., Vandervieren, E.: An adjusted boxplot for skewed distributions. Comput. Stat. Data Anal. **52**(12), 5186–5201 (2008)
10. Inchley, J., Currie, D., Cosma, A., Samdal, O.: Health behaviour in school-aged children (HBSC) study protocol: background, methodology and mandatory items for the 2017/18 survey. International report (2018)
11. Ježowicz, T., Gajdoš, P., Uher, V., Snášel, V.: Classification with extreme learning machine on GPU. In: 2015 International Conference on Intelligent Networking and Collaborative Systems, pp. 116–122. IEEE (2015)
12. Jiang, F., Chen, Y.M.: Outlier detection based on granular computing and rough set theory. Appl. Intell. **42**, 303–322 (2015)
13. Jiang, F., Sui, Y., Cao, C.: Some issues about outlier detection in rough set theory. Expert Syst. Appl. **36**(3), 4680–4687 (2009)
14. Komorowski, J., Pawlak, Z., Polkowski, L., Skowron, A.: Rough sets: a tutorial. Rough fuzzy hybridization: a new trend in decision-making, pp. 3–98 (1999)
15. Kriegel, H.P., Kroger, P., Schubert, E., Zimek, A.: Interpreting and unifying outlier scores. In: Proceedings of the 2011 SIAM International Conference on Data Mining, pp. 13–24. SIAM (2011)

16. Maciá-Pérez, F., Berna-Martinez, J.V., Oliva, A.F., Ortega, M.A.A.: Algorithm for the detection of outliers based on the theory of rough sets. Decis. Support Syst. **75**, 63–75 (2015)

17. Mahalanobis, P.C.: On the generalized distance in statistics. National Institute of Science of India (1936)

18. Ng, K., Cosma, A., Svacina, K., Boniel-Nissim, M., Badura, P.: Czech adolescents' remote school and health experiences during the spring 2020 COVID-19 lockdown. Prev. Med. Rep. **22**, 101386 (2021)

19. Otey, M.E., Ghoting, A., Parthasarathy, S.: Fast distributed outlier detection in mixed-attribute data sets. Data Min. Knowl. Disc. **12**, 203–228 (2006)

20. Pawlak, Z.: Rough Sets: Theoretical Aspects of Reasoning About Data, vol. 9. Springer, Dordrecht (1991). https://doi.org/10.1007/978-94-011-3534-4

21. Saris, W.E., Gallhofer, I.N.: Design, Evaluation, and Analysis of Questionnaires for Survey Research. Wiley, Hoboken (2014)

22. Schubert, E., Wojdanowski, R., Zimek, A., Kriegel, H.P.: On evaluation of outlier rankings and outlier scores. In: Proceedings of the 2012 SIAM International Conference on Data Mining, pp. 1047–1058. SIAM (2012)

23. Shannon, C.E.: A mathematical theory of communication. Bell Syst. Tech. J. **27**(3), 379–423 (1948)

24. Shao, C., Zheng, S., Gu, C., Hu, Y., Qin, X.: A novel outlier detection method for monitoring data in dam engineering. Expert Syst. Appl. **193**, 116476 (2022)

25. Suri, N.R., Murty, M.N., Athithan, G.: Detecting outliers in categorical data through rough clustering. Nat. Comput. **15**(3), 385–394 (2016)

26. Tukey, J.W., et al.: Exploratory Data Analysis, vol. 2. Reading, Mass (1977)

27. Uher, V., Dráždilová, P., Platoš, J., Badura, P.: Automation of cleaning and ensembles for outliers detection in questionnaire data. Expert Syst. Appl. **206**, 117809 (2022)

28. Wilcox, R.R.: Robust regression: testing global hypotheses about the slopes when there is multicollinearity or heteroscedasticity. Br. J. Math. Stat. Psychol. **72**(2), 355–369 (2019)

29. Yuan, K.H., Gomer, B.: An overview of applied robust methods. Br. J. Math. Stat. Psychol. **74**(S1), 199–246 (2021)

30. Yuan, Z., Chen, H., Li, T., Sang, B., Wang, S.: Outlier detection based on fuzzy rough granules in mixed attribute data. IEEE Trans. Cybern. **52**(8), 8399–8412 (2021)

31. Yuan, Z., Chen, H., Li, T., Zhang, X., Sang, B.: Multigranulation relative entropy-based mixed attribute outlier detection in neighborhood systems. IEEE Trans. Syst. Man Cybern. Syst. **52**(8), 5175–5187 (2022)

32. Zijlstra, W.P., Van Der Ark, L.A., Sijtsma, K.: Outlier detection in test and questionnaire data. Multivar. Behav. Res. **42**(3), 531–555 (2007)

Modelling and Optimization

Optimization of Bread Production Using Neuro-Fuzzy Modelling

Tomasz Boiński and Julian Szymański(✉)

Gdansk University of Technology, Narutowicza 11/12, 80-233 Gdansk, Poland
tomboins@pg.edu.pl, julian.szymanski@eti.pg.edu.pl

Abstract. Automation of food production is an actively researched domain. One of the areas, where automation is still not progressing significantly is bread making. The process still relies on expert knowledge regarding how to react to procedure changes depending on environmental conditions, quality of the ingredients, etc. In this paper, we propose an ANFIS-based model for changing the mixer speed during the kneading process. Although the recipes usually indicate the time for which the mixing should be done using slow and fast mixing speeds, however, it is the human, who makes the final decision as the mixers differ in terms of the mixing quality, speed, etc. Furthermore, unexpected differences in flour quality or room conditions can impact the time required to mix the ingredients. In the paper, different methods for fuzzy modeling are described and analyzed. The tested models are compared using both generated and real data and the best solution is presented.

Keywords: bread production optimization · ANFIS · neuro-fuzzy modelling

1 Introduction

Food production is one of the most important aspects of industry. A big part of it is taken by bread-making, which follows humanity for thousands of years. Due to the rising numbers of human beings automation of food production, including bread-making, became crucial for sustained production.

The basic procedure for bread making is relatively simple. We need to mix flour, water, salt, yeast or leaven, allow it to rise, and finally bake it at the correct temperature. On an industrial scale even small deviations from the correct procedure errors can lead to wasting a big amount of resources. Also the correct procedure need to be modified according the additional parameters, external conditions like the quality of the components, ambient temperature, humidity, etc. that should be compensated to obtain a high-quality final product. So far such modifications are applied manually based on the expertise of the baker master.

In this paper, we propose a method for automation of modification of the kneading procedure. In our work, we base our model on expert knowledge and sensor data acquired during the kneading process. As a result we propose a model that allows to automate the process of wheat dough making and control the process with mixer speed.

The structure of the paper is as follows. Section 2 describe dough-making process. Section 3 introduces fuzzy modeling and ANFIS. Next, Sect. 4 presents fuzzy logic and ANFIS applications. Section 6 describes the experiment performed and the obtained results both for the generated and real data. Finally, conclusions and future works are discussed.

2 Dough Making Process

The are numerous types of bread recipes, however, most of them are divided into three stages: dough preparation; loaf formation; baking.

In this paper, we focus on the first stage, i.e. the process of preparing the dough. During this stage the raw materials are mixed which is also referred to as dough kneading. The aim is to combine the flour with water and the remaining ingredients into a homogeneous mass and to give the dough appropriate physical properties. Errors made during this process cannot be compensated in subsequent production stages and results in a low quality final product. The most important parameters of kneading are [1]: kneading time, dough temperature, mixing speed, airing the dough, water absorption by flour, water temperature and total water content in the dough.

To obtain a dough with optimal properties it is required that the flour will be mixed with the right amount of water in a proper temperature. In addition, the dough must exhibit adequate air saturation. The volume of air that enters the dough as a result of kneading is estimated to be 10–15% of the dough volume [2].

When mixing the dough, there are significant relationships between the properties of the dough and the temperature of the dough, and the speed of mixing [3]. It turns out that part of the mechanical energy from the mixer is transferred to the dough, increasing its temperature at the same time. However, it has been observed that this energy helps in the development of the gluten network and gives the dough appropriate properties, in particular the ability to retain gases, making the dough more resistant and stable. It was also confirmed that when the speed of the stirrer's rotation increases, the process of kneading the dough is shortened because the dough reaches the appropriate temperature faster. However, when the dough is over-mixed, it tends to become sticky and lose its elasticity. Therefore, it is very important to stop mixing before the dough loses its best consistency. The recipes for each type of bread usually specify the time for two types of mixing, the first for slow rotation to combine the ingredients, and then for the fast rotation to obtain the best dough consistency and aeration. It is worth noting that the mixing time will change depending on the temperature, humidity of the room, and other external factors. That is why bakers use their experience when kneading the dough to choose the right moment to switch from slow to fast speed and to stop the mixing process.

The dough kneading mathematical simulation is described in [4]. The proposed mathematical model was created for the spiral mixer. The authors experimentally obtained distributions of the bread dough flow velocity vectors in the vertical and horizontal directions. In [5], where 66 wheat flours were mixed according to the appropriate recipes, and then bread, biscuits, and crackers were baked. As a result of the experiment, a close relationship was found between such parameters as development time, dough stability, and the parameters of the alveograph. All the observed relationships significantly differed depending on the quality of the flour and its gluten content. Those observations were confirmed in [6], where the authors, using two Argentinean wheat flours, investigated the mixing time needed to obtain the best rheological parameters of the dough. As a result it can be stated that the physical properties of flour are one of the most important variables significantly influencing the dough mixing process.

The second important aspect is the amount and temperature of the water added to the dough as it influences the development of gluten, the rheological properties of the dough, and the final quality of bakery products [1]. The production processes of some bakery products require hot water to mix the dough to promote gluten development. This is due to the technological properties of hot water, which is a much more effective and efficient gluten plasticizer than colder water. Flours, which can absorb more than 60% of their weight in water, create a slowly fermenting bread dough that retains its shape during final fermentation and baking. In contrast, flours that absorb less than 54% of their weight in water result in a dough that forms quickly and degrades just as quickly during final fermentation and produces an inferior finished bread product. Cappelli et. al. [7], using Chopin's alveograph, which is a tool to study flour quality and rheological properties of the dough, observed that an increase in the total water content of the dough increases the dough extensibility and the swelling ratio, and reduces the dough strength, the deformation energy, and the curve configuration factor, i.e. of the dough strength to extensibility ratio. On the other hand, a poorly hydrated dough would show exactly the opposite tendency for all of the aforementioned properties.

3 Fuzzy Modeling

Fuzzy sets, and fuzzy logic in general, were first formalized by Lotfi Zadeh [8] in 1965. Its origins, however, reach the early 20ties of the XX century, when Jan Łukasiewicz presented three-valued logic, in which, besides the true and false states, he added a third value understood as possible, which was a numerical value between true and false. That started a series of research aiming at representing problems with inaccurate state descriptions, until then not possible to describe them with a precise mathematical model. Fuzzy logic and fuzzy sets have proven themselves very well in nonlinear mathematical problems and, in addition to neural models, it has become the most commonly used method in the 90s [9], and it has found its application in such areas as economics, law, medicine, answering questions, most of all probability theory and decision analysis [10]. Fuzzy set theory also introduce the concept of linguistic variable [11], which values can be described by words. The degree of belonging of the element to the set or class is assigned to each such value, and it is determined by the membership function. Given element can belong to multiple fuzzy sets at once and each such membership is determined by the degree of the belonging.

Fuzzy sets are often used where it is necessary to define fuzzy rules. Fuzzy rules set is a representation of expert knowledge. As the knowledge can contain unknown nonlinear relations usually each fuzzy rule represents simple, observable relation. Such a set is combined into a so-called fuzzy model. During the inference, we deduce the final, nonlinear outcome by the composition of such simple rules. As such they seem to suit perfectly the problem of bread-making as the relations between the mixing speed and time and the environment conditions are nonlinear and cannot be easily modelled using deterministic rules.

Multiple fuzzy models were defined. The most commonly used are *Mamdani* [12], *Sugeno* [13] and *Tsukamoto* [14] models. Independent from the model selected one of the biggest problems when creating the rule-set is the proper definition of rules and their weights. In general, in fuzzy inference systems, the rule set and the membership function are based on expert knowledge and adjusted manually to fit the criteria needed for the proper solving of a given problem. To automate the process of the model tuning adaptive neuro-fuzzy inference system (ANFIS) approach can be applied [15]. ANFIS serves as a means of integration between neural networks and *Sugeno* model.

4   Fuzzy Logic and ANFIS Applications

Fuzzy logic and ANFIS systems are used to solve problems in which the exact mathematical solution is difficult or impossible. In [16], the authors proposed the ANFIS system for non-invasive temperature prediction in lower limb prostheses, which is a very complicated process. The system results were also compared with the Gauss process in machine learning, which showed that the results returned by both methods are very similar - they differed by only 0.5 °C. The authors however state that the ANFIS approach is not universal – the best results are obtained while the dataset is for one patient only and the trained model will adequately predict only that person. Another example is the work [17]. The authors aimed at checking the usefulness and capabilities of the ANFIS systems for interpreting the results of three-axis shear tests on clay soils. It has been shown that the shear strength parameters are significantly influenced by the variables tested during the experiments and the physical parameters of a given soil sample. Finally, the results obtained from the ANFIS model did not differ significantly from the results obtained directly during the execution of physical tests and allowed to take into account the multifaceted mutual relations of the input parameters. In our previous research, we also implemented the ANFIS system within a Mrowisko game [18]. The game implemented a simplified model of the living organisms' environment, namely an ant colony. The ANFIS approach was used to control the resources in the game, which, by limiting the available food, kept the environment in a state of equilibrium.

5   Bread Kneading Fuzzy Model

5.1   Expert Knowledge

An important aspect of fuzzy model creation is gathering expert knowledge. For that, we performed an interview with a renowned Polish bread expert. During the interview the following facts were obtained: the type and size of the mixer influences the kneading process; we cannot constantly add water to the dough, this can only be done once after half of the total mixing time; if the flour does not meet quality standards the mixing will not finish correctly no matter the time and method of mixing; for wheat and wheat/rye dough two mixing modes are required as after the mixing of ingredients the dough needs to be heated up, however too long mixing will overheat the dough and destroy the gluten structure; rye dough does not need high speed mixing as there is not gluten mesh creation involved; changing the mixing speed from slow to fast should take place as soon as the water on the surface of the dough is no longer visible – thus it is enough to observe the difference (delta) of humidity of the dough in the last time window.

The main goal in the mixing process is that the flour should absorb as much water as possible. Water absorption decreases throughout mixing, so it should be added at the beginning of the process. One can add 3–5% water later if needed. It is assumed that the dough at 32 °C loses its properties, which will stop the fermentation process. The water should be at an appropriate temperature and the mixing process should stop before the dough overheats. The water temperature can be calculated according to formula 1, where T_w is water temperature, T_t is a dough target temperature, T_r is room temperature, T_f is flour temperature, and ΔT is the increase of the dough temperature during the kneading process, it is assumed that it should take between 24 and 26 °F (13,3 to 14,4 °C) [3].

$$T_w = T_t * 3 - T_r - T_f - \Delta T \tag{1}$$

5.2   Fuzzy Model for Changing the Mixing Mode

Based on the expert knowledge, we can observe that changing the speed of kneading and adding water are independent and rely on other characteristics of the dough. In this paper, we focus on changing the mixing mode. The proposed automated dough kneading process follows the procedure:

1. A dough recipe is selected (e.g. Kaiser roll or wheat bread).
2. All ingredients required by the recipe are added to the mixer.
3. Mixer is started in *SLOW* speed mode.

4. Controller checks if the maximum time for *SLOW* mode has been exceeded, if so go to step 8.
5. Readings are taken from the sensors and the data is transferred to the controller.
6. The controller makes a prediction based on the data obtained in the previous step using the fuzzy model.
7. If the prediction result is *FAST* mode go to step 8, otherwise go to step 4.
8. Change mode to *FAST*.
9. Controller checks if the maximum time for *FAST* mode has been exceeded, if so go to step 13.
10. Readings are taken from the sensors and sent to the controller.
11. The controller makes a prediction based on the data obtained in the previous step using the fuzzy model.
12. If the prediction result is *STOP* mode go to step 13, otherwise go to step 9.
13. Change the mode to *STOP*.

The model fuzzy model consisted of 4 fuzzy input variables and 6 fuzzy rules. The model is based on the Sugeno approach so the output can take one of the three fixed values defining the mixer mode - SLOW, FAST, and STOP. The input variables of the model are: time [s] (from the start of the mixing - values: introductory, proper, final), dough temperature [°C] (values: low, good, high), dough density (values: low, good, high) and dough humidity delta (values: small, high). The fuzzy rules, based on the expert knowledge, are as follows (the values in the parenthesis denote the degree of belonging):

– if dough humidity delta is high then mixing speed is SLOW(1)
– if dough humidity delta is small then mixing speed is FAST(0.4)
– if time is final and dough temperature is high then mixing speed is STOP(1)
– if time is proper and dough temperature is high then mixing speed is STOP(0.7)
– if time is proper and dough density is high then mixing speed is STOP(0.7)
– if time is final and dough density is high then mixing speed is STOP(1)

6   The Experiments

We tested the proposed model both on the data generated based on the expert knowledge, resources found in the literature and on real data gathered during the dough kneading process.

6.1   Generated Data

The first test was done using generated data, as there are no mathematical models describing the dough mixing and the kneading process itself uses a lot of components. Thus, based on the literature and expert knowledge, we generated data fitting the kneading process as much as possible. This approach generated a lot of input variables as described in the literature (time, room temperature,

Table 1. Value ranges of the variables

Variable	Min value	Max value	Average value	Unit	source
time (form the start of mixing)	0,0	10,0	8,0	$minutes$	[3,19]
room temperature	16,0	30,0	26,0	°C	[3]
dough temperature	17,0	30,0		°C	[3]
flour temperature	21,0	22,0		°C	[3]
dough temperature delta	13,0	15,0		°C	[3]
room humidity	50,0	60,0		%	[3]
dough humidity	34,0	42,0		%	[20]
flour humidity	14,0	14,5		%	[20]
dough density	1 100,0	1 200,0		kg/m^3	[21]
dough acidity	4,8	5,4	5,0	pH	[22,23]
dough humidity delta	no information found				

dough temperature, dough density, dough acidity, dough humidity delta, dough temperature, flour humidity, room humidity - Table 1). Unfortunately, the data is prone to errors, as some information is not available and some are presented only in a form of a graph.

6.2 Mixing Mode Fuzzy Model for Generated Data

Based on the knowledge described in the previous section we generated test data. Next, we tested the data with the mixing model created as described in Sect. 5.2. The model always stays between the best time to change mixing mode and the maximum time. In the case of the switch from SLOW to FAST mode, the time delay is small, changing from FAST to STOP is near the maximum mixing stop time (after this time the bough might overheat and the gluten mesh is broken). The data and the model results can be seen in Fig. 1, where the yellow color denotes the best time to change kneading mode, the green color denotes the max time when kneading mode can be changed and the purple color denotes the time pointed by the fuzzy model.

6.3 Mixing Mode ANFIS Model for Generated Data

Using the generated data we trained an ANFIS model to check the possibility for improvement over the standard fuzzy model. The ANFIS model consisted of 4 input variables and 1 output variable. We compared the approaches where the partition grid was a constant, liner function and obtained using subtractive clustering. The parameters of the models are presented in Table 2.

First, we trained the model using a partition grid with output in form of a constant value. The error tolerance was zero, and the training itself was run for 10 epochs. The smallest RMSE training error was achieved after the second

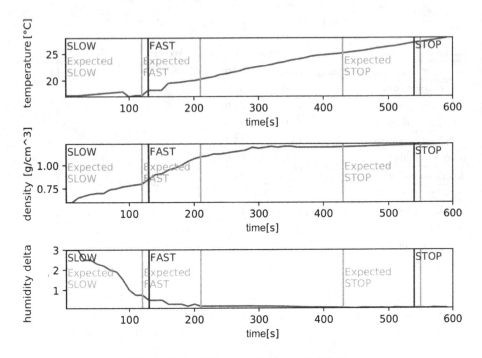

Fig. 1. Fuzzy inference for generated data.

Table 2. ANFIS model parameters for generated data.

	Partition grid with constant output	Partition grid with linear output	Subtractive clustering
Min. RMSE training error	0,079	0,018	**0,011**
Best epoch	2	3	7
Number of nodes	137	137	77
Linear parameters	54	270	35
Non-linear parameters	44	44	56
Total number of parameters	98	314	91
Fuzzy rules	54	54	7

epoch with a value of 0.0785397. Then, we trained the model once again, but in this case, the values of the output variable were in a form of a linear function. This time the smallest RMSE training error was achieved after epoch 3 and was 0.0178692. Finally we tested input data division using substractive clustering algorithm. We tuned the parameters experimentally to minimize the error. The best results were obtained for the following parameter values: Range of impact - 0.3; Minimization factor - 1.25; Acceptance ratio - 0.5; Unacceptable ratio - 0.15. The RMSE training error achieved was 0.011.

The best results (marked with bold in Table 2) were obtained using subtractive clustering. The RMSE training error was 0.011. The model was verified by running simulation on the generated data. The change from *SLOW* to *FAST* mixing mode happened within the appropriate time frame, however, the change from *FAST* to *STOP* happened much too quickly. This could have a significant impact on the state and the quality of the final dough. Compared to the defined model based on expert knowledge, this model fared worse.

6.4   Real Data

The data was gathered using an industrial dough mixer equipped with a series of sensors. The kneading procedure was supervised by an expert judging when to switch the mixing mode and perform any other changes to the procedure. 2 types of dough were made – wheat roll (experiment 1) and wheat-rye bread (experiment 2). During the procedures signal from the pressure transducer located on the side surface of the sword, signal from the pressure transducer located on the cutting edge of the sword and signal from the current transducer were read via the sensors and room, flour, water and dough temperature was read manually. The sensor data was read every 0.001 s. The room ($28\,°C$), flour ($23,5\,°C$), and the water temperature ($6,1\,°C$ for experiment 1 and $5,1\,°C$ for experiment 2) were read once as they are constant during the whole kneading process.

The dough temperature, depending on the current mixing stage, was measured using 3 sensors – the one built into the mixer, a touch-less thermometer, and a probe thermometer. The measured values and current mixing speed for experiments 1 and 2 are presented in Table 3 and 4 respectively.

During both experiments, we recorded the signals from the sensors. Visualization for experiment 2 can be seen in Fig. 2. In both cases, we can observe,

Table 3. Dough temperature and mixing mode for experiment 1

Time [min]	Mixing mode	Dough temperature		
		Mixer thermometer	Touch-less thermometer	Probe thermometer
0	SLOW	25 °C		
1	SLOW	19 °C		
1.5	SLOW	Added water (2 litres)		
6	FAST	21 °C		24 °C
11	FAST	Gluten mesh fully created		
13	STOP	24 °C		27.7 °C

Table 4. Dough temperature and mixing mode for experiment 2

Time [min]	Mixing mode	Dough temperature		
		Mixer thermometer	Touch-less thermometer	Probe thermometer
1	SLOW	17 °C	17.5 °C	
2	SLOW	Added water (2.6 litres)		
10	FAST			
12	FAST	Gluten mesh fully created		
14	STOP			22.8 °C

primarily on channel 1, the point when water was added (sudden, short decrease in dough density). We can also observe the time when gluten mesh was created. It is visible both in signals from channels 0 and 1.

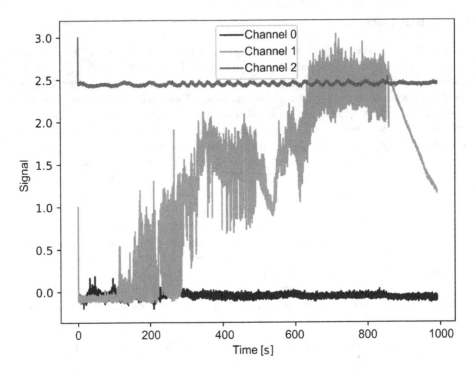

Fig. 2. Graph of sensor values during the kneading process in the experiment 2.

6.5   Mixing Mode ANFIS Model for Real Data

During the aforementioned experiments, the temperature was checked at certain points in time and than interpolated for the whole kneading process period. The total number of samples for experiment 1 was 668,300 and for experiment 2 990,900 (with 0,001 second sampling). For each output class (SLOW, FAST, STOP) we selected 333 equally spaced samples. Such sample set was further divided into training (80%) and test (20%) sets.

For experiment 1 the best results were obtained in epoch 108 for triangular functions with constant output (RMSE equal 0.152). Similarly, the training was done using substractive clustering. We also trained models with different minimization factors (1.125, 1.3, 2 and 2.5). The smallest RMSE error was obtained for coefficient values of 2 and 2.5 (RMSE equal 0.094). This approach proved better than that obtained using the partition grid approach. It is worth noting that this model is very small, having only 30 nodes and only 3 fuzzy rules.

This model has been validated against the decisions made by the expert during the kneading process. As can be seen in Fig. 3 the obtained results (purple) are similar to mode switching points decided by the expert (yellow).

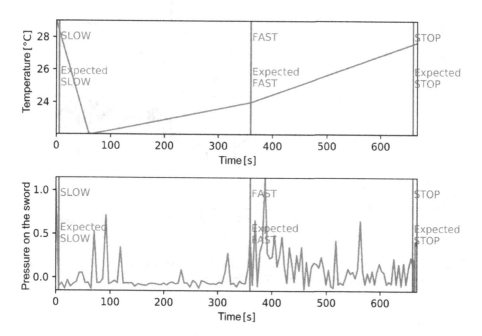

Fig. 3. Inference using ANFIS model for data from experiment 1. Purple - model prediction, yellow - expert decision (Color figure online)

We repeated the training for the data from experiment 2. For the partition grid, the best results were obtained for constant output and triangular function with RMSE error equal 0.208. For subtractive clustering, the best results were for model minimizing factor equal 2 (RMSE equal 0.19). This model was tested in kneading simulation. The results can be seen in Fig. 4. The model predictions are marked in purple, whereas the expert decisions are marked in yellow. The model suggested switching from SLOW to FAST mode a bit earlier than the expert (by 35 s) and suggested turning off mixing (STOP mode) 5 s earlier than the expert. Such differences were judged by the expert as fully acceptable.

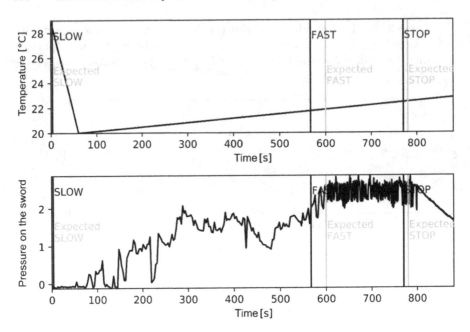

Fig. 4. Inference using ANFIS model for data from experiment 2. Purple - model prediction, yellow - expert decision (Color figure online)

7   Conclusions

The industry relies on expert knowledge in many aspects. On the other hand, there are fewer and fewer experts in some fields requiring automation, not to opt-out human involvement, but rather to fill the gaps created by a lack of skilled workers. Food production is an excellent example of such a problem.

Some of the aspects of dough kneading can be described mathematically (like the temperature of the water added). Other aspects rely on non-obvious, nonlinear relationships between the kneading process and the dough state. We believe that fuzzy logic allows capturing and automation of such relations, thus automating bread production, especially during the dough kneading process.

The models presented in the paper showed that the ANFIS-based models using the Sugeno approach and subtractive clustering prove accurate and potentially useful. The process needs to be split into smaller tasks like: How long should we mix the dough?; How much water should be added during mixing? Each of those questions should be answered by a dedicated model.

Our future work will focus on the creation of the additional model and tries to generalize them. Our current tests show, however, that each device type requires fine-tuning and the creation of a dedicated model. This can be costly, as dough mixers use a lot of resources (up to 40–50 kg of wheat). The modeling process however should require no more than one or two correct kneadings.

Acknowledgments. The work has been supported partially by founds of the Department of Computer Architecture, Faculty of Electronics, Telecommunications and Informatics, Gdańsk University of Technology and the project POIR.01.01.01-00-1449/19-00 entitled "Opracowanie systemu, dedykowanego branży piekarniczej, pełniącego funkcje nadzorowania i sterowania powtarzalnym procesem produkcji ciasta". The Authors would like to thank Joanna Woźna for her help in implementation of the models.

References

1. Cappelli, A., Bettaccini, L., Cini, E.: The kneading process: a systematic review of the effects on dough rheology and resulting bread characteristics, including improvement strategies. Trends Food Sci. Technol. (2020). https://doi.org/10.1016/j.tifs.2020.08.008
2. Dziki, D.: Miesienie ciasta chlebowego - praktyczne uwagi," Mistrz Branży (2014). http://mistrzbranzy.pl/artykuly/pokaz/Miesienie-ciasta-chlebowego-praktyczne-uwagi-2258.html
3. Hamelman, J.: Bread: a Baker's Book of Techniques and Recipes. Wiley, Hoboken (2018). ISBN 9781118132715
4. Luchian, M.I., Stefanov, S., Litovchenko, I., Mihailov, I., Hadjiiski, W.: Simulation of the mixing bread dough process using computational techniques, Technical Report (2013)
5. Osella, C.A., Robutti, J., Sánchez, H.D., Borrás, F., de la Torre, M.A.: Análisis de componentes principales entre propiedades de masa y productos panificados," Ciencia y Tecnologia Alimentaria (2008). https://doi.org/10.1080/11358120809487633
6. Gómez, A., Ferrero, C., Calvelo, A., Añón, M.C., Puppo, M.C.: Effect of mixing time on structural and rheological properties of wheat flour dough for breadmaking. Int. J. Food Properties, 2011. https://doi.org/10.1080/10942910903295939
7. Cappelli, A., Cini, E., Guerrini, L., Masella, P., Angeloni, G., Parenti, A.: Predictive models of the rheological properties and optimal water content in doughs: An application to ancient grain flours with different degrees of refining. J. Cereal Sci. **83**(April), 229–235 (2018). https://doi.org/10.1016/j.jcs.2018.09.006
8. Zadeh, L.: Fuzzy sets, Information and Control (1965). https://doi.org/10.1016/S0019-9958(65)90241-X, https://www.sciencedirect.com/science/article/pii/S001999586590241X
9. Piegat, A.: Modelowanie i sterowanie rozmyte (1999)
10. Zadeh, L.A., Klir, G.J., Yuan, B.: Fuzzy sets, fuzzy logic, and fuzzy systems: selected papers. World Scientific, vol. 6 (1996)
11. Zadeh, L.A.: Fuzzy logic = computing with words. IEEE Trans. Fuzzy Syst. (1996). https://doi.org/10.1109/91.493904
12. Mamdani, E.H., Assilian, S.: An experiment in linguistic synthesis with a fuzzy logic controller. Int. J. Man-Mach. Stud. (1975). https://doi.org/10.1016/S0020-7373(75)80002-2
13. Takagi, T., Sugeno, M.: Fuzzy identification of systems and its applications to modeling and control. IEEE Trans. Syst. Man Cybern. (1985). https://doi.org/10.1109/TSMC.1985.6313399
14. Jang, J.S.R., Sun, C.T.: Neuro-fuzzy modeling and control. In: Proceedings of the IEEE (1995). https://doi.org/10.1109/5.364486
15. Jang, J.S.R.: ANFIS: Adaptive-Network-Based Fuzzy Inference System. IEEE Trans. Syst. Man Cybern. (1993). https://doi.org/10.1109/21.256541

16. Mathur, N., Glesk, I., Buis, A.: Comparison of adaptive neuro-fuzzy inference system (ANFIS) and Gaussian processes for machine learning (GPML) algorithms for the prediction of skin temperature in lower limb prostheses. Med. Eng. Phys. (2016). https://doi.org/10.1016/j.medengphy.2016.07.003

17. Daniszewska -Mazurski, E.: Zastosowanie ANFIS w analizie wyników badań gruntów, Technical Report (2014)

18. Litwin, J., Łuczak, D., Kosiński, S.: Gra w życie z zastosowaniem logiki rozmytej i ANFIS (2021)

19. Munteanu, M., Voicu, G., Stefan, E.M., Constantin, G.A., Popa, L., Mihailov, N.: Farinograph characteristics of wheat flour dough and rye flour dough. In: International Symposium ISB-INMA TEH 2015 (2015)

20. Canja, C.M., Lupu, M., Tăulea, G.: The influence of kneading time on bread dough quality, Bulletin of the Transilvania University of Brasov, Series II: Forestry. Wood Industry, Agricultural Food Engineering (2014)

21. Calderón-Domínguez, G., Vera-Domínguez, M., Farrera-Rebollo, R.: Rheological changes of dough and bread quality prepared from a sweet dough: effect of temperature and mixing time. Int. J. Food Prop. (2004). https://doi.org/10.1081/JFP-120025393

22. Cauvain, S.: Speciality fermented goods. In: Technology of Breadmaking. Springer, Cham, pp. 253–277 (2015). https://doi.org/10.1007/978-3-319-14687-4_9

23. Tyl, C., Sadler, G.D.: pH and titratable acidity. In: Nielsen, S.S. (ed) Food analysis. Springer, Cham, pp. 389–406 (2017). https://doi.org/10.1007/978-3-319-45776-5_22

Applications of Graph Topology in Manufacturing of Anti Cancer Drugs

Debasis Chanda[1]📧, Prosanta Sarkar[2](✉)📧, and Anita Pal[3]📧

[1] MDI Murshidabad, West Bengal, India
dc@mdim.ac.in
[2] Department of Basic Science and Humanities (Mathematics),
Ramgarh Engineering College, Ramgarh, Jharkhand, India
prosantasarkar87@gmail.com
[3] Department of Mathematics, National Institute of Technology Durgapur,
Durgapur, India
anita.pal@maths.nitdgp.ac.in

Abstract. In chemical graph theory, a graph is used to represent a molecule by considering atoms as vertices and the covalent bonds between the atoms as edges. Topological indices are numerical parameters of a molecular graph which characterise bonding topology of a molecule and are necessarily structure invariant. It is known that the characteristics of drugs have a good correlation with their molecular structures. Drug properties are obtained by studying the molecular structure of corresponding drug. The computation of topological indices of a drug structure helps the researchers to predict the physicochemical properties and biological activities of the drug. Cancer is one of the primary causes of mortality globally, and the discovery of new anticancer drugs is the most important need in recent times. In this paper, we focused on the hyaluronic acid-paclitaxel conjugates molecular structure which is used in anticancer drugs manufacturing.

Keywords: General fifth M-Zagreb polynomial · Neighbourhood degree based topological indices · Hyaluronic acid-paclitaxel conjugates

1 Introductions

Chemical graph theory, is the branch of mathematical chemistry that uses graph theory to mathematical modelling of chemical phenomena. A graph-theoretical representation of a molecule is known as a chemical graph which consists of atoms as vertices and bonds between the atoms as edges. A chemical graph is finite, simple and connected. A graph is denoted by $G \equiv (V(G), E(G))$, where $V(G)$ denote the vertex set of G and edge set of G is denoted by $E(G)$ respectively. The number of vertices and edges of a graph G are called the order of G and size of the graph G which are denoted by $|V(G)|$ and $|E(G)|$ respectively. The degree of a vertex $a \in G$, is the number of edges associated with a in G.

K. Saeed et al. (Eds.): CISIM 2023, LNCS 14164, pp. 341–353, 2023.
https://doi.org/10.1007/978-3-031-42823-4_25

Generally, the degree of a vertex $a \in G$ is denote by $d_G(a)$. In this paper, we use the term $S_G(a)$ is the sum of degrees of neighbour vertices of any vertex a in G. In the field of chemical graph theory, a topological index is calculated based molecular descriptor of the chemical graph of a chemical compound. Topological indices are used in the development of quantitative structure-activity relationships (QSARs) in which a large number of molecular properties ranging from physicochemical and thermodynamic properties to chemical activity and biological activity are correlated with their chemical structure. Yet more than hundreds of topological indices are investigated by various researchers which are expected to contain important information that can be useful in predicting biological activities, physical and chemical properties such as the boiling point, entropy, enthalpy, etc. of the molecules. [6, 11, 16, 17, 19–21]. To develop a new drug at the initial stage it requires a large number of experiments to detect their chemical properties, toxicity and degrees of side effects on the human body. For these reasons, the study of topological indices on the molecular graph of a chemical compound has been welcomed by the medical and pharmaceutical researchers to understand their medical properties [4, 12, 18]. In this work, we modified general fifth M-Zagreb indices and defined a new version of general fifth M-Zagreb index $M_{\alpha,\beta}G_5(G)$ and its corresponding polynomial $M_{\alpha,\beta}G_5(G,x)$ and compute it for hyaluronic acid-paclitaxel conjugates molecular structures which used in cancer treatment. Hence, we computed fifth M-Zagreb polynomials, hyper M-Zagreb polynomials, general fifth M-Zagreb polynomials and their corresponding topological indices, first NDe index (ND_1), second NDe index (ND_2), third NDe index (ND_3), and forth NDe index (ND_4) with the help of this new version of general fifth M-Zagreb polynomial.

1.1   Various Neighbourhood Degree Based Topological Indices

Fifth $M-$Zagreb indices were first introduced by Graovac et al. [5], in 2011. They defined these indices as

$$M_1 G_5(G) = \sum_{ab \in E(G)} (S_G(a) + S_G(b))$$

and

$$M_2 G_5(G) = \sum_{ab \in E(G)} (S_G(a) S_G(b)).$$

Then, V.R. Kulli [8], in 2017 generalized these indices as

$$M_1^{\alpha} G_5(G) = \sum_{ab \in E(G)} (S_G(a) + S_G(b))^{\alpha}$$

and

$$M_2^{\alpha} G_5(G) = \sum_{ab \in E(G)} (S_G(a) S_G(b))^{\alpha}.$$

In the same paper [8], he also introduced fifth hyper $M-$Zagreb indices as

$$HM_1G_5(G) = \sum_{ab \in E(G)} (S_G(a) + S_G(b))^2$$

and

$$HM_2G_5(G) = \sum_{ab \in E(G)} (S_G(a)S_G(b))^2.$$

Sourav et al. in [14], first investigated that the correlation coefficient of $M_2G_5(G)$ and $HM_1G_5(G)$ with acentric factor and entropy for octane isomers is almost 1. They also introduced some other neighbourhood degree based topological indices such as first NDe index (ND_1), second NDe index (ND_2), third NDe index (ND_3) and forth NDe index (ND_4) in [15]. They defined these indices as:

$$ND_1(G) = \sum_{ab \in E(G)} \sqrt{S_G(a)S_G(b)},$$

$$ND_2(G) = \sum_{ab \in E(G)} \frac{1}{\sqrt{S_G(a) + S_G(b)}},$$

$$ND_3(G) = \sum_{ab \in E(G)} S_G(a)S_G(b)(S_G(a) + S_G(b)),$$

and

$$ND_4(G) = \sum_{ab \in E(G)} \frac{1}{\sqrt{S_G(a)S_G(b)}}.$$

Based on fifth $M-$Zagreb indices Kulli in [8], defined fifth $M-$Zagreb polynomials as:

$$M_1G_5(G, x) = \sum_{ab \in E(G)} x^{(S_G(a) + S_G(b))}$$

and

$$M_2G_5(G, x) = \sum_{ab \in E(G)} x^{S_G(a)S_G(b)}$$

where, x is a variable. In his paper [8], he also defined fifth hyper $M-$Zagreb polynomials as:

$$HM_1G_5(G, x) = \sum_{ab \in E(G)} x^{(S_G(a) + S_G(b))^2}$$

and

$$HM_2G_5(G, x) = \sum_{ab \in E(G)} x^{(S_G(a)S_G(b))^2}.$$

Similarly, he defined generalized fifth $M-$Zagreb polynomials as

$$M_1^\alpha G_5(G, x) = \sum_{ab \in E(G)} x^{(S_G(a) + S_G(b))^\alpha}$$

and

$$M_2^{\alpha}G_5(G,x) = \sum_{ab\in E(G)} x^{(S_G(a)S_G(b))^{\alpha}}$$

where, $\alpha \in \mathbb{R}$, $\alpha \neq 0$ and x is a variable. Based on general fifth M-Zagreb indices in this paper, we defined a new version of general fifth M-Zagreb index as

$$M_{\alpha,\beta}G_5(G) = \sum_{ab\in E(G)} (S_G(a)S_G(b))^{\alpha}(S_G(a) + S_G(b))^{\beta}$$

and its corresponding polynomial as

$$M_{\alpha,\beta}G_5(G,x) = \sum_{ab\in E(G)} x^{(S_G(a)S_G(b))^{\alpha}(S_G(a)+S_G(b))^{\beta}}.$$

Where, $\alpha, \beta \in \mathbb{R}$, α, β together not equal to zero and x is a variable. We encourage our reader to [1,2,7,9,22,23], for further study about some polynomials and their corresponding topological indices.

Table 1. Relations between $M_{\alpha,\beta}G_5(G)$ index with some other neighbourhood degree based topological indices:

Topological index	Corresponding $M_{\alpha,\beta}G_5(G)$ index
$M_1G_5(G)$	$M_{0,1}G_5(G)$
$M_2G_5(G)$	$M_{1,0}G_5(G)$
$M_1^{\alpha}G_5(G)$	$M_{0,\alpha}G_5(G)$
$M_2^{\alpha}G_5(G)$	$M_{\alpha,0}G_5(G)$
$HM_1G_5(G)$	$M_{0,2}G_5(G)$
$HM_2G_5(G)$	$M_{2,0}G_5(G)$
$ND_1(G)$	$M_{\frac{1}{2},0}G_5(G)$
$ND_2(G)$	$M_{0,-\frac{1}{2}}G_5(G)$
$ND_3(G)$	$M_{1,1}G_5(G)$
$ND_4(G)$	$M_{-\frac{1}{2},0}G_5(G)$

1.2   Hyaluronic Acid-Paclitaxel Conjugates

Hyaluronic acid (HA) is a non sulphated glycosaminoglycan composed of repeating polymeric disaccharides of D-glucuronic acid and N-acetyl-D-glucosamine linked via alternating $\beta(1 \rightarrow 3)$ and $\beta(1 \rightarrow 4)$ glycosidic bonds and it is a substance that is naturally present in the highest concentrations in fluids in the eyes and joints in the human body. Hyaluronic acid has been approved by the FDA to treat during certain eye surgeries, repair of a detached retina, and osteoarthritis via intra-articular injection. It is a key molecule involved in skin moisture that has the capacity in retaining water. Paclitaxel is an effective anti-cancer drug it is well known for its antimitotic activity that promotes tubulin assembly into stable microtubules. Though paclitaxel has limited widespread use in cancer treatment because of its poor solubility and relevant side effects. Hyaluronic acid paclitaxel conjugates were synthesized by utilizing a novel HA solubilization method in a single organic phase. Hydroxyl groups of paclitaxel were directly conjugated to carboxylic groups of hyaluronic acid in a single organic phase using $DCC/DMAP$ as a coupling agent. A hyaluronic acid paclitaxel conjugate is a promising drug conjugate for the intravesical treatment of refractory bladder cancer [3]. The small molecular weight hyaluronic acid paclitaxel conjugates can enhance widespread chemotherapeutic drug efficacy in a preclinical model of brain metastases of breast cancers [10,13]. The molecular structures of hyaluronic acid-paclitaxel conjugates $HA[m]$ for $m = 1, 3$ are depicted in Fig. 1.

2   Main Results

In this section, we first compute the new version of general fifth M-Zagreb polynomial of hyaluronic acid-paclitaxel conjugates molecular structure. Hence, using this new version of general fifth M-Zagreb polynomial we computed fifth $M-$Zagreb polynomials, hyper $M-$Zagreb polynomials, general fifth M-Zagreb polynomials. Also, we computed the new version of general fifth M-Zagreb index from the new version of general fifth M-Zagreb polynomial by using first derivative with respect to x at $x = 1$. Then using the Table 1 we compute various neighbourhood degree based topological indices. The edge partitioned of $HA[m]$ based on degree sum of neighbour vertices of end vertices of every edge is shown in Table 2. To avoid confusion let us consider G = HA[m]

Table 2. The edge partitions with respect to degree sum of neighbour vertices of end vertices of every edge of $HA[m]$

$(S(a), S(b)) : ab \in E(G)$	Total number of edges	$(S(a), S(b)) : ab \in E(G)$	Total number of edges
(2,4)	m	(5,8)	m
(3,4)	$6m$	(6,6)	$4m$
(3,6)	$4m$	(6,7)	$11m - 1$
(3,7)	$5m + 1$	(6,8)	$9m - 1$
(3,8)	m	(6,9)	m
(4,4)	$6m$	(6,10)	m
(4,5)	$6m$	(7,7)	$7m + 1$
(4,6)	$2m$	(7,8)	$4m$
(4,7)	$2m$	(7,10)	$4m$
(4,9)	$2m$	(8,8)	$3m - 1$
(4,10)	$2m$	(8,10)	$3m$
(5,6)	m	(9,10)	$3m$
(5,7)	$6m$	(10,11)	$2m$

Theorem 1. *The new version of general fifth* $M-Zagreb$ *polynomial of hyaluronic acid-paclitaxel conjugate molecular structure is given by*

$$M_{\alpha,\beta}G_5(G,x) = mx^{8^\alpha \times 6^\beta} + 6mx^{(12)^\alpha \times 7^\beta} + 4mx^{(18)^\alpha \times 9^\beta}$$
$$+(5m+1)x^{(21)^\alpha \times (10)^\beta} + mx^{(24)^\alpha \times (11)^\beta} + 6mx^{(16)^\alpha \times 8^\beta}$$
$$+6mx^{(20)^\alpha \times 9^\beta} + 2mx^{(24)^\alpha \times (10)^\beta} + 2mx^{(28)^\alpha \times (11)^\beta}$$
$$+2mx^{(36)^\alpha \times (13)^\beta} + 2mx^{(40)^\alpha \times (14)^\beta} + mx^{(30)^\alpha \times (11)^\beta}$$
$$+6mx^{(35)^\alpha \times (12)^\beta} + mx^{(40)^\alpha \times (13)^\beta} + 4mx^{(36)^\alpha \times (12)^\beta}$$
$$+(11m-1)x^{(42)^\alpha \times (13)^\beta} + (9m-1)x^{(48)^\alpha \times (14)^\beta} + mx^{(54)^\alpha \times (15)^\beta}$$
$$+mx^{(60)^\alpha \times (16)^\beta} + (7m+1)x^{(49)^\alpha \times (14)^\beta} + 4mx^{(56)^\alpha \times (15)^\beta}$$
$$+4mx^{(70)^\alpha \times (17)^\beta} + (3m-1)x^{(64)^\alpha \times (16)^\beta} + 3mx^{(80)^\alpha \times (18)^\beta}$$
$$+3mx^{(90)^\alpha \times (19)^\beta} + 2mx^{(110)^\alpha \times (21)^\beta}. \tag{1}$$

Proof. From the definition of $M_{\alpha,\beta}G_5(G,x)$ we get,

$$M_{\alpha,\beta}G_5(G,x) = \sum_{ab\in E(G)} x^{(S_G(a)S_G(b))^\alpha (S_G(a)+S_G(b))^\beta}$$

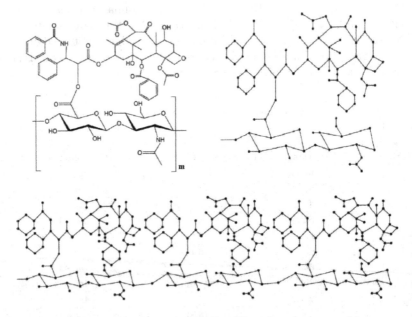

Fig. 1. Molecular structure of hyaluronic acid-paclitaxel conjugates and its corresponding molecular graphs $HA[m]$ for $m=1$ and $m=3$.

$$= \sum_{ab\in E_1(G)} x^{(2\times4)^{\alpha}(2+4)^{\beta}} + \sum_{ab\in E_2(G)} x^{(3\times4)^{\alpha}(3+4)^{\beta}} + \sum_{ab\in E_3(G)} x^{(3\times6)^{\alpha}(3+6)^{\beta}}$$

$$+ \sum_{ab\in E_4(G)} x^{(3\times7)^{\alpha}(3+7)^{\beta}} + \sum_{ab\in E_5(G)} x^{(3\times8)^{\alpha}(3+8)^{\beta}} + \sum_{ab\in E_6(G)} x^{(4\times4)^{\alpha}(4+4)^{\beta}}$$

$$+ \sum_{ab\in E_7(G)} x^{(4\times5)^{\alpha}(4+5)^{\beta}} + \sum_{ab\in E_8(G)} x^{(4\times6)^{\alpha}(4+6)^{\beta}} + \sum_{ab\in E_9(G)} x^{(4\times7)^{\alpha}(4+7)^{\beta}}$$

$$+ \sum_{ab\in E_{10}(G)} x^{(4\times9)^{\alpha}(4+9)^{\beta}} + \sum_{ab\in E_{11}(G)} x^{(4\times10)^{\alpha}(4+10)^{\beta}} + \sum_{ab\in E_{12}(G)} x^{(5\times6)^{\alpha}(5+6)^{\beta}}$$

$$+ \sum_{ab\in E_{13}(G)} x^{(5\times7)^{\alpha}(5+7)^{\beta}} + \sum_{ab\in E_{14}(G)} x^{(5\times8)^{\alpha}(5+8)^{\beta}} + \sum_{ab\in E_{15}(G)} x^{(6\times6)^{\alpha}(6+6)^{\beta}}$$

$$+ \sum_{ab\in E_{16}(G)} x^{(6\times7)^{\alpha}(6+7)^{\beta}} + \sum_{ab\in E_{17}(G)} x^{(6\times8)^{\alpha}(6+8)^{\beta}} + \sum_{ab\in E_{18}(G)} x^{(6\times9)^{\alpha}(6+9)^{\beta}}$$

$$+ \sum_{ab\in E_{19}(G)} x^{(6\times10)^{\alpha}(6+10)^{\beta}} + \sum_{ab\in E_{20}(G)} x^{(7\times7)^{\alpha}(7+7)^{\beta}} + \sum_{ab\in E_{21}(G)} x^{(7\times8)^{\alpha}(7+8)^{\beta}}$$

$$+ \sum_{ab\in E_{22}(G)} x^{(7\times10)^{\alpha}(7+10)^{\beta}} + \sum_{ab\in E_{23}(G)} x^{(8\times8)^{\alpha}(8+8)^{\beta}} + \sum_{ab\in E_{24}(G)} x^{(8\times10)^{\alpha}(8+10)^{\beta}}$$

$$+ \sum_{ab\in E_{25}(G)} x^{(9\times10)^{\alpha}(9+10)^{\beta}} + \sum_{ab\in E_{26}(G)} x^{(10\times11)^{\alpha}(10+11)^{\beta}}$$

$$= |E_1(G)|x^{8^{\alpha}\times6^{\beta}} + |E_2(G)|x^{(12)^{\alpha}\times7^{\beta}} + |E_3(G)|x^{(18)^{\alpha}\times9^{\beta}}$$

$$+ |E_4(G)|x^{(21)^{\alpha}\times(10)^{\beta}} + |E_5(G)|x^{(24)^{\alpha}\times(11)^{\beta}} + |E_6(G)|x^{(16)^{\alpha}\times8^{\beta}}$$

$$+ |E_7(G)|x^{(20)^{\alpha}\times9^{\beta}} + |E_8(G)|x^{(24)^{\alpha}\times(10)^{\beta}} + |E_9(G)|x^{(28)^{\alpha}\times(11)^{\beta}}$$

$$+ |E_{10}(G)|x^{(36)^{\alpha}\times(13)^{\beta}} + |E_{11}(G)|x^{(40)^{\alpha}\times(14)^{\beta}} + |E_{12}(G)|x^{(30)^{\alpha}\times(11)^{\beta}}$$

$$+ |E_{13}(G)|x^{(35)^{\alpha}\times(12)^{\beta}} + |E_{14}(G)|x^{(40)^{\alpha}\times(13)^{\beta}} + |E_{15}(G)|x^{(36)^{\alpha}\times(12)^{\beta}}$$

$$+ |E_{16}(G)|x^{(42)^{\alpha}\times(13)^{\beta}} + |E_{17}(G)|x^{(48)^{\alpha}\times(14)^{\beta}} + |E_{18}(G)|x^{(54)^{\alpha}\times(15)^{\beta}}$$

$$+ |E_{19}(G)|x^{(60)^{\alpha}\times(16)^{\beta}} + |E_{20}(G)|x^{(49)^{\alpha}\times(14)^{\beta}} + |E_{21}(G)|x^{(56)^{\alpha}\times(15)^{\beta}}$$

$$+ |E_{22}(G)|x^{(70)^{\alpha}\times(17)^{\beta}} + |E_{23}(G)|x^{(64)^{\alpha}\times(16)^{\beta}} + |E_{24}(G)|x^{(80)^{\alpha}\times(18)^{\beta}}$$

$$+ |E_{25}(G)|x^{(90)^{\alpha}\times(19)^{\beta}} + |E_{26}(G)|x^{(110)^{\alpha}\times(21)^{\beta}}$$

$$= mx^{8^{\alpha}\times6^{\beta}} + 6mx^{(12)^{\alpha}\times7^{\beta}} + 4mx^{(18)^{\alpha}\times9^{\beta}} + (5m+1)x^{(21)^{\alpha}\times(10)^{\beta}}$$

$$+ mx^{(24)^{\alpha}\times(11)^{\beta}} + 6mx^{(16)^{\alpha}\times8^{\beta}} + 6mx^{(20)^{\alpha}\times9^{\beta}} + 2mx^{(24)^{\alpha}\times(10)^{\beta}}$$

$$+ 2mx^{(28)^{\alpha}\times(11)^{\beta}} + 2mx^{(36)^{\alpha}\times(13)^{\beta}} + 2mx^{(40)^{\alpha}\times(14)^{\beta}}$$

$$+ mx^{(30)^{\alpha}\times(11)^{\beta}} + 6mx^{(35)^{\alpha}\times(12)^{\beta}} + mx^{(40)^{\alpha}\times(13)^{\beta}} + 4mx^{(36)^{\alpha}\times(12)^{\beta}}$$

$$+ (11m-1)x^{(42)^{\alpha}\times(13)^{\beta}} + (9m-1)x^{(48)^{\alpha}\times(14)^{\beta}} + mx^{(54)^{\alpha}\times(15)^{\beta}}$$

$$+ mx^{(60)^{\alpha}\times(16)^{\beta}} + (7m+1)x^{(49)^{\alpha}\times(14)^{\beta}} + 4mx^{(56)^{\alpha}\times(15)^{\beta}}$$

$$+ 4mx^{(70)^{\alpha}\times(17)^{\beta}} + (3m-1)x^{(64)^{\alpha}\times(16)^{\beta}} + 3mx^{(80)^{\alpha}\times(18)^{\beta}}$$

$$+ 3mx^{(90)^{\alpha}\times(19)^{\beta}} + 2mx^{(110)^{\alpha}\times(21)^{\beta}}.$$

Hence, the result follows as in Eq. 1. □

Note: From Eq. 1, it can be noted that fifth M-Zagreb polynomials, hyper M-Zagreb polynomials and general fifth M-Zagreb polynomials are easily obtained for different values of α and β. For $\alpha = 0$ and $\beta = 1$ we get $M_1G_5(G, x)$, in case of $M_2G_5(G, x)$ the value of $\alpha = 1$ and $\beta = 0$. The fifth hyper M-Zagreb polynomials are obtained by putting $(\alpha, \beta) = (0, 2)$ and $(\alpha, \beta) = (2, 0)$ respectively. In the case of general fifth M-Zagreb polynomials the value of $(\alpha, \beta) = (0, \alpha)$ and $(\alpha, \beta) = (\alpha, 0)$ respectively.

Proposition 1. *Now, we obtained new version of general fifth $M-Zagreb$ index $(M_{\alpha,\beta}G_5(G))$ by differentiating the counting polynomial as shown in Eq. 1, with respect to x at $x = 1$ as follows:*

$$
\begin{aligned}
M_{\alpha,\beta}G_5(G) = {}& m \times 8^\alpha \times 6^\beta + 6m \times (12)^\alpha \times 7^\beta + 4m \times (18)^\alpha \times 9^\beta \\
&+ (5m + 1) \times (21)^\alpha \times (10)^\beta + m \times (24)^\alpha \times (11)^\beta \\
&+ 6m \times (16)^\alpha \times 8^\beta + 6m \times (20)^\alpha \times 9^\beta \\
&+ 2m \times (24)^\alpha \times (10)^\beta + 2m \times (28)^\alpha \times (11)^\beta \\
&+ 2m \times (36)^\alpha \times (13)^\beta + 2m \times (40)^\alpha \times (14)^\beta \\
&+ m \times (30)^\alpha \times (11)^\beta + 6m \times (35)^\alpha \times (12)^\beta \\
&+ m \times (40)^\alpha \times (13)^\beta + 4m \times (36)^\alpha \times (12)^\beta \\
&+ (11m - 1) \times (42)^\alpha \times (13)^\beta + (9m - 1) \times (48)^\alpha \times (14)^\beta \\
&+ m \times (54)^\alpha \times (15)^\beta + m \times (60)^\alpha \times (16)^\beta \\
&+ (7m + 1) \times (49)^\alpha \times (14)^\beta + 4m \times (56)^\alpha \times (15)^\beta \\
&+ 4m \times (70)^\alpha \times (17)^\beta + (3m - 1) \times (64)^\alpha \times (16)^\beta \\
&+ 3m \times (80)^\alpha \times (18)^\beta + 3m \times (90)^\alpha \times (19)^\beta \\
&+ 2m \times (110)^\alpha \times (21)^\beta.
\end{aligned}
$$

Corollary 1. *From Proposition 1, we compute various neighbourhood degree based topological indices which are mentioned earlier in this paper, for some particular values of α and β respectively as follows:*

(i) $M_1G_5(G) = M_{0,1}G_5(G) = 1214m - 19$,

(ii) $M_2G_5(G) = M_{1,0}G_5(G) = 3954m - 84$,

(iii) $HM_1G_5(G) = M_{0,2}G_5(G) = 16404m - 325$,

(iv) $HM_2G_5(G) = M_{2,0}G_5(G) = 208082m - 5322$,

(v) $M_1^\alpha G_5(G) = M_{0,\alpha}G_5(G) = m \times 6^\alpha + 6m \times 7^\alpha + 6m \times 8^\alpha + 10m \times 9^\alpha$
$\qquad + (7m + 1) \times (10)^\alpha + 4m \times (11)^\alpha + 10m \times (12)^\alpha$
$\qquad + (14m - 1) \times (13)^\alpha + 18m \times (14)^\alpha + 5m \times (15)^\alpha$
$\qquad + (4m - 1) \times (16)^\alpha + 4m \times (17)^\alpha + 3m \times (18)^\alpha$
$\qquad + 3m \times (19)^\alpha + 2m \times (21)^\alpha$,

(vi) $M_2^\alpha G_5(G) = M_{\alpha,0} G_5(G) = m \times 8^\alpha + 6m \times (12)^\alpha + 4m \times (18)^\alpha$
$$+(5m+1) \times (21)^\alpha + 3m \times (24)^\alpha + 6m \times (16)^\alpha$$
$$+6m \times (20)^\alpha + 2m \times (28)^\alpha + 2m \times (36)^\alpha$$
$$+3m \times (40)^\alpha + m \times (30)^\alpha + 6m \times (35)^\alpha$$
$$+4m \times (36)^\alpha + (11m-1) \times (42)^\alpha + (9m-1) \times (48)^\alpha$$
$$+m \times (54)^\alpha + m \times (60)^\alpha + (7m+1) \times (49)^\alpha$$
$$+4m \times (56)^\alpha + 4m \times (70)^\alpha + (3m-1) \times (64)^\alpha$$
$$+3m \times (80)^\alpha + 3m \times (90)^\alpha + 2m \times (110)^\alpha,$$

(vii) $ND_1(G) = M_{\frac{1}{2},0} G_5(G) = 596.96742m - 9.82637,$

$(viii)$ $ND_2(G) = M_{0,-\frac{1}{2}} G_5(G) = 27.78946m - 0.29794,$

(ix) $ND_3(G) = M_{1,1} G_5(G) = 56500m - 1346,$

(x) $ND_4(G) = M_{-\frac{1}{2},0} G_5(G) = 18.11397m - 0.06257.$

(Taking up to 5 decimal places)

The comparative analysis of topological indices of hyaluronic acid-paclitaxel conjugates molecular structure for different values of m is shown in Fig. 2, Fig. 3, Fig. 4, Fig. 5, and Fig. 6 respectively using line graphs.

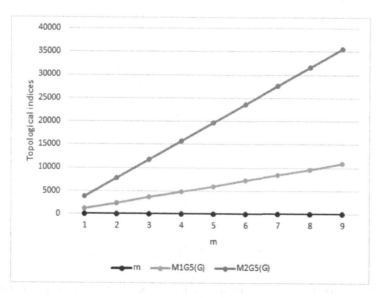

Fig. 2. The comparative analysis between $M_1 G_5(G)$ and $M_2 G_5(G)$ of $HA[m]$ for different values of m.

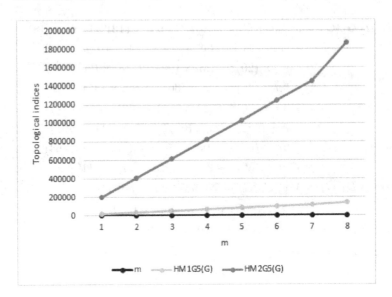

Fig. 3. The comparative analysis between $HM_1G_5(G)$ and $HM_2G_5(G)$ of $HA[m]$ for different values of m.

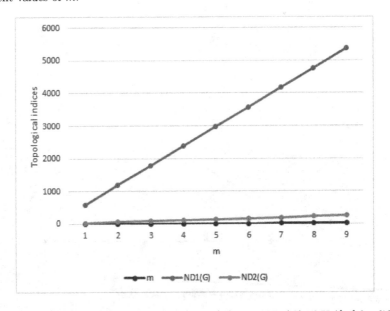

Fig. 4. The comparative analysis between $ND_1(G)$ and $ND_2(G)$ of $HA[m]$ for different values of m.

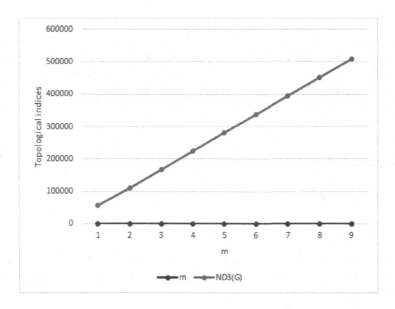

Fig. 5. The line graph of ND_3 of $HA[m]$ for different values of m.

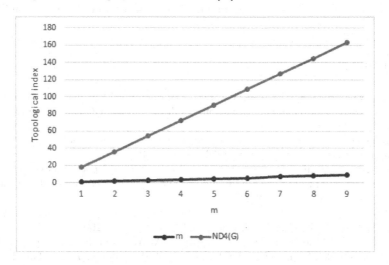

Fig. 6. The line graph of ND_4 of $HA[m]$ for different values of m.

3 Conclusions

In this paper, we studied general fifth M-Zagreb polynomial and computed it for hyaluronic acid-paclitaxel conjugates molecular structures which is used in manufacturing of anti cancer drugs. We also computed various neighbourhood degree based topological indices of hyaluronic acid-paclitaxel conjugates molecular structures such as fifth M-Zagreb indices, general fifth M-Zagreb indices, fifth hyper M-Zagreb indices, first NDe index (ND_1), second NDe index (ND_2), third NDe index (ND_3), and forth NDe index (ND_4) by using our derived result. Also, we have done a comparative analysis of topological indices of hyaluronic acid-paclitaxel conjugates molecular structure for different values of m using line graphs as shown in Fig. 2, Fig. 3, Fig. 4, Fig. 5, and Fig. 6. In the future study, we want to compute this new version of general fifth M-Zagreb index for some chemically important molecular structures.

Declaration

Competing interests

The authors declare that they have no competing interests.

Acknowledgements. We thank the anonymous reviewers for their careful reading of our manuscript and their many insightful comments and suggestions to improve the manuscript.

Author contributions. DC-Reviewing and Editing; PS-Conceptualization, Writing-Original draft preparation; AP-Supervision, Validation, Writing- Reviewing and Editing.

References

1. Baig, A.Q., Naeem, M., Gao, W., Liu, J.B.: General fifth m-zagreb indices and fifth m-zagreb polynomials of carbon graphite. Eurasian Chem. Commun. **2**(5), 634–640 (2020)
2. Bindusree, A., Cangul, I.N., Lokesha, V., Cevik, A.S.: Zagreb polynomials of three graph operators. Filomat **30**(7), 1979–1986 (2016)
3. Campisi, M., Renier, D.: Oncofid^{TM}-p a hyaluronic acid paclitaxel conjugate for the treatment of refractory bladder cancer and peritoneal carcinosis. Curr. Bioact. Compound. **7**(1), 27–32 (2011)
4. Estrada, E., Uriarte, E.: Recent advances on the role of topological indices in drug discovery research. Curr. Med. Chem. **8**(13), 1573–1588 (2001)
5. Graovac, A., Ghorbani, M., Hosseinzadeh, M.A.: Computing fifth geometric-arithmetic index for nanostar dendrimers. J. Math. Nanosci. **1**(1–2), 33–42 (2011)
6. Gutman, I., Tošović, J.: Testing the quality of molecular structure descriptors. vertex-degree-based topological indices. J. Serbian Chem. Soc. **78**(6), 805–810 (2013)
7. Kang, S.M., Yousaf, M., Zahid, M.A., Younas, M., Nazeer, W.: Zagreb polynomials and redefined zagreb indices of nanostar dendrimers. Open Phys. **17**(1), 31–40 (2019)
8. Kulli, V.: General fifth m-zagreb indices and fifth m-zagreb polynomials of pamam dendrimers. Int. J. Fuzzy Math. Arch. **13**(1), 99–103 (2017)
9. Kulli, V.: The product connectivity gourava index. J. Comput. Math. Sci. **8**(6), 235–242 (2017)

10. Lee, H., Lee, K., Park, T.G.: Hyaluronic acid- paclitaxel conjugate micelles: synthesis, characterization, and antitumor activity. Bioconjugate Chem. **19**(6), 1319–1325 (2008)

11. Ma, Y., Cao, S., Shi, Y., Gutman, I., Dehmer, M., Furtula, B.: From the connectivity index to various randic-type descriptors. MATCH Commun. Math. Comput. Chem. **80**(1), 85–106 (2018)

12. Mekenyan, O., Bonchev, D., Sabljic, A., Trinajstić, N.: Applications of topological indices to qsar. the use of the balaban index and the electropy index for correlations with toxicity of ethers on mice. Acta Pharmaceutica Jugoslavica **37**, 75–86 (1987)

13. Mittapalli, R.K., et al.: Paclitaxel-hyaluronic nanoconjugates prolong overall survival in a preclinical brain metastases of breast cancer model. Mol. Cancer Ther. **12**(11), 2389–2399 (2013)

14. Mondal, S., De, N., Pal, A.: Onsome new neighbourhood degree based indices. Acta Chemica Iasi **27**(1), 31–46 (2019)

15. Mondal, S., Dey, A., De, N., Pal, A.: QSPR analysis of some novel neighbourhood degree-based topological descriptors. Complex Intell. Syst. **7**(2), 977–996 (2021). https://doi.org/10.1007/s40747-020-00262-0

16. Mondal, S., De, N., Pal, A.: On neighborhood zagreb index of product graphs. J. Mol. Struct. **1223**, 129210 (2020)

17. Natarajan, R., Kamalakanan, P., Nirdosh, I.: Applications of topological indices to structure-activity relationship modelling and selection of mineral collectors. Indian J. Chem. Section A: Inorg. Phys. Theor. Anal. **42**(6), 1330–1346 (2003)

18. Pyka, A.: Application of topological indices for prediction of the biological activity of selected alkoxyphenols. Acta Poloniae Pharmaceutica **59**(5), 347–352 (2002)

19. Ramane, H.S., Yalnaik, A.S.: Status connectivity indices of graphs and its applications to the boiling point of benzenoid hydrocarbons. J. Appl. Math. Comput. **55**(1–2), 609–627 (2017)

20. Randić, M.: Characterization of molecular branching. J. Am. Chem. Soc. **97**(23), 6609–6615 (1975)

21. Randić, M.: On history of the randić index and emerging hostility toward chemical graph theory. Match Commun. Math. Comput. Chem. **59**, 5–124 (2008)

22. Sarkar, P., Pal, A.: General fifth m-zagreb polynomials of benzene ring implanted in the p-type-surface in 2d network. Biointerface Res. Appl. Chem. **10**(6), 6881–6892 (2020)

23. Siddiqui, M.K., Imran, M., Ahmad, A.: On zagreb indices, zagreb polynomials of some nanostar dendrimers. Appl. Math. Comput. **280**, 132–139 (2016)

An Approach Toward Congestion Management for Improved Emergency Vehicle Management in Intelligent Urban Traffic Network

Abantika Choudhury[1], Suparna Das Gupta[2(✉)], and Rituparna Chaki[3]

[1] RCC Institute of Information Technology, Kolkata, India
abantikachoudhury@gmail.com
[2] JIS College of Engineering, Kalyani, India
suparnadasguptait@gmail.com
[3] University of Calcutta, Kolkata, India
rituchaki@gmail.com

Abstract. Intelligent traffic management in the urban area faces several challenges such as prioritizing emergency vehicles, handling time-of-the-day/season-dependent traffic load changes, etc. The researchers aim to maintain a low waiting time for vehicles in general to improve overall travelers' experience. There is much research work done on improving the situation for a non-emergency vehicle but very little for emergency vehicle management. In this paper, we have proposed optimized scheduling of traffic lights for improved emergency vehicle management considering the general vehicles as well. We have categorized the emergency vehicles depending on their emergency level to provide a better quality of service for congestion management in the overall scenario. We have used the SUMO (Simulation of Urban Mobility) simulator for simulating the urban traffic scenario to evaluate our proposed logic. Our proposed logic showed better performance than that of existing research works.

Keyword: VANET · TMC · ML · RL · RSU · Phase · Vehicle · Traffic Light · Emergency Vehicle

1 Introduction

Nowadays, most growing cities in the world are facing a drastic increment in road traffic congestion due to fast-growing urbanization throughout the world. That is why; traffic congestion becomes one of the leading challenges for traffic management worldwide. Frequent congestion occurs when a large number of vehicles simultaneously use a limited road during peak hours of the day. This kind of problem can be solved with the help of some planned actions. Non-frequent congestions like accidental conditions or bad weather etc. are hard to deal with, where designing appropriate planning and its response is challenging. Traffic congestions generally result in huge economic losses, including delivery disruption, productivity troubles, and increased fuel consumption. In VANET many different methodologies are followed to reduce the congestion of vehicles. To

© The Author(s), under exclusive license to Springer Nature Switzerland AG 2023
K. Saeed et al. (Eds.): CISIM 2023, LNCS 14164, pp. 354–369, 2023.
https://doi.org/10.1007/978-3-031-42823-4_26

achieve the desired objective, Machine Learning (ML) is an effective approach for the accurate prediction of dynamic data and finding out the hidden part through repeated learning from those data. The contribution of this work is:

a. Efficiently control the traffic length to reduce traffic congestion in the urban area networks.
b. Assigning priority to the emergency vehicles to provide quality service.

The rest of the paper is organized as follows. Section 2 narrates the recent related works in this specific field. Section 3 describes the system design. Section 4 describes the proposed methodologies. Section 5 narrates the performance analysis and Sect. 6 is the concluding article.

2 Related Work

Many research works are going on to reduce traffic congestion in urban areas. Few of the research are discussed in this literature review. In [1, 2], the methods provide a solution to reduce congestion by providing intelligent optimized traffic light control. The authors have considered 4-pt intersections only along with fixed lanes other types of intersections are not been considered here. In the research work [3], the authors designed a dynamic traffic light scheduling algorithm that adjusts the green phase time of each traffic flow, based on real-time traffic distribution. The shortcoming of the work is that it increases overall congestion for other vehicles. Authors [4] proposed secure intelligent traffic light control schemes using fog computing. But no emergency vehicles are considered here. The paper [5] reviews control techniques for emergency vehicles. The scheme [6], dynamically determines the priority of the road segment as critical, high, medium, and low using fuzzy logic. Here the authors have not considered the normal vehicle delay. In article [7], two traffic light strategies to control traffic and avoid traffic jams in urban networks are proposed for a traffic light scheduling system that controls traffic lights using local variables. The scheme is designed to serve normal vehicles only excluding emergency vehicles. The research work surveys [8, 9] the existing research works in the field of congestion control and it provides a conclusion with possible future extensions in this field. A pipeline model based on vehicle-to-infrastructure communication [10] is proposed in this work. The technique enables the acquisition of the correct traffic information in a real-time system through message exchange between vehicles and roadside units. Data overhead is high in this scheme. An application of NDN in VANET [11] for smart traffic light systems reduces traffic congestion issues to reduce the waiting time of vehicles in road intersections. The scheme introduces virtual traffic lights here. Here, emergency vehicles are not treated for consideration. The article [12] focuses on traffic light-aware routing protocol with Soft Reservation Multiple Access with Priority Assignment routing protocols at intersections and traffic light signals during the time of congestion. The authors have not considered the emergency vehicle here. A messaging scheme [13, 14] uses vehicles' density and speed and helps RSUs (Road Side Units) and emergency vehicles. The work produces data overhead. A traffic management application [15] is introduced using logical centralization of the SDN control plane to improve traffic management. Only normal vehicles are treated here for consideration.

Overall in the study, we observed that the old methodologies are performing some sort of deficiencies like cost, time, overhead, etc. Unlike the existing research works, the proposed methodology considers the above-mentioned limitations to take care of. We focus on congestion reduction for the emergency vehicle and congestion reduction for normal vehicles in urban area road networks.

3   Categorization of the Intersection

The system is proposed for vehicular congestion reduction considering the urban area road network. Here, it is assumed that all the intersections in a road network are connected. Connected intersection means the intersection is connected via network connectivity of VANET with all its adjacent intersections i.e. two intersections are connected if messages obtained from one intersection can be delivered to the other intersection via VANET infrastructure (maybe fixed infrastructure or vehicles) without loss of data, and vice versa. Figure 1 shows such kind of intersection.

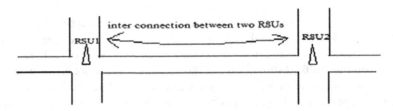

Fig. 1. Connected intersection

In this research work, a variety of intersections in an urban area is considered. The intersection is categorized depending on its various properties.

Case 1: Type of Intersection

i. Type 1 intersection: 4-point intersection is such kind of intersection where 4 roads are connected. These intersections are a very common type of intersection. Most of the intersections in an urban area are 4-point intersections.
ii. Type 2 intersection (3-point, 5-point, 7-point intersections): The intersection where three roads are connected is known as the 3-point intersection. Whereas the intersection that joins 5 roads is known as a 5-point intersection and the intersection that joins 7 roads is known as a 7-point intersection. These intersections are few.

Case 2: Width of the Road

i. Homogeneous intersection- Connected roads of such intersection have the same width.
ii. Heterogeneous intersection- Connected roads of such intersections have different widths.

We define phases for efficient traffic management. A phase is a collection of routes of various directions in an intersection that never collide with each other while occurring simultaneously. Figure 2, and Fig. 3 show the phases of 4-point, and 3-point intersections respectively. Here, it is assumed that all the right turn routes are always open and vehicles can turn toward the right side. That is why the right turn is not taken into consideration for this work. The arrows given in the diagrams denote the routes with definite directions. If the number of roads connected to an intersection is rd_i and the number of phases is (rt_p) then,

$$rt_p = rd_i \tag{1}$$

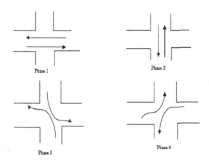

Fig. 2. Phases in a 4-point intersection

Fig. 3. Phases in a 3-point intersection

4 Proposed Methodology

Two methodologies are proposed in this article. One method deals with emergency vehicle management to improve the quality of service. Another method is proposed to improve the movement of normal vehicles in absence of an emergency v vehicle. Both

Table 1. Description of notations

Notation	Description
l	A load of an intersection
wt_max	Maximum waiting time
wt_pev	Waiting time of phase having the emergency vehicle
iv_d	Inter vehicular distance (distance between two consecutive rows of vehicles)

(*continued*)

Table 1. (*continued*)

Notation	Description
t_a	Acceleration time required for a vehicle
t_s	Start time required for a vehicle
q_len	Queue length (Number of rows of vehicles)
e_d	The message was given by emergency vehicle along with the destination
I_{high}	Highly loaded intersection i.e. huge number of vehicles passing through it
I_{low}	Low-loaded intersection i.e. less number of vehicles passing through it
ev_typ	Type of emergency vehicle
q_len_ba	Queue length before action
q_len_aa	Queue length after action
T_g	Green signal time duration
T_{wt}	Waiting time duration of a phase
P_T_{wt}	Waiting time of phase P

methods are described in Sects. 4.1 and 4.2 respectively. The notation used in the method is described in Table 1.

4.1 Traffic Light Scheduling for Emergency Vehicles

The method deals with emergency vehicle management for improving the quality of service in an urban area road network. There is different kind of emergency vehicles passes through the roads in cities. Firstly, emergency vehicles have been categorized into three levels depending upon their level of emergency. The categories are given below.

(i) Level_1 emergency vehicle (ev1)
(ii) Level_2 emergency vehicle (ev2)
(iii) Level_3 emergency vehicle (ev3)

Description of Different Categories of Emergency Vehicle

(i) Level_1 Emergency vehicle (ev1): The vehicle possessing this level of emergency achieves maximum priority to acquire the facility of green traffic signal e.g. ambulance, fire brigade, rescue vehicles, and military vehicles.

We have assigned zero (0) to be the waiting time (wt_ev1) for such kinds of vehicles. Queue length (q_len_ev1) of ev1 is the number of rows of vehicles waiting before ev1. The allotted green signal time duration is calculated by the equation given below.

$$\text{Green signal time}(Tg) = t_a + t_s + (iv\_d \times (q\_len\_ev1 + 1)/\text{speed}). \qquad (2)$$

(ii) Level_2 Emergency vehicle (ev2): The vehicles possessing this level of emergency, achieves the second highest priority to acquire the facility of the green traffic signal. Eg. Administrative vehicle, Police vehicle, water Supply, milk van.

The queue length of ev2 (q_len_ev2) is the number of rows of the vehicle waiting before ev2.

The duration of waiting time and allotted green signal time are calculated by the given equations below.

$$\text{Wait time for emergency vehicle (wt\_ev2)} = \left[wt\_p_{ev2}/2 \right] \qquad (3)$$

where wt_p_{ev2} is the waiting time faced by the phase possessing ev2.

$$\text{Green signal time}(T_g) = t_a + t_s + (iv\_d \times (q\_len\_ev2 + 1))/\text{speed}. \qquad (4)$$

(iii) Level_3 Emergency (ev3): The vehicle possessing this level of emergency achieves the third level of priority to acquire the facility of green traffic signal e.g. School bus and office bus etc.

Let wt_p_{ev3} be the waiting time of the phase facing ev3 and the queue length (q_len_ev3) of ev3 is the number of rows of the vehicle waiting before ev3.

$$\text{Waiting time for emergency vehicle (wt\_ev3)} = \left[wt\_p_{ev3}/3 \right] \qquad (5)$$

$$\text{Green signal time } (T_g) = \left[t_a + t_s + (iv\_d \times (q\_len\_ev3 + 1)/\text{speed} \right] \qquad (6)$$

For all other types of vehicles, we calculate the waiting time as:

$$Wt_k = Wt(i) + \sum\nolimits_{j=1; j \neq k}^{n-1} \left(wt_j \right) \qquad (7)$$

where 'k' is the sequence number of waiting phases and 'm' is the number of emergency vehicles and 'n' total number of phases. The proposed algorithm for traffic signal allotment for an emergency vehicle is given in Algorithm 1 below-

Algorithm 1. Allotting traffic light signals in case of the existence of emergency vehicles in all kinds of intersection

1. Input e_d, ev_typ, phase,
2. Output T_g, wt_p_k, phase
3. Vehicle sends the emergency message (e_d) to the RSU and also the direction.
4. If (ev1)
    4.1. Allot green signal time duration $(T_g) = t_a + t_s + (iv\_d \times q\_len\_ev1+1)/$ speed for ev1.
    4.2. Allot red signal time duration for running phase

$$Wt_k = Wt(i) + \sum\nolimits_{j=1;j\neq k}^{n-1} (wt_j)$$

5. Else if (ev2)
    5.1. Allot waiting time [wt_p_{ev2} /2] for the phase facing ev2.
    5.2. Allot green signal time duration
    $(T_g) = [wt\_p_{ev2} / 2] + [t_a + t_s + (iv\_d \times q\_len\_ev2+1)/$ speed]
    5.3. Allot red signal time duration for running phase

$$Wt_k = Wt(i) + \sum\nolimits_{j=1;j\neq k}^{n-1} (wt_j)$$

6. Else if (ev3)
    6.1. Allot waiting time [wt_p_{ev3} /2] for the phase facing ev3.
    6.2. Allot green signal time duration
    $(T_g) = [wt\_p_{ev3} / 2] + [t_a + t_s + (iv\_d \times q\_len\_ev3)/speed]$
    6.3. Allot red signal time duration for running phase

$$Wt_k = Wt(i) + \sum_{j=1;j\neq k}^{n-1} (wt_j)$$

7. Connected intersections send the message to the next intersection where the vehicle is going.

4.2 Traffic Light Scheduling for Normal Vehicles Without the Existence of Emergency Vehicles

Different terms used in the proposed scheme along with their description are listed in Table 1 below-

The second proposed method considers two parameters for traffic congestion management. One is vehicular density and the other one is intersection load.

Vehicular Density
The vehicular density of an intersection is defined as the number of vehicles with the same moving pattern that passes through the intersection regularly. Vehicular density is measured as inflow density (dI) and outflow density (dO). dI is measured by the number of inflow vehicles (towards the intersection) from other adjacent intersections and dO is measured by the number of outflow vehicles towards other adjacent intersections from that particular intersection. For a particular intersection (I), peak hours (t_p) are considered for a few consecutive days. t_p is divided into different time slots like t_1, t_2, t_3... etc. dI and dO are collected in different time slots like t_1, t_2, t_3, and so on. dI and dO can vary

with respect to time. So, the average connectivity (d) of intersection (I) is

$$d = (dI + dO)/2 \qquad (9)$$

Intersection Load

A load of an intersection means its level of average vehicular density with the same movement pattern. An intersection having high vehicular density gets a higher load and low vehicular density gets a lower load. The load factor is calculated as follows:

$$l = d/d_{max}; \qquad (10)$$

(Where l = load of Intersection I, d = average vehicular density of I, and d_{max} corresponds to the maximum of 'd' among different time intervals) (Table 2).

Table 2. The function of RSU and TMC

Function of RSU	Function of TMC (Traffic Managing Centre)
a. Receives beacon signal from vehicles	a. Receives message from RSU
b. Increments the count of vehicles of each route on receiving the beacon	b. Decides to provide green signal and red signal to corresponding phases
c. In presence of emergency vehicles, RSU receives emergency messages from emergency vehicles	c. Calculate the timing for the green signal and red signal
d. In presence of an emergency vehicle, RSU calculates the distance of the emergency vehicle from the traffic signal	
e. Calculates the distance of the vehicle in the last row of the ready area (RA) from the traffic signal	

For allotting the TLS when no emergency vehicle is present, we have determined the ready area (RA) in terms of the queue length of the phase.

For homogeneous intersections,

Queue length (q_len) = number of rows of vehicles waiting in a phase (rp).   (11)

where a number of rows are defined as (number of vehicles/2);

[Since it is assumed that 2 vehicles in a single row of a lane in a homogeneous inter section];

For heterogeneous intersections,

$$q\_len = \text{(number of vehicles waiting in a phase)}/\text{(average width of the lane)} \quad (12)$$

Algorithm 2. Calculating queue length

1. Input number of vehicles, lane_no, lane_width, phase
2. Output q_len for the phases
3. if (homogeneous intersection)
    3.1. q_len= number of rows of vehicles
4. else
    4.1. q_len= (number of vehicles) / (average lane_width of the phase)
5. Calculate q_len for all the lanes.
6. Add q_len for all the lanes of every phase of the intersection.

Prioritizing of Intersections Depending on Their Load: The load of all the intersections in a given urban area road network is calculated and sorted accordingly. Intersections are prioritized after sorting. The intersection that has a higher load than a pre-defined threshold value (l_{th}) is considered a highly prioritized intersection. Otherwise, it is considered a low-prioritized intersection.

Algorithm 3. prioritization of intersection based on its load

1. Input intersection I[], load l[]
2. initialize i, j, p, q, n
3. for i= 1 to n
    3.1. sort (l[])
    3.2. l_{th}= avg (l)
    3.2 if l[i] >= l_{th} then l[i] is high prioritized
        else l[i] is low prioritized
    3.3. map l in I
4. Output sorted I, high load I_{high}, low load I_{low}

Traffic Light Scheduling Method: The traffic light scheduling method is described in Algorithm 4. In this method, the time duration of green traffic light is being calculated for a selected phase. The dynamic queue-length is considered for the calculation of green traffic light signal time duration.

Algorithm 4: Traffic light scheduling algorithm

Input: phases.
Output: T_g, P_T_g, q_len, T_{wt}
if (phase)
    If beacon signal ($D_{L\text{-}I}$, direction to move)
        q_len <- q_len + 1
        Return Q_len
    End
    Sort q_len from highest to lowest
End
while q_len is highest
    Calculate $T_g = t_s + t_a + D_{L\text{-}I} /S$
    Calculate V_{new} in time T_g
    New_q_len <- q_len + V_{new}
    Calculate new_$T_g = T_g + $ del_T_g
    Calculate V_{new} of next highest q_len in time new_T_g
    if ((highest q_len)/ (next highest q_len)<=0.5)
    calculate gren signal time TG = 0.9*(new_Tg)
    Allot T_g for selected phase to pass 90% of queued vehicles
    else
    while Q_len is next highest
    New_Q_len <- Q_len + V_{new}
    Calculate new_$T_g = T_g + $ del_T_g
    calculate gren signal time TG = 0.9*(new_Tg)
    Allot TG for selected phase to pass 90% of queued vehicles
    End
End
Calculate $T_{wth} = T_{max}$ x (q-len$_{max}$/ q-len)
if ($T_{wt\_p} = T_{wth}$) then
    if p_T_{wt} < 2 then
        allot T_g for P_T_{wt} and $T_r = T_{wth}$ for P_T_g
    else if p_T_{wt}_Q_len1 > p_T_{wt}_Q_len2
        allot T_g for P_T_{wt}_Q_len1 and T_r for P_T_g
        else allot T_g for P_T_{wt}_Q_len2 and T_r for P_T_g
    End
End

---

5 Performance Analysis

To evaluate the algorithm, the simulation has been set up on randomly generated data. It is assumed that the average speed of the vehicles is 60 km/h, acceleration speed is 6 km/h^2, and starts time is 2 s, inter-vehicular distance is 2 m. The simulation is evaluated on a road network of six intersections. The intersections consist of 5-point intersection,

7-point intersection, 4- point intersection, 3- point intersection, and 2-point intersection as well. A road is divided in two lanes (one is incoming and another one is outgoing). A random number of vehicles are generated per hour for a particular lane. Each of the traffic has a random departure and a destination lane. The performance criteria for the simulation are given in Table 3. Each intersection can tune its traffic lights by the intersection TMC. It is assumed that all the right turn routes are always open and not considered for the method. Vehicles can turn toward the right side of any road. The parameters taken for comparison are the average waiting time of the vehicles vs the average number of vehicles at the end of the simulation. The comparison graphs are given below. It is shown that our method shows better results than that of [2] and [7].

5.1 Case Study of the Proposed Method

The case study is taken on a smaller scale to simulate the method shown in Table 3 and Table 4. It is assumed that the initial waiting time of phase having an emergency vehicle (wt_p_{ev}) is 120 s, t_a is 0.6, and t_s 0.2. Performance criteria are shown in Table 5 below.

Table 3. A simulation case study in presence of an emergency vehicle

Intersection	1
Phase	2
Total number of vehicles in phase 1	20
Total number of vehicles in phase 2	30
ev1	1
ev2	1
Queue length of phase 1	5
Queue length of phase 2	7
Waiting time for phase 1	40 s
Waiting time for phase 2	54.93 s
Average waiting time	47.5 s

For performance analysis, the parameters queue length and waiting time of vehicles are taken for comparison with the number of traffic in road networks. The queue length measures the number of vehicles left after the completion of the green traffic light signal. The waiting time depicts the amount of time the vehicles wait for their clearance in intersections. The comparative study shows that the proposed methodologies provide a better result than that of the other research works.

Figure 4, depicts the comparison between the total number of vehicles in the intersections and the average waiting time of the vehicle due to traffic signals. Average waiting time shows the delay time of vehicles in intersection. The blue bar is showing the result of the proposed method. We have gradually increased the number of vehicle in road network. It is shown in the graph that when the number of vehicles are less i.e. 300, the

Table 4. A simulation case study in absence of an emergency vehicle

Intersection	1
Phase	2
Total number of vehicles in phase 1	20
Total number of vehicles in phase 2	30
Queue length of phase 1	5
Queue length of phase 2	7
Waiting time for phase 1	37 s
Waiting time for phase 2	52 s
Average waiting time	44.5 s

Table 5. Performance Criteria

Simulation Parameter	Value
Simulation Tool	SUMO 25.0.0, TraCI extension
Simulation Area	1500 m × 1500 m
Simulation time	2000 ms
Number of Vehicles	300, 600, 900, 1200
Speed of Vehicle	60 km/h
Vehicle type	Passenger vehicle, Emergency vehicle
Number of lanes	2
Data Source	Random Generated Data
Comparison parameter	Average waiting time, Average Queue Length Vs Number of Vehicles, Average waiting time of Emergency Vehicles

difference between the results is not much. The increased number of vehicle (i.e. 600, 900, 1200, 1800) shows larger difference between the results of proposed method and comparing methodologies. The result of proposed method is shown better than other methods because of its traffic signaling scheme is developed by learning the environment and setting dynamic thresholding value of waiting time of vehicles in intersection. Whereas the other methods only deal with a fixed waiting time of the vehicles. As a result, the proposed method provides more reduced waiting time for the vehicles gives better quality of service. The reduced waiting time always improves the quality of service and also reduces the congestion in road network as well.

Figure 5 depicts the comparison between the total number of vehicles and the average waiting time of emergency vehicle in an intersection. Here also the blue bar is showing the result of proposed method. This is clearly visible that the proposed method provides better result than that of other methodologies. Less average waiting time means less delay.

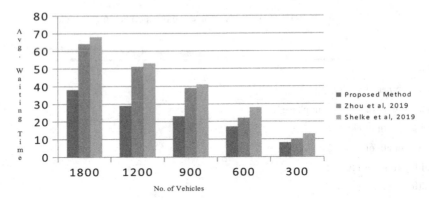

Fig. 4. Average waiting time vs. Number of vehicles (no Emergency vehicle)

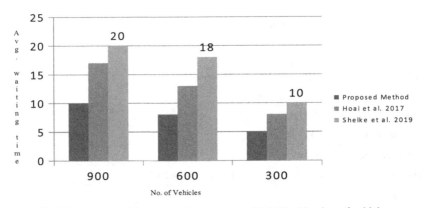

Fig. 5. Average waiting time of emergency vehicle Vs. Number of vehicles

It is always desired that the emergency vehicle always pass through without delay to reach their destination. The proposed method categorizes the emergency vehicles depending on its level of emergency and set prioritizing rules to pass through the intersection. On the other hand the method also takes care of other general vehicles. Whereas the other comparing methods do not consider the different kind the emergency vehicles. They only consider one type of emergency vehicle so other categories are not getting prioritized. The proposed method reducing the delay of all kind of emergency vehicles more than the other methods.

Figure 6 shows, the comparison results of the total number of vehicles passing through all the intersections of the road network, in a selected time period (peak hours) and the average queue length (i.e. the leftover vehicles of the intersections after traffic signal clearance) of the vehicles. Queue length has been calculated in Eq. (12). The graph shows that the proposed methods gives better result than that of other two mentioned here. The improvement is done by using dynamic traffic light signaling scheme by considering dynamic waiting time of vehicles. A reduced queue length means less number of vehicles

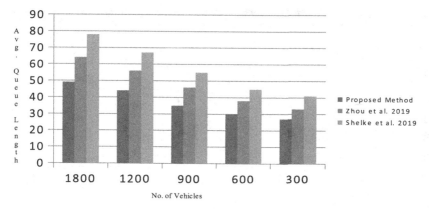

Fig. 6. Average queuing length vs Number of vehicles (no emergency vehicles)

in waiting phase. Reduced queue length always enrich the quality of service in road networks and reduce the congestion.

Figure 7, shows an intersection having number of vehicles. The simulation environment is created in SUMO. The Red-colored vehicle is an emergency vehicle, yellow vehicles are cars and long yellow vehicles are buses.

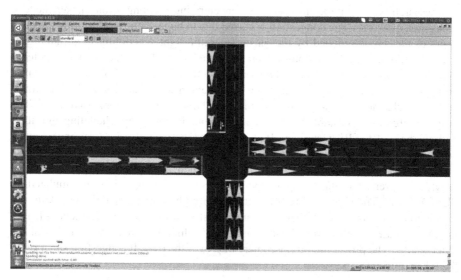

Fig. 7. Simulation environment

In Fig. 8, a road network of the city of Kolkata has been fetched from OSM. Real-time traffic data are tracked from the road network for the simulation.

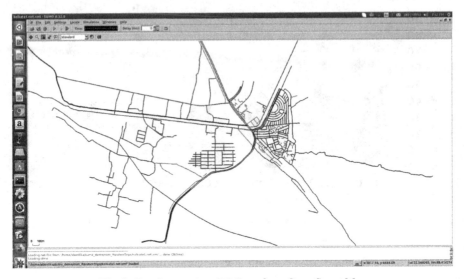

Fig. 8. Road networks of Kolkata from Open Street Map

6 Conclusion

The research work done in this paper is concentrating on congestion management in urban area networks. The congestion occurred due to huge traffic loads during the peak hours of the day is reduced by the means of traffic light scheduling in an intelligent transport system. The methodology proposed here has used the machine learning technique to get more accurate results of our desired output. The proposed scheme also takes an important role to provide preferences to the emergency vehicles so that the emergency vehicles need not wait much during peak hours or highly congested hours. The proposed algorithm is established by the implementation of a new scheduling algorithm with the help of the RL technique. It also provides the idea of prioritization the emergency vehicles depending upon their level of emergency. The proposed scheme targets to reduce the queuing length of road traffic, and their average waiting time, and also provide preferences to the emergency vehicles as well. The algorithm is simulated on SUMO 0.25.0. The simulated result is compared with other methodologies. After the simulation, the output shows that the average waiting time and average queuing length in both the cases (normal vehicle and emergency vehicle) are reduced than that of the older results. The procedure proposed here improves the overall congestion situation in the urban area network.

References

1. Zhou, P., Braud, T., Alhilal, A., Hui, P., Kanjash, J.: ERL: edge-based reinforcement learning for optimized urban traffic light control, pp. 849–854. IEEE (2019). https://doi.org/10.1109/PERCOMW.2019.8730706
2. Bui, K.H.N., Jung, J.E., Camacho, D.: Game theoretic approach on Real-time decision making for IoT-based traffic light control (2017). https://doi.org/10.1002/cpe.4077

3. Younes, M.B., Boukerche, A.: An efficient dynamic traffic light scheduling algorithm considering emergency vehicles for intelligent transportation systems. J. Wirel. Netw. **24**, 2451–2463 (2018). https://doi.org/10.1007/s11276-017-1482-5

4. Liu, J., Li, J., Zhang, L., Dai, F., Zhang, Y., Meng, X., Shen, J.: Secure intelligent traffic light control using fog computing. J. Future Gener. Comput. Syst. **78**, 817–824 (2017). https://doi.org/10.1016/j.future.2017.02.017

5. Hussin, W.M., Rosli, M.M., Nordin, R.: Review of traffic control techniques for emergency vehicles. Indones. J. Electr. Eng. CS **13**, 1243–1251 (2019)

6. Shelke, M., Malhotra, A., Mahalle, P.N.: Fuzzy priority-based intelligent traffic congestion control and emergency vehicle management using congestion aware routing algorithm. J. Ambient Intell. Humaniz. Comput. (2019). https://doi.org/10.1007/s12652-019-01523-8

7. Sarvestani, M.A.S., Azimifar, Z., Wong, A., Safavi, A.A.: An innovative eigenvector-based method for traffic light scheduling. J. Adv. Transp. **6** (2020)

8. Giripunje, L.M., Masand, D., Shandilya, S.K.: Congestion control in vehicular ad-hoc networks (VANET's): a review. In: Abraham, A., Shandilya, S., Garcia-Hernandez, L., Varela, M. (eds.) HIS 2019. AISC, vol. 1179, pp. 258–267. Springer, Cham. https://doi.org/10.1007/978-3-030-49336-3_26

9. Ghazi, M.U., Khan, A.M., Shabir, K.B., Malik, A.W., Ramzan, M.S.: Emergency message dissemination in vehicular networks: a review. J. Mag. IEEE Access **8**, 38606–38621 (2020). https://doi.org/10.1109/ACCESS.2020.2975110

10. Wu, L., Nie, L., Khan, S.U., Khalid, O., Wu, D.: A V2I communication-based pipeline model for adaptive urban traffic light scheduling. Front. Comput. Sci. **13**(5), 929–942 (2018). https://doi.org/10.1007/s11704-017-7043-3

11. Alqutwani, M., Wang, X.: Smart traffic lights over vehicular named data networking. J. Inf. **10** (2019). https://doi.org/10.3390/info10030083

12. Devi, K.S., Selvam, N.S.: Effective traffic management system for vehicular network. Int. J. Innov. Technol. Explor. Eng. **9**, 2278–3075 (2019). https://doi.org/10.35940/ijitee.A4186.119119

13. Banikhalaf, M., Alomari., S.A. Alzboon, M.S.: An advanced emergency warning message scheme based on vehicles speed and traffic densities. Int. J. Adv. Comput. Sci. Appl. **10**, 201–205 (2019). https://doi.org/10.14569/IJACSA.2019.0100526

14. Al-Mayouf, Y.R.B., Mahdi, O.A., Taha, N.A., Abdullah, N.F., Khan, K.S., Alam, M.: Accident management system based on vehicular network for an intelligent transportation system in urban environment. J. Adv. Transp. (2018). https://doi.org/10.1155/2018/6168981

15. Bideh, P.N., Paladid, N., Hell, M.: Software defined networking for emergency traffic management in smart cities. Veh. Ad-hoc Netw. Smart Cities, 59–70 (2020). https://doi.org/10.1007/978-981-15-3750-9_5

Proposal of an Algorithm for Solving the Component Assignment Problem of an Adjacent Triangle-(m, n):F Triangular Lattice System

Taishin Nakamura[✉] [ID]

School of Information Science and Technology, Tokai University,
4-1-1 Kitakaname, Hiratsuka, Kanagawa 259-1292, Japan
nakamura@tsc.u-tokai.ac.jp

Abstract. In this article, we investigate the component assignment problem, which involves determining the optimal component arrangement for maximizing system reliability, given individual component reliabilities. Establishing the optimal arrangement is crucial for the cost-effective design of dependable systems. We focus on the adjacent triangle-(m, n):F triangular lattice system, characterized by mn components arranged in a triangular grid. The system fails when three neighboring components located at the vertices of a triangle fail simultaneously. Applications of this system extend to surveillance camera systems, sprinkler systems, and sensing systems. To date, no algorithm has been reported for finding the optimal arrangement of the adjacent triangle-(m, n):F triangular lattice system. Therefore, this paper aims to develop an algorithm using the branch-and-bound method to determine the optimal arrangement of the adjacent triangle-(m, n):F triangular lattice system. To efficiently acquire the optimal arrangement, we derived three pruning conditions and devised an optimal arrangement search algorithm incorporating them. Computational experiments revealed that all pruning conditions decreased computation time. Specifically, the pruning condition based on necessary conditions reduced computation time on average by approximately 1/9, as demonstrated experimentally. The solutions provided by the proposed algorithm ensure optimality, enabling the assessment of approximation methods, such as metaheuristics.

Keywords: adjacent triangle-(m, n):F triangular lattice system · component assignment problem · exact method · branch-and-bound

1 Introduction

In contemporary society, large and complex systems are integral to daily life. Nevertheless, the escalating scale and intricacy of these systems can lead to system failures with substantial societal impacts. As a result, the importance of reliability engineering has grown.

Supported by Grant-in-Aid for JSPS KAKENHI Grant Numbers 21K14370.

K. Saeed et al. (Eds.): CISIM 2023, LNCS 14164, pp. 370–381, 2023.
https://doi.org/10.1007/978-3-031-42823-4_27

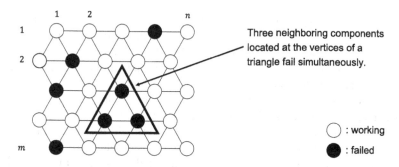

Fig. 1. Tri/(m, n):F system.

This study addresses a primary issue in reliability theory: the component assignment problem (CAP). The CAP entails determining the component arrangement that optimizes system reliability, given component reliabilities. The arrangement that yields maximum system reliability is termed the optimal arrangement. Identifying the optimal arrangement is essential for the cost-effective design of reliable systems.

The consecutive-k-out-of-n:F system (henceforth, Con/k/n:F system) refers to a linearly arranged system of n components, which fails upon the consecutive failure of at least k components. Salvia and Lasher [13] initially extended this system to a two-dimensional context, while Boehme et al. [3] introduced the connected-(r, s)-out-of-(m, n):F lattice system (subsequently, Lin/(r, s)/(m, n):F system). This system comprises mn components organized in an $m \times n$ square grid, failing if all components within any $r \times s$ rectangular region fail. Representative applications include square grid-based surveillance camera systems [3]. However, considering the circular surveillance range of each camera, arranging cameras in a triangular grid rather than a square grid might be preferable for maximizing density and uniformity, such as in circle tiling scenarios.

Yamamoto and Miyagawa [17] devised the adjacent triangle-(m, n):F triangular lattice system (subsequently, Tri/(m, n):F system). This system features mn components in a triangular grid formation, and the system fails when three neighboring components located at the vertices of a triangle fail simultaneously (Fig. 1). Applications span not only surveillance camera systems but also sprinkler and sensing systems [16]. Additionally, the triangular grid can be extended into three dimensions. For instance, Akiba et al. [1] proposed a regular icosahedron-shaped system comprising components in a triangular grid arrangement, approximating a spherical system.

Metaheuristics, despite not guaranteeing optimal solutions, have been applied to the CAP [5,14,15,18]. Prominent examples include simulated annealing, genetic algorithms, and ant colony optimization, which have demonstrated effectiveness in numerous optimization problems. In certain situations, obtaining an exact solution is necessary, even if time-consuming. For instance, when evaluating metaheuristics' performance, calculating the error between approximate and optimal solutions requires an exact solution with guaranteed accuracy.

Exhaustive enumeration is a traditional method for accurately solving the CAP. This approach generates all possible component arrangements, assesses system reliability under each arrangement, and identifies the optimal arrangement. However, when dealing with a large number of components, this method faces the combinatorial explosion problem, potentially failing to find the optimal arrangement within a reasonable timeframe. Thus, the branch-and-bound (B&B) framework is a fundamental and widely utilized methodology for efficiently finding optimal arrangements in small to medium-sized systems. This method systematically enumerates all potential solution candidates and effectively locates solutions by discarding suboptimal candidates, referred to as "branch pruning" in this paper. To enhance the B&B method's speed, maximizing branch prunings is essential. In the CAP, there are three basic branch pruning methods:

(a) Pruning based on system reliability
(b) Pruning to eliminate symmetrical arrangements
(c) Pruning based on necessary conditions

For Con/k/n:F systems, Hanafusa and Yamamoto [6] developed a B&B-based algorithm that finds optimal arrangements and incorporates (a), (b), and (c) branch pruning methods while using Hwang's [7] derived recursive equation to compute system reliability.

Omura *et al.* [12] leveraged the property that allows the Lin(r, s)/(m, n):F system with $r = m$ and $s = 2$ to be transformed into the Con/2/n:F system, proposing an algorithm that searches for optimal arrangements by utilizing the invariant optimal arrangement. Nakamura *et al.* [11] introduced a specialized algorithm for the case when $r = m - 1$ and $s = n - 1$, while Nakamura and Yamamoto [10] formulated an algorithm to efficiently search for the optimal arrangement of Lin(r, s)/(m, n):F systems in general.

To date, an algorithm for finding the optimal arrangement of the Tri/(m, n):F system has not been reported. Hence, this paper aims to develop an algorithm utilizing the B&B method for obtaining the Tri/(m, n):F system's optimal arrangement. To efficiently acquire the optimal arrangement, we derive pruning conditions for the B&B method and assess the effectiveness of these conditions through numerical experiments. The solutions obtained by the proposed algorithm guarantee optimality, thereby enabling the evaluation of approximation methods, such as metaheuristics.

2   Component Assignment Problem for Tri/(m, n):F Systems

In this study, we make the following assumptions:

(a) components and the system can be either working or failed,
(b) components fail independently,
(c) component reliabilities are given, and
(d) components can be assigned to any position.

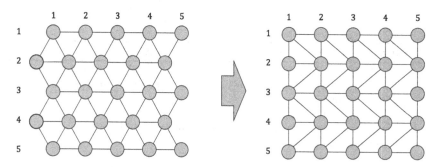

Fig. 2. Tri/(m,n):F system with a square lattice.

2.1   Formulation of the CAP

In this subsection, we present the formulation of the CAP for Tri/(m,n):F systems. To simplify the description, we assume components are arranged in an m-by-n square grid (refer to Fig. 2). The position of the i-th row and j-th column of the system is denoted by (i,j). We assign the component number $\pi(i,j)$ to the position (i,j), and the reliability of the τ-th component is represented by p_τ, where $p_1 < p_2 < \cdots < p_{mn}$. The reliability of the Tri/(m,n):F system is expressed as $R((m,n), \boldsymbol{p}; \Pi)$, where $\boldsymbol{p} = (p_1, p_2, \ldots, p_{mn})$. The CAP for the Tri/$(m,n)$:F system involves finding the optimal arrangement Π^* that maximizes the system's reliability, which can be formulated as:

$$\Pi^* = \operatorname*{argmax}_{\Pi \in \Omega} R((m,n), \boldsymbol{p}; \Pi), \tag{1}$$

where Ω is the set of all arrangements Π.

2.2   Birnbaum Importance

In this subsection, we discuss the concept of Birnbaum Importance (hereinafter referred to as B-importance), which was proposed by Birnbaum [2]. B-importance serves as an indicator to measure the significance of a component assigned to a particular position.

Let $I_B((i,j), \boldsymbol{p}; \Pi)$ represent the importance of the component assigned to position (i,j) in a Tri/(m,n):F system, given the configuration Π and the vector $\boldsymbol{p}$. In this case, $I_B((i,j), \boldsymbol{p}; \Pi)$ can be computed as follows:

$$I_B((i,j), \boldsymbol{p}; \Pi) = R((m,n), (1_{\pi(i,j)}, \boldsymbol{p}); \Pi) - R((m,n), (0_{\pi(i,j)}, \boldsymbol{p}); \Pi), \tag{2}$$

where,

$$(\alpha_\tau, \boldsymbol{p}) = (p_1, p_2, \ldots, p_{\tau-1}, \alpha, p_{\tau+1}, \ldots, p_{mn}),$$

with ($\alpha \in [0,1]$). For instance, $R((m,n), (1_{\pi(i,j)}, \boldsymbol{p}); \Pi)$ represents the reliability of the Tri/(m,n):F system when the reliability of the component assigned to position (i,j) is 1. Equation (2) implies that assigning components with high

---

Procedure 1. LKA procedure for Tri/(m,n):F system [9]

1: For $i = 1, 2, \ldots, m$ and $j = 1, 2, \ldots, n$, set $\pi(i,j) \leftarrow 1$ and $p_{\pi(i,j)} \leftarrow p_1$
2: Initialize $S \leftarrow \{(i,j) | i = 1, 2, \ldots, m, j = 1, 2, \ldots, n\}$ (S: set of positions not yet assigned a component)
3: **for** $\tau = mn, mn - 1, \ldots, 2$ **do**
4:     For each $(i,j) \in S$, compute $I_B((i,j), \boldsymbol{p}; \Pi)$ using Equation (2)
5:     Find the position (s,t) ($\in S$) that satisfies

$$I_B((s,t), \boldsymbol{p}; \Pi) = \max_{(i,j) \in S} I_B((i,j), \boldsymbol{p}; \Pi)$$

6:     Update $S \leftarrow S \backslash \{(s,t)\}$
7:     Assign component τ to position (s,t)
8: **end for**

---

reliability to positions with large $I_B((i,j), \boldsymbol{p}; \Pi)$ values can significantly improve the overall system reliability.

Next, we describe the LKA heuristics, a greedy algorithm that employs B-importance, as proposed by Lin and Kuo [9]. LKA heuristics are used to generate initial solutions for the CAP. Following Kuo and Zuo [8], Procedure 1 presents the steps to obtain the quasi-optimal arrangement for the Tri/(m,n):F system using LKA heuristics. Without loss of generality, note that: $p_1 < p_2 < \cdots < p_{mn}$.

3   Algorithm for Finding the Optimal Arrangement

In this section, we propose an algorithm for finding the optimal arrangement. Recall that previous studies [6,10] employed three types of pruning conditions to reduce the number of arrangements, namely:

- Pruning based on system reliability
- Pruning to eliminate symmetrical arrangements
- Pruning based on necessary conditions

For this study, we derive three types of pruning conditions for the CAP of the Tri/(m,n):F system.

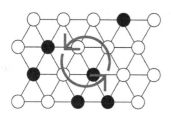

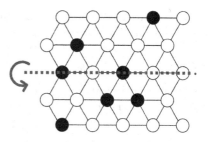

Fig. 3. Rotational symmetry.   **Fig. 4.** Reflectional symmetry

3.1 Pruning Based on System Reliability

Solving the CAP demands a large number of reliability calculations, which can be time-consuming even with an efficient reliability calculation method [16]. Thus, it is crucial to reduce the calculation time of system reliability, even by a small amount. In the proposed algorithm, we partially calculate system reliability using the recursive equation [16] when a component is assigned to position (m, j) $(j = 1, 2, \ldots, n)$. By focusing on the fact that only a few components differ in successive enumerations of different arrangements in the branching operation, we reduce the calculation time by computing the difference between the parts.

Moreover, bounding operations are performed using system reliability. As the system reliability is a non-increasing function concerning the column, if the system reliability of a partially configured system at position (m, j) is less than the system reliability corresponding to the best arrangement found in the previous search, further assignment of components will not increase reliability. In other words, there is no need to assign any more components. Thus, in the proposed algorithm, we perform pruning based on system reliability.

Pruning condition 1. *When a component is assigned to position* (m, j) *for* $j = 2, 3, \ldots, n$, *and if*

$$\boldsymbol{Rmax} > R((m, j), \boldsymbol{p}; \varPi), \tag{3}$$

then prune the branch. Here, $\boldsymbol{Rmax}$ *is the incumbent value (the maximum system reliability obtained so far).*

3.2 Pruning Conditions for Eliminating Symmetric Arrangements

In the Tri/(m, n):F system, system reliability is determined by the relative arrangement of components, given their reliabilities. As a result, multiple arrangements that are essentially equivalent and possess the same system reliability can be obtained through rotations and reflections. When seeking the optimal arrangement, it is not necessary to enumerate all such arrangements; only one representative arrangement from each set of essentially equivalent arrangements needs consideration. In the $\mathrm{Tri}/(m,n)$:F systems, rotational symmetry appears for even m (Fig. 3), while reflectional symmetry appears for odd m (Fig. 4). To accommodate this, the proposed algorithm considers only the arrangements satisfying the following conditions:

Pruning condition 2. *(1) For odd m: When a component is assigned to position $\left(\frac{m+1}{2}+1,1\right)$, and if*

$$\pi\left(\frac{m+1}{2}-1,1\right) > \pi\left(\frac{m+1}{2}+1,1\right), \tag{4}$$

then prune the branch.
(2) For even m and odd n: When a component is assigned to position $\left(\frac{m}{2}+1,\frac{n+1}{2}\right)$, and if

$$\pi\left(\frac{m}{2},\frac{n+1}{2}\right) > \pi\left(\frac{m}{2}+1,\frac{n+1}{2}\right), \tag{5}$$

then prune the branch.
(3) For even m and even n: When a component is assigned to position $\left(\frac{m}{2},\frac{n}{2}+1\right)$, and if

$$\pi\left(\frac{m}{2}+1,\frac{n}{2}\right) > \pi\left(\frac{m}{2},\frac{n}{2}+1\right), \tag{6}$$

then prune the branch.

3.3 Pruning Conditions Based on Necessary Conditions

Arrangements that fail to meet the necessary conditions cannot be optimal, as there exist arrangements with higher objective function values (system reliability). Employing the necessary conditions allows for the elimination of suboptimal arrangements and a reduction in the search space when seeking the optimal arrangement. The pruning conditions based on the necessary conditions are as follows:

Pruning condition 3. *(1) When a component is assigned to position $(2,2)$, and if*

$$\pi(2,2) < \pi(1,1), \tag{7}$$

then prune the branch.
(2) When a component is assigned to position $(1,n)$, and if

$$\pi(1,n-1) < \pi(1,n), \tag{8}$$

then prune the branch.
(3) When a component is assigned to position $(2,n)$, and if

$$\pi(2,n) < \pi(1,n), \tag{9}$$

then prune the branch.

(4-a) When m is odd and a component is assigned to position $(m-1,2)$, and if

$$\pi(m-1,2) < \pi(m,1), \tag{10}$$

then prune the branch.

(5-a) When m is odd and a component is assigned to position (m,n), and if

$$\pi(m,n-1) < \pi(m,n), \tag{11}$$

then prune the branch.

(6-a) When m is odd and a component is assigned to position (m,n), and if

$$\pi(m-1,n) < \pi(m,n), \tag{12}$$

then prune the branch.

(4-b) When m is even and a component is assigned to position $(m,1)$, and if

$$\pi(m-1,1) < \pi(m,1), \tag{13}$$

then prune the branch.

(5-b) When m is even and a component is assigned to position $(m,2)$, and if

$$\pi(m,2) < \pi(m,1), \tag{14}$$

then prune the branch.

(6-b) When m is even and a component is assigned to position (m,n), and if

$$\pi(m-1,n-1) < \pi(m,n), \tag{15}$$

then prune the branch.

Pruning conditions 3 are proved using the Permutation importance introduced by Boland et al. [4].

3.4 Overview of the Algorithm

In this subsection, we provide a brief overview of the proposed algorithm's procedure, which utilizes the B&B method. In maximization problems, the efficiency of the limiting operation increases with the value of the provisional solution. Hence, approximate solution methods are occasionally employed as initial solutions. In the proposed algorithm, the arrangement obtained by LKA [9] serves as the initial solution, and **Rmax** is initialized with its system reliability. When assigning components sequentially, DFS(v) is employed as a processing routine to assign a component to the v-th position for $v = 1, 2, \ldots, mn$. Procedure 2 illustrates the flow of the DFS(v) function, which is a recursive routine for assigning components to each position in the grid. We begin with DFS(1) and output the incumbent solution after enumerating all arrangements.

Procedure 2. DFS(v) Function

1: **if** all components are assigned and the corresponding system reliability of the arrangement exceeds the current maximum reliability value **Rmax then**
2:    the arrangement is saved, and **Rmax** is updated
3: **end if**
4: **for** unassigned component τ **do**
5:    assign component τ to position v
6:    **if** the resulting arrangement does not meet pruning conditions 1 or 2 **then**
7:       **if** the component is assigned to the m-th row **then**
8:          calculate the system reliability
9:          **if** the resulting arrangement does not meet pruning condition 3 **then**
10:             DFS($v + 1$)
11:          **end if**
12:       **else**
13:          DFS($v + 1$)
14:       **end if**
15:    **end if**
16: **end for**
17: **return**

---

4   Numerical Experiment

In this study, we assess the optimal arrangement search algorithm for the Tri/(m, n):F system through numerical experiment. The computational environment comprises the following specifications:

- OS: Windows 11 Pro
- CPU: Intel Core i9-12900K
- Memory: 32.0 GB
- Language: C++
- Development environment: Visual Studio Community 2022

For the experiment, problem instances are generated using a uniform distribution of component reliability within the intervals $[0.0, 1.0]$, $[0.5, 1.0]$, and $[0.9, 1.0]$ for systems with 12 components. The effectiveness of the three pruning conditions integrated into the proposed algorithm is investigated. To achieve this, the computation times of four algorithms listed in Table 1 are compared. The checkmark ($\checkmark$) in the table signifies that the corresponding pruning condition was employed.

Algorithm A incorporates all three pruning conditions, while Algorithm B, Algorithm C, and Algorithm D each remove one pruning condition from Algorithm A. Algorithm B omits the pruning condition based on system reliability, Algorithm C removes pruning symmetric arrangements, and Algorithm D excludes the necessary conditions.

Table 1. Four algorithms for evaluation experiments.

	pruning condition[1]	pruning condition[2]	pruning condition[3]
Algorithm A	✓	✓	✓
Algorithm B		✓	✓
Algorithm C	✓		✓
Algorithm D	✓	✓	

[1] Pruning based on system reliability
[2] Pruning to eliminate symmetrical arrangements
[3] Pruning based on necessary conditions

Table 2. Mean computation times and system reliabilities.

(m,n)	Comp. Rel.	Alg. A	Alg. B	B/A	Alg. C	C/A	Alg. D	D/A	Sys. Rel.
$(2,6)$	$[0.0, 1.0]$	161.9	270.8	167%	318.2	197%	914.3	565%	0.4769
$(2,6)$	$[0.5, 1.0]$	141.1	300.0	213%	283.5	201%	753.5	534%	0.9284
$(2,6)$	$[0.9, 1.0]$	79.8	299.4	375%	163.9	205%	365.0	457%	0.9994
$(3,4)$	$[0.0, 1.0]$	216.2	320.0	148%	398.7	184%	583.4	270%	0.5346
$(3,4)$	$[0.5, 1.0]$	171.6	304.3	177%	341.4	199%	478.0	279%	0.9379
$(3,4)$	$[0.9, 1.0]$	114.8	303.5	264%	229.2	200%	261.5	228%	0.9995
$(4,3)$	$[0.0, 1.0]$	162.1	197.6	122%	499.5	308%	2648.9	1634%	0.4943
$(4,3)$	$[0.5, 1.0]$	131.8	198.4	151%	441.3	335%	1869.0	1418%	0.9339
$(4,3)$	$[0.9, 1.0]$	71.9	198.5	276%	242.2	337%	680.2	946%	0.9995
$(6,2)$	$[0.0, 1.0]$	592.7	628.0	106%	1153.3	195%	8773.1	1480%	0.5743
$(6,2)$	$[0.5, 1.0]$	584.2	584.8	100%	1081.7	185%	8703.2	1490%	0.9460
$(6,2)$	$[0.9, 1.0]$	549.9	575.5	105%	1044.1	190%	7981.7	1452%	0.9996

Table 2 displays the mean computation times and system reliabilities for each problem instance, based on ten runs. In all cases, the optimal values (system reliabilities) determined by each algorithm were identical. As demonstrated in Table 2, all problem instances experienced reduced computation times due to each pruning condition.

The average execution time ratio for B/A was 184%, C/A was 228%, and D/A was 896%, indicating that excluding the necessary conditions for pruning from the proposed algorithm significantly increased computation time relative to other pruning conditions. Notably, the average ratio of D/A was 896%, signifying that incorporating necessary pruning conditions reduced computation time to approximately 1/9 on average. It is concluded that the pruning based on necessary conditions is the most effective in the proposed algorithm.

Additionally, since most of the C/A values were around 200%, pruning symmetric arrangements was found to decrease computation time by approximately half. Moreover, pruning based on system reliability was more effective for problem instances with a larger number of columns n. This can be attributed to the fact that pruning based on system reliability necessitates $n - 1$ evaluations, resulting in an increased pruning frequency as n increases.

5 Conclusion

In this study, we addressed the CAP for Tri/(m, n):F systems. To efficiently obtain the optimal arrangement, we derived three pruning conditions and constructed an optimal arrangement search algorithm that incorporates them. Computational experiment results demonstrated that all pruning conditions reduced computation time. In particular, the pruning condition based on necessary conditions reduced the computation time on average by approximately 1/9, as experimentally shown.

However, even with the proposed algorithm, obtaining the optimal arrangement for systems composed of many components remains challenging. Therefore, acquiring a quasi-optimal arrangement for Tri/(m, n):F systems using metaheuristics is necessary. Incorporating pruning conditions based on necessary conditions derived in this study is anticipated to enhance the algorithm's performance.

References

1. Akiba, T., Yamamoto, H., Kainuma, Y.: Reliability of a 3-dimensional adjacent triangle: F triangular lattice system. In: Proceedings of the 5th Asia Pacific Industrial Engineering and Management Systems, pp. 1–10 (2004)
2. Birnbaum, Z.W.: On the importance of different components in a multicomponent system. Washington Univ Seattle Lab of Statistical Research, Technical Report (1968)
3. Boehme, T.K., Kossow, A., Preuss, W.: A generalization of consecutive-k-out-of-n: f systems. IEEE Trans. Reliabil. **41**(3), 451–457 (1992)
4. Boland, P.J., Proschan, F., Tong, Y.L.: Optimal arrangement of components via pairwise rearrangements. Naval Res. Logist. **36**(6), 807–815 (1989) https://doi.org/10.1002/1520-6750(198912)36:6<807::AID-NAV3220360606>3.0.CO;2-I
5. Cai, Z., Si, S., Sun, S., Li, C.: Optimization of linear consecutive-k-out-of-n system with a Birnbaum importance-based genetic algorithm. Reliabil. Eng. Syst. Saf. **152**, 248–258 (2016). https://doi.org/10.1016/j.ress.2016.03.016
6. Hanafusa, T., Yamamoto, H.: Branch and bound algorithm for the optimal assignment problem in linear consecutive-k-out-of-n: F system. Reliabil. Eng. Assoc. Japan (in Japanese) **22**(7), 641–661 (2000)
7. Hwang, F.K.: Fast solutions for consecutive-k-out-of-n: F system. IEEE Trans. Reliabil. **31**(5), 447–448 (1982). https://doi.org/10.1109/TR.1982.5221426
8. Kuo, W., Zhu, X.: Importance Measures in Reliability, Risk, and Optimization: Principles and Applications. Wiley, Hoboken (2012)
9. Lin, F.H., Kuo, W.: Reliability importance and invariant optimal allocation. J. Heuristics **8**(2), 155–171 (2002). https://doi.org/10.1023/A:1017908523107
10. Nakamura, T., Yamamoto, H.: Algorithm for solving optimal arrangement problem in connected-(r, s)-out-of-(m, n):f lattice system. IEEE Trans. Reliabil. **69**(2), 497–509 (2020). https://doi.org/10.1109/TR.2019.2925142

11. Nakamura, T., Yamamoto, H., Akiba, T.: Fast algorithm for optimal arrangement in connected-$(m-1, n-1)$-out-of-(m, n): F lattice system. IEICE Trans. Fundam. Electron. Commun. Comput. Sci. **101**(12), 2446–2453 (2018)

12. Omura, T., Akiba, T., Yamamoto, H., Xiao, X.: Algorithm for obtaining optimal arrangement of a connected-(r, s)-out-of-(m, n): F system – the case of $m = r$ and $s = 2$ –. IEICE Trans. Fundam. Electron. Commun. Comput. Sci. **E98-A**(10), 2018–2024 (2015). https://doi.org/10.1587/transfun.E98.A.2018

13. Salvia, A.A., Lasher, W.C.: 2-dimensional consecutive-k-out-of-n: F models. IEEE Trans. Reliabil. **39**(3), 382–385 (1990). https://doi.org/10.1109/24.103023

14. Shingyochi, K., Yamamoto, H., Yamachi, H.: Comparative study of several simulated annealing algorithms for optimal arrangement problems in a circular consecutive-k-out-of-n: F system. Q. Technol. Quant. Manage. **9**(3), 295–303 (2012). https://doi.org/10.1080/16843703.2012.11673293

15. Wang, W., Cai, Z., Zhao, J., Si, S.: Optimization of linear consecutive-k-out-of-n systems with Birnbaum importance based ant colony optimization algorithm. Journal of Shanghai Jiaotong University (Science) **25**(2), 253–260 (2019). https://doi.org/10.1007/s12204-019-2125-z

16. Yamamoto, H., Akiba, T., Wakagi, Y.: Efficient algorithm for the reliability of an adjacent triangle: F triangular lattice system. Reliabil. Eng. Assoc. Japan (REAJ) **28**(1), 63–73 (2006)

17. Yamamoto, H., Miyakawa, M.: The reliability of the adjacent triangle: F triangular lattice system. J. Reliabil. Eng. Assoc. Japan (in Japanese) **7**(18), 97–105 (1996)

18. Yao, Q., Zhu, X., Kuo, W.: A Birnbaum-importance based genetic local search algorithm for component assignment problems. Ann. Oper. Res. **212**(1), 185–200 (2014). https://doi.org/10.1007/s10479-012-1223-1

Music Recommender System Considering the Variations in Music Selection Criterion Using an Interactive Genetic Algorithm

Tairyu Saito$^{(\boxtimes)}$ and Eri Sato-Shimokawara(iD)

Graduate School of Systems Design, Tokyo Metropolitan University, Tokyo, Japan
saito-tairyu@ed.tmu.ac.jp, eri@tmu.ac.jp

Abstract. With growing popularity of music distribution services, there has been a lot of research on a music recommender system that suggests music that matches a user's preference. Conventional recommender systems employ parameters such as personal listening history and similarities among users. However, these system needs user's preference data to obtain most suitable recommendation results. Hence, we focus on a music recommender system using an interactive genetic algorithm (iGA) that adopts variations in music selection criteria of an individual. Our proposed method reflects and optimizes music recommendation based on a user's evaluation acquired interactively. In this paper, we described our proposed method, reported influences on its recommendation under some music selection criteria, and verified how adequate music was recommended by iGA based on criteria differences by simulation. The results showed that our system suggested the most suitable music under any music selection criteria. In the future, we will investigate iGA selection methods that applies data distribution and variable-length GA for efficient optimization.

Keywords: ICBAKE · music recommender system · genetic algorithm

1 Introduction

In recent years, popularization of music distribution services has made it easier for users to access large amounts of data. Under these circumstances, there is a growing demand for recommender systems that provides music that matches user's preferences. Conventional music recommender methods are collaborative filtering method [1], which applies listening history of other users with similar tastes, and content-based music recommendation method [8], which applies result of analysis of acoustic feature preference of a user. While above research have focused on improving its accuracy of adequate recommendations, recent research focus on recommendation methods that adopts serendipity [6] with elements such as novelty and unexpectedness.

K. Saeed et al. (Eds.): CISIM 2023, LNCS 14164, pp. 382–393, 2023.
https://doi.org/10.1007/978-3-031-42823-4_28

We previously proposed a fusion-based recommender method which provided serendipity in music from two types of music selected by a user [11]. However, due to diversity of users, we considered that serendipity in music recommendation is not necessarily the best method to improve users' satisfaction. For example, for non-music listeners, music is one of tools to communicate with people because it can be a common topic, and such people may prefer music merely based on its popularity, not on their preferences or satisfactions. Therefore, the purpose of this research is to develop a music recommender system that applies music selection criteria of a user and recommends the most appropriate music interactively with the user.

2 Related Work

2.1 Music Recommender Systems

As the representative of many music recommendation methods, the collaborative filtering [1] method and the content-based recommendation method [8] can be cited. In the collaborative filtering method, the listening history of users stored in a database is used to analyze similarities among users based on their listening patterns, and music is recommended by referring to the patterns of other users who are associated with the target user. While this method has the advantage that it does not need to use acoustic feature data of music, it has some problems such as the fact that it requires a certain amount of listening history of the target user and the fact that music not listened to by anyone is not a candidate for recommendation (cold-start problem).

In the content-based recommendation method, acoustic features of music data are analyzed to recommend music that is similar to the user's preferred one. Since only the user's preferred music and acoustic features are required for the recommendation, this method avoids the cold-start problem in the collaborative filtering method described above. On the other hand, there are some issues such as the discussion on what kind of acoustic features should be used to calculate the appropriate similarity between music, and the fact that the method only recommends similar music, so there is no surprise to the user. Other recommendation methods that focus on improving usability are "context-aware music recommendation" and "interactive music recommendation".

2.2 Interactive Music Recommender Systems

In this section, we present case studies of recent research on methods and systems for recommending optimal music through interaction with a user. Liang investigated methods to promote users to abstain from their current preferences and explore new music genres [4]. As a nudging technique, they employed a method which adopts default genre selection to promote users' own spontaneous actions and experimented with a system that allows users to adjust their level of personalization freely according to their choices. They found that default-based methods were effective for users' searching actions, but less effective for users with musical knowledge. In further research, they focused on the impact of searching with the system over a longer period and conducted a six-week experiment [5]. The results showed that the default initial playlists and visual anchors used as nudging methods were not effective in the long-term aspect. However, an analysis focusing on changes in Spotify profiles showed that the combination of nudging and personalization might be effective in supporting users' long-term genre exploration.

Petridis [9] proposed TastePaths, an interactive web tool for users to explore music genre space. Users explore within a search space clustered by genre, with features such as "guide" that connect key artists in each cluster. They conducted an experiment to compare a personalized version built on a dataset of artists preferred by the user with a non-personalized version built on a dataset of popular artists. They found that users preferred the personalized version and were more willing to interact with the graph screen which reflect their own preferences.

In above research, web interfaces have been developed to allow users to "explore", though it is difficult to display all the music from the world as nodes in such search space. Therefore, a simplified method using music genres has been employed. However, the variety of music nowadays is increasing, and genre-based recommendation methods are considered to have limitations. Therefore, our research focuses on improving the method using an interactive genetic algorithm that optimizes the feedback to each music.

2.3 Interactive Genetic Algorithm in Music Recommender System

In the proposed method, Yamaguchi [12] newly created user-preferred music using an interactive genetic algorithm and recommended the best music based on similarity between the created music and the music in the database. The results of his experiment showed that the evaluation of the created music had increased, but the effectiveness of the recommendation method using the created music had been found as not effective. Yamaguchi believed that one of the reasons for these results was that the number of music data was too small, but also hoped there would be a possibility that future experiments would show the effectiveness of this method.

Kim [2] proposed a recommender system for music data that combines two methodologies: content-based filtering techniques and interactive genetic algorithms. By evaluating the fitness of each recommendation item according to the user's own preferences, the recommendation is gradually adapted based on each user's subjective evaluation. User experiments show that the average score objectively collected by the user's evaluation gradually increases with the number of generations.

3   Proposed Method

3.1   iGA in Our Research

We adopted an interactive genetic algorithm (iGA) as a method to determine a user's current music selection criteria interactively with the system, and to switch recommended music dynamically. There are three reasons. First, the algorithm can dynamically reflect user feedback as an evaluation function in the system. Second, there are various extension methods, such as variable-length GA, which dynamically changes the gene length itself based on the user feedback. Third, compared to machine learning such as Deep Learning, iGA allows optimization to be done with less evaluation data. Table 1 shows the parameters of the iGA used in this research.

Referring to the work of Kim [2], we determined the processing configuration of the iGA as below. Furthermore, since BLX-alpha crossover used in this research is an alternative to mutation, we did not use mutation in this system.

Evaluation:
A user listens to music from list displayed on the website and rates the music on a scale of 1 to 5. The user rating obtained here is used as the fitness of the individual.

Selection:
Truncation Selection: Selects individuals with the top T% of fitness.

Crossover:
BLX-α Crossover: Randomly determines the features of a new individual from an interval defined by the features of the two parent individuals and α. For example, in the case of the i-th feature when the individuals to be crossover are $m1$ and $m2$, the feature $m3_i$ of the new individual is selected in range (MIN, MAX) as follows:

$$MIN = min(m1_i, m2_i) - (\alpha * D_i) \tag{1}$$

$$MAX = max(m1_i, m2_i) + (\alpha * D_i) \tag{2}$$

$$D_i = |m1i - m2i| \tag{3}$$

Matching:
The system calculates the Euclidean distance between the features of the individuals obtained by crossover and the music data registered in the database, and the music with the closest distance of all the music data is selected as the new individual.

3.2 Overview of Our System

Figure 1 shows the diagram of the system we developed, and Fig. 2 show the assumed display screen. The user listens to a 30-second preview of 10 songs on the website, then rates each music on a scale of 1 to 5 from a pull-down menu and presses a submit button. The operation up to this point is one generation, and the objective is to have the system recommend the most suitable music for the user by overlapping these generations.

Table 1. The parameters of the iGA

Parameter	Value	Description
Gene Length	4	the values, valence, energy, popularity and release_date from Spotify
Number of individuals	10	The number of individuals in each generation
Number of generations	18	The number of times the algorithm is repeated
Truncation Selection	$T = 60$	The individuals with the top T% fitness are retained for the next generation
BLX-α Crossover	$\alpha = 0.1$	determined from within the range defined by the two parents and α

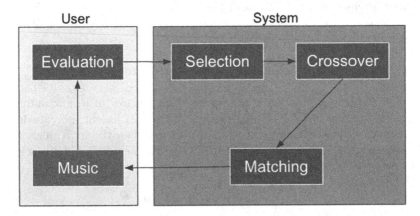

Fig. 1. The diagram of the system

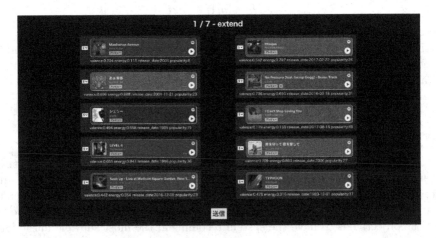

Fig. 2. The assumed display screen

4   Experiment

4.1   Dataset

We procured 40,300 of music data for our system from Spotify. Considering diversity of user preferences, we used search endpoint of the Spotify API[1] to obtain approximately 1,000 music track-identifiers, each released from 1980 to 2023. In this research, we adopted four real numbers from the music data as genes: valence and energy using the audio-features endpoint[2], popularity and release date using the tracks endpoint[3]. In this process, to eliminate duplicating music, those with the same music identifier which were already retrieved were removed. If music with the same valence and energy values exists, the music with the smallest unique ID in the database is selected. The unique ID is a sequential identifier of the music data registered by the experimenter.

The popularity and the release_date were normalized in the range of 0 to 1 to align the scale with valence and energy. In this case, only the year of release was used as the release_date, and month of release was truncated. The distributions of each feature in a data set were important factors in implementing iGA.

The distribution of (valence, energy), popularity, and release_date of the music data are shown in Fig. 3, Fig. 4, and Fig. 5, respectively. Figure 3 shows that the lighter-colored areas have more music, and the darker-colored areas have less music, indicating a slight bias toward music with more (valence, energy). Figure 4 shows that the bias is more visible, indicating that much of the music has low popularity. Figure 4 shows that although there are some partial years with a large amount of music, the overall distribution of release_date is relatively uniform.

4.2   Music Selection Criteria

Assumption. We divided user preferences into three categories: "particular about music," "not particular," and "can't say for sure," and assigned the following music selection criteria to each of these categories.

Content-oriented type:
   This is the most common selection criterion, evaluating whether a listener feels the music is good or bad based on what they hear through their ears. It is a music selection criterion that reflects a neutral preference for music.

Novelty-oriented type:
   We asked six experienced instrumentalists, "In your daily life, do you ever actively seek out music that you have never heard before?" and all of them answered "yes" to this question. This suggests that if one's preference is particular about music, it is likely that one prefers new music.

---

[1] https://developer.spotify.com/documentation/web-api/reference/search.
[2] https://developer.spotify.com/documentation/web-api/reference/get-audio-features.
[3] https://developer.spotify.com/documentation/web-api/reference/get-track.

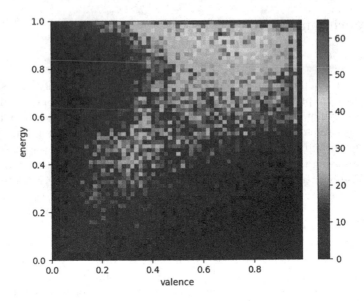

Fig. 3. The distribution of (valence, energy)

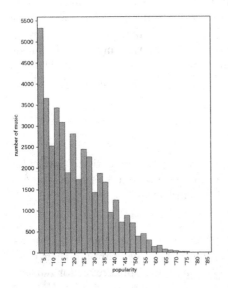

Fig. 4. The distribution of popularity

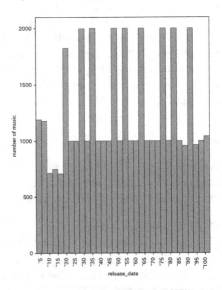

Fig. 5. The distribution of release_date

Popularity-oriented type:

One of the psychological phenomena that create fashion is the bandwagon effect [3]. This is an effect in which more people will choose an option that has been chosen by many other people, and it is considered to work more strongly for people who are not particular about music and may prefer popular music.

In addition, we believe that none of the above music selection criteria is fixed by a single person and that the music selection criteria expresses fluctuation with the passage of time. The reason for this is that even users who normally select music based on their actual listening impression in accordance with the content-oriented type may, at other times, feel an interest in listening to music that is new to them or show interest in music that is advertised as trendy.

Application to Music Data. In the music selection criteria defined in Sect. 4.2, we assume that satisfaction with the recommended music improves as the values of valence and energy reach the ideal value in the content-oriented type. Similarly, we focus on the values of popularity for the popularity-oriented type and release_date for the novelty-oriented type. In addition, since previous research has shown the validity of valence and energy for the content-oriented type [7], we considered that applying these values to Russell's sentiment model [10] would allow us to quantify the content information of the music.

4.3 Simulation

In this section, we describe the simulations we conducted to verify that our system works effectively. In the simulations, ideal values are set for the genes of focus in each music selection criteria, and the fitness is determined by the Euclidean distance between the genes and the suggested music genes. The ideal values refer to the Sect. 4.1 and are set to a value with an even distribution for the content-oriented type and the maximum value in the data set for the popularity-oriented and novelty-oriented types. The ideal values for each gene set are shown in the Table 2. Although it is difficult to determine from the properties of the dataset which music is unknown to the user, we used release_date as an indicator of novelty in this experiment, considering that newly released music is more likely to be unknown.

Table 2. Ideal value in the simulation

gene	value	music selection criterion
valence	0.3	content-oriented
energy	0.2	content-oriented
popularity	0.84(maximum)	popularity-oriented
release_date	1.0(maximum)	novelty-oriented

Considering that music selection criteria change during use, we conducted simulations using the following patterns. Simulations were conducted for 10 people per pattern, and the generational average of the amount of music with a fitness level of 4 or higher was calculated.

pattern 1 content-oriented type
pattern 2 novelty-oriented type
pattern 3 popularity-oriented type
pattern 4 content-oriented type → novelty-oriented type
pattern 5 content-oriented type → popularity-oriented type
pattern 6 novelty-oriented type → popularity-oriented type
pattern 7 novelty-oriented type → content-oriented type → popularity-oriented
    type

4.4 Result

Figures 6, 7, 8, 9 and 10 show the results of calculating the average amount of
music with a fitness level of 4 or higher in each pattern for each generation.
Figure 6 shows that the optimal music was recommended for each of the three
music selection criteria. We also found a significant difference in the rising process
between novelty-oriented and popularity-oriented. Figures 7, 8 and 9 show that
some degree of optimization was achieved even when the music selection criteria
were changed to another one. However, there was not much increase in the
popularity-oriented case. Figure 10 shows that when the music selection criteria
are changed two times, the optimization becomes insufficient.

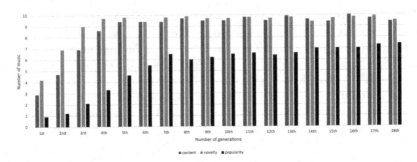

Fig. 6. The amount of music evaluated over fitness level of 4 (pattern 1, 2, 3). Only a
single music selection criterion of content, novelty, and popularity, respectively

5 Discussion

The simulation results show that there are two issues with our system. One is
that it was difficult to increase the fitness of the popularity-oriented type in
all patterns as shown in Fig. 6 and Fig. 8, 9 and 10. We assume the uniformity
of the distribution of popularity (see Fig. 4) is the cause of this issue. In the
future, we will develop selection methods that match the distribution of features.
Second, once the music selection criteria were changed, optimization could not
be achieved unless enough generations were passed each time. To address this
issue, we will investigate by introducing a variable-length GA, in which the

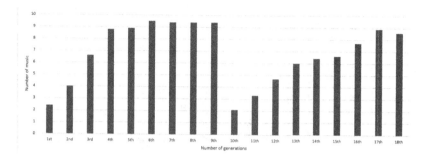

Fig. 7. The amount of music evaluated over fitness level of 4 (pattern 4). From 1st to 9th is evaluated following content-oriented type, From 10th to 18th is evaluated following novelty-oriented type

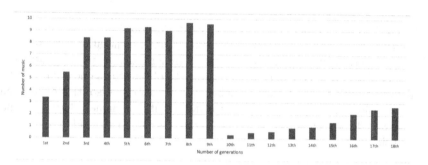

Fig. 8. The amount of music evaluated over fitness level of 4 (pattern 5). From 1st to 9th is evaluated following content-oriented type, From 10th to 18th is evaluated following popularity-oriented type

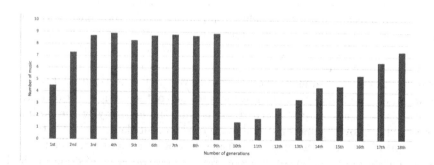

Fig. 9. The amount of music evaluated over fitness level of 4 (pattern 6). From 1st to 9th is evaluated following novelty-oriented type, From 10th to 18th is evaluated following popularity-oriented type

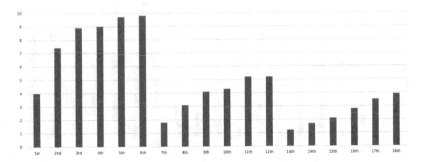

Fig. 10. The amount of music evaluated over fitness level of 4 (pattern 7). From 1st to 6th is evaluated following novelty-oriented type, From 7th to 12th is evaluated following content-oriented type, From 13th to 18th is evaluated following popularity-oriented type

gene length varies to increase the efficiency of optimization. In the simulation experiment, the number of generations was set at 18 generations. However, in the case of actual situations, this number of generations may cause fatigue to users. Therefore, it is necessary to find a way to obtain the same quality of the simulation results with a smaller number of generations. Also, this experiment did not consider the case where there was music with the same values of valence and energy. Along with above issues, we need to consider a method for classifying such music.

6 Conclusion

In this research, we developed a system that considers changes in music selection criteria of users and utilizes them to recommend the most suitable music for users. First, we classified music selection criteria into three types from the viewpoint of "interest in music", namely, "content-oriented", "popularity-oriented", and "novelty-oriented". Next, we adopted an interactive genetic algorithm as a method for determining which of these music selection criteria the user is currently in and recommending music suitable for each criterion through interaction with the system. The simulation conducted to verify the effectiveness of the algorithm showed that our system can respond to each of the music selection criteria, however, two issues were revealed. First is that the accuracy of the optimization is reduced by the uneven distribution of the music data. Second is that the optimization is reset each time the music selection criteria are switched, resulting in low usability. In future research, we will develop iGA selection methods that consider the distribution unevenness and introduce variable-length GA as a method to improve the efficiency of optimization.

References

1. Ekstrand, M.D., Riedl, J.T., Konstan, J.A., et al.: Collaborative filtering recommender systems. Found. Trends® Hum.-Comput. Interact. 4(2), 81–173 (2011)

2. Kim, H.T., Kim, E., Lee, J.H., Ahn, C.W.: A recommender system based on genetic algorithm for music data. In: 2010 2nd International Conference on Computer Engineering and Technology, vol. 6, pp. V6–414-V6-417 (2010). https://doi.org/10.1109/ICCET.2010.5486161

3. Leibenstein, H.: Bandwagon, snob, and veblen effects in the theory of consumers' demand. Q. J. Econ. **64**(2), 183–207 (1950)

4. Liang, Y., Willemsen, M.C.: The role of preference consistency, defaults and musical expertise in users' exploration behavior in a genre exploration recommender. In: Proceedings of the 15th ACM Conference on Recommender Systems, pp. 230–240 (2021)

5. Liang, Y., Willemsen, M.C.: Exploring the longitudinal effects of nudging on users' music genre exploration behavior and listening preferences. In: Proceedings of the 16th ACM Conference on Recommender Systems, pp. 3–13 (2022)

6. McNee, S.M., Riedl, J., Konstan, J.A.: Being accurate is not enough: how accuracy metrics have hurt recommender systems. In: CHI'06 Extended Abstracts on Human Factors in Computing Systems, pp. 1097–1101 (2006)

7. Panda, R., Redinho, H., Gonçalves, C., Malheiro, R., Paiva, R.P.: How does the spotify api compare to the music emotion recognition state-of-the-art? In: Proceedings of the 18th Sound and Music Computing Conference (SMC 2021), pp. 238–245. Axea sas/SMC Network (2021)

8. Pazzani, M.J., Billsus, D.: Content-based recommendation systems. In: Brusilovsky, P., Kobsa, A., Nejdl, W. (eds.) The Adaptive Web. LNCS, vol. 4321, pp. 325–341. Springer, Heidelberg (2007). https://doi.org/10.1007/978-3-540-72079-9_10

9. Petridis, S., Daskalova, N., Mennicken, S., Way, S.F., Lamere, P., Thom, J.: Tastepaths: enabling deeper exploration and understanding of personal preferences in recommender systems. In: 27th International Conference on Intelligent User Interfaces, pp. 120–133 (2022)

10. Russell, J.A.: A circumplex model of affect. J. Pers. Soc. Psychol. **39**(6), 1161 (1980)

11. Saito, T., Sato-Shimokawara, E., Chen, L.H.: Fusion-based music recommender system using music affective space based on serendipity. In: 2022 International Conference on Technologies and Applications of Artificial Intelligence (TAAI), pp. 171–176 (2022). https://doi.org/10.1109/TAAI57707.2022.00039

12. Yamaguchi, G., Fukumoto, M.: A music recommendation system based on melody creation by interactive GA. In: 2019 20th IEEE/ACIS International Conference on Software Engineering, Artificial Intelligence, Networking and Parallel/Distributed Computing (SNPD), pp. 286–290. IEEE (2019)

Fault Detection of Moore Finite State Machines by Structural Models

Valery Salauyou[(✉)] [iD]

Bialystok University of Technology, Wiejska 45A, 15-351 Bialystok, Poland
v.salauyou@pb.edu.pl

Abstract. The fault detection is an important task in the design of fault-tolerant finite state machines (FSMs). The paper describes structural models of Moore FSM for detecting multiple faults in various elements of the FSM and preventing their negative impact on the controlled object. The considered structural models allow detecting invalid transitions between FSM states, invalid input and output vectors, both in each state and for the whole FSM, invalid codes of the present FSM state and the next FSM state. Estimates of the area and performance of the proposed structural models are presented. Experimental results showed that the area overhead for the proposed structural models is from 3 to 26%, which is significantly less than that of the known approaches.

Keywords: fault detection · structural models · finite state machine (FSM) · area · performance · state encoding · unmanned aerial vehicles (UAVs)

1 Introduction

In recent years, unmanned aerial vehicles (UAV) are having an increased popularity in all fields of applications including military conflicts. One method of neutralizing UAV is to use a powerful electromagnetic pulse (EMP) [1]. An effective way to protect the UAV from the impacts of the EMP is to implement the control device of the UAV as a fault-tolerant finite state machine (FSM).

Figure 1 shows the traditional structural model of FSMs, where X is the input vector, R is the state register that stores the code *state* of the present state, Φ is the next state logic that produces the code *next* of the next state, and Ψ is the output logic that produces the output vector Y. The Moore FSM outputs are functions of present state whereas the Mealy FSM outputs are functions of present state and the inputs. The clock signal *clk* for the register R is generated using the generator Oscillator.

The following faults may occur in the FSM as a result of the EMP impact:

- at the inputs: an invalid input vector X;
- in the register R: an invalid present state code *state*;
- in the feedback circuit: an invalid present state code *state*;
- in the logic Φ: an invalid next state code *next*;
- in the logic Ψ: an invalid output vector Y;

K. Saeed et al. (Eds.): CISIM 2023, LNCS 14164, pp. 394–409, 2023.
https://doi.org/10.1007/978-3-031-42823-4_29

- in the generator Oscillator: no clock signal *clk*.

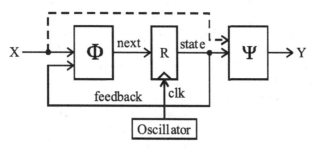

Fig. 1. The traditional structural model of FSMs.

In addition, there may be erroneous behavior of the FSM: transition of the FSM to invalid states, as well as invalid transitions to valid states (Fig. 2).

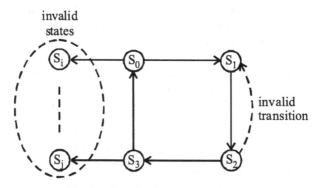

Fig. 2. The behavior errors of the FSM.

A lot of research has been done to build fault-tolerant FSMs. Most methods provide protection from single event upsets (SEUs), which are caused by radiation and cosmic rays. The SEUs change the contents of flip-flops or memory cells, while the primary inputs always considered as correct. However, the EMP is characterized by the following features when it impacts on FSMs:

- significant duration of the exposure time, compared to a space particle;
- impacts simultaneously on all elements of the FSM;
- generates not short-lived SEUs, but long-lasting multiple faults;
- affects mainly on wires (inputs, outputs, a feedback circuit);
- rarely changes the contents of registers or memory cells.

Note that modern development techniques of digital devices [2] differ significantly from the approaches used a few decades ago. As a result, the synthesis of the device is reduced to a correct description of the device behavior in some hardware description language (HDL) [3]. At the same time, the traditional stages of the FSM synthesis are eliminated: encoding of states; forming of logical (Boolean) equations for the combinational circuit Φ and Ψ; minimization, factorization and decomposition of the logic. All these stages are performed automatically by the synthesis tools. However, the redundant logic aimed at building a fault-tolerant FSM can be removed from the design as a result of automatic optimization performed by synthesis tools. Therefore, new approaches to the design of fault-tolerant FSM are needed. But before correcting the FSM failure by any method, the failure must be detected.

Since the model of the Moore FSM is most often used in engineering practice, the purpose of this paper is to present structural models for detecting faults of the Moore FSMs. The proposed structural models allow to detect multiple faults in various FSM elements and to prevent their negative impact on the controlled object.

The novelty of the proposed approach is as follows:

- the FSM faults are considered, which are the result of exposure by an EMP, and not radiation or cosmic rays;
- the number of faults is not limited for the state codes as well as for the input and output vectors;
- the faults can be detected not only in the state register R, but also in the input vector X, in the logic Φ of generating the next state code, in the logic Ψ of generating the output signals, as well as in the feedback circuit;
- the invalid transitions of FSMs and the transitions to invalid states are also detected;
- the proposed structural models not only detect FSM failures, but also prevent their negative impact on the controlled object;
- combined structural models allow simultaneously detect faults in all elements of the FSM;
- the proposed approach can be used to detect faults in both field programmable gate arrays (FPGAs) and application-specific integrated circuits (ASICs).

The objective of this work is to solve at the structural level the problem of detecting multiple faults, which can be caused by an EMP in various components of Moore FSMs.

The paper is organized as follows. In Sect. 2, related works on designing fault-tolerant FSMs are discussed. Section 3 describes an example of the Moore FSM, which is used to demonstrate the proposed approach. The structural models for detecting faults of Moore FSMs are represented in Sect. 4. Section 5 provides estimates of the area and performance of the proposed structural models. Section 6 shows and discusses experimental results. Conclusions and the direction of further research are presented in Sect. 7.

2 Related Works

The problem of fault-tolerant computing is as old as the first computers. However, much greater requirements to the FSM protection from cosmic rays were posed by the space program in the early 1960s. The traditional solution to the problem is a multiple duplication of the FSM architecture, with the triple modular redundancy (TMR) method being the most common for protection against SEU [4] (the area overhead is 220%). In general, the fault tolerance of a digital system can be provided by the architecture redundancy, the runtime increase, and the data redundancy [5].

A lot of research has been done to improving the TMR method. In [6], a single error correction (SEC) code is used to implement the FSM, which allows the SEU in the logic of the next state and in the state register (the area overhead is 233–274%). The traditional solution to the problem is a multiple duplication of the FSM architecture, with the triple modular redundancy (TMR) method being the most common for protection against SEU [4]. The work in [7] compares architectures of the fault-tolerant FSMs (TMR, SEU-ITRM, duplex, EEC, modified EEC, and IEC), which admit single errors when states are switched (the area overhead is 45–514%).

The use of FPGAs to design FSMs offers several advantages over ASICs: small size, low power consumption and low cost, short time to market, possibility of reprogramming, etc. However, FPGAs are more susceptible to SEUs caused by space particles than ASICs. For this reason, Xilinx has released the special FPGAs of the Virtex family, which support the TMR method at the hardware level [8] (the area overhead is 220%). The work in [9] proposes in systems on a chip (SoC), when a fault is detected in the FPGA, the FPGA generates an interrupt for the microcontroller, which triggers the procedure of partial reprogramming of the FPGA. The method for improvement the TMR approach, which combines duplication with comparison (DWC) and concurrent error detection (CED) based on the runtime redundancy, is proposed in [10] (the area overhead is 142–267%).

Separate works use methods of encoding states in the synthesis of fault-tolerant FSMs. The work in [11] considers four methods of the state encoding for fault-tolerant FSMs: binary, one-hot, Hamming with distance 2 (H2) and Hamming with distance 3 (H3); it compares the fault tolerance and the resource utilization (the area overhead is 11–43%). The methods of state encoding (binary, one-hot, and H3) to eliminate SEU in the state register are investigated in [12]; it is recommended to manually set the logic for recovery from an invalid state.

Many methods based on the state encoding have been developed to improve the TMR approach. The dual modular redundancy (DMR) method and the use of a parity bit in the FSM implementation in the embedded memory blocks of FPGAs were presented in [13] (the area overhead is 126%). The work in [14] evaluates two methods of the fault-tolerant FSM synthesis are evaluated: duplication with self-check and TMR. Here the following state coding methods are used: binary, one-hot and Gray (the area overhead is 277–488%). The method to improve the TMR is proposed in [15]; it uses Hamming code to implement the FSM in embedded FPGA memory blocks. The work in [16] improves the TMR method from Xilinx [8]. To do this, the system is represented as a set of FSMs, the control points are introduced to detect the faulty domain. When the fault is detected, only the faulty domain is restored and the rest of the system continues to work. As a result, the system recovery time after the failure is reduced (the area overhead is 284%).

Some methods propose to introduce additional states into the FSM. In [17], the redundant equivalent states are added into the FSM to protect the states with a high probability of the failure (the area overhead is 130–175%). The synthesis method for fault-tolerant FSMs based on single error correction and double error detection (SEC-DED) code is proposed in [18]; it involves returning the FSM to the known safe state or to the reset state (the area overhead is 400%).

Recently, the interest in the design of fault-tolerant FSMs has not weakened. In [19], three synthesis methods of fault-tolerant FSMs are investigated: TMR, H3 and safe synthesis. The work in [20] improves the fault tolerance of FSMs by selectively applying the TMR method according to the importance of the state (the area overhead is 400%). In [21], the quasi-delay-sensitive architecture of an FSM is compared to TMR (the area overhead is 80%).

This analysis shows that almost all methods of fault-tolerant FSM synthesis are aimed at improving the TMR method to correct the SEU in the state register. Most of the methods assume that the primary inputs, the logic of generating the next state code, logic of forming outputs, as well as additional logic for detecting and correcting errors do not have failures.

On the other hand, the different from traditional structural models of FSMs are very effective for improving performance, reducing area and power consumption in implementing FSMs on FPGAs [22]. This paper presents structural models of the Moore FSM for detecting multiple faults in various elements of the FSM and preventing their negative impact on the controlled object.

3   The Demonstration Example

As an example, consider the Moore FSM, the state transition graph (STG) of which is shown in Fig. 3. Our FSM has 5 states, 3 inputs, and 3 outputs. The vertices of the STG correspond to the states S_0, …, S_4, and the edges of the STG correspond to the transitions of the FSM. The input vector that initiates the transition is written near each edge of the STG. Near each vertex of the STG is written the output vector, which is formed in this state. Here the hyphen ("-") can take any bit value: 0 or 1.

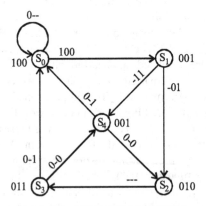

Fig. 3. The STG of the Moore FSM.

The valid transitions between states (Table 1) and the valid output vectors in each state (Table 2) can be determined directly from the STG of the FSM. The valid input vectors in each state are defined by the developer based on the behavior of the device. Let for our FSM the valid input vectors in each state are defined by the Table 3.

Table 1. The valid transitions of the FSM.

Present state	Next state
S0	S_0 S_1
S1	S_2 S_4
S2	S3
S_3	S_0 S_4
S_4	S_0 S_2

Table 2. The valid output vectors of the FSM in each state.

State	Output vector
S0	100
S_1	001
S_2	010
S_3	011
S_4	001

Table 3. The valid input vectors of the FSM in each state.

State	Input vectors
S0	—
S_1	001 101 011 111
S_2	—
S_3	000 010 001 011
S_4	000 010 001 011

4 Proposed Structural Models of the Moore FSMs

Structural models of FSMs for fault detection and prevention of negative impacts of faults on the controlled object are shown in Fig. 4.

The structure in Fig. 4a allows to detect the invalid input vector X for the whole FSM. For this purpose the combinational circuit TVI (total valid inputs) is added to the traditional FSM structure in Fig. 1. The input vector X arrives on the input of the combinational circuit TVI, and the signal tvi is formed on the output of the combinational circuit TVI. The signal tvi = 1 if input vector X is valid, otherwise tvi = 0. The signal tvi controls the input CE (clock enable) of the state register R. The invalid input vectors for the entire FSM are determined by the developer based on the behavior of the controlled object. Let 110 and 111 be the invalid input vectors for our example. If the invalid input vector is detected, the FSM will remain in the present state until the fault is eliminated.

The structure in Fig. 4b allows to detect an invalid input vector for a particular state. For this purpose the combinational circuit VI (valid inputs) is added to the traditional FSM structure. The input of the combinational scheme VI receives the code *state* of the present state as well as the input vector X. For our example the functioning of the combinational circuit VI is defined in Table 3. The output of the combinational circuit VI is the signal vi, which controls the input CE of the state register R. If the input vector is valid in the present state, the signal vi = 1, otherwise vi = 0. If the invalid input vector is detected in some state (vi = 0), the FSM will remain in the present state until the fault is eliminated.

The structure in Fig. 4c allows to detect the invalid code *state* of the FSM present state. For this purpose the combinational circuit VS (valid states) and the output register R_O are added to the traditional structure of the FSM. The input of the combinational circuit VS is the code *state*, and the output of the combinational circuit VS is the signal vs. If the code of the present state of the FSM is valid, then vs = 1, otherwise vs = 0. The signal vs controls the inputs CE of the registers R and R_O. For our example, the valid codes are the codes of the states S_0, ..., S_4. If the invalid present state code is detected, the output signals generated by logic Ψ do not go to the external outputs of the FSM and the FSM remains in the present state until the fault is eliminated.

The structure in Fig. 4d allows to detect the invalid code *next* of the FSM next state. For this purpose, the combinational circuit VNS (valid next states) is added to the traditional FSM structure. The input of the combinational circuit VNS is the next state code *next* generated by the logic Φ. The output of combinational circuit VNS is the signal vns. The signal vns = 1 if the next states code is valid, and vns = 0 otherwise. The signal vns controls the input CE of the state register R. For our example, the valid codes are the codes of the states S_0, ..., S_4. If an invalid next state code is detected, the FSM will remain in the present state until the fault is eliminated.

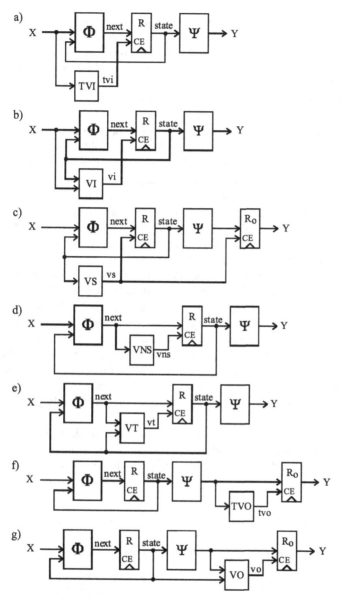

Fig. 4. The structural models of Moore FSMs for detecting: a – valid input vectors for the whole FSM (the structure TVI); b – valid input vectors in each state (the structure VI); c – a valid code of a present state (the structure VS); d – a valid code of a next state (the structure VNS); e – valid transitions between states (the structure VT); f – valid output vectors for the whole FSM (the structure TVO); g – valid output vectors in each state (the structure VO).

The structure in Fig. 4e allows to detect invalid FSM transitions. For this purpose the combinational circuit VT (valid transitions) is added to the traditional FSM structure

(Fig. 1). The input of the combinational circuit VT receives the code *state* of the present state, which is stored in the register R, and the code *next* of the next state, which is generated by the logic Φ. For our example, the functioning of the combinational circuit VT is defined in Table 1. The output of the combinational circuit VT is the signal vt, which controls the input CE of the state register R. If the transition is valid, the signal vt = 1, otherwise vt = 0. If an invalid transition is detected (vt = 0) the FSM remains in the present state until the fault is corrected.

The structure in Fig. 4f allows to detect the invalid output vector for the whole FSM. For this purpose the combinational circuit TVO (total void outputs) is added to the traditional FSM structure. The inputs of the combinational circuit TVO are the signals generated by the logic Ψ, and the output of the combinational circuit TVO is the signal tvo. The signal tvo = 1 if the generated output vector is valid, and tvo = 0 otherwise. The signal tvo controls the input CE of the output register R_O. For our example the valid output vectors are the output vectors generated in the states of the FSM: 100, 001, 010, 011, and 001. If the invalid output vector is detected, the register R_O will retain its previous value until the fault is corrected.

The structure in Fig. 4g allows to detect the invalid output vector in each state. For this purpose the combinational circuit VO (valid outputs) is added to the structure in Fig. 1, as well as the output register R_O. The input of the combinational circuit VO receives the code *state* of the present state and the values of outputs generated by logic Ψ. For our example the functioning of the combinational circuit VO is defined in Table 2. The output of the combinational circuit VO is the signal vo, which controls the input CE of the registers R and R_O. If the output vector is valid, the signal vo = 1, otherwise vo = 0. If an invalid output vector is detected (vo = 0) the invalid output vector does not go to the external outputs of the FSM and the FSM will remain in the present state until the fault is eliminated.

Table 4 summarizes the possible causes of faults that are detected by the structural models in Fig. 4, where Φ is a failure in the logic Φ; X is the invalid input vector; *feedback* is a failure in the feedback circuit; Ψ is a failure in the logic Ψ; R is a failure in the state register R.

Table 4. Possible causes of the faults detected by the FSM structural models.

Causes of failure	TVI	VI	VS	VNS	VT	TVO	VO
X	*	*		¤	¤		
Φ				*	*		
R		*	*	¤	*	¤	*
feedback		*	*	¤	*		*
Ψ						*	*
transition					*		

*–The fault that is detected directly.
¤–The fault that is detected indirectly.

Note that one structure can detect several faults at once. So, some faults are detected by the structure directly, i.e. the invalid value directly arrives to the input of the combinational circuit, while other faults are detected by the structure indirectly, when the wrong value does not arrive directly to the input of the additional combinational circuit. For example, the structure VNS directly detects a fault in the logic Φ of the next state code formation. But the fault can be caused by failures in the input vector X, in the state register R, and in the feedback circuit whose values arrive at the input of the combinational circuit Φ. Therefore, the fault detection does not always indicate the specific element of the FSM, in which the failure occurred.

All the FSM structural models considered are not targeted for implementation on a particular electronic component: each structural model can be implemented on both ASICs and FPGAs.

The structures in Fig. 4 can be arbitrarily combined together at will for the most efficient FSM fault detection. Note that the structure TVI is covered by the structure VI, i.e., if an FSM fault is detected using the TVI structure, that fault will necessarily be detected by the VI structure. Similarly, the structure TVO is covered by the structure VO, and the structures VNS and VS are covered by the structure VT.

Figure 5 shows the generalized structure VI_VT_VO that combines the structures VI, VT and VO.

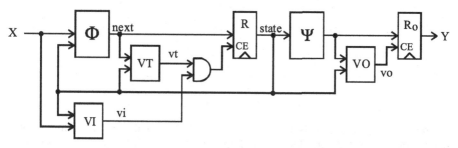

Fig. 5. The generalized structure VI_VT_VO for detecting failures of the Moore FSM.

The diagnostic signals tvi, vi, vs, vns, vt, tvo, and vo generated in the FSM structural models in Fig. 4, can be output to external FSM pins to detect the location of a fault in the ASIC. If necessary, the diagnostic signals can be combined together by an NAND gate to indicate an error, for example to reconfigure the FPGA.

5 Evaluation of the Area and Performance of the Proposed Structural Models

In the case of FSM implementation in FPGA based on LUT (look-up table), the area of the additional combinational circuit can be determined using the following expression:

$$C = \left\{ \begin{array}{l} 1 \ when \ r \leq n, \\ ]\frac{r-n}{n-1}[\ + 1 \ when \ r > n \end{array} \right\}, \tag{1}$$

where n is the number of LUT inputs; r is the rank (number of inputs) of the additional combinational circuit; $]A[$ is the smallest integer greater or equal to the number A.

For the considered structural models, the ranks of the additional combinational circuits are given in Table 5, where i is the number of FSM inputs, o is the number of FSM outputs, and k is the number of FSM state code bits. Note that the ranks of the additional combinational circuits depend on the number k of the FSM state code bits, i.e., on the method of encoding states. For example, the area of the proposed FSM structural models will be different in the case of using one-hot and binary coding.

In the case of FSM implementation on LUT-based FPGAs, the performance of the additional combinational circuits can be estimated by the number of LUT levels required for their implementation [23].

Table 5. The ranks of the additional combinational circuits.

Combinational circuits	Ranks
TVI	$r = i$
VI	$r = i + k$
VS	$r = k$
VNS	$r = k$
VT	$r = 2k$
TVO	$r = o$
VO	$r = o + k$
VI_VT_VO	$r = i + o + 4k$

The number of LUT levels depends on the method of combinational circuit decomposition, which is used in the design tool. For example, in case of sequential decomposition the number l_s of LUT levels is determined by expression (2), and in case of parallel decomposition the number l_p of LUT levels is determined by expression (3):

$$l_s = \left\{ \begin{array}{l} 1 \ when \ r \leq n, \\ ]\frac{r-n}{n-1}[+ 1 when r > n \end{array} \right\}, \tag{2}$$

$$l_p =]\log_n r[. \tag{3}$$

Note that the area C of an additional combinational circuit (1) and the number l_s of LUT levels in the case of sequential decomposition (2) are determined by the same expression. Therefore, in the case of using a sequential decomposition of combinational circuits by a design tool, an optimization by area is simultaneously an optimization by performance and vice versa.

6 Experimental Results

All the considered structural models of the FSM for our example were described in the Verilog HDL and implemented in the Cyclone 10 LP FPGA family using the Quartus Prime design tool version 22.1 from Intel. The experimental results in case one-hot and binary state encoding are shown in Table 6, where L is the number of used LUTs or area, F is the maximum operating frequency (in MHz) or performance, L_b and F_b are similar parameters for the basic structural model (Fig. 1), and L/L_b and F/F_b are relations of corresponding parameters.

Table 6 shows that in the case of using one-hot encoding, the structures VS, VNS, TVO, and VO do not increase the area of the base structure. The area overhead for the TVI structure is 9%, for the VI structure is 36%, for the VT structures is 73%, and for the VI_VT_VO structure is 109%. Note that the area overhead increases significantly for the combinatorial circuits VI and VT. This is because these combinational circuits detect more complex faults, for example, the structure VI detects invalid input vectors in each state, and the structure VT detects an invalid present state code, an invalid next state code, as well as invalid transitions between states.

Table 6. Results of experimental studies of the structural models for the FSM from our example.

FSM	i	o	s	Cb	VS, VNS		TVO		VO		VT		VI		TVI	
					C	C/Cb	C	C/Cb	C	C/Cb	C	C/Cb	C	C/Cb	C	C/Cb
bbase	7	7	24	44	53	1.20	46	1.05	54	1.23	60	1.36	54	1.23	46	1.05
cse	7	7	29	103	112	1.09	105	1.02	115	1.12	122	1.18	115	1.12	105	1.02
ex1	9	19	78	256	280	1.09	262	1.02	288	1.13	308	1.20	285	1.11	259	1.01
ex2	2	2	23	47	55	1.17	48	1.02	55	1.17	62	1.32	55	1.17	48	1.02
ex3	2	2	13	31	34	1.10	32	1.03	36	1.16	40	1.29	36	1.16	32	1.03
ex5	2	2	16	30	35	1.17	31	1.03	36	1.20	41	1.37	36	1.20	31	1.03
ex6	5	8	14	59	63	1.08	62	1.05	65	1.10	68	1.15	65	1.10	61	1.03
ex7	2	2	14	30	34	1.13	31	1.03	35	1.17	39	1.30	35	1.17	31	1.03
keyb	7	2	20	66	72	1.09	67	1.02	73	1.11	79	1.20	75	1.14	68	1.03
planet	7	19	95	173	210	1.21	179	1.03	211	1.22	236	1.36	207	1.20	175	1.01
pma	8	8	49	153	168	1.10	156	1.02	172	1.12	186	1.22	172	1.12	156	1.02
s386	7	7	23	50	57	1.14	52	1.04	60	1.20	65	1.30	60	1.20	52	1.04
sand	11	9	84	213	237	1.11	215	1.01	244	1.15	269	1.26	245	1.15	217	1.02
styr	9	10	57	165	181	1.10	168	1.02	187	1.13	203	1.23	187	1.13	168	1.02
tma	7	6	38	118	129	1.09	120	1.02	133	1.13	143	1.21	133	1.13	120	1.02
mid						1.12		1.03		1.16		1.26		1.16		1.03

Conclusion: in the case of one-hot coding and if detecting invalid transitions between states is not required, the structures VS and VNS can be used instead of the structure VT for area optimization.

In the case of one-hot coding, the structure TVI slightly reduces performance (by 8%), while the structure VI increases performance (by 10%) of the basic structure.

Unexpectedly, the structures VS, TVO, and VO significantly increase the performance of the FSM (from 28% to 36%). This is explained by the addition of the output register R_O into the basic structure, which, despite the delay of the output signals by one clock cycle, increases the clocking frequency of the FSM. The structure VT reduces the performance of the basic structure by 35%. This is due to the complexity of the combinational circuitry VT. The combined structure VI_VT_VO also reduces the performance of the FSM by 35%.

Conclusion: to prevent a significant decrease in performance, when one-hot encoding is used and detecting of invalid FSM transitions is not required, the structures VS and VNS should be used instead of the structure VT.

In the case of binary coding, the structures TVI, VNS, and VT do not increase the area, and the structures VS, TVO, and VO even decrease the area of the base structure. This is explained by the effectiveness of the synthesis methods of the design tool. For our example, the area of the base structure increases only when using structure VI (by 20%). The area overhead for the combined structure VI_VT_VO is 10%, These results are expected. Note that the VT structure in the case of binary encoding does not increase the area.

Conclusion: if it is necessary to detect invalid transitions of the FSM (using the VT structure), binary encoding should be used to save area.

In the case of binary encoding, the performance of all structures either coincides (structures VNS and VT), or exceeds the performance of the basic structure. The greatest increase in performance is observed for structures VS, TVO, and VO (from 35% to 37%), which contain the output register R_O. The performance of the combined structures VI_VT_VO exceeds the performance of the base structure by 36%.

Conclusion: the use of binary coding contributes to increasing the performance of the proposed structural models of the FSM.

General conclusion: if it is necessary to detect invalid transitions of the FSM, binary encoding should be used, if detection of invalid transitions is not required, then any method to encode the FSM states can be used.

The consideration of one example of the Moore FSM does not allow to fully evaluate the proposed structural models, for this reason the structural models have been investigated using FSM benchmarks from MCNC [24]. The results of such studies are shown in Table 7 for one-hot encoding, where i is the number of the FSM inputs; o is the number of the FSM outputs; s is the number of the FSM states; C_b is the area (number of LUT) of the basic FSM structure; C is the FSM area in case using one of proposed structural models; C_b/C is the ratio of corresponding parameters; mid is the arithmetic mean value. The benchmark examples of Mealy FSMs were previously reduced to Moore FSMs using the method of [25].

Table 7 shows that structures TVO and TVI are the least costly by area (area increases on average 3%). The structure TVI defines invalid input vectors for the whole FSM, which may not exist at all, since most FSMs have no constraints on input vectors. There can also be few or no invalid output vectors for the whole FSM, which the structure TVO detects. The structures VS and VNS are next in terms the area overheads (area increases on average 12%), then follow the structures VO and VT (area increases on average 16%), and the most area-consuming structure is VT (area increases on average 26%).

Table 7. Comparison of the area (in number of LUTs) of the basic FSM structure with the proposed structural models.

FSM	i	o	s	Cb	VS, VNS		TVO		VO		VT		VI		TVI	
					C	C/Cb	C	C/Cb	C	C/Cb	C	C/Cb	C	C/Cb	C	C/Cb
bbase	7	7	24	44	53	1.20	46	1.05	54	1.23	60	1.36	54	1.23	46	1.05
cse	7	7	29	103	112	1.09	105	1.02	115	1.12	122	1.18	115	1.12	105	1.02
ex1	9	19	78	256	280	1.09	262	1.02	288	1.13	308	1.20	285	1.11	259	1.01
ex2	2	2	23	47	55	1.17	48	1.02	55	1.17	62	1.32	55	1.17	48	1.02
ex3	2	2	13	31	34	1.10	32	1.03	36	1.16	40	1.29	36	1.16	32	1.03
ex5	2	2	16	30	35	1.17	31	1.03	36	1.20	41	1.37	36	1.20	31	1.03
ex6	5	8	14	59	63	1.08	62	1.05	65	1.10	68	1.15	65	1.10	61	1.03
ex7	2	2	14	30	34	1.13	31	1.03	35	1.17	39	1.30	35	1.17	31	1.03
keyb	7	2	20	66	72	1.09	67	1.02	73	1.11	79	1.20	75	1.14	68	1.03
planet	7	19	95	173	210	1.21	179	1.03	211	1.22	236	1.36	207	1.20	175	1.01
pma	8	8	49	153	168	1.10	156	1.02	172	1.12	186	1.22	172	1.12	156	1.02
s386	7	7	23	50	57	1.14	52	1.04	60	1.20	65	1.30	60	1.20	52	1.04
sand	11	9	84	213	237	1.11	215	1.01	244	1.15	269	1.26	245	1.15	217	1.02
styr	9	10	57	165	181	1.10	168	1.02	187	1.13	203	1.23	187	1.13	168	1.02
tma	7	6	38	118	129	1.09	120	1.02	133	1.13	143	1.21	133	1.13	120	1.02
mid						1.12		1.03		1.16		1.26		1.16		1.03

Note that for the structures VS and VNS, the implementation area is the same.

7 Conclusions

This paper provides novel structural models of the Moore FSM, which allow detecting multiple faults in the input vector, in the logic of forming the next state code, in the logic of forming the values of output signals, in the state register, as well as invalid transitions of the FSM. The presented structural models also prevent the negative impact of faults on the controlled object. Moreover, the estimates of the area and performance of the structural models are given. The guidelines for using considered structural models in order to optimize the area and performance of the FSM are proposed. The experimental results for the benchmark examples showed that the area overhead for the proposed structural models is from 3 to 26%, which is significantly less than that of the known approaches (see Sect. 2).

Future research will focus on developing a methodology for detecting faulty elements of the FSM, as well as developing structural models that correct the FSM faults.

Acknowledgements. The present study was supported by a grant WZ/WI-III/5/2023 from Bialystok University of Technology and founded from the resources for research by Ministry of Science and Higher Education.

References

1. Park, S., Kim, H.T., Lee, S., Joo, H., Kim, H.: Survey on anti-drone systems: components, designs, and challenges. IEEE Access **9**, 42635–42659 (2021)
2. Solov'ev, V.V.: ASMD–FSMD technique in designing signal processing devices on field programmable gate arrays. J. Commun. Technol. Electron. **66**(12), 1336–1345 (2021)
3. Salauyou, V., Zabrocki, Ł.: Coding techniques in verilog for finite state machine designs in FPGA. In: Saeed, K., Chaki, R., Janev, V. (eds.) CISIM 2019. LNCS, vol. 11703, pp. 493–505. Springer, Cham (2019). https://doi.org/10.1007/978-3-030-28957-7_41
4. Lyons, R.E., Vanderkulk, W.: The use of triple-modular redundancy to improve computer reliability. IBM J. Res. Dev. **6**(2), 200–209 (1962)
5. Aviziens, A.: Fault-tolerant systems. IEEE Trans. Comput. **100**(12), 1304–1312 (1976)
6. Rochet, R., Leveugle, R., Saucier, G.: Analysis and comparison of fault tolerant FSM architecture based on SEC codes. In: Proceedings of 1993 IEEE International Workshop on Defect and Fault Tolerance in VLSI Systems, Venice, Italy, pp. 9–16. IEEE (1993)
7. Niranjan, S., Frenzel, J.F.: A comparison of fault-tolerant state machine architectures for space-borne electronics. IEEE Trans. Reliab. **45**(1), 109–113 (1996)
8. Carmichael, C.: Triple module redundancy design techniques for Virtex FPGAs. Xilinx Application Note XAPP197, 1 (2001)
9. Pontarelli, S., Cardarilli, G.C., Malvoni, A., Ottavi, M., Re, M., Salsano, A.: System-on-chip oriented fault-tolerant sequential systems implementation methodology. In: Proceedings 2001 IEEE International Symposium on Defect and Fault Tolerance in VLSI Systems, San Francisco, USA, pp. 455–460. IEEE (2001)
10. Lima, F., Carro, L., Reis, R.: Designing fault tolerant systems into SRAM-based FPGAs. In: Proceedings of the 40th Annual Design Automation Conference, Anaheim, USA, pp. 650–655. Machinery (2003)
11. Burke, G.R., Taft, S.: Fault tolerant state machines. – nasa.gov (2004)
12. Berg, M.: A simplified approach to fault tolerant state machine design for single event upsets. In: Mentor Graphics Users' Group User2User Conference (2004)
13. Tiwari, A., Tomko, K.A.: Enhanced reliability of finite-state machines in FPGA through efficient fault detection and correction. IEEE Trans. Reliab. **54**(3), 459–467 (2005)
14. Cassel, M., Lima, F.: Evaluating one-hot encoding finite state machines for SEU reliability in SRAM-based FPGAs. In 12th IEEE International On-Line Testing Symposium (IOLTS 2006), Lake Como, Italia, 6p. IEEE (2006)
15. Frigerio, L., Salice, F.: RAM-based fault tolerant state machines for FPGAs. In: 22nd IEEE International Symposium on Defect and Fault-Tolerance in VLSI Systems (DFT 2007), Rome, Italy, pp. 312–320. IEEE (2007)
16. Azambuja, J.R., Sousa, F., Rosa, L., Kastensmidt, F.L.: Evaluating large grain TMR and selective partial reconfiguration for soft error mitigation in SRAM-based FPGAs. In: 2009 15th IEEE International On-Line Testing Symposium, Lisbon, Portugal, pp. 101–106. IEEE (2009)
17. El-Maleh, A.H., Al-Qahtani, A.S.: A finite state machine based fault tolerance technique for sequential circuits. Microelectron. Reliab. **54**(3), 654–661 (2014)
18. Sooraj, S., Manasy, M., Bhakthavatchalu, R.: Fault tolerant FSM on FPGA using SEC-DED code algorithm. In: 2017 International Conference on Technological Advancements in Power and Energy (TAP Energy), Kollam, India, pp. 1–6. IEEE (2017)
19. Nidhin, T.S., Bhattacharyya, A., Behera, R.P., Jayanthi, T., Velusamy, K.: Verification of fault tolerant techniques in finite state machines using simulation based fault injection targeted at FPGAs for SEU mitigation. In: 2017 4th International Conference on Electronics and Communication Systems (ICECS), Coimbatore, India, pp. 153–157. IEEE (2017)

20. Choi, S., Park, J., Yoo, H.: Area-efficient fault tolerant design for finite state machines. In: 2020 International Conference on Electronics, Information, and Communication (ICEIC), Barcelona, Spain, pp. 1–2. IEEE (2020)
21. Verducci, O., Oliveira, D.L., Batista, G.: Fault-tolerant finite state machine quasi delay insensitive in commercial FPGA devices. In: 2022 IEEE 13th Latin America Symposium on Circuits and System (LASCAS), Santiago, Chile, pp. 1–4. IEEE (2022)
22. Klimowicz, A. S., Solov'ev, V.V.: Structural models of finite-state machines for their implementation on programmable logic devices and systems on chip. J. Comput. Syst. Sci. Int. **54**(2), 230–242 (2015)
23. Solov'ev V.V.: Synthesis of fast finite state machines on programmable logic integrated circuits by splitting internal states. J. Comput. Syst. Sci. Int. **61**(3), 358–369 (2022)
24. Yang, S.: Logic synthesis and optimization benchmarks user guide: version 3.0. Research Triangle Park, NC, USA: Microelectronics Center of North Carolina (MCNC), pp. 502–508 (1991)
25. Klimovich, A.S., Solov'ev V.V.: Transformation of a mealy finite-state machine into a Moore finite-state machine by splitting internal states. J. Comput. Syst. Sci. Int. **49**(6) 900–908 (2010)

Investigation of Subjective Impression Perceived from Agent that Expresses Multiple Opinions Simultaneously

Rin Takenowaki and Jun-ichi Imai[✉][iD]

Chiba Institute of Technology, 2–17–1 Tsudanuma,
Narashino-shi, Chiba 275–0016, Japan
imai@cs.it-chiba.ac.jp

Abstract. A personified agent is often evaluated based not only on its convenience but also on a subjective impression of it. If an interaction between the agent and users is interrupted due to a feeling of resistance, it will lose an opportunity to demonstrate its performance. Therefore, improving users' impression of the agent is essential for promoting continuous interaction between the agent and the users and, consequently, for demonstrating the agent's original performance. We aim to realize that by imitating humans' perceptible behaviors to lead them to imagine the agent's inner state. In this paper, as one of such perceptible behaviors, we focus on humans' styles of expressing their opinions to others. Humans often express several opinions at one time, especially before making a decision. Such behavior can be interpreted as a sign of hesitation in making a decision and is expected to work as clues to lead people to imagine the person's mind. In this paper, we investigate the effects of the implemented styles of expressing multiple opinions simultaneously, based on the theory of motivational conflicts, on the impression through an evaluation experiment. Experimental results show that a part of the implemented styles improves the impression of the agent.

Keywords: Human-agent interaction · Subjective impression · Simultaneous expression of multiple opinions · Motivational conflict

1 Introduction

We sometimes regard artifacts as autonomous entities with their own intentions just like humans. For example, when something has gone wrong with computers or machines, we often feel as if they are in a bad mood and ask them to regain their good mood. We unconsciously perceive a feeling of human-likeness from an object due to its behavior or factors in its surroundings, even though we know well that it is just an artifact. Interaction with the object is supposed to affect perceiving its own intention or animacy from it [1,2]. Therefore, it is considered that a personified agent in the human-agent interaction (HAI), which aims to interact with humans actively, is more likely to be perceived as a subject than other kinds of artifacts.

The agent is often evaluated based not only on its convenience but also on a subjective impression of it. Depending on the situation, users prefer human-like behaviors to rational but inorganic behaviors pursuing only the best results. For example, several previous studies have shown that the agent that does not necessarily provides the best information for users tends to be highly evaluated under particular situations [3–5]. The well-designed impression of the agent, such as human-likeness, is expected to reduce users' feelings of resistance to interacting and improve their affinity for it. No matter how excellent the agent's performance is, if an interaction between the agent and users is interrupted due to the feeling of resistance, it will lose an opportunity to demonstrate its performance. Therefore, knowledge of means to improve users' impression of the agent is essential for promoting continuous interaction between the agent and the users and, consequently, for demonstrating the agent's original performance. This importance is further increasing along with the widespread of agent technology in our daily life.

Although an ideal mean to give human-likeness to the agent is to precisely simulate a pseudo-mental activity like us humans as its inner state, of course, this is very difficult. Instead, we aim to realize that by a more straightforward method, namely imitating humans' perceptible behaviors to lead them to imagine the agent's inner mental activity.

In this paper, as one of such perceptible behaviors, we focus on humans' styles of expressing their opinions to others. When a conventional agent recommends something to a user during a conversation, it usually expresses only one opinion, which is judged to be the most appropriate among several candidates. On the other hand, humans often express several opinions at one time, especially before making a decision. These expressed opinions are sometimes even contradictory to each other. Such a behavior can be interpreted as a sign of hesitation in making a decision and is expected to work as clues to lead people to imagine the person's mind. In this paper, we implement these styles of simultaneous expression of multiple opinions into the agent, based on the theory of motivational conflicts defined by Lewin [6]. These behaviors are expected to lead users to imagine the agent's inner mental activity and affect their subjective impression. In this paper, we adopt scores of Godspeed Questionnaire Series (GQS) [7] as metrics to quantify the impression perceived from the agent. We investigate the effects of the implemented styles of expressing multiple opinions simultaneously on the impression through an evaluation experiment to obtain new knowledge concerning a policy on the design of the agents.

2   Godspeed Questionnaire Series

As mentioned in Sect. 1, we adopt scores of the Godspeed Questionnaire Series (GQS) proposed by Bartneck et al. [7] as metrics to quantify the impressions perceived from personified agents. It is said that the GQS is one of the most

Table 1. Godspeed Questionnaire Series

	Adjective Pairs		Factors
Q1	Fake	– Natural	Anthropomorphism
Q2	Machinelike	– Humanlike	
Q3	Unconscious	– Conscious	
Q4	Artificial	– Lifelike	
Q5	Moving Rigidly	– Moving Elegantly	
Q6	Dead	– Alive	Animacy
Q7	Stagnant	– Lively	
Q8	Mechanical	– Organic	
Q9	Artificial	– Lifelike	
Q10	Inert	– Interactive	
Q11	Apathetic	– Responsive	
Q12	Dislike	– Like	Likability
Q13	Unfriendly	– Friendly	
Q14	Unkind	– Kind	
Q15	Unpleasant	– Pleasant	
Q16	Awful	– Nice	
Q17	Incompetent	– Competent	Perceived Intelligence
Q18	Ignorant	– Knowledgeable	
Q19	Irresponsible	– Responsible	
Q20	Unintelligent	– Intelligent	
Q21	Foolish	– Sensible	
Q22	Anxious	– Relaxed	Perceived Safety
Q23	Agitated	– Calm	
Q24	Quiescent	– Surprised	

frequently used questionnaires in the field of human-robot interaction (HRI) [8]. Although the GQS was originally designed to evaluate the HRI, Nomura explains that it can also be applied to the evaluation not only of robots but also of personified agents in the field of HAI without any problems [9].

Table 1 shows the contents of the GQS in detail. It consists of twenty-four question items corresponding to one of five factors (anthropomorphism, animacy, likability, perceived intelligence, and perceived safety). Each question is in the style of a semantic differential scale and asks a respondent to rate their impression of an object on a 5-point scale between the adjective pairs with opposite meanings to each other. A larger score means that the impression described by the positive adjective is stronger, and a smaller score means the opposite. (Only Q22–Q24 ask them to rate their emotional state.) All answers will be summarized into the five factors by calculating the average score among all the related questions. We investigate the effects of the expression styles mainly based on the scores of these five factors.

3 Styles of Expressing Multiple Opinions Simultaneously

In this paper, we focus on styles of expressing multiple opinions simultaneously instead of only one (the best) opinion.

When the agent gives multiple opinions at one time, how to express them will become a problem. In the scene where the agent assists a user's decision-making, expressed opinions correspond with the agent's advice to the user. Simply repeating two single opinions, such as "A is good, B is good," results in emphasizing a contradiction between them and making the agent's advice unnatural. To avoid this problem, in this paper, we focus on the theory of motivational conflicts. The motivational conflict is a situation in which there are two or more options based on conflicting motives, and choosing one is not easy. The agent in this paper expresses multiple opinions simultaneously based on this concept of motivational conflicts. By modeling the perceptible style of expressing opinions based on the psychological theory, it is expected that the agent reduces its unnaturalness, leads users to try to imagine its inner state, and thereby makes them perceive a "better" impression such as more human-likeness from it.

Lewin described that motivational conflicts could be classified into the following three types [6].

Approach-Approach Conflict: This is a conflict state within a person where they need to choose one of two equally desirable options. For example, we suppose that a person cannot decide between ice cream and cake for dessert at dinner. In this case, they are in the approach-approach conflict.

Avoidance-Avoidance Conflict: This is a conflict state within a person where they need to choose one of two equally undesirable options. For example, we suppose that a person needs to pass an examination. To pass the examination, they have to study very hard. However, they do not feel like studying at all. In this case, they are in the avoidance-avoidance conflict.

Approach-Avoidance Conflict: This is a conflict state within a person where they need to do something with both desirable and undesirable motives. For example, we suppose that a person wants to watch the sunrise at the top of a mountain but hesitates to set off because being afraid to get hurt on the way. In this case, they are in the approach-avoidance conflict.

In this paper, based on the types of motivational conflict described above, we let the agent express two opinions simultaneously according to one of the following three styles. In each style, the agent states an option to be chosen or avoided after a reason to do so. The second opinion begins with an adversative conjunction or phrase such as "however" or "on the other hand" to make it contextually natural. This paper assumes that the agent's opinions are shown in the text format.

Approach-Approach Expression: In this style, the agent simultaneously expresses two opinions based on motives in the approach-approach conflict. Since the agent evaluates both options as desirable, it recommends taking two different actions simultaneously.

[Example] *"I recommend a cup of ice cream for dessert because you can enjoy many flavors. On the other hand, I also recommend a piece of cake because you can try a muscat flavor for a limited time."*

Avoidance-Avoidance Expression: In this style, the agent simultaneously expresses two opinions based on motives in the avoidance-avoidance conflict. Since the agent evaluates both options as undesirable, it recommends avoiding both two different actions simultaneously.

[Example] *"I don't recommend choosing ice cream because it cools your body too much. However, I also don't recommend choosing cake because it is too high in calories."*

Approach-Avoidance Expression: In this style, the agent simultaneously expresses two opinions based on motives in the approach-avoidance conflict. The agent expresses both positive and negative opinions at one time. That is, it recommends taking action from one viewpoint, and simultaneously it recommends avoiding the same action from the other.

[Example] *"I recommend choosing a cup of ice cream because it's cold and delicious. However, I don't recommend choosing it because your teeth may be sensitive when you eat it."*

From the viewpoint of the agent's performance, introducing these expression styles will not necessarily improve it. In the worst case, they can even reduce it. Since the agent actually does not choose one of two opinions, the simultaneous expression of two opinions will not make any recommendations to the user. It merely provides information from different viewpoints to help the user's decision-making.

4   Experiment

In this section, we carry out an experiment to investigate the effects of the agent's simultaneous expression of multiple opinions on users' impressions.

4.1   Hypotheses

We expect that the simultaneous expression of multiple opinions implemented in this paper leads a user to imagine the agent's inner state and thereby makes them perceive a "better" impression, such as more human-likeness, from it. We therefore formulated the following two hypotheses and carried out an experiment to verify them.

Hypothesis 1: The agent expressing two opinions simultaneously gives users a better impression than the conventional agent expressing only one.

Hypothesis 2: The agent expressing two opinions simultaneously gives users a feeling of easy-to-use than the conventional agent expressing only one.

4.2 Method

Experimental Task. This paper employs a "gem mining game" as an experimental task. Figure 1 shows an example screenshot.

In this game, a participant is asked to collect gems while traveling in a cave on a minecart. There are twenty forks into two paths in the cave, and the participant proceeds while repeating to choose one of two paths. And an agent, which knows the structure of the cave well in advance, plays a role in advising the participant on which path to choose. Figure 2 shows the structure of the cave.

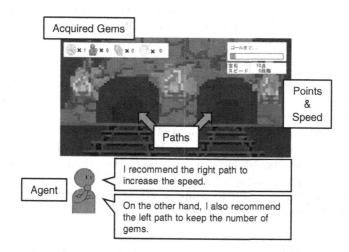

Fig. 1. Screenshot of "Gem Mining Game"

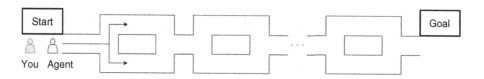

Fig. 2. Structure of Cave

This game has two criteria to be met, and the participant aims to exceed both. The first criterion is a score of acquired gems. In this game, four kinds of gems with different points will appear (diamond: 10 pts., ruby: 5 pts., silver: 3 pts., glass ball: 1 pt.). The participants can acquire new gems on the path in the cave and may also drop the ones already acquired. Points are converted according to the number of gems when they reach the goal. The second criterion is the speed of the minecart at the goal point. The speed of the minecart is set to the 0th level at the beginning of the game, and it may increase or decrease depending on the path chosen at each fork. It is required that the speed of the minecart exceeds a certain level when it reaches the goal.

There are the following two patterns of forks in the cave.

Fork Pattern 1 (Speed or Gems): If the participant chooses one of the forked paths, the speed of the minecart increases by n levels, but they drop n from already acquired gems at that point. If they choose the opposite path, the speed of the minecart remains the same or decreases by n levels.

Fork Pattern 2 (Quality or Quantity of Gems): If the participant chooses one of the forked paths, they get new n gems with higher points than those they would have gotten in the other path. If they choose the opposite path, they get $n + 1$ or more gems with lower points than those they would have gotten in the other path. The total score of gems is set so that the former is higher.

Both paths will bring both an advantage from one viewpoint and a disadvantage from another viewpoint for the participant. Therefore, it cannot be decided which path is better sweepingly.

The participant is not given any clues as to know the consequences of choosing each path except for the advice provided by the agent. The agent's advice suggests to the participant which path to choose, but the participant does not have to obey it. The participant repeats the choice of paths at the forks 20 times. The goal is to get both the gems' scores and the minecart's speed above the predefined levels at the end of the game.

Experimental Conditions. In this experiment, we set four conditions regarding the agents. The first one is the conventional agent that expresses only one opinion at one time. The remaining three conditions correspond with the agents that express multiple opinions simultaneously.

Single Expression (SGL) Condition: In this condition, the agent expresses only an opinion motivated by changes either in the number of gems or in speed levels. The expressed opinion recommends the choice of only one of two paths based on the following basic format:

"Because of (motive), I recommend choosing this path."

Approach-Approach Expression (App-App) Condition: In this condition, the agent simultaneously expresses two opinions, motivated by changes both in the number of gems and in speed levels (or by changes both in quality and quantity of gems), based on the style of the approach-approach expression. One of two opinions recommends choosing one path, and another recommends choosing another path, based on the following basic format:

"Because of (motive #1), I recommend choosing this path. However, because of (motive #2), I recommend choosing this (the opposite) path."

Avoidance-Avoidance Expression (Avo-Avo) Condition: In this condition, the agent simultaneously expresses two opinions, motivated by changes both in the number of gems and in speed levels (or by changes both in quality and quantity of gems), based on the style of the avoidance-avoidance expression. One of two opinions recommends avoiding one path, and another recommends avoiding another path, based on the following basic format:

"Because of (motive #1), I recommend avoiding this path. However, because of (motive #2), I recommend avoiding this (the opposite) path."

Approach-Avoidance Expression (App-Avo) Condition: In this condition, the agent simultaneously expresses two opinions, motivated by changes both in the number of gems and in speed levels (or by changes both in quality and quantity of gems), based on the style of the approach-avoidance expression. One of two opinions recommends choosing one path, and another recommends avoiding the same path, based on the following basic format:

"Because of (motive #1), I recommend choosing this path. However, because of (motive #2), I recommend avoiding this (the same) path."

To prevent the impression evaluation from being affected by differences in performance among the conditions regarding the agents, the parameter settings for the experiment were adjusted to make the expected scores that participants would realize under each experimental condition the same. We can therefore compare the impressions of the agents regardless of the conditions.

4.3   Questionnaires

In this experiment, the participant is asked to complete two different questionnaires.

Table 2. Questionnaire on Relative Evaluation between Agents

	Question Items
Q25	Which agent did you feel human-like?
Q26	Which agent did you feel having its own opinion?
Q27	Which agent did you feel more friendly?
Q28	Which agent did you feel more annoying?
Q29	Which agent did you feel more competent?
Q30	Which agent did you feel easier to use?
Q31	Which agent would you want to ask for advice if you played the same game again?

The first one is the GQS described in Sect. 2. After the task under each experimental condition, the participant is asked to evaluate the impression of the agent by answering the questions shown in Table 1 in the manner of the semantic differential method.

The second one is a questionnaire on relative evaluation between the agent that expresses multiple opinions simultaneously and the agent that expresses only one opinion shown in Table 2. The participant is asked to compare the two agents from each viewpoint described in each question and evaluate them numerically in a range of -2 to $+2$ at the end of the experiment. A positive score means that the style of expressing multiple opinions obtains a better evaluation, and a negative score means the opposite. In particular, Q28–Q31 will be used as metrics to evaluate a feeling of easy-to-use described in Hypothesis 2.

4.4   Procedure

Each participant is assigned to two of the four experimental conditions in this experiment. One is the SGL condition, and the other is one of three conditions for the styles of expressing multiple opinions. The participants are grouped as follows.

App-App Group: A group in which participants are assigned to the SGL and App-App conditions.

Avo-Avo Group: A group in which participants are assigned to the SGL and Avo-Avo conditions.

App-Avo Group: A group in which participants are assigned to the SGL and App-Avo conditions.

Therefore, the comparison within each group (SGL vs. App-App/Avo-Avo/App-Avo) is conducted as a within-participants design, and the comparison among three conditions App-App, Avo-Avo, and App-Avo is conducted as a between-participants design.

Forty-two people (29 males and 13 females) participated in this experiment. Their ages ranged from 20 to 59 years. They were randomly assigned to one of the three experimental groups mentioned above. Fourteen participants were therefore assigned to each group.

The experimental procedure is as follows.

1. The experimenter explains the experimental task to the participant.
2. The participant is asked to perform the task with either the agent in the SGL condition or that in the condition for expressing multiple opinions.
3. The participant is asked to complete the GQS shown in Table 1 regarding the agent used in Step 2.
4. The participant is again asked to perform the task with the other agent, which was not used in Step 2.
5. The participant is again asked to complete the GQS regarding the agent used in Step 4.
6. The participant is asked to answer the relative evaluation questionnaire shown in Table 2.

4.5   Results

Figure 3 shows the evaluation scores (mean values for all participants) of the GQS for each experimental group. The error bars denote the standard error.

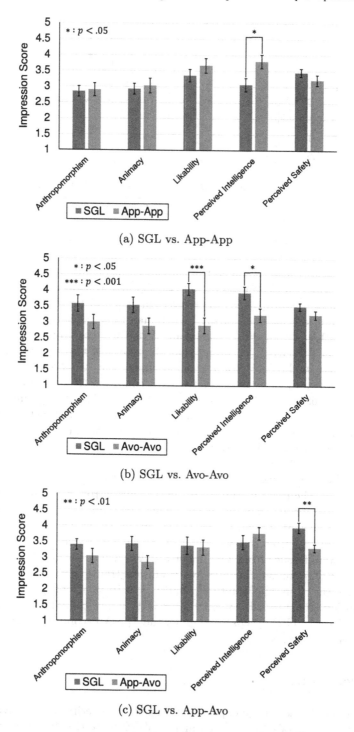

(a) SGL vs. App-App

(b) SGL vs. Avo-Avo

(c) SGL vs. App-Avo

Fig. 3. Results of GQS

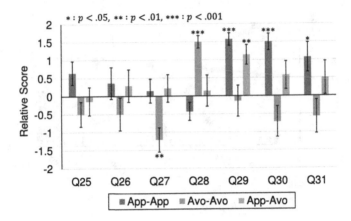

Fig. 4. Results of Relative Evaluation (SGL vs. App-App/Avo-Avo/App-Avo)

The statistical difference was determined using a two-sided paired t-test. From the result of the App-App group (SGL vs. App-App) shown in Fig. 3 (a), we found that the score of the factor "perceived intelligence" for the agent under the App-App condition was statistically higher than that under the SGL condition ($t(13) = -3.01$, $p < .05$). From the result of the Avo-Avo group (SGL vs. Avo-Avo) shown in Fig. 3 (b), we found that the scores of the factors "likeability" and "perceived intelligence" for the agent under the Avo-Avo condition were statistically lower than those under the SGL condition ($t(13) = 4.68$, $p < .001$ and $t(13) = 2.68$, $p < .05$). From the result of the App-Avo group (SGL vs. App-Avo) shown in Fig. 3 (c), we found that the score of the factor "perceived safety" for the agent under the App-Avo condition was statistically lower than that under the SGL condition ($t(13) = 3.51$, $p < .01$).

Figure 4 shows the evaluation scores (mean values for all participants) of the relative evaluation between the SGL condition and the App-App/Avo-Avo/App-Avo condition. The error bars denote the standard error. As mentioned above, a positive score means that the agents under the App-App/Avo-Avo/App-Avo condition are evaluated better, and a negative score means the opposite. The statistical difference from zero was determined using a two-sided t-test. We found the statistical difference from zero under the Avo-Avo condition ($t(13) = -3.63$, $p < .01$) for Q27, under the Avo-Avo condition ($t(13) = 8.63$, $p < .001$) for Q28, under the App-App condition ($t(13) = 9.10$, $p < .001$) and the App-Avo condition ($t(13) = 4.16$, $p < .01$) for Q29, under the App-App condition ($t(13) = 6.56$, $p < .001$) for Q30, and under the App-App condition ($t(13) = 2.60$, $p < .05$) for Q31, respectively.

5   Discussion

In this section, based on the experimental results, we verify the two hypotheses regarding the style of expressing opinions. We evaluate the "better impression" in Hypothesis 1 from the scores of five factors in the GQS and the "feeling of easy-to-use" in Hypothesis 2 from the relative scores for Q28–Q31.

5.1   Approach-Approach Expression

We can see from Fig. 3 (a) that the agent in the style of the approach-approach expression was evaluated statistically higher than the agent that expresses only one opinion regarding the factor "perceived intelligence." Furthermore, we can also see from Fig. 4 that the agent in the style of the approach-approach expression was evaluated statistically higher than the agent that expresses only one opinion for Q29–Q31. These results support both Hypotheses 1 and 2 under the approach-approach condition.

We can consider that the reasons for these results are that both agents made positive recommendations to the participants, but there was a difference in the amount of information between them. The single opinion expressed under the SGL condition and the multiple opinions expressed under the App-App condition were all positive advice on which path should be chosen. However, there was a difference in that the style of the approach-approach expression provided more information to the participants because it referred to both options. From the participants' viewpoint, it is considered that they felt the agent was more intelligent and easier to use due to the large amount of provided information. Therefore, implementing the simultaneous expression of multiple opinions in the approach-approach manner in agents is effective.

5.2   Avoidance-Avoidance Expression

We can see from Fig. 3 (b) that the agent in the style of the avoidance-avoidance expression was evaluated statistically lower than the agent that expresses only one opinion regarding both of the factors "likability" and "perceived intelligence." Furthermore, we can also see from Fig. 4 that the agent in the style of the avoidance-avoidance expression was evaluated statistically higher than the agent that expresses only one opinion for Q28, which asked the participants which agent was more annoying. These results clearly do not support both Hypotheses 1 and 2 under the avoidance-avoidance condition.

We can consider that the reasons for these results are that the disadvantage of low readability of expressed opinions outweighed the advantage of a large amount of provided information. The style of the avoidance-avoidance expression made negative recommendations concerning both options. It is possible that the negative expressions interfered with the participants' understanding meanings of the opinions smoothly and gave a feeling of annoyance.

5.3   Approach-Avoidance Expression

We can see from Fig. 3 (c) that the agent in the style of the approach-avoidance expression was evaluated statistically lower than the agent that expresses only one opinion regarding the factor "perceived safety." Furthermore, we can also see from Fig. 4 that the agent in the style of the approach-approach expression was evaluated statistically higher than the agent that expresses only one opinion for Q29, which asked the participants which agent was more competent. These results do not support Hypothesis 1 under the approach-avoidance condition. On the other hand, we may say that these weakly support Hypothesis 2.

We can consider that the reasons for these results are that the participants interpreted the agent as a system or machine expressing information rather than as a subject due to the perception of its competence. The convenience of expressing multiple opinions simultaneously from different viewpoints might have been too emphasized and suppressed the perception of human-likeness from the agent.

In this paper, a positive opinion was expressed first and a negative one later. It is an important issue to investigate whether the results change when they are expressed in reverse order.

6   Conclusion

This paper focused on humans' styles of expressing their opinions to others. We implemented the styles of simultaneous expression of multiple opinions into the agent based on the theory of motivational conflicts. We investigated the effects of the styles of expression on the impression through an evaluation experiment. Experimental results support our hypotheses that the agent in the style of the approach-approach expression gives users a better impression, such as more intelligence and a feeling of easy-to-use than the conventional agent that expresses only one opinion. On the other hand, it should be noted that the results in this paper were obtained under the conditions of playing a game, and different results could be obtained in a more general context.

In future works, we need to analyze the impression of the agents further. In this paper, we discussed it based only on the scores of the five factors of the GQS. It is expected that a more detailed impression evaluation can be performed by analyzing the evaluation of the scores of original adjective pairs. Furthermore, it is also essential to investigate the case of three or more options.

References

1. Arita, A., Hiraki, K., Kanda, T., Ishiguro, H.: Can we talk to robots? Ten-month-old infants expected interactive humanoid robots to be talked to by persons. Cognition **95**, B49–B57 (2005)
2. Fukuda, H., Ueda, K.: Interaction with movements of robot influences animacy perception. In: Proceedings of Human-Agent Interaction Symposium 2007, 1F–2 (2007)
3. Sakumoto, K., Imai, J.: Effects of provision of neither-good-nor-bad information on trustworthiness of agents. IEICE Trans. Inf. Syst. J103-D (3), 82–91 (2020) (in Japanese)
4. Yokoyama, S., Imai, J.: Conditions under which neither-good-nor-bad information works effectively on user's trust in agents. Int. J. Affect. Eng. **20**(4), 199–208 (2021)

5. Suzumura, Y., Imai, J.: Effectiveness of neither-good-nor-bad information on user's trust in agents in presence of numerous options: IEICE Trans. Inf. Syst. E105-D (3), 557–564 (2022)
6. Lewin, K.: A dynamic theory of personality. McGraw-Hill, New York (1935)
7. Bartneck, C., Kulić, D., Croft, E., Zoghbi, S.: Measurement instruments for the anthropomorphism, animacy, likeability, perceived intelligence, and perceived safety of robots. Int. J. Soc. Robot. 1(1), 71–81 (2009)
8. Weiss, A., Bartneck, C.: Meta analysis of the usage of the Godspeed Questionnaire Series. In: Proceedings of the 24th IEEE International Symposium on Robot and Human Interactive Communication (RO-MAN 2015), pp. 381–388 (2015)
9. Nomura, T.: Humans' subjective evaluation in human-agent interaction (HAI). J. Jpn Soc. Artif. Intell. 31 (2), 224–229 (2016) (in Japanese)

ICBAKE 2023 Workshop: Wellbeing and Affective Engineering

Facial Expression Estimation Using Convolutional Neural Network with Upper and Lower Segmented Face Images

Koichi Mitsumura$^{(\boxtimes)}$ and Hiroki Nomiya

Kyoto Institute of Technology, Kyoto, Japan
m3622038@edu.kit.ac.jp

Abstract. In a convolutional neural network (CNN) for facial expression recognition, it is important to focus attention on the parts of a face where facial expressions are likely to be expressed. We propose two methods to focus on the parts of a face where facial expressions are likely to be expressed: one is to merge face images divided into the upper and lower parts by facial feature points as inputs to separate convolutional layers, and the other is to superimpose the two divided images and use them as 6-channel inputs to the convolutional layer. We evaluated the performance of the two methods by comparing the facial expression estimation results of the model trained with the two methods and the model trained without image segmentation. By segmenting the image, we were able to improve the accuracy of the proposed model with respect to anger, disgust, and neutral.

Keywords: facial expression recognition · convolutional neural network · segmented face images · affective engineering

1 Introduction

Facial expression recognition plays an important role in human-computer interaction and human-human communication by recognizing facial information and analyzing human psychological emotions. It is also expected to be applied in various fields such as multimedia content evaluation and virtual reality [1].

Conventional facial expression recognition methods [2, 10, 11] use manually defined features that are considered important for facial expressions extracted from facial images. Furthermore, with the rise of deep learning, many researchers have attempted to solve the problem of facial expression recognition by using neural networks. In addition, convolutional neural networks allow us to find characteristic patterns in images during training, and to set features by learning instead of manually considering features [3, 12, 13].

When facial expression recognition is performed using manually defined features, limited numerical data are extracted from the facial image, resulting in the problem of ignoring features of the entire facial image that are difficult to be converted into numerical data, such as wrinkles on the eyebrows or a tense face. By using a convolutional

K. Saeed et al. (Eds.): CISIM 2023, LNCS 14164, pp. 427–439, 2023.
https://doi.org/10.1007/978-3-031-42823-4_31

neural network, we expect to improve accuracy by extracting features that are difficult to manually convert into numerical data. On the other hand, when using features obtained by a convolutional neural network, there is a possibility of learning information that is unnecessary for facial expression recognition due to the large amount of information in the image. To solve this problem, we expect to focus on the areas around the eyes and mouth, where facial expressions are more likely to be expressed, by dividing the face image into upper and lower parts and narrowing down the area for convolution.

In this study, a face image is divided into an upper region around the eyes and a lower region around the mouth and input into a convolutional neural network to estimate the facial expression of the face image. This can be achieved by using the two segmented images as inputs to separate convolutional layers and merging them in the full concatenation layer, or by superimposing the two segmented images and using them as 6-channel inputs to the convolutional layer. We evaluate the performance of the model trained with these two methods by comparing the facial expression estimation results of the model trained with these two methods and the model trained without image segmentation.

The paper is organized as follows:

Section 2 introduces related works.
Section 3 describes how the image is segmented and how the model is configured.
Section 4 describes the methods and results of the experiment.
Section 5 discusses the experimental results.
Section 6 presents our conclusions and future work.

2   Related Works

2.1   Upper, Middle and Lower Region Learning for Facial Action Unit Detection

In this work, a face is divided into three regions (upper, middle, and lower) and the presence or absence of movements of various facial muscles called Action Units (AU) is detected [4].

After a face image is input to the backbone CNN to obtain a feature map, the feature map is divided into upper, middle, and lower regions centered at the midpoint between the tip and root of the nose in the face image, and each region is masked to hide the other regions. The feature maps are used to detect the AUs corresponding to the regions. The upper region is responsible for detecting AU1, AU2, and AU4, the middle region for AU6 and AU9, and the lower region for AU12, AU25 and AU26.

After the convolution layer of the CNN model, SEblock [5] is inserted to account for the importance of the feature maps.

Although we agree in that we also segment face images based on facial feature points, our objective is to estimate facial expressions, not to detect AUs.

2.2   Recognizing Facial Expressions of Occluded Faces Using Convolutional Neural Networks

In this work, the task is to recognize facial expressions of a person wearing a virtual reality (VR) headset that covers the upper part of the face. A training example is modified to focus on the upper half of the face by intentionally hiding the upper part of the face [1].

This study fine-tunes a network of pre-trained CNN models in two steps. In the first stage, the CNN model is fine-tuned by training on an image that shows the entire face. In the second stage, the model is further fine-tuned for images in which the upper half of the face is hidden. Learning in the second stage focuses attention on the lower half of the face, and the CNN model is as accurate for images in which the upper half of the face is hidden as it is for images in which the entire face is visible.

We expect that by using the upper and lower parts of the face as input to the CNN model, the model will obtain features of the upper and lower parts of the face where facial expressions are likely to be expressed.

3   Proposed Method

This section describes the image segmentation method and the CNN model used in the proposed method.

3.1   Face Image Segmentation

Facial Landmark

In this study, facial landmarks are used in the segmentation of face images. The facial landmarks are detected using Dlib [6].

The upper left and lower right points of the rectangle obtained by the face detector are P_a and P_b (see Fig. 1), and 68 facial landmarks are detected for the detected faces (see Fig. 2). Facial landmarks are as follows:

Contour: 17 points $(P_0, \cdots, P_{16})$.
Eyebrows: 10 points $(P_{17}, \cdots, P_{26})$.
Nose: 9 points $(P_{27}, \cdots, P_{35})$.
Eyes: 12 points $(P_{36}, \cdots, P_{47})$.
Mouth: 20 points $(P_{48}, \cdots, P_{67})$.

Segmentation

For the upper part of the face, a rectangle is formed with the x-coordinate of P_0 at the left end, the x-coordinate of P_{16} at the right end, the y-coordinate of P_a at the top end, and the y-coordinate of P_{29} at the bottom end. For the lower part of the face, a rectangle is formed with x-coordinate of P_0 at the left end, x-coordinate of P_{16} at the right end, y-coordinate of P_{29} at the top end, and y-coordinate of P_8 at the bottom end.

Since the size of the segmented image changes from image to image, the images are filled in black so that they are square and then resized to 244-pixel x 244-pixel to match the size of the image (see Fig. 3).

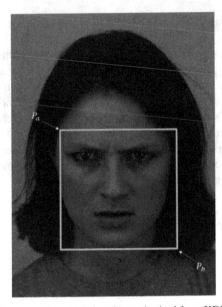

Fig. 1. An example of face detection (This face image is cited from KDEF dataset [8]. The image id is AF01ANS)

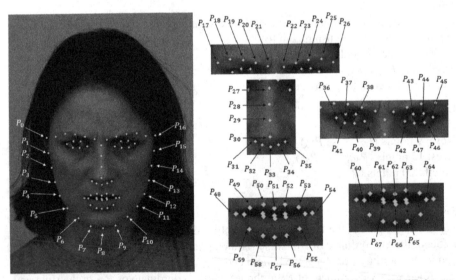

Fig. 2. An example of facial landmark extraction (This face image is cited from KDEF dataset [8]. The image id is AF01ANS)

3.2 Squeeze-and-Excitation Block

Squeeze-and-Excitation block [5] (SEblock) is used in this study. SEblock allows us to determine the importance of each channel.

Facial Landmark Detection

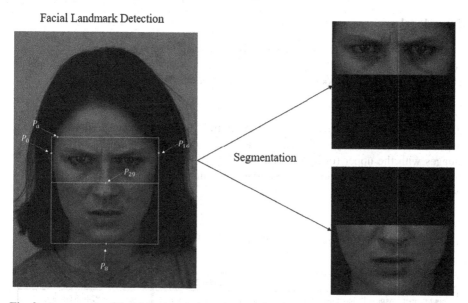

Fig. 3. An example of facial landmark detection and face image segmentation (This face image is cited from KDEF dataset [8]. The image id is AF01ANS)

For feature $U \in \mathbb{R}^{H \times W \times C}$ (H, W denote the vertical and horizontal sizes of the feature map, and C denotes the number of channels), the spatial dimensions $H \times W$ were squeezed into one dimension using a global average pooling function as shown in Eq. (1).

$$z_c = \frac{1}{H \times W} \sum_{i=1}^{H} \sum_{j=1}^{W} u_c(i,j) \tag{1}$$

where u_c denotes the c-th element of feature U. $u_c(i,j)$ is the element in row i and column j of u_c.

Then $Z = [z_1, \cdots, z_C]$ is fed into two dimensionality-reduction fully connected (FC) layers with reduction ratio r as shown in Eq. (2).

$$S = \sigma(W_2 \delta(W_1 Z)) \tag{2}$$

where W_1 denotes a fully connected layer with $1/r$ times the number of outputs, W_2 denotes a fully connected layer with r times the number of outputs, δ donates a Relu function and σ is a sigmoid function.

The output $S \in \mathbb{R}^{1 \times 1 \times C}$ is expanded into $S_e \in \mathbb{R}^{H \times W \times C}$, where the value of every pixel in the same channel is equal. S_e can be regarded as the channel-wise weights, and the output $O \in \mathbb{R}^{H \times W \times C}$ of SEblock with residual structure can be calculated by Eq. (3).

$$O = (S_e \otimes U) \oplus U \tag{3}$$

where $\otimes$ denotes the element-wise multiplication, and $\oplus$ denotes the element-wise addition.

3.3 Models

In this study, we propose two types of CNN models using segmented face images as input. Both models refer to VGG-16 [7]. The configuration of the proposed model is shown in Fig. 4. These models insert SEblock after every convolution layer.

Model 1

The two segmented images are merged in the fully connected layer, each as input to a separate convolution layer. The two inputs for Model 1 are two 244-pixel x 244-pixel images with the upper (or lower) half masked in black. Since the number of features obtained by the convolution layer is 4096, the number of nodes in the merging fully connected layer is doubled to 8192 (see Fig. 4).

Model 2

The two segmented images are superimposed and used as the 6-channel input to the

Model 1		Model 2	Model 3 (VGG-16)
input (upper image)	input (lower image)	input (6-channel image)	input (244×244 RGB image)
conv3-64	conv3-64	conv3-64	conv3-64
conv3-64	conv3-64	conv3-64	conv3-64
maxpool	maxpool	maxpool	maxpool
conv3-128	conv3-128	conv3-128	conv3-128
conv3-128	conv3-128	conv3-128	conv3-128
maxpool	maxpool	maxpool	maxpool
conv3-256	conv3-256	conv3-256	conv3-256
conv3-256	conv3-256	conv3-256	conv3-256
conv3-256	conv3-256	conv3-256	conv3-256
maxpool	maxpool	maxpool	maxpool
conv3-512	conv3-512	conv3-512	conv3-512
conv3-512	conv3-512	conv3-512	conv3-512
conv3-512	conv3-512	conv3-512	conv3-512
maxpool	maxpool	maxpool	maxpool
conv3-512	conv3-512	conv3-512	conv3-512
conv3-512	conv3-512	conv3-512	conv3-512
conv3-512	conv3-512	conv3-512	conv3-512
maxpool	maxpool	maxpool	maxpool
FC-8192		FC-4096	FC-4096
FC-4096		FC-4096	FC-4096
FC-7		FC-7	FC-7
softmax		softmax	softmax

Fig. 4. Model Configuration. The convolutional layer parameters are denoted as "conv(receptive field size)-(number of channels)". The fully connected layer parameters are denoted as "FC-(number of nodes)". The ReLU activation function is not shown for brevity.

convolution layer. We superimpose the two segmented images so that they match the same row and column elements. The fundamental configuration is the same as in VGG-16, but the input is a 6-channel input consisting of superimposed RGB images of the upper and lower parts of the face (see Fig. 4).

Model 3

For comparison, we also prepare a newly trained VGG-16 with unsegmented face images as input. In the same way, SEblock is inserted after the convolution layer.

4 Experiment

The purpose of this study is to compare Model 1, Model 2, and Model 3 to see if image segmentation leads to improved accuracy. The following sections describe the details and results of the experiment.

4.1 Dataset and Settings

Dataset

The dataset used in this study is Karolinska Directed Emotional Faces (KDEF) dataset [8]. The KDEF dataset consists of a total of 4900 images of human facial expressions. It consists of 70 images of each of 35 males and 35 females showing seven different emotional expressions: happiness, surprise, anger, sadness, disgust, fear, and neutral. Each facial expression was captured from five different angles.

The 980 frontal face images in the KDEF dataset were divided into 784 images for training and 196 images for testing. The dataset was randomly split using the ramdom_split in PyTorch's torch.utils.data class [9].

Settings

We insert SEblock of $r = 16$ after all convolution layers of the three models shown in Fig. 4.

The optimization method for all models is Adam. Learning rates were determined by preliminary experiments. Using the training data, we trained the three models without SEblock insertion for 100 epochs with learning rates of 10^{-3}, 10^{-4}, and 10^{-5}. The learning rate for all models was determined to be 10^{-5} because the errors were smallest when the learning rate was 10^{-5} for all three models.

The loss function is Cross Entropy Error. We compare the accuracy after all models have been trained for 100 epochs.

4.2 Experimental Results

Table 1 shows the accuracy of all models. As a comparison of overall accuracy, Model 3 with SEblock inserted produced the best results. For Model 2, the accuracy is lower than Model 3, except for neutral. For Model 1, compared to Model 3, the accuracy of anger, disgust, and neutral increased, while the accuracy of fear, sadness, and surprise decreased significantly. For SEblock, all models are more accurate when inserted.

We can see that the model with SEblock converges faster per epoch than the model without SEblock. Model 1 with SEblock converges the fastest per epoch (see Fig. 5).

Table 1. Accuracy for each expression of each model. Accuracy is defined as the number of output results that match the correct label divided by the number of data.

	anger	disgust	fear	happiness	neutral	sadness	surprise	overall
Model 1 without SEblock	**0.79**	**0.86**	0.47	0.96	**0.92**	0.59	0.64	0.73
Model 1 with SEblock	**0.79**	**0.86**	0.67	0.96	0.85	0.69	0.50	0.74
Model 2 without SEblock	0.61	0.71	0.45	0.87	0.86	0.45	0.75	0.66
Model 2 with SEblock	0.64	0.71	0.62	0.91	0.89	0.52	0.75	0.71
Model 3 without SEblock	0.73	0.79	**0.76**	0.93	0.68	0.81	**0.89**	0.80
Model 3 with SEblock	0.78	0.83	0.72	**0.97**	0.85	**0.85**	0.86	**0.84**

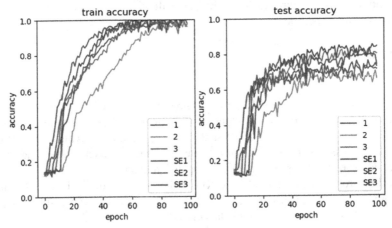

Fig. 5. Accuracy per epoch. 1, 2, and 3 represent Model 1, Model 2, and Model 3 without SEblock inserted, respectively. SE1, SE2, and SE3 represent Model 1, Model 2, and Model 3 with SEblock inserted, respectively.

5 Discussion

Tables 2 through 7 show confusion matrixes with actual labels for the row items and predicted labels for the column items in each model (Tables 3, 4, 5 and 6).

In common with Model 1 and Model 2, the accuracy of fear, sadness, and surprise is significantly low. Fear and sadness tend to be misidentified in various facial expressions. It is thought that by segmenting the image, no features useful for estimating fear or sadness were extracted. Surprise tends to be more easily misidentified as fear when the image is segmented. Surprise and fear are similar expressions, with the main difference being whether the entire face is relaxed or not. Figure 6 shows an example of facial expressions of surprise and fear. Since facial expression recognition is performed by segmenting the image, the convolution of the entire face is not possible, thus it is difficult to recognize facial expressions that have slight features on the entire face.

On the other hand, for facial expressions that easily express emotion, such as anger, disgust, and happiness, the accuracy was improved because we were able to focus on the parts of the face that showed the characteristics of these facial expressions. The lack of facial muscle movement is also a major characteristic of neutral, and we were able to focus on the areas around the mouth, nasolabial folds, and eyes where these characteristics are expressed.

As for overall accuracy, Model 3 has the highest accuracy, which means that the impact of the expressions with decreased accuracy is greater than the expressions with increased accuracy. Therefore, when one wants to detect only anger or disgust, one may benefit from the technique of segmenting face images.

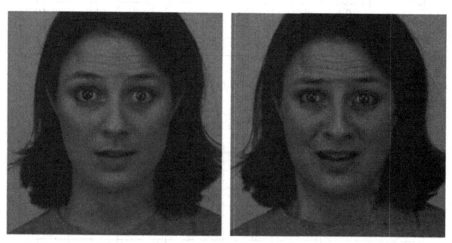

Fig. 6. An example of a look of surprise and fear. On the left is surprise (The image id is AF01SUS), on the right is fear (The image id is AF01AFS). (The face images are cited from KDEF dataset [8])

Table 2. Confusion matrix with actual labels for the row items and predicted labels for the column items in Model 1 without SEblock

		Predicted					
		anger	disgust	fear	happiness	neutral	sadness	surprise
Actual	anger	0.792	0.083	0.083	0.000	0.000	0.042	0.000
	disgust	0.000	0.864	0.045	0.000	0.000	0.091	0.000
	fear	0.133	0.100	0.667	0.000	0.033	0.033	0.033
	happiness	0.000	0.000	0.038	0.962	0.000	0.000	0.000
	neutral	0.000	0.000	0.000	0.000	0.846	0.154	0.000
	sadness	0.031	0.063	0.094	0.000	0.125	0.688	0.000
	surprise	0.028	0.000	0.472	0.000	0.000	0.000	0.500

Table 3. Confusion matrix with actual labels for the row items and predicted labels for the column items in Model 2 without SEblock

		Predicted						
		anger	disgust	fear	happiness	neutral	sadness	surprise
Actual	anger	0.643	0.107	0.036	0.036	0.036	0.107	0.036
	disgust	0.194	0.710	0.000	0.032	0.000	0.065	0.000
	fear	0.069	0.069	0.621	0.000	0.034	0.069	0.138
	happiness	0.000	0.000	0.043	0.913	0.000	0.043	0.000
	neutral	0.036	0.000	0.000	0.000	0.893	0.071	0.000
	sadness	0.138	0.034	0.138	0.000	0.172	0.517	0.000
	surprise	0.000	0.000	0.250	0.000	0.000	0.000	0.750

Table 4. Confusion matrix with actual labels for the row items and predicted labels for the column items in Model 3 without SEblock

		Predicted						
		anger	disgust	fear	happiness	neutral	sadness	surprise
Actual	anger	0.783	0.130	0.000	0.000	0.043	0.043	0.000
	disgust	0.042	0.833	0.042	0.000	0.000	0.083	0.000
	fear	0.000	0.000	0.720	0.000	0.040	0.040	0.200
	happiness	0.000	0.000	0.000	0.966	0.034	0.000	0.000
	neutral	0.059	0.000	0.000	0.000	0.853	0.088	0.000
	sadness	0.074	0.000	0.000	0.000	0.074	0.852	0.000
	surprise	0.000	0.000	0.143	0.000	0.000	0.000	0.857

Table 5. Confusion matrix with actual labels for the row items and predicted labels for the column items in Model 1 with SEblock

		Predicted						
		anger	disgust	fear	happiness	neutral	sadness	surprise
Actual	anger	0.792	0.083	0.083	0.000	0.042	0.000	0.000
	disgust	0.045	0.864	0.000	0.000	0.000	0.091	0.000
	fear	0.067	0.067	0.467	0.100	0.100	0.067	0.133
	happiness	0.000	0.000	0.038	0.962	0.000	0.000	0.000
	neutral	0.000	0.077	0.000	0.000	0.923	0.000	0.000
	sadness	0.094	0.063	0.063	0.031	0.156	0.594	0.000
	surprise	0.028	0.000	0.333	0.000	0.000	0.000	0.639

For all models, the overall accuracy was better for the model with the SEblock inserted, and the convergence per epoch was also faster, indicating that the weights per channel of the output were correctly learned in the convolution layer.

Table 6. Confusion matrix with actual labels for the row items and predicted labels for the column items in Model 2 with SEblock

	Predicted						
	anger	disgust	fear	happiness	neutral	sadness	surprise
anger	0.607	0.036	0.107	0.000	0.071	0.107	0.071
disgust	0.161	0.710	0.000	0.032	0.000	0.097	0.000
fear	0.103	0.069	0.448	0.000	0.034	0.138	0.207
happiness	0.000	0.000	0.000	0.870	0.087	0.043	0.000
neutral	0.000	0.036	0.000	0.000	0.857	0.107	0.000
sadness	0.207	0.034	0.034	0.000	0.241	0.448	0.034
surprise	0.000	0.000	0.214	0.000	0.036	0.000	0.750

(Actual)

Table 7. Confusion matrix with actual labels for the row items and predicted labels for the column items in Model 3 with SEblock

	Predicted						
	anger	disgust	fear	happiness	neutral	sadness	surprise
anger	0.739	0.130	0.043	0.000	0.000	0.087	0.000
disgust	0.042	0.792	0.000	0.125	0.042	0.000	0.000
fear	0.000	0.000	0.760	0.000	0.040	0.040	0.160
happiness	0.000	0.000	0.034	0.931	0.000	0.034	0.000
neutral	0.059	0.000	0.029	0.000	0.676	0.235	0.000
sadness	0.074	0.000	0.037	0.000	0.074	0.815	0.000
surprise	0.000	0.000	0.114	0.000	0.000	0.000	0.886

(Actual)

6 Conclusions

We proposed a method to segment face images into upper and lower parts using facial landmarks, and to use the segmented face images as input to a convolutional neural network. Although we expected to extract features around the eyes and mouth, where facial expressions are more likely to be expressed, the two proposed models did not improve the overall accuracy compared to models trained without image segmentation. However, for Model 1, we confirmed that some facial expressions were more accurate than those in the model trained without image segmentation. In all models, SEblock insertion improved the accuracy, suggesting that SEblock is useful for facial expression recognition.

Future work includes improving the face segmentation method. The segmentation method used in this study assumes that the face is facing the front and does not consider the tilt of the face. By using a segmentation method that considers the tilt of the face, it is possible to handle images in which the face is tilted, which has the advantage of increasing the number of datasets that can be handled. By increasing the number of datasets, not only can more universal facial features be learned, but the hyperparameters can be adjusted by dividing the dataset into training, validation, and test datasets. Improving the performance of the model by adjusting the hyperparameters is also a future challenge. And as a comparison, we used Model 3, a newly trained VGG-16, but we will compare it with other methods to further clarify the issues in order to improve the accuracy of fear, sadness, and surprise.

References

1. Georgescu, M.I., Ionescu, R.T.: Recognizing facial expressions of occluded faces using convolutional neural networks. Int. Conference on Neural Information Process. **1142**(4), 645–653 (2019)
2. Kobayashi, H., Hara, F.: The recognition of basic facial expression by neural network. Trans. Society of Instrument Control Engineers **29**(1), 112–118 (1993)
3. Nishime, T., Endo, S., Toma, N., Yamada, K., Akamine, Y.: Feature acquisition and analysis for facial expression recognition using convolutional neural networks. J. Japanese Society for Artificial Intell. **32**(5), F-H34_1–8 (2017)
4. Xia, Y.: Upper, Middle and Lower Region Learning for Facial Action Unit Detection. arXiv preprint arXiv:2002.04023 (2020)
5. Hu, J., Shen, L., Albanie, S., Sun, G., Wu, E.: Squeeze-and-excitation networks. IEEE Trans. Pattern Anal. Mach. Intell. **42**(8), 2011–2023 (2020)
6. Dlib C++ Library. http://dlib.net/. Accessed 07 Mar 2023
7. Simonyan, K., Zisserman, A.: Very Deep Convolutional Networks for Large-Scale Image Recognition. arXiv preprint arXiv:1409.1556 (2015)
8. Lundqvist, E.D., Flykt, A., Öhman, A.: The Karolinska Directed Emotional Faces - KDEF (CD ROM), Department of Clinical Neuroscience, Psychology Section, Karolinska Institutet, Stockholm (1998)
9. PyTorch torch.util.data. https://pytorch.org/docs/stable/data.html 07 Mar 2023
10. Shiga, Y., Ebine, H., Nakamura, O.: On extraction of the feature amounts from facial parts for the recognition of expressions. IPSJ SIG Technical Reports IM **1999**(69), 97–104 (1999)

11. Ghimire, D., Lee, J., Li, Z.N., Jeong, S.: Recognition of facial expressions based on salient geometric features and support vector machines. Multimedia Tools and Appl. **76**(6), 7921–7946 (2017)

12. Mollahosseini, A., Chan, D., Mahoor, M.H.: Going deeper in facial expression recognition using deep neural networks. In: 2016 IEEE Winter Conference on Applications of Computer Vision, pp. 1–10. IEEE, Lake Placid, NY, USA (2016)

13. Shehu, H.A., Sharif, H., Uyaver, S.: Facial expression recognition using deep learning. AIP Conference Proceedings **2334**(1), 070003–1–5 (2021)

Two-Step Classification Method for Sadness and Fear Facial Expression Classification Using Facial Feature Points and FACS

Mao Segawa[✉] and Hiroki Nomiya

Kyoto Institute of Technology, Kyoto, Japan
gatti1030@gmail.com, nomiya@kit.ac.jp

Abstract. Although systems have been developed to automatically estimate the evaluation of a work (e.g., comics, movie, etc.) based on the facial expressions of people viewing the work, they are insufficient for estimating the evaluation of moving or horror works, for which sadness and fear are less likely to be expressed in facial expressions and these expressions are thought to lead to evaluation. In this paper, we propose a new method to improve the accuracy of classification of facial expressions of sadness and fear. Facial feature points and Action Units (AUs) are extracted from facial images to set facial features and classify facial images into seven facial expressions: six basic facial expressions (anger, disgust, fear, happiness, sadness, and surprise) and neutral. First, the expressions of anger and sadness, which are easily confused, are merged into a single category, and similarly fear and surprise are merged to convert seven categories into five. Then, two-step classification was performed by reclassifying each of the merged facial expressions into two categories. Furthermore, the importance of each feature was compared, and the feature most suitable for each classification step was used to improve the classification accuracy. The results of a random forest model classification experiment using 490 face images from the Karolinska Directed Emotional Faces (KDEF) dataset showed that two-step classification performed better than one-step classification in the classification of sadness and fear. The accuracy was further improved by carefully selecting features.

Keywords: Facial expression · OpenFace · Facial Action Coding System

1 Introduction

In recent years, it has become common to view and distribute many works on the Internet, and not only moving images such as movies and animations, but also paper-based works such as novels and manga are often distributed and viewed as e-books. The evaluation of such works depends on their sales and the number of views.

However, it is difficult to say that these indicators are directly evaluated by consumers, since they are largely influenced by the advertising efforts of companies. Many people do not take the time to answer questionnaires or are not interested in evaluating works, and the percentage of those who answer questionnaires after viewing or watching a work

K. Saeed et al. (Eds.): CISIM 2023, LNCS 14164, pp. 440–452, 2023.
https://doi.org/10.1007/978-3-031-42823-4_32

is not considered large. Therefore, it can be said that the current evaluation criteria are insufficient for obtaining viewer's evaluations of the works.

To solve this problem, research has been conducted to automatically evaluate works based on viewer's facial expressions. Sakaue et al. used facial expression intensity, which represents the degree of facial expression, to estimate impressive scenes in lifelog videos [1]. Based on this theory of facial expression intensity, Shinohara proposed a method to calculate the evaluation of comics using the intensity of reader's facial expressions [2], and Sun proposed a method to estimate the evaluation of a comic dialogue (it is called Manzai in Japanese) based on viewer's facial expressions [3].

However, since both studies evaluated works based on the intensity of happiness, which is highly accurate in facial expression classification, and can only evaluate fun (how much it makes you laugh or smile), it is impossible to evaluate works with attractions other than fun. For example, the intensity of sadness when viewing a moving work or the intensity of fear when viewing a horror work can be used as an evaluation index for each work.

The purpose of this study is to improve the classification accuracy of sadness and fear facial expressions, which have low classification accuracy, with the aim of estimating the evaluation of a work based on the intensity of the viewer's sadness or fear facial expressions. We propose a two-step classification method that first performs a rough classification by grouping together expressions that are easily confused, and then reclassifies each of them. Utilizing the Action Unit (AU) included in the Facial Action Coding System (FACS) [4], we set up facial features specific to the classification of sadness and fear. Using these facial features as input, we constructed a facial expression classification model based on random forests and conducted experiments to classify a frontal face image into seven facial expressions: six basic facial expressions (anger, disgust, fear, happiness, sadness, and surprise) and neutral.

The structure of this paper is as follows. Section 2 introduces related studies, and Sect. 3 provides an overview of previous studies. Section 4 describes the proposed methodology, and Sect. 5 describes the objectives and results of the experiments. Section 6 discusses the experimental results, and Sect. 7 concludes and discusses future issues.

2 Related Research

The following studies are related to facial expression recognition using FACS.

2.1 Detection of Abnormal Facial Expressions Based on Long Short-Term Memory Using the Facial Action Coding System (FACS)

In detecting abnormal human facial expressions, Onishi et al. have proposed a feature extraction method using FACS, which is less susceptible to individual differences in facial structure and more universal. Compared to conventional methods that extract features using Convolutional Neural Network (CNN), feature extraction based on FACS was shown to have certain effectiveness in detecting abnormal facial expressions [5].

Our study uses FACS in the same way, but classifies single face images instead of time series images.

2.2 Image Preference Estimation Using Facial Expression Features in Multiple Image Domains

With the evolution of the Internet and mobile devices, techniques for estimating and recommending subjective preferences for image content are becoming increasingly important. Sato et al. developed a method for recommending user preferences for images posted on SNS. A predictive model of image preferences was constructed based on facial features obtained from AUs of face images and image features extracted from the images themselves in multiple domains to be evaluated, and an importance analysis using Shapley Additive Planations (SHAP) values was performed to identify the features that are important in each domain [6].

In our study, we use the random forest function to analyze importance.

3   Previous Method

In the previous study by Shinohara [2], a method for determining the type of facial expression based on facial expression intensity values derived from facial feature values was proposed. In this chapter, we first explain facial expression intensity and then describe the method for deriving facial feature values.

3.1   Facial Expression Intensity

The greater the degree of expression, the greater the change in face, and facial expression intensity is a quantification of the degree of expression. It is obtained using facial features, which are calculated from changes in the positional relationship of facial feature points. In the previous study [2], facial expression intensity is defined as the sum of the difference between the feature values for an expressionless face and those for a face with a certain expression.

In the previous study [2], facial expression intensity values were used to classify expressions, but in this study, that is not derived because classification is performed by machine learning using facial features.

3.2   Facial Features

Facial features are calculated from facial feature points, and in this study, OpenFace [7] is used to extract facial feature points. OpenFace is an open source toolkit that can extract not only facial feature points, but also AUs, which can be used to characterize each facial expression better than previous methods. In the previous study, facial feature points were extracted using dlib [8], but since similar points can be obtained with OpenFace, this study treats facial feature points in the same way as the previous study by Sun [3].

Figure 1 shows the facial feature points of the entire face. Each feature value is described below. The left eye, right eye, etc., are defined as the left and right eyes viewed from the front of the face. L used for normalization is the distance between the left and right eyes; L is the distance between the midpoints of the two ends $P37$ and $P40$ of the left eye and the two ends $P43$ and $P46$ of the right eye.

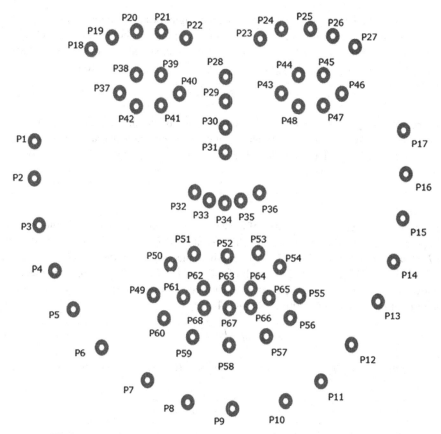

Fig. 1. Facial feature points $P1$ to $P68$ that can be extracted by OpenFace

$f1$ Slope of Left and Right Eyebrows. The slope is obtained from each of the five facial feature points of the eyebrows using the least-squares method, and then by taking the inverse tangent of the mean as in Eq. (1).

$$f_1 = tan^{-1}\left(\frac{a_l-a_r}{2}\right) \tag{1}$$

where a_l is the slope of the left eyebrow and a_r is the slope of the right eyebrow.

$f2$ Distance between Eyebrows and Eyes. The midpoint of two points $P38$ and $P39$ ($P44$ and $P45$) on the upper side of the left eye (right eye) is taken as a tentative facial feature point Pa (Pb). Then, calculate the average length of the line segment connecting the 10 points $P18,\ldots, P27$ on both eyebrows and the 10 points $P37,\ldots, P40, Pa, P43,\ldots,$ $P46, Pb$ on the upper eyelid including the midpoint, from the left, in one-to-one correspondence. Finally, it is divided by L to be normalized as shown in Eq. (2). Note that L_i is the length of the line segment connecting points $P18,\ldots, P27$ and the 10 points $P37,\ldots, P40, Pa, P43,\ldots, P46, Pb$ in one-to-one correspondence from left to right.

$$f_2 = \frac{1}{10L} \sum_{i=1}^{10} \|L_i\| \tag{2}$$

***f*3 Area between Eyebrows.** The area of the rectangle formed by connecting the points $P22$, $P23$, $P40$, and $P43$ closest to the midpoint of the face for both eyes and eyebrows, respectively, and divided by L^2 for normalization, is obtained by Eq. (3). Note that S $(Pi,\dots, Pj)$ is the area of the polygon formed by connecting points Pi to Pj.

$$f_3 = \frac{S(P_{22},P_{23},P_{40},P_{43})}{L^2} \tag{3}$$

***f*4 Area of an Eye.** The area of the hexagon formed by connecting the six points $P37$ to $P42$ ($P43$ to $P48$) around the left eye (right eye) is calculated, averaged as in Eq. (4), and normalized by L^2. Note that b_l is the area of the left eye and b_r is the area of the right eye.

$$f_4 = \frac{b_l+b_r}{2L^2} \tag{4}$$

***f*5 Ratio of the Length and Width of an Eye.** The point P_{ltm} (P_{rtm}) is defined as the midpoint of $P38$ and $P39$ ($P44$ and $P45$). The point P_{lbm} (P_{rbm}) is defined as the midpoint of $P42$ and $P41$ ($P48$ and $P47$). Let the length connecting the point P_{ltm} (P_{rtm}) and the point P_{lbm} (P_{rbm}) be the vertical length of the eye, l_{vl} (l_{vr}). Let the length connecting the two leftmost and rightmost points be the horizontal length of the eye, l_{hl} (l_{hr}). Then, the ratio of the length and width is obtained by Eq. (5).

$$f_5 = \frac{1}{2}\left(tan^{-1}\frac{l_{vl}}{l_{hl}} + tan^{-1}\frac{l_{vr}}{l_{hr}}\right) \tag{5}$$

Note that $l_{vl}, l_{vr}, l_{hl}, l_{hr}$ are obtained using Eqs. (6) and (7) respectively.

$$\begin{cases} l_{vl} = \|P_{ltm} - P_{lbm}\| \\ l_{vr} = \|P_{rtm} - P_{rbm}\| \end{cases} \tag{6}$$

$$\begin{cases} l_{hl} = \|P_{37} - P_{40}\| \\ l_{hr} = \|P_{43} - P_{46}\| \end{cases} \tag{7}$$

***f*6 Area of Inner Circumference of a Mouth.** The area of the octagon formed by connecting the eight facial feature points on the inner circumference of a mouth, divided by L^2 and normalized to obtain Eq. (8).

$$f_6 = \frac{S(P_{61},P_{62},P_{63},P_{64},P_{65},P_{66},P_{67},P_{68})}{L^2} \tag{8}$$

***f*7 Area of Outer Circumference of a Mouth.** This is the area obtained in the same way as $f6$ using the points on the outer circumference of the mouth. It is obtained by Eq. (9).

$$f_7 = \frac{S(P_{49},P_{50},P_{51},P_{52},P_{53},P_{54},P_{55},P_{56},P_{57},P_{58},P_{59},P_{60})}{L^2} \tag{9}$$

***f*8 Ratio of the Length and width of the Inner Circumference of a Mouth.** The length connecting the uppermost and the lowermost points on the inner circumference of the mouth is the vertical length m_in_v, and the length connecting the two leftmost and rightmost points is the horizontal length m_in_h, $f8$ is calculated as shown in Eq. (10).

$$f_8 = tan^{-1}\frac{m\_in_v}{m\_in_h} \tag{10}$$

Note that m_in_v and m_in_h are obtained using Eq. (11).

$$\begin{cases} m\_in_v = \|P_{63} - P_{67}\| \\ m\_in_h = \|P_{61} - P_{65}\| \end{cases} \tag{11}$$

$f9$ Ratio of the Length and Width of the Outer Circumference of a Mouth. This is the aspect ratio obtained in the same way as $f8$ using the points on the outer circumference of the mouth. It is obtained by Eq. (12).

$$f_9 = tan^{-1} \frac{m\_out_v}{m\_out_h} \tag{12}$$

Note that m_out_v and m_out_h are obtained using Eq. (13).

$$\begin{cases} m\_out_v = \|P_{52} - P_{58}\| \\ m\_out_h = \|P_{49} - P_{55}\| \end{cases} \tag{13}$$

$f10$ Degree of Elevation of the Corners of a Mouth. The degree of elevation of the corners of the mouth is obtained from the points $P49$ and $P55$ at the two ends of the mouth and from the points $P52$ and $P58$ at the top and bottom of the mouth, respectively, using Eq. (14). Note that $y(P)$ is the y-coordinate of the feature point P.

$$f_{10} = \frac{(y(P_{49})+y(P_{55}))-(y(P_{52})+y(P_{58}))}{\|y(P_{52})+y(P_{58})\|} \tag{14}$$

$f11$ Angle of a Mouth. This facial feature is the average of the angles of two-line segments formed by connecting the leftmost (rightmost) point $P49$ ($P55$) and one medial point $P50$ or $P60$ ($P54$ or $P56$) at the top and bottom of the mouth, respectively, and is calculated using Eq. (15). Note that $A(p, q, r)$ is the angle between the two-line segments formed by connecting the facial feature points p, q and q, r respectively.

$$f_{11} = \frac{A(P_{50},P_{49},P_{60})+A(P_{54},P_{55},P_{56})}{2} \tag{15}$$

$f12$ Slope of a Nasolabial Fold. It is the slope of the line connecting point $P49$ ($P55$) at the edge of the mouth and point $P32$ ($P36$) at the edge of the nose. It is obtained by dividing the difference in y-coordinates by the difference in x-coordinates for the left and right sides, and then averaging the two sides as in Eq. (16). Note that b_l is the slope of the left nasolabial fold and b_r is the slope of the right nasolabial fold.

$$f_{12} = tan^{-1} \left(\frac{b_l - b_r}{2} \right) \tag{16}$$

$f13$ Area of a Triangle Formed by Connecting the Two Ends of a Mouth and the Apex of a Nose. The area of the triangle formed by connecting the leftmost and rightmost points $P49$ and $P55$ of the mouth and the vertex of the nose $P31$ is found and divided by L^2 to normalize. The result is obtained by Eq. (17).

$$f_{13} = \frac{S(P_{49},P_{55},P_{31})}{L^2} \tag{17}$$

ƒ14 Distance between a Mouth and a Nose. The five points $P50,\ldots,P54$ on the outside of the upper lip and the five points $P32,\ldots,P36$ on the bottom of the nose are connected one-to-one from the left to form five line segments. This feature value is obtained by taking the average of those lengths and dividing it by L for normalization as shown in Eq. (18).

$$f_{14} = \tfrac{1}{5L} \sum_{i=32}^{36} \|P_i - P_{i+18}\| \tag{18}$$

ƒ15 Area of the Quadrangle Connecting the Ends of a Nose and a Mouth. The normalized area of the rectangle connecting the points $P32$ and $P36$ at the end of the nose and the points $P49$ and $P55$ at the end of the mouth obtained using Eq. (19).

$$f_{15} = \tfrac{S(P_{32},P_{36},P_{55},P_{49})}{L^2} \tag{19}$$

ƒ16 Area of Eyebrows and Eyes. The average of the normalized area of the rectangle formed by connecting the leftmost and rightmost points $P37$ and $P40$ ($P43$ and $P46$) of the left eye (right eye) and the leftmost and rightmost points $P18$ and $P22$ ($P23$ and $P27$) of the left eyebrow (right eyebrow) as shown in Eq. (20).

$$f_{16} = \tfrac{S(P_{37},P_{40},P_{22},P_{18})+S(P_{43},P_{46},P_{27},P_{23})}{2L^2} \tag{20}$$

3.3   Problem

Since this study deals only with facial expression classification, we omit the discussion on facial expression intensity estimation.

Table 1 shows the accuracy of facial expression classification in the previous study by Shinohara [2]. In the previous study, facial expression intensity estimation was performed on videos labeled with the types of facial expressions. The facial expressions with the largest intensity in the video were classified as the expressions estimated from the video. However, the three expressions of anger, disgust, and sadness were more likely to be confused, and the same was true for fear and surprise. In the previous study, the estimation accuracy was improved by dividing the expressions into three categories: positive (happiness), negative (anger, disgust, fear, and sadness), and surprise.

In the previous study by Sun [3], the estimation of facial expression intensity was limited only to the expressions of happiness and was targeted at comic works that were evaluated for "fun."

However, for example, the intensity of facial expressions of sadness and fear when viewing emotional or horror works is considered a valid evaluation index for these works. The classification accuracy of sadness and fear facial expressions needs to be improved in order to estimate the evaluation of these works.

4   Proposed Method

In this study, we use AU to classify seven facial expressions, including six basic facial expressions and neutral (i.e., expressionless), based on random forests. First, a new feature set was created by combining AU and conventional features. To improve the accuracy of classification of fear and sadness expressions, we perform two-step classification and carefully select features based on their importance in each classification.

Table 1. Accuracy of facial expression classification (F1-score) in previous study [2]

Expression	F1-score
anger	0.571
disgust	0.609
fear	0.450
happiness	0.813
sadness	0.615
surprise	0.733

4.1 Extraction of Facial Feature Points and AUs by OpenFace

The FaceLandmarkImg project of OpenFace extracts the coordinates of facial feature points and the intensity of AUs from a face image. Since the facial feature point extraction function of OpenFace is equivalent to that of dlib, which was used in the previous study [3], the facial features from $f1$ to $f16$ can be used without modification.

4.2 Setting New Facial Features

Based on the existing features and the intensity of the AU, new features $f17$ to $f25$ were set. Each feature was subjectively set to have a larger value for a certain facial expression based on the characteristics of each facial expression described by Paul Ekman Group [9]. The reasons for setting each feature and the target expressions are as follows.

$f17$ **"AU9: Wrinkle Nose"** → **"Disgust"**. The wrinkling of the nose is considered to be the most significant change in the expression of disgust.

$f18$ **"AU12: Lips pulled up at both Ends"** → **"Happiness"**. This was chosen because the movement of pulling up both ends of the lips is a change in facial expression seen only in happiness.

$f19$ **Product of "AU5: Raise uoper eyelid" and "f8: Ratio of Length and Width of the Inside of the Mouth"** → **"Surprise"**. Fear and surprise are listed as expressions that cause the upper eyelids to lift, and we set this expression because we thought that only surprise would cause the mouth to widen vertically.

f20 Product of "AU5: Raise upper eyelid" and "AU20: Pull both Ends of Lips to the Side" → **"Fear"**. Among the expressions for raising the upper eyelids, contrary to $f19$, we set $f20$ to "pull the mouth to the side" because it is considered to be seen only in fear.

$f21$ **"AU1: Raise the inside of the eyebrows" Divided by "f8: Ratio of the Length and Width of the Inside of the Mouth"** → **"Sadness"**. The eyebrows are raised in fear, sadness, and surprise, whereas the value of $f8$ is smaller for sadness because the mouth is not opened.

$f22$ **"AU15: Lowering the ends of the lips" divided by "AU9: Wrinkling the Nose"** → **"Sadness".** Since the lowering of both ends of the lips was observed in disgust and sadness, and the wrinkling of the nose was observed only in disgust, the value was set to be larger in sadness.

$f23$ **Product of "AU4: lowering eyebrows" and "AU23: Lips Tightly Closed"** → **"Anger".** Both lowering the eyebrows and closing the lips have been cited as characteristics of angry facial expressions, and we set the product of the two to be large only for angry facial expressions.

$f24$ **"AU2: Lifting the outer part of the eyebrows"** → **"Surprise".** Fear and sadness are also mentioned as expressions that raise the eyebrows, but in both cases the inner part of the eyebrows is raised, and the expression that raises the outer part of the eyebrows is limited to surprise.

$f25$ **Product of "AU26: lowering the chin and opening the lips" and "f6: Inner Mouth Area"** → **"Surprise".** Both are related to the opening of the mouth, and are set because they are considered to have a large value in the expression of surprise.

Since the scale differs between the conventional features and the added features, all features are standardized at this stage.

4.3 Facial Expression Classification in Two Steps

Classification is performed using a random forest trained with features $f1$ to $f25$ as input. We performed two-step classification of facial expressions because we believe that direct classification of sadness and fear, as in previous studies, would result in inaccurate classification of sadness and fear.

First, anger, sadness, fear, and surprise, which are easily confused, are grouped together to form the five categories of anger + sadness, fear + surprise, disgust, happiness, and neutral. Next, those classified as "anger + sadness" are classified into either "anger" or "sadness," and those classified as "fear + surprise" are classified into either "fear" or "surprise." We thought that the two-class classification using the new features would improve the accuracy of facial expressions, which are considered to be easily confusable.

4.4 Careful Selection of Features by Importance

The importance of the features is calculated at each classification stage using the random forest function. The number of features used is varied to check the classification accuracy in each of one-step classification (i.e., classification into seven classes), the first step of two-step classification, the second step of two-step classification (anger + sadness), and the second step of two-step classification (fear + surprise), and to find the optimal features. Since the simpler the classification, the more limited the number of important features is considered to be, we carefully select features with the policy of omitting some less important features in one-step classification and the first step of two-step classification and using only some highly important features in the second step of two-step classification.

5 Experiment

5.1 Dataset

The experiment uses face images from the Karolinska Directed Emotional Faces (KDEF) dataset [10], which contains face images of 35 males and 35 females from five different angles, each with seven different facial expressions (six basic facial expressions and neutral). In this experiment, however, only the front-facing face images are used. The data consist of 490 images (70 images for each of the seven facial expressions) with feature values $f1$ to $f25$ labeled with the respective facial expression labels, divided into 343 sets of training data and 147 sets of test data. The data was split using the train_test_split function of scikit-learn, a Python machine learning library, so that the ratio of training data: test data = 7:3. The value of random_state is fixed so that the data are split in the same way for one-step classification and two-step classification.

5.2 Expression Classification Without Consideration of Importance

We test whether two-step classification is superior to one-step classification for sadness and fear.

We construct the seven-class classification model for one-step classification, five-class classification model for the first step of two-step classification, two-class classification model (anger + sadness) for the second step of two-step classification, and two-class classification model (fear + surprise) for the second step of two-step classification using Scikit-learn's RandomForestClassifier (using default values for parameters). The test data are classified by training these models with features $f1$ to $f25$ of the training data. The classification accuracy is compared based on the F value (F1-score).

The classification accuracies for each of one-step classification and two-step classification are shown in Table 2.

Table 2. Classification accuracy without considering importance (F1-score)

	One-step Classification	Two-step Classification
anger	0.870	0.785
disgust	0.889	0.889
fear	0.652	0.847
happiness	0.878	0.878
sadness	0.585	0.676
surprise	0.622	0.905
neutral	0.821	0.632

Table 2 shows that two-step classification improves the accuracy of classification of fear, sadness, and surprise, and decreases the accuracy of classification of anger and neutral.

5.3 Facial Expression Classification Based on Importance

We test how much classification accuracy can be improved by carefully selecting features based on their importance. Features used in each classification (seven-class, five-class, and two-class) are carefully selected. As a result of comparing the accuracy, the classification accuracy was the best when the following combinations of features were used.

Seven-Class Classification. Excluding four features of lower importance ($f23, f12,$ $f13, f15$).

Five-Class Classification. Excluding eight features of lower importance ($f23, f20,$ $f22, f12, f13, f15, f24, f14$).

Two-Class Classification (anger + sadness). Using the top five most important features ($f3, f2, f16, f1, f21$).

Two-Class Classification (fear + surprise). Using the top seven most important features ($f24, f3, f2, f9, f16, f20, f22$).

Classification is performed by a random forest trained with only carefully selected features as input. Table 3 shows the classification accuracy for each of one-step classification and the two-step classification.

Table 3. Classification accuracy based on importance (F1-score)

	One-step Classification	Two-step Classification
anger	0.870	0.706
disgust	0.865	0.889
fear	0.667	0.868
happiness	0.878	0.900
sadness	0.683	0.758
surprise	0.651	0.936
neutral	0.829	0.651

Comparing Tables 2 and 3, there is no significant change in one-step classification except for the classification accuracy of sadness. Two-step classification also shows an improvement in the classification accuracy for sadness, but there is no significant improvement for the other facial expressions, and a decrease in the classification accuracy for anger. In both Tables 2 and 3, two-step classification is superior in classifying fear, sadness, and surprise, while one-step classification is superior in classifying anger and neutral.

6   Consideration

From the experimental results, it can be confirmed that the proposed method can classify facial expressions with higher accuracy than the classification accuracy of the previous studies. Two-step classification is effective for improving the classification accuracy of sadness and fear expressions, which is the objective of this study, and the overall accuracy is considered to be improved by considering the degree of importance. In particular, the improvement in the classification accuracy of sadness is remarkable. The use of AUs such as AU9 as features was shown to be useful. In one-step classification, there was little improvement in classification accuracy after careful selection of features. For example, if "anger, surprise, and neutral" were grouped together as "others" and then features were carefully selected, the accuracy would be improved.

7   Conclusion

In this study, we proposed two-step classification method using FACS and random forests to improve the accuracy of classification of sadness and fear in facial expression classification. The classification of seven facial expressions, including six basic facial expressions and neutral, was performed using a random forest trained with these features as input. The classification accuracy of sadness and fear was improved by first classifying five expressions that are easily confused, and then classifying two expressions individually. The classification accuracy of disgust, which was considered difficult to classify using conventional features, was also improved by using AU, and the accuracy of happiness was maintained at a high level. However, there was no significant improvement in the classification accuracy of expressions other than the target expressions, and the classification accuracy of anger and neutral was noticeably lower than that of the target expressions.

Future issues include devising a method for deriving facial expression intensity based on feature bias, identifying the causes of poor accuracy in anger and neutral and improving accuracy, and verifying the versatility of the method using a variety of data sets. It is also necessary to examine the difference between sad or fearful facial expressions that lead to good evaluations and those that lead to bad evaluations in the evaluation of works.

References

1. Sakaue, S., Nomiya, H., Hochin, T.: Estimation of emotional scene from lifelog videos in consideration of intensity of various facial expressions. Studies in Comput. Intell. **721**, 121–136 (2016)
2. Shinohara, Y.: A Study on Evaluation Methods of Images and Movies by Estimating Facial Expression Intensity. Master's thesis, Kyoto Institute of Technology, Kyoto, Japan (2020)
3. Sun, Y.: Proposal of a Smile Intensity Estimation Model for Video Rating Estimation. Master's thesis, Kyoto Institute of Technology, Kyoto, Japan (2021)
4. Facial Action Coding System - Paul Ekman Group. https://www.paulekman.com/facial-action-coding-system/. Accessed 30 Jan 2023

5. Onishi, Y., Matsukawa, T., Suzuki, E.: Detection of Abnormal Facial Expressions Based on Long Short-Term Memory Using the Facial Action Coding System (FACS). FIT2021, 2nd Division, no.F-014, pp. 381–382 (2021) (in Japanese)
6. Sato, Y., Horaguchi, Y., Vanel, L., Shioiri, S.: Image Preference Estimation Using Facial Expression Features in Multiple Image Domains. JSAI2021, no.4D2-OS-4a-03 (2021) (in Japanese)
7. Baltrušaitis, T., Zadeh, A., Lim, Y., Morency, LP.: OpenFace 2.0: facial behavior analysis toolkit. IEEE International Conference on Automatic Face and Gesture Recognition (2018)
8. Dlib C++ Library. http://dlib.net/. Accessed 30 Jan 2023
9. Universal Emotions I What are Emotions? I Paul Ekman Group. https://www.paulekman.com/universal-emotions/. Accessed 30 Jan 2023
10. Lundqvist, D., Flykt, A., Öhman, A.: The Karolinska Directed Emotional Faces – KDEF. CD ROM from Department of Clinical Neuroscience, Psychology section, Karolinska Institutet, Stockholm, Sweden, ISBN 91–630–7164–9 (1998)

Positiveness Calculation of Japanese POPS Using Music Features Extracted from Acoustic Data

Ryosuke Toi[1] and Teruhisa Hochin[2](✉)

[1] Graduate School of Information Sciences, Kyoto Institute of Technology, Matsugasaki, Sakyo-ku, Kyoto 606-8585, Japan
m3622028@edu.kit.ac.jp
[2] Information and Human Sciences, Kyoto Institute of Technology, Matsugasaki, Sakyo-ku, Kyoto 606-8585, Japan
hochin@kit.ac.jp

Abstract. In recent years, with the spread of music streaming services, listening to music has become a part of everyday life for many people. In the field of music therapy, there is a principle that listening to music that is homogeneous to one's psychological state at the time is soothing to the human body (ISO-Principle). In this paper, we propose a method to calculate a simple measure of positiveness using music features extracted from acoustic data of Japanese POPS for obtaining music pieces matching the psychological situation. We adopt the Thayer model, in which impression words are mapped onto a two-dimensional plane. Two axes are Valence and Arousal. The values of each axis of the Thayer model were determined by using the fuzzy clustering as the feature extracted from the music piece, and the positiveness was calculated by summing the weighted values of each axis. In the subject experiment, 20 subjects were asked to fill out a questionnaire regarding the positiveness of the music piece. The error between the calculated positiveness and the actual one was verified. As a result, relatively good results were obtained for songs whose measured positiveness was high or low, indicating the effectiveness of the proposed method.

Keywords: Thayer model · Valence · Arousal · ISO-Principle

1 Introduction

Psychological wellbeing describes the state of mental health and well-being of human beings. Positive computing is also a term used to describe technology that improves psychological wellbeing by using technology. Ogino [1] defines positive computing as (1) the measurement of human emotional responses to emotional information expressed by objects, things, and people based on brain science, psychology, and physiology, (2) modeling the relationship between emotional information and emotionality, and (3) using emotionality technology to design and develop products and information systems that enable humans to become emotionally positive. In the field of psychotherapy using

K. Saeed et al. (Eds.): CISIM 2023, LNCS 14164, pp. 453–465, 2023.
https://doi.org/10.1007/978-3-031-42823-4_33

music, it has been reported that, based on the "ISO-Principle", listening to music that is homogeneous with the psychological situation is healing to humans [2]. Today, music listening has become even more prevalent in people's daily lives due to the spread of music streaming services such as iTunes and Spotify. If the relationship between music and sensitivity can be modeled and people can select and listen to music according to their mood, this could have a healing effect on many people. Although there have been studies on musical impressions [3–7], most of them categorize songs into words expressing impressions. From the perspective of music retrieval, this has the disadvantage that it imposes on the user the complicated task of searching for impression words according to mood from a huge vocabulary and selecting songs from them.

In this paper, we attempt to quantify the relationship between music and sensitivity by calculating a simple scale defined as "positiveness" by using music features of J-POP songs.

The remainder of this paper is organized as follows. Section 2 describes the proposed and experimental methods. Section 3 evaluates the proposed method through experiments. Section 4 presents the conclusions of this paper.

2   Methods

2.1   Thayer Model

The language of human emotions is so varied that it is difficult to define them on a single scale. Russell defined emotions as "all emotions can be described in terms of a circular plane with two dimensions: pleasant-displeased and aroused-drowsy" [8]. Thayer then conducted psychoacoustic experiments based on Russell's circular model and created the Thayer model [9]. Thayer's model consists of Arousal on the vertical axis, which indicates how much emotion-calm a piece of music has, and Valence on the horizontal axis, which indicates the quality of emotion (positive-negative) (Fig. 1), and the degree of each axis expresses the emotion. The mood of a song is classified into four clusters according to the level of Arousal and Valence: delighted, relaxed, depressed, and angry/anxious, which are defined as C1, C2, C3, and C4 in this paper in this order.

2.2   Extraction of Music Features

Music features were extracted from the entire music piece in WAVE file format by using librosa [10], a sound analysis package tool for Python. The sampling frequency was 22,050 Hz. Pre-processing was performed by using Studio One 4 [11] to normalize the volume and to cut off the silence at the beginning and the end of the sound source.

2.3   Extraction of Music Features Related to the Arousal Axis

RMS (Root Mean Square Root) is used as the music feature for the Arousal axis. STFT (Short-Time Fourier Transform) is applied to the music data to construct seven subbands (Eq. (1)), from low to high frequencies in the frequency domain of the signal, and the RMS is calculated for each. The RMS of each sub-band and the RMS of the entire piece,

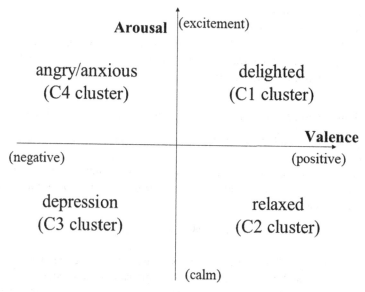

Fig. 1. Thayer model

for a total of 8 dimensions, are used as the features of the piece concerning the Arousal axis.

$$\left(0, \frac{F_s}{2^n}\right), \left(\frac{F_s}{2^n}, \frac{F_s}{2^{n-1}}\right), \cdots \left(\frac{F_s}{2^2}, \frac{F_s}{2^1}\right), (Fs : 22050, n = 7) \tag{1}$$

2.4 Extraction of Music Features Related to the Valence Axis

The music features for the Valence axis are MFCC (5 dimensions), Spectral centroid, spectral variation, spectral roll-off, tonality, and BPM, for a total of 10 dimensions.

- MFCC (Mel-Frequency Cepstral Coefficient)
  MFCCs were extracted from the entire sound source data using librosa.feature.mfcc(). The number of dimensions was 13, and the discrete cosine transform type 3 was used. Averages were taken for each of the dimensions from the lowest to the fifth and used as the MFCC.
- Spectral centroid
  The spectral centroid of gravity was extracted for the entire sound source data using librosa.feature.spectral_centroid() and the average of each frame was used.
- Spectral variation
  The temporal power change between frames was calculated for the entire sound source data using librosa.onset.onset_strength() and the average value was used.
- Spectral roll-off
  The spectral roll-off was calculated for the entire sound source data using librosa.feature.spectral_rolloff() and the average value was used. The threshold was set to 95%.

- BPM (Beat Per Minute)

    BPM is extracted from the sound source data as much as possible. For those that could not be obtained, the BPM was calculated using librosa.beat.beat_track(), and any incorrect BPM extracted was manually corrected. The integer part of the obtained BPM was used as the music features.
- Tonality

    The following procedure was performed on the entire sound source data.

Step 1 Separate the sound source data into harmonic and percussion sounds by using librosa.effects.hpss().

Step 2 Based on the obtained BPM, the hop length is determined based on eighth notes (Eq. (2)). Decimal places are rounded off. The BPM shown here is the same value as the BPM used as the music feature value.

$$x = \frac{sr*60}{BPM*2}(sr = 22050) \tag{2}$$

Step 3 A chromagram is created using librosa.feature.chroma_cqt(). The input is the harmonic tone separated in Step 1 and the hop length calculated in Step 2.

Step 4 Assign 0 to the value of the fifth highest-valued tone in the chromagram that is lower in value than the fifth highest-valued tone (sparsification).

Step 5 Chord estimation is performed by taking the inner product of the previously created chord template and the chromagram. If the template with the highest inner product corresponds to a major chord, set 1 as a parameter, if it corresponds to a minor chord, set -1.

Step 6 Extract the values of the notes comprising the estimated chord from the chromagram and take the product of the values of the three notes and the parameters set in Step 5.

Step 7 Perform Step 4 to Step 6 for each frame of the chromagram, take the average of all frames, and use it as the music feature.

2.5 Calculation of Values

The procedure for calculating the degree of positiveness based on the extracted music features is described here. This procedure can be divided into the calculation of the values corresponding to each axis of the Thayer model through fuzzy clustering and the calculation of positiveness by using the values of each axis. While previous studies [3, 4] used GMM-based clustering, fuzzy clustering is employed in this study because the degree of belonging to a cluster can be flexibly adjusted according to the membership values.

Calculation of the Values Corresponding to Each Axis of the Thayer Model. Fuzzy clustering is used to determine the degree of belongingness of clusters G1 and G2, which are estimated to have high and low psychometric (or emotional) values, respectively, for the features obtained in Sects. 2.2 and 2.3 (Eq. (3)).

$$Arousal(Valence)\ Feature \Rightarrow \begin{cases} P(G1) \\ P(G2) \end{cases} \tag{3}$$

Here, P(G1) and P(G2) are the degrees of belongingness of each cluster calculated by fuzzy clustering, Arousal and Valence values are calculated by subtracting these two values (Eq. (4)).

$$Arousal(Valence)\ Score = P(G1) - P(G2) \tag{4}$$

Fuzzy clustering was conducted through skfuzzy [12], a tool for Python. The membership values were adjusted to six patterns with $m = 2.0, 3.0, 4.0, 5.0, 6.0,$ and 7.0. The error rate, which adjusts the degree of convergence, was set to 0.005.

Calculation of Positiveness. The final positiveness is calculated by using Eq. (5)

$$Positive\ Score = \{\alpha * (Arousal\ Score) + \beta * (Valence\ Score)\} * 50 + 50 \tag{5}$$

Here, α and β are weighting values, satisfying the conditions of Eq. (6).

$$\alpha + \beta = 1\ (0 \leq \alpha, \beta \leq 1) \tag{6}$$

The values of α and β are decided by solving the problem of minimizing the Mean Absolute Error (MAE) under the constraints of Eq. (6) for the positiveness, Valence, and Arousal values obtained in the experiment (Eq. (7)).

$$\frac{\sum_{i=1}^{n} |True\ Score_i - \{\alpha * (True\ Arousal_i) + \beta * (True\ Valence_i)\}|}{n} \tag{7}$$

Here, the values of n, True Score, True Arousal, and True Valence are the experimentally obtained positiveness, valence, and arousal values scaled from 0 to 100, where n is 10 (the total number of song data obtained in the experiment).

The α and β determined in this way are substituted into Eq. (5) to determine the membership value m that minimizes the MAE between the estimated positiveness value and the experimentally obtained positiveness value.

2.6 Music Material

The proposed method was applied to 20 songs. A total of 20 songs were subjectively selected based on the Thayer model, four songs in each of the clusters C1, C2, C3, and C4, and four songs that were felt not to fall into any of the clusters, of which 10 songs were used in the evaluation experiment. In a reference study, Ono et al. [2] raised the issue of the impression of songs changing depending on the characteristics of the singing voice, so the songs in each cluster and the four songs that did not correspond were selected so that there were two songs for each male and female singing voice. The songs used in the experiment were randomly selected so that 10 of the 20 songs to which the proposed method was applied would satisfy the conditions described above, with two songs in each of the clusters C1–C4 and none of the clusters, and one song for each male and female voice. The 10 songs used in the experiment and their corresponding cluster numbers are listed as follows:

- C1

    "Peace sign" - Kenshi Yonezu

    "Try & Try" - Malcolm Mask Mclaren

- C2
    "Highway Star, Speed Star" - Cymbals
    "mayonnaise" - ego apartment
- C3
    "Tsukimiso" - Novelbright
    "Gekko" - Chihiro Onitsuka
- C4
    "Usseewa" - Ado
    "Matomo na sekai" - eastern youth
- None
    "How to be loved" - yureru landscape
    "Kids In The Park feat. PUNPEE" – RHYMESTER

2.7 Evaluation Experiment

In order to evaluate the proposed method of calculating positiveness, an evaluation experiment was conducted on 10 auditory materials using the following procedure. A total of 10 songs were used in the experiment, selected from the 20 songs listed in Sect. 2.5, two songs from each cluster and two songs that did not seem to fit into any of the clusters (one male and one female singing voice).

Step 1 Listening to the music material.
Step 2 Answering a questionnaire about the impressions received from the music material.
Step 3 One-minute interval.
Step 4 Step 1 to Step 3 repeated for each material.
Step 5 Answers to a post-questionnaire.

BOSE SoundTrue Around-Ear II headphones were used for listening to the music. The material was cut into one chorus by using Studio One 4 and processed to fade out in the last five seconds. The order of listening was determined randomly in order to avoid bias in impressions due to the order of the songs.

A total of 20 undergraduate and postgraduate students (10 males and 10 females, mean age 21.9 years) joined in the experiment.

Questionnaire Item. We prepared an impression survey questionnaire. In this questionnaire, the eight items shown in Table 1 were presented to the subjects. The ratings on Arousal and Valence axes were made with reference to Ohno et al. [13].

3 Results

The means of the evaluation values of the items on the C1, C2, C3, C4, Arousal axis, Valence axis, and Positiveness of the questionnaire are shown in Table 2. Next to the material number, it indicates which cluster the song corresponds to. Figure 2 shows the results of mapping the 10 songs used in the experiment to the Thayer model by using the Valence and Arousal values obtained from the experiment.

Table 1. Impression evaluation questionnaire items for the music.

Item	Rating scale
Positiveness felt from the song	0 (negative) - 10 (positive)
Fun, Exciting (corresponding to C1)	1 (not applicable) - 5 (applicable)
Relaxed, Calm (corresponding to C2)	
Sad, Depressed (corresponding to C3)	
Angry, Anxious (corresponding to C4)	
Arousal axis: intensity of the song	1 (calm) - 5 (intense)
Valence axis: Mood felt from the song	1 (dark mood) - 5 (light mood)
Have you heard this song before?	Yes or No

3.1 Relevance of the Selected Songs

The validity of the song selection is evaluated with reference to the impression word questionnaires corresponding to each cluster as the songs used in the experiment were selected subjectively. Although the C1, C3, and C4 clusters had the highest ratings for the corresponding impression words, there was some confusion with the C1 cluster regarding the materials 3 and 4 belonging to the C2 cluster and material 8 belonging to the C4 cluster. This result also corresponds to Fig. 2 using Valence and Arousal values.

Table 2. Results of questionnaire (average)

Number	C1	C2	C3	C4	Arousal	Valence	Positive
1 (C1)	3.9	1.75	1.5	1.65	4.05	4.2	7.25
2 (C1)	4.55	1.95	1.05	1.25	4.5	4.8	8.3
3 (C2)	4.15	2.95	1.35	1.1	3.05	4.2	7.1
4 (C2)	4	3.35	1.5	1.35	2.6	4	6.5
5 (C3)	1.7	3.1	3.55	2.35	1.85	2.15	3.8
6 (C3)	1.4	3.35	3.75	2.65	1.25	1.9	2.75
7 (C4)	2.65	1.25	2.15	3.85	4.85	2.8	3.9
8 (C4)	2.75	2	1.7	2.8	3.75	3.6	5.9
9 (None)	2.8	3.65	2.35	1.7	1.95	3.4	5.55
10 (None)	3.95	2.5	1.55	1.65	3	3.9	7.3

However, all songs were selected as intended, since the corresponding impression words were the first (or second) highest in the evaluation for material numbers 2, 3, and 8.

In the C2 cluster, the material 3, which had a corresponding impression word rating of less than 3, was compared with the material 9, which had a high impression word

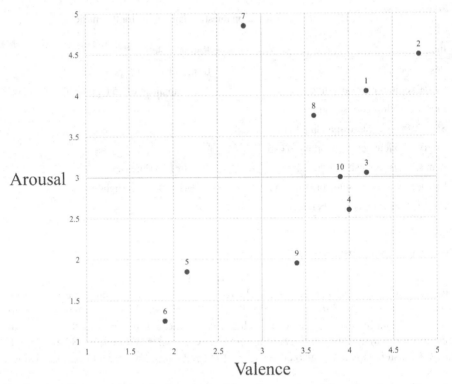

Fig. 2. The Valence and Arousal values obtained from the experimental results were used to map the songs used in the experiment to the Thayer model.

Table 3. Relationship between BPM and Arousal/Valence (average).

Number	BPM	Valence	Arousal
1 (C1)	200	4.2	4.05
2 (C1)	206	4.8	4.5
3 (C2)	184	4.2	3.05
4 (C2)	96	4	2.6
5 (C3)	78	2.15	1.85
6 (C3)	76	1.9	1.25
7 (C4)	178	2.8	4.85
8 (C4)	136	3.6	3.75
9 (None)	89	3.4	1.95
10 (None)	96	3.9	3

rating corresponding to the C2 cluster, in terms of features. As a result, there was a large difference in BPM between the material 3 and 9 (184 and 89) (Table 3).

When the correlation coefficient between BPM and Arousal value was calculated for all songs, a strong positive correlation (0.858, p-value is 0.00151) was observed. This suggests that the large BPM value is one of the reasons for the confusion with the C1 cluster. This discussion is related to Hevner's experiment [14] in which he used eight adjective clusters to show the relationship between the impression and the tempo of the songs. The C1 cluster in this paper corresponds to the cluster represented by "merry" among the adjective clusters presented by Hevner, and the C2 cluster corresponds to the cluster represented by "calm". In a previous study, music with a fast tempo was strongly associated with the "merry" cluster, while music with a slow tempo was strongly associated with the "calm" cluster. This result suggests that BPM may have contributed to the cluster confusion.

The correlation coefficient between BPM and Valence value was 0.629 (p-value is 0.0515), indicating that there was a correlation, but weaker than that of the Arousal value. This result contradicts the method of using rhythmic features as features of the Valence axis, which was shown in a previous study [2].

3.2 Determination of Weighting and Membership Values

Based on the values obtained from the questionnaire, the method proposed in Sect. 2.4 was carried out. The results were $\alpha = 0.87586...$, and $\beta = 0.12413...$ The MAE (mean absolute error) was 6.08449.... Membership values were calculated based on the obtained α and β.

As a result, both Valence and Arousal values were 7.0, and the MAE was 20.00707.... The reason for this may be that there were several calculated values for both Valence and Arousal that were far from the experimentally obtained values, and as a result, membership values with calculated positiveness concentrated in the 35–65 range were calculated as the smallest MAE values. In other words, this is because the accuracy of the Valence and Arousal values calculated for each piece of music differs greatly, and it is difficult to determine the appropriate membership value at this stage. Therefore, we will estimate plausible membership values by examining the calculation accuracy of each Valence and Arousal value for each piece of music.

3.3 Accuracy of Valence and Arousal Values

The absolute error between the Valence value and the value obtained from the questionnaire at each membership value (m) is shown in Table 4, and the absolute error of the Arousal value is shown in Table 5. The calculated Valence and Arousal values were scaled according to the stage (1–5) of the questionnaire items, and those with absolute errors exceeding 1 were grayed out.

For the Valence values, the membership values with the highest number of materials with an absolute error within 1 were 3.0 and 7.0. For the Arousal value, the membership values were 3.0, 6.0, and 7.0. The Valence and Arousal values tend to converge to 50 as the membership value increases, since the size of the membership value is proportional to the ambiguity of the attribution to a cluster. Therefore, the errors in the cases of m

Table 4. Absolute error between Valence values and questionnaire evaluation values at each membership value (m)

Number	m=2.0	3.0	4.0	5.0	6.0	7.0
1(C1)	0.501977	0.886969	1.009439	1.065543	1.094867	1.113008
2(C1)	0.202821	0.839541	1.139601	1.298854	1.394008	1.458162
3(C2)	3.077034	2.667996	2.379211	2.186572	2.043158	1.931323
4(C2)	2.933192	2.476923	2.05827	1.792088	1.625195	1.51521
5(C3)	1.077859	0.618741	0.203898	0.060208	0.226219	0.335779
6(C3)	0.553261	0.074867	0.407752	0.589537	0.698824	0.769927
7(C4)	1.999193	1.422648	1.077655	0.87984	0.757179	0.672516
8(C4)	1.963063	1.442559	1.219865	1.09515	1.011496	0.950769
9(None)	2.3579	2.108397	1.885892	1.72433	1.586136	1.456441
10(None)	1.066739	0.754103	0.401856	0.140427	0.045875	0.180176

Table 5. Absolute error between Arousal values and questionnaire evaluation values at each membership value (m)

Number	m=2.0	3.0	4.0	5.0	6.0	7.0
1(C1)	0.791957	0.206925	0.200066	0.439993	0.585352	0.67974
2(C1)	0.160271	0.775575	1.037254	1.171576	1.249857	1.300097
3(C2)	1.618588	0.97719	0.647634	0.474837	0.373526	0.308549
4(C2)	2.123788	1.495989	1.130423	0.924343	0.800356	0.71976
5(C3)	0.665972	0.08182	0.329658	0.56254	0.702126	0.792236
6(C3)	0.3448	0.964167	1.248396	1.393882	1.478641	1.532941
7(C4)	0.065191	0.678611	1.058585	1.275297	1.407054	1.493439
8(C4)	1.811906	1.305493	1.131782	1.036846	0.978104	0.938315
9(None)	0.288918	0.286092	0.490809	0.605618	0.679649	0.732262
10(None)	1.669383	1.056781	0.72971	0.543129	0.4267	0.348435

= 6.0 and 7.0 are caused by the convergence of the values of large or small (above 4 or below 2) material to the middle values (2–4) due to the membership value. On the other hand, the error in the case of $m = 3.0$ can be attributed to two factors: firstly, the number of samples for the clustering was insufficient, so that items that should have been calculated as around the middle value were calculated as more extreme values. This tendency was seen in the absolute error in the Arousal value. Another factor is that the calculated values are the opposite of the values obtained in the questionnaire and the scale. This tendency was seen in the absolute error in the Valence value. This may be due to the low precision of some of the features and the small number of features. The correlation between the features used to determine the Valence values, and the Valence values obtained from the questionnaire was investigated about the low accuracy of the features.

As a result, the correlation coefficients were 0.19115... and 0.20634... For spectral variation and tonality, respectively, and no correlation could be confirmed. In particular, the implementation of the tonality was focused on the detection of major and minor triads, which resulted in the misrecognition of major and minor chords in the Seventh and Fractional chords. Therefore, more detailed implementation of tonality is in future work. On the other hand, the correlation coefficients between MFCC and Valence values were 0.69732..., -0.68158... and 0.69963... For the third component from the lowest dimension, respectively, showing a rather strong correlation. In terms of the number of features, there were six comments after the experiment that the number of features was often influenced by the lyrics, suggesting that one possible improvement measure would be to incorporate features related to the lyrics. It is therefore considered that the errors occurring at $m = 6.0$ and 7.0 are due to excessive ambiguity in the attributional nature of the clustering, while the errors occurring at $m = 3.0$ are due to the accuracy of the features. As there is considerable room for improvement about the latter, error verification of positiveness at $m = 3.0$ is carried out for each song in the next section to find more detailed problems.

3.4 Positiveness Error Verification for Each Song

Table 6 shows the absolute error between the positiveness estimated using α, β and the calculated Valence and Arousal values from the experiment and the positiveness obtained from the questionnaire. Material numbers 9 and 10 were selected without any specific cluster in mind, but the cluster number corresponding to the impression word that was most highly rated in the questionnaire is indicated in brackets. For songs in the C2 and C4 clusters, a large error of 29–56 was observed, while for songs in the C1 and C3 clusters, a relatively high accuracy was obtained with an error of 2–11, except for material number 5.

Table 6. Absolute error between estimated positiveness and questionnaire ratings at $m = 3.0$

Number	Estimated value	Measured value	Absolute error
1 (C1)	60.8	72.5	11.7
2 (C1)	73.3	83.0	9.7
3 (C2)	15.0	71.0	56.0
4 (C2)	21.1	65.0	43.9
5 (C3)	14.0	38.0	24.0
6 (C3)	25.1	27.5	2.4
7 (C4)	80.4	39.0	41.4
8 (C4)	29.8	59.0	29.2
9 (C2)	10.2	55.5	45.3
10 (C1)	82.9	73.0	9.9

The positive and negative values of the Valence and Arousal axes in the Thayer model are identical for the songs in the C1 and C3 clusters, so the high and low positiveness levels tend to be extreme. This is thought to be the reason why the positiveness of songs in the C2 and C4 clusters, where the positive and negative values of the axes do not match, was calculated with less error than in the C1 and C3 clusters. Many of the songs in the C2 and C4 clusters with large errors had a positiveness of around 40–60, so increasing the number of samples and reviewing the features is an issue to improve the accuracy around the clustering boundaries.

In an interview-style impression questionnaire conducted after the experiment, it was found that there was a discrepancy in impressions of experimental material 1, depending on whether or not the music was recognized, such as "Generally, this song has a positive image, but it is the theme song of an anime, and whenever I hear it, I remember sad scenes from the anime" and "This song is often played at my workplace, so I have a bigger image of it from other sources than from other songs" for the experimental material 5. The respondents also commented that the influence of the voice quality was greater than that of the sound source. This suggests that the addition of features that focus on the singing sound may be useful for improving accuracy.

4 Conclusion

With the aim of improving positive computing technology by quantifying the relationship between music and sensitivity, we proposed a method for calculating positiveness by using J-POP. Music features were extracted from the sound source data in WAVE format, and the values of the Valence and Arousal axes in the Thayer model were determined by using fuzzy clustering. Positiveness was calculated by using the experimentally determined weighting values and the Valence and Arousal values. An experiment was conducted on a total of ten songs, two songs in each quadrant of the Thayer model and two songs that did not seem to fall into any of the quadrants. The results showed that the quadrants in which the positive and negative Valence and Arousal values were consistent had relatively small positiveness errors. On the other hand, significant errors were observed in the quadrants where the positive and negative values of each axis did not match. Possible sources of error include poor clustering performance due to insufficient number of samples and low accuracy of the music features. Particularly with regard to the second factor, no correlation was found with the measured values for spectral variation and tonality. In the impression questionnaire, there were also opinions pointing out the influence of the music's recognizability and lyrics on the impression, so further examination of the music features is an issue to be addressed in the future.

Acknowledgement. This work was partially supported by JSPS KAKENHI Grant Number JP21K12084.

References

1. Ogino, A.: Positive computing using kansei technology: kansei engineering for well-being. J. Japan Society of Kansei Eng. **18**(2), 55–62 (2020) (In Japanese)
2. Altschuler, I.M.: The past, present and future of musical therapy. Music in Therapy, pp. 24–35 (1954)

3. Ono, Y., Katto, J.: An automatic estimation method of music emotion based on musical psychology. IPSJ SIG Technical Reports **2009**(23), 61–66 (2009) (In Japanese)
4. Lu, L., Liu, D., Zhang, H.J.: Automatic mood detection and tracking of music audio signals. IEEE Trans. Audio Speech Lang. Process. **14**(1), 5–18 (2006)
5. Kumamoto, T., Ohta, K.: Design, implementation, and opening to the public of an impression-based music retrieval system. The Japanese Society for Artificial, Intelligence **21**, 310–318 (2006). (In Japanese)
6. Bischoff, K., Firan, C.S., Paiu, R., Nejdl, W., Laurier, C., Sordo, M.: Music mood and theme classification – a hybrid approach. 10th International Society for Music Information Retrieval Conference, pp. 657–662 (2009)
7. Tzanetakis, G.: Musical genre classification of audio signals. IEEE Trans. Speech and Audio Process., **10**(5) (2002)
8. Russell, J.A.: A circumplex model of affect. J. Pers. Soc. Psychol. **39**(6), 1161–1178 (1980)
9. Thayer, R.E.: The Biopsychology of Mood and Arousal. Oxford University Press, Oxford (1989)
10. Librosa Homepage. https://librosa.org. Accessed 19 Mar 2023
11. Studio One | Presonus Homepage. https://www.presonus.com/products/Studio-One. Accessed 19 Mar 2023
12. skfuzzy 0.4.2 docs. https://scikit-fuzzy.github.io/scikit-fuzzy/. Accessed 19 Mar 2023
13. Ohno, N., Nakamura, S., Yamamoto, T., Goto, M.: Construction of impression evaluation dataset for music videos and investigation of its characteristics (Translated from Japanese). IPSJ Technical Report, vol. 2015-MUS-108, no. 7 (2015) (In Japanese)
14. Hevner, K.: The affective value of pitch and tempo in music. Am. J. Psychol. **49**(4), 621–630 (1937)

Machine Learning Using Biometric Data and Kansei Data

Classification of Programming Logic Understanding Level Using Mouse Tracking Heatmaps and Machine Learning Techniques

Attaporn Khaesawad[1]([✉]) [iD], Vibol Yem[2] [iD], and Nobuyuki Nishiuchi[1] [iD]

[1] Faculty of Systems Design, Tokyo Metropolitan University, Tokyo, Japan
22960602@ed.tmu.ac.jp, nnishiuc@tmu.ac.jp
[2] Faculty of Engineering, Information and Systems, University of Tsukuba, Ibaraki, Japan
yem@iit.tsukuba.ac.jp

Abstract. Programming skill is one of the essential basic experience that each student in the field of computer science has to acquire. To potentially train all students such a skill, teachers should know every student understanding level during the practice of a programming for individually supporting. Conducting a test is a common method to classify the understanding level of the students. However, it would be a heavy burden for teachers and the student levels are known after the test. The purpose of our study is to classify the understanding level of programming during the practice. In this study, we focus on a block coding learning platform, and we propose a classification method by using mouse tracking heatmaps and machine learning techniques. As a first step of the study, we conduct a test with 18 participants. The results had shown that using mouse click heatmap image and decision tree algorithm was observed to classify students based on their programming logic understanding level through activity on a block coding learning platform. In our future work, we will increase the accuracy of classification and develop a model that can classify the understanding levels almost in real time of during programming practice.

Keywords: Understand Level Classification · Block Coding Learning Platform · Mouse Tracking Heatmap · Classification · Machine Learning · Teacher Support

1 Introduction

Over the past few years, we have witnessed a drastic change in the way computer technology is applied in our daily lives. Software and machine learning have been increasingly paid attention and careers in software development have become in high demand and consistently ranked in the Top 10 in the job market demand report [1, 2]. Accordingly considering the opportunity for students' careers, many fields of study put programming practice as one of the basic skills in their majors. To train programming to students with various levels, it is important to classify their understanding group; especially during the practice; thus, teachers can provide individual support effectively. By conducting a programming test, it is possible to classify the understanding levels of the students.

However, it is not only making a heavy burden for teachers, but such a method provides the result after the test and the result might vary according to the problem items.

This study aims to classify the programming understanding level using mouse tracking heatmap images and machine learning techniques. Our method can reduce the workload of teachers as well as for our further study in which we will classify the understanding level almost in real-time during training. In this study, we focus on the programming logic understanding level through the block coding learning platform [3, 4]. We conducted three steps for mouse tracking heatmap classification using the proposed framework as shown in Figs. 1, 2 and 3 respectively.

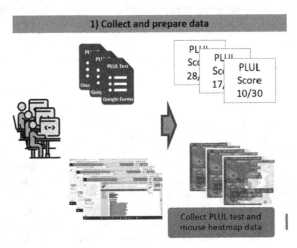

Fig. 1. The first step: collect and prepare data from PLUL Test and mouse tracking heatmaps.

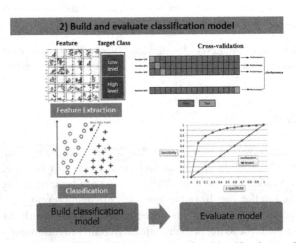

Fig. 2. The second step: build and evaluate four classification models.

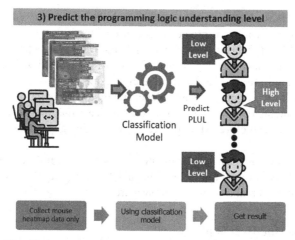

Fig. 3. The third step: Predicting the programming logic understanding level.

2 Related Work

2.1 Programming Logic Understanding Level

The programming logic understanding level (PLUL) refers to the degree to which a person understands the basic concepts and principles of programming logic. It is an essential aspect of computer programming, enabling individuals to write efficient and effective code. Basic programming logic refers to the process of designing a sequence of steps or instructions that a computer can follow to perform a specific task. Examples of programming logic concepts [5] that a person should understand include: variables are used to store data values and how using variables correctly is crucial for writing effective code; conditional statements are used to control the flow of a program based on specific conditions; loops are used to repeat a block of code a specific number of times or until a particular condition is met, and functions are blocks of code that can be called from other parts of a program for organizing code and avoiding repetition.

A person with a high programming logic understanding level can write efficient and effective code that achieves the desired outcome. They will also be able to debug and troubleshoot code more easily. Several studies have proposed the use of machine learning methods for programming level classification. For example, Çetinkaya and Baykan [6] have predicted the middle school students' programming aptitude using artificial neural network (ANN) algorithms by taking a survey of the 20-level Classic Maze course (CMC) on the Code.org website. Their results showed that ANN was an appropriate machine learning method for forecasting participants' skills, such as analytical thinking, problem-solving, and programming aptitude. Sagar et al. [7] have evaluated students' performance in two programming environments – the HackerEarth was a competitive programming website and the IGDTUW university-based programming portal. Their study aimed to assist students in self-assessment and help educators evaluate their students' progress by supervised learning namely, XGBoost and Random Forests and to predict students' performance for both dataset. The highest accuracy from XGBoost obtained for the HackerEarth dataset was 80%, while the accuracy for the University dataset was 91%. Sivasakthi [8] predicted the introductory programming performance of first-year bachelor students in a computer application course by a predictive data mining model using Multilayer Perception (MLP), Naïve Bayes, SMO, J48 and REPTree as classification algorithms. The collected data contains the students' demographics, grades in introductory programming at college, and grade on the introductory programming test that contains 60 questions. The results indicate that the MLP performs best with 93% accuracy. Therefore, MLP proves to be a potentially effective and efficient classifier algorithm.

Though these studies may help to identify the students who are novice programmers in introductory programming, they did not focus on mouse tracking data and classification almost in real time was not considered.

2.2 Mouse Tracking Heatmap

In this study, we focus on using a mouse tracking heatmap [9]. It is one of the popular data visualizations used to evaluate the mouse usage behaviours of users to interact with elements on a website. It is generated from the mouse movement, mouse click, mouse stop time activities or others. Commonly, positions with high mouse activity are hot colors (e.g., red) and positions with low mouse activity are cold colors (e.g., blue). It helps us to know the level of user attention shown in any component or content of the website to serve as data for improving the website's user experience. For example, Kirsh [10] proposes a new type of web page heatmap, Word Attention Heatmap (WAH), that shows a user's attention level to words or sentences in web content using data from mouse movements. As a result, our web page heatmap generated from mouse movement data can highlight words or sentences based on the user's attention level and can be used to improve web content to be more readable and understandable. In another example, Navalpakkam and Churchill [11] have used mouse movement heatmaps versus eye gaze heatmaps to analyze the mouse tracking data has a similar potential to the eye tracking data for measuring and predicting the user experience of a web content. The benefit of using mouse tracking data is that it is cheaper and has fewer lab settings compared to the use of eye tracking data. Figure 4 had shown a mouse tracking heatmap can be generated from the user's mouse movements on the code block learning platform to determine the understanding level of the programming logic. This indicates that the user has to move the mouse in a large number of positions. (shown in red) to successfully solve the programming logic problem in that activity.

2.3 Block Coding Learning Platform

The block coding learning platform is an online platform that provides resources and tools to help users learn and develop skills in block coding. Block coding involves programming by dragging and dropping visual blocks representing code functions, rather than typing out text-based code. The block coding learning platforms can be conducted for different age ranges and skill levels. The platforms may offer different features such as interactive tutorials, challenges, and community forums. For example, Scratch [12] is a block coding platform developed by MIT for children and teenagers. It allows users to

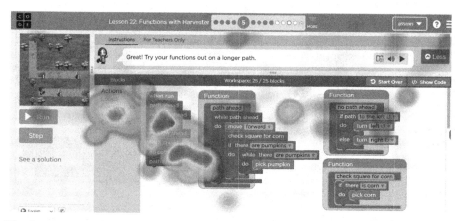

Fig. 4. An illustration example shown how a mouse tracking heatmap can be generated from the user's mouse movements on the code block learning platform.

create interactive stories, games, and animations by dragging and dropping code blocks. Code.org [13] is a nonprofit organization for all computer science accessible students. It offers block coding tutorials for beginners and more advanced courses on programming languages like JavaScript and Python. Tynker [14] is a block coding platform for children aged from seven to 14 years old. It offers interactive coding courses, puzzles, and games to help users learn coding concepts and develop programming skills. Blockly [15] is an open-source project that provides a visual programming language for creating web applications. It can be integrated into other platforms to provide block coding functionality.

In this study, we chose a block coding learning platform from the Code.org website because it has some advantages such as free use, multilingual support, large user community, the ability of student groups management, and enables learning activities choosing which suitable for students. It also has a system to track learning progress, and there are a variety of learning activity topics such as introductory programming concepts, robot control simulators, learning principles of AI, developing apps on mobile devices, etc. The activity screen on the Code.org website consists of six parts: 1) The display result area of running all block codes that the user has placed. 2) The problem that requires the user to solve this activity. 3) The recommended number of block codes to solve the problem in this activity. 4) The button to run all placed block codes and adjust the speed of display results. 5) All block codes that the user can use. 6. The area for placed block codes that will be used to solve this problem, as shown in Fig. 5.

2.4 Principal Components Analysis

Principal Components Analysis (PCA) [16, 17] is a statistical technique that is commonly used in the field of machine learning to recognize patterns and reduce the dimensionality of high-dimensional data. The data are converted into a new set of variables, known as principal components, which are linear combinations of the features that were initially collected. This is how the method works. The ability of the principal components to

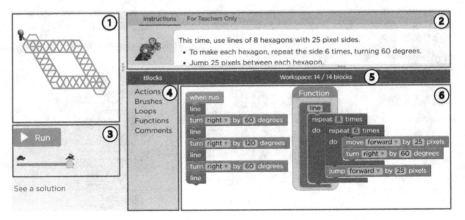

Fig. 5. The activity screen on the Code.org website consists of six parts.

explain the variation in the data is used to determine the order in which they are presented. The first principal component explains the most variation in the data, followed by the second principal component, which explains the second most, and so on. The principal component analysis (PCA) is a useful tool for simplifying high-dimensional data while preserving the majority of the information. It is possible to simplify models and make them more efficient by reducing the dimensionality of the data while still preserving the overarching structure of the data. Consider the following scenario: we have a dataset that contains ten features, and we want to lower the dimensionality of the data so that it only contains three features. PCA allows us to transform the data into three principal components, which are linear combinations of the original features. These principal components can then be analyzed independently. There is a possibility that a linear combination of the first five features, the next three features, and the last two features would make up the first, second, and third principal components, respectively.

3 Methodology

3.1 Proposed Procedure

We created a machine learning process to classify the programming logic understanding level through the block coding learning platform into two groups: a high-level group is a group with a high level of understanding of programming logic, and a low level group is a group with a low level of understanding of programming logic. We used three mouse tracking heatmap images from the mouse tracking data of 18 participants two times as dataset. However, we employed principal component analysis (PCA) as a means of reducing the dimensionality of the mouse tracking heatmap image. This approach was adopted to train classification models with the aim of mitigating overfitting issues and minimizing execution time.

3.2 Gathering of Dataset

The dataset in this study is collected from first-year university students in the information technology and business innovation program, Faculty of Science and Social Sciences, Burapha University, Sa Kaeo campus, Thailand. 18 participants took this study for 2 times: the beginning and the end of the information technology and business innovation fundamentals course. The dataset consists of two parts: the first part is the data that the participants took the programming logic understanding level test to be used to validate the results of programming logic understanding level classification. The second part is the mouse tracking data generated by a given activity in the block coding learning platform (code.org website), converted those data into mouse tracking heatmap images and brought those images into the classification models to classify a group of programming logic understanding levels.

The programming logic understanding level test has three types of questions that were sequenced and conditional execution, loops and iterations, and functions. This test had 30 questions representing a PLUL score were 30 points, which this score was used as a criterion to divide the programming logic understanding level into two groups: low-level and high-level. The criterion for categorizing such groups was based on the average PLUL score of all participants as shown in Fig. 6.

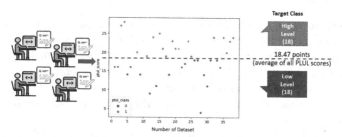

Fig. 6. A scattering chart of the criterion for categorizing such groups was based on the average PLUL score of all participants.

The activity in the block coding learning platform for collecting mouse tracking data was selected based on the instructor's recommendations to appropriate the programming logic understanding level evaluation and according to the programming logic understanding level test. The mouse tracking data consists of four parts: mouse timestamp, x-axis position, y-axis position, the amount of time the mouse stops at each position, and mouse click status. These data are converted into three types of mouse tracking heatmap image: mouse movement heatmap image, mouse click heatmap image, and mouse duration time heatmap image. Participants set their display resolution to 1280 x 720 with, a scale of 100%, and carried out the data collection procedure as follows: we introduce tools to collect mouse tracking data to participants, participants do a programming logic understanding level test, participants get familiar with tools to collect mouse tracking data, and participants collect actual mouse tracking data in a given activity as shown in Fig. 7.

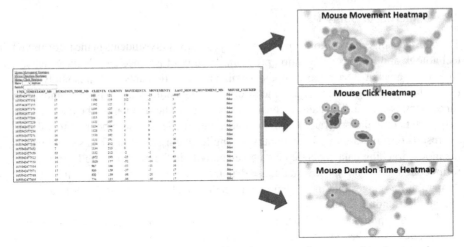

Fig. 7. The mouse tracking data are converted into three types of mouse tracking heatmap image: mouse movement heatmap image, mouse click heatmap image, and mouse duration time heatmap image.

3.3 Data Preparation

We calculated the average scores of all participants who tested their programming logic understanding level test. And took this average score as a criterion to divide the level of comprehension of programming logic into two levels: low level and high level. The part of mouse behavior data obtained from learning activities in the form of visual blocks was converted into three types of mouse heatmap image: mouse movement heatmap image (MM_HM), mouse click heatmap image (MC_HM), and mouse duration time heatmap image (MD_HM).

To prepare the heatmap data for building the classification model, we followed a three-step process as follows:

- Firstly, we resized all the images to make them suitable for processing and reduce the required processing time.
- Secondly, we transformed the 3-dimensional heatmap files (RGB) of individual images into a feature matrix represented as multi-dimensional arrays.
- Finally, we utilized the principal component analysis (PCA) to reduce the high-dimensional feature vectors into lower-dimensional vectors. The process of PCA involved flattening the feature matrix and computing the eigenvectors and eigenvalues of the covariance matrix to identify the principal components. The step of PCA transformed those sets of one-dimension arrays to PCA dataset as shown in Fig. 8. Each of the heatmaps dataset was processed and transformed by these techniques before building classification model.

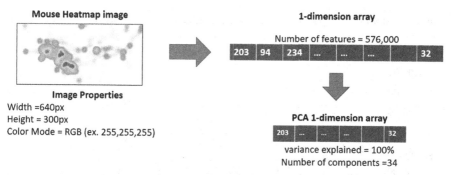

Fig. 8. Process of principal components analysis (PCA).

3.4 Building Classification Models

We used four types of machine learning algorithm to build the models and used the Grid Search (GS) method for parameter tuning of those algorithms. The tuned parameters of each algorithm were as follows: 1) Support Vector Machine (SVM) [18, 19] was kernel function, regularization parameter, degree of the polynomial kernel function and kernel coefficient. 2) K-nearest neighbors (k-NN) [20] was leaf size, number of neighbors and power parameter for the Minkowski metric. 3) Decision Tree [21] was maximum depth of the tree and max leaf nodes. 4) Random Forest [22] was tree number of trees in the forest, number of features to consider when looking for the best split and max leaf nodes, maximum depth of the tree and max leaf nodes. Table I shown the parameters values of each algorithm explored in this study. Then brought the prepared mouse heatmap image data to train each model.

3.5 Evaluating Classification Models

We employed Leave-one-out cross-validation (LOOCV) [23] to assess the efficacy of all classification models. This method was deemed appropriate due to its ability to effectively evaluate classification models with a limited number of datasets. The leave-one-out cross-validation technique is a variant of cross-validation, wherein the number of folds is equivalent to the number of instances present in the dataset. The application of the learning algorithm involves a singular iteration for each instance. During this process, the remaining instances are utilized as a training set, while the chosen instance is utilized as a test set consisting of a single item.

4 Results and Discussion

We compared different classification models which generated using four types of classification algorithms, namely SVM, k-NN, decision tree and random forest. Then we evaluated the performance of all classification models using LOOCV as shown in Fig. 9. The Y-axis represents the percentage accuracy of LOOCV and the X-axis shown the pattern of using input data to train the model and classification algorithm in each model. Among the models tested, the machine learning classification model produced good accuracy, as demonstrated in Fig. 9. These results have several research implications as follows:

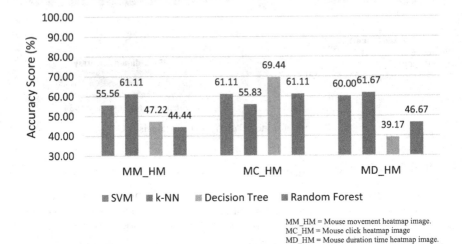

MM_HM = Mouse movement heatmap image.
MC_HM = Mouse click heatmap image
MD_HM = Mouse duration time heatmap image.

Fig. 9. Performance of each classification algorithm on three datasets.

Firstly, a comparison was made among three types of mouse heatmap image, namely mouse movement heatmap image (MM_HM), mouse click heatmap image (MC_HM), and mouse duration time heatmap image (MD_HM). The results of our study indicate that the LOOCV accuracy score of mouse click heatmap images was observed to be the highest among all heatmap images because it could pinpoint the location of objects as critical components for successfully solving given problems better than other mouse heatmap images. Secondly, the decision tree algorithm that utilised mouse click heatmap images and set max_depth = 1 and max_leaf_nodes = 2 was observed to be the highest LOOCV accuracy score at 69.44%.

5   Conclusion

This paper proposed a method to classify the understanding level of programming logic through a block coding learning platform using mouse tracking heatmaps and machine learning techniques. The accuracy score of using mouse click heatmap image and decision tree algorithm was tuned parameters by the Grid Search method was 69.44%. The findings of this study indicate that using mouse click heatmap image and decision tree algorithm was observed to classify students based on their programming logic understanding level through activity on a block coding learning platform.

The limitation of this study is the very small number of samples in the dataset used for training a classification model. Future work focuses on increasing the number of datasets, using other feature selection techniques, using data augmentation techniques, and using a combination of three type mouse tracking heatmap images as a new dataset to increase the reliability and accuracy score of the results. Furthermore, we will develop an effective model that can classification student's programming logic understand level during the programming practice.

References

1. Lauer, D.C.: Exploring Workplace Learning for Software Developers from the Perspectives of Software Developers and Managers of Software Developers. Drake University (2022)
2. Verma, A., et al.: An investigation of skill requirements in artificial intelligence and machine learning job advertisements. Ind. High. Educ. **36**(1), 63–73 (2022)
3. João, et al.: A cross-analysis of block-based and visual programming apps with computer science student-teachers. Educ. Sci. **9**(3), 181 (2019). https://doi.org/10.3390/educsci9030181
4. Carlos Begosso, L., et al.: An analysis of block-based programming environments for CS1. In: 2020 IEEE Frontiers in Education Conference (FIE), pp. 1–5 IEEE, Uppsala, Sweden (2020). https://doi.org/10.1109/FIE44824.2020.9273982
5. Zelle, J.M.: Python Programming: An Introduction to Computer Science. Franklin, Beedle & Associates Inc, Portland, Oregon (2017)
6. Çetinkaya, A., Baykan, Ö.K.: Prediction of middle school students' programming talent using artificial neural networks. Eng. Sci. Technol., an Int. J. **23**(6), 1301–1307 (2020). https://doi.org/10.1016/j.jestch.2020.07.005
7. Sagar, M., et al.: Performance prediction and behavioral analysis of student programming ability. In: 2016 International Conference on Advances in Computing, Communications and Informatics (ICACCI), pp. 1039–1045 IEEE, Jaipur, India (2016). https://doi.org/10.1109/ICACCI.2016.7732181
8. Sivasakthi, M.: Classification and prediction based data mining algorithms to predict students' introductory programming performance. In: 2017 International Conference on Inventive Computing and Informatics (ICICI), pp. 346–350 IEEE, Coimbatore (2017). https://doi.org/10.1109/ICICI.2017.8365371
9. Koonsanit, K., Tsunajima, T., Nishiuchi, N.: Evaluation of Strong and Weak Signifiers in a Web Interface Using Eye-Tracking Heatmaps and Machine Learning. In: Saeed, K. and Dvorský, J. (eds.) Computer Information Systems and Industrial Management. pp. 203–213. Springer International Publishing, Cham (2021). https://doi.org/10.1007/978-3-030-84340-3_16
10. Kirsh, I.: Using mouse movement heatmaps to visualize user attention to words. In: Proceedings of the 11th Nordic Conference on Human-Computer Interaction: Shaping Experiences, Shaping Society, pp. 1–5 ACM, Tallinn Estonia (2020). https://doi.org/10.1145/3419249.3421250
11. Navalpakkam, V., Churchill, E.: Mouse tracking: measuring and predicting users' experience of web-based content. In: Proceedings of the SIGCHI Conference on Human Factors in Computing Systems, pp. 2963–2972 ACM, Austin Texas USA (2012). https://doi.org/10.1145/2207676.2208705
12. Scratch - Imagine, Program, Share. https://scratch.mit.edu/. Accessed 21 Mar 2023
13. Learn computer science. Change the world. https://code.org/. Accessed 21 Mar 2023
14. Coding For Kids, Kids Online Coding Classes & Games | Tynker. https://www.tynker.com. Accessed 21 Mar 2023
15. Blockly. https://developers.google.com/blockly. Accessed 21 Mar 2023
16. Principal component analysis for special types of data. In: Principal Component Analysis, pp. 338–372 Springer-Verlag, New York (2002). https://doi.org/10.1007/0-387-22440-8_13

17. Koonsanit, K., Hiruma, D., Nishiuchi, N.: Dimension reduction method by principal component analysis in the prediction of final user satisfaction. In: 2022 12th International Congress on Advanced Applied Informatics (IIAI-AAI), pp. 649–650. IEEE, Kanazawa, Japan (2022). https://doi.org/10.1109/IIAIAAI55812.2022.00128

18. Cristianini, N., Shawe-Taylor, J.: An Introduction to Support Vector Machines and Other Kernel-based Learning Methods. Cambridge University Press (2000).https://doi.org/10.1017/CBO9780511801389

19. Koonsanit, K., Nishiuchi, N.: Predicting final user satisfaction using momentary UX data and machine learning techniques. J. Theor. Appl. Electron. Commer. Res. **16**, 3136–3156 (2021). https://doi.org/10.3390/jtaer16070171

20. Zhang, Z.: Introduction to machine learning: k-nearest neighbors. Ann. Transl. Med. **4**(11), 218–218 (2016). https://doi.org/10.21037/atm.2016.03.37

21. Priyanka, N.A., Kumar, D.: Decision tree classifier: a detailed survey. IJIDS. **12**(3), 246 (2020). https://doi.org/10.1504/IJIDS.2020.108141

22. Speiser, J.L., et al.: A comparison of random forest variable selection methods for classification prediction modeling. Expert Syst. Appl. **134**, 93–101 (2019). https://doi.org/10.1016/j.eswa.2019.05.028

23. Webb, G.I., et al.: Leave-one-out cross-validation. In: Sammut, C., Webb, G.I. (eds.) Encyclopedia of Machine Learning, pp. 600–601 Springer US, Boston, MA (2011). https://doi.org/10.1007/978-0-387-30164-8_469

Investigating the Use of Machine Learning Methods for Levels of Sense of Presence Classification Based on Eye Tracking Data

Peerawat Pannattee[1]([✉]) [ID], Shogo Shimada[1] [ID], Vibol Yem[2] [ID],
and Nobuyuki Nishiuchi[1]

[1] Faculty of Systems Design, Tokyo Metropolitan University, Tokyo, Japan
{pannattee-peerawat,shimada-shogo}@ed.tmu.ac.jp, nnishiuc@tmu.ac.jp
[2] Faculty of Engineering, Information and Systems,
University of Tsukuba, Ibaraki, Japan
yem@iit.tsukuba.ac.jp

Abstract. This paper presents a study aimed at developing a framework for classifying levels of user satisfaction in Immersive Virtual Environments (IVEs). As an initial step, we conducted an experiment to explore the potential for using machine learning methods to classify levels of Sense of Presence (SOP). Participants performed a task in two virtual environments with varying levels of SOP, and their eye tracking data were analyzed. Our study found that Support Vector Machine (SVM) achieved the best performance based on pupil dilation-based features, with an accuracy of 79.1%. However, relying solely on pupil dilation-based features may not be reliable due to the sensitivity of pupil dilation to light intensity. Eye movement-based features were also analyzed, and Random Forest achieved the best result with an accuracy of 64.6%. In addition, we confirmed that texture resolution affects the perception of SOP by analyzing participants' IPQ scores. Our results showed that higher resolution leads to a higher perception of SOP. These findings suggest the potential for using machine learning methods to classify levels of SOP based on eye tracking data and provide a positive step towards developing a framework for classifying levels of user satisfaction in IVEs.

Keywords: Sense of Presence · Virtual Reality · Virtual Environment · User Satisfaction · User Experience

1 Introduction

The Metaverse is a concept that refers to a shared 3D virtual space where people can interact with each other in real-time through avatars, engage in activities such as gaming or socializing, and even buy and sell virtual goods and services [9]. Although it has been around for decades, it has recently gained a lot of

K. Saeed et al. (Eds.): CISIM 2023, LNCS 14164, pp. 481–495, 2023.
https://doi.org/10.1007/978-3-031-42823-4_35

attention, as demonstrated by the involvement of giant technology companies, either by directly investing in building Metaverse platforms or investing in related technologies such as Virtual Reality and Augmented Reality. The recent hype and rapid growth of the Metaverse make it a promising new form of future online social media that is expected to offer a new level of immersion and interactivity beyond what traditional social media platforms can provide.

Immersive Virtual Environments (IVEs) are defined as 3D computer-based simulations that have a near true-to-life level of immersion [10], in which users can navigate and interact with worlds that are otherwise not accessible or may not even exist. As a result, they are a fundamental component for building the Metaverse's 3D virtual spaces. In addition to its role in helping to bring about the emergence of the Metaverse, IVEs can provide a more enhanced, immersive, and realistic experience compared to traditional 2D user interfaces. Due to this potential, IVEs have been widely embraced by various industries for a variety of applications [6,13,19].

Due to the hype surrounding the Metaverse, IVE has become highly attractive to users, leading to a rapid increase in the development of IVE-based applications. As a result, understanding user satisfaction after using these applications has become important in evaluating and improving them to better meet user needs. However, the study of evaluating IVEs is quite limited. Some studies have made an effort to build models to evaluate IVEs, but most of them rely on using questionnaires, which have many steps and are difficult to evaluate. Furthermore, they also require much human effort to analyze and interpret. These limitations make it difficult to utilize as tools for evaluating IVEs in real-world scenarios. As a result, there is a lack of efficient tools for obtaining feedback to enhance user experience in IVEs, which is the opposite of the rapidly increasing content in Metaverse and IVE-based applications.

Our study has a long-term objective of developing a framework that can automatically classify the levels of user satisfaction in IVEs. User satisfaction is a subjective measurement that involves multiple components. Therefore, we are conceptualizing the framework as a multimodal machine learning-based framework that can classify levels of user satisfaction considering on various factors. With this scheme, we can create an efficient and comprehensive method for evaluating IVEs. Furthermore, we intend to employ biological data such as physiological responses and behavioral patterns to gain insights into users' emotions and attitudes. Machine learning algorithms will identify patterns and make classifications about levels of user satisfaction based on this data. The ultimate outcome will be a flexible and adaptable framework that can be used as a tool for evaluating content in Metaverse and IVE-based applications, allowing creators to obtain user feedback to enhance their products and services. Figure 1 shows an illustration of the conceptualized framework.

This paper presents the initial step of our long-term study, which aims to develop an automatic framework for classifying the levels of user satisfaction. Specifically, we explore the feasibility of using machine learning methods to classify subjective measurements based on biological data, such as eye tracking data. Since user satisfaction is a complex construct, we focus our attention on

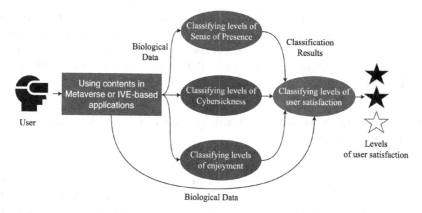

Fig. 1. An illustration of the conceptualized framework for classifying levels of user satisfaction.

the Sense of Presence (SOP) in this study. SOP is the sense of being present in a 3D virtual space and is a known contributor to user satisfaction. To assess our approach, we asked participants to complete a task in two virtual environments that differed in levels of SOP, which were controlled by the resolution of object textures. We collected eye tracking data while participants interacted with these virtual environments. We employed four classical machine learning algorithms - Logistic Regression, Random Forest, K-Neighbors, and Support Vector Machine (SVM) - to classify two levels of SOP based on the eye tracking data, including pupil dilation-based and eye movement-based features.

2   Related Works

2.1   Evaluation Models for Immersive Virtual Environments

The rapid growth in the number of immersive virtual environment (IVE)-based applications and content in the Metaverse platform has led to an increased interest in understanding user satisfaction and experience. As a result, the research community has been developing methods to evaluate the quality of IVEs. Several models have been proposed to measure user experience, including Tcha-Tokey et al.'s comprehensive model [16] that consists of various aspects and Wienrich et al.'s model [18] that includes factors such as presence, social presence, discomfort, and simulator sickness, as well as investigates the correlation with general aspects of 2D User Experience (UX) evaluation. Additionally, Damme et al. proposed the Overall Immersiveness Index [17] as a model for evaluating IVEs, and some research has focused solely on the sense of presence (SOP) as a vital measurement for user experience and satisfaction. For example, Servotte et al. investigated the factors of SOP in IVE-based medical training simulations and proposed a model to measure SOP [15].

However, these methods are limited to using questionnaires, which can be difficult to evaluate due to their many steps and the human effort required to analyze and interpret them. Consequently, these limitations make it is impractical to use these tools for evaluating contents in Metaverse and IVE-based applications in real-world scenarios.

2.2 Automatic Methods for Evaluating Immersive Virtual Environments

Due to the limitations of using questionnaires for evaluating IVEs, some researchers have proposed automatic methods. For example, Ochs et al. proposed a method [11] for evaluating SOP in medical training simulations based on the lexical richness and linguistic complexity. Their hypothesis was that users who perceive higher levels of SOP will use a richer vocabulary to interact with the intelligent agent. However, this method is limited to a specific task. Kim et al. also proposed an automatic method [7] for evaluating SOP in IVEs using a statistical model of frame changing. Unfortunately, this method only considers system factors and does not take user-centric measurements into account, which may not be practical for various applications.

2.3 Using Eye Tracking Data for Subjective Measurement in Immersive Virtual Environments

Eye tracking data has been used for behavioral and psychological measurement research for many years, and recently it has become widely used for subjective measurement in the VR and IVE research community. For instance, Zheng et al. proposed using machine learning methods to classify four classes of emotions in IVEs based on pupil diameter [20], demonstrating that pupil dilation has a significant correlation with different emotions. However, although this work showed the potential of using machine learning to classify subjective measurements based on eye tracking data, the classification of emotions may not be directly relevant to our study's ultimate goal of developing a framework for classifying levels of user satisfaction. It is worth noting that negative emotions, such as fear and sadness, can sometimes lead to satisfaction, as in horror or drama movies. Additionally, some research has explored measuring user satisfaction or experience directly based on eye tracking data. For example, Gao et al. employed machine learning to classify levels of user experience in different locomotion techniques [4]. Although this work is highly relevant to our study's ultimate goal, it is limited to a specific experience, which is the locomotion method. While our study aims to build a comprehensive framework that can classify levels of overall user satisfaction. Moreover, in this paper, we only focus on classifying levels of SOP, so the method proposed in [4] cannot be directly used here. Nevertheless, we adapt some useful techniques for utilizing eye-tracking data.

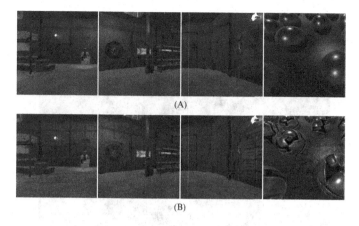

Fig. 2. An illustration of the two virtual environments used in the study, which had different levels of SOP that were achieved by adjusting the object texture resolution: (A) Low SOP Environment; (B) High SOP Environment.

3   Experimental Design for Data Collection

3.1   Virtual Environment and Task

The main focus of this study is to classify the levels of SOP using a machine learning models based on eye tracking data. To collect data for training the model, we conducted an experiment that used two virtual environments with differing levels of SOP: one with high SOP and the other with low SOP. We created the different levels of SOP by adjusting the object texture resolution, as shown by Kim et al.'s experiment [7], which demonstrated that texture resolution affects SOP perception. Specifically, the high SOP environment was set at 2048 × 2048 resolution, while the low SOP environment was set at 32 × 32 resolution. It is important to note that all aspects of these two environments were kept the same except for the object texture resolution, in order to ensure that the level of SOP was controlled. An illustration of the two virtual environments is shown in Fig. 2.

In the experiment, participants were tasked with a "pick and place" task in both virtual environments. The environments had two desks, and participants were required to move a total of 40 balls from one desk to the other. Each environment was approximately 3–5 minutes long. To control the degree of movement, which may impact the levels of SOP, the two desks were positioned very close together. As a result, participants were only required to rotate and make slight sideways movements, rather than changing their location in the virtual space. Figure 3 shows an illustration of the two desk positions.

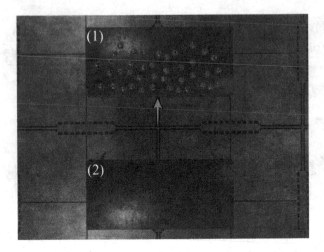

Fig. 3. An illustration of the two desk positions. The task involved moving 40 balls from the desk (1) to the desk (2). The arrow shows the starting position and direction of participants at the beginning of the experiment.

3.2 Participant

The experiment involved six male participants who were graduate students studying computer science. Their ages ranged from 23 to 42 years old, and all of them were confirmed to be healthy with no history of eye disease.

3.3 Questionnaire for Making Ground-Truth Labels

To determine the level of Sense of Presence (SOP) experienced by participants in each environment after completing the task, we utilized the Igroup Presence Questionnaire (IPQ) to create ground-truth labels. The IPQ is a widely used standard questionnaire that comprehensively measures SOP in virtual environments. It consists of four subscales: General Presence, Spatial Presence, Involvement, and Experience Realism. The score of IPQ ranging from 0 to 6.

3.4 Device

For this study, we used the HTC Vive Pro Eye VR headset, which is equipped with Tobii® eye tracking technology. The headset has a dual organic light-emitting diode screen with a resolution of 1440 × 1600 pixels per eye, a field of viewing angle of 110°, and a refresh rate of 90 Hz. The experiments were conducted using Steam VR and Unity 3D software, and eye tracking data was collected with the SRanipal SDK provided by HTC.

3.5 Experimental Procedure

Prior to beginning the experiment, participants were briefed on the details of the study as well as the task that they would be performing in each environment. In addition, participants were requested to provide personal information including their age, gender, and prior experience with IVE-based content. Participants were given 3–5 min to calibrate the eye tracking sensor and to prepare themselves for the experiment.

Participants were instructed to complete the assigned task in each environment sequentially, with the order of the environments being randomized. The task required participants to use hand controllers to pick up balls from one desk and place them on another desk. Eye tracking data, including pupil position and diameter, were collected during participant interactions with the virtual environments.

Upon completing the task in each environment, participants were prompted to assess their levels of SOP by means of the IPQ to generate the ground-truth labels. Figure 4 shows an overview of the experimental procedure.

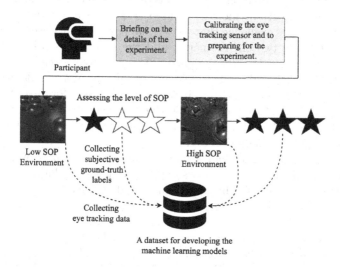

Fig. 4. An overview of the experimental procedure. Note that the order of the environments was randomized.

4 Sense of Presence Classification Using Machine Learning

4.1 Preprocessing and Feature Extraction

During the participants' interactions with the virtual environments, eye tracking data were collected in two forms: pupil position and pupil diameter. Both forms were collected separately for each eye and with a sampling rate of 50 samples per second. The pupil diameter was recorded as the actual size of the pupil in millimeters, while the pupil position was recorded as pairs of x and y coordinates in the normalized sensor area. This can be represented as follows:

$$X_d = \{d_n\}_{n=1}^{N}, \tag{1}$$

$$X_p = \{(x_n, y_n)\}_{n=1}^{N}. \tag{2}$$

where d_n represents the nth sample of pupil diameter, and X_d is a time sequence of the pupil diameter. Meanwhile, (x_n, y_n) represents the pair of x and y positions of the pupil in the normalized sensor area for the nth sample, and X_p is the time sequence of the pupil position. Note that, N is the total length of the recorded time sequences information. To obtain a more accurate measurement, we applied the Savitzky-Golay filter [14] to smooth the 1D signal of the time sequence of pupil diameter from both eyes. The window length of the filter was set to 75 samples or around 1.5 s. However, we did not apply any smoothing filter to the time sequence of pupil position.

In this study, we focused on only 2 levels of SOP - low and high. To train the supervised machine learning models, we used IPQ scores as ground-truth labels. However, we faced the challenge that the virtual environments used in our study were limited to only two environments, and the IPQ scores collected did not range from 0 to 6 as originally designed. Thus, we divided the collected IPQ scores into two levels based on their median. Specifically, if a sample had an IPQ score lower or equal to the median, it was identified as a low-level SOP class. Conversely, if a sample had a score higher than the median, it was identified as a high-level SOP class. As a result, our dataset consisted of 6 samples for low-level SOP and 6 samples for high-level SOP.

Since the original dataset had a limited number of samples, we performed data augmentation by splitting each sample's eye-tracking data sequences, X_d and X_p, into two sequences. This approach helped create a more robust dataset and avoid overfitting. We should note that the ground-truth labels of the augmented data were the same as the original data since the participants performed the same task and perceived the same setting in both the original and augmented data. Consequently, we obtained a dataset of 24 samples, consisting of 12 samples for the low-level SOP class and 12 samples for the high-level SOP class.

We computed a set of features that we hypothesized would be effective in classifying levels of SOP using machine learning. The feature set consists of two main types of features: 1.) Pupil dilation type, which includes pupil diameter change rate and pupil diameter change rate in percent, and 2.) Eye movement type, which includes pupil angle change rate and number of saccades. Each of these features is further divided into sub-features based on statistical values, such as mean, maximum, and variance, except for number of saccades, which was not divided into sub-features. A summary of these features is presented in Table 1.

Table 1. List of features

Feature name	Description	Sub-feature
1.) Pupil diameter change		
Pupil diameter change rate	Pupil diameter change rate in millimeters per sampling	Mean, Maximum, Variance
Pupil diameter change rate in percent	Pupil diameter change rate in percent per sampling.	
2.) Eye movement		
Pupil angle change rate	Pupil angle change rate in degree per sampling.	
Number of saccades	The total number of saccades in the entire eye tracking sequence (using the method proposed in [3])	None

4.2 Machine Learning Training and Validation Details

We utilized four classical machine learning methods, including Logistic Regression [8], Random Forest [2], K-Neighbors [1], and Linear Support Vector Machine (Linear SVM) [5], to classify the levels of SOP. The default settings from the Scikit-learn Library [12] were used for all methods except for K-Neighbors, where we set the number of neighbors to 3 for better alignment with our dataset. Since our dataset is small, train/test splitting was not appropriate. Therefore, we employed Leave-One-Out Cross-Validation (LOOCV) to validate our models. LOOCV involves using each sample as a test set and the remaining samples as a training set. The results of LOOCV were averaged over all the results for each test sample. We trained and validated each method using LOOCV 100 times and averaged the results to prevent misinterpretation due to different random seeds. We utilized four classical machine learning methods, including Logistic Regression [8], Random Forest [2], K-Neighbors [1], and Linear Support Vector Machine (Linear SVM) [5], to classify the levels of SOP. The default settings from the Scikit-learn Library [12] were used for all methods except for K-Neighbors, where we set the number of neighbors to 3 for better alignment with our dataset. Since our dataset is small, train/test splitting was not appropriate. Therefore, we employed Leave-One-Out Cross-Validation (LOOCV) to validate our models. LOOCV involves using each sample as a test set and the remaining samples as a training set. The results of LOOCV were averaged over all the results for each test sample. We trained and validated each method using LOOCV 100 times and averaged the results to prevent misinterpretation due to different random seeds.

5   Experimental Results

5.1   Effect of Object Texture Resolution on Sense of Presence

To analyze the effect of the texture resolution on SOP, we used the Mean Opinion Score (MOS) and conducted a t-test to investigate the statistical significance between the two environments. Figure 5 displays the MOS of the overall IPQ scores in the two different virtual environments that used different resolutions, as well as the statistical significance of the overall IPQ scores between the two environments. The results indicate that in the high SOP environment, which employed a higher resolution, participants tended to rate a higher perception of SOP (higher MOS), and the resulting p-value from the t-test was 0.059. This suggests that the resolution of the object texture tends to affect the perception of SOP, with a higher resolution leading to a greater perception of SOP. As mentioned in Sect. 3.3, the IPQ questionnaire consists of four subscales. We also examined the effect of the texture resolution on these subscales using MOS and the t-test. Figure 6 presents the results, indicating that all subscales showed a trend towards an increase as the texture resolution increased. However, statistical significance was not observed for the General Presence and Spatial Presence subscales, resulting in p-values of 0.21 and 0.70, respectively. On the other hand, the Involvement and Experienced Realism subscales showed statistical significance, with p-values of 0.017 and 0.030, respectively. Based on these findings, it can be concluded that the resolution of the object texture tends to affect SOP perception, with statistical significance observed for the Involvement and Experienced subscales.

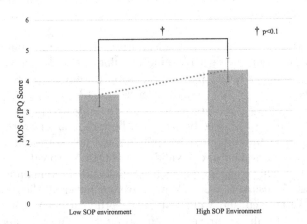

Fig. 5. Comparison of the mean opinion scores (MOS) of IPQ scores in the two different environments.

However, despite the resolution of object texture can affect the overall perception of SOP, it is important to note that SOP is an individual perception. Some participants in our study rated their perception of SOP as nearly identical

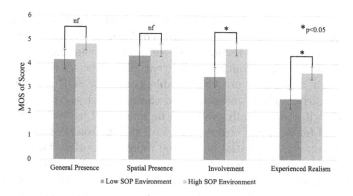

Fig. 6. Comparison of the mean opinion scores (MOS) of the IPQ subscales in the two different environments.

in both environments, shown in Fig. 7, indicating that the resolution of each environment may not accurately reflect individual perceptions. To obtain a better understanding of individual perceptions of SOP, it would be appropriate to use machine learning methods to classify levels of SOP.

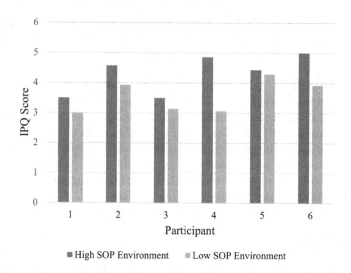

Fig. 7. Each participant's IPQ score in different virtual environments.

5.2 Levels of Sense of Presence Classification Using Machine Learning

We utilized four machine learning methods to classify levels of SOP by employing the feature set detailed in Table 1. However, including unhelpful features in the feature set can have adverse effects on classification performance and lead to overfitting. Therefore, we utilized Analysis of Variance (ANOVA) to calculate p-values and eliminate such features. We selected the four best features based on the four lowest p-values, but we found that all four best features were based on pupil dilation, which may not be a reliable feature for SOP perception. Pupil diameter is sensitive to light intensity, and changes in object texture resolution can also impact it. Additionally, SOP can be influenced by various factors such as the degree of freedom and engagement with the environment, making factors that do not solely rely on spatial perception more appropriate for various applications. Hence, we also considered features that are not influenced by light intensity, such as eye movement-based features, which are more commonly observed behavioral features across various settings. The utilized features from both feature types, pupil dilation, and eye movement, are listed in Table 2. We compared the classification results using different machine learning methods based on both feature types, and the results are presented in Table 3. The results indicate that machine learning methods have the potential to classify levels of SOP based on eye tracking data, and the best result was achieved from SVM, with a 79.1% accuracy using the pupil dilation features. Furthermore, using features that are free from light intensity effects, such as eye movement features, also reveals the potential of using machine learning to classify levels of SOP. The best result from eye movement features was 64.6% by Random Forest.

In our opinion, the reason for the results of each feature type not appearing in the same direction is that pupil dilation-based features exhibit fewer non-linear properties compared to eye movement-based features. Consequently, methods that perform well with linear data, such as Logistic Regression, are likely to provide higher accuracy. Although SVM generally excels with non-linear data, it can also yield high accuracy in this case. On the other hand, K-Neighbors is a straightforward method that typically requires a larger amount of data, resulting in poor performance with our small dataset. Additionally, eye movement-based features possess more non-linear properties, causing Logistic Regression to perform poorly. However, our dataset is very small, which amplifies the impact of external factors like random seed, making it challenging to observe the true characteristics of different machine learning methods.

6   Discussion

The results of the experiment indicate that machine learning methods have the feasibility to be used to classify different levels of SOP based on eye tracking data. SVM achieved the best performance with an accuracy of 79.1%. The selected features for this result were based on pupil dilation and were chosen from the four lowest corresponding p-values. However, using only pupil dilation-based features may not be a reliable indicator of SOP perception because pupil dilation can be sensitive to light intensity, and it is unclear whether changes in the resolution of object texture in our experiment affect the light intensity. Additionally, SOP can be influenced by various other factors, such as the degree of freedom

Table 2. The utilized features from both feature types and their corresponding p-value.

Feature name	P-value
1.) Pupil diameter change	
*Average pupil diameter change rate in percent	0.048
*Varience of pupil diameter change rate in percent	0.137
*Average pupil diameter change rate	0.222
*Varience pupil diameter change rate	0.309
2.) Eye movement	
Number of saccades	0.420
Maximum pupil angle change rate	0.497
Average pupil angle change rate	0.923
Variance of pupil angle change rate	0.979

* The four lowest p-value features.

and engagement with the environment. Therefore, the study also investigated eye movement-based features, which are more commonly observed behavioral features across various settings. The study found that Random Forest achieved the best result with an accuracy of 64.6%.

Although the classification results from both feature types are relatively low, they demonstrate the potential of using machine learning methods to evaluate subjective measurements. This finding contributes to the ongoing development of a framework for classifying levels of user satisfaction in IVEs. However, the study was limited by a small dataset (24 samples from 6 participants), and future studies with larger sample sizes are necessary to obtain more accurate results. Furthermore, while texture resolution was used to control SOP, real-world scenarios can be influenced by various other factors beyond texture realism. Therefore, further studies are required to explore the impact of other factors on eye tracking data and develop a more comprehensive framework that can be applied in different settings. Finally, it is important to note that the study only examined two levels of SOP, and more complex levels should be considered to create a more practical framework.

Table 3. Comparison of the classification results using different machine learning methods.

Method	Accuracy (Percent)	
	Pupil Diameter	Eye Movement
Logistic Regression	75.0	50.0
Random Forest	76.1	64.6
K-Neighbors	62.5	58.3
Support Vector Machine	79.1	58.3

7   Conclusion

To conclude, this paper introduces the concept of a long-term study aimed at developing a framework for classifying levels of user satisfaction in IVEs. Our experiment explored the potential of machine learning methods to classify levels of SOP based on eye tracking data. We confirmed that the perception of SOP is significantly influenced by object texture resolution, with higher resolution leading to higher SOP perception. We applied machine learning methods to classify levels of SOP and found that SVM achieved the best performance with an accuracy of 79.1%, using pupil dilation-based features. However, relying solely on these features may not be a reliable indicator of SOP perception due to the sensitivity of pupil dilation to light intensity. Thus, we also investigated eye movement-based features and found that Random Forest achieved an accuracy of 64.6%. Our study provides evidence of the potential of using machine learning methods to classify levels of SOP based on eye tracking data, which represents a significant step towards developing a framework for classifying levels of user satisfaction in IVEs.

References

1. Altman, N.S.: An introduction to kernel and nearest-neighbor nonparametric regression. Am. Stat. **46**(3), 175–185 (1992)
2. Breiman, L.: Random forests. Mach. Learn. **45**, 5–32 (2001)
3. Engbert, R., Rothkegel, L.O.M., Backhaus, D., Trukenbrod, H.A.: Evaluation of velocity-based saccade detection in the SMI-ETG 2W system (2016)
4. Gao, H., Kasneci, E.: Eye-tracking-based prediction of user experience in VR locomotion using machine learning (2022)
5. Hearst, M.A., Dumais, S.T., Osuna, E., Platt, J., Scholkopf, B.: Support vector machines. IEEE Intell. Syst. Appl. **13**(4), 18–28 (1998)
6. Kilmon, C.A., Brown, L., Ghosh, S., Mikitiuk, A.: Immersive virtual reality simulations in nursing education. Nurs. Educ. Perspect. **31**(5), 314–317 (2010)
7. Kim, W., Lee, S., Bovik, A.C.: VR sickness versus VR presence: a statistical prediction model. IEEE Trans. Image Process. **30**, 559–571 (2020)
8. Kleinbaum, D.G., Klein, M.: Logistic Regression. SBH, Springer, New York (2010). https://doi.org/10.1007/978-1-4419-1742-3
9. Lee, L.H., et al.: All one needs to know about metaverse: a complete survey on technological singularity, virtual ecosystem, and research agenda. arXiv preprint arXiv:2110.05352 (2021)
10. Loomis, J.M., Blascovich, J.J., Beall, A.C.: Immersive virtual environment technology as a basic research tool in psychology. Behav. Res. Methods Instrum. Comput. **31**(4), 557–564 (1999)
11. Magalie, O., Sameer, J., Philippe, B.: Toward an automatic prediction of the sense of presence in virtual reality environment. In: Proceedings of the 6th International Conference on Human-Agent Interaction, pp. 161–166 (2018)
12. Pedregosa, F., et al.: Scikit-learn: Machine learning in python. J. Mach. Learn. Res. **12**(Oct), 2825–2830 (2011)
13. Roussou, M.: Learning by doing and learning through play: an exploration of interactivity in virtual environments for children. Comput. Entertainment (CIE) **2**(1), 10–10 (2004)

14. Schafer, R.W.: What is a savitzky-golay filter?[lecture notes]. IEEE Signal Process. Mag. **28**(4), 111–117 (2011)
15. Servotte, J.C., et al.: Virtual reality experience: Immersion, sense of presence, and cybersickness. Clin. Simul. Nurs. **38**, 35–43 (2020)
16. Tcha-Tokey, K., Christmann, O., Loup-Escande, E., Richir, S.: Proposition and validation of a questionnaire to measure the user experience in immersive virtual environments. Int. J. Virtual Reality **16**(1), 33–48 (2016)
17. Van Damme, S., Torres Vega, M., De Turck, F.: Enabling user-centric assessment and modelling of immersiveness in multimodal multimedia applications. In: IMX 2022-Doctoral Consortium. pp. 1–10 (2022)
18. Wienrich, C., Döllinger, N., Kock, S., Schindler, K., Traupe, O.: Assessing user experience in virtual reality – a comparison of different measurements. In: Marcus, A., Wang, W. (eds.) DUXU 2018. LNCS, vol. 10918, pp. 573–589. Springer, Cham (2018). https://doi.org/10.1007/978-3-319-91797-9_41
19. You, S., Kim, J.H., Lee, S., Kamat, V., Robert, L.P., Jr.: Enhancing perceived safety in human-robot collaborative construction using immersive virtual environments. Autom. Constr. **96**, 161–170 (2018)
20. Zheng, L.J., Mountstephens, J., Teo, J.: Four-class emotion classification in virtual reality using pupillometry. J. Big Data **7**, 1–9 (2020)

Personalized Beverage Blending System Using Interactive Genetic Algorithm and Its Search Analysis

Miko Yokoi[1], Yuki Fujioka[1], Yoshiko Hanada[1(✉)], and Makoto Fukumoto[2] (iD)

[1] Faculty of Engineering Science, Kansai University, Osaka, Japan
hanada@kansai-u.ac.jp
[2] Department of Computer Science and Engineering, Fukuoka Institute of Technology, Fukuoka, Japan
fukumoto@fit.ac.jp

Abstract. In this study, we improved the dispensing accuracy of the automatic juice blending system in the previous study to optimize the mixing ratio of juices that match the preference of each user using an interactive genetic algorithm (IGA). We verify the properties of the solution obtained by IGA by conducting subject experiments under an improved experimental environment that allows adjustment of the discharging of each juice with an accuracy of 100 ms. In addition, we analyze the difference in convergence tendency from the experimental results of the subject experiments when the design variable space is expanded.

Keywords: Interactive Genetic Algorithm · Blending Juice

1 Introduction

Interactive Evolutionary Computation (IEC) [1, 2] is a method to support the creation of media content that reflects the user's preferences by having the human user play the role of the evaluation function in evolutionary computation which is one of approximation method for optimization. Human sensibility, *kansei*, is difficult to be formulated, so that by leaving directly the evaluation step of EC to each user, it is possible to search according to the bias of each user's preferences, i.e., to search for the optimal solution of a function with black-box characteristics. Due to these characteristics of search of IEC and input/output devices in general computers, such as displays and speakers, can be used as evaluation interfaces, IEC that involves the user's visual and auditory senses for content search has been developed intensively [3–7]. In recent years, by introducing special equipment, IEC has been applied to the generation of a wide range of content, not only for audiovisual media, but also for tactile [6, 7] and olfactory [8] senses.

In our previous work, we have focused on the creation of taste content by IEC, and have developed an automatic blender for juices and optimized the blending of beverages to suit users' preferences using an Interactive Genetic Algorithm (IGA). Through subject experiments, by optimizing the ratio of blending five source juices, a continuous increase in evaluation values was observed, indicating that it is possible to optimize the taste to suit the user by IGA [9]. However, a simple water pump was used there, and it was difficult to control the flow corresponding to the accuracy indicated by each design variable of IGA, and it was accompanied by operational failures such as backflow.

In this study, we adopt a peristaltic pump for food with high accuracy in order to realize more accurate search, and improve the extraction accuracy of each source juice without a failure in flow control. In addition, to re-evaluate the search behavior of IGA, we significantly increase the number of trials of the subject experiments. In the experiments, we verify how the convergence tendency changes from day to day by conducting trials with the same subjects on different days. Furthermore, we verify the characteristic in convergence trends from the experimental results of the subject experiments when the number of source juices is increased to eight which expands the design variable space.

2 Beverage Blending System with Interactive Genetic Algorithm

2.1 Outline of the System

In this study, the blending ratio of N source juices is optimized according to the user's preference using an IGA. In the juice blending system, N pumps are arranged in parallel and one juice is assigned to each pump; the Arduino controls the drive time of each pump to adjust the amount of source juice extracted. Each source juice is extracted for a drive time proportional to the mixing ratio obtained by the IGA described below to produce a mixed beverage. The user inputs his/her evaluation of solution candidates, mixed beverages, into the IGA. This process is repeated to produce a beverage that meets the user's preferences. Figure 1 shows this process.

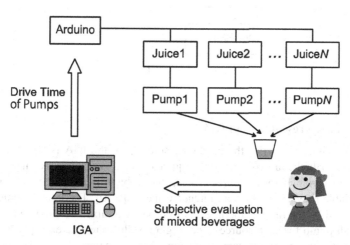

Fig. 1. Outline of the blending system

2.2 Interactive Genetic Algorithm

Figure 2 shows a flowchart of a typical IGA. While Genetic Algorithm evaluates individuals (candidate solutions) using an evaluation function based on numerical calculations, IGA evaluates individuals by human users. Therefore, IGA is expected to obtain a solution that suits the user. Selection, crossover, and mutation are main search operations of IGA, but the number of individuals in the population is usually set small to avoid users' fatigue.

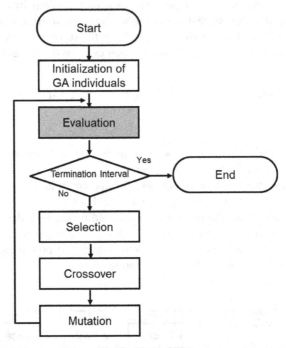

Fig. 2. Flow of IGA

2.3 Solution Representation in IGA

As in the previous study [9], the candidate solution of the IGA is represented as an integer vector with the ratio of each source juice blended to produce the mixed beverage as the design variable; for N source juices, the problem is N design variables. Each design variable (beverage) takes an integer value of [0,20]. The total beverage output is then divided by the ratio of the integers to produce a mixed beverage with the drive time of each pump for each source juice. Figure 3 illustrates the example to calculate the drive times for each pump from the design variables in the case of $N = 5$ with a total dispense time of 5000 ms. This example shows the design variables of $\{11, 3, 2, 5, 4\}$ to be converted to each drive time.

If an integer value in the design variable is divisible by the greatest common divisor, it is divided by that number to simplify the blend ratio.

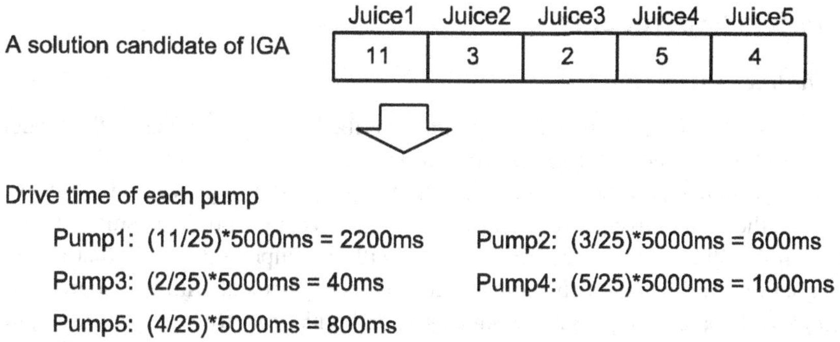

	Juice1	Juice2	Juice3	Juice4	Juice5
A solution candidate of IGA	11	3	2	5	4

⇩

Drive time of each pump

Pump1: (11/25)*5000ms = 2200ms   Pump2: (3/25)*5000ms = 600ms

Pump3: (2/25)*5000ms = 40ms   Pump4: (5/25)*5000ms = 1000ms

Pump5: (4/25)*5000ms = 800ms

Fig. 3. Calculation of each drive time of pump corresponding to a solution candidate of IGA (Total drive time: 5000 ms)

2.4 Experiment Equipment

In our previous study [9], when the above IGA was employed to optimize the mixed beverage of five source juice, a continuous increase in the evaluation value was observed, indicating that optimization of the taste suited to the users' preference is possible. However, although the experiments were conducted on subject experiments using a simple water pump with the bottles of each source juice in a sealed condition, the pump motor malfunctioned and backflow occurred when switching the drive, requiring adjustment by the experimenter each time. Therefore, a peristaltic pump is used in this study, which can be controlled more precisely.

Figure 4 shows a circuit diagram of pump control using an Arduino. In the figure, M indicates the pump. A peristaltic pump from Switch Science [10] was used as the pump. This pump works with 5 V and 500 mA so that a PNP transistor, 2SC2120-Y [11], was used to drive the pump motor, and a 470 kΩ resistor was placed on the base side and adjusted by a DC power supply. An Arduino Leonard, ARDUINO-A000057 [12], was used for motor drive control as in the previous study. Through preliminary experiments, we have confirmed that the liquid extraction can be adjusted in 100 ms increments by using this device.

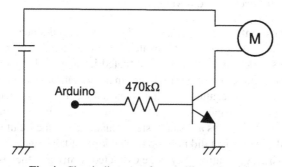

Fig. 4. Circuit diagram of controlling one pump

3 Subject Experiments

3.1 Outline of Experiments

Here, we use the beverage blending system described in Sect. 2 to verify the tendency of the search for mixed beverage generation with IGA.

First, through a mixed beverage generation experiment using five source juices, we verify whether the convergence trend of IGA obtained in a previous study [9] is the same or not as the convergence trend of IGA with the improved system that increases the extraction accuracy of each source juice. In this experiment with five source juices, we employed apple, orange, grape, pineapple, and pink grapefruit as the source juices. Next, under the same IGA settings, we tested the search performance of the IGA when the search space was expanded by using eight source juices: apple, orange, grape, pear, peach, grapefruit, coconuts water and bitter gourd. The total extraction time was set to 5000 ms for the experiment with 5 source juices and 8000 ms for the experiment with 8 source juices; all of source juices were 100% fruit juices. All subjects participated in the study with prior knowledge of the source juices that made up the mixed beverage.

Ten subjects participated in the experiments, which consisted of two stages: a search experiment and an evaluation experiment. The search experiment is a solution search using IGA that repeats the evaluation of mixed beverages, and the evaluation experiment is an experiment to examine whether the solution obtained by the search of IGA is better than the solution before the search. In both experiments, each subject participated separately from the other subjects. The details are described below.

Search Experiment. In this experiment, subjects optimize a mixed beverage to their own preferences through the IGA system. The parameters of the IGA are shown in Table 1. For each trial, initial individuals were randomly generated within the domain of definition. In the process of the search by IGA, subjects rated eight individuals to be converted to mixed beverages presented by the system on a 7-step Likert scale [13], with 1 being "very tasteless", 4 being "neither" and 7 being "very tasty", every generation. Figure 5 shows the form of the evaluation GUI that the subjects were asked to fill out. The subjects were allowed to drink water to reset their mouth during the repeated evaluation. The subjects were asked to refrain from eating or drinking for 30 min prior to the start of the experiment. The mixed beverages were placed in plastic cups for tasting, and a new cup was used for each mixed beverage.

Evaluation Experiment. After at least one day had elapsed since one search experiment, each subject participated in the evaluation experiment. Among the candidate solutions that the subject him/herself had evaluated in the search experiment, the best candidate solution from each of the initial and final generations was extracted from the population and subjected to evaluation. That is, the subject re-evaluated the two solution candidates created in the first and last generations of the search. As in the search experiment, the evaluation index was a 7-step taste evaluation, and the input interface shown in Fig. 6 was used. The subject did not know what kind of beverages the two beverages were (including which generation they were extracted from), and they were required to taste both beverages before evaluating them. The order of presentation was randomly counterbalanced to account for order effects.

Table 1. Settings of IGA

Item	Details
Number of generations	7 generations from the 0th to 6th
Number of individuals	8
Selection	Roulette Shuffle and Elitism Strategy
Crossover	One-point crossover with 95%
Mutation	One variable was changed in a range 3 point with 5%

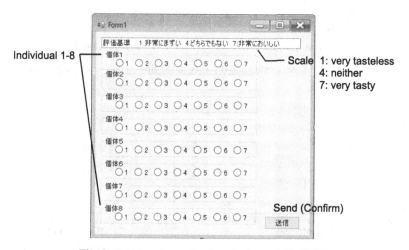

Fig. 5. Interface for evaluations in the search of IGA

Fig. 6. Interface for the evaluation experiment comparing the solutions of the initial and the final generations

3.2 Five Source Juices Experiments.

Convergence Tendency of IGA. A search experiment was conducted on 10 subjects, with two trials for each subject on different days, so that 20 trials were conducted. The results of the search experiment for the first and second trials are shown in Fig. 7 and Fig. 8, respectively. These values shown in (a) were averaged across subjects after calculating the average, maximum, and minimum evaluation values for each subject in each generation. The inter-solution distance shown in (b) is the average value of 28 pairs of distances for all 8 individuals in each generation of one trial, with smaller values indicating a convergence of the population of IGA.

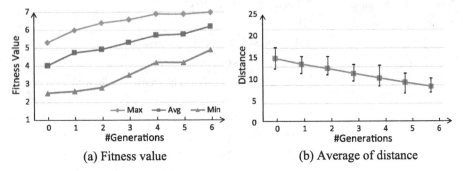

(a) Fitness value   (b) Average of distance

Fig. 7. Histories of fitness value and distance at the first trial of search experiments

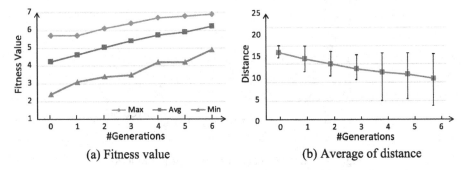

(a) Fitness value   (b) Average of distance

Fig. 8. Histories of fitness value and distance at the second trial of search experiments

As shown in Fig. 7 and Fig. 8 (a), the average, maximum, and minimum evaluation values increased in both the first and second trials. A statistical comparison between the initial and final generations showed significant increases (P < 0.01). These results show the same trend as in the previous study [9]. In addition, the distance trends in Fig. 7 and Fig. 8 (b) show that the distances for both trials decreased rapidly with the progress of the generation, indicating that the population of IGA generally converged. A statistical comparison of the average distance between the initial and final generations also shows a significant increase (P < 0.01). The maximum distance in the second trial is larger than in the first one. This was due to the presence of trials where the population contained two very different solutions through 7 generations, in search experiments in the second trial.

Results of Evaluation Experiments. In the search experiment with the five source juices, the 10 subjects participated in 13 additional trials in addition to the 20 trials described in the previous section. Each subject was limited to one search experiment per day and participated in at least two and at most five trials. Among the total of 33 search trials, 20 trials of evaluation experiments were conducted after those search experiments.

The result of the search experiment for 33 trials are shown in Fig. 9. Figure 10 shows the averaged values and standard deviations for the 20 trials of the evaluation experiment conducted after search experiments.

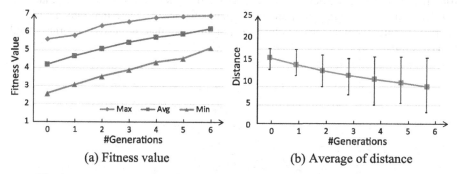

(a) Fitness value   (b) Average of distance

Fig. 9. Histories of fitness value and distance of all trials of the search experiment

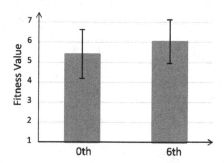

Fig. 10. Average and standard deviation of fitness value in the initial and final generations in the evaluation experiment

Figure 9 shows that the same trends as in Fig. 7 and Fig. 8 were obtained even when the same subject continued the search multiple times, indicating that the IGA enables stable search. A statistical comparison between the initial and final generations in the search experiment confirmed a significant increase in the average, maximum, and minimum evaluation values ($P < 0.01$). On the other hand, no significant difference was observed in the evaluation experiment after the search experiment shown in Fig. 10. These results are similar to the trends observed in the previous study [9].

From the above, we can see that IGA is capable of local search in the taste content, while global search is difficult. This is because of the difficulty of obtaining a sufficient population size and number of search generations due to the limitation of user fatigue, as well as the possibility that the convergence trend might change depending on the condition of the user during the experiment.

Distribution of Obtained Solutions. Here we verify the convergence trend of the individuals obtained in the IGA. Figure 11 shows the classification of the solutions with the maximum score of 7 points in the last generation of 33 trials, using self-organizing maps (SOM) [14]. To generate SOM, we used *Somoclu* [15]. The amount of each source juice discharged was used to determine the classification of individuals. The alphabets in the figure are the initial letters of the subjects, and a number was assigned according to each trial. In the figure, light color to red areas are relatively small in scale that indicate high density areas, while dark (blue) areas are relatively large in scale that indicate sparse areas. In addition, points located close each other mean that the mixed beverages tend to have similar tastes.

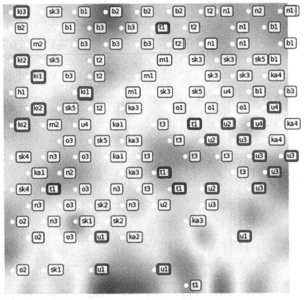

Fig. 11. Distribution of all best solutions (five source juices): Red boxed result means an example of a similar convergence trend for all trials in one user (ki*). Blue boxed result means an example of the subject's preference changing between days (u*). Purple boxed result means an example where multiple types of solutions exist in the population in one trial (t1).

From Fig. 11 we can observe that there are three patterns in the distribution of the same subject: 1) solutions are placed close to each other in all trials, 2) solutions are placed close to each other in each trial, and 3) solutions are dispersed to distant positions even in the same trial. In the first pattern, the subject's preference is fixed and the mixing ratio converges close each other; in the second pattern, the subject's preference might change from day to day, or the distribution of initial population might affect the search, leading to a local solution. The third case means that the IGA does not converge due to several subject preferences.

3.3 Eight Source Juices Experiments

In the search experiment with the eight source juices, a total of 16 search trials were conducted on 10 subjects. Each subject was limited to one search experiment per day and participated in one or two trials of the search experiment. Among 16 search trials, 13 evaluation experiments were conducted. The result of the search experiment for 16 trials are shown in Fig. 12. Figure 13 shows the average and standard deviation for the 13 trials of the evaluation experiment.

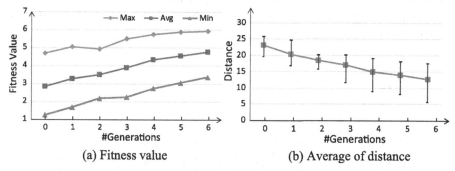

(a) Fitness value   (b) Average of distance

Fig. 12. Histories of fitness value and distance of all trials of the search experiment

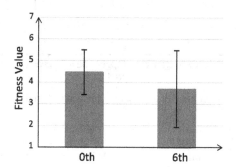

Fig. 13. Average and standard deviation of fitness value in the initial and final generations in the evaluation experiment

From the results in Fig. 12 (a), it is shown that the average, maximum, and minimum evaluation values also increased in the search experiment for the eight source juices. However, the search space is larger than that of the five source juices problem, and the average, maximum and minimum of evaluation values in the search experiment for the eight source juices are all about 1 point lower than those in the search experiment for the five source juices shown in Fig. 9 (a). From the results in Fig. 12 (b), the distance between individuals also decreases, indicating that the search is moving toward convergence. However, while the search experiment showed an increase in the evaluation values, as shown in Fig. 13, the evaluation experiment conducted after the search experiment showed a reversal in the evaluation values of the best of the initial and final generations. The standard deviation was also larger in the final generation.

Figure 14 shows the average of 16 trials of the discharge amount of each source juice in the 0th generation and the 6th generation. From the result of Fig. 14, it is shown that the searches were concentrated in the direction of decreasing the ratio of bitter gourd in common among the subjects. According to the opinions of several subjects, although an increase in the evaluation value was accepted, unlike the search experiments for five source juice, the bitter taste of the bitter gourd was strong, and the taste of candidate solutions was not improved from the initial generation so that a satisfactory solution was not obtained in the final generation. In addition to the difficulty of the exploration due to the large design variable space, there was a large difference in taste intensity between the bitter gourd and the other seven source juices, and all seven source juices tasted light. These might be reasons that make the stable search difficult.

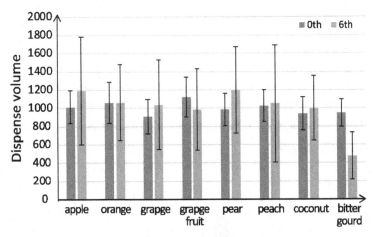

Fig. 14. Dispense volume of each source juice at 0-th and 6-th generations

Figure 15 shows the convergence trend of the solutions obtained in the mixed optimization of the eight source juices using the SOM; since there are few individuals with a score of 7, solution candidates with the highest score in the final generation are plotted.

From the distribution trend in Fig. 15, it can be confirmed that there are two patterns: one is placed close to each other in each trial, and the other is distributed at a distance even in the same trial. From the evaluation experiment, the search for the user's favorite flavor failed in the experiment of mixing 8 types of source juices, but on the other hand, the trend of obtained solutions observed on SOM was similar to that of the experiment of mixing 5 types of source juices, suggesting that the IGA is effective in the search on the design variable space.

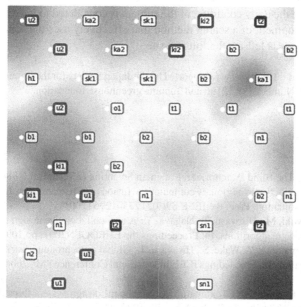

Fig. 15. Distribution of all best solutions (eight source juices): Red and blue boxed results mean examples where one trial of IGA converged to relatively similar taste but the subject's preference changing between days (ki* and u*). Purple boxed result means an example where multiple types of solutions exist in the population in one trial (t2).

4 Conclusion

In this study, we conducted a subject experiment to verify the convergence trend in the optimization of beverage blending according to users' preferences using IGAs by using an improved automatic blender for juices. In the search experiments for five source juices, a continuous increase in the evaluation value was observed during the search for IGAs, as in previous studies. In addition, the distance between individuals in the population also showed a general convergence trend, confirming that the search in the design variable space is effectively working by IGA. In the evaluation experiment conducted after the search experiments, the difference between the evaluation values before and after the search was not large. Some typical trends in the convergence were observed in the classification on the SOM; converged solutions were different for each trial even for the same user, or there were several different solutions within one trial in the population. Also in the search experiments for eight source juices, continuous increase in the evaluation value was observed, but the evaluation values of the final generation became worse than that of the initial generation in the evaluation experiments. However, the convergence of distance in the population was observed and convergence in distribution of obtained solution in some trials on SOM, indicating that IGA achieves the local search. The global search is difficult due to the limitation of the number of evaluations caused by subject fatigue in IGA. The distribution of initialized individuals may also affect the search. For a problem with large solution space, it would be effective to exchange information on good solutions and search space through IGA [16] in which multiple people participate.

In addition, since the daily condition of the subject is considered to have an effect on the search, the development of a search method that effectively uses the solutions obtained from multiple trials is left for the future issue.

Acknowledgement. This work was supported by the Japan Society for the Promotion of Science, KAKENHI Grant Number 19K12196 and Tanuma greenhouse foundation.

References

1. Dawkins, R.: The Blind Watchmaker. Longman Scientific & Technical (1986)
2. Takagi, H.: Interactive evolutionary computation: fusion of the capabilities of EC optimization and human evaluation. Proc. the IEEE **89**(9), 1275–1296 (2001)
3. Ogawa, Y., Miki, M., Hiroyasu, T., Nagaya, Y.: A new collaborative design method based on interactive genetic algorithms. In: Proceedings the EUROGEN2001, pp.109–114 (2001)
4. Miki, M., Yamamoto, Y., Wake, S., Hiroyasu, T.: Global asynchronous distributed interactive genetic algorithm. In: Proceedings IEEE International Conference SMC2006, pp. 3481–3485 (2006)
5. Takenouchi, H., Inoue, H., Tokumaru, M.: Signboard design system through social voting technique. In: Proceedings ISIC2014, pp. 14–19 (2014)
6. Fukumoto, M., Hatanaka, T.: A proposal for distributed interactive genetic algorithm for composition of musical melody. IEE **3**(2), 56–68 (2017)
7. Nomura, K., Fukumoto, M.: Music melodies suited to multiple users' feelings composed by asynchronous distributed interactive genetic algorithm. Int. J. Software Innov. **6**(2), 26–36 (2018)
8. Fukumoto, M., Inoue, M., Koga, S., Imai, J.: Interactive differential evolution using time information required for user's selection: in a case of optimizing fragrance composition. In: Proceedings 2015 IEEE Congress on Evolutionary Computation (CEC) (2015). https://doi.org/10.1109/CEC.2015.7257155
9. Fukumoto, M., Hanada, Y.: A proposal for creation of beverage suited for user by blending juices based on interactive genetic algorithm. In: Proceedings IEEE International Conference SMC2019 (2019). https://doi.org/10.1109/SMC.2019.8914494
10. Peristaltic Liquid Pump with Silicone Tubing - 5V to 6V DC Power. https://www.adafruit.com/product/3910
11. NPN transistor 2SC2120-Y. https://akizukidenshi.com/catalog/g/gI-13829/
12. Arduino Leonard (ARDUINO-A000057). https://www.switch-science.com/catalog/968/
13. Osgood, C.E., Suci, G.K., Tannenbaum, P.: The Measurement of Meaning. University of Illinois Press, USA (1957)
14. Kouhonen, T.: Self-organization and associative memory. Springer Series in Information Sciences 8 (1984)
15. Somoclu. https://somoclu.readthedocs.io/en/stable/
16. Fukumoto, M., Hanada, Y.: Improvement of multi-user IEC for creating beverage on the assumption of taste-communication. IPSJ Magazine, **62**(5), Digital Practice (2021) (in Japanese)

Author Index

© The Editor(s) (if applicable) and The Author(s), under exclusive license
to Springer Nature Switzerland AG 2023
K. Saeed et al. (Eds.): CISIM 2023, LNCS 14164, pp. 509–511, 2023.
https://doi.org/10.1007/978-3-031-42823-4

Printed in the United States
by Baker & Taylor Publisher Services